French Prose and Criticism through 1789

Titles in the CRITICAL COSMOS series include

THE CRITICAL COSMOS SERIES

French Prose and Criticism through 1789

Edited and with an introduction
by *HAROLD BLOOM*
Sterling Professor of the Humanities
Yale University

CHELSEA HOUSE PUBLISHERS
New York ◇ *Philadelphia*

Printed and bound in the United States of America

10 9 8 7 6 5 4 3 2 1

Library of Congress Cataloging-in-Publication Data

French prose and criticism through 1789 / edited with an
introduction by Harold Bloom.
    p.   cm.—(The Critical cosmos series)
  Bibliography: p.
  Includes index.
  ISBN 1-555-46080-1
  1. French prose literature—18th century—History and
criticism. 2. French prose literature—17th century—History
and criticism. 3. French prose literature—16th century—
History and criticism. 4. Criticism—France—History.
I. Bloom, Harold. II. Series: Critical cosmos.
PQ611.F74 1987
848'.08—dc19   87–18360
                                       CIP

Contents

Editor's Note

This book brings together a representative selection of the best criticism available upon the principal writers of French nonfictional prose and criticism from Montaigne through the Revolution of 1789. I am grateful to Chantal McCoy and James Swenson for their assistance in editing this volume.

My introduction centers upon Montaigne and Pascal, contrasting Montaigne's relation to Seneca and Plutarch to Pascal's more anxious influence-relation to Montaigne. The essay by Timothy J. Reiss on Montaigne concerns the effect of the great essayist's sense of the self's instability upon his desire for a strong social order.

Descartes, the other authentic founder of French intellectuality, is read in his *Discours de la méthode* by Jean-Luc Nancy as having inaugurated "the pure *I* . . . who utters myself uttering," which became the *I* of Louis XIV, Victor Hugo, Flaubert, and Stendhal.

The Port-Royal *Grammar* and *Logic*, a crucial context for Pascal, is analyzed by the great linguist Noam Chomsky as part of the history of Cartesian linguistics. La Rochefoucauld, ironic moralist and prince of aphorists, is discussed by Philip E. Lewis as a social psychologist of self-love and its consequences.

Pascal's theory of rhetoric is illuminated by the late Paul de Man, the leading rhetorical critic of our era. Louise K. Horowitz, in an overview of Madame de Sévigné, discourses upon the relation between love and language, and upon the tensions between Jansenism and idolatry.

The orator Bossuet is analyzed by Domna C. Stanton as a bold confronter of "the problematics of utterance and reception." Kirsti Simonsuuri treats Perrault's criticism as a dialectic of individual genius playing against cultural influences, while Wilbur Samuel Howell, historian of rhetoric, charts the relations between poetry and oratory in the literary theory of Fénelon.

Roland Barthes considers La Bruyère as a theorist of writing, after which Herbert Dieckmann presents Fontenelle's theory of poetry. Saint-Simon's vision of Louis XIV is eruditely examined by Leo Spitzer, in a critical mode very different from the Marxist Structuralism of Louis Althusser's study of Montesquieu and Herbert Lüthy's informed exegesis of Quesnay's sense of the economics of society.

Voltaire's rationalist excursions into history writing constitute the subject of Suzanne Gearhart's essay, while Blair Campbell restores La Mettrie to his importance as *philosophe* as well as biologist. Paul de Man returns with his influential deconstruction of the rhetoric of Rousseau's *Social Contract*, after which Michael Fried presents Diderot as aesthetician, and the theorist of deconstruction, Jacques Derrida, reads Condillac as an instance of everything problematical in the work of reading.

D'Alembert's rhetoric is surveyed by Peter France, while Ronald L. Meek gives an overview of Turgot and the idea of progress. Condorcet's elitism is examined by Keith M. Baker, after which this volume concludes properly with the French Revolution as mirrored in Carol Blum's study of Rousseau's influence upon the political rhetoric of Robespierre and Saint-Just.

Introduction

I

Montaigne, until the advent of Shakespeare, was the great figure of the European Renaissance, comparable in cognitive power and in influence to Freud in our century. His mordant essay "Of Books" is marked by a genial irony that is profoundly skeptical of the Humanist program that ostensibly (and rather off-handedly) is endorsed:

> Let people see in what I borrow whether I have known how to choose what would enhance my theme. For I make others say what I cannot say so well, now through the weakness of my language, now through the weakness of my understanding. I do not count my borrowings, I weigh them. And if I had wanted to have them valued by their number, I should have loaded myself with twice as many. They are all, or very nearly all, from such famous and ancient names that they seem to identify themselves enough without me. In the reasonings and inventions that I transplant into my soil and confound with my own, I have sometimes deliberately not indicated the author, in order to hold in check the temerity of those hasty condemnations that are tossed at all sorts of writings, notably recent writings of men still living, and in the vulgar tongue, which invites everyone to talk about them and seems to convict the conception and design of being likewise vulgar. I want them to give Plutarch a fillip on my nose and get burned insulting Seneca in me. I have to hide my weakness under these great authorities. I will love anyone that can unplume me, I mean by clearness of judgment and by the sole distinction of the force and beauty of the remarks. For I who, for lack of memory, fall short at every turn in picking them out by knowledge of their

origin, can very well realize, by measuring my capacity, that my
soil is not at all capable of producing certain too rich flowers that
I find sown there, and that all the fruits of my own growing could
not match them.

This hardly seems a matter of "classical courage" but rather of cunning,
humor, skill, and a deliciously bland disarming of one's critics. It is also,
rather clearly, a knowingly defensive irony, directed against a literary anxiety that Montaigne insists is universal, and not merely individual. Montaigne at this time (1578–80) is well under way to his final stance, where
he forsakes the high Humanist doctrine in favor of the common life, so as
to affirm the exuberance of natural existence, and the enormous virtue of
being the *honnête homme*, thus establishing a new norm against which Pascal
would rebel, or perhaps an influence that Pascal could neither escape nor
accept. What "Of Books" subverts most audaciously is the Humanist
scheme of benign displacement by imitation. When Montaigne writes of
his unsavory critics, "I want them to give Plutarch a fillip on my nose and
get burned insulting Seneca in me," he not only accurately names his prime
precursors, but he asserts his own power of contamination. In contrast,
consider Ben Jonson, more truly Greene's hero of "classical courage":

The third requisite in our poet or maker is imitation, *imitatio*, to
be able to convert the substance or riches of another poet to his
own use. To make choice of one excellent man above the rest, and
so to follow him till he grow very he, or so like him as the copy
may be mistaken for the principal. Not as a creature that swallows
what it takes in, crude, raw, or undigested; but that feeds with
an appetite, and hath a stomach to concoct, divide, and turn all
into nourishment. Not to imitate servilely, as Horace saith, and
catch at vices for virtue, but to draw forth out of the best and
choicest flowers, with the bee, and turn all into honey, work it
into one relish and savour; make our imitation sweet; observe how
the best writers have imitated, and follow them: how Virgil and
Statius have imitated Homer; how Horace, Archilochus; how
Alcæus, and the other lyrics; and so of the rest.

Here one imitates precisely as the precursors imitated, which seems
to me an apt reduction of the Humanist argument. It is no surprise that
Jonson goes on to say of reading that it "maketh a full man," borrowing
from his truest precursor Sir Francis Bacon in the essay "Of Studies."
Admirable essayist in his narrow mode, Bacon is about as adequate to
compete with Montaigne as Jonson was to challenge Shakespeare. It takes
a singular perversity to prefer Bacon's essays to Montaigne's, and yet Jonson could insist persuasively that he was being loyal to the Humanist
doctrine of imitation:

Some that turn over all books, and are equally searching in all papers; that write out of what they presently find or meet, without choice. By which means it happens that what they have discredited and impugned in one week, they have before or after extolled the same in another. Such are all the essayists, even their master Montaigne. These, in all they write, confess still what books they have read last, and therein their own folly so much, that they bring it to the stake raw and undigested; not that the place did need it neither, but that they thought themselves furnished and would vent it.

Bacon's essays certainly do not "confess still what books they have read last," and Montaigne is anything but formalist in his use of quite immediate reading. Greene is wiser, I think, when he recognizes that ambivalence and the antithetical haunt all imitation, however Humanist:

The process called imitation was not only a technique or a habit; it was also a field of ambivalence, drawing together manifold, tangled, sometimes antithetical attitudes, hopes, pieties, and reluctances within a concrete locus.

At the heart of Humanism was an ambivalence, even an antithetical will that perhaps still makes the phrase "Christian Humanist" something of an oxymoron. Most simply, Humanism entailed a love of Greek and Latin wisdom and humane letters, a desire to know qualities uniquely available in antiquity. Christianity, in the early Renaissance, indeed became Greek and Latin in its culture, at a certain cost. The morality of the Christian Bible is scarcely Greek or Latin, and the God of Christianity remained the God of Abraham, Isaac, and Jacob, rather than the gods of Achilles, Odysseus, and Aeneas. Imitation or mimesis, whether of nature or of a precursor, is a Greek notion, rather than a Hebraic postulate. We cannot image an ancient Greek or Latin author confronting the stark text of the Second Commandment.

Erich Auerbach, in his *Mimesis: The Representation of Reality in Western Literature*, finds in Rabelais and Montaigne an early Renaissance freedom of vision, feeling, and thought produced by a perpetual playing with things, and hints that this freedom began to decline not so much in Cervantes as in Shakespeare, the two writers who by paradox may be the only Western authors since antiquity clearly surpassing the powers of even Rabelais and Montaigne. As Auerbach emphasizes:

In Rabelais there is no aesthetic standard; everything goes with everything. Ordinary reality is set within the most improbable fantasy, the coarsest jokes are filled with erudition, moral and philosophical enlightenment flows out of obscene expressions and stories.

This extraordinary freedom of representation in Rabelais is matched by Montaigne in Auerbach's description of his emancipation not only from the Christian conceptual schema but from the cosmological view of his precursors Cicero, Seneca, and Plutarch:

> His newly acquired freedom was much more exciting, much more of the historical moment, directly connected with the feeling of insecurity. The disconcerting abundance of phenomena which now claimed the attention of men seemed overwhelming. The world—both outer world and inner world—seemed immense, boundless, incomprehensible.

Shakespeare, "more consciously aristocratic than Montaigne" in Auerbach's view, grants the aesthetic dignity of the tragic only to princes, commanders, and eminent figures in Roman history. To the Humanist heritage Auerbach attributes Shakespeare's sense that there is more than a temporal gap between contemporary life and the heroic past:

> With the first dawn of humanism, there began to be a sense that the events of classical history and legend and also those of the Bible were not separated from the present simply by an extent of time but also by completely different conditions of life. Humanism with its program of renewal of antique forms of life and expression creates a historical perspective in depth such as no previous epoch known to us possessed.

Of Cervantes Auerbach beautifully remarks: "So universal and multilayered, so noncritical and nonproblematic a gaiety in the portrayal of everyday reality has not been attempted again in European letters." It is as though Humanist perspectivism—not yet developed in the rambunctious Rabelais, a powerful shadow in Shakespeare, forsaken for the common life by Montaigne—had been set aside by a genial power of acceptance of the mundane in Cervantes. But these in any case are the Renaissance writers as strong as Homer, Dante, and Chaucer. With lesser writers (lesser only as compared with these), the opening to the past carried with it a perspectivism that generated anxieties both of influence and of representation. Paradoxically, Humanism both exalted and burdened writers by proclaiming that the vernacular could achieve what the ancients had achieved by the aid of an antique greatness that carried its own implicit force of inhibition.

The literary criticism of the sixteenth century, since it is so entirely part of what can be called a Humanist manifesto, now demands to be read in a certain spirit of affectionate de-idealization. The greatest writers of the century accomplish this de-idealization by themselves, and if such an activity be considered criticism (and it is), then Montaigne, rather than du Bellay or Sidney or Tasso, becomes the great critic of the early Renaissance. To call the *Essays* a vast work of literary criticism is a revisionary act of judgment, but only in the sense of seeing now that Sigmund Freud, who died in 1939, appears in 1986 to have been the crucial critic of the twentieth century. Montaigne's defense of the self is also an analysis of the self, and Montaigne appears now to have been the ancestor not only of Emerson and Nietzsche, both of whom acknowledged him, but also of Freud, who did not.

Returning to Montaigne then, in a wider compass than just the essay "Of Books," is to encounter a poetics of the self that is also a relentless (for all its casual mode) critique of the Humanist, idealized poetics of the self. Petrarch, du Bellay, even the more pragmatic Sidney, and most of all the tormented Tasso—all of them idealize their stance in relation to vernacular precursors, and also in regard to ancient wisdom. Montaigne, once past his Humanist first phase and his skeptical transition, does not deceive either himself or others when it comes to the problems of writing:

> I have not had regular dealings with any solid book, except Plutarch and Seneca, from whom I draw like the Danaïds, incessantly filling up and pouring out. Some of this sticks to this paper; to myself, a little or nothing.

This, from near the start of the 1579–80 essay "Of the Education of Children," is one of the most astonishing sentences even in Montaigne. Terence Cave, in *The Cornucopian Text*, reads this sentence in the manner of Derrida and Barthes:

> The fullness of two model-texts is here designated, it would seem, as a source; the labour of the Danaides would thus represent the activity of transmission or exchange ("commerce"), by which the textual substance of Plutarch and Seneca is displaced into a discourse bearing the signature "Montaigne." But this sentence is marked from the beginning by a negation. Plutarch and Seneca appear in a concessive phrase made possible only by the absence of any "livre solide": a characteristically Montaignian insistence on the emptiness of discourse (particularly the written discourses of pedagogy) allows provisional access to certain privileged texts whose unsystematic, open-ended form endorses that of the *Essais* themselves. The negation is not, however, limited to the unnamed texts Montaigne claims to have neglected. The Danaides are, after all, not a wholly reassuring figure of plenitude. Rabelais cites them as a counter-example of cornucopian productivity, a sign of despair, and the uselessness of their labours is made explicit in the following sentence: "J'en attache quelque chose à ce papier; à moy, si peu que rien." The *locus* is closed, as it began, in negation. The *moi*, in a place outside discourse, is scarcely touched by the language even of Plutarch and Seneca; its integrity is preserved, as at the beginning of the passage, by a repudiation of books. Alien

discourse cannot be "attached" to the self, is external to it. Hence the gesture of transference, endlessly repeated, appears as an empty mime. The only thing to which fragments of another text may be attached is "ce papier," a mediate domain which clearly concerns the *moi* (since the sentences inscribed on it have a habit of beginning with "je"), but is no less clearly different from it. The paper on which the text of the *Essais* appears is, indeed, a place of difference: it allows the rewriting and naturalization of foreign texts; it thereby permits the search for the identity of a *moi* in contradistinction from what is "other"; but at the same time it defers any final access to the goal of the search, since the self is expressly an entity dissociated from the activity of writing.

If read in that deconstructionist manner, then Montaigne is achieving an awareness that the experimental fullness he seeks outside language, and which he hopes to represent in his own language, is no more a true presence in Plutarch and Seneca than in his own pages, or in his own self. Like the Danaïds, all writers are condemned to carry the waters of experience in the sieve of language. But Montaigne (unlike Cave) *does* regard the *Moral Essays* of Plutarch and the *Epistles* of Seneca as "solid books." They are not merely privileged texts or sources, but pragmatically, experientially, they have, *for Montaigne*, a different status than his own writing possesses. They are the fathers, true authors and authorities; they do augment because they do not go back to the foundations, but for Montaigne they *are* the foundations. And some of their reality does stick to Montaigne's manuscript and printed page, even if some does not. Montaigne's self is as formidable as the selves of Plutarch and Seneca; his self repels influences. Yet he does grant priority to the text of the fathers, because his text, as opposed to his self, cannot have authority without some transference from the fathers.

Cave concludes his very useful study of Montaigne by turning to the text of the culminating essay, the magnificent "Of Experience" (1587–88). After observing that there is envy and jealousy between our pleasures, so that they clash and interfere with one another, Montaigne opposes himself to those who therefore would abandon natural pleasures:

> I, who operate only close to the ground, hate that inhuman wisdom that would make us disdainful enemies of the cultivation of the body. I consider it equal injustice to set our heart against natural pleasures and to set our heart too much on them. Xerxes was a fool, who, wrapped in all human pleasures, went and offered a prize to anyone who would find him others. But hardly less of a fool is the man who cuts off those that nature has found for him. We should neither pursue them nor flee them, we should accept them. I accept them with more gusto and with better grace than most, and more willingly let myself follow a natural inclination. We have no need to exaggerate their inanity; it makes itself

felt enough and evident enough. Much thanks to our sickly, kill-joy mind, which disgusts us with them as well as with itself. It treats both itself and all that it takes in, whether future or past, according to its insatiable, erratic, and versatile nature.

> Unless the vessel's pure, all you pour in turns sour.
>
> Horace

I, who boast of embracing the pleasures of life so assiduously and so particularly, find in them, when I look at them thus minutely, virtually nothing but wind. But what of it? We are all wind. And even the wind, more wisely than we, loves to make a noise and move about, and is content with its own functions, without wishing for stability and solidity, qualities that do not belong to it.

Cave deconstructs this:

Full experience is always absent: presence is unattainable. All that the *Essais* can do, with their ineradicable self-consciousness, is to posit paradigms of wholeness as features of a discourse which, as it pours itself out, celebrates its own inanity. The Montaignian text represents the emptying of the cornucopia by the very gesture of extending itself indefinitely until the moment of ultimate *egressio* or elimination: the figures of abundance play a prominent part in the closing pages of *De l'experience*. Whatever plenitude seems to have been proper to the past, whatever festivity is assigned to these terminal moments, Montaigne's writing is both the only place in which they can be designated, and a place from which they remain inexhaustibly absent.

The plenitude of the textual past, of Plutarch, and of Seneca, and of Horace, is certainly present here, but so is the pragmatic presence of an achieved text, a newness caught in its annunciation. If we are all wind, and Montaigne's *Essays* nothing but wind, why then let us be as wise as the wind. The text, like ourselves, makes a noise and moves about. Like the wind, we and our texts ought not to seek for qualities not our own. But an unstable and fluid text, always metamorphic, can be viewed as positively as a mobile self. If Montaigne declares limitation, he also asserts a freedom, both for his text and for himself.

Montaigne, like the characters of Shakespeare's plays, changes because he listens to what he himself has said. Reading his own text, he becomes Hamlet's precursor, and represents reality in and by himself. His power of interpretation over his own text is also a power over the precursors' texts, and so makes of his own belatedness an earliness. What Petrarch and du Bellay and Tasso longed for vainly, what Sidney urbanely courted, is what Rabelais first possessed in the Renaissance and is what culminates in Montaigne's "Of Experience," before it goes on to triumph again in Don Quixote, Falstaff, and Hamlet. Call it a Humanist reality rather than a Humanist idealization: an exaltation of the vernacular that authentically carried representation back to its Homeric and biblical strength. In that exaltation, the writer makes us see regions of reality we could not have seen without him. As Wallace Stevens said of the poet, the enterprise of the Renaissance Humanist author:

> tries by a peculiar speech to speak
> The peculiar potency of the general,
> To compound the imagination's Latin with
> The lingua franca et jocundissima.

II

Pascal never loses his capacity to offend as well as to edify. Contrast his very different effects upon Paul Valéry and T. S. Eliot. Here is Valéry:

> I hate to see a man using artifice to turn others against their lot, when they are in it in spite of themselves and are doing what they can to make the best of it; to see a man trying to persuade others that they must expect the worst, must always keep in mind the most intolerable notion of their predicament, and be alert to whatever is most unbearable in it—which is precisely the notion of suffering and risk, and anxiety about the risk—using the notion of eternity as an almighty weapon, and developing it by the artifice of repetition.

This is to accuse Pascal of being an obscurantistic rhetorician, rather resembling the T. S. Eliot of the religious prose writings. Here is Eliot on Pascal:

> But I can think of no Christian writer, not Newman even, more to be commended than Pascal to those who doubt, but who have the mind to conceive, and the sensibility to feel the disorder, the meaninglessness, the mystery of life and suffering, and who can only find peace through a satisfaction of the whole being.

I suspect that Valéry and Eliot are saying much the same thing, the difference being the rival perspectives towards Pascal of a secular intellectual and a Christian polemicist. Pascal essentially is a polemicist, rather than a religious or meditative writer. The *Pensées* ultimately are not less tendentious than the *Provincial Letters*. A Christian polemicist in our time ought to find his true antagonist in Freud, but nearly all do not; they either evade Freud, or self-defeatingly seek to appropriate him. Pascal's Freud was Montaigne, who could not be evaded or appropriated, and who scarcely can be refuted. But Pascal's case of influence-anxiety, in regard to

Montaigne, was hopelessly overwhelming. Eliot, putting the best case for Pascal, insisted that Montaigne simply had the power to embody a universal skepticism, in which Pascal necessarily shared, though only to a limited degree. Doubtless Eliot attributed to Montaigne one of the essayist's plethora of authentic powers, but a secretly shared (and overcome) skepticism hardly can account for the full scandal of Montaigne's influence upon Pascal. Tables of parallel passages demonstrate an indebtedness so great, extending to figuration, examples, syntax, actual repetition of phrases, that Pascal would be convicted of plagiarism in any American school or university with their rather literal notions of what constitutes plagiarism. The frequent effect in reading Pascal is that he begins to seem an involuntary parody of his precursor. This is particularly unfortunate whenever Pascal overtly denounces Montaigne, since sometimes we hear the pious son castigating the unbelieving father in the father's inescapable accents.

It has been surmised that Pascal jotted down his *Pensées* with his copy of Montaigne's *Essays* always lying open before him. Whether this was literally true or not, we may say that Montaigne was for Pascal quite simply a presence never to be put by. Eliot speaks of Montaigne's readers as being "thoroughly infected" by him, and certainly Pascal must have known inwardly the anguish of contamination. What are we to do with *Pensées* 358, one example out of many:

> Man is neither angel nor brute, and the unfortunate thing is that he who would act the angel acts the brute.

That would have been admirable, had it not been lifted from the best essay ever written, Montaigne's "Of Experience," where it is expressed with rather more force and insight:

> They want to get out of themselves and escape from the man. That is madness: instead of changing into angels, they change into beasts; instead of raising themselves, they lower themselves.

It is an ancient commonplace, but Montaigne plays variations upon his sources, since his sense of self is his own. What is distressing is that Pascal neither evades nor revises Montaigne, but simply repeats him, presumably unaware of his bondage to his skeptical precursor. Since Pascal's mode is polemic, and Montaigne's is rumination and speculation, the rhetorical edge is different; Pascal emphasizes moral action, while Montaigne centers upon moral being. Yet the reader is made uncomfortable, not because Pascal has appropriated Montaigne, but because Pascal has manifested a paucity of invention. Voltaire and Valéry would seem to be confirmed. Pascal writes as a pragmatic enemy of Montaigne, and this necessarily makes Pascal, as Valéry said, into an enemy of humankind. We are in a difficult enough situation, without being castigated by Pascal merely for being what we have to be. Do we still need Pascal? We read Montaigne as we read Shakespeare and Freud. How can we read Pascal?

Nietzsche insisted upon finding in Pascal an antithetical precursor, and shrewdly located Pascal's major error in the famous "wager":

> He supposes that he proves Christianity to be true because it is necessary. This presupposes that a good and truthful providence exists which ordains that everything necessary shall be true. But there can be necessary errors!

Later Nietzsche observed that "one should never forgive Christianity for having destroyed such men as Pascal." Yet Nietzsche also remarked, in a letter to George Brandes, that he almost loved Pascal for having been "the only *logical* Christian." The true link between the two was in their greatness as moral psychologists, a distinction they share with Montaigne and with Kierkegaard and, in another mode, with Swift. Pascal's strong swerve away from Montaigne, which transcends his guilt of obligation to a naturalistic and skeptical master, is manifested in the development of a new kind of religious irony. Montaigne urges relativism because we are opaque to ideas of order other than our own, but this is precisely Pascal's motivation for our necessary surrender to God's will. Since God is hidden, according to Pascal, our condition is no less than tragic. A hidden God is doubly an incoherence for us; intolerable if he exists and equally intolerable if he does not. We are thus reduced to an ironic quietism, in which we are best off doing nothing in regard to worldly realities. We reject the order of society so thoroughly that pragmatically we can accept it totally.

The extraordinary ironies of the *Provincial Letters* are founded upon this Pascalian stance that allows him to chastise the Jesuits for worldliness while defending society against them:

> What will you do with someone who talks like that, and how will you attack me, since neither my words nor my writings afford any pretext for your accusation of heresy and I find protection against your threats in my own obscurity? You feel the blows of an unseen hand revealing your aberrations for all to see. You try in vain to attack me in the persons of those whom you believe to be my allies. I am not afraid of you either on behalf of myself or of anyone else, as I am attached to no community and no individual whatsoever. All the credit you may enjoy is of no avail as far as I am concerned. I hope for nothing from the world; I fear nothing from it, I desire nothing of it; by God's grace I need no one's wealth or authority. Thus, Father, I entirely escape your clutches. You cannot get hold of me however you try. You may well touch Port-Royal, but not me. Some have indeed been evicted from the Sorbonne, but that does not evict me from where I am. You may well prepare acts of violence against priests and doctors, but not against me who am without such titles. You have perhaps never had to deal with anyone so far out of your range and so well fitted

to attack your errors, by being free, without commitments, without allegiance, without ties, without connexions, without interests; sufficiently acquainted with your precepts and determined to drive them as far as I may believe myself obliged by God to do, without any human consideration being able to halt or check my pursuit.

Implicit in this superbly polemical paragraph is the unassailable rhetorical position of the ironic quietist, beyond this world yet its only true defender. One calls this "unassailable" in Pascal's stance because his rhetoric and psychology are so intimately related to his cosmology, and the three indeed are one. We have fallen into figuration, psychic division, and the eternal silence of the infinite spaces, and all these ought to terrify us equally. Sara Melzer usefully emphasizes Pascal's difference from negative theology, to which I would add Gnosticism, as the most negative of all theologies. God's otherness, the Pascalian version of which is hiddenness, has nothing in common with the alien God of the Gnostics and the Hermeticists. For Pascal, the hiddenness leads to the wager of faith, rather than to a negation of all tropes, terms for order, and scientific postulates.

If this is error, it is at least one of the necessary errors, psychologically speaking. Pascal never found his way out of the shadow of Montaigne, not I think because Montaigne spoke also for Pascal's own skepticism, but because Montaigne was too authentic a self and too strong a writer to need wagers of any kind. A paragraph like this, from the *Apology for Raymond Sebond*, must have been a permanent reproach to Pascal:

> Furthermore, it is here in us, and not elsewhere, that the powers and actions of the soul should be considered. All the rest of its perfections are vain and useless to it; it is for its present state that all its immortal life is to be paid and rewarded, and for man's life that it is solely accountable. It would be an injustice to have cut short its resources and powers; to have disarmed it, and to pass judgment and a sentence of infinite and perpetual duration upon it, for the time of its captivity and imprisonment, its weakness and illness, the time when it was forced and constrained; and to stop at the consideration of so short a time, perhaps one or two hours, or at worst a century, which is no more in proportion to infinity than an instant; in order, from this moment of interval, to decide and dispose definitively of its whole existence. It would be an inequitable disproportion to receive eternal compensation in consequence of so short a life.

Against this, Pascal's eloquence and psychic intensity must fall short, even in the most notorious of the *Pensées:*

205

When I consider the short duration of my life, swallowed up in the eternity before and after, the little space which I fill, and even can see, engulfed in the infinite immensity of spaces of which I am ignorant, and which know me not, I am frightened, and am astonished at being here rather than there; for there is no reason why here rather than there, why now rather than then. Who has put me here? By whose order and direction have this place and time been allotted to me? *Memoria hospitis unius diei prætereuntis.*

206

The eternal silence of these infinite spaces frightens me.

"It is here in us, and not elsewhere, that the powers and actions of the soul should be considered." Montaigne remains in our mind, Pascal in our heart. Freud, the Montaigne of our era, reminded us that the voice of reason was not loud, but would not rest until it gained a hearing. Montaigne's voice is never-resting, while Pascal's voice is restless. As Montaigne's involuntary and perpetual ephebe, Pascal always knew which voice was stronger.

Montaigne and the Subject of Polity

Timothy J. Reiss

> *I sent your Grace*
> *The parcels and particulars of our grief,*
> *The which hath been with scorn shoved from the court,*
> *Whereon this Hydra son of war is born,*
> *Whose dangerous eyes may well be charmed asleep*
> *With grant of our most just and right desires,*
> *And true obedience, of this madness cured,*
> *Stoop tamely to the foot of majesty.*
> —SHAKESPEARE, *Henry IV, Part 2*, 4.11 (c. 1597–98)

It might seem that the question of the subject (of any subject) in the work of Montaigne lies on such well-worn terrain that it is scarcely worth the trouble to cover it again. Indeed, much has been said regarding the "ambiguities" and "contradictions" of Montaigne in this regard. He has been seen sometimes as the precursor of the voluntarist Cartesian subject, and other times as the sign of a moment in which something like a "subject" still remains to be constituted. There have been disputes between those who emphasize the all-too-famous phrase "Each man bears the entire form of man's estate" (*Complete Works*, trans. Donald Frame [Stanford, 1957], book 3, essay 2; hereafter styled as 3.2) and those who favor another, less well-known, one, "I do not share that common error of judging another by myself" (1.37), or the warning that follows it immediately: "I have a singular desire that we should each be judged in ourselves apart, and that I may not be measured in conformity with the common patterns." At times Montaigne is viewed as a conservative, as the loyal and even intolerant subject of his prince; at others he is praised as a (secretly) radical or even revolutionary thinker—the intrepid successor of what is then interpreted as the "leftist" text of his friend La Boetie, the *Discours de la servitude volontaire*. Thus it is that recently (we need not venture into the interpretive tradition) there has been talk of Montaigne's "dialectic" of the self (which is no dialectic at all), of the "wager" of exemplarity that is taken to inform his thought, or again, to avoid the suggestion of extremism in this latter, of the "paradox" of this appellation, "Michel de Montaigne," which names a "universal being" one minute, but which cannot name anything at all the next.

I do not want to extend this field of ambiguity, of contradiction, of paradox and extreme. Such views seem to me to emerge from a refusal to situate Montaigne in a specific historical moment, and from a desire to read him as an exemplary representative of the "human"—as if this concept of the human were not itself the product of a certain history (a matter to which I will return). Yet it is not a question here of situating him in any "social" or "biographical" sense (this latter work having already been accomplished magisterially by Donald Frame). Rather, I want to consider Montaigne insofar as he belongs to a certain moment of what is called more and more nowadays "the history of mentalities"; and this with reference to a particular field of thought—that of political theory. Thus I shall attempt not only to cut across the question of the subject in Montaigne and that of a certain political thought, but as well to place the problem with relative precision in a current of political thought leading from the Middle Ages through a "first" definitive questioning (dating from the period of Machiavelli's work) toward an eventual consolidation of the liberal theory of the state in Hobbes and Locke.

In a general fashion, though without special reference to political theory, this development has been examined more closely in my *Discourse of Modernism*. There I make considerable use of Michel Foucault's work in order to analyze a certain textual corpus to show how what he calls the *episteme,* what I prefer to call the sociocultural environment, gradually develops and consolidates into a sphere of action and thought under the sway of what I term the dominant discursive model. Because this analysis seeks to show how contradictions and occultations, emergent and residual elements in one such model force a relatively gradual *transformation* toward another, it differs considerably from Foucault's notion of epistemic rupture, though it can make use of his tools for the analysis of a sociocultural environment once it has in fact been consolidated. The difference from Foucault's analysis, however, goes further than what has just been suggested. For the concept of the sociocultural environment is used to enable us to escape from an analysis that remains essentially bound to a linguistic order and views all human processes as in some fundamental way languagelike. All human actions, I would propose, may be conceived as forms of discourse. But "discourse," here, is positively *not* to be understood as in any way coterminous with language. Rather does it refer to the meaningful process ordering *any* sign material, where language (for example) is simply one such material. With this in mind, once we begin to see all human actions as sociocultural ways of producing meanings, and history as a process of environmental transformations and consolidations, then the very terms of such actions take on new meanings. If Montaigne, for example, is viewed as participating in a period of transformation, then we begin to realize that certain key terms recurring constantly in the *Essays* may well have been fundamentally misinterpreted—in the light of meanings they have taken on under the sway of a discursive model that Montaigne may have helped bring into being but which is quite foreign to his own and his contemporaries' thought and action. Trying to analyze Montaigne in such a light, to fit such terms at once into their particular history and into the practical and theoretical environment that was Montaigne's, will oblige us, I think, to see the *Essays* in a completely new light and as playing an emblematic role in the consolidation of an eventually new discursive dominance of unexpected importance and significance.

Instead of seeing the ambiguities and contradictions, I shall propose simply that in Montaigne there are "two" subjects: one which scarcely constitutes itself as such, which marks an attempt to seize thought in process and which is rigorously "private" (to use a word employed constantly by Montaigne); the other by which the "public" individual is "subject" to his prince—in the first case the private "subject," in the second the social and political subject. It is this double constitution of the subject which I shall pursue briefly. Yet I must stress right away that *in no way* is this duality a question of opposition. On the contrary, one is absolutely essential to the other. If the political subject has a "being," one must find it in the constant movement of thought that alone constitutes the private subject; if this latter has an "existence," it is thanks to its projection (in a geometrical or logical sense) into the concrete world of the social. (These terms of "being" and "existence" are of course anachronistic here in this sense, but they serve to underline the relationship that seems to be at issue.) Even more important than this absence of contradiction: we find ourselves here faced with a schema rigorously analogous to that which exists in the case of the sovereign prince. Indeed, in this double subject we find the form of "the King's double body" as symbolized in the phrase of succession, "The King is dead, long live the King," and definitively elucidated by Ernst Kantorowicz. In the king's case it is a question of the "mystical" and immortal body, guaranteeing the stability and permanence of the state, as against the present, particular and mortal body, subject to the laws and punctual relations of a given society and historical moment (*The King's Two Bodies: A Study in Medieval Political Theology*). This idea is found in Montaigne, as in this addition to the 1595 edition:

> We owe subjection and obedience equally to all kings, for that concerns their office; but we do not owe esteem, any more than affection, except to their virtue. Let us make this concession to the political order: to suffer them patiently if they are unworthy, to conceal their vices, to abet them by commending their indifferent actions if their authority needs our support.

> (1.3)

The relationship here is not simply made up out of thin air. The duality of the mystical body and the material body of the king is a concept essential to a certain order of sovereignty. Coming down from the Middle Ages and affirming itself especially in theories of divine right toward the end of the sixteenth century, the theory of the double body is one way of guaranteeing the stability of a certain type of social and political order (in fact, one should speak less of "theory" and more of "mentality," for Kantorowicz's explication of the theory relies less upon great theoretical texts than upon juridical and polemical documents—the reflections of a certain concrete practice). The mystical body guarantees the continuity of the state, the immutable existence of the social. In Montaigne this notion corresponds as well to the public subject, servant of the established political order, maintained by the legitimate government and guaranteed by God through the mystical body of the king. But the king, insofar as he is a living being, has his own real body—a body that by the same token moves, changes, and dies. It is there that we find this "perennial movement" (3.2) that is proper to everything in the lower world and that is above all the "proper" characteristic of the private person: "Seeing that the slightest pinprick, or passion of the soul, is sufficient to deprive us of the pleasure of being monarch of the world. At the first twinge of the gout, there is no comfort in his being Sire and Majesty" (1.42). Montaigne is expressing his agreement with Xenophon, who in his *Hieron* (also used by La Boetie) shows the king of the title role affirming that "even in the enjoyment of pleasures kings are worse off than private citizens" (ibid.).

This state of affairs comes about because the king, as living symbol of the order of state, cannot shed his political role, whereas the specific ("private") individual can easily withdraw: "For anyone who wants to ensconce himself by his hearth, and who can manage his house without quarrels and lawsuits, is as free as the Doge of Venice" (ibid.). Like Diocletian, a king may indeed want "to retire to the pleasure of a private life" (ibid.), but he cannot escape from the requirement of being always visibly present in his political aspect. The private being of the king, says Montaigne, is secondary and must be suppressed. All other members of society have a certain choice:

> In truth, our laws are free enough, and the weight of sovereignty scarcely touches a French nobleman twice in his life. The real and essential subjection is only for those among us who go seeking it and who like to gain honors and riches by such service.
>
> (ibid.)

Through this idea of liberty, then, we come back to the double subject. For here we are in fact dealing, on the social level, with the "liberty" and unobstructed movement of thought as a *process*, as ongoing thinking: "Things in themselves may have their own weights and measures and qualities; but once inside, within us, she [the soul] allots them their qualities as she sees fit" (1.1). But the freedom to withdraw from the social is no more than that, for if this freedom of reason becomes mixed in with the public domain of the sociopolitical, one ends up with complete confusion. I shall cite here a passage that is, to be sure, very famous, but one that permits us to situate Montaigne within a whole itinerary of the political thought of his age:

> I have observed in Germany that Luther has left as many divisions and altercations over the uncertainty of his opinions, and more, as he raised about the Holy Scriptures. Our disputes are purely verbal. I ask what are "nature," "pleasure," "circle," "substitution." The question is one of words, and is answered in the same way. "A stone is a body." But if you pressed on: "And what is a body?"—"Substance."—"And what is substance?" and so on, you would finally drive the respondent to the end of his lexicon. We exchange one word for another word, often more unknown. I know better what is man than I know what is animal, or moral, or rational. To satisfy one doubt, they give me three; it is the Hydra's head.
>
> (3.13)

This passage follows a long discussion of the multiple interpretations given of the laws by legal theoreticians, and it precedes a long appeal for the simplification of these same laws as well as the elimination of learned glosses that only augment "doubts and ignorance" and lead to "an irregular, perpetual motion, without model and without aid." For this reason the very "commandment" of the laws, he says, is "confused and inconstant."

We find a whole series of preoccupations thrown together here: the question of right and law, that of religious opinion and thus of the civil wars, a question concerning language and its relationship to things and concepts, another regarding inconstancy and yet another, implicit, on the subject and what it is capable of knowing. It will be useful to link this passage immediately with another dating from the same edition (1588)— a passage that addresses the same series of questions and which, like the one above, will facilitate my insertion of Montaigne into a certain theoretical "development" concerning the state and power, the subject and sovereignty. I believe I can show that Montaigne occupies a place at once interesting and important in this development, to which the literary criticism normally concerning itself with Montaigne has paid little or no attention.

This time Montaigne speaks explicitly of the civil wars to the extent that he is considering those who seek to "upset the state":

> All sorts of new depravity gleefully draw, from this first and fertile source, examples and models to trouble our government. Men read in our very laws, made for the remedy of this first evil, an apprenticeship and excuse for all sorts of wicked enterprises; and we are experiencing what Thucydides says of the civil wars of his time, that men baptized public vices with new milder names to excuse them, adulterating and softening their true titles.
>
> (1.23)

This well-known passage by the Greek historian had become a sort of cliché in the political thought at the close of the wars of religion and we will return to Montaigne's use of it very soon. But let us move on, for a few moments, to other writers known by Montaigne, some of whom played considerable roles as much in public life as in what Pierre Mesnard has rather felicitously called the launching of political philosophy (*L'Essor de la philosophie politique au XVIᵉ siècle*). Then we shall be able to situate more easily Montaigne's considerations on the subject, on sovereignty and the relationships of force within the state.

In August of 1570 Louis Le Roy signed at Saint-Germain-en-Laye the dedication to his *Exhortation aux François pour vivre en concorde, et iouir du bien de la Paix*. The text is dedicated to King Charles IX, who, at the same place and in the same month, had signed the pact known as "The Peace of Saint Germain," putting an "end" to the second war of religion. In his work, Le Roy stresses that a single sovereignty, concretized in the person of the king, is essential to the continued existence of "all the Kingdom." The stability that necessarily follows such sovereignty (an idea possibly culled from Bodin's *Method for the Easy Comprehension of History*, published in 1556—but the question was in any case becoming a burning one) he sets against the complete upheaval resulting from political sedition, a principal consequence, he says, of the discontent of the nobles. The major sign of this upheaval is the complete confusion of the sense of language: on this subject he quotes at great length the passage from Thucydides which we have just seen mentioned by Montaigne. We shall come back to this, not only because we will find the reference elsewhere, but because the relationship between political sedition, the overthrow of state sovereignty, inconstancy of the subject, and linguistic confusion is no less central for Montaigne. This relationship is closely linked to all the debates surrounding the question of sovereignty and political power.

Louis Le Roy, in 1570, sets the concept of the prince's unique sovereignty against another—that of a dispersed sovereignty represented at the time by the discontent of the nobles. It had already become clear that the so-called wars of religion masked a completely different struggle: the one between an old "feudal" concept of relations of force and a new concept yet to be found. In the meantime a confusion reigned which all found disquieting, but by which few commentators were deceived: what was at issue, the complaint ran, was not at all the religious question, or not primarily, but rather the "interest" of one side or the other. The diversity of these interests sowed confusion. At the level of political relations this confusion was perceived as a question of sovereignty. For, affirms Montaigne, it stems from according an unwonted identity and privilege to the private subject: "Society in general can do without our thoughts; but the rest—our actions, our work, our fortunes, and our very life—we must lend and abandon to its service and to the common opinion. . . . For it is the rule of rules, and the universal law of laws, that each man should observe those of the place he is in" (1.23). Or, again, he adds, "it takes a lot of self-love

and presumption to have such esteem for one's own opinions that to establish them one must overthrow the public peace and introduce so many
inevitable evils" (ibid.). Anyone who opts to place the private realm first,
"meddles with choosing and changing, usurps the authority to judge"
(ibid.). Montaigne thus considers the intervention of the private into the
public domain as a usurpation of sovereignty.

I would like to take another example whose considerable interest for
the case of Montaigne we shall see shortly. In his *Second Discours sur l'estat
de France* (in *Quatre Excellens Discours sur l'estat présent de la France*), published in 1593, Michel Hurault de l'Hôpital denounces the ambition and
self-interest of the house of Lorraine. According to him, it has resulted in
thirty years of war: "For religion was not yet at stake; they took it only for
want of a better pretext." He continues with a short history of the civil
wars, shortly thereafter giving a specific example of struggles between
various interested groups which shows how, concretely, these struggles
were played out. He stresses that what is at stake is indeed sovereignty:

> Just man, if at this moment you wanted to see the image of con-
> fusion and disorder, you would find it clearly painted in that party.
> To begin with, the Duke of Mayenne calls himself *Lieutenant general
> of the Royal State and of the crown of France*. This is a great illusion:
> can there be a *Lieutenant*, if there is no head? And who is head if
> not the King? Yet the majority of their party doesn't want any
> king. *As to the State:* formerly one heard talk of the States of France,
> but never of the State: or if one heard it named it was when one
> said, "the King and his State." In that case the state was named
> in terms of obedience and not of command: and these madmen
> place it at the head.

Montaigne, who is doubtless less interested by the Huguenot party in
and of itself than by the idea of a legitimate king, leans in the same direction
in a passage added in 1595:

> See the horrible impudence with which we bandy divine reasons
> about, and how irreligiously we have both rejected them and taken
> them again, according as fortune has changed our place in these
> public storms. This proposition, so solemn, whether it is lawful
> for a subject to rebel and take arms against his prince in defense
> of religion—remember in whose mouths, this year just past, the
> affirmative of this was the buttress of one party, the negative was
> the buttress of another; and hear now from what quarter comes
> the voice and the instruction of both sides, and whether the weap-
> ons make less din for this cause than for that.
>
> (2.12)

The question being debated is indeed that of rebellion and sovereignty.
Furthermore, we find ourselves manifestly at a moment of change in the
very concept of the state: this is not a new finding, but it is important to

notice that this change takes place not simply on the basis of some theoretical abstraction. It does so through reference to actual conditions and applies itself *immediately* to concrete life.

According to Hurault, the Catholic League affirms that the head of state is nothing more than the guardian ("lieutenant general") of *a state that is itself sovereign.* It would be easy indeed to find examples of the phrase "State of France" before this date: the argument proposed by Hurault is that this phrase had always signified the king's domain over which he is sovereign—an inalienable domain in some sense the "proper" characteristic of the immortal body of the king. This is the meaning of the doctrine of the king's two bodies. If sovereignty is characteristic of the state itself (thus an abstract concept, not personified by the king, which will eventually need the ascendency of the doctrine of contract in order to fix and explain the relationship of the sovereign state to its individual members), then what counts is the immortality of the state, so to speak, and not that of the mystical body of the king. The consequence of this, says Hurault, is very serious: the complete confusion of a state that no longer has a language. Since there is no longer a sovereign prince, the officers of the ex-king no longer know "how to pronounce, they dare not speak in the name of the King [i.e., Henry IV], they do not want to speak in the name of the people and even less in that of Monsieur de Mayenne, for by the statutes of the Kingdom they can recognize no one but he who has absolute command."

Thus one is up against a fundamental disorder and confronts a "divided multitude of authorities." It is the birth of anarchy in the strictest sense of the term: the loss of a single head leads in the long run to an infinite multiplication. And so Hurault complains of the creation of kinds of communes ("councils of certain persons of low degree in whose hands all authority has been placed") in the cities, saying that this "new democracy has undermined" the principal "Royal column," which is "justice": "Following the example of the capital city of Paris, all the other cities are doing the same thing; we have a Republic in every town." If events continue to unfold in this way, all the other cities, big and small, will do the same: "And thus by degrees there will eventually be no village in France that has not made itself into a sovereign state." It is worth following a bit further the interesting perspectives opened up by Michel Hurault's commentaries (which were of a type quite widespread at the time). They have a certain importance regarding the interpretation of Montaigne that I shall propose, especially, as concerns the historical role I shall attempt to show him playing.

Hurault thus argues that the League finds itself in a contradictory position. On the one hand it assumes the total sovereignty of the state, while on the other it confronts a real splintering of this very same state, a disintegration of the country's local units into a bunch of tiny sovereignties. His argument turns around the essential idea that the state and its prince are inextricably linked. Royal sovereignty (inherent in the immortal and mystic body) forms the keystone of the state as a single unit: remove this stone (by denying the king or his unique sovereignty) and the state disintegrates. Each part is driven into independence, and chaos ensues—whence the constant call of a Montaigne for "natural and simple obedience," an obedience that must be through "subjection" and not through "discretion" (1.17).

Such an obedience is essential: "The ordinary discipline of a state that is in a healthy condition does not provide for these extraordinary accidents; it presupposes a body that holds together in its principal parts and function and a common consent to its observance and obedience" (1.23). And in 1595 he adds that: "The law-abiding pace is a cold, deliberate and constrained one, and is not the kind that can hold up against a lawless and unbridled pace." One of the principal merits of the Christian religion is its "precise recommendation of obedience to the magistrate and maintenance of the government" (1.23). To this statement from 1588 he adds in 1595 that it seems

> very iniquitous to want to subject public and immutable institutions and observances to the instability of a private fancy (private reason has only a private jurisdiction), and to attempt against divine laws what no government would endure against civil laws. These last, although human reason has much more to do with them, are still supremely the judges of their judges; and the utmost ability serves at best to expound and extend their accepted use, not to turn it aside and innovate.
>
> (ibid.)

Divine laws, social laws, sovereignty of the "magistrate"—together these form a network, a "coherent body" that dissolves under the pressure of any usurpation "of mastery" (1.17: addition in 1595), of any usurpation of the "authority to judge" (1.23). For him as for Hurault the consequence of such usurpation is concretely visible on all sides: "the unity and contexture of this monarchy, this great structure, having been dislocated and dissolved" (ibid.: addition in 1588).

The doctrine of sovereignty as it is found in the *Six Books of the Republic* (1576) of Jean Bodin does not differ fundamentally from this type of argument. It lies at the base of every response given to the question posed most clearly by La Boetie regarding what he calls "la servitude volontaire": How can one explain the fact that millions of people obey one? This question was asked both by the Huguenots following the Saint Bartholomew Massacre and by the League following the death of Henry III (as we have seen Montaigne lament: 2.12) as a way of justifying sedition. The final response of a Hobbes would be the same as Montaigne's: to give free rein to "private fantasy" already assumes that the state does not exist, that there is no legitimate order and hence no society, since, as Hobbes says in his *Behemoth*, the latter depends upon the former. For the one as for the other the response would thus be to place the accent on the *volontaire*, rather than the *servitude*. Thus sovereignty lies for Hobbes (though not for Montaigne, since for him voluntary obedience has nothing to do with people's "rights" but instead with their "duties") not in the prince as an individual but in the state as a collective enterprise *represented by* princely authority. It will be Locke, soon after in his *Treatise of Civil Government* (1689), who will confirm the idea that sovereignty belongs to the state, whatever forms of representation it may now take (thereby giving the necessary theoretical support to the effects of the 1688 revolution).

At the time of the close of the religious wars, we are still very far from any such solution, even if we are at the center of the debates that will lead to it. Moreover, Hurault seems to perceive such a solution, though he disputes it and considers it impossible:

> This is not all, for even when the capital cities of the provinces have chased out the King, killed all the nobles, conquered each their own province and bailiwick, they will still have to form some sort of government afterwards and some judiciary link will have to be found to hold them together.

> ["Ce n'est pas tout, car quand bien les villes capitales des Provinces auroient chassé le Roy, auroient tué tous les nobles, conquis chacune son ressort & son bailliage, il faut encores qu'entre elles, apres elles prenent quelque forme de gouuernement & qu'il se trouue vn lien de justice qui les tienne ensemble."]

This idea of a "judiciary link" [*lien de justice*] is interesting indeed, for what can such a "link" be if it is not a contract? Equally interesting is the fact that Hurault describes it as an abstraction. Indeed, he does not say "they will have to find" (the construction one would expect considering what precedes it), but "will have to be found." The phrase *qu'il se trouve* implies that the link will, so to speak, find itself. The formula suggests that in Hurault's eyes the question is not one of a concrete alliance or of a person but of an abstract doctrine that would permit the return of an ordered civil structure. Equally "Hobbesian" is his idea that the lack of such a link leads necessarily to evil, since malice is the chief characteristic of natural man en masse: "I do not believe that they could ever agree on anything except doing evil; for good action is not to be found amid such confusion." And he adds that "the nature of man is malicious [*meschant*]." Confusion, disorder, malice, and finally death ("you won't last long this way") will of necessity follow the destruction of the "ruling lord's" sovereignty. I cannot but recall Hobbes's famous phrase from the beginning of *Leviathan* (1651), according to which in the state of nature "the life of man is solitary, poore, nasty, brutish, and short."

This is why, according to Hobbes, voluntary surrender of the individual's power to a central authority is absolutely essential. Hurault says nothing else. According to Hobbes the absolutely fundamental natural right is the protection and conservation of one's own life. It follows, for a rational being, that the fundamental natural law is the law of peace (*Leviathan*, 1.14). For Hobbes the "natural" consequence of this is the contract that founds civil society and which emerges from a rational accord among individuals possessed each of the same free will and, at least until the moment they relinquish it freely and willingly, of their own complete power. For Hurault exactly the same condition depends upon an act of the king and the subject's recognition of the advantage of obedience: this is the difference I noted earlier between a will linked to right and one linked to duty. Hurault transforms a call to peace directed at all combatants in the present wars of religion into an affirmation of the king's sovereignty within his state. Let the king think of peace, he says,

> for perhaps this is one of the great secrets of his state. Peace offers the advantage that subjects necessarily bring their will and assent into obedience of the Prince, otherwise there would be no peace. War and force cannot achieve this end. For true obedience relies upon free will and not force. When a king commands peoples who are voluntarily obedient, he possesses in himself alone the force of his scepter and needs no one else but himself.

He underscores the fact that the king will hence have no need of the many kinds of officers, captains, princes, nobles, and so on to whom he would then owe the maintenance of his crown, and he will thus provide no element that could lead to the present confusion, the cause of the loss of sovereignty and of chaos. On his subjects' part, will corresponds to duty, and this duty appears as the mark of a fixed position within a social hierarchy. Such difference in rank in no way affects the equality of the subjects with regard to royal sovereignty, provided only that the sovereignty be absolute. This notion of mutual dependence and utility seems to contain something "proto-contractual" (in the Hobbesian sense of the contract, a sense having little to do with the Huguenot contractual theory, which implies a kind of constitutive accord between two separate entities, people and prince, ratified by their mutual relationship to God).

For both Hurault and Montaigne it is duty that cements this mutual relationship of utility and dependence. When he speaks of the teacher's need to train his pupil for his social obligations, Montaigne affirms: "If his tutor is of my disposition, he will form his will to be a very loyal, very affectionate, and very courageous servant of his prince; but he will cool in him any desire to attach himself to that prince otherwise than by a sense of public duty" (1.26). This idea is no mere theoretical abstraction. It answers a real need for mediation between extremes, between the Huguenot party of Henry of Navarre and the League, between Protestantism and Catholicism (an opposition treated increasingly by commentators of the period as a hypocritical pretext), between the old high feudal nobility and the new high (often ennobled) bourgeoisie, between a desire to maintain a fragmentation of centers of power—be they Protestant cities or the great old fiefs—and an ever stronger tendency toward the centralization of power and the consolidation of the state into a nation. The perfect symbol of this last tendency will be the transformation of Henry of Navarre into Henry IV, his conversion for political reasons from Protestant to Catholic (which corresponds perfectly to Montaigne's oft-repeated idea that public duty requires the suppression of "private fantasy"), his passage from the Béarn and Pau, his native city, to the Ile de France and Paris, capital of the country.

The theoretical notion of duty finds its practical counterpart in that group of thinkers, statesmen, highly placed functionaries, and lawyers known as the *Politiques*. They functioned in fact not only as mediators between opposing parties but also between old and new conceptions of the state. The case of the man I have just cited at such length is in many ways exemplary. Michel Hurault de l'Hôpital was grandson of the chancellor of France. Both men must have been well known to Montaigne. As regards his relationship to the great chancellor (himself a friend of La Boetie long before Montaigne), we have the essayist's own testimony, as well as others'. As for the grandson, circumstances are sufficient indication: he had been chancellor to Henry of Navarre. Among other tasks, he had undertaken missions to Holland and Germany on his behalf. His duties were such that he was obviously suspected of Calvinism, though no one could discover exactly which religion he followed. We know that Montaigne, on missions for Henry, had to undergo the same kind of annoyances. When Henry became King of France, Hurault was named governor of Guillebeuf. He died in 1592. Montaigne's relations with Henry of Navarre, his court, his diplomacy, and his political interventions are today well known (even if not in every detail), so we should not be surprised if there are profound coincidences between his thought and Hurault's.

This situation is not simply of anecdotal interest. What is at issue are discussions and struggles that led directly to the modern concept of the liberal state. In this light we may look at the specific case that we have seen both Hurault and (though less explicitly) Montaigne consider: that of the Duke of Mayenne. Mayenne was the second son of François of Lorraine, Duke of Guise and brother of Henry of Guise. Following the assassination of his brother in 1588 (on order of Henry III), Mayenne sparked a revolt in Burgundy and Champagne, then entered Paris on February 15, 1589. Once in the capital he organized a local government, called the *Conseil general d'union*—the very pattern for the disintegration of sovereignty deplored by Montaigne and Hurault. Throughout this entire period, or at least for the duration of the Estates of Blois in 1588, which ended with the assassination of Mayenne's brother, Montaigne was present—along with Etienne Pasquier, who mentions him in this context. (*Les Lettres d'Estienne Pasqvier Conseiller & Advocat general du Roy a Paris. Contenans plusieurs belles matieres & discours sur les affaires d'Estat de France, & touchant les guerres ciuiles,*

2 vols. "We were, [Montaigne] and I, familiars and friends, thanks to a meeting of minds and a common culture. We were together in the city of Blois at the time of that famous assembly of the Three Estates in 1588, whose end brought about so many of France's misfortunes.")

To show these personal connections is important, for one may describe all these personages—Pasquier, Hurault, Montaigne, Henry IV himself—with the words Horkheimer uses in speaking of Bodin:

> The tendency to remain neutral in religious questions, and to subordinate religion to reasons of state, the recourse to a strong state which would be the guarantor of the security of commerce and exchange, corresponds to the conditions of existence of the *parvenue* bourgeoisie and its alliance with absolute monarchy.
>
>   ("Montaigne et la fonction du scepticisme," in
>   *Théorie critique: Essais*)

The question is thus first of all one of stability and certitude. When Le Roy speaks of sedition, of the dispersal of sovereignty and of the confusion of language, he cites at length the passage from Thucydides in which the historian comments upon the false use of language as both symptom and cause of the social upheaval of the civil wars. For Le Roy, the sovereignty of the principal subject, the king himself, is on the one hand set against the disintegration of sovereignty among the nobles and in the city councils, but it is also opposed on the other to the uncertainty of a language that false usage is destroying—along with the social fabric.

I spoke earlier of a cliché, and indeed the idea of a rapport between language and the social realm is very widespread. Le Roy's own work enjoyed an international renown. Already in the 1580s the Englishman Gabriel Harvey stated that it would be difficult to find a scholar who was not reading "Le Roy on Aristotle or the *Six Books* of Bodin" (Quentin Skinner, *The Foundations of Modern Political Thought*). But the relationship in question goes way back. In texts from the close of the sixteenth century one finds quotations, not only from Thucydides, but also from, among others, Plato, Aristotle, and Xenophon. Let me take up another instance in which Thucydides is quoted, because it is relatively short and especially because it appeared the year before the edition of the *Essays* containing the first appearance of both the reference to Thucydides and the famous passage that I cited toward the outset of this essay comparing the multiplicity of linguistic interpretations with "the Hydra's head." I am referring to the *Discours politiques et militaires* of François de la Noüe (1587):

> The wise historian Thucydides describes summarily how the Greeks governed themselves during civil discord. . . . As soon as an insolent remark was made somewhere, he says, everyone else found the nerve to say something worse, either in order to do something new or to show that they were more assiduous than

the others, or more insolent and eager to avenge themselves: and all the evils which they committed they disguised with praise-worthy titles, calling temerity magnanimity; modesty pusilla-nimity; precipitate indignation virility and boldness; consultation and prudent deliberation pale tergiversation. In this way, whoever showed himself always furious was reputed a loyal friend; and whoever contradicted him was held suspect. . . . Today I ask if in similar actions we have not equalled the Greeks?

La Noüe was obviously a considerable personage; he was a famous soldier (known as "Iron Arm" [*Bras de fer*]) and one of the chief lieutenants of Gaspard de Coligny. Still, he deserves a place alongside the other "me-diators." Although he was one of the leaders of the Huguenots, it was to him that Charles IX turned in order to attempt a reconciliation with his party after the Saint Bartholomew Massacre. Thus, like Montaigne or Hu-rault, he was perceived at least potentially as a mediator, as a participant in the launching of a different kind of future. And like them he understood the confusion of language, of social relations, and of political life as one and the same problem.

The same can be said of the Duke of Alençon (Henry III's brother, the fourth son of Henry II), who, complaining of foreign (i.e., Italian) influence at court, allied himself with the Protestant forces at Dreux on September 15, 1575. He, too, could thus be presented as a mediator, one to whom Innocent Gentillet can address his "Souhait pour la France" at the end of his *Anti-Machiavel* of 1576: "That he will extinguish the fires of our civil wars in the countryside and the cities: And like a French Hercules cut off the heads of this monster who still today shows itself sworn enemy to our laws." Twenty years earlier in his *Arraisonnement* of 1569, François de Belle-forest had called these confusions "the tortuous hydra of rebellions." In his text of 1593, Hurault would apply this same metaphor very precisely to the League:

> It is thus that we must consider generally the Party of the League today, this monster having been formed of many members which, for having been ill-proportioned from the outset, have rendered it so terrifying that it is no wonder if it has been seen to have several heads, like a serpent engendered out of the earth's putrescence.

We have seen this same idea expressed by Shakespeare in my epigraph taken from 2 *Henry IV*, especially if we recall that the archbishop's com-mentary (concerned with a rebellion, though of course he pretends other-wise) precedes a whole series of deceptions, traps, and even an apparent betrayal: that of John of Lancaster toward the rebels and that of Hal toward Falstaff and then his father, Henry IV, when he "removes" his crown.

The metaphor is thus applied at once to the disintegration of the political and linguistic orders. Pasquier applies it to a situation of most specific interest to us because it concerns the actual case of the Guises of which I spoke before: it again links Montaigne and himself, Guise and Mayenne, the real situation of France to this metaphor concerning state and language and thus to a particular political-theoretical movement. In a letter written to "Monsieur Airault Lieutenant Criminel d'Angers," Pasquier speaks of the assassination of the Duke of Guise and of his uncle the Cardinal during the meeting of the Estates-General at Blois. This is how he explains the situation:

> You should know that the King was enraged by several matters which occurred to his disadvantage during our assembly, and which he thought were only due to the direction of these two Princes. He felt that the more flexible he showed himself toward our members, the more intractable they became toward him (such that it was truly a Hydra, one of whose heads cut off gave birth to seven others; so much so that three or four days before Monsieur de Guise had quarrelled with him both about his status as Lieutenant General and about the town of Orleans [which was *ligueur*]). He thus decided [*il se delibere*] to have the two Princes done to death, considering that their death would also be that of all these new Councils.

The comparison is here of enormous significance, not simply because of the complexity of the elements mentioned before and which it composes together, but because it links in detail the birth of political factionalism with the birth of too many words (*nouueaux Conseils, une dispute, il se delibere,* and so forth): not to mention that the Estates of November and December 1588 were themselves a matter of discussions. The use of the hydra metaphor thus coincides with the use made everywhere of the passage from Thucydides: subject, sovereignty, power, language, right, law, war, and peace are thus all so many concepts concealed within these texts of Montaigne. And he is a link of prime importance in the discussions that eventually lead to the solution of certain of these issues. In Montaigne's eyes one cannot separate language from reason, and both share in the inconstancy proper to all human things: " 'We reason rashly and inconsiderately,' says Timaeus in Plato, 'because, like ourselves, our reason has in it a very large element of chance' " (1.47). Montaigne says in fact that human reason, "ridiculous" and "risible" as it is, cannot guarantee language, on which the sociopolitical order nonetheless depends. But neither is the opposite the case, for language too takes part in this constant movement. Only *the law* (itself, however, prey to a multiplicity of interpretations) can resist: "The commonwealths that kept themselves regulated and well governed, like the Cretan and the Lacedaemonian, made little account of orators" (1.51).

In opposition to the law, speech (the use made of language) serves to "manipulate and agitate a crowd and a disorderly populace"; it serves to persuade "the herd" and "the ignorant" in a state where "things were in perpetual turmoil." In such a case, speech *can* offer itself as "a medicine," though a very dangerous one, for it appeals precisely to the constant oscillation of the private being and not to the loyalty of the public one. Either it sets off anarchy (Mayenne in Paris, for example) or it is of use only where anarchy already reigns, for instance in Rome at the time of the civil wars, "when affairs were in the worst state and agitated by the storm of civil wars" (1.51). So we come back again to the commonplace of Thucydides. Thus Montaigne affirms that the best way to obstruct these pernicious developments is to secure the power of one man: "it is easier to safeguard him, by good education and advice, from the effects of that poison" (ibid.). This power "of a monarch" will in turn guarantee the "good government" of the state.

The law and the order of the state thus rest on the king's unique sovereignty, itself "situated" in his mystical body, whose guarantor is God himself and God's reason. The latter's stability stands in direct opposition to human reason: "Now our human reasons and arguments are as it were the heavy and barren matter; the grace of God is their form; it is that which gives them shape and value" (2.12). The plenitude of divine reason stands in opposition to "the inanity, the vanity and nothingness of man" (ibid.). "Divine majesty" stands as the only true reason over against the nothingness and instability of human reason: "It is to this alone that knowledge and wisdom belong; it alone that can have some self-esteem, and from which we steal what we account and prize ourselves for" (ibid.).

We should not believe that we are dealing here with scepticism pure and simple. On the contrary, we are faced with a complex schema of the human situation in the natural, social, and divine orders. On one side stands weak human reason, largely useless except in that it allows reasoning individuals to come to an awareness of their own universal weakness; on the other side—but not infinitely removed—stand God and his reason. Between the two lies the space occupied by the society of the organized state, which is best guaranteed by a king who partakes to a certain degree of both divine permanence and reason (the doctrine of the mystical body) and the domain of the human (the real body). The king's participation in both of these realms assures the functioning of the law: the divine secures the role of duty, the human leaves a space for "will." What is lacking in this schema for the moment is the placing of the ordinary person, characterized by inconstancy and incertitude. This question can be answered by means of a discussion of the subject, the notion of a "self."

We are all familiar—too familiar—with Montaigne's statement, quoted at the outset, according to which "each man bears the entire form of man's estate." But considerable difficulties arise when we seek to understand it, and even more appear when we try to extricate *the* sense of it. Three and a half centuries of a certain mode of thought have led us to believe that, essentially at least, the human being is everywhere and always the same. And we have a strong tendency to place this sameness and its essence at the level of a subjectivity that, even if it cannot always be located, is always solidly grounded. Such is the case even if we believe that ontologically it is unseizable in "itself" (the case of the Sartre of *Being and Nothingness*, for example) and psychologically unable to be held onto (by Freudian psycho-analysis). The existence of this subjectivity, as such, nonetheless presents itself in the form of a clear and distinct concept. It is human being in itself, given as the origin of all human activity, of whatever kind. And all other activity always appears as posterior to it.

It is true that Marxism thought it had escaped from such a concept of subjectivity. Yet perhaps the most considerable crisis of Marxist theory (at least in the West) has come precisely from the perception of a renewed need to make room for such a concept—while comprehension of it has not yet found a way to move beyond Hegel. This is to say that our concept of the subject still remains in a line stemming directly from Cartesianism. And if I am compelled to mention the name of Descartes here it is just because he marks the moment at which Western philosophy took on a certain inflection. Now Montaigne may indeed be one of the precursors of this inflection, but he has not yet reached it; and one must beware before launching into anachronism. Let me say right away, and with a certain abruptness, that this Cartesian idea of the subject is not to be found in Montaigne.

The context of the affirmation of this "entire being" (*estre universel* 3.2), of this "entire form," which Montaigne could easily "dislike" (as he says himself, ibid.), seems to leave no doubt regarding its signification—though the English translation, changing the terms, loses it entirely. The essential characteristics of this universal condition of the "human" are indeed the "perennial movement," this "stability itself" which is "nothing but a more languid motion." Montaigne could never paint this universal "being," because in itself it exists nowhere; he can only paint the "passage." He insists that "we go hand in hand and at the same pace, my book and I" (3.2); the phrase was added for the 1595 edition, as was this other one: "I have no more made my book than my book has made me—a book consubstantial with its author" (2.18). All of this is old hat. Still, one can only conclude from it that the "universal being" is universal by virtue of its movement and inconstancy. The universal character of the world, of "all things," is indeed this constant instability. The universal being is universal because it conforms to this universal character of the world. The movement of being, the passage that is thus painted by Montaigne, is the essential form of the human: whence also follows, precisely, the fact that one can "tie up all moral philosophy with a common and private life just as well as with a life of richer stuff" (3.2).

The sentence, then, that "each man bears the entire form of man's estate," so often used as proof of Montaigne's discovery of the modern concept of subjectivity (that of the willful and self-possessive subject, doubt-less, but above all of a self that is always and everywhere the same and constant in itself) is entirely caught up in contradiction in the very passage where Montaigne introduces it. To be sure, something like a "confirmation" of this concept of the self seems to present itself a little later: "There is no one who, if he listens to himself, does not discover in himself a pattern all his own [une forme sienne], a ruling pattern [une forme maistresse], which struggles against education and against the tempest of the passions that oppose it" (3.2). A ruling pattern, therefore, a deep self that struggles not simply against customary forms and those imposed by education—against the social—but even against all those irrational passions stemming from the very humanity of the individual of which this subjectivity would com-pose the "still, quiet center of being." To the modern mind this seems quite admirable: here we are before an almost Cartesian subject.

Yet here we are again in complete contradiction, for the very next paragraph insists on "corruption and filth," on disease, guilt, sin, vice, and ugliness, the constant companions of humankind (2.2), that is to say on the fact that humans in their social relations never escape the rule of pas-sions nor everything vicious in their social relations. In practice, therefore, the "ruling pattern" remains quite hidden, fitfully glimmering perhaps as a kind of hope—what we might nowadays call a *desire*, but a permanent and forever unsatisfied desire. Far from some innate structure of mind, this would be a sign of the *absence* of such a subject rather than one of its presence. In Montaigne's text itself its idea is explored only through con-tradiction and opposition.

I am tempted indeed to suggest that in the *Essays*, the "subject" is glimpsed only by these signs of its *absence*. In Descartes the subject is *there* by the certainty of its *presence*. When Montaigne affirms that even "con-science" itself is "born of custom" (1.23), he removes from the subject (before the fact, of course) one of the elements central to its modern concept: the moral sentiment that, for subsequent thought, will be one of the fun-damental marks of the human, central to the thinking of Montesquieu and Rousseau as it will be to that of Adam Smith and Kant. One can even wonder whether it is questioned at all by Freud, since the moral sense is then lodged in the superego as the presence of a socialization fully assumed in and by the psyche, and such an assumption presupposes the psyche's identity, its presence to itself.

Two types of movement govern both "the earth, the rocks of the Cau-casus, the pyramids of Egypt" and the human being: they move "both with the common motion and with their own" (3.2). The sentence is ob-scure: from external and internal motion? From the social motion and the universal motion that is characteristic of all things? For my present concern, there is no difference between the two interpretations. As far as human beings are concerned, the exterior *is* the social, and the interior *is* the pri-vate—and thereby the universal. The private *is* movement, thought in process that is not yet reason since it is by definition disordered. The freedom of the individual resides in keeping a space for the private while at the same time lending oneself to the social order, to the requirements of the law—which moreover is the condition *sine qua non* for maintaining this private freedom. One must learn not to mix the two, and what Montaigne says about inheritances in this respect can be applied generally as well: "it is abusing this liberty unreasonably to make it serve our frivolous and private fancies." One must instead follow "the common and legitimate arrangement" (2.8). Thus do we avoid "the natural instability of our conduct and opinions" (2.1).

On this question Montaigne does not hesitate: on the social level the private (and universal) subject has no function; nor does the language that accompanies such a "subject":

I have the same opinion about these political arguments: whatever part they give you to play, you have as good a chance as your opponent, provided you do not bump up against principles that are too plain and obvious. And therefore, to my mind, in public affairs there is no course so bad, provided it is old and stable, that it is not better than change and commotion.

He says this in spite of the present corruption:

The worst thing I find in our state is instability, and the fact that our laws cannot, any more than our clothes, take any settled form. [Because of the (false) freedom granted to the private] It is very easy to accuse a government of imperfection, for all mortal things are full of it. It is very easy to engender in a people contempt for their ancient observances; never did a man undertake that without succeeding. But as for establishing a better state in place of the one they have ruined, many of those who have attempted it have achieved nothing for their pains.

(2.17)

The sole means whereby things become a bit more stable (or continue so, if one has the good luck to be in some stable state) is custom, *la police*, and the recognition that in the realm of public affairs "frivolous and private fancy" must be replaced by a public subjectivity: "I give my prudence small share in my conduct; I readily let myself be led by the general way of the world" [*l'ordre public du monde*] (ibid.). It is only the authority of political power—and its acceptance by everyone—only the state in the power of a single individual which can guarantee a certain constancy: this is what law is. It does not concern the private subject, which is characterized only by "inconstancy" and about which law can do nothing, but a public subject, which secures itself through appurtenance to an order of custom.

This law of state assumes then the acceptance by the subject, as sociopolitical function, of a certain order—both out of a ("voluntary") duty and out of interest. This law will guarantee not only the material well-being of the subject in question, but also its ordered use of reason, which without law is mere directionless wandering unable to help anyone except "by accident" (2.6). This is doubtless why Montaigne insists upon the movement of the *Essays* and upon the fact that they do not concern his public being: "It is not my deeds that I write down; it is myself, it is my essence" (ibid.). He may indeed set himself forth as an example of the universal being, but social and political being depend upon an order of custom which is visible (at least in principle) to all.

Thus, like the entire group of the *Politiques* (they were never exactly a party), Montaigne affirms that obedience to accepted custom, to law, and to familiar authority is essential: "In this controversy on whose account France is at present agitated by civil wars, the best and soundest side is undoubtedly that which maintains both the old religion and the old government of the country" (2.19). For him what dominates is the concept of a local, particular society. The notion of a society that would correspond to some concept of universal justice is impossible: the universal is either human inconstancy or a divine constancy to which the human has no access: "Justice in itself, natural and universal, is regulated otherwise and more nobly than that other, special, national justice, constrained to the need of our governments" (3.1). A utopia founded upon this universal justice remains forever unobtainable, and any attempt to reach it will lead only to anarchy; and even tyranny is preferable to anarchy. The worst of evils is not the failure to attain "universal" justice—that in any case belongs to God; it is disorder. And yet natural human reason is only a disordered drift of no possible use to the social domain (even though the "grace of God" could give it a "form" directing it toward his universality)—whence the "Machiavellianism" of Montaigne, which leads him to affirm, for example, that under certain conditions the prince may find himself obliged to give up "his [private, and thus universal] reason to a more universal and powerful reason [here, that of the state]" (3.1).

The comparative "more" here signals clearly the three following steps: (1) universal nature, private subject, inconstant reason; (2) society ordered and customary, public subject, reason of state, king sovereign by virtue of his "human body"; (3) God, divine reason, king sovereign by virtue of his "mystical body." The private subject is related to the second step by will; the public subject is related to the third by duty, with the king functioning as mediator. The order of law is obviously essential in this schema: "It is neither handsome nor honorable . . . to keep oneself wavering and half-and-half, to keep one's allegiance motionless and without inclination in one's country's troubles and in civil dissension" (3.1). The individual has a social obligation to maintain this order. For a certain period this type of relationship will remain central to the concept of divine right and to the (official) theory regarding the relationship between the social realm and the individual, the king and the divinity. The royalist poet Abraham Cowley will articulate this notion clearly in 1639, after the Pacification of Berwick and the consequent peace between England and Scotland, in a poem to Charles I: "Welcome, great Sir, with all the joy that's due/To the return of *Peace* and *You,*/Two greatest *Blessings* which this age can know:/For *that* to *Thee,* for *Thee* to Heav'n we ow."

So the state, coherence, law, and ordered reason form a whole. The corruption of reason, visible for example in the "false" use of language, leads to the ruin of the state—in fact it signals it. Since mutual understanding is brought about solely by way of words, whoever breaks a promise betrays human society. Speech is the only instrument by means of which our wills and thoughts communicate; it is the interpreter of our soul. If it fails us, we have no more hold on each other, no more knowledge of each other. If it deceives us, it breaks up all our relations and dissolves all the bonds of our society (2.18). A good linguistic order guarantees a reasonable subject, and this subject is thus inseparable from the sociohistorical situation; whence derives Montaigne's insistence upon participation in government and in "public society," as he says that "our very life—we must lend and abandon to its [public society's] service and to the common opinions" (1.23). To accept "treachery, lewdness, avarice, and every sort of inhumanity and cruelty" (3.6) as the French did during the wars of religion and as the natives of America were forced to do by European conquerors is to accept a condition counter to ordered reason since it goes hand in hand with the acceptance of anarchy and the destruction of discourse.

Thus the social subject itself becomes guarantor of a well-ordered society and historical process to the precise extent that it denies its own "universality." This subject is in no way Cartesian; it could never remove itself from the here and now, either politically, socially, or temporally. Reason and social equity conform strictly to each other—so says a remonstrance addressed to Henry III in 1593 which Montaigne and the *jurats* of Bordeaux all signed. In Montaigne there is no concept of anything like a "self" that can grow into self-realization. There are two subjects: one is nothing more than an inconstant passage; the other is reasonable and is defined only by its insertion into the sociopolitical realm. He says this himself, in fact, in a passage added to the 1595 edition:

> These supple variations and contradictions that are seen in us have made some imagine that we have two souls, and others that two powers accompany us and drive us, each in its own way, one toward good, the other toward evil; for such sudden diversity cannot well be reconciled with a simple subject.
>
> (3.1)

If by the word "good" here we understand *order,* and by "evil" we understand *disorder*—a change authorized by the text—we come back to my own argument. For order in Montaigne is always that which conforms to what he calls the "well-governed" [*bien policé*] state, whereas evil, disorder, is always anarchy, a release of human passions and desires, always drawing us toward extremes that are necessarily vicious. On the level of the state we have seen the terms into which this opposition is translated. As Shakespeare's Henry V says with reference to precisely such a political context: "Every subject's duty is the King's, but every subject's soul is his own" (*Henry V* [1598–99], 4.1).

In speaking of the normative grammars of the second half of the seventeenth century, Michel Foucault writes that "it is in the very nature of grammar to be prescriptive, not because it would like to impose the norms of language, beautiful and faithful to the rules of taste, but because it ascribes the radical possibility of speaking to the setting in order of representation" (*The Order of Things*). I have myself affirmed that the nearly "metaphysical" necessity of such grammars at that time (recalling the demand for order that one finds in all realms of knowledge) responds to a loss of order in the world—or more precisely to the loss of a certain type of order, an order owing nothing to humans and whose guarantor lay "elsewhere," as "divine will," or the "world-soul." As long as people and the world of which they are a part are subsumed into an order that transcends and contains them, human classifications can go on being diverse, multiform, and polysemic at will. The disappearance of such an order, however, imposes the need for a will to order that is properly human (*The Discourse of Modernism*).

The sixteenth century lived through the progressive loss of such an external order: and first of all there where it had been at once the most "visible" and the most closely experienced—in the social and political domains. The Machiavellian analysis of political practices and realities had driven aside any need for divine intervention, a development of which Cardinal Reginald Pole had warned Charles V as early as 1539. The French religious wars raised the same problem in the most acute of forms: a close reading of commentators of the age quickly convinces one of the influence of Machiavelli's analysis—even when the contrary is affirmed. In the domain of the *res publica*, as it was called, civil war, ever-increasing inflation, constantly expanding unemployment, the collapse of feudal bonds, and the uncertainty of mutual obligation between monarch and subject were all strikingly patent signs, lived in the very flesh, of the recognized order's dissolution.

One of the responses brought by the next century would be the hypostasis of the subject into a willful and possessive individual, with its own recognized rights, a subject that would succeed in imposing *its* order. The new knowledge would be nothing but the imposition of the individual's own power onto nature. All the forces necessary to the social disposition would be invoked by the new centralized state, eventually legitimized by the concept of the contract and of its presupposition: the cession of the power of each in favor of one who, since he represents all, will guarantee the peace and good order of the new civil society. Such a solution was unavailable to the thinkers of the sixteenth century. If, as early as 1576, Jean Bodin could elaborate the theoretical bases of an absolute sovereignty (and, as we have seen, he was followed by a whole swarm of writers), it would be a very long time before the arrival of a sociopolitical conjuncture that could respond to his formulation. In France it came with the age of Louis XIV—once he had won his victories in the Frondes—built upon terrain prepared by Richelieu. In England it would come with the brief "dictatorship" of Cromwell in the mid-1650s and then the short reign of James II leading up to his expulsion in 1688. These, however, are only the extreme forms of a model built upon a concept of the subject as fixed, as the originator of all action, of all knowledge, of all power, and so on.

Without the constitution of such a fixed subject, disorder could not be eliminated in this way: "I paint the passing"; "stability itself is nothing but a more languid motion" (and so many other famous lines from Montaigne). A private subject (such as that of seventeenth-century individualism will be, but then in a quite different manner) could never fix itself, could never take a position once and for all—let alone impose itself. Thus Montaigne offers a particular response to the question of his friend La Boetie: Why do millions of people allow themselves to be crushed by the power of a single man, when one only need do nothing to bring such power tumbling down? Even such an abstention, Montaigne implies, would suppose that these ("voluntary," La Boetie would say) slaves, these "serfs" could fix themselves as subjects. If they could act in such a way, then they would no longer be the subjects of a prince, but rather his equal—a status already at least implicit in Machiavelli. But for Montaigne, as we have seen, the political subject receives its being from its relationship to a sovereignty incarnate in the person of the prince. This subject of the state may in some sense "keep," free and "for itself," the inconstant and constantly mutable subject, but as a constant subject one has a duty toward society and the common good. In the private realm the "individual" *is not properly speaking a subject*, nothing but this constant motion. As a subject one becomes in some sense the "function" of the prince. In a letter to Henry IV, dated January 18, 1589, in which he counsels the new king on the proper comportment to exercise toward his new "subjects," Montaigne makes this idea explicit. One need only be a little attentive, he writes, for "popular inclinations go in waves; if the leaning in your favor is once established, it will gather its own momentum and go all the way." It is enough for the king to show his people "a paternal and truly royal affection."

If the private being could constitute itself as a fixed subject, it would necessarily go against the civil order—whence come the commentaries of Hurault, Le Roy, Montaigne, and many others regarding the members of the House of Lorraine and sovereign cities; whence also doubtless (at least if the tradition upholding the story is well founded) Montaigne's reputed advice to Henry of Navarre following his victory at Coutras not to follow the forces of Henry III and thus take on a rebel's status. The king need not abuse his subjects; he has only to show himself. The metaphor of the father/ son relationship that we have just seen Montaigne use is rigorous and exact: whence as well the horror of the Saint Bartholomew Massacre. In that case the king had completely perverted his relationship to the people. Until that date it had always been possible to maintain that violence was being perpetrated only by those seeking to oppose the legitimate power of the king on the grounds of religion, by the overthrow of feudal obligations, and so forth. The massacre risked bringing on total confusion and cutting away all possible points of stability. This explains why Montaigne constantly extols a "return" (which would in fact be no return at all), the recovery of the old stability, of the old union of church and state, the establishment of a royal sovereignty and a well-defined state power.

Contrary to what Richard Sayce has suggested, there is no contradiction between the concept of the subject's inconstancy and the desire for a stable political order in Montaigne (*The Essays of Montaigne: A Critical Exploration*). Nor is it simply the case, as I have just suggested, that the latter guarantees the possibility of the former. It is just as much that the lack of fixity of the private subject guarantees the stability of the state and the place of the public subject: for that becomes the *only* possible place in which something like an "individual" with a more or less secure status can situate itself. In the face of a political and social crisis, Montaigne seeks to keep from losing his footing by redeeming a certain number of elements placed at his disposal by the political theory and practice of his age which seemed pertinent to the stabilization of civil life. It becomes clear that it is an anachronism to argue (as the critical tradition continues to do) about the conservatism, the liberalism, or the radicalism of Montaigne. It makes little sense either to speak of a "democratic" Montaigne (as Donald Frame and many after him have done), and still less to speak (with Sayce and others) of a "revolutionary" Montaigne. He is resolutely of his age and can be inserted fully into a current running from Machiavelli to Locke.

Montaigne affirms the necessity of obedience to the laws and customs of a particular local society. At the same time he is convinced that what guarantees the functioning of voluntary duty and of the political subject's loyalty to the sovereign prince is the conformity of sociopolitical reason and equity. We have seen a moment of mediation in this conjuncture. In synchronic terms it is a question of opening a path between two extremes of political thought. In diachronic terms the point is to pass between two different concepts of universal order: one that would be external to the human and to which it would submit, and another that would in some sense be due to humanity. One manifestation of this latter concept at the close of the seventeenth century would be the quest for a universal grammar, conceived as conforming exactly to the structure of human reason, universal but at the same time individual and particular—Cartesian "good sense."

Now it happens that there is an intermediary theoretical step, quite widespread and typified by Montaigne, leading directly to this new concept of order. For the essayist, we have also seen, the only point of solid anchorage for the political subject lies in a constant, fixed public order. The close of the sixteenth century was in fact precisely a moment of passage when jurists and historians believed that they had found the certainty of universal reason in the political and legal order itself instead of in a divine system or in individual reason: I am referring to the movement known as "neobartolism." In a commentary on the *Anti-Tribonian* of François Hotman (1567), J. G. A. Pocock has noted that the jurist "proposes a project for legal apprenticeship in which students undertake a comparative study of all known and valued juridical systems with the aim of extracting from them the essential principals of juridical reason common to them all." We have here, he adds, "the principle known by the name of "neo-bartolism" which came to dominate French juridical thought toward the end of the [sixteenth] century, and whose fundamental principle is that of discovering the basic principles of all systems of law" (*The Ancient Constitution and the Feudal Law: A Study of English Historical Thought in the Seventeenth Century*).

We can see clearly here the conceptual resemblance between this project and the attempt that will develop three quarters of a century later to find a universal grammar capable of providing for the constants of reason and human discourses. The difference between them, however, is no less essential. The neobartolists (and Montaigne with them) envisage a sociopolitical and juridical universal. Universal grammar assumes instead *the universality of the structure of individual reason:* for Montaigne such a structure could never be found nor literally even imagined. Montaigne—and I insist upon this essential fact—considers that the sociopolitical order, the reason of state, is a "superior reason," since individual reason in the Cartesian sense does not even really exist yet. It seems to me that this is the sense of the "universal reason" in terms of which the prince sometimes finds himself obliged to act.

For Hobbes and Locke, this superior reason will become the "function" of individual reason, which could in effect be characterized according to the laws furnished by a universal grammar. And indeed, those are the very terms with which Hobbes prefaces the *Philosophical Rudiments concerning Government and Society:* "not to point which are the laws of any country, but to declare what the laws of all countries are." Such general and universal laws will then be possible because they stem from a single rationality, from a human mind whose act of creating civil society is exactly equivalent to the divine *Fiat* of the Creation in Genesis—as Hobbes will himself write in the Introduction to *Leviathan.* The double "subject" of Montaigne then easily generates a more general and even more central reading. The subject as "passage" (though, as I have indicated, we cannot really yet use the term "subject" for it) will be transformed into cognitive reason (though it is not yet such for Montaigne); it will be that reason conscious of the continuity and certainty of its own functioning—in short, the *cogito* of Descartes. The political subject will take instead the form of the Cartesian or Baconian "provisional morality," which renders possible the social being's action while keeping aside the being of "method" and of the "new reason," which is not yet in a position to oversee a change in the political or social order. For the time being such a separation doubtless seemed essential. It has been well understood by Max Horkheimer who, in a comparison of Montaigne to the Protestant thinkers of his age, notes their shared notion of the weakness of human reason: "Both of them reject reason only to the extent that it enters into opposition with what is legally established, with the existing order, they don't reject science as such."

Thus there are, so to speak, two types of thought. One represents the movement of the private realm, transported into the social domain; it is upon this base that La Boetie would have liked to situate his (utopian) society founded on what he called amicable "mutual recognition" [*entre-cognoissance*]—the very idea of which Montaigne rejects (for him, in a rather untypical anti-Ciceronian move, friendship is a *private* affair). The other represents what will become the provisional ethics of Descartes. The question for the future became that of articulating the two together. Once again, it was the theory of the contract that succeeded in doing so, making possible the combination of the two subjects into one. The thought in process of the *Discourse of Method* or of the *Meditations* would become the voluntary subject of the *Passions of the Soul,* and *this* subject would become the fixed subject able to enter into the Hobbesian (and then Lockean) contract.

The concept of universal laws in the sociopolitical and juridical domain—a necessary concept given the permanent inconstancy of private reason on the one hand and the gradual disappearance of belief in direct divine intervention into human affairs on the other—would be replaced by the conception of universal laws that govern individual reason and *produce and create* the civil society of the state. Thus reason would become *originative.* The neobartolist idea had hardly been satisfactory, since it was difficult to perceive the fundamental unity of social systems whose diversities were more striking than their similarities. Once individual reason had been raised to an originative position, the whole thing became much "easier," and after Locke the way is opened to the *Spirit of Laws,* to the exploration of diversity subject to a human thought that is structurally everywhere and always identical with itself. For Montesquieu the relationship between this thought and the sociopolitical structure would be, in an ideal system, of the most immediate kind—and thus superior to what one finds elsewhere. Within this development the complex thought of Montaigne occupies a place both representative and important.

Descartes: *Mundus Est Fabula*

Jean-Luc Nancy

"The apologue is composed of two parts, one of which may be called the body, the other the soul; the body is the fable, the soul the morality." So states La Fontaine in the preface to his *Fables*. This doctrine is unmistakably Cartesian. But it is Cartesian in a greater and far different sense than might be suspected. Descartes' soul—or to be more precise, what for the moment could be called the human soul considered in its substantial qualification of *thinking* soul—is proposed and exhibited as the morality of a fable. (The soul considered in entirety and in its relation to the body will have to be discussed in another study: "Unum Quid" in *Ego Sum*.) This does not take place for reasons of convenience, expediency or literary ornamentation, but by virtue of a fundamental necessity of the *cogito*. This fable itself is the story of Descartes's thinking life, his intellectual autobiography. And this in turn can obey no other logic than that of the invention of its own fable. The *cogito's* structure and function are governed through and through by this "fabulatory" law. This is what must be proven.

As frontispiece let us take one of the portraits of Descartes, the one made by J. B. Weenix around 1647. (Not to mention here the other portrait that is the *Discours* itself, which we described in "*Larvatus pro Deo*.") It shows René Descartes holding an open book, the left page of which is visible. Upon it is written *mundus est fabula*. In other words, according to the Latin and the modern acceptation, "the world is a play," and "the world is a fable." Certain traditions situate the origin of this maxim—at least as it concerns the comparison of the world to a theater—as far back as Pythagoras. Thus, as far back as the origin itself (of philosophy). According to this emblematic portrait, Descartes' entire doctrine lies in the

From *MLN* (French Issue) 93, no. 4 (May 1978), special issue editor, Rodolphe Gasche. © 1978 by The Johns Hopkins University Press.

reinscription of this timeless maxim. What if philosophy indeed began anew with Descartes in the reappearance of this expression, which henceforth acquires a status equal to that of science and the subject?

But this is no hypothesis. *Mundus est fabula* effectively becomes with Descartes the expression of the science of the world. And since this science is such only through that which constitutes it, first of all, as science of the subject—science that the subject possesses, and science he has of himself (science that he possesses only through and according to his self-knowledge)—the expression becomes that of the ontology of subjectivity. This is to say, of the "firm ground" that metaphysics reaches, according to Hegel, with Descartes, this firm ground upon which we are still walking, especially when we walk on the moon, upon which we continue to build our cities, our States, our factories. This is the firm ground of the subject, upon which we are founded. Today, since Descartes, the subject is the world and vice versa. The maxim must be taken to mean as well that *mundus*—he who is pure, proper—*est fabula*. The Subject, the Self's own pure self-possessing, is a fable.

This is not word play, but the same word, *mundus*, pure, clean/proper, well ordered, well arranged, world [*monde*]. According to Plutarch, this is what Pythagoras meant by the word *kosmos*: the world is a fine arrangement, orderly, pure and proper. The world is that which is not impure [*immonde*].

Thus we must prove the following: what is absolutely not impure, what is absolutely world, that which can draw upon itself in its self-possession is a fable. Or rather, is Fable itself.

We shall not limit ourselves to the way in which this term is almost always understood: "it's merely a fable." Quite possibly the painter Weenix understood the expression he painted (who chose it then? the painter? the model?) in its most banal, proverbial sense, a commonplace in Baroque thought: the world we see and in which we live is no more real than fable, the illusion of which is provided us by theater. Descartes probably agrees with this, for he too is part of the Baroque banality. He even produces the theory of the unreality of the world we know. *Le Monde* begins thus:

> Proposing to treat here of light, the first thing I would point out to you is that there may exist a difference between the feeling we have of it, that is, the idea of it formed in our imagination through the intermediary of our eyes, and what there is in objects that produces this feeling in us, that is, that which is in fire or the Sun, and takes the name of light.

The distinctive characteristic of the Cartesian enterprise will be, however, to shatter the illusion and establish the truth upon which may draw this same subject who perhaps does not know things themselves, namely, *certitude*. This has nothing at all to do with the subjectivism in relation to which "*mundus est fabula*" is commonly understood concerning Descartes. The doctrine of ideas in the *Méditations* is on the contrary the doctrine of the *resemblance* of ideas, which are "like paintings," to their originals. This resemblance is the effect less of an imitation, which would still have us in theater, than of a communication of being through an idea-producing causation.

> That an idea contain one such objective reality rather than another it doubtless owes to some cause, in which there occurs at least as much formal reality as objective reality contained by this idea.
>
> (Third *Méditation*)

(It should be recalled that Descartes specified the meaning of the words "objective" [the object's reality in my mind] and "formal" [the equivalent of "actual," thus the reality of the thing existing in itself].)

Therefore, although I cannot know everything, or know everything perfectly, "it is certain . . . that I have within me the means of knowing with certitude" everything in the world (Sixth *Méditation*).

Cartesian knowledge abolishes the subjectivism that takes the world for mere fable. In this respect the portrait painted by Weenix is a gross error.

But this knowledge causes subjectivism to turn short only because the Subject of this knowledge, the possessor of certitude, wins himself and lays himself open by presenting his own veridicle fable. This is the *Discours de la méthode*.

> My design is not to teach here the method that everyone must follow in order to direct his reason rightly, but only to show how I have attempted to direct my own. Those who take it upon themselves to furnish precepts must consider themselves to be cleverer than those to whom they furnish them; and if they fail in the smallest point, they must bear the blame. But offering this work only as a story, or if you prefer, a fable, in which are perhaps to be found, among a few examples that may be imitated, several others that it will be well not to follow, I hope that it will be useful to some without being harmful to any, and that all will be grateful to me for my frankness.

Descartes proposes his *Discours as a fable*. This is not a comparison; his text does not imitatively borrow the traits of a literary genre. But it is presented as fable, and it is precisely as fable that one must deal with it. Hence what we find here is not exactly the motif of a fiction, which, although opposed in its essence to truth, would serve as its instrument or its ornament. If fable here then is to introduce *fiction*, it will do so through a completely different procedure. It will not introduce fiction 'upon' truth or beside it, but *within* it.

From the outset the "fable" of the *Discours* exceeds the theme of fiction, perhaps even turns it completely back upon itself. Moreover, and if one may say, in truth, henceforth all that will be in question concerns the way in which a certain turning back of fiction is the operator of the truth of the subject.

This is why the fable's prefatory position in the *Discours* is related only distantly to what should be called the *literary* trappings of fiction of which Descartes avails himself in several other texts. Either, as in the *Principes*, he suggests this literary aspect to the reader by inviting him to peruse this treatise "first in its entirety as one would a novel," or he sets it up expressly as a way of staging as in the unfinished dialogue entitled *La Recherche de la vérité,* or perhaps, as in the comedy or "sylvan fable" the text of which has been lost, he wanted to write a literary work with philosophical content. In all these cases—whose frequency, moreover, cannot fail to alert us to the unexpected insistence in Descartes upon these literary techniques, which incidentally were very common at the time—what is at stake is a fable insofar as it must not be believed, the fable referred to in the twelfth of the *Regulae* to serve as a comparison to the illusions of the senses, the fable that is not a "true story," a *res gesta.*

The same motif of the fable was presented with a different function before the *Discours* in *Le Monde.* When Descartes takes up the description of the structure and elementary matter of the world such as he knows it— that is to say, when he takes up the description of the scientific truth of the world—he states (at the end of chapter 5):

> But so that you will find the length of this discourse less tedious,
> I should like to envelop a part of it with the invention of a fable,
> through which I hope that truth will be always sufficiently visible,
> and that it will be no less pleasant to behold than if I exposed it
> in all its nakedness.

According to this presentation the fable of the World is an "envelope" or cover, an embellishment intended to please. Such a statement, however, deserves to be looked into. Descartes mentions the risk that fable may hide the truth a bit too much. But beginning with the *Regulae*, the truth of Cartesian science is precisely such that it *requires* a covering (that of "common mathematics") in order to show itself. This first function, which because of its very principle cannot be reduced to the function of literary ornament, becomes even more complicated in *Le Monde.* The fable in question (or the *feint,* as it will be called later) is that of God's creating a new world. Or more precisely, what we have here *at the same time* is Descartes' invention of a world ("that I shall bring into being in imaginary space"), God's creation of a new world ("let us suppose that God creates again"), and the repetition of the creation of our world (we must go back beyond the "five or six thousand years" that mark the age of the earth). Thus we have a fiction intended to display the truth of this world through the explanation of its constitution. But this is no longer possible unless fiction enters into an intrinsic relation with explanation. And it enters into such a relation through its own invention of fiction. It is not a question of presenting the "things that are actually in the true world," but of "feigning one at random . . . that nevertheless could be created just as I will have feigned it." The fable of *Le Monde* is thus far less the instrument of an exposition than the *organ of an equivalent of creation.* In *inventing* this fable I make—I make and I feign, I "fiction," I fashion—a world. It is perhaps not that of actuality, yet it does not run counter to the laws of the actual creation. It thus can be the learned truth of this world.

The question for Descartes is not to provide a fictive yet probable equivalent of the real world; this verisimilitude could be established only through previous knowledge of the "real" world. The question is rather to provide the true invention of a world. For if the worlds of fiction and of reality are not identical, what instead is identical—yielding Descartes' very identity—is the activity of invention and creation. One does not exist in a relation of verisimilitude with the other, yet the two are the same inaugural truth. The fable's inventor is the God of a world that, while not the world itself, is nonetheless *another true world,* and this, *because it is invented.* Thus, it meets the conditions of a possible creation. (This is the foundation of the scientificity of the modern sciences, whose very functioning Descartes thinks as follows: from the invention of the fable (theory) to the institution of the experiment [the instrumental construction of the fabulous arrangement], it is always the *mise en oeuvre* of the subject, the subject who is indistinguishable from his operation as artist-technician.) The subject of true knowledge must be the inventor of his own fable.

The *Discours* radicalizes this exigency, fulfilling it to the point of ontology.

The *fable* of the *Discours* has nothing of literary ornamentation about it. It has even abandoned the fiction or the feint of being a simple ornament, like that covering the fable of *Le Monde.* It is the very pattern according to which the *Discours* is proposed. The text therefore leaves no doubt as to how we are to understand the term "fable" ("offering this work . . . as a fable in which, among a few examples that may be imitated . . ."). At stake here is the fable as moral genre, as that which teaches or imparts a "morality." What properly makes the fable here is the exemplary story.

The literary theory of the fable implied by the *Discours* is the one developed after Descartes (to what extent should one say *"because of him"*?) by classical poetics.

1. The first thing one must do in making a Fable is choose the instruction and the moral issue, which must serve as foundation in accordance with the purpose and the goal one chooses.

2. This moral truth then must be reduced to an action; a general and imitated action must be simulated from singular and authentic actions. This is the moment of the fable's invention: it must disguise the "moral issue"; the instruction must remain hidden.

3. The names one gives to characters begin to specify a Fable.

4. It must always be remembered that the epic poem is a fable, that is, not the *narrative* of the action of some hero, told to shape behavior on his example, but rather a *discourse* invented to shape behavior by the story of a simulated action carefully described, borrowing the name of an illustrious person, selected after the action attributed to him has already been outlined.

(Le Bossu, *Traité du poème épique* [1675], quoted by A. Kibédi-Varga, in "L'Invention de la fable," *Poétique*, 25 [1976]. Parenthetically, one can see the extent to which Nietzsche's *Zarathustra* will always answer this same philosophical poetics.)

Let us assume for the moment that the reader of the *Discours* can appeal to no other conception of fable than this. "Discours de la méthode" thus means in a very rigorous sense "Fable de la méthode."

At the same time, however, it is apparent how Descartes' poetics differs from literary poetics: his character is anonymous first of all, and thus his fable is not "specified." It is Fable *in genere*, a general fable, or generative of all fable and thus of all discourse.

Moreover, and inversely, the "general action" the fable will propose is not "simulated from" a "singular action": it is nothing other than the singular action of the author, who in turn is the (anonymous) character. The *Discours* is the fable of the generality of a singular and authentic action. Thus it proposes a veridical story, and in its composition the choice of a "moral issue" merges completely with "the reduction of this moral truth to action." In other words, all the compositional operations of the fable are annulled or reabsorbed in a "moment of invention," which itself is one with the simple decision to state what I have lived. What we are given to read is the discourse of truth in act, the discourse of truth's action.

What we are dealing with here is by no means a fable, and this poetics is exactly the opposite of the poem's. Why then "propose this work as a fable"? This is the question that must be answered slowly, patiently, in accordance with the order of the action of the *Discours* itself.

The commentaries concerning this proposition of Descartes' that can be made independently of the *Discours*—of the *philosophy* of the *Discours*—lead to dead ends. This is the case with most of the hitherto classic readings of Descartes when, as happens rarely enough, the attempt is made at least to single out and interpret this proposition (that is, to treat it as other than a pure and simple background ornament). (For the following we have used the monumental commentary of Etienne Gilson: René Descartes, *Discours de la méthode: texte et commentaire*.)

One might remark, for example, that the fable, an instructive narrative, is situated halfway between an ethics as such and a simple narration. But if this be the case then we are unconditionally unable to understand how this intermediary form can be suitable for the exposition of a method that presents itself as nothing other than the method of truth in the sciences.

And henceforth we are given up to a series of hypotheses that are all untenable: either we must consider the *Discours* as a preliminary stage that precedes the properly metaphysical exposition of the *Méditations* (but this conception, which proves unacceptable, moreover, once we turn to the texts, prevents us in any case from asking why this preliminary and narrative stage was able to be established, and why the definitive stage of the *Méditations* takes on in turn the traits of a narrative); or else we must conclude that this method claims to propose itself for René Descartes and for him alone (and we shall see how the *Discours* unequivocally refutes such a hypothesis); or else we must abandon the motif of a moralizing fable and return to the conception of a literary covering—a feigned story here cloaks a universal truth.

Now this hypothesis in turn troubles the classic interpretation, which finds that it must ask itself whether or not the intellectual autobiography of the *Discours* is a fiction. If the classic interpretation wishes to acknowledge the authenticity of the *cogito* (and it must acknowledge it, at the risk of opening up a discussion of its universal validity and being faced with the prospect of being able to consider the *Discours* merely as a jest), it must state that this autobiography for the most part is not fictive. This, however, in no way affects the question of its metaphysical status. Yet nothing would be gained by submitting an opposing thesis, stating (as one would probably be more than willing to do today) that the autobiography is but fiction. In both cases the motif of the fable, as it is brought into play by Descartes, becomes contradictory and even absurd.

The fable of the *Discours* cannot be treated as a literary covering, nor can it be questioned in terms of a truth-relation with an experience exterior to the *Discours* itself. The question of the fable of the *Discours*, of the Fable-Discourse, cannot be broached by distinguishing between truth and fiction. This distinction, which Descartes practices elsewhere (as does everybody, one is tempted to say, in other words to the extent that he takes it over from the entire philosophical tradition), can have only a secondary and derived status with respect to the inaugural gesture of the *Discours*. This is one of the conclusions we must draw once we have taken up the Fable by way of the only path remaining, the *Discours* itself. (Which is to say as well that one of the questions that necessarily must be asked is the following: in the course of any attempt to complicate the division between truth [or theory] and fiction, or even to identify them, however this is done [and it has been done in more than one way, from the Romantics to the present], must the question not inevitably be raised, at one point or another and whether one wants to or not, whether and to what extent such an attempt is not fundamentally derivative of Descartes?)

Why a fable? Descartes furnishes the first answer at the same time as the proposition. Although the fable is defined as exemplary story, all of such a story's examples are not necessarily worthy of imitation. This gives this fable quite a special status: either that which (the figure that) in a fable carries its morality must be called *example,* and no fable could include more than one example (more than one truth, more than the necessarily unique truth), or all the fable's figures must be called "examples." But in this latter case we must understand the possibility of several figures within the single character of this fable, and especially why it is, contrary to all other fables, that this one does not indicate in and of itself which is the *right* example.

In a fable the narrative must lead to the same point as the discourse, the "hidden instruction" must be identified with and by a character. But here everything joins to perturb this pattern: there is but one character, and he is not completely exemplary. We shall see that the remainder of the story sheds no further light on how to go about eventually dividing what is imitable from what is not.

However, the proposition of the fable also contains the instructive decision we have been expecting. Descartes says in effect, I am giving this story only as a fable for I do not give absolute "precepts," which would imply that I possess an authority superior to ordinary men. I have nothing more to communicate than the path I have followed. I do not *teach* (which invalidates the fable's function as defined by the adage *fabula docet*), I *show.* What one can show when one does not teach is oneself. There is no "hidden instruction" here; the instruction itself, the motif or the subject of instructing is as if withdrawn from the fable. Here authority, truth as authority, *withdraws itself.* It is thus that *fabula docet:* I teach above all that I am not teaching.

We must reverse anew the reversal of the poem that appeared to make up the poetics of the *Discours.* Here "discourse" is withdrawn from the "narrative." *Discourse withdraws itself* is perhaps the statement, although still enigmatic, that characterizes this Discourse.

There remains only the narrative, in which the function of exemplarity becomes unclear, undecidable. *Autobiography* is the necessary genre for whoever renounces all teaching authority (all truth that is taught from a position of authority, that in short is taught, in other words that comes from the outside to a "subject"), yet not the presentation of examples. Here at least this means whoever does not renounce presenting something that can be imitated, and consequently an *originality,* in all senses of the word. Or put more precisely, the autobiographical gesture in general—including the one that would give nothing to imitate either by excess or lack of "originality" in the common sense—cannot by definition be conceived of otherwise than as the gesture of originality.

Our difficulty lies then in bringing to light the *original* of the *Discours:* what it proposes for imitation, what distinguishes it in this respect from all other discourse, but also its writer. And the originality of this original resides most surely in the fact that in this fable the narrative becomes discourse.

The story of my life becomes discourse: the moral issue resides in that I relate quite simply and plainly the path I followed, unconcerned with separating the more recommendable from the less. This, then, is how the originality of the fable is indicated to us: it is in that for which "all will be grateful" to its author, it is in his *frankness*. The question here is not that of the distinction between good and less good examples: the *Discours* has essentially only one exemplarity, and the fable only one morality, which is frankness. It is through frankness that Descartes distinguishes himself from all those who deal in doctrines and precepts. Because he proposes no teaching of truth, his work must be taken as a fable; and that is also its whole lesson. Just as La Fontaine's "The Wolf and the Lamb," for example, is the fable of the right of the most powerful, the *Discours* is *the fable of frankness*.

As such, the *Discours* is certainly not like a fable whose instruction would be in behalf of the moral virtue of frankness. For such a fable would amount to hiding beneath some example a lesson that would establish the value of that virtue. But here, the value of frankness is obviously presupposed: it is self-evident that nothing is worthier of esteem than a frank work (which relates everything from the biography in question) and a frank writing (transposing the "free-will" [*franc-arbitre*] found elsewhere in Descartes), in other words, a discourse that in relating everything *frees itself from the fabulatory condition of doctrinal and authoritative discourses.*

The advantage—or the exemplarity—of the fable does not stem from an ethic nor does it lie in this "morality." The only discourse of truth is the discourse freed from the story plots of "those who must think themselves cleverer." The presupposition of the moral value of frankness allows for this fable's *gnoseological* "morality." The freeing of the fable constitutes all the instruction (at once hidden and evident, as we see) of the fable of frankness: the advantage is truth itself.

It is indeed this theoretical morality that shall be drawn from the autobiography that begins here ("I was nurtured on letters from my childhood on") and that shall be drawn in particular from an entire critique of *fables* and *examples*.

Fabulation and exemplarity comprise in the first part of the *Discours* the constant motif of Descartes' denunciation of the education he received in school as well as from books and in "the great book of the world." In the end Descartes will have resolved "to study within myself" and "to build upon a ground that is all my own." For in books and in the world, in the examples that they are and contain, he will have encountered essentially forms of "extravagance."

But what is extravagance? Fables furnish us with its model and structure.

> Besides that fables make us imagine several events as being possible when such is not at all the case, and that even the most faithful of stories, while perhaps neither changing nor heightening the value of things in order to make them worthier of being read,

nevertheless almost always omit the lowest and least illustrious circumstances. This is why the rest does not appear such as it is, and why those who fix their actions according to the examples they draw therefrom are likely to fall into the extravagance of the paladins of our novels, and to conceive of plans that go beyond their powers.

The extravagance of fables thus is defined quite precisely by the omission of what the fable of the *Discours* does not omit. The *Discours* recounts everything: the fable of frankness is a frank fable. It is more faithful than the "most faithful of stories"; it is veridical.

Hence this fable is not only the opposite of fables, it is also their perfection, if indeed it is the *fable of fidelity* in the sense that its narrative (or its feint) is absolutely and rigorously faithful to its discourse (to its veracity, which because of this *is* veracity). It is that towards which all fables tend, yet are unable to reach. (Why? This is what Descartes does not say. Because of their very principle this is what is lacking in all fables but one—this Discourse.) This fable is the original of all fables, to which every fable should conform. It is the fabulous example of the veritable fable, the true fable.

Thus it must be understood that these "paladins of our novels" are bad examples not because of an excess but a lack. They are not true enough, that is, they do not succeed in showing *everything*. And showing everything, hiding nothing, is an enterprise that surpasses these paladins' prowess, or rather the prowess their authors attribute to them. But no paladin will ever be able to show everything if he is not the author himself. He who says "I" here is the paladin of an infinitely more modest and infinitely more illustrious adventure: the fabulous truth of him who recounts himself. But clearly not in the name of the empirical singularity of one life among others (the modern value of *sincerity* will never be more than a psychological and literary by-product of the ontology articulated here), for in this case the narrative would not be a discourse, in other words a fable. We confront the unique, exceptional case where *there is discourse only when there is nothing more than the narrative.*

This is why what is at stake here can be only the life—by its own principle exemplary—of him who is through himself *the* truth, not that of him who exposes *his* truth; nor is it the life of him who would be the truth so as to be "cleverer than the others." What is at stake here is the life of him who is truth insofar as he is frankly himself. Doubtless this implies eventually that what is involved here is truth insofar as it is for itself the story (the veridical narrative) of its life, of its own *res gesta*. The Discourse is truth's deed, the Absolute Novel (*absolute* meaning, above all, freed and absolved of all fabulation).

It follows inevitably that if the paladins are not fit to be imitated, Descartes' example is *inimitable* (which puts an end to the obscuring—or the elucidating—of the distinction between those examples that can and cannot be recommended in the *Discours*).

If I am rather pleased with my work and show you its model here, it is not because I wish to advise anyone to imitate it. Those upon whom God's bounty has been more generously given will perhaps have higher designs. Yet I do fear that for many the present work is already too bold. The single resolution to rid oneself of all opinions one has previously come to believe is not an example that each must follow. The world is composed roughly of two kinds of minds to which it is not at all suited.

(The "two sorts of minds," explains the rest of the passage, are those who precipitate their judgments, and those who follow others' opinions. In other words those who have not recognized Method. As we read, the world is "roughly composed" of them. Only I remain.)

The model is withdrawn—it withdraws to its original. What I show you does not constitute a *model*. It if did, it would have to be a narrative feigned so as to make my discourse understood. But what I show you is my discourse itself, in the pure identity of its narrative.

Mundus, the pure, the all-to-itself, the in-itself-well-ordered—*ego*—*est fabula*: I am fabulous, and can even less than any paladin become an example.

The reason for this is not that my example is even more extravagant. Or rather, it functions according to the logic of the passage to the limit, which is constantly at work here. What is fabulously inimitable is ridding oneself of all fables and all examples, and maintaining *oneself* in this divestment—set up as a model that can no longer constitute an example *since in order to imitate it one first of all can no longer come to believe it*. Discourse can neither teach itself nor believe itself. Its own communication passes to the limit.

In the *Discours* narrative, discourse and fable all pass together to the limit, in their own limit. They are accomplished through their withdrawal. The passage to the limit of extravagance no longer extravagates, it no longer goes beyond the fable's *subject*. The passage to the limit of example cannot be imitated, for it is the original, an original that each person can (perhaps) produce, but that no one can reproduce. Such then is the *cogito*, in other words (finally) the content of this story.

The *cogito* resists extravagance:

And observing that this truth, *I think therefore I am*, was so fast and assured that even the skeptics' most extravagant suppositions could not shake it, I judged that I could accept it without hesitation as the first principle of the philosophy I sought.

What we are dealing with is not a chance encounter of words, nor a distant analogy between the *cogito* and the fable. Consistent with all that came before, the *cogito* (which is the fable's "instruction" and "activity," its instructive action and its active instruction) has exactly the same structure as the fable that shows it.

The *cogito's* demonstrative procedure—which instead might be called *monstrative*, for we know Descartes will later explain that there exists therein no "science well-considered or acquired by demonstration"—is familiar enough that we can call upon it without awaiting the final point: if the *cogito* is unshakable, it is because it forms the point where I can no longer feign, *the point of an impossible feint or fiction*, or rather, the point of the feint's passage to its limit. ("Responses to the Sixth Objections." Such a science could and should be able to be *taught*, as is not the case with the Method.)

Initially we can recognize, at least formally, the very position of the Fable-Discourse: the extreme point, exceeding any novel or treatise, where "it" withdraws itself in truth.

This correspondence is not a formal one however: only the *content* of the *cogito* is to be this point. It is not *at* the extremity of the feint, as if it were its absolute exteriority of truth, rather it *is* this extremity *itself*. The height of feint—or of fiction, for they are the same word and have the same function, that of the Fable beginning with *Le Monde*—is that *I am feigning*.

Descartes does not write, "I am feigning." Not really. He immediately substitutes, or has already-always sustituted "I think." But this *thought* is rigorously nothing other than *feint*: "I was mindful that while I wished to think that all was false, I who thought this necessarily had to be something." What is *being* here, or this *something*? It is of course the subject of the fiction, the sub-stance that supports and engenders it. To feign one must think, and to think one must be. That however cannot be proven. It cannot be proven because truly what is involved is neither a logical consecution nor an ontological subordination. Or rather, what can be exhibited only in the form of a logical implication ("necessarily had to be") is given actually through an immediate apprehension requiring no operation of thought. Being as thought is given not through a thought but through

> that force of interior knowledge that always precedes what is ac-
> quired, and which is so natural to all men as far as thought and
> existence are concerned, that although perhaps blinded by some
> prejudices and more heedful of the sound of words than of their
> true meaning, we are capable of feigning that we do not possess
> it, nevertheless it is impossible that in fact we do not.
>
> (ibid.)

(The second *Méditation* will proceed according to the feint's [indis-sociable] reverse side: "there is some sort of very powerful and clever deceiver, who sets all his industry always to deceive me. Thus there can be no doubt that I am, if he deceives me." Thus *I am feigned*, and I am feigned by my *fiction* of the Malus Genius.)

Even though I feign, at this farthest point of feint I cannot not know that I am. And all my fictions can in a sense only heighten the certitude of this being, for fiction is nothing then (except that here it is the fiction that nothing exists) if not that I fiction "I think." Therefore I am, but this "therefore" is nothing other than a "force of knowledge" that is always already given at the opening (or the closing) of my fiction: I feign, I *am* feigning.

Premise or substance (being) are coeval with consequence or accident (thought), just as *lux* and *lumen* are coeval. What is reached here in the double light of fiction is this luminous coevality; consequently it is less light, luminous matter or elucidation of a thing, than that which makes light (and which as we know will throw it upon everything). What is reached here is *illumination*.

At the farthest point where feint blinds itself (in the fiction of seeing no world), *the feint is self-illuminating*. This does not mean it is brought to light, revealed as feint and denounced. It does not melt like the wax of fiction in the light of truth. It is self-illuminating for being my fiction, and thus it is self-illuminating for *being*. At this very moment feint withdraws of itself: only truth is there. But truth withdraws as well. It does not offer itself unclothed, but as the infinitely drawn out point of the feint (and this point is its nudity, a truth so naked that one sees its feint). At this farthest point that is always withdrawn and yet always in excess of what could stop it, the light of being illuminates itself.

"Thought" only appears to be a predicate that bestows quality upon this being. At the point of the *cogito*—the point of the feint—thought can be identified only through this structure of the feint, by the structure of *extreme withdrawal*.

The structure of the withdrawn fiction thus does not properly belong to what we consider under the name of "thought" (a term that Descartes specifies moreover in the moment of the *cogito* by *nothing* other than the illumination of being just described). Its first model was given concerning the primary *matter* of the fable of *Le Monde*. This matter was situated in the fiction as "the most confused and entangled chaos that Poets can describe."

> But before I explain this in greater length, stop once again for a moment to consider this chaos and observe that all things it contains are known to you so perfectly that you could not even feign not knowing it. . . . As for the matter from which I have formed it, there is nothing simpler or more easily known in inanimate creatures. Its idea is contained to such an extent in those that our imagination can form that necessarily either you must conceive of it or you must never imagine anything.

The Fable of the invention of the World thus included its material *cogito*, its *chaogito*, situated at the extreme, in other words initial point of fiction, at the point where the first deed of creation was fictioned, where fiction withdraws. If then, as we have established, the fable's truth is in its invention, this truth is not merely parallel or homologous to the truth of what it contains (fictive creation). It functions only insofar as it invents in itself—or invents itself as—the veritable creation, the unfictionable origin of a world in general. True or feigned, an invented world remains the invention of a world. This is the point of the fable. In this point you cannot feign, you cannot be feigned: you are and cannot not be, just as the chaos, out of which the world—or its fable—can come, cannot not be conceived.

The last model of this structure will be the primordial position in the *Méditations* not of the "I think," but of the "I am, I exist." Between *Le Monde* and the *Méditations*, the *Discours* represents in this respect the weakest model in that the extremity of the withdrawal here is simultaneously covered over, saturated and guaranteed by the word of thought and by the formal mark of reasoning (*therefore*, I am). (Once again, after the *Méditations*, this will be the expression of the didactic exposition of the *Principes*. But didactic exposition excludes by definition exposing *invention* (and hence narration), which constitutes in Descartes however everything there is to expose as far as truth is concerned.) But this word's "concept" and its demonstrative "reason" reside in fact as we now can see in the conjunction of the two other models, in their impossible articulation.

Chaos—I am. *I am*—chaos.

What in turn operates the inoperable predication that we comprehend thus without comprehending is the fabulous arrangement of the *Discours*. The fable is told here as the fable of him who passes to the farthest point of fiction, *who passes to the point of the fable's invention, where he withdraws.*

Such a point can only be the point where the fable is inaugurated, the point of fabulation itself, or of the invention of a fable such that no poetics is capable of describing it, and still less of prescribing it—and such that it can be assigned only by the illumination of an autobiographical ontology.

Such an ontology is bound up indistinguishably with the invention of the discourse on my life, the invention of my life *as* discourse (or fable). The ontological locus, the locus of substance is the point from which I pronounce this discourse. Invention becomes one with *énonciation*. It cannot take place in any place, in any anterior or subjacent instance at the farthest point of feint, since this extremity bears the generalized fiction of the absence of all being and all truth. Substance here is thus not sub-jacent, it *speaks itself*. Or rather it is the sub-jacency of *énonciation* to itself: the empty depth, the withdrawn cavity from which a voice is heard, which says "I fabulate." We know moreover that if the *cogito* makes me know *that* I am substance, it does not make me know however *what* this substance is. Unless it is "thinking," that is, "feigning."

The subject takes place in that he says *I feign*, in that he says *I fabulate*—or *I am fabulating*—and that he says it at such a distance that he brings himself to the fable's origin, in other words that he transports *fable* itself, withdrawn from fiction as well as from truth, to the illumination of its own etymology—"*fari*," to speak, to say.

"*For*," I say, says he who invents the fable, who invents himself fable, or whom his fable invents. I discourse, says Method. I free myself from all fabulation as well as from all verification. I speak myself, I am. The second *Méditation* will mark the mutual relation of being and the moment of *énonciation*.

> This proposition, *I am, I exist*, is necessarily true each and every time I pronounce it or conceive of it in my mind.

"I am" is *true* only when I say "I am." But "I am" says only that "I am feigning," and "I am feigning" finally means, or begins to mean (instantaneously) *for*, "I say." And this means nothing [*ne veut rien dire*], or rather it means the will-to-express itself [*veut dire le vouloir-dire lui-même*] (reference to Jacques Derrida's *Speech and Phenomena*). The Discourse-Fable speaks being—or knowledge—as the expression of the will to express. The autobiography that constitutes the text's narrative is the autobiography of this desire. The fable that makes discourse of this has as its "instruction" this expression. From this comes its lesson the *lectio*, recitation, repetition of *I*—invents expression.

The lesson is the pure *lectio*, and this is why the example of the *Discours* is inimitable and its fable incredibly veridical: one cannot imitate the *cogito* whose *thought* is equivalent to the utterance [*l'énoncé*] or more precisely to the act of uttering [*l'énoncer*]. "I pronounce it *or* conceive it" establishes this equivalence, which the entire fable implied and out of which it grew. Utterances may be imitated, but not uttering: the *cogito* cannot be spoken by an actor, only by Descartes, character of his fable.

Mundus est fabula: the pure *I* is I who utters myself uttering. A pure and truthful fiction indeed, at this height of purity. All at once the subject withdraws. Throughout centuries of subjectivity there will never be any other I than the I withdrawn from his own discourse, and who will recite his fables, saying "I am the State," or "Ego, Hugo," or "I am Madame Bovary," or even "Good Lord, why is it that I am I?"

Deep and Surface Structure in the Port-Royal *Grammar* and *Logic*

Noam Chomsky

The study of the creative aspect of language use develops from the assumption that linguistic and mental processes are virtually identical, language providing the primary means for free expression of thought and feeling, as well as for the functioning of the creative imagination. Similarly, much of the substantive discussion of grammar, throughout the development of what we have been calling "Cartesian linguistics," derives from this assumption. The Port-Royal *Grammar* [*Grammaire générale et raisonée*], for example, begins the discussion of syntax with the observation that there are "trois operations de nostre esprit: concevoir, juger, raisonner," of which the third is irrelevant to grammar (it is taken up in the Port-Royal *Logic*, which appeared two years later, in 1662). From the manner in which concepts are combined in judgments, the *Grammar* deduces what it takes to be the general form of any possible grammar, and it proceeds to elaborate this univeral underlying structure from a consideration of "la manière naturelle en laquelle nous exprimons nos pensées." Most subsequent attempts to develop a schema of universal grammar proceed along the same lines.

James Harris's *Hermes*, which does not bear the imprint of the Port-Royal *Grammar* to the extent usual in eighteenth-century work, also reasons from the structure of mental processes to the structure of language, but in a somewhat different way. In general, he maintains, when a man speaks, "his Speech or Discourse is *a publishing of some Energie or Motion of his soul.*" The "powers of the soul" are of two general types: perception (involving the senses and the intellect) and volition (the will, passions, appetites— "all that moves to Action whether rational or irrational". It follows that there are two kinds of linguistic acts: to assert, that is, "to publish some

From *Cartesian Linguistics: A Chapter in the History of Rationalist Thought.* © 1966 by Noam Chomsky. Harper & Row, 1966.

Perception either of the Senses or the Intellect"; or to "publish volitions," that is, to interrogate, command, pray, or wish. The first type of sentence serves "to declare ourselves to others"; the second, to induce others to fulfill a need. Continuing in this way, we can analyze the volitional sentences in terms of whether the need is "to have some perception informed" or "some volition gratified" (the interrogative and requisitive modes, respectively); the requisitive is further analyzed as imperative or precative, depending on whether the sentence is addressed to inferiors or noninferiors). Since both interrogatives and requisitives serve "to answer to a need," both types "require a return"—a return in words or deeds, to the requisitive, and in words alone, to the interrogative. Thus the framework for the analysis of types of sentences is provided by a certain analysis of mental processes.

Pursuing the fundamental distinction between body and mind, Cartesian linguistics characteristically assumes that language has two aspects. In particular, one may study a linguistic sign from the point of view of the sounds that constitute it and the characters that represent these signs or from the point of view of their "signification," that is, "la manière dont les hommes s'en servent pour signifier leurs pensées" (*Grammaire générale et raisonnée*). Cordemoy announces his goal in similar terms (*Discours physique de la parole*, 1666, preface): "je fais en ce discours un discernement exact de tout ce qu'elle [la Parole] tient de l'Ame, et de tout ce qu'elle emprunte du Corps." Similarly, Lamy begins his rhetoric by distinguishing between "l'ame des paroles" (that is, "ce qu'elles ont de spirituel," "ce qui nous est particulier"—the capacity of expressing "les idées") from "leur corps" ("ce qu'elles ont de corporel," "ce que les oyseaux qui imitent la voix des hommes ont de commun avec nous," namely, "les sons, qui sont les signes de ses idées") (*De l'art de parler*, 1676).

In short, language has an inner and an outer aspect. A sentence can be studied from the point of view of how it expresses a thought or from the point of view of its physical shape, that is, from the point of view of either semantic interpretation or phonetic interpretation.

Using some recent terminology, we can distinguish the "deep structure" of a sentence from its "surface structure." The former is the underlying abstract structure that determines its semantic interpretation; the latter, the superficial organization of units which determines the phonetic interpretation and which relates to the physical form of the actual utterance, to its perceived or intended form. In these terms, we can formulate a second fundamental conclusion of Cartesian linguistics, namely, that deep and surface structures need not be identical. The underlying organization of a sentence relevant to semantic interpretation is not necessarily revealed by the actual arrangement and phrasing of its given components.

This point is brought out with particular clarity in the Port-Royal *Grammar*, in which a Cartesian approach to language is developed, for the first time, with considerable insight and subtlety. The principal form of thought (but not the only one—cf. below) is the judgment, in which something is affirmed of something else. Its linguistic expression is the proposition, the two terms of which are the "*sujet*, qui est ce dont on affirme" and the "*attribut*, qui est ce qu'on affirme." The subject and the attribute may be *simple*, as in *la terre est ronde*, or *complex* ("composé"), as in *un habile Magistrat est un homme utile à la République* or *Dieu invisible a créé le monde visible*. Furthermore, in such cases as these, the complex subject and the complex attribute

> enferment, au moins dans nostre esprit, plusieurs jugemens dont on peut faire autant de propositions: Comme quand je dis, *Dieu invisible a créé le monde visible*, il se passe trois jugemens dans mon esprit renfermez dans cette proposition. Car je juge premierement que *Dieu est invisible*. 2. Qu'*il a créé le monde*. 3. Que *le monde est visible*. Et de ces trois propositions, la seconde est la principale et l'essentielle de la proposition. Mais la première et la troisième ne sont qu'incidentes, et ne font que partie de la principale, dont la première en compose le sujet, et la seconde l'attribut.

In other words, the deep structure underlying the proposition *Dieu invisible a créé le monde visible* consists of three abstract propositions, each expressing a certain simple judgment, although its surface form expresses only the subject-attribute structure. Of course, this deep structure is implicit only; it is not expressed but is only represented in the mind:

> or, ces propositions incidentes sont souvent dans nostre esprit, sans estre exprimées par des paroles, comme dans l'exemple pro-posée (viz., *Dieu invisible a créé le monde visible*).

It is sometimes possible to express the deep structure in a more explicit way, in the surface form, "comme quand je reduis le mesme exemple à ces termes: *Dieu QUI est invisible a créé le monde QUI est visible*." But it constitutes an underlying mental reality—a mental accompaniment to the utterance—whether or not the surface form of the utterance that is produced corresponds to it in a simple, point-by-point manner.

In general, constructions of a noun with a noun in apposition, an adjective, or a participle are based on a deep structure containing a relative clause: "toutes ces façons de parler enferment le relatif dans le sens, et se peuvent resoudre par le relatif." The same deep structure may be realized differently in different languages, as when Latin has *video canem currentem*, and French *je voy un chien qui court*. The position of the relative pronoun in the "proposition incidente" is determined by a rule that converts deep structure to surface structure. We see this, for example, in such phrases as *Dieu que j'ayme, Dieu par qui le monde a esté créé*. In such cases,

> on met tousjours le relatif à la tête de la proposition (quoy que selon le sens il ne deust estre qu'à la fin) si ce n'est qu'il soit gouverné par une preposition [in which case] la preposition pre-cede au moins ordinairement.

In the case of each of the sentences just discussed, the deep structure consists of a system of propositions, and it does not receive a direct, point-by-point expression of the actual physical object that is produced. To form an actual sentence from such an underlying system of elementary propositions, we apply certain rules (in modern terms, grammatical transformations). In these examples, we apply the rule preposing the relative pronoun that takes the place of the noun of the incident proposition (along with the preposition that precedes it, if there is one). We may then, optionally, go on to delete the relative pronoun, at the same time deleting the copula (as in *Dieu invisible*) or changing the form of the verb (as in *canis currens*). Finally, we must, in certain cases, interchange the order of the noun and the adjective (as in *un habile magistrat*).

The deep structure that expresses the meaning is common to all languages, so it is claimed, being a simple reflection of the forms of thought. The transformational rules that convert deep to surface structure may differ from language to language. The surface structure resulting from these transformations does not directly express the meaning relations of the words, of course, except in the simplest cases. It is the deep structure underlying the actual utterance, a structure that is purely mental, that conveys the semantic content of the sentence. This deep structure is, nevertheless, related to actual sentences in that each of its component abstract propositions (in the cases just discussed) could be directly realized as a simple propositional judgment.

The theory of essential and incident propositions, as constituent elements of deep structure, is extended in the Port-Royal *Logic* with a more detailed analysis of relative clauses. There, a distinction is developed between *explicative* (nonrestrictive or appositive) and *determinative* (restrictive) relative clauses. The distinction is based on a prior analysis of the "comprehension" and "extension" of "universal ideas," in modern terms, an analysis of meaning and reference. The comprehension of an idea is the set of essential attributes that define it, together with whatever can be deduced from them; its extension is the set of objects that it denotes:

> The comprehension of an idea is the constitutent parts which make up the idea, none of which can be removed without destroying the idea. For example, the idea of a triangle is made up of the idea of having three sides, the idea of having three angles, and the idea of having angles whose sum is equal to two right angles, and so on.
>
> The extension of an idea is the objects to which the word expressing the idea can be applied. The objects which belong to the extension of an idea are called the inferiors of that idea, which with respect to them is called the superior. Thus, the general idea of triangle has in its extension triangles of all kinds whatsoever.
>
> (*La Logique, ou l'art de penser*, trans. *The Art of Thinking*)

In terms of these notions, we can distinguish such "explications" as *Paris, which is the largest city in Europe* and *man, who is mortal* from "determinations" such as *transparent bodies, wise men* or *a body which is transparent, men who are pious*:

> A complex expression is a mere *explication* if either (1) the idea expressed by the complex expression is already contained in the comprehension of the idea expressed by the principal word of the complex expression, or (2) the idea expressed by the complex expression is the idea of some accidental characteristic of all the inferiors of an idea expressed by the principal word.

> A complex expression is a *determination* if the extension of the idea expressed by the complex term is less than the extension of the idea expressed by the principal word.

In the case of an explicative relative clause, the underlying deep structure actually implies the judgment expressed by this clause, when its relative pronoun is replaced by its antecedent. For example, the sentence *men, who were created to know and love God, . . .* implies that men were created to know and love God. Thus an explicative relative clause has the essential properties of conjunction. But in the case of a restrictive relative clause (a determination), this is obviously not true. Thus in saying *men who are pious are charitable*, we do not affirm either that men are pious or that men are charitable. In stating this proposition,

> we form a complex idea by joining together two simple ideas— the idea of man and the idea of piety—and we judge that the attribute of being charitable is part of this complex idea. Thus the subordinate clause asserts nothing more than that the idea of piety is not incompatible with the idea of man. Having made this judgment we then consider what idea can be affirmed of this complex idea of pious man.

Similarly, consider the expression *The doctrine which identifies the sovereign good with the sensual pleasure of the body, which was taught by Epicurus, is unworthy of a philosopher*. This contains the subject *The doctrine which . . . taught by Epicurus* and the predicate *unworthy of a philosopher*. The subject is complex, containing the restrictive relative clause *which identifies the sovereign good with the sensual pleasure of the body* and the explicative relative clause *which was taught by Epicurus*. The relative pronoun in the latter has as its antecedent the complex expression *the doctrine which identifies the sovereign good with the sensual pleasure of the body*. Since the clause *which was taught by Epicurus* is explicative, the original sentence does imply that the doctrine in question was taught by Epicurus. But the relative pronoun of the restrictive clause cannot be replaced by its antecedent, *the doctrine*, to form an assertion implied by the full sentence. Once again, the complex phrase containing the restrictive relative clause and its antecedent expresses a single complex idea formed from the two ideas of a doctrine and of identifying the sovereign good with the sensual pleasure of the body. All this information must be represented in the deep structure of the original sentence, according to the Port-Royal theory, and the semantic interpretation of this sentence must proceed in the manner just indicated, utilizing this information.

A restrictive relative clause is based on a proposition, according to the Port-Royal theory, even though this proposition is not affirmed when the relative clause is used in a complex expression. What is affirmed in an expression such as *men who are pious*, as noted above, is no more than the compatibility of the constituent ideas. Hence in the expression *minds which are square are more solid than those which are round*, we may correctly say that the relative clause is "false," in a certain sense, since "the idea of being square" is not compatible with "the idea of mind understood as the principle of thought."

Thus sentences containing explicative as well as restrictive relative clauses are based on systems of propositions (that is, abstract objects constituting the meanings of sentences); but the manner of interconnection is different in the case of an explicative clause, in which the underlying judgment is actually affirmed, and a determinative clause, in which the proposition formed by replacing the relative pronoun by its antecedent is not affirmed but rather constitutes a single complex idea together with this noun.

These observations are surely correct, in essence, and must be accommodated in any syntactic theory that attempts to make the notion "deep structure" precise and to formulate and investigate the principles that relate deep structure to surface organization. In short, these observations must be accommodated in some fashion in any theory of transformational generative grammar. Such a theory is concerned precisely with the rules that specify deep structures and relate them to surface structures and with the rules of semantic and phonological interpretation that apply to deep and surface structures respectively. It is, in other words, in large measure an elaboration and formalization of notions that are implicit and in part expressly formulated in such passages as those just discussed. In many respects, it seems to me quite accurate, then, to regard the theory of transformational generative grammar, as it is developing in current work, as essentially a modern and more explicit version of the Port-Royal theory.

The relative pronoun that occurs in the surface form does not always have the dual function of standing for a noun and connecting propositions, in the Port-Royal theory. It may be "depoüillé de la nature de pronom" and may thus serve only the latter role. For example, in such sentences as *je suppose que vous serez sage* and *je vous dis que vous avez tort*, we find that, in the deep structure, "ces propositions, *vours serez sage, vous avez tort,* ne font que partie des propositions entières: *je suppose,* etc., *je vous dis,* etc." (*Grammaire*).

The *Grammar* goes on to argue that infinitival constructions play the same role in the verbal system that relative clauses play in the nominal system, providing a means for extending the verbal system through the incorporation of whole propositions: "l'Infinitif est entre les autres manières du Verbe, ce qu'est le Relatif entre les autres pronoms"; like the relative pronoun, "l'Infinitif a pardessus l'affirmation du Verbe ce pouvoir de joindre la proposition où il est à un autre." Thus the meaning of *scio malum esse fugiendum* is conveyed by a deep structure based on the two propositions expressed by the sentences *scio* and *malum est fugiendum*. The transformational rule (in modern terms) that forms the surface structure of the sentence replaces *est* by *esse*, just as the transformations that form such sentences as *Dieu (qui est) invisible a créé le monde (qui est) visible* perform various operations of substitution, reordering, and deletion on the underlying systems of propositions. "Et de là est venu qu'en François nous rendons presque tousiours l'infinitif par l'indicatif du Verbe, et la particule *que. Je scay que le mal est a fuir.*" In this case, the identity of deep structure in Latin and French may be somewhat obscured by the fact that the two languages use slightly different transformational operations to derive the surface forms.

The *Grammar* goes on to point out that indirect discourse can be analyzed in a similar way. If the underlying embedded proposition is interrogative, it is the particle *si* rather than *que* that is introduced by the transformational rule, as in *on m'a demandé si je pouvois faire cela*, where the "discours qu'on rapport" is *Pouvez-vous faire cela?* Sometimes, in fact, no particle need be added, a change of person being sufficient, as in *Il m'a demandé: Qui estes-vous?* as compared with *Il m'a demandé; qui j'estois.*

Summarizing the Port-Royal theory in its major outlines, a sentence has an inner mental aspect (a deep structure that conveys its meaning) and an outer, physical aspect as a sound sequence. Its surface analysis into phrases may not indicate the significant connections of the deep structure by any formal mark or by the actual arrangment of words. The deep structure is, however, represented in the mind as the physical utterance is produced. The deep structure consists of a system of propositions, organized in various ways. The elementary propositions that constitute the deep structure are of the subject-predicate form, with simple subjects and predicates (i.e., categories instead of more complex phrases). Many of these elementary objects can be independently realized as sentences. It is not true, in general, that the elementary judgments constituting the deep structure are affirmed when the sentence that it underlies is produced; explicative and determinative relatives, for example, differ in this respect. To actually produce a sentence from the deep structure that conveys the thought that it expresses, it is necessary to apply rules of transformation that rearrange, replace, or delete items of the sentence. Some of these are obligatory, further ones optional. Thus *Dieu qui est invisible a créé le monde qui est visible* is distinguished from its paraphrase, *Dieu invisible a créé le monde visible,* by an optional deletion operation, but the transformation that substitutes a relative pronoun for the noun and then preposes the pronoun is obligatory.

This account covers only the sentences based exclusively on judgments. But these, although the principal form of thought, do not exhaust the "operations de nostre esprit," and "on y doit encore rapporter les conjonctions, disjonctions, et autres semblables operations de nostre esprit; et tous les autres mouvemens de nostre ame; comme les desirs, le commandment, l'interrogation, etc." In part, these other "forms of thought" are signified by special particles such as *non, vel, si, ergo,* etc. But with respect to these sentence types as well, an identity of deep structure may be masked through divergence of the transformational means whereby actual sentences are formed, corresponding to intended meanings. A case in point is interrogation. In Latin, the interrogative particle *ne* "n'a point d'object hors de nostre esprit, mais marque seulement le mouvement de nostre ame, par lequel nous souhaittons de sçavoir une chose." As for the interrogative pronoun, "ce n'est autre chose qu'un pronom, auquel est jointe la signification de *ne,* c'est a dire, qui outre qu'il tient la place d'un nom, comme les autres pronoms, marque plus ce mouvement de nostre ame, qui veut sçavoir une chose, et qui demande d'en estre instruitte." But this "mouvement de l'ame" can be signified in various ways other than by the addition of a particle, for example, by vocal inflection or inversion of word order, as in French, where the pronomial subject is "transported" to the position following the person marker of the verb (preserving the agreement of the underlying form). These are all devices for realizing the same deep structure.

Notice that the theory of deep and surface structure as developed in the Port-Royal linguistic studies implicitly contains recursive devices and thus provides for infinite use of the finite means that it disposes, as any adequate theory of language must. We see, moreover, that in the examples given, the recursive devices meet certain formal conditions that have no a priori necessity. In both the trivial cases (e.g., conjunction, disjunction, etc.) and the more interesting ones discussed in connection with relatives and infinitives, the only method for extending deep structures is by adding full propositions of a basic subject-predicate form. The transformational rules of deletion, rearrangement, etc., do not play a role in the creation of new structures. The extent to which the Port-Royal grammarians may have been aware of or interested in these properties of their theory is, of course, an open question.

In modern terms, we may formalize this view by describing the syntax of a language in terms of two systems of rules: a *base system* that generates deep structures and a *transformational system* that maps these into surface structures. The base system consists of rules that generate the underlying grammatical relations with an abstract order (the rewriting rules of a phrase-structure grammar); the transformational system consists of rules of deletion, rearrangement, adjunction, and so on. The base rules allow for the introduction of new propositions (that is, there are rewriting rules of the form: A → . . . S . . . , where S is the initial symbol of the phrase-structure grammar that constitutes the base); there are no other recursive devices. Among the transformations are those which form questions, imperatives, etc., when the deep structure so indicates (i.e., when the deep structure represents the corresponding "mental act" in an appropriate notation).

The Port-Royal grammar is apparently the first to develop the notion of phrase structure in any fairly clear way. It is interesting, therefore, to notice that it also states quite clearly the inadequacy of phrase-structure description for the representation of syntactic structure and that it hints at a form of transformational grammar in many respects akin to that which is being actively studied today.

Turning from the general conception of grammatical structure to specific cases of grammatical analysis, we find many other attempts in the Port-Royal grammar to develop the theory of deep and surface structure. Thus adverbs are analyzed as (for the most part) arising from "le desir que les hommes ont d'abreger le discours," thus as being elliptical forms of preposition-noun constructions, for example, *sapienter* for *cum sapientia* or *hodie* for *in hoc die*. Similarly, verbs are analyzed as containing implicitly an underlying copula that expresses affirmation; thus, once again, as arising from the desire to abbreviate the actual expression of thought. The verb, then, is *"un mot dont le principal usage est de signifier l'affirmation: c'est à dire, de marquer que le discours où ce mot est employé, est le discours d'un homme qui ne conçoit pas seulement les choses, mais qui en juge et qui les affirme."* To use a verb, then, is to perform the act of affirming, not simply to refer to affirmation, as an "objet de nostre pensée," as in the use of "quelques noms qui signifient aussi l'affirmation; comme *affirmans, affirmatio*." Thus the sentence *Petrus vivit* or *Pierre vit* has the meaning of *Pierre est vivant*, and, in the sentence *Petrus affirmat*, "*affirmat* est la mesme chose que *est affirmans*." It follows, then, that in the sentence *affirmo* (in which subject, copula, and attribute are all abbreviated in a single word), two affirmations are expressed: one, regarding the act of the speaker in affirming, the other, the affirmation that he attributes (to himself, in this case). Similarly, "le verbe *nego* . . . contient une affirmation et une negation."

Formulating these observations in the framework outlined above, what the Port-Royal grammarians are maintaining is that the deep structure underlying a sentence such as *Peter lives* or *God loves mankind* (*Logic*) contains a copula, expressing the affirmation, and a predicate (*living, loving mankind*) attributed to the subject of the proposition. Verbs constitute a subcategory of predicates; they are subject to a transformation that causes them to coalesce with the copula into a single word.

The analysis of verbs is extended in the *Logic*, where it is maintained that, despite surface appearances, a sentence with a transitive verb and its object "expresses a complex proposition and in one sense two propositions." Thus we can contradict the sentence *Brutus killed a tyrant* by saying that Brutus did not kill anyone or that the person whom Brutus killed was not a tyrant. It follows that the sentence expresses the proposition that Brutus killed someone who was a tyrant, and the deep structure must reflect this fact. It seems that this analysis would also apply, in the view of the *Logic*, if the object is a singular term; e.g., *Brutus killed Caesar.*

This analysis plays a role in the theory of reasoning developed later on in the *Logic*. It is used to develop what is in effect a partial theory of relations, permitting the theory of the syllogism to be extended to arguments to which it would otherwise not apply. Thus it is pointed out that the inference from *The divine law commands us to honor kings* and *Louis XIV is a king* to *the divine law commands us to honor Louis XIV* is obviously valid, though it does not exemplify any valid figure as it stands, superficially. By regarding *kings* as "the subject of a sentence contained implicitly in the original sentence," using the passive transformation and otherwise decomposing the original sentence into its underlying propositional constituents, we can finally reduce the argument to the valid figure *Barbara*.

Reduction of sentences to underlying deep structure is resorted to elsewhere in the *Logic*, for the same purpose. For example, Arnauld observes that the sentence *There are few pastors nowadays ready to give their lives for their sheep*, though superficially affirmative in form, actually "contains implicitly the negative sentence *Many pastors nowadays are not ready to give their lives for their sheep.*" In general, he points out repeatedly that what is affirmative or negative "in appearance" may or may not be in meaning, that is, in deep structure. In short, the real "logical form" of a sentence may be quite different from its surface grammatical form.

The identity of deep structure underlying a variety of surface forms in different languages is frequently stressed, throughout this period, in connection with the problem of how the significant semantic connections among the elements of speech are expressed. Chapter VI of the Port-Royal *Grammar* considers the expression of these relations in case systems, as in the classical languages, or by internal modification, as in the construct state in Hebrew, or by particles, as in the vernacular languages, or simply by a fixed word order, as in the case of the subject-verb and verb-object relations in French. These are regarded as all being manifestations of an underlying structure common to all these languages and mirroring the structure of thought. Similarly, Lamy comments in his rhetoric on the diverse means used by various languages to express the "rapports, et la suite et la liaison de toutes les idées que la consideration de ces choses excite dans notre esprit" (*De l'art de parler*). The encyclopedist Du Marsais also stresses the fact that case systems express relations among the elements of discourse that are, in other languages, expressed by word order or specific particles, and he points out the correlation between freedom to transpose and wealth of inflection (*Logiques et principes de grammaire*).

Notice that what is assumed is the existence of a uniform set of relations into which words can enter, in any language, these corresponding to the exigencies of thought. The philosophical grammarians do not try to show that all languages literally have case systems, that they use inflectional devices to express these relations. On the contrary, they repeatedly stress that a case system is only one device for expressing these relations. Occasionally, they point out that case names can be assigned to these relations as a pedagogic device; they also argue that considerations of simplicity sometimes may lead to a distinction of cases even where there is no difference in form. The fact that French has no case system is in fact noted in the earliest grammars.

It is important to realize that the use of the names of classical cases for languages with no inflections implies only a belief in the uniformity of the grammatical relations involved, a belief that deep structures are fundamentally the same across languages, although the means for their expression may be quite diverse. This claim is not obviously true—it is, in other words, a nontrivial hypothesis. So far as I know, however, modern linguistics offers no data that challenges it in any serious way.

As noted above, the Port-Royal *Grammar* holds that for the most part, adverbs do not, properly speaking, constitute a category of deep structure by function only "pour signifier en un seul mot, ce qu'on ne pourroit marquer que par une preposition et un nom." Later grammarians simply drop the qualification to "most adverbs." Thus for Du Marsais, "ce qui distingue l'adverbe des autres espèces de mots, c'est que l'adverbe vaut autant qu'une préposition et un nom: il a la valeur d'une préposition avec son complément: c'est un mot qui abrège." This is an unqualified characterization, and he goes on to analyze a large class of items in this way—in our paraphrase, as deriving from a deep structure of the form: preposition-complement. This analysis is carried still further by Beauzée. He, incidentally, maintains that, although a "phrase adverbiale" such as *avec sagesse* does not differ from the corresponding adverb *sagement* in its "signification," it may differ in the "idées accessoires" associated with it: "quand il s'agit de mettre un acte en opposition avec l'habitude, l'Adverbe est plus propre à marquer l'habitude, et la phrase adverbiale à indiquer l'acte: et je dirois: *un homme que se conduit* sagement *ne peut pas se promettre que toutes ses actions seront faites* avec sagesse" (*Grammaire générale, ou exposition raisonnée des éléments nécessaires du langage*). This distinction is a particular case of "l'eloignement que toutes les langues ont naturellement pour une synonymie entière, qui n'enrichiroit un idiome que de sons inutiles à la justesse et à la clarté de l'expression."

Earlier grammarians provide additional instances of analysis in terms of deep structure, as, for example, when imperatives and interrogatives are analyzed as, in effect, elliptical transforms of underlying expressions with such supplementary terms as *I order you . . .* or *I request. . . .* Thus *venez me trouvez* has the deep structure *je vous ordonne (prie) de me venir trouver; qui a trouvé cela?* has the meaning of *je demande celui qui a trouvé cela;* etc.

Still another example that might be cited is the transformational derivation of expressions with conjoined terms from underlying sentences, in the obvious way; for example, in Beauzée. Beauzée's discussion of conjunctions also provides somewhat more interesting cases, as, for example, when he analyses *comment* as based on an underlying form with *manière* and a relative clause, so that the sentence *je sais comment la chose se passa* has the meaning, *je sais la manière de laquelle manière la chose se passa*; or when he analyzes *la maison dont j'ai fait l'acquisition* as meaning *la maison de laquelle maison j'ai fait l'acquisition*. In this way, the underlying deep structure with its essential and incident propositions is revealed.

An interesting further development, along these lines, is carried out by Du Marsais in his theory of *construction* and *syntax*. He proposes that the term "construction" be applied to "l'arrangement des mots dans le discours," and the term "syntaxe," to the "rapports que les mots ont entre eux." For example, the three sentences *accepi litteras tuas, tuas accepi litteras,* and *litteras accepi tuas* exhibit three different constructions, but they have the same syntax; the relations among the constituent elements are the same in all three cases. "Ainsi, chacun de ces trois arrangemens excite dans l'esprit la même sens, *J'ai reçu votre lettre.*" He goes on to define "syntaxe" as "ce qui fait en chaque langue, que les mots excitent le sens que l'on veut faire naître dans l'esprit de ceux qui savent la langue . . . la partie de la Grammaire qui donne la connoissance des signes établis dans une langue pour exciter un sens dans l'esprit." The syntax of an expression is thus essentially what we have called its deep structure; its construction is what we have called its surface structure.

The general framework within which this distinction is developed is the following. An act of the mind is a single unit. For a child, the "sentiment" that sugar is sweet is at first an unanalyzed, single experience; for the adult, the meaning of the sentence *le sucre est doux,* the thought that it expresses, is also a single entity. Language provides an indispensable means for the analysis of these otherwise undifferentiated objects. It provides a

> moyen d'habiller, pour ainsi dire, notre pensée, de la rendre sensible, de la diviser, de l'analyser, en un mot, de la rendre telle qu'elle puisse être communiquée aux autres avec plus de précision et de détail.
>
> Ainsi, les pensées particulières sont, pour ainsi dire, chacune un ensemble, un tout que l'usage de la parole divise, analyse et distribue en détail par le moyen des différentes articulations des organes de la parole qui forment les mots.

Similarly, the perception of speech is a matter of determining the unified and undifferentiated thought from the succession of words. "[Les mots] concourent ensemble à exciter dans l'esprit de celui qui lit, ou qui écoute, le sens total ou la pensée que nous voulons faire naître." To determine this thought, the mind must first discover the relations among the words of the sentence, that is, its syntax; it must then determine the meaning, given a full account of this deep structure. The method of analysis used by the mind is to bring together those words that are related, thus establishing an "ordre significatif" in which related elements are successive. The actual sentence may, in itself, have this "ordre significatif," in which case it is called a "construction simple (naturelle, nécessaire, significative, énonciative)." Where it does not, this "ordre significatif" must be reconstructed by some procedure of analysis—it must be "rétabli par l'esprit, qui n'entend le sens que par cet ordre." To understand a sentence of Latin, for example, you must reconstruct the "natural order" that the speaker has in his mind. You must not only understand the meanings of each word, but, furthermore,

> vous n'y comprendriez rien non plus, si par une vue de l'esprit vous ne rapprochiez les mots qui ont relation l'un à l'autre. Ce que vous ne pouvez faire qu'après avoir entendu toute la phrase.

In Latin, for example, it is the "terminaisons relatives, qui après que toute la Proposition est finie, nous les [that is, les mots] font regarder selon l'ordre de leurs rapports, et par consequent selon l'ordre de la *construction simple, nécessaire* et *significative*." This "construction simple" is an "ordre toujours indiqué, mais rarement observé dans la construction usuelle des langues dont les noms ont des cas." Reduction to the "construction simple" is an essential first step in speech perception:

> Les mots forment un tout qui a des parties: or la perception simple du raport que ces parties ont l'une à l'autre, et qui nous en fait concevoir l'ensemble, nous vient uniquement de la construction simple, qui, énonçant les mots suivant l'ordre successif de leurs raports, nous les présente de la manière la plus propre à nous faire apercevoir ces raports, et à faire naitre la pensée totale.

Constructions other than the "constructions simples" (namely, "constructions figurées")

> ne sont entendues, que parce que l'esprit en rectifie l'irrégularité, par le secours des idées accessoires, qui font concevoir ce qu'on lit et ce qu'on entend, comme si le sens étoit énoncé dans l'ordre de la construction simple.

In short, in the "construction simple" the relations of "syntaxe" are represented directly in the associations among successive words, and the undifferentiated thought expressed by the sentence is derived directly from this underlying representation, which is regarded, throughout, as common to all languages (and, typically, as corresponding to the usual order of French).

The transformations which form a "construction figurée" effect reordering and ellipsis. The "principe fondamental de toute syntaxe" is that reordering and ellipsis must be recoverable by the mind of the hearer; that is, they can be applied only when it is possible to recover uniquely "l'ordre sec et métaphysique" of the "construction simple."

Many examples of reduction to "construction simple" are presented to illustrate this theory. Thus the sentence *qui est-ce qui vous l'a dit?* is reduced to the "construction simple" (*celui ou celle*) *qui vous l'a dit est quelle personne?*; the sentence *Aussitôt aimés qu'amoureux, On ne vous force point à répandre des larmes* is reduced to *comme vous êtes aimés aussitôt que vous êtes amoureux . . .* ; the sentence *il vaut mieux être juste, que d'être riche; être raisonable que d'être savant* is reduced to four underlying propositions, two negative, two positive, in the obvious way (Gunvor Sahlin, *César Chesneau du Marsais et son rôle dans l'évolution de la Grammaire générale*).

A rather different sort of example of the distinction between deep and surface structure is provided by Du Marsais in his analysis of such expressions as *j'ai une idée, j'ai peur, j'ai un doute*, etc. These, he says, should not be interpreted as analogous to the superficially similar expressions *j'ai un livre, j'ai un diamant, j'ai une montre*, in which the nouns are "noms d'objets réels qui existent independamment de notre manière de penser." In contrast, the verb in *j'ai une idée* is "une expression empruntée," produced only "par une imitation." The meaning of *j'ai une idée* is simply *je pense, je conçois de telle ou telle manière.* Thus the grammar gives no license for supposing that such words as *idée, concept, imagination* stand for "objets réels," let alone "êtres sensibles." From this grammatical observation it is only a short step to a criticism of the theory of ideas, in its Cartesian and empiricist forms, as based on a false grammatical analogy. This step is taken by Thomas Reid, shortly after.

As Du Marsais indicates with abundant references, his theory of syntax and construction is foreshadowed in scholastic and renaissance grammar. But he follows the Port-Royal grammarians in regarding the theory of deep and surface structure as, in essence, a psychological theory, not merely a means for the elucidation of given forms or for analysis of texts. As indicated above, it plays a role in his hypothetical account of the perception and production of speech, just as, in the Port-Royal *Grammar*, the deep structure is said to be represented "dans l'esprit" as the utterance is heard or produced.

As a final example of the attempt to discover the hidden regularities underlying surface variety, we may mention the analysis of indefinite articles in chapter 7 of the Port-Royal *Grammar*, where it is argued, on grounds of symmetry of patterning, that *de* and *des* play the role of the plural of *un*, as in *Un crime si horrible mérite la mort, des crimes si horribles méritent la mort, de si horribles crimes méritent la mort*, etc. To handle the apparent exception, *il est coupable de crimes horribles* (*d'horribles crimes*), they propose the "rule of cacophony" that a *de de* sequence is replaced by *de*. They also note the use of *des* as a realization of the definite article, and other uses of these forms.

Perhaps these comments and examples are sufficient to suggest something of the range and character of the grammatical theories of the "philosophical grammarians." As noted above, their theory of deep and surface structure relates directly to the problem of creativity of language use, discussed in the first part of the present work.

From the standpoint of modern linguistic theory, this attempt to discover and characterize deep structure and to study the transformational rules that relate it to surface form is something of an absurdity; it indicates lack of respect for the "real language" (i.e., the surface form) and lack of concern for "linguistic fact." Such criticism is based on a restriction of the domain of "linguistic fact" to physically identifiable subparts of actual utterances and their formally marked relations. Restricted in this way, linguistics studies the use of language for the expression of thought only incidentally, to the quite limited extent to which deep and surface structure coincide; in particular, it studies "sound-meaning correspondences" only in so far as they are representable in terms of surface structure. From this limitation follows the general disparagement of Cartesian and earlier linguistics, which attempted to give a full account of deep structure even where it is not correlated in strict point-by-point fashion to observable features of speech. These traditional attempts to deal with the organization of semantic content as well as the organization of sound were defective in many ways, but modern critique generally rejects them more for their scope than for their failures.

The Social Ethic of "Honnêteté" in La Rochefoucauld's *Maximes* and *Réflexions*

Philip E. Lewis

It has been said that La Rochefoucauld adopts psychology as his prime field of investigation; it is no less evident, however, that his psychology, and especially the theory of self-love, is inextricably intertwined with the elucidation of human relationships in society. . . . The psychological insights of the *Maximes* and the *Réflexions* open onto a sociological perspective in at least two respects. First, the observation of human motivations appears to be on firmer ground in a social sphere, where the ego of the observer is less immediately involved than in introspective analysis. Second, it is in the social sphere that man's efforts to exert control over himself and his environment can be observed and evaluated. Once the individual is placed in an interpersonal situation, the comprehension of egocentric activity becomes, to be sure, more complicated. To perceive man as a creature of self-love is to detect, over and beyond his fidelity to possessive instincts, the critical influence that other people exert upon his conduct and to appreciate the difference between a man acting by himself and the same man acting under observation. As a factor in the determination of a course of action, the anticipated response of witnesses functions as a coercive presence to which man's capacity for action can ordinarily be traced: "Perfect valor consists in doing without witnesses what one would be capable of doing before the world at large" (Max. 216). Such perfect valor is rare (see Max. 213, 215); it requires a man capable of acting virtuously on his own, for himself; it supposes a degree of independence and self-control that La Rochefoucauld associates with the mythical *élévation* of the hero (cf. Max. 217), whose ethical purity requires the exclusion of public opinion from his concerns.

From *La Rochefoucauld: The Art of Abstraction.* © 1977 by Cornell University. Cornell University Press, 1977.

Beneath the *Maximes* and the *Réflexions* some readers sense an uneasy ambivalence with respect to the hero, who appears as the object of both exaltation and demystification. The prevailing current of La Rochefoucauld's thinking does, without question, lead away from adherence to a heroic outlook and toward a practical decision to come to grips with the particular characteristics of human nature that determine societal normality. Over and over the *Maximes* invoke, as matters of fact, the fundamentally egotistical motivations that govern human relationships.

> Self-love increases or decreases the good qualities we see in our friends in accord with the degree to which we are satisfied with them; and we determine their worth by the way they get on with us.   (Max. 88)

> Humility is often just a feigned submissiveness, used to gain the submission of others; it is an artifice of pride which lowers itself in order to gain ascendancy; and although pride transforms itself in a thousand ways, it is never better disguised and more capable of deceit than when hiding behind the face of humility.
>   (Max. 254)

These maxims represent two sides of the same coin, man's self-serving judgment of others and his self-protecting concern to manage the judgments to be conferred upon him by others. In each case, self-love instinctively assumes the right to subject (*soumettre*) others, to give priority to its own centrality and satisfaction in preference to fair judgment and genuine understanding. Maxime 254 marks emphatically the deceptive capability ("*feigned* submissiveness," "*artifice* of pride," "better *disguised* and more capable of *deceit*," "*hiding* behind the face") that self-love deploys when faced with its counterpart in other men.

Acquiring the pervasive force of an unquestioned habit, the social pattern of deception naturally carries over into the psychological pattern of self-deception. The latter is rooted in the internal histrionics of a deceitful self-love that escapes direct awareness and fosters man's false perception of his own motives: "We are so accustomed to disguising ourselves from others that we end up disguising ourselves from ourselves" (Max. 119). By the same token, one can suspect man of profiting from his mastery of self-deception as he goes about deceiving others: "What shows that men know their own faults better than one may think is that they are never mistaken when heard discussing their own behavior: the same self-love which ordinarily blinds them then opens their eyes and gives them such clear perceptions that they are led to omit or to disguise the slightest things which might be condemnable" (Max. 494). Here we catch the outlines of a simple dialectic between the public and the private self within which the degree of self-deception decreases as the concern with deceiving others increases, and vice versa. Even if openly exposed in a momentary lucidity required by social circumstance, self-love can expect to recuperate its guise of secrecy upon the return to privacy.

Thus the scheming of self-love situates man in a role—deceiver of self, of others, of self and others together—and sets in motion a social comedy revolving around the confrontation of conflicting egotistical drives. The nature of social interaction has to be redefined in terms of the predominant and ubiquitous pursuit of private interest: "What men have called friendship is merely an association, a reciprocal balancing of interests, and an exchange of good offices; it is finally just a business arrangement in which self-love always envisages something to be gained" (Max. 83). On a purely semantic level, this maxim plays off a conventional concept (*amitié*) against other, more empirical notions in a verbal conflict, the result of which is the debunking so characteristic of the *Maximes*. Viewed in terms of game theory, word games of this type throw into question the relationship between linguistic signs and the realities they purport to designate. The phrase "what men have called friendship" points to the temerity of naming any human conduct whatsoever, *dis*-plays the word in its fundamentally functional and relational, rather than representational, aspect and reminds us that for the interpreter of human behavior the referential function of language is continually problematical.

Yet as soon as we move beyond the perspective of verbal conflict to include the realities brought into question by the words, we realize that the referential function remains paramount in the moralist's statement—that, for example, friendship as a human relation is quite as problematical as the use of the term *friendship*. Certainly its existence as a real experience is not questioned. The suggestion is, rather, that our notion of friendship should be cleansed of fantasies and supported by hard-nosed observation. This observation furnishes a version of interpersonal relationships that has intrinsic interest as a view of society. What is implied by the equivalence of four terms—*une société, un ménagement réciproque d'intérêts, un échange de bons offices, un commerce*—that form a sphere within which self-love is the driving force? To depict social intercourse as exchange, reciprocity, trading, arrangement, and so forth, amounts to underscoring its entrenchment in interchange and interdependence: communal existence inevitably constitutes an *economy*, within which the participants naturally pursue their own interests and in so doing tend to treat one another as adversaries, contestants seeking a reward: "Each person wants to find his own satisfaction and advantages at the expense of others; we always prefer ourselves over those with whom we seek to live, and we almost always make them sense our preference; this is what unsettles and destroys society" (Réfl. II, "De la société"). Social interaction appears to reproduce unceasingly an interplay of differing preferences within which individuals run the risk of upsetting society by following their egotistical impulses.

Rational understanding of this conflict of interest leads to what game theory terms a game of *strategy*: "Interest speaks all sorts of languages, and plays all sorts of roles, even that of the disinterested party" (Max. 39); "In all walks of life each person puts on an air and an outward appearance in order to look the way he wants others to believe that he is. Thus we can say that society is composed only of airs" (Max. 256). Unlike games of skill or games of pure chance, games of strategy require the player to assume a role that he conceives and acts out with regard to other players, who are likewise rational actors playing their roles. Thus the human comedy, staged in a world composed of guise and pretense where calculation presides over the acting, absorbs and accommodates a host of conflicting motivations (as many as there are players), each of which bypasses the dangerous (potentially tragic) clash of unmediated drives, anticipating the gain available with lower risk through ingenuity and artifice, relying upon the utility—and relative security—of controlled appearances.

Notwithstanding the pervasive empire of the traditional antitheses, appearance/reality, mask/truth, and the like, these categories acquire no substantive ontological status in the *Maximes*. Since maxim after maxim works to unsettle "realities" perceived at all levels of human experience, when the *Maximes* are viewed as a collection they seem to demonstrate almost endlessly that one debunking merely lays bare another notion to be reduced, that critical analysis can subvert any reality, even basic phenomena uncovered deep within the self. Although unmarked by didactic asseveration, a crucial lesson for society does arise from such destructive analysis: man must agree to deal with appearances, must accept the interplay of "truth" and artifice without arbitrarily depreciating the latter: "There are disguised falsehoods which represent the truth so well that not allowing oneself to be deceived would be an error of judgment" (Max. 282). The wise man chooses to play the game and does so willingly because he admits that the scandalous realness of appearances cannot be overcome. Rather than a hierarchical scheme based upon the axiological subordination of illusion to truth, we confront in society a game in which both participate as functions whose interplay will determine value, which—no longer preconceived as an immanent property of the "true"—relates to the quality of play and/or to the outcome of the game.

The emerging sociological reality here pertains not to the still vulnerable, metaphysically tinted essence or principle that exploded illusions leave exposed, but to the observable relationship between the factual and the fictive—it is the reality of their *jeu* (game, play, interplay, interaction, interacting), whose rules govern the ongoing concatenation of fact and fiction, disallowing the triumph of one over the other. Barren "essential" truth about men, were it accessible, would be unbearable, undermining all human contacts: "Men would not last long in social existence if they were not one another's dupes" (Max. 87). Conscious of his own reticence, the *honnête homme* tends to institutionalize a regulation of social relations, protecting the individual against inexpedient exposure: "The relation which can be found among minds would not uphold society for long if society were not *controlled* and *supported* by common sense, by good humor, and by the consideration which must obtain among persons who want to live together" (Réfl. II, "De la société," italics added). Regulating the perpetuation of mutual deception, the rules of *honnêteté* correspond to a strategy of cooperation or coalition designed to secure the pleasures of the game itself, to nurture the connection between minds by conditioning their (inter) play, forbidding subversive conquest: "The wise man finds greater advantage in forgoing battle than in winning" (Maxime posthume [hereafter cited as MP] 50). Yet solitude offers no escape from the search for an absolute truth: "It is sheer folly to wish to be wise all by oneself" (Max. 231). What then is the lot of the "wise dupe" who elects to play the game, to participate in society? Pursuing his interest through cooperation, each player enters into the jurisdiction of the game, commits himself to continue playing, accords his undivided attention to the action, and resists at all costs the disillusion and isolation of either victory or defeat. Caught up in their roles, the players incorporate—and simultaneously incorporate themselves into—the dominion of the game. Their renunciation of victory connotes a subtle triumph that ultimately belongs to the game itself, whose control over all the forces in play sustains the enaction of a successful social strategy.

Recognizing that La Rochefoucauld must be considered one of the theoreticians of *honnêteté*, Bénichou traces his originality to the experience behind the adoption of this relatively conventional position: "His originality is that he is aware, more than anyone else, of the ruins upon which it is constructed" ("L'Intention des *Maximes*"). This is not to suggest, of course, that La Rochefoucauld's personal sensitivity to the erosion of aristocratic values suffices in itself to account for the particular articulation of the theory of *honnêteté* that we find in the *Maximes* and the *Réflexions*. The originality of this elaborative enterprise should also be related to the possibility of drawing out the internal logic of these works along two separate tracks. On the one hand, *honnêteté* may represent a willful response, the last resort of lucid nobles who seek to preserve their society from the iconoclastic menace of a heroic thrust toward individual glory and self-fulfillment. Numerous passages in the *Réflexions* lend credence to this idea. On the other hand, the theory may be understood as directly correlative to the theory of self-love insofar as it envisages the practice of *honnêteté* as an instinctive tactic consistent with the self's concentration upon its own preservation and dignity. Taken together, these strains of analysis offer an intriguing interplay of voluntaristic and fatalistic perspectives, a variation of emphasis corresponding loosely to a fluctuation of viewpoint between individual (psychological) and collective (sociological) concerns. Regardless of the viewpoint, however, the advocacy of *honnêteté* reflects a logic of counteraction (not one of resolution or overcoming), for the *honnête homme* readily accepts a modus vivendi with aggressive and/or destructive tendencies and seeks to balance them through regulation rather than to eradicate or transform them. Within his highly polished, urbane community, he can engage simultaneously in verbal and social play, having the opportunity to bring both conceptual and interpersonal conflict under the control of endlessly renewable games.

Whether words or people, the "opponents" in these games are functionally interdependent, can only exist in *co*existence, as parts of a system wherein the adversary is also a partner and the "players" enter into an openly ambivalent relation corresponding to what Schelling terms a "mixed-motive game" (Thomas C. Schelling, *The Strategy of Conflict*)—an intersection of partnership and competition, concordance and contradiction. Beneath the conventions and tactics that allow the games to endure lie the structural axes of language and society, rules of grammar and rules of conduct, indispensable frames of reference for an analytic assessment of the quality of play. In their respective domains the rules both set limits and open possibilities: projecting a formal construct of boundaries, procedures, errors, and conventions, they provide the players with an opportunity to develop patterns of contention, to channel their conflicts into the realm of artistic expression, to deal with the threat of impotence or destruction by subjecting it to what Starobinski calls an esthetic transmutation, a displacement of moral imperatives by esthetic values. La Rochefoucauld thus links the subduing of pessimism to a necessarily communal objective: to make social relationships, as well as verbal ones, a work of art, to judge an impoverished society and its players by artistic criteria instead of applying unattainable moral standards. Starobinski asserts that the recourse to artful play—to the diversion criticized by Pascal—is fully conscious, the choice of a disabused moralist: "The spirit of play, the concern with elegance and exact expression will in no way change the pessimistic conviction. They will only cover it over with a veneer of hedonism ("La Rochefoucauld et les morales substitutives"). Man remains fundamentally the aggressive creature of self-love, achieving his humanistic identity only as a player in the ongoing game of cultural refinement.

It is self-evident that the principal instrument for playing this game is language and that the play of the salon thrives on the exhibition of elegance and subtle, precise expression. The fourth of the *Réflexions diverses*, "De la conversation," reads like a manual of strategy for permanent success in polite society, treating skillful conversation as an end in itself, a gratifying concurrence of social stability and genteel pleasures. As if to crystallize the difference of La Rochefoucauld from Pascal, Starobinski adopts the perspicuous formula "a wager for speech," a commitment that not only precludes taking refuge in divine mysteries but also discredits in advance any call to practical action. Although language may enter into cooperative efforts as an effective force, when discourse becomes a communal art cultivated by men as the crucial element of their interrelations, language can assume a profoundly conservative role in society. If we ordain that social intercourse be concentrated in verbal exchange, in a sort of fanciful or sportive negotiation with the primary objective of preserving the advantages of negotiating, we may derive a prolonged sense of satisfaction from manipulating the multiple resources of language so as to structure the functioning of society. Yet this institutionalized exploitation of language summarily discounts much of society's potential for compounding other relationships and activities. In short, we may promote linguistic refinement at the expense of meaningful social development.

Perhaps the crucial divergence tending to vitiate the correlation of linguistic games and social games lies in the relatively greater mediative power of the rules of grammar vis-à-vis the rules of conduct: the incomparable flexibility of language provides a unique instrument for absorbing, restructuring, and expressing conflict, whereas polite society presupposes telling circumstantial restrictions both on the nature and scope of conflict and on the identity of the players. This drift toward a narrowing of the social context (to the exclusive world of an articulate elite) suggests that the operational parallelism heretofore supposed between mixed-motive games in language and those in society breaks down precisely at the point where the games are perceived in their natural conjunction and interpenetration. Word games in society—social games in language: their integration obviously entails a reciprocal determination which language and society exert on one another. This interaction results in another, more complex mixed-motive game that redistributes the forces in play, polarizing conflict in society and mediation in language, evincing the predictable concentration of *free play* at the locus—in speech—where mediation occurs. Recognizing that the articulation of conflict in Maxime 83 goes beyond a mere challenge to the meaning (fulness) of a word, one might simply have supposed that the social game takes place in the extralinguistic reality that the maxim, as a vehicle of observation, evokes. The *Réflexions* make it clear, however, that the play with and on words does not merely take control of conflict within the maxim while referring to a comparable regulation of conflict in society, but that the word play actually implements the mediation of the social conflict, that it meets directly the dual requirement of developing checks and balances for social as well as conceptual oppositions. Responding concretely to the mediative power of language, the theory of *honnêteté* frequently takes the form of a theory of language use, plying the rules of the game not only to the conception of proper and appropriate speech, but also to the art of interpreting speech and refraining from speech:

One must say natural, easy, and more or less serious things according to the mood and inclination of the persons who are conversing, and not press them to approve of what one says, nor even to reply. . . . One must never put on airs of authority while speaking, nor use words and terms more imposing than the things. One can hold to his opinions if they are reasonable, but in doing so should never offend the beliefs of others nor appear to be shocked by what they have said. . . . But if there is a great deal of art in speaking, there is no less in keeping quiet. There is an eloquent silence, which sometimes serves to approve and to condemn; there is a scornful silence; there is a respectful silence.

(Réfl. IV, "De la conversation")

One can speak (to friends) of things which concern them, but only insofar as they allow it, and one must maintain great circumspection; it is polite, and sometimes even humane, to refrain from penetrating too far into the recesses of their hearts; they are often hurt by the unveiling of all that they know, and are hurt still more when one sees through what they do not understand.

(Réfl. II, "De la société")

Since they move beyond a straightforward penetration into the deeper realities of other personalities and explicitly incorporate a knowledgeable assessment of that penetration, such overtly normative principles of the theory of *honnêteté* shed a curious light on the trenchant psychological insights of the *Maximes*. They lead to the inescapable implication that the sociology of La Rochefoucauld rests on a quasi renunciation of his psychological perspicacity; or, more precisely, they suggest that the sociological understanding supported by psychological insight places significant restrictions on the use of the latter and complies with these restrictions by integrating the articulation of psychological insights into the linguistic play of the *honnête homme*. In other words, the theory of *honnêteté* displaces the uncompromisingly "pure" psychology of the theory of self-love—articulated with obdurate severity in the *Maximes*—with a "practical," circumstantially oriented psychology that stops short of driving home every disarming lesson of acute discernment. This restriction on the pursuit of demystification is all the more certain to be observed because the "rules of the game" in polite society do not merely discourage direct, indictive intrusions upon another person's ego, but ultimately provide for a measured interpretation of and reaction to any statement.

"The true gentleman [*honnête homme*] is never excited [*se pique*] by anything" (Max. 203). The import of this celebrated dictum allows for a dual appreciation of the role of incisive maxims in the society of *honnêtes gens*. In addition to circumventing, by virtue of its generality, some embarrassments of pointedly personal reference, the maxim assumes, by virtue of its distinctive form, the status of an artistic (or linguistic) object, open to interpretive discussion. Once the maxim is identified as a statement, it is possible to play with it without taking it too seriously, without dwelling excessively upon its stark implications. Perhaps the most important internal guide to understanding La Rochefoucauld's work lies in the warning against appearing to be shocked, which amounts to a warning against being diverted from concentration on upholding the quality of play—in the game of reading as well as in society.

While, in the last analysis, La Rochefoucauld accords a certain logistical priority to sociological over psychological perspectives, this priority does not stem simply from the acknowledged necessity of society to human life. As the sole theater in which life can be acted out for and with others and not just experienced for oneself, society takes on an existence and a character of its own that transcend the individual player, relegating him to support of the community and of social values: "The man who thinks he can find within himself the wherewithal for doing without everyone else makes a bad mistake; but the man who thinks that others cannot do without him is still more mistaken" (Max. 201); "As it is hard for several persons to have the same interests, it is at least necessary, for the tranquility of society, that they not have opposing ones" (Réfl. II, "De la société"). Inclusion in the community of *honnêtes gens* requires a modicum of conformity from each member, whose individuality will be protected primarily by his reserve, secondarily by the consideration that the others afford him. Admission to the game means playing a position or a part, as opposed to "being oneself," precisely because the private self does not automatically attune its interests to the pattern of acceptability that defines the area of public interest.

Despite the relatively modern note struck by the attribution of primacy to the social order, La Rochefoucauld's adherence to the theory of *honnêteté* upholds a profoundly reactionary view of society, consonant with the separatism of a cultural elite, a self-conscious community of disabused minds bent upon securing an equilibrium among egotists that will allow for an optimum of truth, freedom, and pleasure. The distinction of "les *vrais* honnêtes gens" epitomizes the alliance of cultural perfection with social exclusivism: "False *honnêtes gens* are those who disguise their failings to others and to themselves. True *honnêtes gens* are those who are well aware of their failings and admit to them" (Max. 202). As a special group, "les vrais honnétes gens" presumably possess a moral superiority, attained by those whose mastery of the game engenders a confidence allowing them to air the truths of private identity—almost as if they were actors in a metatheatrical setting who regain some sense of the distance between themselves and their roles. The ambivalence of the term *honnête,* which clearly takes on a moral connotation in the second sentence of Maxime 202, reflects a permanent tension within the theory of *honnêteté* between the choices of withholding or of expressing personal truths. The whole normative apparatus of the theory represents an attempt to divert the notion of honesty away from simple candor toward civility in the social sphere, where the observance of diplomatic procedures should facilitate the free exchange of general opinions and objective truths.

Yet the exchange of private, confesssional truths and personal views unspotted by the falsehood of omission clearly requires a degree of confidence that can only prevail in a still smaller, more exclusive community of kindred spirits. In Réflexion V, "De la confiance," La Rochefoucauld emphasizes the necessity of singling out those persons in whom one can confide without restraint. Although trust is "the bond of society and of friendship," the opening characterization of trust via comparison to sincerity suggests that the frame of reference for "true" *honnêteté* is actually a model of intimate, rather than group, relationships. Common to the entire reflection is the assumption that the "true" *honnête homme*, in refusing to violate a confidence, whatever the price of his fidelity, must be a man of rare virtue and fortitude, must belong to a kind of moral elite. At any rate, the size of the elite seems destined to diminish when its members are themselves implicated in the exchange of truths.

Within this narrowing sphere of interpersonal contacts, the ultimate case is necessarily that of relationships between two individuals. And on the surface this seems to be a privileged case in La Rochefoucauld's meditation on human nature. Invoked in five of the nineteen *Réflexions diverses* and in some sixty-four maxims, the nature of love is, at least in its frequency, the most prominent theme of his work, which also devotes considerable attention to the nature of friendship. Moreover, the perceptions relayed by maxims dealing with love display such remarkable variety and acuity that La Rochefoucauld has been typed "the first clinician of love" (Jean Rostand, "La Rochefoucauld," in *Hommes de vérité*), a worthy predecessor of Stendhal and Proust. Yet the real significance of intimate relationships in La Rochefoucauld's work has to do with the latent consent, within the theory of *honnêteté*, to a necessarily narrow conception of community. As in the case of social relationships, the value of close personal relationships derives from their role in man's efforts to balance or divert the forces of selfish instincts and to attain a measure of humanity. These efforts presumably have a better chance to achieve permanent, deeply satisfying success and to attain a high degree of honesty (in the sense of veracity) when channeled into the sphere of love and friendship.

If there is one indubitable lesson to be garnered from La Rochefoucauld's meditation on love and friendship, it is simply that even very private relationships cannot easily transcend the natural patterns of human behavior. In a reflection remarkable for its emphasis on the passage of time (Réfl. IX, "De l'Amour et de la vie"), the correlation between the temporal experiences of love and those of life suggests that many of the moralist's pronouncements on the nature of love may be treated as analogues to comparable insights into life, or vice versa:

> Love is an image of our life: each of them is subject to the same about-faces and the same changes. . . . This involuntary inconstancy is an effect of time, which in spite of us makes itself felt in love as in our lives. . . . Jealousy, mistrust, the fear of growing weary, the fear of being abandoned are troubles which accompany the aging of love, as illnesses accompany the excessive duration of life: one no longer feels alive because he feels sick, and one no

longer has the feeling of being in love except by feeling all the
pains of love.

(Réfl. IX)

Beyond its status as a mode of correlation, the march of time is recognized
as an active force in this reflection, for it *puts its hold* on love and life, which
are *subjected* to the irreversible process of change. Thus, as Freudmann
points out, the effects of time enter La Rochefoucauld's arsenal of critical
tools alongside the effects of self-love and other natural forces ("La
Rochefoucauld and the Concept of Time"). In combination, the various
implements for debunking supply the impetus for a disenchanting picture
of love, marred by impurity, futility, and suffering, or still worse, a hypocritical exercise of intrigue and coquetry.

Nevertheless, La Rochefoucauld fails to maintain a uniformly skeptical
view of love, allowing a certain ambivalence to creep into it by admitting
the possibility of "*le véritable* amour": "As for true love it is like the ap-
parition of the spirits: everyone talks about them, but few people have seen
any" (Max. 76; see also Max. 376, 473, 477). Although the definition of love
proves to be difficult (Max. 68), there are occasional, if somewhat indirect,
statements that associate it with the "passions violentes" (Max. 266, 466)
or "belles passions" (self-portrait), as an irrational and miraculous attraction, endowed with the strength to be lasting: "The same resoluteness
which helps ward off love also serves to make it violent and lasting, and
weak persons, who are always stirred up by the passions, are almost never
really possessed by them" (Max. 477). In addition to the force of passionate
desire, steadfastness in love demands a capacity for renewal, for the *re-
generation* of passion: "Constancy in love is a perpetual inconstancy, owing
to which our heart is drawn to all the qualities, one after another, of the
person whom we love, sometimes giving preference to one, sometimes to
another; so that this constancy is just an inconstancy which has been arrested and confined to the same object" (Max. 175; see also Max. 75, 176).
Not that love is solely an affair of the heart, for all the inventive power of
self-love comes into play: "An *honnête homme* can love life like a madman,
but not like a dolt" (Max. 353). By no means, however, does the intellectual
or spiritual component of love—"in the mind it is mutual understanding"
(Max. 68)—override the predominance of self-love, which triumphs in the
fulfillment of desire and in the pleasure of its own passion, not in the
passion that it provokes (Max. 259, 262).

If, then, love seems perfectly compatible with self-interest, what makes
it so rare? In the first place, the birth of a burning mutual passion is a
matter of chance; then, in the long run, the maintenance of love requires
that it be genuine, not staged: "Where there is love, no disguise can hide
it for long; neither can love be feigned where there is none" (Max. 70; see
Max. 74). Recognizing that "love's greatest miracle is to cure coquetry"

(Max. 349; cf. Max. 376), La Rochefoucauld links the miracle of love to a withdrawal from the artifice of play. The truth of love lies in the bond of confidence and sincerity, in that "openness of heart" which, instead of a "subtle dissimulation for drawing the confidence of others" (Max. 62; cf. Max. 116), is "a love for truth, a repugnance for disguise, a desire to overcome one's faults, and even to diminish them by virtue of admitting them" (Réfl. VI, "De la confiance"). Here again it is clear that egotistical motives are not totally suppressed, since sincerity allows one to fulfill a desire for absolution or moral elevation; what is suppressed is the dependency on rules, the sense of restraint and "justes limites" that the intersection of multiple interests imparts to less intimate relationships of trust. When, in love, the power of egotism reaches its apogee (Max. 262), self-love arrives at the stage that allows it to give up its histrionic stance in favor of free play and to identify directly with its passion. The ultimate, if transitory, miracle of the love relationship is to harbor the coexistence of unfettered passion and candor, to achieve interpersonal harmony without normative regulation and in conjunction with unmitigated self-satisfaction.

True love opens the way to a kind of liberation, an occasion to "be oneself." Can the same be said of true friendship, to which La Rochefoucauld apparently attaches still greater value? Two facts make this a surprisingly delicate question. First, in its consistency and uncompromising tone, the debunking of friendship surpasses that of love, leaving us with the barest minimum of suggestions as to the nature of true friendship. Second, "la véritable amitié" is invariably invoked concurrently with "le véritable amour"—"However rare true love may be, it is still less rare than true friendship" (Max. 473; see Max. 376, Réfl. XVII). Furthermore, in Réflexion XVII ("De l'inconstance"), the comparison of friendship to love (an analysis of the latter providing the basis for the comparison) unequivocally rules out the notion that men should prefer friendship because it is more durable than love: "But time, which changes temperament and interests, destroys each of them in almost the same way. Men are too weak and too given to change to sustain for long the weight of friendship." Confronted with the extreme rarity of true friendship and a host of unsettling insights into the falsities and weaknesses of common friendship, one can only proceed, at least for the most part, to envisage true friendship negatively in terms of what it is not, especially since the absence of violent passion in friendship works to restrict the analogy of friendship and love.

As Truchet points out, our main guidepost in this area is this single maxim, "which dates from 1678, [and] gives, in short, La Rochefoucauld's ultimate thought on friendship" ("Introduction" to Garnier edition of the *Maximes*). "We can love nothing except in relation to ourselves, and we are only following our taste and our pleasure when we prefer our friends to ourselves; it is nevertheless by this preference alone that friendship can be true and perfect" (Max. 81). In friendship as in love, egocentricity remains the fundamental factor; yet friendship differs from love in one crucial respect—it does entail a real preference for the friend, whereas in love the lover continues to prefer himself: "There is no passion in which love of oneself reigns so powerfully as in love; and we are always more inclined to sacrifice the tranquillity of our loved one than to lose our own" (Max. 262). If sincerity and perfection in friendship are difficult and rare, it is because they require a strong commitment from self-love to achieve satisfaction through its capacity for self-denial and devotion to others rather than to cultivate intense passion or to pursue the self-centered promotion of a praiseworthy self-image. For the moralist who enunciates this principle of friendship, there is clearly no way to cleanse friendship of all egotism, to achieve pure altruism. True friendship, in order to avoid the hypocrisy and inconstancy discovered in the *Maximes* behind "what men call friendship," must embody a directed egocentricity, lucidly affirmed and, in the company of an equally lucid friend, shamelessly relished. The force and sustenance of such friendship depend upon a rare combination: two individuals whose tastes and pleasures coincide. For it is precisely in the solidarity achieved by sharing one's egotism with another, by perceiving and experiencing it in and through the other, that self-satisfaction can attain its fullest authentication. Just as the *honnête homme* accepts, in society, the realness of appearances, he accepts, in friendship, the inescapable truth of egotism. Whereas in society he casts his lot for the ego-shielding interplay of truth with illusion, in friendship he cultivates a less prescriptive, less distracting game, the ego-building interplay of selfishness and selflessness, which is the reality of unmitigated personal truth. The triumph of sustaining this truth in friendship is reserved to individuals who find in themselves, without support from societal sanctions, sufficient strength to keep their egotism under control. Whence the extreme rarity of this exceptional achievement, securing in the narrowest of human relationships the bond through which *honnêteté* and veracity ultimately coincide.

If La Rochefoucauld's work holds out precious little hope for attaining "real" love or friendship, does it not put forth the solution of *honnêteté* as a kind of compensation, a more reasonable goal? To the somewhat simplistic thesis according to which the theory of *honnêteté* represents a positive outcome of La Rochefoucauld's thinking and at least a partial antidote to his so-called pessimism, one can obviously oppose the arsenal for debunking that the *Maximes* assemble. Countless texts restate the judgment that man is too weak, ignorant, and inconstant to play the game of social adjustment consistently, to persist in the exercise of prudence or honor. Nevertheless, since the solution of *honnêteté* is developed in sociological terms, it is against the background of society that it must finally be tested. The artisans of polite society ultimately ignore the pessimistic implications of their recourse to a cultural and/or moral elite, to a complacently antisocial perspective that overlooks the plight of humanity while legislating the satisfaction of a happy few. As La Rochefoucauld depicts it, the standard of the *honnête homme* makes such great demands upon its bearers that it remains out of reach to the average egotist, holds out little real hope for "humanization." While acknowledging the potential for controlling self-love through the checks and balances of social interaction, the theory of *honnêteté* does not give form to a societal design capable of reversing the broader implications of the theory of self-love, for the latter sets forth a psychology of Man in general, whereas the theory of *honnêteté* presents, not a sociology of Man, but a social creation—historically precarious—of privileged men.

For the individual, the unresolved tension between the general theory of self-love and the particular theory of *honnêteté* gives rise to an ethical dilemma. To ply oneself to the regimen of *honnêteté* (and even more, to act with heroism) is at once to commit oneself to a laudable search for human perfection and to succumb to an egological drift toward alienation. To opt for elevation is, in a restricted sense, to opt against humanity, to ground a claim of superiority to those who remain victims of their egotism. Faced with this choice, which eventually exposes the moralist to the charge of bad faith, La Rochefoucauld unequivocally elects to pay the price of distinction, and in so doing, implicitly posits the conjoint expression and sublimation of the ego as the primary moral act upon which can ethic can be built. Abstracted from the immediate historical setting in which it was elaborated, the code of *honnêteté* can still be read as enabling legislation, as a general call for adherence to a program for cultural upliftment. At any rate, La Rochefoucauld's ethic should not be dismissed as the mere corollary of social elitism, but should be examined as a response to the difficulty of opening the possibilities of moral conduct in the face of the constraints imposed by self-love.

The *Maximes* contain only a small number of precepts concerned with deportment. The *Réflexions*, however, in elaborating the theory of *honnêteté*, necessarily include many normative statements, most of which reflect an overall concern with securing harmony in human relationships. The code of prudence and self-control developed in the theory of *honnêteté* sanctions the practice of consideration and indulgence for others: "We must stand ready to excuse our friends when their faults were born with them and when these add up to less than their good qualities; we must often avoid revealing to them that we have noticed their faults and been shocked by them, and we must try to act so as to enable them to correct them [see also Max. 319]. . . . We should seek our own contentment and that of others, make allowance for their self-love and always refrain from offending it" (Réfl. II, "De la société"). The explicit point of departure for the enunciation of these precepts is man's inclination, which the achievement of true friendship has to reverse, always to prefer himself to his fellow men: "We should at least know how to hide this preferential desire, since it is too natural in us for us to get rid of it" (Réfl. II). Within a reflection based on the premise that society is necessary to man, this acknowledgment that covering up the self-preference is necessary to society draws the connection between the theories of self-love and *honnêteté*. In the context of the social comedy, it clearly implies the moral acceptability of the mask.

As we might well expect, however, La Rochefoucauld hardly allows the social necessity of play to take on the semblance of a moral absolute, for here again a measure of theoretical caution intervenes to establish limits and constraints that govern the recourse to dissimulation and the scope of its use: "Complaisance is necessary in society, but it must have limits: it becomes a servitude when it is excessive; it must at least appear to be free, and when we comply with the opinion of our friends, they must be persuaded that we are also following our own opinion" (Réfl. II). This proposition terminates a substantial paragraph that focuses on the importance of maintaining enough distance from society to conserve one's personal freedom, to uphold respect for the individual and his private identity. What should impress the player who sets out to conform to this part of the code of *honnêteté* is the way in which tacit recognition of independence as a human value is carried over into the realm of appearances: necessary amenity must appear free. This apparent contradiction mirrors the wider contradiction assumed by the *honnête homme* when he adopts the devices of playacting in order to facilitate the exchange of truth and frank opinion. By requiring this incongruity of appearance and reality, the code marks the inescapable precedence of basic ethical values, calling for disinterested judgment and action, with which the social and esthetic values of polite society should not openly conflict. Far from displacing such traditional virtues as honesty, sincerity, trust, generosity, independence, and so forth, the normative enterprise of the *Réflexions* represents an attempt to legislate conditions within which they can be put into "practice" and be said to govern human conduct. Just as the code of *honnêteté* works to further both honesty and civility, it favors the advance of humanity in both a moral and a cultural sense, disallowing the pursuit of the esthetic at the expense of the ethical, and vice versa.

In principle, then, it should be possible to attach a positive moral value to the practice of *honnêteté*, which has frequently been identified as La Rochefoucauld's definitive ethical doctrine. A reading of the *Maximes*, though, does not allow such a view to pass uncontested: "However even the world of *honnêtes gens* lacks perfect wisdom, it is neither difficult nor meritorious to comply with its rules." Coulet proceeds to invoke the hero's moral superiority over the *honnête homme*, arguing that the values to which La Rochefoucauld accords his ultimate allegiance pertain to a hero's view of humanity, one that discredits the false virtues of common mortals: "It is in the eye of that hero that humanity is self-love, vanity, the puppet of chance, blind passions" ("La Rochefoucauld et la peur d'être dupe").

Moreover, with or without the stance of the hero, shedding doubt upon the moral value of the theory of *honnêteté* hardly exacts a herculean effort from the composer of maxims. Since the theory is directed toward a conciliation of conflicting egos and includes neither discreditation nor approbation of self-love, its development can be attributed to the workings of self-love and interest that the *Maximes* expose—whence the possibility of deeming the code immoral in its very foundations. Of greater weight, to be sure, is the charge that *honnêteté* gives rise to a masquerade of false virtues, allowing its followers to content themselves with the facile artifice of virtuous action and thereby doing violence to the cause of "real"—and necessarily more difficult—moral uprightness. Insofar as resorting to false virtue creates still another triumph of self-love, these doubts about the moral value of *honnêteté* resolve into a single central question: does the critical appraisal of virtue in the *Maximes* hinge upon the advocacy of a *true* virtue that is incompatible with the prudential ethic of the *honnête homme*? In other words, does a higher, if not heroic, morality emanate from the *Maximes*?

The analysis of virtue stands out as the archetype of critical reduction in the *Maximes*. To define virtue is to expose the morally deficient nature of its source:

> Our virtues are usually just vices in disguise.
>
> (Epigraph)

> What we take for virtues are often just a collection of diverse actions and interests which fortune or our ingenuity is able to contrive; and it is not always through valor and through chastity that men are valiant and women chaste.
>
> (Max. 1)

> What an Italian poet has said of the honor of women can be said of all our virtues: it is often nothing more than an art of appearing to be honorable.
>
> (Maxime supprimée [hereafter cited as MS] 33)

> What society calls virtue is usually just a phantom conjured up by our passions to which we give a respectable name in order to be able to do what we wish with impunity.
>
> (MS 34)

Now in each of these four texts we note that the restrictive *n'est . . . que* ("is . . . just," etc.) is itself restricted by an adverbial qualifier ("often," "usually"), which leaves open the possibility of an irreducible virtue. In some instances the use of the vice/virtue antithesis appears to imply the same possibility, suggesting that vice takes on the guise of virtue in imitation of something that is superior to and innately different from itself: "Hypocrisy is a tribute which vice pays to virtue" (Max. 218). By comparison however, vice clearly holds a more fundamental ontological position than virture, if only because—as the basic fact of "moral life"—it is never thrown into question. Virtue may consist of vice in disguise, but not vice versa, and only vice is represented as an inevitable experience of life:

> It might be said that the vices await us in the course of life like hosts with whom we must stay one after the other; and I doubt

that experience would lead us to avoid them if it were possible for us to pass two times along the same path.

(Max. 191)

Nothing is so contagious as example, and we never do very good or very bad deeds which fail to inspire similar ones. We imitate good actions by emulation, and bad ones because of the malevolence of our nature, which shame held in check and which example sets free.

(Max. 230; see also Réfl. VII, "Des exemples")

At first glance, the image of vices as hosts (in Max. 191) may overshadow the larger image of the course of life, a conventional metaphor that incorporates the attentiveness to succession and to necessity that recurs throughout La Rochefoucauld's meditation on human experience. As a host, a vice is already present, waiting for errant men who have to accept its hospitality; and if a man, having already paid one visit to an evil host, nonetheless returns, his return does not merely reflect an innocent haplessness, for the necessity of the visit cannot depend simply on the availability of the lodging, but has to be seconded by the visitor's inborn inclination to evil—"the malevolence of our nature." The distinction between imitating good actions by emulation and imitating bad actions by dint of human nature rests upon the referential disparity of the two adverbial phrases: "par émulation" picks up the notion of mimetic or competitive response, which the verb "imiter" carries over from the opening remark on the function of examples, whereas in the second half of the comparison "par la malignité de notre nature" is conceptually affiliated with the object "mauvaises actions." To turn this construction into a straight parallelism, it suffices to substitute for "par émulation" the notion that we imitate good actions "because of the *goodness* of our nature," but it is precisely this goodness that La Rochefoucauld is not prepared to concede without reservations: "It is quite difficult to distinguish goodness in all things, extended to everyone, from consummate cleverness" (MS 44). There is little need to illustrate La Rochefoucauld's (in)famous propensity to point out the contamination of goodness and virtue by interest, vanity, passion, or vice in general, a contamination that virtue naturally incurs because it can appear only in a corruptive atmosphere—in the course of man's recurrent dealings with the well-ensconced innkeepers of vice. The image of the hosts suggests that the predominance of vice over virtue or evil over good might well be represented in institutional terms; the former enjoys the unquestioned prerogatives of the establishment, while the latter has to confront the pull of absorption into the establishment.

Although the cards are heavily stacked against the existence of real virtue, men continue to believe in it, or at least in their own: "What often prevents us from appreciating maxims which prove the falseness of the virtues is that we believe too readily that they are genuine in ourselves"

(MP 7). Thus La Rochefoucauld's analysis takes him beyond the falsehood of virtues per se and points to the presence of falsehood—especially self-deception—in the process of assessing and reacting to virtue. The same individual who readily overlooks the flaws in his own supposed virtue will probably affirm those of his fellow men with unwarranted haste: "Quickness to assume wrongdoing, without sufficient examination, is an effect of pride and laziness: we want to find culprits, and we do not want to go to the trouble of examining the crimes" (Max. 267). That the most fundamental moral or polemical structure inherent to the analysis of virtue resides in the indictment of inadequate understanding can be seen in the original version of the epigraph (Max. 181 of the first edition): "We are preoccupied with our own advantage in such a way that we often take for virtues what are actually just a number of vices which resemble them, and which pride and self-love have disguised from us" (see also MS 19). What is left out when this maxim is geared down to the more categorical pronouncement of the epigraph is not merely the clause referring to the source of the disguise. The original text also places a more concerted emphasis on the misapprehension of virtue, that is, in addition to disclosing the alliance of self-love with vice, the text points to an excess of egotism, which is its inattention to itself. Man's initial derelection consists in failing to see or in ignoring the vitiating ingredient of self-love in the makeup of virtue. Men cannot be guilty of their natural egotism, only of failing to discern and restrain it. In exposing the fraudulent attitude that men adopt toward virtue, the *Maximes* impugn their unwillingness to acknowledge the predominance of evil: "However wicked men might be, they would not dare appear to be enemies of virtue, and when they wish to do harm to it, they pretend to believe that it is spurious, or they attribute crimes to it" (Max. 489). If they were honest, men would admit their wickedness and carry out their opposition to virtue without feigned disbelief or misrepresentation. Their distaste for the beneficent acts of others (see Max. 14, 29) testifies to the untimeliness of goodness and virtue in an interest-dominated society.

As they expose man's hostile attitude to real virtue along with his investment in false virtue, the *Maximes* seem to put into practice the "ethic of lucidity" with which La Rochefoucauld is often associated. It is necessary to recognize, however, that the virtue of lucidity could not constitute, by itself, the real virtue that, in theory if not in fact, has to serve as the counterpart to false virtue and as the positive pole in the vice/virtue antithesis. Lucidity is but a starting point—an awareness of egotism in which an ethic like the code of *honnêteté* can well be grounded and back to which the *honnête homme* must continually refer in order to maintain the moral integrity of his position. True virtue, free from the inroads of vice, demands the ability to appropriate the lessons of lucidity in opposition to the prevailing force of vice. As we have come to expect, the motif of authenticity is accompanied here, as in maxims that invoke true love and friendship, by an awareness of its extreme rarity and of the necessary possession of strength: "Nothing is rarer than genuine goodness; the very ones who believe that they possess it ordinarily have only weakness" (Max. 481).

Reflecting his skepticism toward the so-called "pacific virtues" (Max. 398; see also Max. 16, 169, 266, 293), the dissociation of true goodness from weakness invokes an important leitmotiv of La Rochefoucauld's thought: "Weakness is more opposed to virtue than is vice" (Max. 445; see also Max. 130, 316, 479). Given the undeniable power of vice in the human arena, virtue cannot stand up against it without commensurable strength: "No one deserves to be praised for goodness if he lacks the force to be wicked: all other goodness is most often just a laziness or an impotence of the will" (Max. 237; see also MS 45). The vigor of denunciation in the *Maximes* reaches its apex with the characterization of sloth, in an extraordinary text that deserves, stylistically and conceptually, to be classed with the famous reflection on self-love (MS 1):

> Of all the passions the one which is the least well known to ourselves is sloth; it is the most zealous and the most malicious of all, although its violence is imperceptible and its ravages are well hidden; if we consider its power attentively, we shall see that in every eventuality it assumes mastery over our feelings, our interests, and our pleasures; it is the remora strong enough to stop the greatest ships, it is a calm more dangerous to important affairs than reefs and the greatest storms; the repose of sloth is a secret charm of the soul which suddenly suspends the most ardent pursuits and the most unyielding resolutions; to give in conclusion the true idea of this passion, it is necessary to say that sloth is, as it were, a blissful state of the soul which consoles it for every loss and which takes the place of its every good.
>
> (MS 54)

The paradox of sloth, like that of self-love, stems from the stealth of its activity, from its seeming ability to work mightily and purposefully, that is, in contradiction to the observable patterns of indolence. Not only does sloth achieve mastery over opinions, interests, and pleasures, it can also prevail over the violent passions, like love and ambition: "Sloth, however languorous, often exerts mastery over them nonetheless; it encroaches upon every aim and every action in life; it destroys and consumes imperceptibly the passions and the virtues" (Max. 266). Generating an inertia that dissipates the impulse to purposeful exertion, sloth acts as the most insidious opponent to virtue by consolidating in man the conditions under which vice can predominate without challenge. In a sense, as Barthes points out, weakness and sloth represent a scandalous condition for La Rochefoucauld because they effectively put a stop to the dialectic of vice/virtue or good/evil and thereby exclude the very possibility of virtue. In the series of images that compose the second half of MS 54, each of the terms signifying an abeyance of movement ("rémore," "bonace," "repos," "béatitude") is modified by a complement that underscores the extraordinary braking power behind the realization of quiescence. The resulting picture of a listing, tranquilized soul offers a negative image of true virtue, which demands a soul with the strength to overcome the enticing comfort of inaction.

If there are, in reality, bona fide manifestations of such a forceful soul, one obvious reference point must be the glorious ascendancy of the hero: "Intrepidity is an extraordinary strength of the soul which raises it above the troubles, disorders, and emotions that the sight of great perils could stir up in it; and it is by dint of this strength that heroes maintain their inner calm and preserve the free usage of their reason in the most surprising and the most terrible eventualities" (Max. 217). Here the spiritual *force* of the hero serves to guarantee his freedom to commit moral acts, yet this is not to say that his intrepidity, any more than his lucidity, is thus qualified in ethical terms as *good*. On the contrary, the *Maximes* clearly recognize that inherently *great* action remains subject to post facto moral evaluation: "There are heroes in evil as in good" (Max. 185). The hero does not automatically serve as either the model or the judge of true virtue. As is the case with the code of *honnêteté*, the relatively evanescent evocation of heroism in the *Maximes* entails no full-scale redefinition of good and evil. For Nietzsche, who strongly approved of La Rochefoucauld's distaste for weak virtues such as pity, the moralist's critique of virtue failed to go far enough because it merely denied the truth of the motives behind actions, whereas Nietzsche went on to deny that moral judgments are founded upon truths. Far from affirming the strength of the ego as a fundamental value, the heroism invoked in the *Maximes* (and in the *Mémoires*) seems incommensurable with the energy cult of the Nietzschean overman. No more than the *honnête homme* can the classical hero, in striving for his own particular virtue, appropriate to his exceptional role, escape from the predominance of inherited values; at best, he can only hope to reorder them by assigning higher priority to heroic—*traditionally* heroic—values.

La Rochefoucauld, moreover, does not protect the presumed superiority of the hero from the barbs of critical deflation. He indicates that the hero's *élévation* can hardly stem from unique moral attributes since the ascent from the common to the heroic represents an essentially quantitative jump in ambition and vanity: "When great men let themselves be beaten down by long-drawn-out misfortunes, they reveal that they had only borne them through the strength of their ambition, not through that of their soul, and that apart from great vanity heroes are made like other men" (Max. 24). Rather than being an ethical assessment, this maxim brings into play what Starobinski terms "a principle of nonconservation of force," which is to say that heroism is undermined by temporal and material limitations on the generation of passions. The vanity of the hero does not, to be sure, constitute a moral disqualification; it reflects his lucidity with regard to his natural, inborn strength and goes hand in hand with his will to make use of that strength while he possesses it, a volition that separates him from the common lot of men who have "more force than will" (Max. 30).

The passive voice—"Les héros *sont faits*"—is a revelatory construction. Excluding the image of a self-made hero, it situates individual identity as a *product*, reflecting the predominance of natural endowment even in the heroic dimension. On the whole, commentators of the *Maximes* have failed to accord adequate attention to the difference between natural value and acquired value in La Rochefoucauld's outlook. Not only do the *Maximes* expose the being behind appearances, the man behind the facade, they often proceed to qualify that being, to assess the man in terms of his merit and his defects, his good and bad qualities. This process reveals the crucial impact of nature's selectivity in determining the individual's potential: "There are good qualities which degenerate into faults when they are natural, and others which are never perfect when they are acquired. We must, for example, use our reason to keep our wealth and our counsel; but nature, on the other hand, must give us goodness and valor" (Max. 365; see also Max. 53, 153, Réfl. III, "De l'air et des manières," and Réfl. 14, "Des modèles de la nature et de la fortune"). Thus it is necessary to avoid confusing the qualifications of man's nature with the judgment of his action. In large measure, the hero owes his heroism to nature (and to fortune), just as man in general owes to nature his limited potential for vice and virtue: "It seems that nature has prescribed for each man, from the moment of birth, limits for virtues and vices" (Max. 189; see also MS 36). Strictly speaking, it is within the range of this potential for vice and virtue that moral judgment focused on the exercise of reason comes into play.

On what basis, then, do the *Maximes* grant approval to human action? The essential criterion calls for the exercise of will, for "application" (Max. 243). Implicit in the definition of *grandeur d'âme* (the antithesis of weakness or laziness of the soul) as a function of *grands desseins*, and not as a fixed preponderance of virtue over passion (MS 31), is the stipulation that a praiseworthy act must carry out the conscious designs of a naturally meritorious individual: "However astonishing an action may be, it must not be considered great when it is not the effect of a great aim" (Max. 160). This maxim states the principle applied in others (Max. 7, 57, 120, for example) where the discreditation of an action depends upon the individual's lack of conscious intent. Consonant with his insistence on planning or calculation, La Rochefoucauld also shows concern for the modes of action that are selected: "The glory of great men must always be measured against the means which they have used to acquire it" (Max. 157); "It is not enough to have great qualities; they must be well managed" (Max. 159; see also Max. 437). Maxime 157 clearly opens the way to a moral critique of heroism, making the hero subject to condemnation when he succumbs to the temptation to indulge wantonly in the exaltation of superior force. Rather than merely disallowing the possibility of justifying the means by the end, La Rochefoucauld affirms that the end must be measured against the means, that the individual should combine his talents with a view to controlling the relationship between the end and the means. Significantly, the final maxim in this group of texts (156–161) dealing with the value of conduct invites us to envisage this relationship in terms of proportionality: "There must be a certain proportion between actions and intentions if one is to derive from them all the results they can yield" (Max. 161). Hinged upon the search for effects, this text has an almost utilitarian ring: one may obtain a maximum of results from actions that correlate well with intentions—as if the desirability of proportion should derive, not from its intrinsic value, but from a concern with efficiency. What is ultimately sanctioned is nothing else than the deliberate regulation of forceful action.

At first glance, the outlooks of the hero and the *honnête homme* seem to correspond in the commitment to lucidity that they both exhibit. Starting with this common denominator, it suffices to assent to the critique of heroism in order to arrive at the conventional logic by which the hero's (La Rochefoucauld's?) application of lucidity to his own position in a changing society leads him to abandon the hero's role and to adopt the more viable role of the *honnête homme*. To contest this logic, however, it suffices to acknowledge, with Coulet, that the *Maximes* question the viability of the *honnête homme* no less than that of the hero. The alternative—heroism/*honnêteté*—raised in a basically historical context, tends to obscure the possibility of a less categorical view. If the exercise of lucidity is situated in the sphere of moral judgment, the *Maximes* appear to gravitate toward a certain convergence of the decisive modes of action—force and regulation—that distinguish, respectively, the lives of the hero and the *honnête homme*.

To this tentative synthesis it is doubtless pertinent to object that the axiological statements cited earlier (among others, Max. 157, 159, 160) refer uniformly, not to moral acceptability, but to greatness, and thereby imply an ineradicable preference for the supremely demanding, yet triumphant, virtue of the hero. One has to recall—in answer to Coulet's dismissal of *honnêteté* as well—that the *honnête homme* applies himself to an exceedingly difficult regime, to the creation of a "*great* work" (Réfl. II, "De la société"), thoroughly imbued with the conscious design that La Rochefoucauld requires in great action. Furthermore, the correlation of intent, action, and outcome reaches an ideal culmination in the society of *honnêtes gens*, where the goal of harmony—proportion between *actions* and *desseins*—is attained by a veritable fusion of means and end in the quest for linguistic perfection. By preserving his independence and intellectual detachment, the *honnête homme* retains that crucial element of the hero's posture which guarantees the free exercise of reason in trying circumstances—*il ne se pique de rien*. By conceiving of *honnêteté* as an alternative to—and not a replacement of—heroism, one can even think of the true *honnête homme* as a superior individual who, relying less upon the strength of his soul than upon the strength of reason, exercises in his own fashion the functions of a cultural hero. In his fashion he acquires a distinction that sets him above the lot of common men.

When, beyond its social significance, the meaning of *honnêteté* embraces moral connotations, the doctrine assumes its higher and more exclusive function as a summons to a certain authenticity. At this point, where the judgment to be rendered concerns the individual's manner of acquiring extrinsic traits and determining his place in life, both the hero and the *honnête homme* have to be measured by the same universally applicable standard, which cannot be narrowly qualified as either heroic or *honnête:* "I do not intend, by what I say, to enclose us so tightly within ourselves that we do not have the freedom to follow examples and to acquire useful or necessary qualities that nature has not given us: the arts and sciences are good for everyone; but these acquired qualities must have a certain relationship and a certain union with our own qualities, which extend and increase them imperceptibly" (Réfl. III, "De l'air et des manières"). Like the social ethic of harmony and gentility that it subsumes, this precept is essentially classical. Coinciding with the traditional theme of fidelity to one's nature, the authenticity in question here remains distant from the modern emphasis on accepting one's freedom and responsibility in opposition to the notion of a natural self. Yet this hardly furnishes a legitimate basis for accusing La Rochefoucauld of using nature as a refuge from moral accountability. In the wake of his critical assault upon the inadequacies of man's natural qualities, he affirms both the freedom to acquire qualities that nature fails to provide and the necessity of doing so. The observation of men in action reveals the importance of controlling wisely this acquisition process: "It seems that men do not find enough faults for themselves; they still increase them in number with certain peculiar qualities with which they seek to adorn themselves, and they cultivate them with such care that they eventually become natural faults which are no longer within their power to correct" (Max. 493). This maxim, which links the display of discordant qualities (appearances) to a decisively reprehensible result, also suggests the possibility of developing natural merit, grounded in adherence to qualities that can be assumed without undue pretense. The call for a harmonious relationship between the natural and the acquired, which implicitly accords a sanction to the axiological precedence of *le naturel,* does not simply reflect the esthetic prejudice of polite society; it is, for the man who understands that developing such a relationship depends upon a candid perception and evaluation of his nature, a genuine call to honesty and integrity. The *Maximes* go no further than this, offer no delineable ethical system either in opposition or in parallel to that of the *Réflexions:* instead, they bring to bear upon the code of *honnêteté,* as upon heroism, a rigorous axiological perspective that underscores the consummate difficulty of achieving—over and beyond social distinction—moral rectitude.

Pascal's Allegory of Persuasion

Paul de Man

Attempts to define allegory keep reencountering a set of predictable problems, of which the summary can serve as a preliminary characterization of the mode. Allegory is sequential and narrative, yet the topic of its narration is not necessarily temporal at all, thus raising the question of the referential status of a text whose semantic function, though strongly in evidence, is not primarily determined by mimetic moments; more than ordinary modes of fiction, allegory is at the furthest possible remove from historiography. The "realism" that appeals to us in the details of medieval art is a calligraphy rather than a mimesis, a technical device to insure that the emblems will be correctly identified and decoded, not an appeal to the pagan pleasures of imitation. For it is part of allegory that, despite its obliqueness and innate obscurity, the resistance to understanding emanates from the difficulty or censorship inherent in the statement and not from the devices of enunciation: Hegel rightly distinguishes between allegory and enigma in terms of allegory's "aim for the most complete clarity, so that the external means it uses must be as transparent as possible with regard to the meaning it is to make apparent" (*Vorlesungen über die Aesthetik*, de Man's translation). The difficulty of allegory is rather that this emphatic clarity of representation does not stand in the service of something that can be represented.

The consequence, throughout the history of the term *allegory*, is a recurrent ambivalence in its aesthetic valorization. Allegory is frequently dismissed as wooden, barren (*kahl*), ineffective, or ugly, yet the reasons for its ineffectiveness, far from being a shortcoming, are of such all-encompassing magnitude that they coincide with the furthest reaching achievements available to the mind and reveal boundaries that aesthetically more

From *Allegory and Representation: Selected Papers from the English Institute 1979–1980*, New Series, no. 5, edited by Stephen J. Greenblatt. © 1981 by the English Institute.

successful works of art, because of this very success, were unable to perceive. To remain with Hegel a moment longer, the aesthetic condemnation of allegory, which becomes evident in the assumed inferiority of Vergil with regard to Homer, is outdone, in Hegel's own allegory of history, by its assignation to the meta-aesthetic age of Christianity, thus making the triadic procession from Homer to Vergil to Dante characteristic for the history of art itself as the dialectical overcoming of art. The theoretical discussion of the uncertain value of allegory repeats, in the *Aesthetics*, the theoretical discussion of the uncertain value of art itself. In the wavering status of the allegorical sign, the system of which the allegorical is a constitutive component is being itself unsettled.

Allegory is the purveyor of demanding truths, and thus its burden is to articulate an epistemological order of truth and deceit with a narrative or compositional order of persuasion. In a stable system of signification, such an articulation is not problematic; a representation is, for example, persuasive and convincing to the extent that it is faithful, exactly in the same manner that an argument is persuasive to the extent that it is truthful. Persuasion and proof should not, in principle, be distinct from each other, and it would not occur to a mathematician to call his proofs allegories. From a theoretical point of view, there ought to be no difficulty in moving from epistemology to persuasion. The very occurrence of allegory, however, indicates a possible complication. Why is it that the furthest reaching truths about ourselves and the world have to be stated in such a lopsided, referentially indirect mode? Or, to be more specific, why is it that texts that attempt the articulation of epistemology with persuasion turn out to be inconclusive about their own intelligibility in the same manner and for the same reasons that produce allegory? A large number of such texts on the relationship between truth and persuasion exist in the canon of philosophy and of rhetoric, often crystallized around such traditional philosophical topoi as the relationship between analytic and synthetic judgments, between propositional and modal logic, between logic and mathematics, between logic and rhetoric, between rhetoric as *inventio* and rhetoric as *dispositio*, and so forth. In order to try to progress in the precise formulation of the difficulty, I turn to what I find to be a suggestive example, one of the later didactic texts written by Pascal for the instruction of the pupils at Port Royal. The text, which dates from 1657 or 1658 (Pascal died in 1662), remained unpublished for a long time, but did not pass unnoticed, since Arnauld and Nicole incorporated parts of it in the *Logique* of Port Royal. It has since been mentioned by most specialists of Pascal and has been the object of at least one learned monograph. The text is entitled *Réflexions sur la géométrie en général; De l'esprit géométrique et de l'Art de persuader*, a title rendered somewhat oddly, but not uninterestingly, in one English edition of Pascal as *The Mind of the Geometrician*. It is an exemplary case for our inquiry, since it deals with what Pascal calls, in the first section, "l'étude de la verité" or epistemology and, in the second, "l'art de persuader" or rhetoric.

Ever since it was discovered, *Réflexions* has puzzled its readers. Arnauld's and Nicole's way of excerpting from it to make it serve the more narrowly traditional Cartesian mold of the *Logique* considerably simplified and indeed mutilated its Pascalian complexity; the Dominican Father Touttée, who was the first to unearth it from among Pascal's papers, expressed great doubts about its internal coherence and consistency. Despite strong internal evidence to the contrary, the text has often not been considered as a single entity divided in two parts, but as two entirely separate disquisitions; Pascal's early editors, Desmolets (in 1728) and Condorcet (in 1776), gave it as separate fragments, and not until 1844 did it appear more or less in the now generally accepted form of one single unit divided into two parts. The history of the text's philology curiously repeats the theoretical argument, which has compulsively to do with questions of units and pairs, divisibility, and heterogeneity.

The argument of the *Réflexions* is digressive, but not at all lacking in consistency. If it indeed reaches dead ends and breaking points, it does so by excess of rigor rather than for lack of it. That such breaking points are reached, however, cannot be denied. Recent commentators have valiantly tried to patch up the most conspicuous holes by attributing them to historical indeterminations characteristic of Pascal's time and situation. In a text that is historically as overdetermined as this one—and that contains echoes of an almost endless series of disputations which, in the wake of such philosophers as Descartes, Leibniz, Hobbes, and Gassendi, mark the period as one of intense epistemological speculation—the temptation is great to domesticate the more threatening difficulties by historicizing them out of consciousness. Even after this operation has been performed, some anomalies remain that pertain specifically to the nature rather than the state of the question. The most conspicuous break occurs in the second part, in the section on persuasion. Pascal has asserted the existence of two entirely different modes by which arguments can be conducted. The first mode has been established in the first section, in polemical opposition to the scholastic logic of syllogisms, as the method of the geometricians, and it can be codified in the rules that Arnauld and Nicole incorporated in the *Logique*. When these rules are observed, it is the only mode to be both productive and reliable. Because of the fallen condition of man, however, it cannot establish itself as the only way. Though man is accessible to reason and convinced by proof, he is even more accessible to the language of pleasure and of seduction, which governs his needs and his passions rather than his mind. In their own realms, the language of seduction (*langage d'agrément*) and the language of persuasion can rule or even cooperate, but when natural truth and human desire fail to coincide, they can enter into conflict. At that moment, says Pascal, "a dubious balance is achieved between truth and pleasure (*vérité et volupté*), and the knowledge of the one and the awareness of the other wage a combat of which the outcome is very uncertain." Such dialectical moments are, as the readers of the *Pensées* well know, very common in Pascal and function as the necessary precondition for insights. No such resolution occurs at this crucial moment, however, although the efficacy of the entire text is at stake. Pascal retreats in a phraseology of which it is impossible to say whether it is evasive or ironically personal: "Now, of these two methods, the one of persuasion, the other of seduction (*convaincre . . . agrées*), I shall give rules only for the former . . . [the geometrical persuasion]. Not that I do not believe the other to be incomparably more difficult, more subtle, more useful, and more admirable. So, if I do not discuss it, it is because of my inability to do so. I feel it to be so far beyond my means that I consider it entirely impossible. Not that I do not believe that if anyone is able to do so, it is people whom I know, and that no one has as clear and abundant insight into the matter as they do." The reference appears to be to Pascal's friend the Chevalier de Méré, who had already been present by polemical allusion at an earlier and delicate moment in the first part of the treatise, thus enforcing the impression that, at the moment in the demonstration when we are the most in need of clear and explicit formulation, what we get is private obfuscation. For, as is clear from many testimonials and, among many other instances, from the prose of the *Lettres provinciales*, Pascal's claim at being incompetent in the rhetoric of seduction is certainly not made in good faith. The concluding paragraphs of the text never recover from this decisive break in a by no means undecisive argument. What is it, in this argument, that accounts for the occurrence of this disruption? What is it, in a rigorous epistemology, that makes it impossible to decide whether its exposition is a proof or an allegory? We have to retrace and interpret the course of the argument, as it develops in the first section of the *Réflexions* and as it finds its equivalent in the underlying logical and rhetorical structure of the *Pensées*, in order to answer this question.

"De l'esprit géométrique," part 1 of the *Réflexions*, starts out from a classical and very well known problem in epistemology: the distinction between nominal and real definition, *definitio nominis* and *definitio reo*. Pascal insists at once that the superiority and reliability of the geometrical (i.e., mathematical) method is established because "in geometry we recognize only those definitions that logicians call *definitions of name (définitions de nom)*, that is to say, giving a name only to those things which have been clearly designated in perfectly known terms." Nothing could be simpler, in Pascal's exposition, than this process of denomination, which exists only as a kind of stenography, a free and flexible code used for reasons of economy to avoid cumbersome repetitions, and which in no way influences the thing itself in its substance or in its properties. Definitions of name are, says Pascal, "entirely free and never open to contradiction." They require some hygiene and some policing. One should avoid, for example, that the same signifier designate two distinct meanings, but this can easily be assured by public convention. Real definitions, on the other hand, are a great deal more coercive and dangerous: they are actually not definitions, but axioms or, even more frequently, propositions that need to be proven. The confusion between nominal and real definitions is the main cause of the difficulties and obscurities that plague philosophical disputation, and to keep the distinction between them clear and sharp is, in Pascal's own terms, "the (real) reason for writing the treatise, more than the subject with which I deal." The mind of the geometrician is exemplary to the extent that it observes this distinction.

Can it really do so? As soon as it is enunciated, the apparently simple definition of definition runs into complications, for the text glides almost imperceptively from the discussion of nominal definition to that of what it calls "primitive words," which are not subject to definition at all, since their pretended definitions are infinite regresses of accumulated tautologies. These terms (which include the basic *topoi* of geometrical discourse, such as motion, number, and extension) represent the natural language element that Descartes scornfully rejected from scientific discourse, but which reappear here as the natural light that guarantees the intelligibility of primitive terms despite their undefinability. In geometrical (i.e., epistemologically sound) discourse, primitive words and nominal definition are coextensive and blend into each other: in this "judicious science . . . all terms are perfectly intelligible, either by natural light or by the definitions it produces."

But things are not quite so simple. For if primitive words possess a natural meaning, then this meaning would have to be universal, as is the science that operates with these words; however, in one of the sudden shifts so characteristic of Pascal and which sets him entirely apart from Arnauld's trust in logic, this turns out not to be the case. "It is not the case," says Pascal, "that all men have the same idea of the essence of the things which I showed to be impossible and useless to define . . . (such as, for example, time). It is not the nature of these things which I declare to be known by all, but simply *the relationship between the name and the thing*, so that on hearing the expression *time*, all turn (or direct) the mind toward the same entity . . . (*tous portent la pensée vers le même objet*)." Here the word does not function as a sign or a name, as was the case in the nominal definition, but as a vector, a directional motion that is manifest only as a turn, since the target toward which it turns remains unknown. In other words, the sign has become a trope, a substitutive relationship that has to posit a meaning whose existence cannot be verified, but that confers upon the sign an unavoidable signifying function. The indeterminacy of this function is carried by the figural expression "porter la pensée," a figure that cannot be accounted for in phenomenal terms. The nature of the relationship between figure (or trope) and mind can only be described by a figure, the same figure that Pascal will use in the *Pensées* in order to describe figure: "Figure *porte* absence et présence, plaisir et déplaisir" (265–677) (Pascal's *Pensées* exist in different editions with different identifying numbers. I quote the number of the Lafuma classification in the Editions du Seuil volume, followed by the number of the Brunschwieg classification in italics); this is a sentence to which we will have to return later on. This much, at least, is clearly established: in the language of geometry, nominal definition and primitive terms are coextensive, but the semantic function of the primitive terms is structured like a trope. As such, it acquires a signifying function that it controls neither in its existence nor in its direction. Another way of stating this is to say that the nominal definition of primitive terms always turns into a proposition that has to, but cannot, be proven. Since definition is now itself a primitive term, it follows that the definition of the nominal definition is itself a real, and not a nominal, definition. This initial complication has far-reaching consequences for the further development of the text.

The discussion of denomination and of definition leads directly into Pascal's more fundamental and systematic statement about the intelligibility and coherence of mind and cosmos: the principle of double infinity, which also underlies the theological considerations of the *Pensées*. From a traditional point of view, the interest of the *Réflexions* is that it spells out, more explicitly than can be the case in the apologetic and religious context of the *Pensées*, the link between this central principle, so often expressed, in Pascal himself and in his interpreters, in a tonality of existential pathos, and the geometrical or mathematical logic of which it is actually a version. The text helps to undo the tendencious and simplistic opposition between knowledge and faith which is often forced upon Pascal. The *logos* of the world consists of the "necessary and reciprocal link" that exists between the intrawordly dimensions of motion, number, and space (to which Pascal also adds time), the principle asserted in the only quotation from Scripture to appear in the text: *Deus fecit omnia in pondere, in numero, et mensura.* (The assimilation of space to measure (*mensura*) and especially of motion to weight (*pondere*) raises questions leading into Pascal's scientific and experimental concerns with the problems of gravity.)

Pascal is indeed in conformity with his age of science in making the cohesion of arithmetic, geometry, and rational mechanics the logical model for epistemological discourse. He is also in essential conformity with that age, the age of Leibniz and the development of infinitesimal calculus, in designating the principle of double infinity, the infinitely large and the infinitely small, as the "common property (of space, time, motion, and number) where knowledge opens up the mind to the greatest marvels in nature." Thus, when the burden of Pascal's text becomes the assertion of the infinite divisibility of space and of number (it being assumed that infinite expansion is readily granted, but that the mind resists the notion of infinite divisibility), one is not surprised to find the first four of the five arguments designed to overcome that resistance to be traditional assertions that do not stand in need of development. They reiterate such fundamental principles of calculus as the impossibility of comparing finite and infinite quantities and, in general, move between spatial and numerical dimensions by means of simple computation (as in the instance of the irrational number for the square root of two), or by experimental representations in space, without the intervention of discursive language. The text starts to proliferate and to grow tense, however, when it has to counter an objection that is to be attributed to Méré and that compels Pascal to reintroduce the question of the relationship between language and cognition. Méré argued that it is perfectly possible in the order of space to conceive of an extension made up from parts that are themselves devoid of extension, thus implying that space can be made up of a finite quantity of indivisible parts, rather than of an infinity of infinitely divisible ones, because it is possible to make up numbers out of units that are themselves devoid of number. Méré uses the principle of homogeneity between space and number, which is also the ground of Pascal's cosmology, to put the principle of infinitesimal smallness into question. Pascal's retort marks the truly Pascalian moment in the demonstration. It begins by dissociating the laws of number from the laws of geometry, by showing that what applies to the indivisible unit of number, the *one*, does not apply to the indivisible unit of space. The status of the *one* is paradoxical and apparently contradictory: as the very principle of singleness, it has no plurality, no number. As Euclid said, *one* is not a number. It is a mere name given to the entity that does not possess the properties of number, a nominal definition of nonnumber. On the other hand, the one partakes of number, according to the principle of homogeneity enunciated by the same Euclid who decreed the one not to be a number. The principle of homogeneity ("magnitudes are said to be of the same kind or species, when one magnitude can be made to exceed another by reiterated multiplication") is mathematically linked to the principle of infinity in this proposition. *One* is not a number; this proposition is correct, but so is the opposite proposition, namely, that *one is* a number, provided it is mediated by the principle of homogeneity which asserts that *one* is of the same species as number, as a house is not a city, yet a city made up of houses that are of the same species as the city, since one can always add a house to a city and it remains a city. Generic homogeneity, or the infinitesimal, is a synechdocal structure. We again find in the fundamental model of Pascal's cosmos, which is based on tropes of homogeneity and on the notion of the infinite, a system that allows for a great deal of dialectical contradiction (one can say $1 = N$ as well as $1 \neq N$), but one that guarantees intelligibility.

The interest of the argument is, however, that it has to reintroduce the ambivalence of definitional language. The synechodocal totalization of infinitude is possible because the unit of number, the *one*, functions as a nominal definition. But, for the argument to be valid, the nominally indivisible number must be distinguished from the *really* indivisible space, a demonstration that Pascal can accomplish easily, but only because the key words of the demonstration—indivisible, spatial extension (*étendue*), species (*genre*), and definition—function as real, and not as nominal, definitions, as "définition de chose" and not as "définition de nom." The language almost forces this formulation upon Pascal, when he has to say: "cette dernière preuve est fondée sur la *définition* de ces deux *choses*, indivisible et étendue" or "Donc, il n'est pas de même genre que l'étendue, par la *définition* des *choses* du même genre" (italics mine). The reintroduction of a language of *real* definition also allows for the next turn in the demonstration, which, after having separated number from space, now has to suspend this separation while maintaining it—because the underlying homology of space and number, the ground of the system, should never be fundamentally in question. There exists, in the order of number, an entity that is, unlike the *one*, heterogeneous with regard to number: this entity, which is the *zero*, is radically distinct from one. Whereas one is and is not a number at the same time, zero is radically not a number, absolutely heterogeneous to the order of number. With the introduction of zero, the separation between number and space, which is potentially threatening, is also healed. For equivalences can easily be found in the order of time and of motion for the zero function in number: instant and stasis (*repos*) are the equivalences that, thanks to the zero, allow one to reestablish the "necessarily and reciprocal link" between the four intrawordly dimensions on which divine order depends. At the end of the passage, the homogeneity of the universe is recovered, and the principle of infinitesimal symmetry is well established. But this has happened at a price: the coherence of the system is now seen to be entirely dependent on the introduction of an element—the zero and its equivalences in time and motion—that is itself entirely heterogeneous with regard to the system and is nowhere a part of it. The continuous universe held together by the double wings of the two infinites is interrupted, disrupted *at all points* by a principle of radical heterogeneity without which it cannot come into being. Moreover, this rupture of the infinitesimal and the homogeneous does not occur on the transcendental level, but on the level of language, in the inability of a theory of language as sign or as name (nominal definition) to ground this homogeneity without having recourse to the signifying function, the real definition, that makes the zero of signification the necessary condition for grounded knowledge. The notion of language as sign is dependent on, and derived from, a different notion in which language functions as rudderless signification and transforms what it denominates into the linguistic equivalence of the arithmetical zero. It is as sign that language is capable of engendering the principles of infinity, of genus, species, and homogeneity, which allow for synechdocal totalizations, but none of these tropes could come about without the systematic effacement of the zero and its reconversion into a name. There can be no *one* without zero, but the zero always appears in the guise of a *one*, of a (some)thing. The name is the trope of the zero. The zero is always *called* a one, when the zero is actually nameless, "innomable." In the French language, as used by Pascal and his interpreters, this happens concretely in the confusedly alternate use of the two terms *zéro* and *néant*. The verbal, predicative form *néant*, with its gerundive ending, indicates not the zero, but rather the one, as the *limit* of the infinitely small, the almost zero that is the one. Pascal is not consistent in his use of *zéro* and *néant*; nor could he be if the system of the two infinites is to be enunciated at all. At the crucial point, however, as is the case here, he knows the difference, which his commentators, including the latest and most astute ones, always forget. At the end of the most systematic exposition of the theory of the two infinites, at the conclusion of part 1 of the *Réflexions*, we find once again the ambivalence of the theory of definitional language, which we encountered at the start.

The unavoidable question will be whether the model established in this text, in which discourse is a dialectical and infinitesimal system that depends on its undoing in order to come into being, can be extended to texts that are not purely mathematical, but stated in a less abstract, more phenomenally or existentially perceivable form. One would specifically want to know whether the principle of homogeneity implicit in the theory of the two infinites, *as well as* the disruption of this system, can be retraced in the theological and subject-oriented context of the *Pensées*. Since this would involve an extensive reading of a major and difficult work, we must confine ourselves here to preliminary hints, by showing first of all how the principle of totalization, which is implicit in the notion of the infinite, underlies the dialectical pattern that is so characteristic of the *Pensées*. Once this is done, we should then ask whether this pattern is at all interrupted, as the numerical series are interrupted by zero, and how this disruption occurs. As a general precaution, we should be particularly wary not to decide too soon that this is indeed the case, not only because the consequences, from a theological and an epistemological point of view, are far-reaching but also because the remarkable elasticity of the dialectical model, capable of recovering totalities threatened by the most radical contradictions, should not be underestimated. The Pascalian dialectic should be allowed to display the full extent of its feats, and, if a disjunction is to be revealed, it can only be done so by following Pascal in pushing it to its eventual breaking point.

What is here called, for lack of a better term, a rupture or a disjunction, is not to be thought of as a negation, however tragic it may be. Negation, in a mind as resilient as Pascal's, is always susceptible of being reinscribed in a system of intelligibility. Nor can we hope to map it out as one topos among topoi, as would be the case with regular tropes of substitution. It is possible to find, in the terminology of rhetoric, terms that come close to designating such disruptions (e.g., *parabasis* or *anacoluthon*), which designate the interruption of a semantic continuum in a manner that lies beyond the power of reintegration. One must realize at once, however, that this disruption is not topical, that it cannot be located in a single point—since it is indeed the very notion of point, the geometrical zero, that is being dislodged—but that it is all-pervading. The anacoluthon is omnipresent, or, in temporal terms and in Friedrich Schlegel's deliberately unintelligible formulation, the parabasis is permanent. Calling this structure ironic can be more misleading than helpful, since *irony*, like *zero*, is a term that is not susceptible to nominal or real definition. To say then, as we are actually saying, that allegory (as sequential narration) is the trope of irony (as the one is the trope of zero) is to say something that is true enough but not intelligible, which also implies that it cannot be put to work as a device of textual analysis. To discover, in the *Pensées*, the *instances de rupture*, the equivalence of the zero in Pascal's theory of number, we can only reiterate compulsively the dialectical pattern of Pascal's own model or, in other words, read and reread the *Pensées* with genuine insistence. Pascal himself has formulated the principle of totalizing reading, in which the most powerful antinomies must be brought together, in the Pensée headed "Contradiction" (257–684): "One can put together a good physiognomy only by reconciling all our oppositions. It does not suffice to follow a sequence of matched properties without reconciling contraries: in order to understand an author's meaning, one must reconcile all the contradictory passages" (*pour entendre le sens d'un auteur il faut accorder tous les passages contraires*). Applied to Scripture, which Pascal here has in mind, this reconciliation leads directly to the fundamental opposition that underlies all others: that between a figural and a true reading. "If one takes the law, the sacrifices, and the kingdom as realities, it will be impossible to coordinate all passages (of the Bible); it is therefore necessary that they be mere figures." The question remains, of course, whether the pair figure-reality can or cannot be itself thus reconciled, whether it is a contradiction of the type we encountered when it was said that one is a number and is not a number at the same time, or whether the order of figure and the order of reality are heterogeneous.

For all the somber felicity of their aphoristic condensation, the *Pensées* are also very systematically schematized texts that can be seen as an intricate interplay of binary oppositions. Many of the sections are, or could easily be, designated by the terms of these oppositions, as is the case for our first and simplest example, two of the *Pensées* (125–92 and 126–93), which could properly be entitled "Nature" and "Custom": "What are our natural principles if not the principles we have grown accustomed to? In children, they are the principles they have learned from the customs of their fathers, like the hunt in animals. A different custom will produce different natural principles. This can be verified by experience, by observing if there are customs that cannot be erased. . . . Fathers fear that the natural love of their children can be erased. What kind of nature is this, that can thus be erased? Custom is a second nature that destroys the first. But what is nature? Why is custom not natural? I am very much afraid that this nature is only a first custom, as custom is a second nature." This passage turns around a saying of common wisdom (*La coutume est une seconde nature*), as is frequently the case in Pascal, and it thus sets up a very characteristic logical or, rather, rhetorical pattern. A set of binary oppositions is matched in a commonsensical order in terms of their properties: here, custom and nature are matched with the pairs first/second and constant/erasable (*effaç-able*), respectively. Nature, being a *first* principle, is constant, whereas custom, being second or derived from nature, is susceptible to change and erasure. The schema, at the onset, is as follows:

nature	first	constant
custom	second	erasable

The pattern is put in motion by a statement (also based, in this case, on common observation) that reverses the order of association of the entities and their properties. It is said that fathers fear, apparently with good reason, that natural feelings of filial affection can be erased, thus coupling the natural with the erasable and, consequently, with secondness. A first (nature) then becomes a first second, that is, a second; a second (custom) becomes in symmetrical balance, a second first, that is, a first:

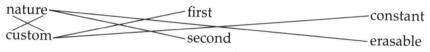

The properties of firstness and secondness have changed places, which results in the undoing or the deconstruction of the binary opposition from which we started. It has now become impossible to decide whether a given experience can be called natural or customary. Since they are able to exchange or cross over, in a chiasmic reversal, their properties, nature, and custom have been brought together to the extent that their opposition has been inscribed into a system of exchange which is structured like a trope (chiasmus). Nature and custom are united within a single system, which, although experienced as negative by the author ("I am afraid that . . ."), is nevertheless a cognition.

The same pattern, with increased complications, reappears time after time and underlies some of the most famous and thematically suggestive of the Pensées. Consider, for example, the section on the nature of man (131–434). It starts out from an opposition that, this time, is historical and, to that extent, empirical: the philosophical debate—to which Pascal has gained access through his closest predecessors, Montaigne and Descartes—between sceptical and dogmatic philosophy, *pyrrhoniens* and *dogmatistes*. The establishment of the original grid, which was obvious in the case of nature and custom as first and second, is more complex in this case, in which scepticism and dogmatic faith have to be matched with truth and nature, respectively. The argument goes back to the example and the logic used by Descartes in the first two meditations. It established the claim for the cognitive value of doubt by reference to the polarity of sleeping and waking, of dream and reality. One normally assumes that the condition of waking is the true condition of man, the first norm from which sleep and dream are derived and displaced, secondary versions. Sleep is grafted upon the condition of awakeness like a secondary upon a primary quality. The original pattern is as follows:

wake	perception	first
sleep	dream	second

Since we think that we are awake when we dream, it follows that the properties can be ordered according to the same symmetrical pattern we encountered in the Pensée on nature and custom. Like Keats at the end of the "Ode to a Nightingale," we should each ask: Do I wake or sleep? For it is no longer certain that our primary consciousness is awake at all, that consciousness is not a palimpsest of dreams, some of them individual, some shared with others, all grafted upon each other. "Is it not possible that this half of our life (day) is itself a mere dream on which the other dreams are grafted, and of which we will awake at death?" This suspicion, which undoes the natural polarities of day and night, wake and sleep, is clearly the product of the sceptical mind and justifies the pairing of scepticism with knowledge. The sceptical position always had knowledge on its side, and the only thing the dogmatists can oppose to this knowledge is the natural conviction that infinite doubt is intolerable. "What will man do in this condition? Will he doubt of everything, doubt that he is awake, that he is being pinched or burned, will he doubt that he doubts, doubt that he is? One cannot reach this condition, and I assert as a fact that there never has been a perfectly consistent and actual sceptic. Nature supports our feeble reason and shelters it from such extravagance." Scepticism and dogmatism are now firmly paired with truth and nature, respectively.

Scepticism	Truth
Dogmatism	Nature

But this original configuration is not a stable one. As is clear from the preceding quotation, one cannot be consistently sceptical, but it is just as impossible to be consistently natural, for however "extravagant" the sceptical position may be, it is nevertheless the only mode of truth accessible to us, and it deprives all claims to natural truth of authority. To the belief "that one cannot doubt natural principles," the sceptics counter "that the uncertainty of our origin includes that of our nature." This argument cannot be refuted: "The dogmatists have been trying to refute it ever since the world began."

The situation is not only unstable, but coercive as well. At this point in the *Pensées*, one moves from the logic of propositions, statements as to what is the case, to model logic, statements of what should or ought to be the case. For one cannot remain suspended between the irreconcilable positions: it is clear that, by not choosing between the two poles of the polarities, one is adopting the sceptical position. The predicament is that of the undecidable: propositional logic is powerless to decide a conflict that has to find a solution, if this logic is to survive.

In a first dialectical reversal, the answer will be to give the predicament a name, which, in this case, will be "man," the being who stands in that predicament. "Man" is then not a definable entity, but an incessant motion beyond itself. "L'homme passe l'homme" says Pascal, in a phrase that has received many pseudo-Nietzschean interpretations of existential transcendence and transgression. Perhaps more important is the numerical formulation of the "definition" of man, which takes us back to the *Réflexions*. For it follows, says Pascal, that man is double, that the one is always already at least a two, a pair. Man is like the *one* in the system of number, infinitely divisible and infinitely capable of self-multiplication. He is another version of the system of the two infinites; immediately after having stated that man surpasses man, and that man is double, Pascal can add that Man *infinitely* surpasses man, "l'homme passe *infiniment* l'homme." As a metaphor of number, man is one and is not one, is a pair and is infinite all at the same time.

The dialectic of the infinite, which starts in the initial doubt, is thus able to unfold itself consistently. For the double, and hence infinitesimal, condition of man, this becomes the key to the knowledge of man's nature. "For who fails to see that without the knowledge of this double condition of nature man was in an irrevocable ignorance of the truth of his nature?" This ruse of reason is purely Cartesian: doubt is suspended by the knowledge of doubt. One sees that the original structure, pairing scepticism with truth and dogmatism with nature, has been chiastically crossed, since now the true knowledge of radical scepticism is paired with nature, through the mediation of the concept of man, standing by implication for the system of double infinitude. The rhetorical pattern that underlies this system is the same as in the previous example.

It is legitimate to "pair" this Pensée with another and more rigorously schematized one, which states the same tension, but empties it of the existential pathos of totalization (122–416). It is headed by the binary opposition "Grandeur et misère": "Since misery is derived from greatness, and greatness from misery, some have decided in favor of misery all the more decisively, since they have taken greatness to be the proof of misery, and others have decided for greatness with all the more power, since they derive it from misery itself. All they were able to say in support of greatness has served as an argument for the others to demonstrate misery, since the higher the station from which one falls the more miserable one will be, and vice versa. They are carried upon each other (*portés les uns sur les autres*) in a circle without end, it being certain that as men gain in enlightenment, they find both greatness and misery in themselves. In a word: man knows he is miserable. He is therefore miserable, since that is what he is, but he is also great because he knows it." (En un mot, l'homme connait qu'il est misérable. Il est donc misérable puisqu'il l'est, mais il est bien grand puisqu'il le connait.)

The end of the text telescopes the chiasmus in a particularly condensed form, starting from the pairing of misery with (self-) knowledge and of greatness with being: "Man *is* great because man *knows* misery" (*l'homme connait qu'il est misérable*). The final sentence has reversed the pattern: misery is paired with being, in the tautology "il est misérable puisqu'il l'est," and greatness with knowledge, the self-knowledge of misery. The mediation is carried out by the apparently deductive prepositions in the sentence: "il est *donc* misérable *puisqu'*il l'est," where the cognitive power is carried by the logical articulations *donc* and *puisque,* and the ontological power by the tautology of the assertion. The dialectic has been flattened out into tautology, in the endlessly circular repetition of the same, and the teleological form of infinite transcendence has been replaced by this monotony. All the same, despite the thematic and tonal difference between the two Pensées on man, the rhetorical pattern remains the same, grounded in the infinitesimal symmetry of the chiasmic reversal. Here, in one of the bleakest of the *Pensées,* this pattern appears perhaps in the purest form (see also Pensée 514–397).

The transition from self-knowledge and anthropological knowledge to teleological knowledge often passes, in Pascal, through the dimension of the political. Louis Marin is right to insist on the close interconnection between epistemology, political criticism, and theology, in the sequence of *Pensées* entitled "Raison des effets" (*La Critique du discours*). This sequence deals primarily with a distinction between popular and scientific knowledge and thus returns to the question that underlies the *Réflexions* as well: the antinomy between natural language and metalanguage. The polarities in Pensées 90–101 (Lafuma classification; Brunschweig: 337–336–335–328–313–316–329–334–80–536–467–324) oppose the language of the people (vox populi) to that of the mathematicians; moreover, Pensée 91 contains a good description of Pascal's own writing style, in its peculiar mixture of popular, nontechnical diction with redoubtable critical rigor: one must have what Pascal calls "une pensée de derrière" (which sees behind the apparent evidence of things), yet speak like the people. Whereas the man of science possesses true knowledge (*episteme*), the people follow the vagaries of opinion (*doxa*). The starting position, then, will be:

people	doxa	false
geometrician	episteme	true

It would be a mistake, however, to dismiss popular opinion as simply false. In a way, the (popular) saying "Vox populi, vox dei" is sound, as are, according to Pascal, the various popular opinions of which he enumerates a rather baffling catalogue of examples. This being the case, a first chiasmic reversal takes place, in which popular opinion has some claims to truth, and the mind of the geometrician, in his scorn for popular wisdom, some taint of falsehood.

people   doxa   false
geometrician   episteme   true

This first chiasmus, however, is only the beginning. Although it is true that the people have sound opinions, it is not really true that they possess the truth. For the people can be counted on to provide the wrong reasons for their sound opinions. "They believe," says Pascal, "that truth is to be found where it is not. There is truth in their opinions, but not where they imagine it to be." This knowledge of error, which is true, is no longer a popular knowledge, but the privileged knowledge of the man who has benefited from the critical rigors of scientific reasoning. A second reversal now associates popular opinion, which to some extent is true, with epistemological falsehood, whereas the knowledge of this falsehood is again true. "We have shown that men are vain in their respect for trivial matters; this vanity reduces all their opinions to nought. We have then shown these opinions to be altogether sound; consequently, the self-esteem of the people is quite legitimate, and the people are not at all as inestimable as one believes. And thus we have destroyed the opinion that destroyed the opinion of the people. But we must now destroy this final proposition and show that it remains true that the people are in error, although their opinions are sound, because they don't locate their truth where it belongs, and by thus locating it where it is not, their opinions are again very erroneous and very unsound."

Many more instances could be listed in an order than would cover the thematic scale of topoi taken up in the *Pensées*, from the most trivial to the most sublime. The same structure, the same "continual reversal from pro to contra" (*renversement continuel du pour au contre*) would reappear in an endless set of variations on chiasmic crossings of binary oppositions. In the process, a wealth of thematic insights would indicate the universal effectiveness of what is a fundamentally dialectical pattern of reasoning, in which oppositions are, if not reconciled, at least pursued toward a totalization that may be infinitely postponed, but that remains operative as the sole principle of intelligibility. Our question remains whether some of the texts from the *Pensées* explicitly refuse to fit this pattern—not because they are structured along a different tropological model (which would diversify but not necessarily invalidate the dialectical model), but because they disrupt the motion of what is demonstrably the same pattern. Consider the Pensée (103–298) headed "Justice, Power" (Justice, force).

> It is just that what is just should be followed; it is necessary that what has the most power should be followed.
> Justice without power is impotent, power without justice is tyrannical.

Justice without power is open to contradiction, because there always are wrongdoers. Power without justice stands accused. Justice and power must therefore be brought together, by making the just strong and the strong just.

Justice is subject to dispute. Power is easily recognizable and without dispute. [Thus it has been impossible to give power to justice, because power has contradicted justice and said that it is unjust, and said that it is itself just.

And thus, not being able to make the just strong, one has made the strong to be just.]

[Ainsi on n'a pu donner la force à la justice, parce que la force a contredit la justice et a dit qu'elle était injuste et a dit que e'était elle qui était juste.

Et ainsi ne pouvant faire que ce qui est juste fût fort, on a fait que ce qui est fort fût juste.]

It is at once clear, on hearing the passage, that, although the chiasmic structure is the same as before, the crossing is no longer symmetrical, since it takes place in one direction but not in the other. A new complication has been introduced and is observable in an opposition that gives each of the key words a double register that is no longer, as in the previous passages, an opposition between two modes of cognition. The opposition is stated at the start in the contrast between "il est juste" and "il est nécessaire," in which the first assertion depends on a propositional cognition, but the second on sheer quantitative power, as in the proverb "La raison du plus fort est toujours la meilleure" or, in English, "Might makes right." Propositional statements line up on the side of cognition, model statements on the side of performance; they perform what they enunciate regardless of considerations of truth and falsehood. Consequently, all words used in the demonstration acquire this ambivalent status: the verb *suivre*, for instance, can be read in its deductive and cognitive sense, in which the necessity is the necessary deductiveness of reason, but it can also be read in the sense of pure coercive power, as in the phrase "la femme doit suivre son mari."

"Suivre" is thus distributed in its double register in the first two sentences of the Pensée. The same is true of justice, which can on the one hand be read as cognitive *justesse*, as the precision of rational argument, but which is clearly also to be read in the sense of the judicial praxis of a court of law. In this latter capacity, it clearly lacks the persuasive power of sheer argument which it possesses in the first sense; it is open to uncertainty and contradiction and therefore lacks power. For the proper of justice to be power, and for the proper of power to be justice, they must be able to exchange the attributes of necessity and of innocence which characterize them. Justice must become necessary by might, might innocent by justice. This would accomplish and demonstrate the homogeneity of propositional statements as cognition and of modal statements as performance. But, unlike all other previous examples from the *Pensées*, the exchange does not take place. Justice refuses to become justesse; it remains pragmatic and inconsistent, "sujet à dispute," unable to fulfill the criterium of necessity as cognitive persuasion. Might, however, has no difficulty whatever satisfying the criterion of necessity; it is "sans dispute" and can therefore *usurp* the consistency of cognition without giving anything in return. The usurpation occurs in the double register of the locution "sans dispute," a quality that pertains to mathematical proof as an indication of epistemological rigor, but which, as in "right makes might," also pertains to force by sheer intolerance and tyranny. Force, which is pure performance, usurps the claim to epistemological rightness. It does so because it can become the subject of the sentence of enunciation and can be said to speak: "la force a contredit . . ." and "la force a dit . . ."; it can pronounce on the lack of epistemological "rightness" of justice, and it can proclaim its own epistemological infallibility. The performative declares itself declarative and cognitive. The "on" in the final sentence: "on a fait que ce qui est fort fut juste" can only be "might," which belongs indeed to the order of the "faire" and not of "savoir." But the unilateral victory of force over justice, if it is to be enunciated, as is the case in this passage, still can only be stated in the mode of cognition and of deduction, as is evident from the use of the deductive "ainsi" coupled with "faire" in the sentence "ainsi on a fait. . . ." The status of this "ainsi" is now very peculiar, however, for the pure act of force is entirely arbitrary and not cognitively consequential at all. The "ainsi" does not belong to Descartes, but to any despot who happens to be in power.

The discomfort one should experience on the reading of this final sentence is the same one should experience on hearing the zero assimilated to the one and thus being reinscribed into a system of cognition in which it does not belong. For at the very moment that might has usurped, by imposition and not by transgression, the authority of cognition, the tropological field of cognition is revealed to be dependent on an entity, might, that is heterogeneous with regard to this field, just as the zero was heterogeneous with regard to number. The break is immediately reinscribed as the knowledge of the break in the "ainsi on a fait . . . ," but this "ainsi" must now be said to be ironical, that is to say disruptive of its own deductive claim. The dialectic starts again, but it has been broken in a way that is essentially different from the transgressive reversals we encountered in the other instances. It is in the realm of practical and political justice, and not of Christian charity, that the equivalence of the mathematical zero reappears in the text of the *Pensées*. What is of considerable importance, from a linguistic point of view, is that the break that in the *Réflexions* was due to the complications of definition is now seen to be a function of the heterogeneity between cognitive and performative language. Language, in Pascal, now separates in two distinct directions: a cognitive function that is right (*juste*) but powerless, and a modal function that is mighty (*forte*) in its claim to rightness. The two functions are radically heterogeneous to each other. The first generates canonical rules of persuasion, whereas the second generates the eudaemonic values that are present as soon as one has to say that the claim to authority is made "at the *pleasure* of" the despot. The first is the language of truth and of persuasion by proof, the second the language of pleasure (*volupté*) and of persuasion by usurpation or seduction. We now know why it is that, in the second half of the *Réflexions*, Pascal had to dodge the question of the relationship between these two modes. To the extent that language is always cognitive and tropological as well as performative at the same time, it is a heterogeneous entity incapable of justice as well as of *justesse*. Even in the transcendental realm of revealed language in Holy Writ, the necessary choice between seduction and truth remains undecidable. Pascal's "definition" of figure retains this complication: when it is said that "Figure porte absence et présence," we recognize the infinitesimal structure of cognitive dialectics, but when it is also said that "Figure porte plaisir et déplaisir," it will be impossible to square, to inscribe the four terms *présence/absence* and *plaisir/déplaisir* into a homogeneous "geometrical" structure. The (ironic) pseudo-knowledge of this impossibility, which pretends to order sequentially, in a narrative, what is actually the destruction of all sequence, is what we call allegory.

Madame de Sévigné

Louise K. Horowitz

"Elle n'a pas de passion au coeur en écrivant: mettons à part toujours l'amour maternel." Gustave Lanson's earnest desire to relegate Mme de Sévigné's passion for her daughter to a substrate level reflects his basic preoccupation with the nonessential side of the voluminous correspondence. Lanson was most fascinated by the anecdotal Mme de Sévigné, the part of the letters given over to describing the multifold events of the time— "Toutes ces anecdotes, ces narrations charmantes ou poignantes, sont un des documents les plus sincères que l'histoire puisse consulter" (*Choix de lettres du dix-septieme siècle*)—and the ambiguous, strange relationship with Mme de Grignan is seen basically as an *écart* from the epistolary norm.

Certainly, Lanson's taste seems to have fixed Mme de Sévigné and her letters into a mold that only recently has been deemed questionable. Most of the *morceaux choisis* collections refer constantly to the letters depicting the death of Turenne, the representation of Racine's *Esther*, and, suspecting perhaps that it was at least necessary to allude once to the feelings of Mme de Sévigné for Mme de Grignan, the editors frequently include the famous episode of the crossing of the Avignon bridge. Seemingly, one reason for easily including the latter piece would be that stylistically, through its reenactment of the little drama, it conforms to the general notion we have of Mme de Sévigné as a tableau painter, gifted in depicting a certain sense of color and movement through the written word.

But in the past few years, critical interpretations have centered on the primary, essential point of the correspondence: the mother-daughter relationship. Reading through the three volumes of the letters in the Pléiade edition, it is evident immediately that the anecdotal approach is more than

From *Love and Language: A Study of the Classical French Moralist Writers.* © 1977 by the Ohio State University Press.

merely limiting. Such analysis actually disfigures the work, for the anecdote serves only as a support, or even sometimes as a foil, for the one element that overwhelmingly dominates the letters to Mme de Grignan—the expression of the great love.

In terms of the general study I have proposed, it is fair to question whether the letters occupy the same position toward society as the works of the other writers [The Chevalier de Méré, La Rochefoucauld, Madame de Lafayette, Saint-Evremond]. Do they offer a general view of man in his universe—both immediate and cosmic? Do they propose a code or style of living? Does the introduction of "je" alter the basic intention of the seventeenth-century moralists: an impersonal negating and subsequent reconstruction of social patterns most necessary to the fundamental well-being of the individual and his society? In reply it must be said that a very powerful view of life, of living, does emerge from the letters of Mme de Sévigné; and in fact, it is one that goes counter to the philosophical and religious thinking of the day. Mme de Sévigné identified living with loving.

The Jansenist, Epicurean, and *mondain* codes are all violated by this other life-view: Jansenism by Mme de Sévigné's heavy emphasis on human love; Epicureanism by her willingness to plunge into a total, highly intense involvement with another, thereby sacrificing repose and emotional liberty; and finally *la mondanité* by her refusal to establish an idiom allowing for the superficial transfer of sentiment without loss of inner control. Unlike the great majority of classical moralists, Mme de Sévigné opted, through her letters, for a radical approach to life, radical in that it embraced the passions without fear.

Nevertheless, her stance is not without ambiguity. Life as love is not exactly what Mme de Sévigné chose, or it is precisely what she chose if living can be completely synonymous with writing. There is a distinction between stressing her passion or stressing the writing that interpreted it, between Mme de Sévigné primarily as active "lover" or passive poet. Recent criticism has tended to emphasize one side at the expense of the other, sometimes forgetting that the feelings and their expression can be separated only with great difficulty. Roger Duchêne in his *Madame de Sévigné et la lettre d'amour* accentuates her passion as a living force, so strong that she had to express it constantly. Left without any other means to do so, she opted for the letter. His study traces the history of Mme de Sévigné's passionate love for Mme de Grignan. Letter-writing is seen as a means to filling in the terrible gap that Mme de Grignan's departure for Provence had created. Beginning with the fateful day, Duchêne skillfully follows the life of Mme de Sévigné's unusually intense love:

> Les lettres à Mme de Grignan permettent de suivre les étapes de l'évolution des sentiments de Mme de Sévigné. Après les lents progrès vers une meilleure entente de 1671 à 1676, vient la brusque rupture de 1677 avec, jusqu'en 1680, des sursauts et des parox-

ysmes. Et c'est enfin, dans une sérénité un peu grave, l'accord que seule attriste la pensée de la mort. La preuve de la vérité de l'amour dans les lettres, c'est cette courbe, dessinée au jour le jour, d'une affection s'étalant sur vingt-cinq années.

Whereas Duchêne is interested primarily in the curve of Mme de Sévigné's love for her daughter and in examining the reasons for such fluctuation, Gérard-Gailly, in his introduction to the Pléiade edition of the letters, offers a Freudian analysis of the passion itself. Duchêne describes from the outside; Gérard-Gailly from the inside. His reading centers primarily upon certain semi-erotic passages of the letters and he concludes: "Passion maternelle! Maternelle, sans doute, mais amoureuse aussi, et passion d'amant pour un autre être humain." His views are reinforced by the fact that the more obvious "love" passages were removed by Mme de Sévigné's earliest editors, who probably recognized their ambiguous value.

For other critics, notably Jean Cordelier, the love relationship between Mme de Sévigné and Mme de Grignan is viewed as the means through which the former was best able to fulfill a calling as a writer. Cordelier seeks to prove that the passion she experienced was only indirectly tied to Mme de Grignan, via the necessity of writing. Thus she loved the person who allowed her to realize her vocation. Interpreting the question of language in a different vein, Bernard Bray explains that the erotic language Mme de Sévigné frequently used in the letters to her daughter was the result of a linguistic impasse. She was forced into the lyric note because "la marquise ne disposait d'aucun autre langage pour exprimer la douleur de l'absence" (*L'Art de la lettre amoureuse*). This interpretation is diametrically opposed to the Freudian analysis of Gérard-Gailly, and the center of focus shifts from the psychological to the socio-linguistic.

All the methods used to analyze the correspondence both succeed and fail in their attempts to understand the strange letters. Roger Duchêne's exhaustive study maintains too strict a parallel between living and writing. He is so interested in the gaps between letters, in what mother and daughter were feeling at all times, that he forgets that Mme de Sévigné's primary identity is through letter-writing, and hence through the domain of the summary, the deliberate exclusion, not through any consecutive, all-inclusive pattern.

As for Gérard-Gailly's Freudian study, it too fails at a certain point. Without a doubt his perceptions do open doors, for very frequently Mme de Sévigné's "maternal" love appears ambiguous. The rivalry with M. de Grignan for control over her daughter, the fascination with Mme de Grignan's physical beauty, the references to kisses and embraces far beyond polite convention, point to a situation that seemingly reflects desires of incest and sapphism. Mme de Sévigné herself, on occasion, found it useful to clarify that her love was *maternel*, as if other thoughts had indeed crossed her mind at some point. But the Freudian bent ultimately fails to tell the whole story, for the letters show that writing was a clear alternative—in fact, even sometimes a clear preference—to physical presence, and their love seemed to express itself most satisfactorily for both parties when the written word could interpret it. Thus a study of psyches and motives cannot reflect the entire problem, for it neglects the very crucial question of the necessity to remain in the domain of written communication, and, going one step further, in the domain of the imagination.

On the other hand, the theories stressing the writing experience are belied by Mme de Sévigné herself. Although in reality her great passion may have fared far better when on paper than at any other time, she nevertheless did believe that writing was a substitute for Mme de Grignan's presence, that it was only second best: "Quand je ne suis pas avec vous, mon unique divertissement est de vous écrire" (1.611). On the conscious plane, the marquise perceived that seeing was highly desirable, and writing, a palliative. Thus Jean Cordelier's neat little system transforming "je vivrai pour vous aimer" into "je vivrai pour vous écrire" (*Mme de Sévigné par elle-même*) stretches the truth. That writing emerges eventually as a superior alternative to being together is clear through the letters, but only at rare moments was it viewed as such by Mme de Sévigné. Most of the time, she yearned for her daughter's presence. Finally, Bernard Bray, in emphasizing that linguistic patterns alone dictated Mme de Sévigné's expression, cannot sufficiently take into account either the nature of the relationship or the view of living that Mme de Sévigné sought to communicate. Ultimately, all aspects involved in Mme de Sévigné's relationship with her daughter must be studied, not only the fundamental ties but also how and why this alliance expressed itself as it did.

It is difficult to ascertain the precise nature of Mme de Sévigné's feeling for her daughter prior to the latter's departure for Provence, shortly after her marriage. In the face of scholarship suggesting that Mme de Sévigné's love for her daughter was an outgrowth only of Mme de Grignan's marriage and subsequent departure, and thus of a loss of a person who for so many years had been dominated and dependent, other critics have attempted to show that the separation of the two women marked only a heightening of an already forceful passion.

There is really no strong evidence either way. But does an understanding of the years that preceded the 1671 departure to Provence shed much light on the correspondence itself? The only important question—that of Mme de Sévigné's possible desire to dominate her child—can be gleaned readily through the letters themselves, and references to past patterns of behavior do little to clarify that problem. However, by no means was the dependence-independence syndrome the sole, or even primary, reason for Mme de Sévigné's faithful correspondence, a view that might be suggested by an overly detailed account of the years previous to Mme de Grignan's departure.

What is significant is that the departure of Mme de Grignan for Provence on 5 February 1671 (where she was to follow her husband, who had just been named *lieutenant-général* by the court) was an abrupt move and a shock that was to release an expression of intense passion that, during the *grand siècle*, was paralleled perhaps only by the *Lettres portugaises*. The opening words of the first letter, written on 6 February 1671, one day after saying farewell to Mme de Grignan, set the note and tone of the twenty-five years of correspondence:

> Ma douleur serait bien médiocre si je pouvais vous la dépeindre; je ne l'entreprendrai pas aussi. J'ai beau chercher ma chère fille, je ne la trouve plus, et tous les pas qu'elle fait l'éloignent de moi. Je m'en allai donc à Sainte-Marie, toujours pleurant et toujours mourant: il me semblait qu'on m'arrachait le coeur et l'âme; et en effet, quelle rude séparation!
>
> (1.189)

Each subsequent separation following a period of reunion evokes a similar outcry; and although as she becomes accustomed to the absence of her daughter Mme de Sévigné consciously attempts to modify her acute misery and to modulate her tone, the letters are nevertheless, with varying degrees of intensity, primarily the vivid expression of the anguish engendered by the "eternal" separation. Through a process of *défiguration* that a collection of letters such as these cannot help but create, the reader is left with the impression that the periods of separation far surpassed in length the number of days when the two women were reunited. It is, however, the reverse that is true; sixteen years, nine months together, eight years, four months apart. But it is not time together or apart, more of one than of the other, that is really at stake here. The nature of the feeling was such that each period of separation seemed "forever" to Mme de Sévigné.

The motives governing Mme de Sévigné's correspondence with her daughter are no clearer than the precise nature of their relationship prior to 1671. At times it appears that the marquise was "engaged in a battle for a resisting heart" (Eva Marcu, "Madame de Sévigné and Her Daughter"), that she sought to maintain her daughter in a state of dependency inconsistent with the newly acquired freedom that marriage and distance had bestowed upon Mme de Grignan. Her frequently haughty, commanding tones suggest that this was at least partially responsible for the highly intense exchange of letters. At certain times—for example, when she unsuccessfully exhorts Mme de Grignan to join her at Vichy and then to return to Paris together for the remainder of the year—it is obvious that a battle of wills was a definite part of their relationship.

In a variation of the above theme, it could be postulated that Mme de Sévigné's obsessive passion for Mme de Grignan illustrates perfectly the fascination with an "absent" person, the fascination that Proust described at such length. Thus Mme de Grignan represents the creature who ultimately escapes total possession, what Albertine was for the *narrateur* of the

Recherche. "Passion proustienne, non pas que la mère de Mme de Grignan ait rien d'une femme damnée . . . mais parce que son aventure apparaît comme l'illustration parfaite de l'analyse que Proust fera de la passion amoureuse, analyse qu'une brève citation de la *Recherche* suffit à rappeler: 'On n'aime que ce qu'on ne possède pas tout entier' " (Cordelier). In this case, Françoise-Marguerite's portrait, which Mme de Sévigné keeps close to her throughout the years and to which she makes frequent reference in her letters, would be the perfect symbol of *l'être de fuite,* she who is both present and absent, the ideal metaphor for possession and lack of it.

But if precise motivation cannot be determined (for doubtless Mme de Sévigné was moved to write by several reasons), other questions can be more readily resolved. Reading through the letters consecutively, one perceives two important points: (1) the letters to Mme de Grignan do not fit in at all with the ongoing trends of *la mondanité* and *la galanterie;* and (2) on the writing level at least, Mme de Sévigné's involvement with her daughter was strikingly absolute and total.

That the marquise's relationship with Mme de Grignan, as she expressed it in her letters, far transcends any notions of simple gallantry or artificial social structures has been most thoroughly documented by Roger Duchêne in his recent comprehensive study of the letters. *La lettre galante* enjoyed much favor in seventeenth-century French society, where the salon life cultivated various socially acceptable "masks." Thus it emerges as an extremely well-perfected means to avoid the more fundamental sentiments of a primarily erotic base. "Parler d'amour s'avère en conséquence à la fois nécessaire et impossible, sauf précisément par le biais de la galanterie, masque commode et qui permet d'oser beaucoup puisqu'elle est réputée jeu d'esprit innocent, admis et même recommandé par les conventions de la vie mondaine" (Duchêne).

Such a code is evident in the letters of the marquise, although not in those to her daughter. Rather, it is in her correspondence with her male admirers that she readily introduces *la galanterie,* particularly in that addressed to Ménage and to Bussy-Rabutin, her cousin. Those letters are filled with wit and teasing grace, with joking ambiguities and puns. Especially in the letters to her cousin, Mme de Sévigné demonstrates a proclivity for a certain equivocal note, where frequent references of a sexual nature contrast with her very restrained, indignant manner when her cousin, provoked by her banter, steps beyond social rules. In the correspondence with her cousin, up until 1658 (in later years this tone is wholly absent from their commerce), the young marquise employs an art of adept word manipulation with great flair, referring to Bussy-Rabutin once, for example, he who had produced no sons, as "le beau faiseur des filles" (1.99).

The letters addressed to her daughter never joke about love or passion. Of course, Mme de Sévigné was writing then to someone of her own sex, and even if latent incestuous desires were present, the male-female element was absent. Hence there is an immediate reduction in any form of *la co-quetterie*. But whereas quarrels or misunderstandings with Bussy-Rabutin or Ménage gave rise to a semi-serious, semi-teasing lilt, any disagreement between Mme de Grignan and her mother was a constant source of pain and bitterness. "Les rapports de la mère et de la fille," writes Jean Cordelier,

> ont tout d'une véritable liaison amoureuse: craintes sans fonde-ment, jalousie sans cause, ergotages tendres, accusations aussi maladroites que sincères, protestations indignées, qui font de la *Correspondance* un chef-d'oeuvre de correspondance amoureuse, digne de figurer en bonne place dans toutes les anthologies de lettres d'amour.

Mutual jealousy did indeed exert a strong influence throughout the letters—Mme de Sévigné's envy of Grignan; Françoise-Marguerite's antip-athy toward Retz and Corbinelli, close friends and confidants of the mar-quise. Mme de Sévigné persistently lashed out at M. de Grignan, feeling that it was indeed her right to regulate even when he slept with his wife, to say nothing of the visits to Paris. The letters suggest, on the other hand, that Mme de Grignan was tormented by worry over her mother's "fidelity":

> Avez-vous bien peur que j'aime mieux Mme de Brissac que vous? Craignez-vous, de la manière dont vous me connaissez, que ses manières me plaisent plus que les vôtres? que son esprit ait trouvé le chemin de me plaire? Avez-vous opinion que sa beauté efface vos charmes? Enfin pensez-vous qu'il y ait quelqu'un au monde qui puisse, à mon goût, surpasser Madame de Grignan, étant même dépouillée de tout l'intérêt que j'y prends?
>
> (1.265–66)

In the opposite vein, there were moments of great tenderness—Mme de Sévigné's pleas to her daughter to take better care of her health; the frequent self-denigration ("j'ai trouvé mille fois que je ne valais pas l'ex-trême peine que vous preniez pour moi" [2.259]) that alternated with pe-riods of frenzied worry when letters failed to arrive on time or when the marquise believed that Mme de Grignan was somehow in danger, anguish that was frequently without cause. Mme de Sévigné's imagination, her almost masochistic pleasure in torturing herself by creating dreaded ad-ventures, demonstrate that the mood of the letters cannot compare with the cajoling, teasing tone of the correspondence with Ménage and Bussy. Mme de Sévigné's letters to her daughter testify to an overwhelming ab-sorption, which had nothing in common with the orchestrations of *la galanterie*.

Time after time, the marquise writes that her love, her obsession, for her daughter, is in a realm separate from any other domain of her life. To permit the development of such emotion, to allow the feelings to attain a purer state, she frequently sought out absolute solitude:

Quoique ma lettre soit datée du dimanche, je l'écris aujourd'hui, samedi au soir; il n'est que dix heures, tout est retiré; c'est une heure où je suis à vous d'une manière plus particulière qu'au milieu de ce qui est ordinairement dans ma chambre: ce n'est pas que je sois contrainte, je sais me débarrasser; je me promène seule, et quoi que vous disiez, ma très chère, je serais bien oppressée si je n'avais pas cette liberté. J'ai besoin de penser à vous avec attention, comme j'avais besoin de vous voir.

(3.18–19)

Solitude, however, necessarily depended upon the absence not only of all who were irrelevant to the passion but also of *l'objet aimé*. Doubtless, a certain amount of fictionalization occurred. What the solitude and the free reign of the imagination offered was the preferred formulation of her sentiments. Being alone allowed for the satisfaction of both the emotional need (constant attention focused on Mme de Grignan) and of the artistic one (perfection of the means of expression). Either way, what is important is the desire to isolate in order to concentrate best on the obsession to the exclusion of all else.

Countless times throughout the long period from 1671 to 1696, Mme de Sévigné explicitly states the degree to which the passion possesses her:

Enfin tout tourne ou sur vous, ou de vous, ou pour vous, ou par vous.

(1.235)

Je vivrai pour vous aimer, et j'abandonne ma vie à cette occupation.

(1.283)

C'est une chose étrange que d'aimer autant que je vous aime: on a une attention et une application naturelle et continuelle, qui fait qu'en nulle heure du jour on ne peut être surprise sans cette pensée.

(1.685–86)

Quelle possession vous avez prise de mon coeur, et quelles traces vous avez faites dans ma tête!

(2.454)

Je pense continuellement et habituellement à vous.

(2.460)

Mon coeur est à vous . . . tout vous y cède et vous y laisse régner souverainement.

(3.10)

Even the infrequent recourse to *précieux* expression—as in the last example—cannot detract from the totality of involvement that left little room for other emotional demands. The preoccupation with Mme de Grignan, or perhaps more precisely with the image of Mme de Grignan, the almost deification of that image, is one of the most remarkable aspects of the entire correspondence. One perceives that the extreme concentration upon her daughter, the quasi-religious fervor with which she endows the other woman's very being, was fundamentally vital to Mme de Sévigné, that this extraordinary effort and immersion was linked to the life flow.

Consciousness of her own body was very much a part of the marquise's passion. The love for her daughter is repeatedly tied to her own respiration—"Je souhaite, ma petite, que vous m'aimiez toujours: c'est ma vie, c'est l'air que je respire" (1.264)—and she "experienced it as consubstantial with her being, with her own identity"(Harriet Ray Allentuch, *Madame de Sévigné: A Portrait in Letters*). What the mail brings and takes away is life itself. As Harriet Ray Allentuch has shown in her study, separation was seen as a period of mourning, of physical pain: "Cette séparation me fait une douleur au coeur et à l'âme, que je sens comme un mal du corps" (1.201). Reunion, on the other hand, was viewed as spiritual and physical rebirth: "Quel voyage, bon Dieu! et quelle saison! vous arriverez précisément le plus court jour de l'année, et par conséquent vous nous ramenez le soleil"(2.259).

In this identification of her love with the life process itself, Mme de Sévigné violates the precepts offered by the Jansenists, the Epicureans, and the *mondain* writers, all of whom placed another ideal—love of God, ataraxia, social perfection—above the intense emotional involvement absolutely vital to the marquise's sense of well-being. Even if, in part, the recourse to letter-writing reveals a decided preference for an attachment to what is absent, rather than a predilection for a permanent, "present" relationship (a second marriage, perhaps), the commitment is nonetheless of a different nature from those proposed by the other writers of the age.

The totality of the involvement, however, created certain problems, the most significant of which is the degree to which Mme de Sévigné altered reality—consciously or subconsciously—to conform to her emotional demands. Time, space, people, all undergo a radical transformation within the context of the letter.

The present is a nonexistent moment in the marquise's writings to her daughter. The passage of time is viewed within her own special confines, dependent upon her own private relativity:

Pour cette négligence et cette joie de voir passer les jours les uns après les autres, je la sens en moi et j'y fais réflexion à toute heure. Quand vous êtes ici, il n'y en a pas un que je ne regrette; je trouve qu'ils m'échappent avec une vitesse qui m'attriste. Une heure, un jour, une semaine, un mois, un an, tout cela court et s'enfuit avec une rapidité qui m'afflige toujours. . . . Présentement, ma bonne, que je ne respire que de vous revoir et vous pouvoir garder et conserver moi-même, je voudrais que tout cet intervalle fût passé;

je jette les jours à la tête de qui les veut, je les remercie d'être
passés. Le printemps et l'été encore me paraissent des siècles; il
me semble que je n'en verrai jamais la fin. Je dors vite; et j'ai de
l'impatience d'être toujours à demain, et puis de recevoir vos
lettres, et puis d'en recevoir encore, et encore d'autres.

(2.572–73)

But more is involved than simply an art of eloquent expression; for Mme
de Sévigné the present assumes form and meaning only in relation to the
past or the future, and is colored completely by either remorse or anticipation. Particularly in the earlier letters to Mme de Grignan, the ones written between 1671 and 1676, she alludes frequently to such states of mind.
Thoughts that revolve upon the past are inevitably filled with great sadness
of time lost: "Hélas! c'est ma folie que de vous voir, de vous parler, de
vous entendre; je me dévore de cette envie, et du déplaisir de ne vous avoir
pas assez écoutée, pas assez regardée" (1.230–31). She turns next to the
future, since the past has not fulfilled and the present is suspended, a non-
moment: "Il faut pourtant que je vous dise encore que je regarde le temps
où je vous verrai comme le seul que je désire à présent et qui peut m'être
agréable dans la vie" (1.282). And in one remarkable passage, written four
years later, she shows with what ease she could make the transition from
past to future, completely negating the present:

Il est vrai que, depuis trois ans, nous n'avons été que quatre mois
séparées, et ce qui s'est passé depuis votre départ. J'ai senti toute
la joie de passer les étés et les hivers avec vous; et je sens encore
plus le déplaisir de voir ce temps passé, et passé pour jamais, cela
fait mourir. Il faut mettre à la place de cette pensée l'espérance de
se revoir.

(1.768–69)

The future reveals itself also as the undisputed answer to all problems,
and, in fact, as a strong counterforce to a reality that is not only unsatisfying
but frequently bitter. Even after a period of reunion that was particularly
acrimonious, the future assumes a rosy glow, as Mme de Sévigné almost
desperately invests time with qualities of transfiguration. The most recent
reunion may have been a disaster, but time alone will change that, installing
a reign of "truth" that the past has failed to achieve: "Eh, mon Dieu, ne
nous reverrons-nous jamais en nous faisant sentir toutes les douceurs de
l'amitié que nous avons? . . . Faisons donc mieux, ma bonne, une autre
fois . . . faisons-nous honneur de nos sentiments, qui sont si beaux et si
bons: pourquoi les défigurer?" (2.280). The problem, of course, lies in determining whether the reunion (in this case, unsuccessful) or the promise
of another encounter (judged successful in advance) is the disfiguration of
the truth. Living versus writing. The essential truth of the relationship, as
Mme de Sévigné saw it, was revealed through the letters. That which did
not adhere to the image was somehow inaccurate, false, *défiguré*.

Space, too, acquires new perspectives. That which is "dead" is really most alive. Through the resuscitative powers of memory, places that have a particularly strong association with Mme de Grignan and the past are those sites that most powerfully live within the marquise: "Il n'y a point d'endroit, point de lieu, ni dans la maison, ni dans l'église, ni dans le pays, ni dans le jardin, où je ne vous aie vue; il n'y en a point qui ne me fasse souvenir de quelque chose de quelque manière que ce soit; et de quelque façon que ce soit aussi, cela me perce le coeur. Je vous vois; vous m'êtes présente"(1.236).

But letter-writing achieves an even stronger transformation of reality. It was necessary, of course, in the correspondence with Mme de Grignan, to have recourse to the outside world, that is, to the world beyond Mme de Sévigné and her daughter. But did the marquise's references truly reflect ongoing reality? On a double level, it appears that by her particular selection of those to be mentioned in her letters, she conferred identity, existence even, to a choice few alone, and that her choice was ultimately guided by her passion for her daughter. As Bernard Bray has shown, the correspondence is a closed work, a perfect reflection of the closed society at its root; and the letters refer constantly to the same basic group of friends, acquaintances, and family, common to both Mme de Sévigné and Mme de Grignan ("Quelques Aspects du système épistolaire de Mme de Sévigné").

And yet the distinction of who enjoys favor—naming—does not stop there. Particularly those friends who are most deeply involved with Mme de Grignan—or who at least give that appearance to her mother—are included in the letters. Mme de Sévigné attempted to render her passion a collective one, to give it a sense of social primacy that it did not, could not, have. She sought to extricate her obsession from the strictly individual by endowing it with qualities of communal preoccupation: "Si je vous disais tous ceux qui vous font des compliments, il faudrait un volume: M. et Mme de Chaulnes, M. de Lavardin, M. le comte des Chapelles, Tonquedec, l'abbé de Montigny, évêque de Léon, M. d'Harouys cinq cent mille fois, Jean Fourché, Chésières, etc." (1.373). Those who refrained from such compliments were far less often alluded to, for Mme de Sévigné transformed the world according to her own highly limited standards.

This is the problem central to the correspondence, and one that at times did not escape Mme de Sévigné herself. Which is "more real"? Living or writing? Furthermore, is it through writing or being together that a more satisfactory version (vision) of life emerges? Although constantly seeking her daughter's presence, on a conscious level at least, as that which would achieve the greatest fulfillment for herself, Mme de Sévigné, on perhaps a deeper plane, was aware that letter-writing offered a viable and perhaps more sustaining alternative to living together. In fact, that perception was shared by Mme de Grignan, according to her mother: "Vous me dites que vous êtes fort aise que je sois persuadée de votre amitié, et que c'est un bonheur que vous n'avez pas eu quand nous avons été ensemble" (1.226). The preceding was written in 1671, and eight years later, a similar tone still prevails: "Je ne me souviens plus de tout ce qui m'avait paru des marques d'éloignement et d'indifférence; il me semble que cela ne vient point de vous, et je prends toutes vos tendresses, et dites et écrites, pour le véritable fond de votre coeur pour moi" (2.451). It is evident that those expressions of tenderness may have been more often written than said, and that Mme de Sévigné was more than willing to replace any signs of indifference or hostility—not uncommon during their periods together—with what was the preferred mark, although expressed in writing.

In a paradoxical way, then, absence allowed for a more satisfactory expression of love than did presence; and it can be said that writing did emerge as superior to being together, although on the conscious level the latter was the expressed, desired goal. But writing was heavily relied upon to communicate "true" feelings, those superior emotions free of any bitterness, which Mme de Sévigné judged to be the real mark of the relationship with her daughter. That she saw the possibility of achieving the perfection she had mentally established as inherent in her involvement with Mme de Grignan is evident in the unusual recourse to writing even when her daughter was in or nearby Paris. Expressing herself via the written word was a means of achieving both a certain liberty and self-constraint through the working over and the manipulation of terms. And it is a rather remarkable piece of writing that the marquise offers to her child while Mme de Grignan was visiting her:

> Il faut, ma chère bonne, que je me donne le plaisir de vous écrire, une fois pour toutes, comme je suis pour vous. Je n'ai pas l'esprit de vous le dire; je ne vous dis rien qu'avec timidité et de mauvaise grâce; tenez-vous donc à ceci. Je ne touche point au fond de la tendresse sensible et naturelle que j'ai pour vous; c'est un prodige. Je ne sais pas quel effet peut faire en vous l'opposition que vous dites qui est dans nos esprits; il faut qu'elle ne soit pas si grande dans nos sentiments, ou qu'il y ait quelque chose d'extraordinaire pour moi, puisqu'il est vrai que mon attachement pour vous n'en est pas moindre. Il semble que je veuille vaincre ces obstacles, et que cela augmente mon amitié plutôt que de la diminuer: enfin, jamais, ce me semble, on ne peut aimer plus parfaitement.
>
> (2.408)

The perfect expression of her sentiments, the harmony, calm, and tranquility which filter into that expression, can be obtained only through a letter. In choosing to communicate via writing, Mme de Sévigné implicitly states that although the relationship may seem imperfect, especially to Mme de Grignan, in essence it is sublime. The rest is appearance, sham, misunderstanding, a failure to relate. If the communication can be made more satisfactory, so too can the relationship; hence, the recourse is to writing. "Mes lettres sont plus heureuses que moi-même; je m'explique mal de bouche, quand mon coeur est si touché" (2.400).

This problem of what is "more real" is paramount in the letters. There is an ambiguity between absence and presence, imagination and reality, that is difficult to resolve. Aware of the possibility of *défiguration*, Mme de Sévigné proceeded, nevertheless, to (re)construct an elaborate, complex relationship far more successfully on the written level than on the "living" one. At the center of the correspondence is the altering of time, space, and the entire system of relating. Mme de Sévigné stressed the satisfaction of the individual psyche as the preeminent element in the structuring of a life "project," and consequently was governed only by that which could conform to it. The organization of her mental world had to fit the emotional demands she imposed upon it. Moreover, her fantasizing, her reconstruction of the world around her through the use of the written word, was exactly the option of an Esprit, of a Saint-Evremond, or of a La Rochefoucauld, although her demands differed considerably from each of those writers. If we feel more keenly her attempt to transform the universe to certain needs, it is perhaps because her effort was so obviously an intimate one, painted as such, with no recourse to an anonymous *on*. The dream somehow seems more fragile, the attempt to rebuild more vulnerable, because she left herself so exposed.

If, however, the marquise's struggle resembles in structure those of other classical moralists, particularly in the firm belief in the power of the word, her desire to live through her love, and the incessant expression of it, was not at all consistent with the three prevailing "moralist" currents: Jansenism, Epicureanism, and *la mondanité*. The latter two were challenged by her refusal—conscious or subconscious—to be guided by desire for repose or social adaptability. The letters to Mme de Grignan are far too intense ever to be considered as part of the gallant code, and in her refusal to live a present-oriented life, uninvolved and *disponible*, she clearly violated the precepts of Saint-Evremond and the Epicureans. In both cases it was the overwhelming totality of her passion—one that left little room for anyone or anything else—that was in opposition to the current vogues.

Nor do either of the codes seem to have obviously affected her. This was definitely not the case, however, for Jansenism, which appears, at first, to have been the greatest obstacle to Mme de Sévigné's involvement with her daughter. Clearly, her love for her child could never be tolerated by the Jansenists, for whom terrestrial love was viewed as a direct rival to man's love of God. However, the marquise's intellectual battle with Jansenism can be seen as the socialized form of her own private guilt, and as the sole force—sufficiently structured and well developed—able to control what she undoubtedly saw as a violent, potentially self-destructive passion. Recourse to the Jansenist ideals was her only means of counterbalancing her obsession, and although its tenets could not destroy her feelings, at least she could use them as a moderating power.

Mme de Sévigné experienced a vague, nebulous guilt concerning her passion for her daughter, although it is impossible to describe the precise source of that feeling. She had grave concern over the emotional demands and sacrifices that the relationship had placed upon both Mme de Grignan and herself. There are allusions to her own anxieties over the nature of her love, for example, when she finds it necessary to clarify for Françoise-Marguerite (and perhaps for herself as well) that when she says "amour" she means "amour maternel" (2.677–78). In any case, whatever the exact cause of the guilt, which runs through the letters, its most satisfactory expression was in religious terms.

The marquise thus came to perceive that her sentiments for her daughter were a violation of God's law. Mme de Sévigné was fully aware that in loving, in adoring, her daughter as she did, she was going counter to the stern Jansenist principles and therefore was not truly surprised when Arnauld d'Andilly scolded her for "idolatry" toward her daughter, or when a priest refused her absolution and communion during Pentecost (1.276, 729). How deeply she was concerned over the reprimands is questionable, as is the entire question of her involvement with Jansenism. What can be said is that the rigorous, Jansenist code served as a slight braking force on what would otherwise have been a totally uncontrolled passion. That she felt guilty, as most critics view the situation, for violating the Jansenist principles is not certain; what seems far more probable, judging from certain tones in the letters, is that she experienced a rather strong sense of guilt, and that Jansenism was a sound philosophy for tempering, even only moderately, her obsessive passion.

But the long, emotional struggle with this braking force was not a very successful one. Aware that her feelings bordered on deification, Mme de Sévigné nevertheless failed to make use of the Jansenist tenets in any substantial way. Ultimately, she opted for idolatry and for the free expression of her emotions. By judging and conceding her failure in advance, by stating multifold times that she was too weak to oppose her passion, she thereby allowed for the liberty of living and expressing herself as passionately as she did: "Et quand nous sommes assez malheureux pour n'être point uniquement occupés à Dieu, pouvons-nous mieux faire que d'aimer et de vivre doucement parmi nos proches et ceux que nous aimons"(2.643). Jansenism was there to serve as a constant reminder to her of the extent of her involvement, to temper the tendencies toward uncontrol, but it was also prejudged unsuccessful.

The only substantial comfort she obtained from the precepts of Jansenism was through the idea of a Providence that she came to see as "willing" the separation of mother and daughter. But this too offered only a means to emotional equilibrium that she could not easily realize. An increasingly strong reliance upon submission to Providence can be detected over the span of twenty-five years, thus giving rise to a theory of religious conversion. Nevertheless, it seems most accurate to conclude, as has Harriet Ray Allentuch, that the heavy dependence upon the ways of Providence was not only "a substitute for painful thoughts" but also a means to absolve both herself and especially Mme de Grignan of any responsibility. "If Madame de Sévigné conceived the suspicion that her daughter might not be doing her utmost to arrange the Grignans' permanent return to Paris, she need only push the phantasm aside."

Too much time has been devoted, however, to the problem of Jansenism in Mme de Sévigné's life and letters. The strict tenets were primarily a means to self-control. The central problem of the correspondence still remains one of penetrating the nature of its origins and expression. A definite choice of structuring life was made, along grounds that were at once personal and general. The obsession with Mme de Grignan was individual, try as the marquise did to endow it with a sense of collective concern. But to base an entire adult life upon this passion, to write about it, to interpret it again and again, to explain, to justify, are needs whose limits are precisely and persistently intertwined in the double domains of love and language.

The Predicatory Mouth:
Problematics of Communication
in Bossuet's *Oeuvres oratoires*

Domna C. Stanton

*Mes Frères . . . ce ne sont pas les prédicateurs qui se font eux-mêmes. Ne
vous persuadex pas qu'on attire du ciel quand on veut cette divine parole.
. . . Voulez-vous savoir, Chrétiens, quand Dieu se plait à parler? Quand
les hommes sont disposés à l'entendre. . . . Que si, au contraire, vous êtes
de ceux qui détournent leur oreille de la vérité . . . Dieu . . . retirera la
saine doctrine de la bouche des prédicateurs. . . . Voilà le mystère que je
promettais. Ce sont les auditeurs fidèles qui font les prédicateurs
évangéliques, parce que, les prédicateurs étant pour les auditeurs, "les uns
reçoivent d'en haut ce que méritent les autres" Aimez donc la vérité,
Chrétiens, et elle vous sera annoncée; ayez appétit de ce pain céleste, et il
vous sera présenté.*

—*Sermon sur la parole de Dieu* in *Oeuvres oratoires*

In *Sermon sur la parole de Dieu* (1661), his most suggestive text on the theory
and practice of predication, Bossuet outlines a process of communication
so paradoxical it constitutes a mystery. According to his scheme, the predicator is not the producer of a message transmitted to the listener; nor,
in the terminology of contemporary reception theory, is his message merely
actualized or realized by the receiver. Rather, it is the receiver who determines the words that the predicator himself receives from the transcendental sender, and them emits. This three-way transactive model of
communication places primary responsibility for the message on the listener's "disposition," and effaces the speaking subject. If listeners do not
hunger for "le pain céleste," the Logos, God "retirera la saine doctrine de
la bouche des prédicateurs."

The image of the human mouth receiving divine nourishment is part
of a semantic network in *Sermon sur la parole de Dieu* that assimilates communication to the rite of communion. Conceptually, "ce secret rapport entre
le mystère de l'Eucharistie et le ministère de la parole" is ascribed to Saint
Augustine. Bossuet goes further, however, exploiting the homophony between *la chair*, the body of Christ, and *la chaire*, the locus from which the
speaker's word emanates, and thus, by analogy, the predicatory mouth:

[Les prédicateurs] y montent pour y célébrer un mystère, et un
mystère semblable à celui de l'Eucharistie. . . . Dans le mystère

From *Papers on French Seventeenth-Century Literature* no. 16, Part 1 (1982). © 1982 by *Papers
on French Seventeenth-Century Literature*.

> de l'Eucharistie, les espèces que vous voyez sont des signes, mais ce qui est enfermé dedans, c'est le corps même de Jésus-Christ. Et dans les discours sacrés, les paroles que vous entendez sont des signes, mais la pensée qui les produit et celle qu'elles vous portent, c'est la vérité même du Fils de Dieu.

Since Christ is the Word become flesh, his utterances, which are carried by the preacher's mouth, comprise "une espèce de second corps . . . et en ce nouveau corps . . . il vit et il converse avec nous." Predicatory discourse, then, re-presents Christ, reincorporates him as a presence. And its transmission from speaker to listener ideally reenacts the rite of the Last Supper, when Christ instructed his disciples: "Celui qui mange ma chair et boit mon sang, demeure en moi et moi en lui." As Bossuet insists: "Il en est de même . . . de la parole céleste."

While it is used to exact a serious reception from the listener, this extended notion of the Word as divine flesh (or Eucharistic bread) also serves to describe the source of the predicator's discourse. His words should reveal "qu'un Dieu [le] nourrit," an alimentary metaphor found in the Scriptures: "Elles nous disent ailleurs que Dieu est une nourriture admirable . . . cette vérité éternelle qui seule est capable de sustenter [nos âmes]. C'est ce qui nous est signifié par ce pain des anges . . . pain céleste que nous désirons par un appétit de vie éternelle, que nous prenons par l'ouïe, que nous ruminons par l'entendement, que nous digérons par la foi" (*Sermon sur les deux alliances*). The listener literally takes in words through his ears, the privileged organ of Christian faith. Bossuet, however, marks the gustatory in such mixed metaphors as "ce pain des oreilles," or, on a deeper level of ingestion, "la bouche du coeur" (*Sur la parole de Dieu*); far from idiosyncratic, this confusion of the gustative and the auditive is a product of what Lévi-Strauss calls their isomorphism (*The Raw and the Cooked*). For the speaker who consumes "[la] nourriture céleste" before he retransmits it, the mouth is the matricial organ, a metonym of the container for the contained. "J'écouterai ce que dira en moi le Seigneur," says the predicator, citing Augustine, "parce qu'il mettra en ma bouche des paroles de paix pour son peuple." Indeed, the epigraph from Matthew that dominates Bossuet's *Sur la prédication évangélique* (1662)—"l'homme ne vit pas seulement de pain, mais il vit de toute parole qui sort de la bouche de Dieu"—pertains not merely to the inscribed listener or narratee [in Genette's sense (*narrataire*) of fictional reader and listener], but also to the predicator's self-representation as the mouth that consumes God's Word, made flesh in the Eucharist.

"Mangez Jésus-Christ, savourez cette viande céleste et divine," intones the priest, "Nourrissez-vous de cet aliment et de cette nourriture sacrée, incorporez-vous à elle" (*Paroles à l'occasion d'une profession*). Commentators from Sir James Frazer to Sigmund Freud have interpreted the Eucharist as a secondary elaboration of the primitive religious rite: eating the body of the god. This essentially cannibalistic act is motivated by a desire to acquire the god's special attributes and powers; but this "incorporation," to use Freud's term from *Totem and Taboo*, exacts in exchange "deferred obedience" to the consumed being. In his rendition of the scene of the primal horde, however, Freud clearly subordinates the cannibalistic to the patricidal urge, a critical notion that Theodore Reik questions in his essay, "You Are Whom You Eat": "I am of the opinion that the cannibalistic part of the primal deed, casually treated in Freud's reconstruction, is of paramount importance and is the central seat of most of the social and religious developments originated in the emotional reactions created by that crime (*Myth and Guilt: The Crime and Punishment of Mankind*). And Reik's evidence includes tribal puberty rites of a monster devouring young boys, classical myths of gods eating their children, the biblical sin of tasting the forbidden fruit, and, finally, the totemic meal of the Eucharist. Extending that idea, the consumption of God's Word by the human mouth, which Christianity particularly valorizes, may be viewed as a tertiary elaboration of the cannibalistic act. Logo is ego, as Christ's locution "hoc est meum corpum" suggests. By eating the Word, the subject will 'incorporate' God's linguistic power, acquire the right to speak for Him, and, concomitantly, become more obedient to Him. In Bossuet's theory of predication, the process centers on the speaker's mouth, and is to be mimetically reproduced in the listener's consumption of the discourse. This *structure en relais* (Barthes), further complicated by the listener's crucial input into the nourishing, uttering mouth of God, underlies the mystery of the predicatory operation and its inherent problematic.

"O Dieu, vous voyez en quel lieu je prêche, et vous savez, ô Dieu, ce qu'il y faut dire," the preacher exclaims in *Sur la prédication évangélique*. "Donnez-moi des paroles sages, donnez-moi des paroles puissantes." Throughout Bossuet's self-reflexive *Oeuvres oratoires*, the predicator implores God to fill him with verbal mana, "cette parole . . . plus douce que le miel à ma bouche" (*Sur la loi de Dieu*). While the mouth is ideally represented as a mere receptacle, an instrument, a canal that conveys the Logos, the speaker remains uncertain that his hunger will be fulfilled. Thus he displaces and multiplies his appeals for inspired nourishment to the Holy Ghost, the Immaculate Mother, but above all, to the Son, sent to offer up the body/word in the wake of human failure:

> Dieu ayant parlé à nos pères en plusieurs façons différentes par la bouche de ses prophètes, nous a parlé enfin par son propre Fils. . . . Il savait bien ce grand Dieu, qu'il n'appartenait pas à des hommes de nous conduire à la vérité, parce que leur autorité n'est pas assez grande pour nous la faire croire sur leur parole. . . . Il nous a donc envoyé son Fils qui . . . s'est revêtu d'une chair humaine, afin de nous enseigner en personne les secrets célestes.
>
> (*Sur la parole de Dieu*)

As the intercessor between humanity and divinity, Christ "a mis dans nos bouches la parole de réconciliation" (*Pour la fête de l'Annonciation de la Sainte Vierge*). The predicatory mouth must feed off that Word as it is incorporated in the Scriptures: "Le prédicateur évangélique, c'est celui qui fait parler Jésus-Christ. Mais il ne lui fait pas tenir un langage d'homme, il craint de donner un corps étranger à sa vérité éternelle; c'est pourquoi il puise tout dans les Écritures, il en emprunte même les termes sacrés" (*Sur la parole de Dieu*).

As the predicator pours over the Scriptures, Bossuet tells us in *Pour former un orateur* (1670), he should fill himself with their substance, choosing and internalizing the most limpid parts or "members." Once "fortified," he can proceed to the "corps de doctrine," especially the texts of Cyprian, Augustine and Chrysostom, "the golden mouth," and digest the art of constituting his own discourse. Its texture must show that the speaker is "plein de la doctrine céleste, [qu'il s'est] . . . nourri et rassasié du meilleur suc du christianisme" (*Oraison furèbre du P. Bourgoing*). His utterance should thus comprise a tissue of disparate fragments—citations and references—taken from the scriptural and doctrinal corpora, but somehow bound together syntagmatically to produce a new entity "qui sorte toute vivante de la bouche" (*Panégyrique de Saint Paul*). From dismemberment and consumption to a reconstitution, a reproduction that is a resurrection, this is the mysterious process that must occur for the predicator to have *une langue*, a tongue, a language and a life. "Demandez pour moi," asks the speaker of his listeners in Bossuet's *Panégyrique de Saint François de Paule* (1600), "que je puisse tous les jours apprendre à traiter saintement et fidèlement la parole de vérité; que non seulement je la traite, mais que je m'en nourrisse et que j'en vive."

The divine corpus is not, however, the sole source of nourishment. The predicatory mouth can also feed off the human body, as Bossuet's funeral orations confirm. "Je puis bien ici répéter devant ces autels les paroles que j'ai recueillies de sa bouche," says the orator of the Prince de Condé (*Oraison funèbre de Louis de Bourbon*). Although the decomposition of the material body is vividly evoked, particular acts and utterances can be disinterred, represented and transubstantiated into an *exemplum* of the eternal Word: "[Marie Thérèse] vous dit par ma bouche . . . que la grandeur est un songe, la joie une erreur, la jeunesse une fleur qui tombe, et la santé un nom trompeur. Amassez donc les biens qu'on ne peut perdre" (*Oraison funèbre de Marie-Térèse d'Autriche*). As the speaker appropriates the dead body to extract and transmit its essential substance, *la scène/la cène* of the funeral oration emblematizes the very process of constitution of predicatory utterance.

Despite these various sources of nourishment, the danger that the mouth will emit "un corps étranger à [la] vérité éternelle" is not dispelled. On the contrary, the predicator's discourse seems doomed to alloy the force of the Logos, since it is bound in the changing, ephemeral matter of human language. "Comment peut-on confier des actions immortelles à des langues toujours incertaines et toujours changeantes?" asks the speaker (*Discours de réception à l'Académie française*). Moreover, there is the ubiquitous problem that any *prise de la parole* asserts a subject, an "I" which appears to speak in its own name, rather than in God's, as His instrument. Whenever that reflexive "I speak" bodies forth sinful pride, it must be checked in the very body of the text. "On doit écouter notre parole, ou plutôt la parole du Fils de Dieu," says the predicator (*Sur la parole de Dieu*); and elsewhere, "Vous m'écoutez, ou plutôt vous écoutez Dieu qui vous parle par ma bouche" (*Sur les rechutes*). This apparent lapsus, which is cancelled and corrected by the phrase "ou plutôt," is part of a pervasive problematic of mimesis as sinful mimicry: the desire to communicate the power of the Logos may generate a powerful mode of speech that suggests presumptuous imitation, an identification with the divine verging on self-apotheosis. As the speaker observers:

> s'il y avait un prédicateur assez téméraire pour attendre [de] grands effects de son éloquence, il me semble que Dieu lui dit comme à Job: ". . . Si tu crois avoir un bras comme Dieu et tonner d'une voix semblable, achève et fais le Dieu tout à fait; élève-toi dans les nues, parais en ta gloire, renverse les superbes en ta fureur, et dispose à ton gré des choses humaines. . . ." Quoi! avec cette faible voix imiter le tonnerre du Dieu vivant!
>
> (*Sur la parole di Dieu*)

Instead, the preacher should strive to reproduce the naive, but majestic humility of Christ's style, which was the concretization of his message: "Faisons . . . des prédications dont la bassesse tienne quelque chose de l'humiliation de la croix" (*Panégyrique de Saint Paul*). Just as Christ disdained the "help of eloquence," so too did his apostles, most notably Saint Paul, reject the artifices, *les affeteries*, of rhetoric: "Tout se fait [chez eux] par une secrète vertu . . . qui, venant du ciel, sait se conserver toute entière dans la bassesse de leurs expressions et dans la simplicité d'un style vulgaire" (*Sur la divinité de Jésus-Christ*). To receive and retain this secret gift, the predicator yearns to strip his utterances of all figures of profane speech: "Que plût à Dieu que nous puissions détacher de notre parole tout ce qui . . . délecte l'esprit, tout ce qui surprend l'imagination, pour n'y laisser que . . . la seule force et l'efficace toute pure du Saint Esprit!" (*Sur la résurrection*). But as he confronts the impossibility of achieving this zero degree, the speaker must find a compromise between the purity of transcendent nourishment and the tainted flesh of mortal words. On the authority of Augustine's *De Doctrina Christiana*, Bossuet incorporates rhetoric in his theory of predication as an ancillary figure that is not sought, but "semble venir comme d'elle-même, attirée par la grandeur des choses" (*Sur la parole de Dieu*), a mysterious, spontaneous by-product of the Logos. At best, rhetorical figures should comprise the surface covering of the body, or, in other words, "l'assaisonnement de la nourriture solide" (*Panégyrique de Saint Paul*).

Bossuet's denial of the rhetorical nature of all speech and scripture, and his definition of eloquence as the corporeal supplement to a spiritual essence compound the problematic tensions in predication. Not only must the speaker debase the absolute purity of the Logos with profane human speech, but, on a secondary axis, the relative purity of his word is further compromised by the receiver's profane desires. The preacher is forced, he tells his listeners, to use "ces ornements étrangers . . . puisque telle est votre délicatesse, que vous ne pouvez goûter Jésus-Christ tout seul dans la simplicité de son Évangile" (*Varies excuses des pécheurs*). Indeed, the speaking subject in the *Oeuvres oratoires* tends to obscure the ontological dilemma of his quest for divine nourishment by stressing the phenomenological problem caused by narratees who desire unholy utterances.

Chief among these negative narratees is "the esthetic receiver" who consumes the predicatory word only as poetic form. "Quoi! cette période n'a pas ses mesures, ce raisonnement n'est pas dans son jour, cette comparaison n'est pas bien tournée!" parodies the speaker. Such an obsessive taste for superficial delectation can contaminate the predicatory mouth that lacks the fortitude of le Père Bourgoing: "O! qu'il était éloigné de ces prédicateurs infidèles . . . qui ne rougissent pas d'acheter . . . des paroles de flatterie par la parole de vérité, des louanges, vains aliments d'un esprit léger, par la nourriture solide et substantielle que Dieu a préparée à ses enfants" (*Oraison funèbre du P. Bourgoing*). In this travesty of holy communication, the predicator mouths words only to have his ego fed by listeners who seek pleasure and play. They want their ears flattered, tickled, and their emotions titillated, like the audience in a theater. "Ce n'est pas ici un théâtre," intones the speaker, "où nous puissions inventer à plaisir des sujets propres à émouvoir et à exciter les passions" (*Aux nouveaux convertis*). Because he is bound in obedience to the corpus that nourishes him, because he refuses to attenuate the austerity of the Christian Word, the predicator, like John the Chrysostom before him, has difficulty competing with his satanic rival, the actor. Through various artifices and subterfuges, the spectator is so thoroughly seduced by the actor that identification, a kind of incorporation, occurs: "Il est donc ému, il est transporté, il se réjouit, il s'afflige de choses qui au fond sont indifférentes. . . . Cette pitié qui causait des larmes, cette colère qui enflammait et les yeux et le visage, n'étaient que des images et des simulacres par lesquels le coeur se donne la comédie en lui-même" (*Sur la parole de Dieu*). Beyond the spectator's self-delusions, the power and pleasure of theatrical effects can arouse contempt for predicatory discourse, even scandalous laughter. No wonder then that the speaker tries to "déraciner tout à fait le goût de la comédie" from his corrupted listeners (*Maximes et réflexions sur la comédie*).

In this persistent effort, Bossuet draws the fine but crucial distinction between theater, which excites the passions, and predication, which should stir the heart; in a word, the difference between *plaire* and *toucher*. Bad listeners, "cherchent partout ce qui les flatte et qui les délecte . . . s' imaginent être innocents de désirer dans les chaires les discours qui plaisent et non ceux qui touchent et qui édifient, et énervent par ce moyen toute l'efficace de l'Évangile" (*Sur la parole de Dieu*). The word is efficacious only when the speaker "parle au coeur par [sa] bouche," and listeners open their hearts to receive it: "ouvrons-lui-en toute l'étendue." Ideally, this transmission to the heart should not pass through the ears, already infected and hardened by profane utterances, but rather, through "les oreilles [du] coeur": "Jésus-Christ savait . . . qu'il y a des oreilles intérieures où la voix humaine ne pénètre pas et où lui seul a droit de se faire entendre. Ce sont ces oreilles qu'il faut ouvrir pour écouter la prédication." The speaker, however, has no access to the inner ear—a metaphor for what Augustine first called "internal predication." "Je ne puis parler qu'aux oreilles," he confesses, "et c'est dans le coeur que vous êtes attentifs, où ma parole n'est pas capable de pénétrer. Je ne sais si cette parole a eu la grâce de réveiller au dedans de vous cette attention secrète à la vérité qui vous parle au coeur. Je l'espère, je le conjecture" ("*Pour la Toussaint*"). Because it is no more than a conjecture, the speaker searches for confirming signs on the listening bodies: "J'ai vu, ce me semble, vos yeux et vos regards attentifs; je vous ai vus arrêtés et suspendus, avides de la vérité et de la parole de vie. Vous a-t-elle délectés? . . . Il me le semble, mes Frères, vous étiez doucement occupés de la suavité de la parole." In other instances, he exhorts the receiver to emit signs—"Donnez des regrets, donnez des soupirs" (*Sermon sur l'endurcissement*)—especially to shed tears, which should attest to the heart's consumption and its compunction. Like John the Chrysostom, however, the preacher knows that such signs may be duplicitous, and merely represent "des affections de théâtre" that can never touch the heart (*Sur le parole de Dieu*).

And yet, even the heart does not constitute the ideal repository of the Word. Both the predicatory mouth and the receiver should seek a more hidden site, "ce lieu caché dans lequel Dieu parle," which is the locus of the production of desire:

> pour être attentif à la parole de l'Évangile, il ne faut pas ramasser son attention au lieu où se mesurent les périodes, mais au lieu où se règlent les moeurs; il ne faut pas se recueillir au lieu où l'on goûte les belles pensées, mais au lieu où se produisent les bons désirs. . . . Enfin, s'il y a quelque endroit encore plus profond et plus retiré où se tienne le conseil du coeur, où se déterminent tous ses desseins, où se donne le branle à ses mouvements, c'est là qu'il faut se rendre attentif pour écouter parler Jésus-Christ.

In this locus, which we would call the subconscious, the listener already possesses the Word. Incorporated by God, it now lies dormant, lifeless in some recess of the memory. "Tu as des conduites si enveloppées, des retraites si profondes et si tortueuses dans lesquelles tes connaissances se recèlent," the speaker instructs the listener. "Souvent ce que tu sais, tu ne le sais pas; ce qui est en toi est loin de toi; tu n'as pas ce que tu possèdes" (*Sur la prédication évangélique*). Expounding on the Augustinian doctrine of anamnesis, Bossuet does not describe this body of truths as forgotten, but repressed: "Nous sommes bien aise de les éloigner par une malice affectée." Thus the predicatory mouth, like the psycho-analytic, must do more than "stir" or "agitate" the internal, alienated body; he must extricate and reproduce it before the listener to ensure a fruitful encounter, "[une] rencontre bienheureuse."

This moment of communion is not achieved, however, and the resulting sense of failure emerges in recurring complaints against resistent listeners. "En quoi donc nous plaignons-nous justement que vous méprisez notre travail?" asks the speaker. "En ce que vous nous écoutez, et que vous ne nous croyez pas" (*Vairies excuses des pécheurs*). Elsewhere, he concludes in despair: "J'ai parlé en l'air, et vous ne croyez rien de ce que j'ai dit" (*Sur la parole de Dieu*). The unbeliever elicits far less criticism, however, than the narratee who is not listening to the predicatory utterance, and "[laisse] tomber à terre la parole de vérité," an act as sacrilegious as dropping the Host during communion. This anti-addressee is characterized as a present absence, a dead being who reduces the preacher to an alien voice crying in the desert. In trying to resuscitate and sustain his attention, the speaking subject emphasizes the phatic function: "Mais quoi!" he exclaims in the middle of a sermon "on ne m'entend plus; tu m'échappes à ce coup, auditeur distrait!" (*Pour la fête de la circoncision*). Indeed, Bossuet pronounces entire discourses on attention, among these, *Sermon sur l'endurcissement* (1669): "Donnez-moi du moins de vos attentions dans un discours où il s'agit de l'attention elle-même". And his sermon *Sur la soumission due à la parole de Jésus-Christ* (1660) is generated and punctuated by the verse from Matt. 17:5: "Celui-ci est mon Fils bien aimé . . . écoutez-le"; *ipsum audite*. Grafted from biblical intertexts, the imperative mode, or the stress on the conative function, is systematically marked in the predicatory text: "il faut seulement écouter et croire" (*Sur la parole de Dieu*). But such illocutionary directives lead to commissive threats before deaf ears and unreceptive hearts: "Mon discours, dont vous vous croyez peut-être les juges, vous jugera au dernier jour; ce sera sur vous un nouveau fardeau . . . et si vous n'en sortez plus chrétiens, vous en sortirez plus coupables" (*Oraison funèbre d'Anne de Gonzague*). Anything but an innocuous substance, the word that is not consumed changes into a body that kills: "Ainsi la divine parole, ce pain des oreilles, ce corps spirituel de la vérité; ceux qu'elle ne touche pas, elle les juge; ceux qu'elle ne convertit pas, elle les condamne; ceux qu'elle ne nourrit pas, elle les tue" (*Sur la parole de Dieu*).

In the face of rejection, the maternal predicatory mouth that yearns to nourish is transformed into a predatory mouth that assaults the intended receiver. An instrument of God, the mouth becomes an aggressive phallic weapon that strikes with the word, *verbum* turned to blows, *verbera*. On the authority of Saint Paul, for whom God's Word is "plus pénétrant qu'un glaive tranchant des deux côtés," the predicatory/predatory organ tries to "penetrate" the occluded bodies, "les abattre à ses pieds . . . les forcer invinciblement au milieu de leurs défenses," and ravish them. Because this is "un ravage salutaire," however, the listener should not simply submit to his violation, but in fact, participate in the act, thrusting the phallic word deeper in the recesses of his being: "Si le coup ne va pas assez loin, prenons nous-mêmes le glaive et enfousons le plus avant. Que plût à Dieu que nous portassions le coup si avant que la blessure allât jusqu'au vif . . ." Still more, the (s)word should dismember the body, annihilate it:

> Il faut prendre ce glaive dont Jésus-Christ parle dans son Évangile
> . . . qui coupe, qui tranche, qui sépare. . . . Quand on veut ouvrir
> un corps, on se sert des rasoirs les plus fins et les plus délicats
> pour couper et séparer les muscles des nerfs, des tendons; on
> fouille partout dans les entrailles. . . . Ainsi il faut prendre cette
> épée à deux tranchants . . . qui sépare et divise, qui anéantisse et
> retranche tout ce qui est contraire à l'obéissance jusqu'aux
> moindres fibres.

Aux Ursulines de Meaux

The dismembered, immolated body is the precondition for the transfiguration, the conversion that the predicatory mouth desires. Only violent death can produce a conversion that resembles a resurrection, or better yet, a profound renewal tantamount to a painful rebirth: "la conversion du pécheur est une nouvelle naissance; et c'est la malédiction de notre nature, 'qu'on ne peut enfanter qu'avec douleur. . . .' Mais, parmi ces douleurs, . . . songez, mes Frères, que vous enfantez; et ce que vous enfantez, c'est vous-mêmes" (*Sur la pénitence*). In this birth trauma, the maternal function is assumed not only by listeners but by predicators as well, the proverbial "mères de Jésus-Christ," who strive to engender, *enfanter*, the Christian corpus in their receivers. But like God, who discharges both the maternal and the paternal functions, the predicatory tongue also possesses the ravaging and inseminating powers of the Father: "ma parole est le glaive tranchant qui vous va arracher au monde. . . . Il y veut tout ensemble tuer et renouveler; il y veut égorger l'homme ancien, mais il y veut faire renaître l'homme tout nouveau" (*Pour la profession de Mme de la Vallière*).

Through the mystical process of transubstantiation, listeners who consume the predicatory word are consumed, annihilated and reborn as obedient children. Incorporating the *corpus Christi*, they are converted into "son corps et ses membres," a body whose actions are the fulfillment of the Logos. The Word become flesh, the new beings are concomitantly the flesh become Word: they gain the divinity's power to speak and transmit the Logos, like Saul, renamed Saint Paul, "le premier des prédicateurs." Thus, when the Princesse Palatine "[se nourrit] de la parole de vie," and underwent a profound conversion, she acquired the gift of predication; in her utterances, says the orator, "j'y ressens la manne cachée et le goût des Écritures divines." The converted tongue converts others in turn: "Presque tous ceux qui lui parlaient se rendaient à elle." Undeniably, the efficacy of her simple speech "[efface] les discours les plus magnifiques." As the predicator ultimately admits, "je voudrais ne parler plus que ce langage."

The conditional mode of that admission introjects the element of self-doubt that must mark any utterance from the predicatory mouth. Throughout the *Oeuvres oratoires*, the speaker never ceases to question his power to consume the listener and engender the Christian: "Esprit saint . . . puissant moteur des coeurs, qu'ai-je donc fait aujourd'hui pour vous et par vous? Ai-je pénétré ces coeurs, ai-je remué ces coeurs? Ai-je du moins fait retentir quelque chose de ce bruit que vous fîtes entendre lorsque vous descendîtes du ciel? . . .Ha! que je crains pour plusieurs que non" (*Pour la profession de Mme de La Vallière*). This self-effacing conclusion may not be inaccurate, observes Jacques Truchet, for Bossuet evinces an inability to condescend to his listeners, understand their needs. His predication has "the allure of a monologue," Truchet maintains, but in its most effective instances, it dramatizes "a pathetic effort" to reach the other. That Bossuet's word may not have converted its receivers is also Peter France's conclusion. In contrast to Truchet, however, France argues that the celebrated seventeenth-century predicator made, or had to make, too many concessions to his audience's taste. As he tried to break through their blasé indifference, Bossuet was forced to become an entertainer, the actor he despised, producing sermons filled with brilliant rhetorical devices, and not the humble bread of the Evangelical word.

However intriguing these comments may be, authorial problematics cannot be reconstructed from texts. What Bossuet's corpus does inscribe is a contradiction between the theory of Eucharistic discourse as a signified and the practice incorporated in the verbal texture, a disjunction that underscores the speaker's failure to be the ideal predicatory mouth. Thus, while the subject of enunciation projects the sinful desire for pleasure onto the narratee, while he imputes the quality of his utterance to this alter ego, "ô pécheurs, mes semblables," he also suggests that the fundamental choice to *plaire* rather than to *convertir* spells his own damnation: "Malheur à moi, si dans cette chair j'aime mieux me chercher moi-même que votre salut, et si je ne préfère à mes inventions, quand elles pourraient vous plaire, les expériences . . . qui peuvent vous convertir" (*Oraison funèbre d'Anne de Gonzague*).

That various constraints and contradictions contaminated Bossuet's predicatory mouth and produced far more pleasures than conversions seems to be diachronically confirmed by readers from Sévigné to Valéry. Esthetic receivers, they have relished the splendidly constructed verbal shapes and figures of Bossuet's texts. "Pour [les] amants de la forme," writes Valéry. "[Bossuet] est un trésor de figures, de combinaisons et d'opérations coordonnées. Ils peuvent admirer passionnément ces compositions du plus grand style, comme ils admirent l'architecture de temples dont le sanctuaire est désert et dont les sentiments et les causes qui les firent édifier se sont dès longtemps affaiblis" ("Bossuet"). Three centuries of "profound changes," insists Valéry, render the substance of Bossuet's work naive, strange, even inconceivable. However, if the substance of those texts is defined as *le drame de l'interlocution,* to use Barthes phrase, then Bossuet's predicatory discourse enacts a primary scene that has consumed and been reproduced by speakers and readers before and after the seventeenth century, irrespective of the "profound changes" claimed by Valéry.

The problematics of utterance and of reception that the author of *Sermon sur la parole de Dieu* confronted when he idealized communication as communion have continued to haunt both religious and so-called secular texts. A century after Bossuet, Hegel repeatedly compared the Last Supper to the consumption of the written word. (see Werner Hamacher, "The Reader's Supper: A Piece of Hegel," *Diacritics* 11 [Summer 1981].) But in *The Spirit of Christianity,* an early text, Hegel also points out that the objective food/word becomes subjective when it is consumed, and thus, that no moment of union ever occurs; the sense of separation always remains. It is surely no accident that almost two centuries later, this "remarkable" passage is cited in *Glas,* as Derrida attempts to deconstruct imperial, Hegelian logocentrism on the left side of his colossal text. That Derrida places on the right side the dismembered texts of Jean Genet does not, however, efface the religious model that generated the criminal's, the deviant's, parodies of the Annunciation, the Last Supper, or even the Gospel according to John. In his own antilogocentric gesture, Derrida emblemetizes *le morceau, le reste,* as Barthes and Blanchot valorize the fragment, but these are still remains of *la cène* when the Word became flesh and was consumed in communion. That ritual scene of communication is not annihilated in *Glas:*

> N'allez surtout pas croire que je vous raconte ici, dans l'arrière boutique de la pharmacie de Jésus, l'histoire d'un genêt dont la teinture, le pharmakon, m'intéresse avant tout. Et il est vrai que je n'aurai rien fait si je n'ai pas réussi à vous affecter de genêt, à vous colorer, barbouiller, encoller, à vous rendre sensible, à vous transformer, par delà tout ce qui se combine ici, depuis l'affect le plus propre de ce texte.

Le glas has not tolled as yet; the communicative mystique remains. Derrida himself validates Sartre's definition of *la grande affaire:* the scandal of theological survivals among the most secular, the most radical of thinkers. Like *Huis-Clos,* which dramatizes a postmortem hell that Sartre, the thinker, denies, we cannot escape the use, and, thus, the hold of myths and metaphors of communication as communion which Bossuet's predicatory mouth forcefully tried to impress upon his listeners. While we may claim with Nietzche to have killed God, Bossuet's supreme nourishment, we are—I am—reenacting the totem meal of the word with ever greater passion. In the words that close Sartre's representation of hell, "Eh bien, continouns."

Opposition to Antiquity: Charles Perrault

Kirsti Simonsuuri

Should modern writers copy the ancients or should they rather follow their own creative talent? That was, in its simplest form, the question debated during the *querelle des anciens et des modernes*. The issue was not a new one. It had been raised during the fourteenth century when the modernists of the early Renaissance had discussed cultural progress. But during the seventeenth-century *querelle*, Perrault and the *modernes* made certain theoretical assumptions about progress which were to prove rich in consequences. It is hardly an oversimplification to say that the *querelle* itself was the most crucial intellectual struggle in the early development of modern Europe. During the *querelle* values derived from classical antiquity were for the first time set in opposition to progress, and the late seventeenth and early eighteenth century hence marked the beginning of a new phase in the history of thought.

Initially, the *querelle* represented the revolt of French and English writers against the traditional acceptance of antiquity as a linguistic, literary and artistic model. The name itself owes its origins to Charles Perrault, whose *Parallèle des anciens et des modernes* (1688–97) gives an account of the issues at stake in support of the modernist position. The origins of the linguistic and literary debate can be traced back to Jean Desmarets de Saint-Sorlin's *La comparaison de la langue et de la poësie françoise avec la grecque et la latine* (1670), where a decided attack on Homer was made. This was the most famous of the many treatises produced in the 1670s which defended the French language and thus could be considered modernist. When de Callières published his account of the *querelle* in 1688, its title, *Histoire poëtique de la guerre nouvellement declarée entre les anciens et les modernes*, indicated

From *Homer's Original Genius: Eighteenth-Century Notions of the Early Greek Epic (1688–1798)*. © 1979 by Cambridge University Press.

the existence of a prolonged debate that had recently gained greater prominence.

In the 1680s the debate moved by slow stages to consider critical, creative, educational and cultural questions in general. Literature constituted the crucial area in which the problem of cultural values was being worked out. Perrault and his friends assumed that a literary work owed its character to the social and cultural conditions that existed at the time of its creation. Their idea that the level of cultural development determines literary productions reflected particularly badly on Homer, since the Homeric epics were the products of a primitive age. Theories implicit in the statements the *modernes* made about classical antiquity and cultural development became the dominant issues of the eighteenth century in the work of Vico and the Scottish primitivists.

During the *querelle* a new humanist concern manifested itself, and the humanistic implications of the debate are still largely with us. The central questions of the *querelle* can be characterized as a series of enquiries into the meaning of culture by an age which was becoming conscious of itself and saw its relation to the past in a more detached way than the previous generation had done. The men of the 1670s and 1680s grouped around the French Academy were increasingly interested in three interconnected questions: the different standards of artistic excellence in ancient and modern culture (the *literary critical* problem), the dependence of creative genius on its culture and environment (the *creative* and *educational* problem) and the debt owed by contemporary arts and sciences to antiquity (the *cultural* problem). Two fundamentally different concepts of man were reflected in the discussion of these problems. Either man could be always the same, as La Bruyère, the supporter of the ancients, put it: "Les hommes n'ont point changé selon le coeur et selon les passions, ils sont encore tels qu'ils étaient alors et qu'ils sont marqués de Théophraste" (*Discours sur Théophraste*); or man was changing and constantly bettering himself, because man was essentially a function of his brain and intellect, not of his heart and emotions, as Fontenelle argued: "l'homme n'est homme que par la raison, et rien n'est plus beau que d'apprendre aux autres comment ils s'en doivent servir à étudier la Nature, et à développer toutes les enigmes qu'elle nous propose" (*Nouveaux dialogues des morts*).

The supporters of the ancients and the moderns, led by Boileau and Perrault respectively, differed also in their views as regards the method and the solution. The ancients saw no essential need for adopting new standards of criticism for value judgments of contemporary works, arguing, as they did, for universality; likewise they largely ignored the importance of environment as a factor in the formation of genius, and stated that a level of perfection had been attained in antiquity which contemporary literature could only imitate.

While the ancients equated classical antiquity with nature in saying that "sed iuxta antiquos naturam imitabere pulchram," and stated that the classics should be imitated because they had imitated nature so well, the moderns viewed humanity as constantly transforming and dependent on cultural and environmental forces largely outside its control. Human phenomena, including individuals, societies and their intellectual and cultural achievements, were set in opposition to nature. Fontenelle argued for nature's continual power to mould human events; there was an abstract principle, not unlike that proposed by Newtonian physics, that was shaping humanity and its history according to natural laws. Classical antiquity represented one stage in the history of humanity that is subject to these forces of nature. However, judgments concerning the individual productions of antiquity had to be rendered in relative, human terms, because the men of genius who had created these works were formed by the early environment.

In literature, the moderns argued emphatically for relative criteria. The evaluation of poetry involved in the first place an attempt to assess the period in which poetry had been produced. Descartes' anti-authoritarianism was evident in the modernist position. Cartesianism wanted to emancipate not only philosophy but also literature, and break the ties that were thought to unite antiquity and the French "esprit" (*Discours sur la méthode*, 1637). Saint-Evremond, who through his personal contacts with England became the mediator of the relativist view to English criticism, argued in his essay "Sur les anciens" (?1685) that the Homeric poetry could not be a guide to modern writers because between antiquity and the modern age "tout est changé: les Dieux, la nature, la politique, les moeurs, le goût, les manières." The moderns denied the value of classical antiquity and its literary and artistic productions as models, while nevertheless perceiving their inherent merits. Here is the crucial difference between the moderns and the ancients; and even though Saint-Evremond was relatively moderate in his arguments—he steered away from the heat of the *querelle* by staying in England—his view of the Homeric epic expressed the position maintained by the moderns until La Motte: "Si Homère vivoit présentement, il feroit des poèmes admirables accomodez au siècle où il écrivoit: nos poëtes en font des mauvais, ajustez à celuy des anciens, et conduits par des règles qui sont tombées avec des choses que le temps a fait tomber."

The imitation of antiquity based on admiration could be positively harmful. Fontenelle, the most notable philosopher among the moderns, argued that it was exactly on this issue that the progress of human knowledge was crucially held back: "Rien n'arrête tant le progrès des choses, rien ne borne tant des esprits, que l'admiration excessive des anciens. Parce qu'on s'était dévoué à l'autorité d'Aristôte, et qu'on ne cherchait la vérité que dans ses écrits énigmatiques, et jamais dans la nature." Fontenelle's influential essay *Digression sur les anciens et les modernes*, appended to his literary piece *Poësies pastorales* in 1688, has relevance to the discussion of human knowledge insofar as this is scientific, for in science we can meaningfully speak of progress based on accumulative knowledge. Seventeenth-century French writers worked out a new attitude to classical antiquity largely because they had to respond to the challenge presented by the progress of experimental science and scientific thought. In these fields of knowledge the superiority of the modern age was obvious even to those who were not scientists. The popularization of science had become a serious aspect of culture by the time of the *querelle*. There was not only the opposition to Aristotle's view of scientific method, expressed here by Fontenelle and maintained, on different grounds, already by Bacon; it was more generally realized that the ancient writers had believed in the Ptolemaic universe, and that even Aristotle and Lucretius had held views about natural phenomena which most educated people found preposterous. Fontenelle capitalized on these shortcomings of ancient science, and in his *Entretiens sur la pluralité des mondes* (1688), which was immediately translated into English, he demonstrated to the public the advancement of modern scientific ideas in relation to the ancient: "The Ancients were pleasant Gentlemen, to imagine that the Celestial Bodies were in their own nature unchangeable, because they observed no change in them: but they did not live long enough to confirm their opinion by their own experience; they were Boys in comparison to Us."

Fontenelle's ideas—and those of the moderns—on natural sciences, physics, chemistry and astronomy and their methodology have only a marginal interest here; but they do have a bearing on the argument of this chapter. During the *querelle*, a confrontation between the ancients and the moderns as regards literary critical, creative, educational and cultural issues was inevitable, because the concept of man presented an infinitely more complex problem than it had done for the thinkers of previous generations. Montaigne is a representative of a century that knew its classics thoroughly and read them primarily for personal reasons and because they revealed a rich and full picture of human nature. Even in the generation after Descartes, scientists could not yet adequately tackle the complexity of man's nature. There were philosophers and sensitive students of man who continued to use classical literature as their material evidence, and the need for a science was echoed by Pope some thirty years later—"Know then thyself, presume not God to scan;/the proper study of mankind is Man"— but a science of man in the modern sense of psychological and social sciences was virtually nonexistent. It was in natural sciences that the advancement from the ancient position could be clearly stated and even shown. The certainty of progress there suggested to moderns that similar development had occurred in the arts and humanities. Only it was much more difficult to prove.

The moderns argued that human nature revealed in contemporary works was in fact much richer and more complex than that in the literature of antiquity. Fontenelle pointed out in his *Digression* that centuries differ in regard to the number of people who have been able fully to realize their potentialities: "Elle [nature] produit dans tous les siècles des hommes propres à être des grands hommes, mais les siècles ne leur permettent pas toujours d'exercer leurs talents" (*Digression*). Perrault in his *Parallèle* . . . expressed most clearly the idea of some slow but steady development in man's intellectual capacities which better qualify him for the study of his own nature.

In the last phase of the *querelle,* at the end of the seventeenth century and the beginning of the eighteenth, the issues expanded to cover every vital aspect of culture. The scope of Perrault's *Parallèle* is evidence for this. Even in that work, though its main attack was directed against classical culture and its men of genius, there were elements which suggested that literary men and scholars alike were beginning to feel that more factual information about antiquity was needed for a proper revaluation of the classical heritage. The existing view of classical literature was dependent on a textual tradition which even the Renaissance scholars had realized to be insufficiently critical, while the physical environment of antiquity was known only through books or through impressionistic travellers' accounts. It was realized that if more factual information were available, in terms of both reliable texts and archaeological findings, the attitudes to the classics might substantially change. Perrault's generation knew its classics very badly and through translations; but it awakened to a new adventurous interest in the reality that had produced classical art and literature. A plea for a kind of imaginative archaeology was made in the *Parallèle*: "Nous naissons au milieu de sphères et des cartes géographiques, qui nous enseignent dès nostre enfance la véritable situation de tous les pays, et nous croyons mal-à-propos qu'il en a esté de mesme du temps d'Homère."

By the time discussion of the issues of the *querelle* had spread outside the circle of the participants, and the controversy itself had ended, the division of labour between the ancients and the moderns was beginning to be settled. The moderns made the practical proposal that contemporary literature and art should proceed independently of what had gone on before, because in their eyes the fact that the classical forms of literature had survived for centuries was evidence of their adaptability and variety, not of their superiority as such. The ancients interested themselves more and more in the practical problems that emerged in the study of classical antiquity. The classical scholars of the late eighteenth century and of the nineteenth can be seen as the descendants of the ancients of the *querelle*. The eighteenth-century contribution to classical studies lay in investigating the philological accuracy of ancient texts and testing the archaeological authenticity of the classical remains; and by this development one of the issues raised during the *querelle* was brought to its material fruition.

"Nothing is more natural and reasonable than to have great veneration for all those things that are truly valuable in themselves and which have the additional merit of being old," begins Charles Perrault's massive four-volume analysis of the two cultures, the classical and the contemporary, his *Parallèle des anciens et des modernes* (1688–97). Considering its scope, the range of its intentions and its immediate impact, the *Parallèle* can be regarded as the culmination of the ideological controversy in which French poets and critics questioned their relation to the values and criteria of classical literature. Perrault's work challenged the traditional valuation of the achievements of classical antiquity, and although its bias is thus decisively on the side of the moderns, it remains the most comprehensive ideological review that has reached us from late-seventeenth-century France.

As we know, Perrault first won notice for his views when he read a small poem entitled "Le siècle de Louis le Grand" at the meeting of the French Academy convened to celebrate the recovery of Louis XIV from a recent illness on 27 January 1687. He could not have chosen a more propitious moment. And although this polemical exercise, intended simply to provoke, was by no means the origin of the *querelle*, the debate was considerably enlivened by it. Perrault argued that classical antiquity and all the notions about it that had become part and parcel of French late-seventeenth-century culture should be taken down from their pedestal and thoroughly re-examined. He did not argue for their dismissal.

> La belle Antiquité fut toujours venerable,
> Mais je ne crus jamais qu'elle fust adorable.
> Je voys les Anciens, sans plier les genoux,
> Ils sont grands, il est vray, mais hommes comme nous.

The re-examination should start with a comparative analysis of the achievements of antiquity and the modern age: "Et l'on peut comparer sans crainte d'être injuste, / Le siècle de Louis au beau siècle d'Auguste." The spearhead of Perrault's criticism was thus directed against that stagnation which respect for the past, seen as an essential element in humanities, might produce in the life of a culture.

The *Parallèle* was a continuation of the line of thought first sketched in the "Siècle," and the poem's argument served as the starting-point for it: "Il m'a paru tant d'aveuglement dans cette prevention et tant d'ingratitude à ne pas vouloir ouvrir les yeux sur la beauté de nostre siècle, à qui le Ciel a départi mille lumières qu'il a refusées à toute l'Antiquité, que je n'ay pu m'empêcher d'en estre ému d'une véritable Indignation: ç'a esté cette Indignation qui a produit le petit poëme du siècle de Louis le Grand." The poem and the *Parallèle*, a work in a more sustained and reflective form, attacked the authority of those who maintained that the imitation of the classics was necessary for contemporary literature and arts. This was the view which Perrault regarded as inimical to him, and the indignation of which he spoke had a curious personal force.

It is ironical that the man who devoted his life to the criticism of traditional values is now considered to be a classic himself. Charles Perrault came of a distinguished family of lawyers, and his elder brothers did very well in their chosen fields, Pierre as a lawyer, Claude as a physician and architect, Nicolas as a classical scholar and theologian. Charles himself had a career apart from his literary achievements as a public administrator and academician. His interest in classical literature had a long if somewhat unusual history. While still in his early twenties, he wrote in collaboration with his brothers Claude and Nicolas a burlesque epic, "Les murs de Troie," which was a parody of Homer, and a burlesque translation of the sixth book of the *Aeneid* (?1648–49), a parody of the *ancien régime*. These poems display in full the raillery that is the disturbing undercurrent of Perrault's later serious writings. All his life, he remained a mixture of an iconoclast manqué and a considerable contributor to the culture of his age. A savage critic of authority, he was at the same time interested in discovering new solutions, so that his fame rests rather on his *Contes* than on the *Parallèle* which has been one of the underestimated masterpieces of French literature.

The *Parallèle* is not an easy work. The ambiguity of Perrault's position is evident in the fact that the book was cast in the form of a literary dialogue, a classical genre made popular by Valla and Erasmus in the Renaissance. But in Perrault's hands it largely served to take the edge off his sharpest arguments, and perhaps intentionally so. There is a complexity which is clearly intended neither to prove nor to disprove. There is little that is originally Perrault's, and yet the *Parallèle* manages to convey a round and at times entertaining picture of late-seventeenth-century French life and ideas. Its conflicting arguments largely recapitulated the complex views of his eminent opponents like Boileau, Arnauld, Fénelon and Huet, who had already protested at the "Siècle," and of his modern supporters like Fontenelle, who was an active accomplice, and the Homeric scholar abbé d'Aubignac, who remained quietly behind the scenes. Despite its dramatic structure, the *Parallèle* does not achieve the artistic unity that characterizes the Platonic dialogues. It is unclassical in the special sense of being unclassifiable; but it bears the endearing stamp of search and research of time past and present, with all the ramifications that this might involve.

The *Parallèle* discusses the fields of ancient and modern poetry, rhetoric, epic literature, philosophy, mathematics, natural sciences, religion, the visual arts and architecture. It thus aims at a comprehensive panorama of culture. These topics are discussed in five dialogues held while the three participants are walking and taking the air in the garden of Versailles. They are le Président, l'Abbé and le Chevalier, each of whom represents a different element in society and a different point of view as regards antiquity. Le Président is a representative of the ancients; he appears to be fearsomely learned, especially in the classics and fine arts, but is in fact the archetypal pedant and a fool, and the perfect caricature of everything he stands for. He defends Homer as the "prince of poets" as tradition since the Renaissance had done, and is shocked at the idea that the Homeric poems might have been compilations, as l'Abbé suggests. L'Abbé is a representative of the moderns, and thus Perrault's most obvious spokesman. He, too, is learned, but feels more at home in philosophy and the sciences than in literature, and likes to throw original ideas into the conversation. Le Chevalier is also a representative of the moderns, although his role is a mediatory one. He captures some of the French liking for "bel esprit" that characterizes the Jesuit tradition, and his comments which support l'Abbé's more serious disquisitions often have a jovial, vivacious style. As the dialogues proceed each new topic defines the roles more closely. In the fourth dialogue the participants discuss Homer and the classical epic, and draw general conclusions about poetry and the dependence of genius on culture. It is on these issues that Perrault comes most clearly into his own and clashes with the ancients and with his arch-enemy Boileau in particular.

Nicolas Boileau was the principal target of Perrault's attack and parody. His popular *L'Art poëtique* (1674) had shown him to be a reasonably flexible critic who was prepared to admit that "poeta nascitur, non fit," or at least must learn to recognize his talent. He had maintained however that it was through imitation of the classics that the poet could achieve excellence.

> C'est en vain qu'au Parnasse un témeraire Auteur
> Pense de l'Art des Vers atteindre la hauteur.
> S'il ne sent point du Ciel l'influence secrète
> Si son Astre en naissant ne l'a formé Poëte,
> Dans son génie étroit il est toujours captif.
> Pour lui Phébus est sourd, et Pégase est rétif.

The crucial difference between Boileau and Perrault was over the question of artistic excellence and originality. Boileau did not deny the value of genius and originality as artistic criteria, but unlike Perrault he saw no obvious contradiction in coupling them with the rules and patterns to be observed within literary tradition, and thus maintained primarily formal criteria in the production and evaluation of literature. The greatest works of antiquity were seen as the models and the storehouses of rules to be imitated. The superiority of Homer and Virgil was unquestioned, as Boileau stated in his "laudatio Homeri." Boileau also set an essential value on the continuous and general esteem and admiration that some works of classical antiquity had earned in European literary tradition. In his *Réflexions critiques* (1694) he answered Perrault's views in the first three volumes of the *Parallèle* and in the "Siècle."

Where Boileau wanted to see excellence in the degree to which a contemporary work of art observed universally valid forms and the general rules of poetry, Perrault argued that all literary works, including the classics, should be approached as products of specific cultural situations. Herein was the true test of originality, and thus in making value judgments the critic should look to the poetry itself.

> Si les ouvrages d'Homère étoient perdus, je serois fort curieux
> d'apprendre ce qu'en auroient dit, et ce qu'en auroient pensé ceux

qui les auroient vus. Mais puisque ses ouvrages sont entre nos mains, pourquoi nous tourmenter tant sur ce que les autres en ont jugé? Voyons-les nous-mesmes et disons ce qui nous en semble.

C'est comme si nous disputions icy des beautés de Versailles sur les descriptions qu'on nous en a données, au lieu d'aller nous-mesmes sur les lieux voir ce qui en est.

Though Perrault maintained from the start that there is progress in the arts and humanities, and admitted that this progress depends on the accumulation of ideas and forms of expression that have been repeatedly found viable, he realized that in literature and the arts creative achievements must be in some way products of their culture, which he regarded as an organic unity. No real assessments could be made without realizing that there was an individual, as well as a specific cultural situation, behind each classical masterpiece. Every work of art or cultural act should be traced back to its human origins.

Hence Perrault belittled the Homeric epics for cultural, and not for exclusively formal reasons.

Pour ce qui est du nom d'Homère, qui signifie Aveugle, ils disent que plusieurs de ces Poëtes étoient de pauvres gens, et la plûpart aveugles, qui alloient de maison en maison reciter leurs poëmes pour de l'argent; et qu'à cause de cela ces sortes de petits poëmes s'appelloient communément, les chansons de l'Aveugle.

Perrault's thesis, that the modern age represented enlightenment in the arts and literature as well as the sciences, and was therefore superior to antiquity, comes out clearly in his discussion of Homer. Homer proved to be his greatest stand-by in his battle against the ancients. The manner of composition of the epics, in which Homer had taken part as one of the many rhapsodists, that is as one of a collective class of blind and poverty-stricken mercenary singers, suggested an essentially inferior age:

ils disent que l'Iliade et l'Odyssée ne sont autre chose qu'un amas, qu'une collection de plusieurs petits Poëmes de divers Auteurs qu'on a joints ensemble.

In order to demonstrate the cultural backwardness of Homer, Perrault utilized as his sources the unfavourable views on Homeric poetry which were available at that time in the work of the abbé d'Aubignac and the Renaissance scholar J. C. Scaliger. Perrault, like all the moderns, showed a keen interest in the authorship question of the Greek epic, as he perceived in it possible ways to discredit some of the most cherished notions about Homer, those of the "prince of poets" and the "father of epic rules." The controversy about the authorship and authenticity of the *Iliad* and the *Odyssey*, which originated with the ancient writers Josephus, Plutarch and Aelian, became topical again at the end of the seventeenth century, partly because it was in the interests of the moderns. D'Aubignac's treatise *Conjectures académiques, ou dissertation sur l'*Iliade (written *c.* 1665) rose out of this background of doubts concerning the personal Homer. Their first exponent in England was Richard Bentley, who in his *Remarks upon a Late Discourse of Free-thinking* (1713) argued that the epics had been collected together in Athens at the time of Pisistratus. D'Aubignac's study was suppressed twice by the public authorities because of its "fausse et pernicieuse" thesis. It was known to the Perrault brothers, however, as the *Parallèle* tells us, and also to a number of contemporary writers and critics through Adrien Baillet's resumé in his *Jugements des savants* in 1685, before it was eventually published in 1715. D'Aubignac's argument was that the author of the *Iliad* could not have been the same person as the author of the *Odyssey*, the poems being too discordant in style and subject matter, and that Homer had been a collective name for a group of rhapsodists. This was the standard view among the moderns, and Perrault, in his eagerness to criticize the ancients, went as far as stating that "il n'y a jamais eu au monde un homme nommé Homère."

In order to demonstrate the unsuitability of the Homeric epics for modern imitation, Perrault exploited J. C. Scaliger's famous disparagement of Homer. The points he made were in the first place related to questions of style and taste. Scaliger in *Poetices Libri Septem* (1561) had claimed that Virgil was superior to Homer on the ground of such qualities as *simplicitas*, *humanitas* and *dignitas*, which were Virgilian, not Homeric, characteristics. The Homeric epic was seen, by contrast, simply as a confused account of the military valour and robust heroism of the early Greeks. Scaliger rejected Homer for his puerility and his lapses of taste. Perrault echoed these views, too. Homeric epics, "quoy qu'admirable en certains endroits, me paroissent pleins de grossiereté, de puerilité, et d'extravagance," whereas the works of Virgil "me semblent remplis de finesse, de gravité, et de raison." Perrault maintained an idea of the epic which incorporated the values of humanity, universality and omniscience. The epic poem should be "le chef-d'oeuvre de l'esprit humain" and should express nature perceived by the individual poetic mind.

> Un Poëte et particulièrement un Poëte épique doit parler pertinemment de toutes les matières qu'il traite dans son poëme, ou bien il se mesle d'un métier dont il est indigne. Il faut qu'il connoisse les choses de la Nature.

But Perrault did not see that the Homeric poems met this idea of the epic, and in this too he differed from the neoclassicists and the ancients. Perrault and the moderns, who maintained the theory of continuous progress in the arts, logically rejected everything they saw to be old and primitive. Naturally they also discarded tradition and authority as the significant shaping forces in literary production. The notion that Homer was omniscient and the father of all arts seemed to them unacceptable in modern times. The common belief that the Homeric poems contained all the rudiments of wisdom, "qu'Homère n'a rien ignoré des choses de la Nature, et qu'il est le père de tous les Arts," was absurd because knowledge itself had had its evolution.

> Visions qu'on a pu avoir dans les siècles passez, mais qui ne sont plus supportables dans le temps où nous sommes.

But insofar as there was a continuity and interdependence between the ancient and modern literatures and arts—which would have been very difficult indeed to disprove—Perrault argued that contemporary literature had an undeniable advantage over classical antiquity because it was created in a far richer and more complex cultural situation. Although there were some differences in the ways arts and sciences had progressed, the modern age was superior to antiquity even in the arts and literature, since the soil in which art grows can be held to be enriched by the progress of scientific knowledge. Moreover, Perrault claimed with Fontenelle that humanity was subject to a steady progress which was reflected in all its cultural achievements.

> Pourquoi voulez-vous, Monsieur le Président, que l'éloquence et la poësie n'aient pas eu besoin d'autant de siècles pour se perfectionner que la physique et l'astronomie? Le coeur de l'homme, qu'il faut connaître pour le persuader et pour lui plaire, est-il plus aisé à pénétrer que les secrets de la Nature, et n'a-t-il pas de tout temps été regardé comme le plus creux de tous les abîmes, où l'on découvre tous les jours quelque chose de nouveau?

Perrault seems to have envisaged a progressive amelioration in man's potentialities; and using literature as his field of enquiry he came to grips with man's complexity more successfully than Fontenelle, who concentrated on the natural sciences. He looked at poetic imagination as the key to the individual mind, and assumed that cultural achievements could be meaningfully explained by the study of the individual. The way he thus came to look at literature and the arts is related to his interest in genius. But he saw genius as the extent to which personal endowments enable an artist to take advantage of the general level of contemporary potentialities, and certainly a genius could produce remarkable work in any age, however backward. There was no reason in principle why a culturally backward poet, such as he saw Homer to have been, should not have possessed genius and imagination and produced work that was valuable on that score. The handicap of detrimental environment should even relatively raise the merit of the individual genius. All this did not however in Perrault's view apply to Homer, as the Homeric poems had a collective authorship.

Perrault regarded literature as an activity essentially dependent on imagination; and his negative attitude to the high valuation of imitation of the ancients was related to his emphasis on poetic imagination. As a poet can give "to airy nothing / a local habitation," it was preposterous to make literary production depend on imitating the classics. Imitation was an abuse of the rich material provided by classical writers—who ought indeed to be valued primarily for their imagination—and betrayed a narrow view of the creative act. For at the moment of writing a real poetic genius will dispense with the models. Poetry is the expression of visual images in the language.

> La Poësie n'est autre chose qu'une peinture agréable, qui repre-
> sente par la parole tout ce que l'imagination peut concevoir, en
> donnant presque toujours un corps, une âme, du sentiment et de
> la vie aux choses qui n'en ont point.

It is a curious fact that whereas visual description, invention and poetic imagery were exactly the qualities for which the eighteenth century came to value Homer, Perrault was unable to perceive them in the Greek poet. He, too, was a product of his age and culture, and was consumed by his indignation at the antiquated robes in which he saw his contemporaries wrap themselves.

In his discussion of seventeenth-century French literature, *Les Hommes illustres* (1697–1700), translated into English as *Characters Historical and Pan-egyrical of the Greatest Men* (1704–5), Perrault evaluated poets and authors in terms of genius. His starting point was that genius is the quality that distinguishes a great author from minor poets and imitators, and he held moreover that it is a quality that cannot be transmitted to others or imitated. "It may even be advanc'd, that those who have thus distinguished them-selves by the single force of their Genius, are more visibly the work of Heaven, than the rest of Mankind." In La Fontaine he praised originality: "Never did a Person merit more to be looked upon as an Original, and as the first in his kind"; Malherbe, he said, had suffered from his environment, as Caën, his birthplace, had not had men of letters "remarkable particularly for the fineness and beauty of their Genius"; and in his essay on Racine, he emphasized that genius is inborn: "Genius is a Gift of Nature which cannot be hid, and which shews itself in Children almost as early as Reason." This appraisal of genius is related to the issues of the *Parallèle*, where Perrault attacked imitation and the uncritical acceptance of classical models. His insistence on the role of genius ran counter to the high value he placed on cultural influences. *Les Hommes illustres* was intended to be a kind of dictionary of famous men of his day, and it develops the same idea as the *Parallèle*, namely the superiority of modern culture to antiquity. The apparent contradiction in the dual emphasis on individual talent and en-vironment in Perrault's criticism can be resolved by the special meaning that he gave to genius. Genius was more than a talent or an aptitude. Whereas an individual poetic genius can appear in any age, there were certain periods that manifestly produced more men of genius.

Oratory and Poetry in Fénelon's Literary Theory

Wilbur Samuel Howell

Fénelon is believed to have written his famous *Dialogues on Eloquence* in the year 1679. At that time he was twenty-eight years old, and his career as priest of the parish of Saint-Sulpice in Paris had just been terminated by his appointment as Superior of the "New Catholics," an institution designed to strengthen the orthodoxy of young women newly converted from Protestantism to Catholicism. Thirty-five years later, his life almost at an end, he composed his *Letter to M. Dacier, Permanent Secretary of the French Academy, on the Occupations of the Academy.* Between those two epochs in his literary career, he distinguished himself in various ways: he served for ten years as preceptor of Louis XIV's grandson, heir presumptive of the throne of France; he became a member of the French Academy and wrote his best-known work, *The Adventures of Telemachus*; he was named Archbishop of Cambrai; and he identified himself with the doctrine of Quietism as advocated by Madame Guyon. This doctrine, with its emphasis upon the annihilation of self and the passivity of the soul as the conditions necessary to achieve a mystical union between man and God, cast a shadow across the last two decades of Fénelon's life. His support of Madame Guyon when she fell from favor at court led to the termination of his productive friendship with the great preacher Bossuet, and caused such other misfortunes as his dismissal from his preceptorship in the royal household and the condemnation of one of his works by Pope Innocent XII. These events occurred during the last three or four years of the seventeenth century. Thereafter Fénelon lived at Cambrai and devoted himself to his duties as Archbishop and his pursuits as writer.

His *Letter to the Academy* was first published at Paris in 1716, the year

From *Quarterly Journal of Speech* 37, no. 1 (February 1951). © 1951 by the Speech Communication Association.

after his death, and it achieved immediate recognition in intellectual circles. At Amsterdam in 1717 it was printed in company with the *Dialogues on Eloquence*, which up to that moment had lain in manuscript. Upon these two works Fénelon's reputation in the field of aesthetics and rhetorical theory pretty largely depends. At no place in the whole body of his writings is oratory analyzed with the care and brilliance that he bestows upon it in the *Dialogues*, where he also has things to say about historical and philosophical composition, poetry, music, dancing, painting, and architecture. The *Letter to the Academy* is concerned with much the same subject matter. It begins by recommending that the Academy complete its dictionary of the French language. It then proposes a grammar and a rhetoric as projects of immediate concern. Next it furnishes a detailed plan for treatises on poetics, tragedy, comedy, and historical writing. It concludes with a contribution to the controversy between ancients and moderns, and with an indication that Fénelon had not lost his earlier preference for Greek architecture as against Gothic.

The *Letter to the Academy* has received more praise than have the *Dialogues*, no doubt because the predominance of aesthetic interests in the former turned out to be more congenial to subsequent taste than did the predominance of rhetorical interests in the latter. But it should be emphasized that Fénelon himself did not in either of these works take the part of the aesthetic interests against the rhetorical. He makes no invidious assumptions about the superiority of poetry to oratory. Nor does he give more care to one than to the other, as if they were of unequal value and deserved unequal kinds of intellectual effort from the theorist who chose to write upon both. He does not see them as so disparate in quality that oratory has to be patronized for claiming a persuasive function and a concern for a practical method, whereas poetry has to be exalted for its capacity to give delight by means veiled in the higher mysteries of genius. He does not account for the differences between the oration and the poem by postulating that they stand in relation to each other in the kingdom of letters as commoner stands to aristocrat in the monarchy of the Bourbons. The fact is, Fénelon sees oratory and poetry as instruments of similar value in human affairs. But he is aware that there are differences between them, and he devotes productive attention to the formulation of these differences.

In this chapter I should like to state what Fénelon's conception of these differences is. I shall not attempt to handle my subject in terms of everything Fénelon had to say upon all matters pertaining to critical and aesthetic theory. My discussion instead will be limited to his analysis of oratory and poetry in the *Dialogues* and the *Letter to the Academy*. These two works, as I have already indicated, represent in concentrated form the essential principles of this aspect of his thinking. This aspect is worthy of attention for three reasons. First, it illustrates a specific application of the views of Plato, Cicero, and St. Augustine to the problems of the seventeenth century. Secondly, it raises issues similar to those involved in the modern question of the relations between propaganda and art. Thirdly, it indicates the frustrations that attend even the most promising distinctions between the rhetorical and the poetic branches of literature.

II

The basic principle in Fénelon's conception of the relations between oratory and poetry is that these two arts, in common with all the others, are persuasive in function. By this he means that the various arts cannot be logically grouped to one side or the other of a dividing line between that which gives pleasure and that which influences thought and action. His belief is that, if there seems to be a class of artistic works devoted wholly to the giving of pleasure, the critic should deal with it, not as something fundamentally unpersuasive, but as a case of concealed persuasion. He insists, in short, that all works of art act to influence the conduct of mankind, pleasure being an intermediate aim, a way station on the road to ultimate persuasiveness.

This view is applied to oratory early in the *Dialogues on Eloquence*. One of the spokesmen, who is called *A*, and whose importance suggests that he expresses Fénelon's own ideas, demands of another spokesman, *B*, the definition of eloquence. *B* replies that eloquence is the art of speaking well. *A* wonders whether men speak simply to speak well, whether talk has no design except that of achieving the status of refinement. This observation leads *B* to declare that men speak in order to please and in order to persuade. Thus are two rival aims of oratory brought into focus, the former being no doubt intended by Fénelon to represent the prevailing conception of rhetoric as derived from the teachings of Peter Ramus, while the latter is the conception of Fénelon himself. What *A* says in reply to *B* is not only a denial that these two aims were in any final sense mutually exclusive, but also a fresh approach to the pleasure-persuasion dichotomy in artistic theory. *A* remarks at once that a careful distinction should be made between "to please" and "to persuade." Then he states how orators proceed in practice:

They speak to persuade—that is what they always do. They also speak to please—that is merely what they too often do. But when they seek to please, they have another, a more distant, aim, which is nevertheless the principal one. The good man seeks to please only that he may urge justice and the other virtues by making them attractive. He who seeks his own interest, his reputation, his fortune, dreams of pleasing only that he may gain the bow and esteem of men able to satisfy his greed or his ambition. Thus, even his case can be reduced like that of the good man to persuasion as the single aim which a speaker has; for the self-interested man wishes to please in order to flatter, and he flatters in order to inculcate that which suits his interest.

Later in the *Dialogues, A* reverts once more to the thesis that pleasure is an effect to be striven for only because it lies athwart the road to persuasion. He demands of *C*, Fénelon's third character, whether anything in a discourse can have any function except that of influencing the hearer. *C* replies that certain things in discourse will contribute to the hearer's pleasure. *A* observes:

> Let us distinguish, if you will. That which serves to please in order to persuade is good. Solid and well-expounded proofs are unquestionably pleasing; the lively and natural movements of the speaker have much charm; faithful and animated portraitures enchant. Thus the three things which we make essential to eloquence give pleasure; but they are not limited to this effect. It is a question of knowing whether we shall approve of thoughts and expressions which have no purpose but to please, and which cannot in any way have a more substantial purpose. These I call conceits. Of course, you are always to keep well in mind, if you will, that I praise in discourse all the pleasing traits which minister to persuasion; and that I reject only those wherein the author, full of self-admiration, has sought to exhibit himself and to amuse the listeners with his wit, rather than to absorb them utterly in his subject.

Oratory in Fénelon's scheme is not the only art that has persuasion as its principal function and pleasure as an intermediate effect. He puts poetry and the other fine arts in the same class. In the *Dialogues C* observes: "But if true orators are poets, it seems to me that poets are also orators, because poetry is by rights persuasive." And *A* replies: "Unquestionably they both have the same end." These statements are made in connection with Fénelon's attempt to differentiate poetry from oratory, and later we shall see what that differentiation amounts to. Just now, however, we need perhaps only to notice that, whatever differences he has in mind, he insists at least upon the complete identity of these two arts in respect to persuasiveness. In the *Letter to the Academy* he attributes the same function to the other fine arts, emphasizing again that pleasure is an auxiliary effect:

> Plato does not permit in his republic any music with the effeminate pitch of the Lydian style. The Lacedaemonians excluded from their republic all the highly complicated instruments which were able to weaken the spirit. Harmony which goes only so far as to flatter the ear is merely an amusement of weak and idle folk. It is unworthy of a well-governed republic. It is good only so far as the sounds of it agree with the sense of the words, and the words of it inspire virtuous sentiments. Painting, sculpture, and the other fine arts, ought to have the same end. Without question eloquence ought to enter into the same design. Pleasure ought to be mingled

in it only to form a counterbalance against evil passions and to make virtue attractive.

The words just quoted echo a passage in the *Dialogues* upon the subservience of pleasure to persuasiveness in ancient art. In the course of a panegyric upon the serious intent of the art of the early Greeks and Hebrews, *A* remarks:

> All the arts which consist in melodious sounds, or in movements of the body, or in the use of language—in a word, music, dancing, eloquence, poetry—were devised only to express the passions and to inspire them in the very act of expressing them. By such means as these, mankind wished to impress great thoughts upon the human soul and to bring to men lively and striking pictures of the beauty of virtue and the ugliness of evil. Thus all these arts appeared to be for pleasure, but were in reality among the ancients a part of their deepest striving for morality and religion.

Thus does Fénelon admit pleasure and persuasion into artistic theory without making these effects mutually exclusive or using them as keys to the difference between the fine and the practical arts. He recognizes, however, that throughout the entire domain of art, practical as well as fine, pleasure may receive more emphasis than persuasion, even though when this happens the effect must still be counted persuasive in the final analysis. In fact, one of his critical principles is that pathologies in the world of art appear as the product of a persuasive intention which is limited on the one hand to the promotion of the artist's personal fortunes and on the other to the excessive exploitation of the spectator's fondness for pleasure. This principle receives some development in the *Dialogues* and the *Letter to the Academy*. I should like to examine it now in order to show that it underlies Fénelon's distinction between health and disease in art rather than his distinction between the poetical and the rhetorical branches of literature.

III

Interpreted in the broadest sense, Fénelon's view of good and bad art, whether oratorical or poetic, stresses the concern of the artist for the interests of mankind as opposed to the interests of himself. If someone were to object that this principle belongs more to the realm of morality than to aesthetics, Fénelon would doubtless answer by denying the desirability or possibility of separating these two realms. Indeed, this phase of his critical thinking derives special support from the theological doctrine of Quietism, which, as I indicated earlier, strives for the annihilation of self as one condition of spiritual perfection. Good art in Fénelon's sense of the term is that which inspires men in the quest for wisdom, good laws, justice, and individual betterment, whereas bad art inspires men to favor their flatterers, to follow their private inclinations, to give rewards on the basis of something less than merit, or to seek personal power, wealth, reputation, at no matter what expense. It is in this latter kind of art where pleasure tends to be the most visible of the possible effects, seeming at times to be the artist's only aim, and at other times to be the aim which but partly masks his desire for personal advancement.

Many passages in the *Dialogues* and the *Letter to the Academy* illustrate this principle. For example, when *A* is mentioning the degeneracy which followed the period of Athenian rule in ancient Greece, he characterizes it as one wherein "pleasure, which ought only to be the means to inculcate wisdom, usurped the place of wisdom herself." Thus is the concept of social decadence linked with the concept of art as mere diversion. The same spokesman had earlier borrowed the Socratic manner and the Platonic doctrine to get *B* to consent to banish from the ideal republic "any of the sciences or any of the arts which serve only for pleasure, for amusement, and for curiosity." And why are they to be banished? Because, as *B* finally concedes, they are not merely indifferent to the struggle between good and evil, but actually are on the side of evil. His words are:

> If anything can assist the cause of virtue, the identification of virtue with pleasure can do so. On the contrary, when you separate them, you strongly invite men to abandon virtue. Besides, everything that pleases without instructing beguiles and softens merely.

But the principle is not developed only in terms of abstract moral precepts. It is made highly concrete in its application to oratory. *A's* unfavorable opinion of Isocrates, a recurrent theme of the *Dialogues*, shows that orator to typify an art devoted, not to national ends, but to self-exhibition, with ostentatious ornaments the artist's means, and amusement his principal, almost his only, goal. Again, a concern for his own fortune, as distinguished from the fate of the Roman republic, is alleged by the same spokesman to be a visible blemish in the works of the youthful Cicero. *A* also remarks that a selfish concern vitiates Pliny's eulogy of Trajan. And in the course of constructing his own theory of oratory, he lays great stress upon the necessity for complete disinterestedness on the part of a speaker both as a matter of good morality and good oratorical strategy.

The issue of preoccupation with self as opposed to preoccupation with the interests of mankind has the same application to poetry as to oratory. *A* cites the *Aeneid* as being open to the charge, if one cared to press it, of showing somewhat more interest in flattering Augustus and his family, and thus in advancing Virgil's own fortune, than in giving the Roman people an unmixed image of their national destiny. This charge against Virgil *A* does not regard seriously. On the contrary, he emphasizes in the same breath that the *Aeneid* is an example of high poetic excellence. But the charge, as a possible line of attack upon Virgil, embodies a precise principle by which criticism may separate good poetry from bad, and that principle is given a general formulation by Fénelon himself in the following words from the *Letter to the Academy*:

> Just in the same degree as one ought to despise bad poets, so ought one to admire and cherish a great poet, who does not make poetry into a play of wit to attract unto himself a vainglory, but uses it to transport men in favor of wisdom, virtue, and religion.

Fénelon's distinction between good and bad art rests upon the teachings of Plato and St. Augustine. He leaves no doubt upon this score, not only because he probably thought it simple honesty to acknowledge his philosophic debts, but also perhaps to suggest that his theory cut across the boundaries between paganism and Christianity, and thus could not be called merely parochial. At any rate, he has *A* emphasize that one does not have to be a Christian to believe in the self-forgetfulness of the artist as the precondition of great art, inasmuch as Socrates and Plato had taken the same position. *A* documents this statement with a lengthy analysis of Plato's *Gorgias* and a shorter reference to the *Phaedrus*. As for St. Augustine, who figures preponderantly in the Third Dialogue by virtue of his authority in the field of sacred rhetoric, he too is used to support Fénelon's view that the aesthetic stature of a work of art is determined by the stature of its selflessness of purpose. In a passage in the First Dialogue made up of borrowings from two separate chapters of St. Augustine's *De Doctrina Christiana*, *A* declares:

> For what do a man's beautiful speeches serve, if fine as they are they contribute no benefit whatever to the public? Words are made for men, as St. Augustine says, and not men for words.

IV

Thus far we have seen that Fénelon does not use the distinction between pleasure and persuasiveness as a means of separating poetry from oratory. He uses it instead to show that there is a kind of bad art devoted seemingly to pleasure but actually to the inculcation of attitudes which suit the artist's material interests. He sees poetry and oratory as alike persuasive in their healthy forms. He sees pleasure as normally common to both in the sense that this effect accompanies persuasion. He sees good oratory and good poetry as kinds of discourse which contribute primarily, and in the first instance, to the public benefit. What, then, is his distinction between the rhetorical and the poetic branches of literature?

His answer to this question is that oratory is almost poetry. This is the simplest way to state his distinction. This is also the way he himself follows when he comes in the *Dialogues* to the problem of maintaining on the one hand that poetry as well as oratory is persuasive and on the other that the well-established habit of thinking these two arts to be somehow different must receive attention in criticism. Let us hear what he says on this matter.

The conversation in the Second Dialogue has paused upon the question of the difference between the genuine and the false ornament of style. *A* has been insisting that persuasion is the end of oratory, and that oratory deserves to be called eloquence only when it really succeeds in persuading men to virtue. Now persuasion, *A* explains, requires that discourse prove something and excite strong feelings toward what it proves. To prove, he goes on, is to convince the auditor that a proposition is true. The method by which this is done is characterized by exactness, dryness, bareness; by an adherence to the forms of good argument; by a sense of order similar to that followed in geometry; and by a speculativeness similar to that found in metaphysics. To excite strong feelings is to be forced to do two things beyond proof: to portray and to strike. "To portray is not only to describe things," remarks *A*, "but to represent their surrounding features in so lively and so concrete a way that the listener imagines himself almost seeing them." The term "to strike" is defined later, after *A* has identified it with "movement" as distinguished from "proof" and "portraiture." "Movement" turns out to be not only the stylistic variation of the speech, as the speaker's linguistic patterns move in accordance with his inner patterns of thought and emotion, but also the physical swing of speaking, as the speaker's voice and body respond to his mind and will.

Of these three elements in persuasive discourse or eloquence, portraiture is of central importance in persuasion; and it is thus a common feature of the oration and the poem. *A* sees a difference in degree, however, between the portraiture produced by the orator and that produced by the poet. Upon this difference in degree he founds his distinction between the two arts. To illustrate portraiture at its best, he points to Virgil's account of the death of Dido. Then he says:

> I have given you an example drawn from a poet, in order to make you better understand the matter; for portraiture is still more lively and stronger among the poets than among the orators. Poetry differs from simple eloquence only in this: that she paints with ecstasy and with bolder strokes. Prose has its paintings, albeit more moderated. Without them one cannot heat the imagination of a listener or arouse his passions.

Versification, *A* proceeds at once to remark, has nothing to do with the question of distinguishing the poetical from the nonpoetical discourse. In either form, genuine effectiveness is the product of portraiture. "If one does not have this genius to portray," insists Fénelon's chief spokesman, "never can one impress things upon the soul of the listener—all is dry, flat, boring." A moment later the whole matter is summed up in this exchange between *A* and *C*:

A: The entire difference [between oratory and poetry] consists in that which I have set forth to you. Over and above orators, poets have ecstasy, and this makes them still more elevated, more lively, and more daring in their utterances. You well remember what I told you yesterday from Cicero?

C: What! Is it . . . ?

A: That the orator ought almost to have the diction of the poet. That "almost" tells the whole story.

Thus poetry and oratory in Fénelon's basic view turn out to have persuasion as their end and portraiture as a common means, the distinction between them being that portraiture in poetry has about it an ecstasy, a heat of genius, not found in oratory. In short, as I suggested before, oratory is almost but not quite poetry. Fénelon himself points out in the passage last quoted that the "almost" comes from Cicero. To be more precise, it comes from *De Oratore,* 1. 28. 128, where oratory, comprehensively defined, is said to demand not only a dialectician's acuteness, a philosopher's knowledge, a lawyer's memory, a tragedian's voice, and an accomplished actor's gesture, but also a diction almost that of the poet.

We might in passing note the relations established by Fénelon among the other traditional kinds of discourse. He strongly intimates that philosophical discourse or learned writing in the field of the scientific disciplines differs from oratory as proof isolated from portraiture and movement differs from proof combined with these things. He also says in effect that historical writing differs from poetry as a moderated and impartial portrait of events and personalities differs from a bolder, more inspired, portrait. But it is only against the background of his concept of eloquence that these distinctions have their full meaning. According to that concept, any discourse which actually succeeds in improving men deserves alone to be called eloquent; and no discourse can have that effect without portraiture. Hence poetry, which is in essence inspired portraiture, becomes eloquent when it acts to make men more perfect. Hence history, which is moderated and impartial portraiture, becomes eloquent when it produces the selfsame result. Hence oratory, which combines proof and movement with a portraiture almost poetic, becomes eloquent when it achieves no different goal. Of the four conventional types of discourse, only philosophy, which has no concern with image-making as a necessity of its own style, fails to achieve the full stature of eloquence. But its emphasis upon conviction as effect and proof as means gives it a primary concern for truth; and thus, when it succeeds in presenting things as they are, it induces knowledge, which is not least among the preconditions of virtue.

V

Three aspects of Fénelon's theory of the relations between oratory and poetry call for attention by way of conclusion.

First of all, his insistence upon the persuasiveness of oratory is in line not only with the best classical and modern emphasis but also with the tendency of the late seventeenth century to abandon the rhetorical teachings of Peter Ramus. At the time when Fénelon wrote the *Dialogues on Eloquence*, the influence of Ramus upon logical and rhetorical theory in France (and in England) was still pronounced, despite the fact that Ramus had died as long before as 1572. One of Ramus's key doctrines was that one art could not claim any function or subject matter belonging to another art. Accordingly, if logic professed to offer to writers and speakers the theory of invention and arrangement, and thus to provide the means of convincing audiences, rhetoric must abandon these subjects and confine itself to other aspects of composition. As a consequence of this doctrine, Ramus's colleague, Talaeus, created a rhetoric limited to style and delivery, and copiously elaborated in terms of all the figures of speech and all the ornamental contrivances of style. This sort of rhetoric, with its emphasis upon antithesis, paradox, word-play, conceit, and epigram, came to have the reputation of being exclusively devoted to amusement. Against the theory that men spoke only to give pleasure, and that they used as means only the conceits of style, Fénelon leveled his heaviest guns. To some extent he also leveled his guns against Ramus's theory that a work on rhetoric could include nothing pertaining to logic or the other liberal arts, although Fénelon's contemporary, Antoine Arnauld, had effectively attacked this aspect of Ramus's doctrine in the famous *Port Royal Logic*, published seventeen years before Fénelon wrote the *Dialogues*. In Fénelon's emphasis that oratory is primarily an instrument of persuasion, and that the orator is an honored partner of the logician and the historian in the enterprise of learning and communication, we see a wholesome restoration of Ciceronian doctrine as well as an imaginative anticipation of modern interests.

The same reminiscence of a classical attitude, the same foretaste of a modern conviction, is visible in a second aspect of Fénelon's theory of the relations between oratory and poetry. This aspect emerges in his insistence that delight is the intermediate and contributory, persuasiveness the ultimate, object of both of these arts. So far as poetical theory is concerned, Fénelon is here suggesting the impossibility of divorcing expression from communication or aesthetics from rhetoric and logic. He is assuming instead that man's response to a work of art springs from a complex of adjustments, some of which are aesthetic, others, intellectual. He sees no point in treating such a response as if one could unerringly separate its pleasurable from its intellectual phases. No doubt he felt that knowledge of either phase by itself would not be the same as knowledge of both phases in all their complicated interactions. At any rate, at one point in the *Dialogues* he has C observe: "As for myself, I wish to know whether things are true before I find them beautiful." If this statement seems to give priority to logic above aesthetics in an act of literary evaluation, Fénelon might have explained his real intention by saying that, in an age which gave the latter more emphasis than the former, counterexaggeration was the approved way to restore the balance between the two.

The third aspect of Fénelon's distinction between oratory and poetry involves a complication which I did not mention earlier for fear of emphasizing it more than our author does. This complication appears both before and after the passages in which he says that poetry differs from oratory only in the superior vividness of its portraiture. There is no doubt that he is convinced of the validity of this major difference; but he seems to realize that it does not completely exhaust the subject. Thus he introduces two terms which suggest that poetical and oratorical portraiture differ not so much in degree as in kind. These two terms are *imitation* and *fiction*. In the *Dialogues*, as *A* is comparing a historian's portrait of the death of Dido with that in the *Aeneid*, he says of the latter: "There one sees the power of imitation and of portraiture." Later, after he has dismissed versification from the list of qualities that poetry must have, *A* remarks: "In the last analysis, poetry is nothing but a lively fiction which portrays nature." In the *Letter to the Academy*, speaking in his own person, Fénelon declares: "Poetry is without doubt an imitation and a portraiture." These passages make it clear that, although Fénelon is insisting upon portraiture as an element in poetry, he half doubts whether oratorical and poetic portraiture differ only in degree, and in his hesitancy he resorts to the terms *imitation* and *fiction*, perhaps to satisfy his subconscious realization that poetry, at least in its epic, dramatic, and narrative forms, portrays situations different from those handled in oratory and history. Had he gone on to show that portraiture in poetry is usually the lifelike representation of an imagined situation, whereas portraiture in oratory and history is usually the lifelike representation of a real situation, he would have been able to preserve his emphasis upon portraiture as an essential characteristic of these three literary forms, and at the same time to preserve his emphasis upon fiction and imitation as the distinguishing conditions of portraiture in poetry.

Without some recognition of the difference between actual and imagined situations, it is hard to see how Fénelon's account of the difference between oratory and poetry can explain distinctions taken for granted by the literary critic on the one hand and the rhetorical and historical critic on the other. The literary critic, speaking of portraiture in a play, a novel, or a narrative poem, uses as a matter of course the machinery of oppositions between the romantic and realistic, the naturalistic and symbolic, the allegorical and nonallegorical, the classical and Gothic, to indicate changing fashions in poetic portraiture. The theory that oratory and history differ from poetry only as the moderated portrait differs from the inspired appears to suggest that the same machinery and the same fashions apply to rhetorical and historical criticism. But do they? Except in a pejorative sense, is there a romantic as opposed to a realistic oratory or history? Is there a school of symbolist and another school of naturalist orators and historians? Hardly. And this answer suggests that some concepts applicable to poetry are not applicable to oratory and history, despite Fénelon's apparent indication to the contrary in the basic phase of his distinction between the oration and the poem.

La Bruyère

Roland Barthes

La Bruyère occupies an ambiguous place in French culture: he is taught as a "major author"; his maxims, his art, his historical role are assigned as dissertation subjects; his knowledge of Man and his premonition of a more equitable society are extolled: *The notion of humanity*, Brunetière used to say, *dawns with La Bruyère*; he is made (O precious paradox!) at once a classic and a democrat. Yet outside our schools, the La Bruyère myth is a meager one: he has not yet been caught up in any of those great dialogues which French writers have always engaged in from one century to another (Pascal and Montaigne, Voltaire and Racine, Valéry and La Fontaine); criticism itself has scarcely bothered to renew our entirely academic image of him; his work has not lent itself to any of the new languages of our age, has stimulated neither historians nor philosophers nor sociologists nor psychoanalysts; in short, if we except the sympathy of a Proust quoting some penetrating maxim ("Being with the people one loves is enough; dreaming, talking to them or not talking to them, thinking about them or about indifferent things in their presence, it is all one." *Du coeur*, No. 23), our modernity, though quite ready to appropriate classical authors, seems to have great difficulty recuperating him: though he stands with the great names of our literature, La Bruyère is nonetheless disinherited, one might almost say *deconsecrated:* he lacks even that final fortune of the writer: to be neglected.

In short, this glory is a little drowsy, and it must be admitted that La Bruyère himself is not a likely agent for great awakenings; he remains, in everything, temperate (Thibaudet used to speak of La Bruyère's *chiaroscuro*), avoids exhausting the subjects he initiates, renounces that radicality of

From *Critical Essays,* translated by Richard Howard. © 1972 by Northwestern University Press.

viewpoint which assures the writer a violent posthumous life; close as it is to La Rochefoucauld's, for example, his pessimism never exceeds the prudence of a good Christian, never turns to obsession; though capable of producing a short, lightninglike form, he prefers the somewhat longer fragment, the portrait which repeats itself: he is a moderate moralist, he does not scald (except perhaps in the chapters on women and money, of an unyielding aggressiveness); and furthermore, although an avowed painter of a society and, within that society, of the most social passion there is, worldliness, La Bruyère does not become a chronicler, a Retz or a Saint-Simon; it is as if he wanted to avoid the choice of a specific genre; as a moralist, he persistently refers to a real society, apprehended in its persons and events (as the number of "keys" to his book testifies); and as a sociologist, he nonetheless experiences this society in its moral substance alone; we cannot really deduce from him the image of man's "eternal flaw"; nor can we find in him, beyond good and evil, the lively spectacle of a pure sociality; perhaps this is why modernity, which always seeks certain pure nutriments in the literature of the past, has difficulty acknowledging La Bruyère: he escapes it by the most delicate of resistances: it cannot name him.

This uneasiness is doubtless that of our modern reading of La Bruyère. We might express it differently: the world of La Bruyère is at once *ours* and *different; ours* because the society he paints conforms so closely to our academic myth of the seventeenth century that we circulate quite comfortably among these old figures from our childhood: Ménalque, the plum lover, the savage beast-peasants, the "everything has been said and we have come too late," the city, the court, the parvenus, etc.; *different* because the immediate sentiment of our modernity tells us that these customs, these characters, these passions even, are not ourselves; the paradox is a cruel one: La Bruyère is ours by his anachronism and alien to us by his very project of eternity; the moderation of this author (what used to be called *mediocrity*), the weight of academic culture, the pressure of contiguous readings, everything makes La Bruyère transmit an image of classical man which is neither distant enough for us to relish its exoticism, nor close enough for us to identify ourselves with it: it is a familiar image which does not concern us.

To read La Bruyère would of course have no reality today (once we have left school), if we could not violate that suspect equilibrium of distance and identity, if we did not let ourselves be swayed toward one or the other; we can certainly read La Bruyère in a spirit of confirmation, searching, as in any moralist, for the maxim which will account in a perfect form for that very wound we have just received from the world; we can also read him and underline all that separates his world from ours and all that this distance teaches us about ourselves; such is our enterprise here: let us discuss everything in La Bruyère which concerns us little or not at all: perhaps we shall then, at last, collect the modern meaning of his work.

And first of all, what is the world, for someone who speaks? An initially formless field of objects, beings, phenomena which must be organized, i.e., divided up and distributed. La Bruyère does not fail this obligation; he divides up the society he lives in into great regions, among which he will distribute his "characters" (which are, roughly, the chapters of his book). These regions or classes are not a homogeneous object, they correspond, one may say, to different sciences (and this is natural enough, since every science is itself a dividing up of the world); first of all, there are two sociological classes, which form the "basis" of the classical world: the court (the nobility) and the city (the bourgeoisie); then an anthropological class: women (a particular race, whereas man is general: he says *de l'homme* but *des femmes*); a political class (the monarchy), psychological classes (heart, judgment, merit), and ethnological classes, in which social behavior is observed at a certain distance (fashion, customs); the whole is framed (an accident, or a secret significance?) by two singular "operators": literature, which opens the work (we shall discuss, later on, the relevance of this inauguration), and religion, which closes it.

This variety of objects manipulated by La Bruyère, the disparity of the classes he has constituted as chapters, suggest two remarks; first of all: *Les Caractères* is in a sense a book of total knowledge; on the one hand, La Bruyère approaches social man from every angle, he constitutes a kind of indirect *summa* (for it is always literature's function to circumvent science) of the various kinds of knowledge of the *socius* available at the end of the seventeenth century (it will be noted that this man is indeed much more social than psychological); and on the other hand, more disturbingly, the book corresponds to a kind of initiatory experience, it seeks to reach that supreme point of existence where knowledge and conduct, science and consciousness meet under the ambiguous name of *wisdom*; in short, La Bruyère has sketched a kind of cosmogony of classical society, describing this world by its aspects, its limits and interferences. And this leads to our second remark: the regions out of which La Bruyère composes his world are quite analogous to logical classes; every "individual" (in logic, we would say every *x*), i.e., every "character," is defined first of all by a relation of membership in some class or other, the tulip fancier in the class *Fashion*, the coquette in the class *Women*, the absent-minded Ménalque in the class *Men*, etc.; but this is not enough, for the characters must be distinguished among themselves within one and the same class; La Bruyère therefore performs certain operations of intersection from one class to the next; cross the class of *Merit* with that of *Celibacy* and you get a reflection on the stifling function of marriage (*Du mérite*, No. 25); join Tryphon's former virtue and his present fortune: the simple coincidence of these two classes affords the image of a certain hypocrisy (*Des biens de fortune*, No. 50). Thus the diversity of the regions, which are sometimes social, sometimes psychological, in no way testifies to a rich disorder; confronting the world, La Bruyère does not enumerate absolutely varied elements like the surveyor writers of the next century; he combines certain rare elements; the man he constructs is always made up of several principles: age, origin, fortune, vanity, passion; only the formula of composition varies, the interplay of intersecting classes: a "character" is always the product of the encounter of at least two constants.

Now this is a treatment of man which to us has become if not alien at least impossible. It has been said of Leibnitz, more or less La Bruyère's contemporary, that he was the last man able to know everything; La Bruyère, too, was perhaps the last moralist able to speak of *all* of man, to enclose all the regions of the human world in a book; less than a century later, this would require the thirty-three volumes of the *Encyclopédie;* today, there is no longer a writer in the world who can treat man-in-society by regions: not all the human sciences combined can manage to do it. To borrow an image from information theory, we might say that from the classical century to our own, the *level of perception* has changed: we see man on another scale, and the very meaning of what we see is thereby transformed, like that of an ordinary substance under the microscope; the chapters of *Les Caractères* are so many brakes applied to the vision of man; today we cannot stop man anywhere; any partition we impose upon him refers him to a particular science, his totality escapes us; if I speak, *mutatis mutandis*, of the city and the court, I am a social writer; if I speak of the monarchy, I am a political theorist; of literature, a critic; of customs, an essayist; of the heart, a psychoanalyst, etc.; further, at least half the classes of objects to which La Bruyère refers have no more than a decrepit existence; no one today would write a chapter on women, on merit, or on conversation; though we continue to marry, to "arrive," or to speak, such behavior has shifted to another level of perception; a new dispatching refers them to human regions unknown to La Bruyère: social dynamics, interpersonal psychology, sexuality, though these realms can never be united under a single kind of writing: narrow, clear, "centered," finite, obsessive, La Bruyère's man is always *here;* ours is always elsewhere; if it occurs to think of someone's character, we do so either in terms of its insignificant universality (the desire for social advancement, for instance), or of its ineffable complexity (of whom would we dare say quite simply that he is a *dolt?*). In short, what has changed, from La Bruyère's world to ours, is what is notable: we no longer *note* the world the way La Bruyère did; our speech is different not because the vocabulary has developed, but because to speak is to fragment reality in an always committed fashion and because our dividing-up refers to a reality so broad that reflection cannot accommodate it and because the new sciences, those we call the human sciences (whose status, moreover, is not clearly defined), must intervene: La Bruyère notes that a father-in-law loves his daughter-in-law and that a mother-in-law loves her son-in-law (*De la société*, No. 45); this is a notation which would concern us more today if it came from a psychoanalyst, just as it is Freud's Oedipus who sets us thinking now, not Sophocles'. A matter of language? But the only *power* history has over the "human heart" is to vary the language which utters it. "Everything has been said now that men have been living and thinking for seven thousand years": yes, no doubt; but it is never too late to invent new languages.

Such, then, is La Bruyère's "world," accounted for by several great classes of "individuals": court, city, Church, women, etc.; these same classes can easily be subdivided into smaller "societies." Merely reread fragment 4 of the chapter *De la ville:* "The city is divided into various societies, which are like so many little republics, each with its own laws, customs, jargon, and jokes." One might say in modern terms that the world is made up of a juxtaposition of *isolates,* impermeable to one another. In other words, the human group, as La Bruyère sees it, is not in the least constituted in a substantial fashion; beyond the purely contingent way in which these little societies are filled with bourgeois or with nobles, La Bruyère seeks out some feature which might define them all; this feature exists; it is a form; and this form is enclosure; La Bruyère is concerned with worlds, with *the* world, insofar as they—and it—are closed. We are dealing here, poetically, with what we might call an imagination of partition which consists in mentally exhausting every situation which the simple enclosure of a space gradually engenders in the general field where it occurs: choice of the partition, different substances of *inside* and *outside,* rules of admission, of exit, of exchange—it suffices that a line be closed in the world for a host of new meanings to be generated, and this is what La Bruyère realized. Applied to the social substance, the imagination of enclosure, whether experienced or analyzed, produces in fact an object which is both real (for it can be derived from sociology) and poetic (for writers have treated it with predilection): this object is worldliness. Before literature raised the problem of political realism, worldliness was a precious means for the writer to observe social reality yet remain a writer; worldliness is indeed an ambiguous form of reality: committed and uncommitted; referring to the disparity of the human condition but remaining in spite of everything a pure form, enclosure guarantees access to the psychological and the social without passing through the political; this is why, perhaps, we have had a great literature of worldliness in France, from Molière to Proust: and it is in this tradition of an entire imaginary world focused on the phenomena of social enclosure that La Bruyère obviously takes his place.

There can exist a great number of little worldly societies, since they need merely be closed in order to exist; but it follows that enclosure, which is the original form of all worldliness, and which we can consequently describe on the level of infinitesimal groups (the coterie of fragment 4 of *De la ville,* or the Verdurin salon), assumes a precise historical meaning when it is applied to the world as a whole; for what is then inside and outside it inevitably correspond to the economic partition of society; this is the case for the general worldliness described by La Bruyère; it has necessarily social roots: what is inside the enclosure are the privileged classes, nobility and bourgeoisie; what is outside are men without birth and money, the people (workers and peasants). La Bruyère, however, does not define social classes; he variously populates an inland and an outland; everything which occurs inside the enclosure is thereby called into Being; everything which remains outside it is rejected into nothingness; one might say, paradoxically, that social substructures are only the reflection of the forms of rejection and admission. The primacy of the form thus renders indirect the notations we would today call political. La Bruyère's democratic sentiments are often hailed, generally supported by fragment 128, *De l'homme*, which is a grim description of the peasants ("Certain wild animals . . . are to be seen about the countryside"). Nonetheless, *the people*, in this literature, has no more than a purely functional value: it remains the object of a charity, of which the subject alone, the charitable man, is called upon to exist; in order to exercise pity, there must be a pitiable object: *the people obliges*. In formal terms (and it has been said how much the closed form predetermined this world), the poor classes, enlightened by no political consideration, are that pure exterior without which bourgeoisie and aristocracy could not realize their own being (see fragment 31, *Des biens de fortune*, in which the people watches the nobility live their emphatic existence, as though on a stage); the poor are the thing starting from which one exists: they are the constitutive limit of the enclosure. And of course, as pure functions, the men of the exterior have no essence. We can attribute to them none of those "characters" which mark the inhabitants of the interior with a full existence: a man of the people is neither a dolt nor absent-minded nor vain nor greedy nor gluttonous (greedy, gluttonous— how could he be?); he is merely a pure tautology: *a gardener is a gardener, a mason is a mason*, no more can be said of him; the only double quality, the only relation to Being which, from the interior and beyond his utensile nature (to tend the garden, to build a wall), he can occasionally be granted is to be a man: not a human being, but a male whom the women of the world discover when they are too sequestered (*Des femmes*, No. 34): the questioner (the torturer who applies the question) is not a bit cruel (that would be a "character"); he is simply "a young man with broad shoulders and a stocky figure, a Negro moreover, a black man" (*Des femmes*, No. 33).

The "character" is a metaphor: it is the development of an adjective. Forbidden definition (being merely a limit), the people can receive neither adjective nor character: therefore the people vanishes from discourse. By the very weight of the formal postulate which consigns what is enclosed to Being, all the writing of *Les Caractères* is focused on the interior plenitude of the enclosure: it is here that characters, adjectives, situations, anecdotes abound. But this abundance is, one might say, rare, purely qualitative; it is not a quantitative abundance; the inland of worldliness, though filled to bursting with Being, is a narrow and sparsely populated territory; there occurs here a phenomenon of which our mass societies are losing all notion: everybody knows everybody else, everyone has a name. This interior familiarity, based on an openly sociological circumstance (nobles and bourgeois were a small minority) suggests what happens in societies of minor demography: tribes, villages, even American society before the great immigration. Paradoxically, La Bruyère's readers could conceive the universal better than the anonymous: thus any description of a character coincides with the sentiment of an identity, even if this identity is uncertain; the many "keys" which followed the publication of *Les Caractères* do not constitute a paltry phenomenon which would indicate, for instance, contemporary incomprehension in the face of the book's general scope; it is perhaps indifferent that the glutton *Cliton* was actually Count de Broussin or Louis de la Trémouille; it is not indifferent that the "characters" were almost all drawn from a personalized society: nomination here is a strict function of enclosure: the worldly type (and it is here that it probably differs from the typical roles of comedy) is not born of abstraction, quintessence of countless individuals: the worldly type is an immediate unit, defined by his place among adjacent units whose "differential" contiguity forms the inland of worldliness: La Bruyère does not purify his characters, he recites them like the successive cases of one and the same worldly declension.

Enclosure and individuation, these are dimensions of a sociality we no longer know anything about. Our world is open, we circulate in it; and above all, if enclosure still exists, it is anything but a rare minority which is confined within it and emphatically finds its being there; on the contrary, it is the countless majority; worldliness, today, is normality; it follows that the psychology of partition has entirely changed; we are no longer sensitive to characters resulting from the principle of vanity (decisive when it is the minority which is associated with both Being and Having), but rather to all the variations of the abnormal; for us, characters exist only marginally: it is no longer La Bruyère who gives a name to men now, it is the psychopathologist or the psychosociologist, those specialists who are called upon to define not essences but (quite the contrary) divergences. In other words, our enclosure is extensive, it confines the majority. There ensues a complete reversal of the interest we can take in characters; in the past, the character referred to a "key," the (general) *person* to a (particular) *personality*; today, it is the opposite; our world certainly creates, for its spectacle, a closed and personalized society: that of the stars and celebrities which we might group under the name of modern Olympians; but this society does not yield characters, only functions or roles (the love goddess, the mother, the queen enslaved by her duty, the vixen princess, the model husband, etc.); and contrary to the classical circuit, these "personalities" are treated as persons in order that the greatest number of human beings can recognize themselves in them; the Olympian society we create for our own consumption is, in short, only a world set within the world so as to represent it—not an enclosure but a mirror: we no longer seek out the typical but the identical; La Bruyère condensed a character in the fashion of a metaphor; we develop a star like a narrative; Iphis, Onuphre, or Hermippe lent themselves to an art of the portrait; Margaret, Soraya, or Marilyn renew that of the epic gesture.

This "structural" distance of La Bruyère's world in relation to ours does not cause our lack of interest in his, but merely exempts us from trying to identify ourselves with it; we must get used to the idea that La Bruyère's truth is, in the full sense of the term, elsewhere. Nothing will prepare us to do this better than a glance at what we would call today his political position. As we know, his century was not subversive. Born of the monarchy, fed by it, entirely immersed within it, writers of the period were as united in approving the establishment as those of today are in contesting it. Sincere or not (the question itself was virtually meaningless), La Bruyère declares himself as submissive to Louis XIV as to a god; not that his submission is not experienced as such; simply, it is inevitable: a man born a Christian and a Frenchman (i.e., subject to the king) cannot, by nature, approach the great subjects, which are the forbidden subjects: nothing remains for him except to write well (*Des ouvrages de l'esprit*, No. 65); the writer will therefore fling himself into the sanctification of what exists, *because it exists* (*Du souverain*, No. 1); it is the immobility of things which shows their truth; the Siamese welcome Christian missionaries but refrain from sending theirs to Europe: this is because their gods are false and "ours" true (*Des esprits forts*, No. 29). La Bruyère's submission to the most emphatic (and therefore to the most banal) forms of the royal cult is of course not at all strange in itself: every writer of his day employed this style; but all the same, there is one singularity about it: it suddenly reins in what today we would call a demystifying attitude: moralism, which is by definition a substitution of rationales for appearances and of motives for virtues, ordinarily operates like vertigo: applied to the "human heart," the investigation of truth seems unable to stop anywhere; yet in La Bruyère, this implacable movement, pursued by means of tiny notations throughout a whole book (which was the book of his life) concludes with the dullest of declarations: that the things of this world remain finally as they were, motionless under the gaze of the god-king; and that the author himself joins this immobility and "takes refuge in mediocrity" (*mediocrity* in the sense of the *juste milieu*; see *Des biens de fortune*, No. 47): it is as if we were hearing a new profession of dharma, the Hindu law which prescribes the immobility of things and of castes. Thus there appears a kind of distortion between book and author, a discrepancy at once surprising and exemplary; surprising because, whatever effort the author makes to submit, the book continues to ignite everything in its path; exemplary because by founding an order of signs on the distance between the witness and his testimony, the work seems to refer to a particular fulfillment of man in the world, a fulfillment which we call, precisely, *literature*. It is, finally, just when La Bruyère seems farthest from us that a figure suddenly appears who concerns us very closely and who is, quite simply, the *writer*.

It is not a question, of course, of "writing well." We believe today that literature is a technique at once more profound than that of style and less direct than that of thought; we believe that it is both language and thought,

thought which seeks itself on the level of words, language which considers itself philosophically. Is that what La Bruyère is?

One might say that the first condition of literature is, paradoxically, to produce an *indirect* language: to name things in detail in order not to name their ultimate meaning, and yet to retain this threatening meaning, to designate the world as a repertoire of signs without saying what it is they signify. Now, by a second paradox, the best way for a language to be indirect is to refer as constantly as possible to objects and not to their concepts: for the object's meaning always vacillates, the concept's does not; whence the concrete vocation of literary writing. Now *Les Caractères* is an admirable collection of substances, sites, customs, attitudes; man here is almost constantly dominated by an object or an incident: clothing, language, movement, tears, colors, cosmetics, faces, foods, landscapes, furniture, visits, baths, letters, etc. Everyone knows that La Bruyère's book has none of the algebraic dryness of La Rochefoucauld's maxims, for instance, which are based on the articulation of pure human essences; La Bruyère's technique is different: it consists of *putting on record*, and always tends to mask the concept under the percept; if he wants to say that the motive of modest actions is not necessarily modesty, La Bruyère will produce a little story of apartments or meals ("The man who, lodged in a palace, with two sets of apartments for the two seasons, comes to the Louvre to sleep in a vestibule," etc. *Du mérite*, No. 41); every truth begins this way, in the fashion of a riddle which separates the thing from its signification; La Bruyère's art (and we know that art, i.e., technique, coincides with the very Being of literature) consists in establishing the greatest possible distance between the evidence of the objects and events by which the author inaugurates most of his notations and the idea which actually seems to choose, to arrange, to move them retroactively. Most of the characters are thus constructed like a semantic equation: the concrete has the function of the signifier; the abstract, that of the signified; and between them comes a suspense, for we never know in advance the final meaning the author will draw from the things he treats.

The semantic structure of the fragment is so powerful in La Bruyère that we can readily attach it to one of the two fundamental aspects which Roman Jakobson so usefully distinguishes in any system of signs: a selective aspect (to choose a sign from a reservoir of similar signs) and a combinatory aspect (to connect the signs thus chosen within a discourse); each of these aspects corresponds to a typical figure of the old rhetoric, by which we can designate it: the selective aspect corresponds to *metaphor*, which is the substitution of one signifier for another, both having the same meaning, if not the same value; the combinatory aspect corresponds to *metonymy*, which is the shift, starting from a same meaning, from one sign to another; esthetically, a resort to metaphorical procedure is at the origin of all the arts of variation; a resort to metonymic procedure is at the origin of all the arts of narrative. A portrait by La Bruyère, then, has an eminently metaphorical structure; La Bruyère chooses features which have the same signified, and he accumulates them in a continuous metaphor, whose unique signified is given at the end; consider, for instance, the portrait of the rich man and of the poor man at the end of the chapter *Des biens de fortune*, No. 83: in *Giton* are enumerated, one right after another, all the signs which make him a rich man; in *Phédon*, all the signs of the poor man; we thus see that everything which happens to Giton and to Phédon, although apparently recounted, does not derive, strictly speaking, from the order of narrative; it is entirely a matter of an extended metaphor, of which La Bruyère himself has very pertinently given the theory when he says of his Ménalque that he is "less a particular character than a collection of examples of distraction" (*De l'homme*, No. 7); by this we are to understand that all the distractions enumerated are not really those of a single man, even one fictively named, as would occur in a real narrative (metonymic order); but that they belong instead to a lexicon of distraction from which can be chosen, "according to taste," the most significant feature (metaphoric order). Here perhaps we approach La Bruyère's art: the "character" is a false narrative, it is a metaphor which assumes the quality of narrative without truly achieving it (we recall moreover La Bruyère's scorn for storytelling: *Des jugements*, No. 52): the indirect nature of literature is thus fulfilled: ambiguous, intermediate between definition and illustration, the discourse constantly grazes one and the other and deliberately misses both: the moment we think we perceive the clear meaning of an entirely metaphorical portrait (lexicon of the features of distraction), this meaning shifts under the appearances of an experienced narrative (one of Ménalque's days).

A false narrative, a masked metaphor: this situation of La Bruyère's discourse perhaps explains the formal structure (what used to be called the composition) of the *Caractères*: it is a book of fragments precisely because the fragment occupies an intermediary place between the maxim which is a pure metaphor, since it defines (see La Rochefoucauld: "Self-love is the worst flatterer"), and the anecdote, which is pure narrative: the discourse extends a little because La Bruyère cannot be content with a simple equation (he explains this at the end of his preface); but it stops as soon as it threatens to turn into a story. *Les Caractères* exploits, in fact, a very special language, one which has few equivalents in a literature so imbued with the excellence of determined genres, fragmented language (the maxim), or continuous language (the novel); yet we might cite precedents—a prosaic reference and a sublime one. The prosaic reference of the fragment would be what we call today the *scrapbook*, a varied collection of reflections and items (press cuttings, for instance) whose mere *notation* leads to a certain meaning: *Les Caractères* is indeed the scrapbook of worldliness: a timeless fragmented gazette whose pieces are in a sense the discontinuous significations of a continuous reality. The sublime reference would be what we call today *poetic language*; by a historical paradox, poetry in La Bruyère's day was essentially a continuous discourse, of metonymic and not metaphoric structure (to return to Jakobson's distinction); it has taken the profound sub-version worked upon language by surrealism to obtain a fragmentary utterance which derives its poetic meaning from its very fragmentation (see for instance Char's *La Parole en archipel*); if it were poetic, La Bruyère's book would certainly not be a poem but, in the manner of certain modern com-positions, a pulverized language: that the example refers us on the one hand to a classical rationality (characters) and on the other to a poetic "irrationality" in no way alters a certain shared experience of the fragment: the radical discontinuity of language could be experienced by La Bruyère as it is experienced today by René Char.

And indeed it is on the level of language (and not of style) that *Les Caractères* can perhaps touch us most closely. Here we see a man conducting a certain experiment upon literature: its object may seem to us anachro-nistic, as we have seen, though the word ("literature") is not. This exper-iment is conducted, one may say, on three levels.

First of all, on the level of the institution itself. It seems that La Bruyère very consciously worked out a certain reflection on the Being of that singular language which we now call *literature* and which he himself named, by an expression more substantial than conceptual, *the works of the mind:* in ad-dition to his preface, which is a definition of his enterprise on the level of discourse, La Bruyère dedicates to literature a whole chapter of his work, and this chapter is the first one, as if all reflection on man must initially establish in principle the language which sustains it. No one at that time, of course, could imagine that *to write* was an intransitive verb, without moral justification: La Bruyère therefore writes in order to instruct. This finality is nonetheless absorbed in a group of much more modern defini-tions: writing is a métier, which is a way of demoralizing it and at the same time of giving it the seriousness of a technique (*Des ouvrages de l'esprit*, No. 3); the man of letters (a new notion at the time) is open to the world yet occupies a place in it shielded from worldliness (*Des biens de fortune*, No. 12); one engages in writing *or* in not-writing, which signifies that writing is a choice. Without trying to force the modernity of such notations, all this suggests the project of a singular language, distant both from the playful-ness of the *précieux* (naturalness is a theme of the period) and from moral instruction, a language which finds its secret goal in a certain way of di-viding up the world into words and of making it signify on the level of an exclusively verbal labor (which is *art*).

This brings us to the second level of the literary experiment, which is the writer's commitment to words. Speaking of his predecessors (Malherbe and Guez de Balzac), La Bruyère remarks: "Discourse has been given all the order and all the clarity of which it is capable (which it can receive): it can now be given only wit." Wit designates here a kind of *ingenuity* between intelligence and technique; such, indeed, is literature: a thought formed by words, a meaning resulting from form. For La Bruyère, to be a writer is to believe that in a certain sense content depends on form, and that by modifying the structure of form, a particular intelligence of things is produced, an original contour of reality, in short, a new meaning: language, to La Bruyère, is an ideology in and of itself; he knows that his vision of the world is somehow determined by the linguistic revolution of the beginning of his century and, beyond this revolution, by his personal utterance, that ethic of discourse which has made him choose the fragment and not the maxim, metaphor and not narrative, the *naturel* and not the *précieux*.

Thus he affirms a certain responsibility of writing which is, after all, quite modern, and which leads to the third determination of the literary experiment. This responsibility of writing is not at all identified with what we now call commitment and what was then called *instruction*. Of course the classical writers could quite well believe that they were instructing, just as our writers believe they are bearing witness. But even though it is substantially linked to the world, literature is elsewhere; its function, at least at the heart of that modernity which begins with La Bruyère, is not to answer the world's questions directly but—at once more modestly and more mysteriously—to lead the question to the verge of its answer, to construct the signification technically without fulfilling it. La Bruyère was certainly not a revolutionary nor even a democrat, as the positivists of the last century used to claim; he had no idea that servitude, oppression, poverty could be expressed in political terms; yet his description of the peasants has the profound value of an awakening; the light his writing casts on human misery remains indirect, issuing for the most part from a blinded consciousness, powerless to grasp causes, to foresee corrections; but this very indirectness has a cathartic value, for it preserves the writer from bad faith: in literature, through literature, the writer has no rights; the solution of human misery is not a triumphant possession; his language is there only to designate a disturbance. This is what La Bruyère has done: because he chose to be a writer, his description of man touches on the real questions.

Fontenelle's Theory
of Poetic Expression

Herbert Dieckmann

When we raise the question of esthetic theory and criticism in the eighteenth century, we do not impose upon the thought of that period ideas of another century. Not only the term *esthetics* but also the theory of esthetics go back to the Age of Enlightenment, and even if their connotations and semantic range vary from the eighteenth to the nineteenth century, the fundamental sense remains consistent. As far as criticism is concerned, be it of literature or the arts, it exists, of course, before the eighteenth century, but only during that period does it become a special field of investigation, a major concern for the speculative mind. This development is a partial aspect of the more general growth of criticism in the eighteenth century: from the role of a preliminary stage of intellectual inquiry, it turns into a predominant activity of the mind.

I take "esthetics" here in the sense of a field of study that comprises more than one art; esthetics may deal with the basic concepts common to literature, the fine arts, and music, or with a comparison of the different arts. I take "criticism" both as theory or doctrine and as practical criticism, i.e., as analysis of specific works of art.

If I use the term "modern," I mean that which is modern in and for the eighteenth century and is, in some measure, still valid or of some concern for our own time. This concept is not imposed upon the period under discussion, for at the beginning of eighteenth-century esthetics and criticism in France is the *Querelle des anciens et des modernes*. In a more general way one may say that the eighteenth century considered itself to be a modern period. It is perhaps the first period to do so, for the Renaissance is, as its very name implies, a rebirth; in the eighteenth century we have the consciousness of a radical new beginning.

From *Introduction to Modernity: A Symposium on Eighteenth-Century Thought,* edited by Robert Mollenauer. © 1965 by the University of Texas Press.

One of the most characteristic features of esthetics and criticism in the eighteenth century is their relationship to philosophy. This relationship can be considered from the point of view of philosophy and of esthetics. In the first case one will then discuss, for example, the influence which ethics and esthetics exerted upon each other; the deep changes in epistemological studies brought about by the analysis of the faculties that participate in artistic creation (the theory of knowledge changes its character when its field of inquiry, the operations of the mind, no longer is limited to the logic of science but also includes the arts); the new evaluation of the particular, the specific, the concrete, and of historical or geographical variability as opposed to the general, the abstract, the permanent and universal; the mutual relationship between esthetics and the new science of biology (this relationship appears not only in Kant's *Kritik der Urteilskraft* [*Critique of Judgment*] but can be traced throughout the eighteenth century). In the second case, i.e., in the case of the influence of philosophy on esthetics, one will discuss the systematization of esthetics in the eighteenth century or, to put it differently, the constitution of esthetics as part of a philosophical system. This development can be traced in Germany as well as France, though in Germany systematization was carried out more thoroughly and completely. I am referring to Baumgarten's *Aesthetica* (1750), and as far as *ars poetica* is concerned, to Gottsched's *Versuch einer critischen Dichtkunst vor die Deutschen* (1730, 1737, 1742, 1751; the systematic trend increased in the later editions). From these works a direct line can be drawn to the transformation of esthetics into the philosophy of art in Kant's *Kritik der Urteilskraft* (1790).

An equally important example of the alliance between philosophic thought and esthetics is to be found in the pervasive influence which British experimental empiricism exerted on the conceptions of art, artistic faculties and the individual's response to works of art. This influence reached its full effectiveness, deepest penetration, and widest application when it combined with the reaction to and progressive turning away from the classical and neoclassical theory of art, its standards, metaphysical assumptions or postulates and normative principles. Historians of English criticism have shown that the empirical, psychological approach was, in its early stages, still combined with the rationalistic tenets of neoclassicism but that its fundamental orientation—opposition to the objectively general and abstract, to universals, to a priori principles—tended to lead it away from those tenets.

The interpenetration of philosophy and esthetics as well as criticism in France follows a distinct and rather complex pattern. Two different currents of thought influence a movement of ideas which is determined by the reaction to the *doctrine classique* (the poetic theory of seventeenth-century French classicism) but which did not liberate itself entirely from the values and criteria of that doctrine. One of these currents is Cartesianism, the role of which is somewhat difficult to define; the other is British empiricism, which played a major role in the undermining of the classical tradition.

In order to clarify the interplay of various factors in the history of that movement, one must first of all avoid the still persistent error that the *doctrine classique* was based upon or resulted fom Descartes' philosophy. The chapter on esthetics in Cassirer's *Die Philosophie der Aufklärung* [*The Philosophy of the Enlightenment*]—a work which since its translation has become highly influential in this country—offers a good example of this erroneous assumption. Cassirer begins his exposé by placing eighteenth-century esthetics in the perspective of a gradual transition from Cartesianism to Newtonianism. It is only fair to add that this perspective is not the only one adopted by Cassirer and that there are excellent parts in his chapter.

There can be no doubt that Descartes himself excluded the field of esthetics from his philosophy, and that the *doctrine classique* was formulated independently from Descartes' philosophy. Neither rationalism nor the high evaluation of the "universal" and the "general," nor the concern for clarity and distinctness, nor the emphasis on method and rules was introduced into esthetics by Descartes. On the other hand, it is equally certain that these tenets of the *doctrine classique* show an affinity or analogy with his thought and that, in the latter part of the seventeenth century and in the beginning of the eighteenth, they became connected with a generalized form of Descartes' philosophy, called Cartesianism. Through this connection they were strengthened and reaffirmed, but they also underwent a certain formalization and transformation. The combination of the humanistic tradition of Classical Antiquity and seventeenth-century culture, the blending of ideal values and social decorum as we find them in the literature, arts, and poetics or art theory of French classicism, lost their force toward the end of the century, and the rationalistic, analytical element became predominant. In the writings of Perrault, Houdar de La Motte, and Fontenelle, "Cartesian" rationalism triumphs over the cultural heritage which is part of French classicism. Certain parts of the *Traité du Beau* (1714–1715) of Crousaz, the *Essai sur le Beau* (1741) by the Père André, and Batteux's *Les Beaux Arts réduits à un même principe* (1746), three works that exerted a deep influence on eighteenth-century esthetics, show the transformation of the classical doctrine by the geometrical spirit of Cartesianism.

In English eighteenth-century esthetics we also notice both a tradition of neoclassical restrictions and regulations and a movement against the confinement of artistic expression. There exists, however, an essential difference between the development in France and England. To be sure, neoclassic poetic theory in England had been formed under a strong influence of French ideas, but it came at a time when undisputed masterworks of creative literature, works written independently from these ideas, already existed, whereas in France the establishment of the *doctrine classique* coincided with the creation of literary masterpieces and was almost contemporary with the renewal of French philosophical thought. If no eighteenth-century French critic can free himself completely from this tradition, we can attribute his failure in great part to the veneration of the classical theater, a veneration which is fully equal to that of Shakespeare and Milton in England. Everyone who studies not only key concepts but also their significance in the minds of individual authors knows that despite striking similarities, eighteenth-century literary theories in France and England manifest widely divergent trends. In England, except in some extreme cases, as that of Rymer (who characteristically influenced Voltaire's critical judgment of Shakespeare), the representatives of neoclassicism tried to reconcile their concepts with their admiration of Shakespeare, Spenser, and Milton, whose works cannot be fitted into classical categories; in France, Corneille, Racine, Molière seemed to exemplify the *doctrine classique*.

It is all the more important to clarify the question of classicism and neoclassicism in eighteenth-century England and France, because the starting point of the reaction to classicism, the form it took, and the role which philosophic ideas came to play in it have been obscured by the trend to present eighteenth-century esthetics as a transition from classicism to romanticism.

This interpretation, which is in some measure a variant of the preromanticism-bias and which replaces the former (end of the nineteenth century) bias that the theater and poetry of the eighteenth century represent a downfall from the height of the *siècle de Louis XIV* and that its *ars poetica* is an aberration, colors all the concepts which express a reaction to classicism or neoclassicism and systematizes these reactions. In reality the esthetic concepts of the eighteenth century are far from having the meaning which they later acquired in romanticism, and they often constitute an opposition to only a few points of the classical doctrine, while other criteria and values of classicism continue to be accepted. The reaction is moreover sometimes directed not against the original *doctrine classique* but a highly formalized or conventionalized version of it. To give an example of the erroneous coloring of a key concept: the term "sentiment" or "feeling" as used in eighteenth-century criticism often does not indicate a current of romanticism nor does it necessarily denote emotionalism—it stands for interior evidence, an immediate awareness of what occurs in our souls or hearts, and for a lower form of judgment or knowledge; it also may simply express a reaction to the restricting of the faculty of reason to logical abstraction and mathematical demonstration, a turning away from predominantly analytical thinking and an antagonism to excessive and endless methodizing. The same observation can be made with regard to other terms, as "concrete," "particular," "imagination."

The evolutionary scheme which underlies the notion "from classicism to romanticism" not only leads to a dangerous simplification, unification, and systematization of both classicism and romanticism, and proceeds by a series of abstract antitheses (such as reason and feeling, mechanic and organic, imitation and creation), but it also presupposes a gradual development from one position to the other, whereas we find in the eighteenth century a reaction to classicism, a revision of some of its tenets, and a subsequent return to a new classicism.

The conclusion to be drawn from these observations is that the criticism of the tenets and criteria of classicism or simply the reaction against them must be studied with respect to individual causes, motives, and manifestations independently from any preassigned goal, and the reasons which determined this criticism in its beginnings must be distinguished from those that intervened later. As far as the development of esthetics during the eighteenth century is concerned, neither the ideas of Leibniz, nor of Locke, nor the entelechy of romanticism and Baudelaire, nor an evolution from Cartesianism to Newtonianism were its determining causes, though Leibniz' and Locke's ideas became part of the movement later, and both influenced it and were influenced by it. Social changes, the growing self-consciousness of the bourgeoisie, played a major role in the turning away from seventeenth-century classicism; so did formalization and conventionalization, though these factors had to be combined with others to become decisive.

I should like to conclude this first part of my paper with a few general reflections on the relationship between philosophy and esthetics as well as criticism. Such a relationship is inherent in esthetics; the thinkers of the eighteenth century did not create it; however, they re-established it. In a slow, highly complex, difficult, at times confused process they re-examined the long tradition of esthetics and *ars poetica* that began in Classical Antiquity. They first confronted this tradition in the historical form that immediately concerned them, but then went beyond that form. The decisive factor in the re-examination is that it was not at first (roughly, the first two-thirds of the eighteenth century) a return to the "true" meaning of Plato, Aristotle, or Horace, and that it was not limited to certain concepts of this tradition while the framework was left intact. It went beyond the point of view of *ars poetica* and rhetoric, and was strongly influenced by the currents of antimetaphysical rationalism and experimental empiricism; in other words, it tended towards a new philosophic foundation of esthetics and criticism. One of the major effects of this twofold rational and empirical criticism was that it put an end to the unreflective, rhetorical usage of the key concepts of esthetic theory. It is not enough to say that these concepts acquired new meaning; they acquired again meaning, thanks to the deliberate effort to make them intelligible instead of using them as self-evident principles, precepts, or values. Critical reexamination means an inquiry into the significance of these concepts, that is, into their logical foundation, their origin, and their genesis; the inquiry is at times rational, at times empirical-psychological, and at times both. It is moreover accompanied by a shift of emphasis, away from the consideration of the work of art itself and the norms to which it has to conform, towards the study of the process of its creation, the faculties that create it, and towards the response to art, that is, towards the nature of esthetic pleasure. The latter shift is connected with the formation of a new public and the spreading of culture in the eighteenth century. The critic as the intermediary between the artist and the work of art on one side and the public on the other asserts himself, and practical criticism as distinguished from art theory and normative esthetics develops.

In this latter development we notice a discrepancy or tension between theory and practice. The speculation on the theory of art, the philosophic clarification of its basic concepts, does not succeed in freeing these concepts on all points from the metaphysical and classical tradition and in establishing a new esthetics that would replace the former one. In practical criticism, however, the modern criteria were applied spontaneously and freely. We find thus that with some critics the idealistic, abstract conception of beauty, a rationalistic idea of nature, the traditional form of the postulates of imitation, norms, and rules, lingers on in some form and coexists with a sensuous, imaginative, impressionistic description and analysis of individual works of art. Criticism as interpretation seems to solve in practice the problems which critical theory could not overcome. It would, however, be erroneous to assume that practical criticism was not affected by philosophic thought. On the contrary: we owe both the development of esthetics and the rapid growth of criticism in the nineteenth century, the enrichment of critical vocabulary and the differentiation of critical categories, to the reexamination and clarification of esthetic concepts which brought about a high degree of consciousness of all questions concerning the nature of artistic creation, artistic expression, artistic criteria, and understanding of art.

After having indicated the general lines of the development of esthetics and criticism in the eighteenth century, I should like to choose as illustration a specific issue, that of metaphoric expression as it is discussed by . . . Fontenelle, . . . in whose thought it is of major significance. As is well known, the evaluation of image and metaphor is a touchstone by which to test a critic's stand on poetics and esthetics. Fontenelle is representative of the early stage of the Enlightenment (roughly, the last two decades of the seventeenth century) and its intransigent rationalism. . . .

The most important source for our knowledge of Fontenelle's ideas on image and metaphor is his treatise entitled *Sur la poésie en général*. It was written in defense of a poet, Houdar de La Motte, who had been accused of being a philosopher, rather than a poet, of having more ideas than images. This positive purpose, which the author states in his *Avertissement*, is important, for Fontenelle is by no means, as has been stated, an enemy of poetry. He deals with questions of poetics and esthetics *en philosophe*, as one said in the eighteenth century; that is, he treats them in a critical spirit, considers them as one of the manifestations of the human mind, and traces them back to questions of principle. In his *Sur la poésie en général* he leads up to the discussion of poetic images by an inquiry into the origin and essence of poetry: one origin he finds in primitive man's desire to remember accurately fundamental laws; man committed them to memory in prosodic form, and later other important and solemn themes were also stated in this manner. The second origin is to be found in man's delight in song. These novel forms of expression were startling, filling listeners with admiration and awe; the poet's claim to be inspired by the gods was readily accepted. As to the essence of poetry, it is to be found in the pleasing effect of its themes, in the qualities that appeal to the ear and those that appeal to the mind. This latter appeal is treated at some length by Fontenelle. He distinguishes two forms of pleasure: the first is that derived from difficulty overcome; whereas man's natural mode of expression is prose, poetry is art and imposes shackles (meter, rhythm, rhyme) upon the natural expression. If these difficulties are conquered, the mind enjoys the mastery of the art and the perfection of the new form. The second appeal to the mind comes from images and it is greater than the first. As to metaphor, it is a necessity in all forms of speech; in poetry, however, it is used voluntarily, and is more highly developed than in prose.

In his discussion of imagery Fontenelle follows the "natural" order: he deals first with "images fabuleuses," mythological images, because they were the first to be used. They are characteristic of the early stages of mankind, when the coarse imagination of ignorant people gave birth to the multitude of the gods. As mythological imagery developed, simple nature almost disappeared under the cover of fabulous beings. The fact that mythological imagery still prevails at present, though we know that the gods and half-gods are imaginary, can be attributed to its appeal to man's nonrational nature and to education which keeps mythology alive. Through this twofold influence we have become so used to mythology that we seem to be born pagans though we claim to be Christians. By yielding to the charm of mythological imagery we fall back into childhood; we adopt again the ideas of the primitive ancient Greeks, "des plus anciens Grecs encore sauvages." Mythology is, as it were, imposed upon a passive mind by tradition and education (cf. Fontenelle's *De l'origine des fables*). Let us notice here that, according to Fontenelle, the poets originally did not invent mythology but adopted it, partly because it supported their claim to be inspired by the gods. In other passages of his treatise, Fontenelle does not altogether reject the "images fabuleuses," provided they are used in a novel way and reveal genuine enthusiasm; he recognizes that they are still pleasing, that they are still considered to give life to everything. However, he recommends replacing them by "images demi-fabuleuses," personifications of inanimate objects or of conceptions, such as glory, fame, death, which are also formed in the mind but have a basis in reality. These would have the same animating power as mythological images and would in addition be new and original.

This latter idea introduces a fresh attack upon mythological images; they are, Fontenelle emphasizes, thoroughly worn out, "extrêmement usées"; everyone can and does use them. It is significant that Fontenelle does not bring up this argument among his first objections, and that he connects it with the question of the originality and activity of the human mind, and with that of the basis which images have in reality. The following comparison which Fontenelle makes between "une image fabuleuse" and "une image demi-fabuleuse" throws an interesting light on his criteria and on eighteenth-century imagery:

> Si je veux présenter un bouquet avec des vers, je puis dire ou que Flore s'est dépouillée de ses trésors pour une autre divinité, ou que les fleurs se sont disputé l'honneur d'être cueillies; et si j'ai à choisir entre ces deux images, je croirai volontiers que la seconde a plus d'âme, parce qu'il semble que la passion de celui qui a cueilli les fleurs ait passé jusqu'à elles.

Fontenelle's preference seems to me to show not only a disdain for mythology and symbolism, but also a strain of intellectual preciosity. To be sure, the first image had become a cliché, but, if taken seriously, Flora personifies nature in bloom and the beloved partakes of divinity. In the second image, the poet makes a conscious transposition: he knows that he uses an analogy and "falsely" treats an object of nature as if it were animate and had passions. The first is an image, the second a conceit; or, the first is a symbol, the second a simile expressing artistry and politeness. We have here a good illustration of the danger inherent in the demand of "thought in poetry." Joseph Trapp knew it well when in his "Of the beauty of thought in poetry" he warned against "pointed turns" and trifling (*Lectures on Poetry*, lecture 8).

Another form of metaphorical expression consists of the "images réelles" which Fontenelle later in his treatise calls "images matérielles"; we might call them descriptive images of great, dramatic events, such as tempests or battles; they are all the more moving, powerful, and magnificent if no divinities are permitted to interfere. Fontenelle does not develop this idea in any detail. The reason for his brief treatment will appear when we now turn to the last two kinds of images, the "images spirituelles" and the "images intellectuelles."

Whereas the "images fabuleuses" speak only to an imagination biased by a wrong philosophy ("prévenue d'un faux système"), and the "images réelles" only to the eyes, the "images spirituelles" speak to the mind. Following the Abbé de Bernis, Fontenelle calls these images also "pensées," thoughts. He quotes two examples from La Motte; we return here to the theme stated in the *Avertissement*:

Quand de la Motte a appellé les flatteurs:

> Idolâtres tyrans des rois.

ou qu'il a dit:

> Et le crime seroit paisible,
> Sans le remords incorruptible
> Qui s'élève encore contre lui.

ces expressions, *idolâtres tyrans, remords incorruptible,* sont des images spirituelles. Je vois les flatteurs qui n'adorent les rois que pour s'en rendre maîtres; et un homme qui, applaudi sur ses crimes par des gens corrompus, porte au-dedans de lui-même un sentiment qui les lui reproche, et qu'il ne peut étouffer. La première image est portée sur deux mots; la seconde sur un seul.

What Fontenelle likes in these images is that they present thoughts in a new, unusual combination and in this way give to the mind ideas which it did not have before; in other words, he finds in them the very function of metaphor, and he perceives, as it were, directly the act of comparison: "I *see* the flatterers" [emphasis mine].

The "images réelles," on the contrary, present to the eyes only what the eyes have already seen; if the concrete image seems pleasant, it is so only thanks to the mind which becomes interested in the visual impression. Taken in themselves, material images do not offer anything new, for everything has been seen for a long time. The latter statement is all the more significant as Fontenelle sharply attacks the dictum that everything has already been *thought*. He conceives here of our sensuous perceptions in a completely static way and isolates them from the mind, which alone develops, grows, and appropriates new domains. The mind's activity is what pleases Fontenelle, even in the use of "images réelles."

The "images spirituelles" in turn not only speak to the mind, but appeal also to the heart; they represent not only thoughts but also feelings and passions; they alone have the power to interest and to move. The feelings to which Fontenelle refers here are, no doubt, highly intellectualized emotions, but it is important to notice that he emphasizes their being present in the "images spirituelles." Not many poets, Fontenelle continues, will be able to reach the heights of these images; we find them above all in dramatic poetry, while epic poetry, the older genre, uses "images réelles." The conception of the "images spirituelles" is linked with the idea of man's higher faculties and of a detachment from all that is coarse and material. It is also linked, as the reference to epic and drama discloses, with the theory of a progressive evolution of literary genres.

Above these images are those that pertain to the order of the universe, to space, time, and the Deity. Fontenelle calls these metaphysical images "images intellectuelles," and the poetry in which they are used, "philosophical poetry." Only a few authors and readers, Fontenelle concedes, can appreciate them and conquer the prejudice that philosophy is necessarily pedantic and academic. To be sure, philosophic terminology has something barbarous that revolts the ear. There is, however, hope that poetry will strive to find a simple language for lofty conceptions. Perhaps even the "images fabuleuses" could be rejuvenated by the great abstractions of philosophical poetry. The task is difficult, but history shows us that poetry and philosophy have often formed an alliance; and, as Fontenelle has stated before, the conquering of difficulties constitutes poetry's charm. (It probably was Fontenelle's deep aversion to enthusiasm and his distrust of all states of rapture that prevented him from connecting his idea of "images spirituelles" and "images intellectuelles" with the conception of the sublime in poetry. He comes, however, close to such a conception, and he does so, as it were, by reason. Fontenelle's rationalism has often been identified with his scepticism, his distrust of delusion, his polite and playful aloofness, and his tendency to find a middle position. This interpretation is only partly justified and must not make us overlook the element of radicalism in his reason. Though he would have considered it poor taste and bad manners to display this radicalism in society, he expressed it occasionally in his writings, in those which he published either late in his life or anonymously, or not at all. It made him push an idea to its last consequences, assert the full independence of thought and make *tabula rasa* of traditional and institutional values or criteria. There was in Fontenelle a strain of the lyricism of reason, and we find it in his reflections on the arts and in some passages of the *Entretiens sur la pluralité des mondes*.)

Even this general outline of Fontenelle's theory of images will have made it clear that for him poetic expression is not a mere ornament and poetry is no pastime. On the contrary, he expects poetic expression to instruct the human mind, not in any didactic manner in which poetry serves as the vehicle for teaching, but by its inherent metaphorical nature. Fontenelle wishes poetry, by its alliance with philosophy, to become again substantial and significant. It is precisely by the use of mythological images, "ces ornaments pris dans un système absolument faux et ridicule," that poetry has ceased to be meaningful. Fontenelle's treatise is a sincere defense of philosophic poetry. It is this purpose and seriousness which give it, among other factors, its great importance.

Fontenelle's philosophic viewpoint appears also in his division of images: he does not follow the tradition of rhetoric or poetics, but establishes a hierarchy based on rational values and formed by the principle of increasing intellectuality. In two instances he seems to use the criterion of reality also, but this criterion depends again on an intellectual one: when he states that the "images demi-fabuleuses" are founded on reality, he means that they are not based on pure invention, as mythological images; despite their abstractness, which shows the working of reason, they are rooted in the experience of inner or outer reality. In the case of the "images réelles" or "matérielles," it is not their reality content, the accurate description, which constitutes their poetic value, but the comprehension of the mind, whose reflection is directed upon the descriptive elements. Though he reasons along different lines, Fontenelle is here in agreement with the eighteenth-century critics of the literal *imitatio naturae* and *ut pictura poesis* principles, to whom descriptive images are not beautiful in themselves but through a comparison between the model and the imitation—a comparison made by the mind. It is thus the activity of the mind, the movement and interplay of our faculties, which is recognized as a source of esthetic pleasure.

Fontenelle's hierarchy of images includes also significant historical elements. It would be an exaggeration to state that he went so far as to transform a hitherto static, timeless hierarchy into an evolutionary pattern, but he certainly prepared the way for such a development. The "images fabuleuses" are to him an expression of the primitive mind, of mankind in its infancy; if we still like them, we show only that we find it difficult to grow up and that a wrong system of education keeps turning our heads backwards. The "images intellectuelles," on the other hand, are clearly connected with the new philosophy which, according to Fontenelle, originates with Descartes.

We have stated above that the long-held thesis of Descartes's influence on the poetics of French classicism is not valid. However, what has been disproved in the case of Descartes and French classicism is not wrong for the Cartesians who followed him and for the classicism of the end of the seventeenth century and the beginning of the eighteenth. Descartes had clearly restricted the domain of philosophy and excluded poetry from the field in which his new method was to be applied. Fontenelle, on the other hand, extended the borderline of this field and generalized the application of the method. One of the chief passages in which he states this principle is to be found, in fact, in our treatise:

> Il n'est pas douteux que la philosophie n'ait acquis aujourd'hui quelques nouveaux degrés de perfection. De là se répand une lumière qui ne se renferme pas dans la région philosophique, mais qui gagne toujours comme de proche en proche, et s'étend enfin sur tout l'empire des lettres. L'ordre, la clarté, la justesse, qui n'étaient pas autrefois des qualités trop communes chez les meilleurs auteurs, le sont aujourd'hui beaucoup davantage, et même chez les médiocres. Le changement en bien, jusqu'à un certain point, est assez sensible partout. La poésie se piquera-t-elle du glorieux privilège d'en être exempte?

Fontenelle's answer to this question is a clear "No"; and he shows it not only in his evaluation of poetic images but throughout his treatise, in the general considerations with which the reflections on imagery are interspersed and which give to these reflections a broad significance. The defense of the "images demi-fabuleuses," the "images spirituelles," and "images intellectuelles" is at the same time a defense of the *poète-philosophe,* a defense which leads to an examination of the preference of "talent" over "esprit." Fontenelle questions this preference: "Le talent est comme indépendant de nous et ses opérations semblent avoir été produites en nous par quelque être supérieur qui nous a fait l'honneur de nous choisir pour ses instruments." Fontenelle is evidently attacking here the idea of the divinely inspired, enraptured poet, the "fous de la façon du feu divin." To this talent he opposes "l'esprit," enlightened reason which is our own, which constitutes our conscious, critical, deliberating, freely choosing, freely acting self. "Pour ce qu'on appelle *esprit*, ce n'est que nous; nous sentons trop que c'est nous qui agissons." He underscores his low esteem of divinely inspired talent even more heavily by establishing, almost without transition, a parallel between talent and animal instinct. Talent, like instinct, dominates and determines us; it shuns the light of reflection. We reach here the very center of Fontenelle's Cartesianism; the animal instinct, however perfect, is outside the domain of the mind; a talent which is given to us and upon which we depend, which unconsciously—Fontenelle says blindly—directs us, is outside the domain of freedom, which is the prerogative of the mind that possesses itself and is capable of perfecting itself. We have, it would seem to me, in this self-affirmation of the mind, the inner link between Fontenelle and Descartes, of whom Wilhelm Dilthey admirably said:

> Descartes ist die Verkörperung der auf Klarheit des Denkens gegründeten Autonomie des Geistes. In ihm lebt eine originale Verbindung von Freiheitsbewusstsein mit dem Machtgefühl des rationalen Denkens. Und hierin liegt wohl die äusserste Steigerung des Souveränitätsbewusstseins, zu der sich je ein Mensch erhoben hat.

> [Descartes is the embodiment of the autonomy of spirit which is grounded in the clarity of thought. There lives in him an original combination of the consciousness of freedom with the sense of power resulting from rational thought. That may well be the farthest advance of the consciousness of sovereignty to which man has ever raised himself.]

(trans. Michael Shane)

Fontenelle differs, however, from Descartes in that he establishes an analogy and, at times, a connection between philosophic and poetic knowledge, and he goes beyond Descartes in formulating with great directness what is only *implicite* in Descartes' thought: the idea of progress and, connected with it, the rejection of Classical Antiquity and of tradition as model, authority, and criteria of truth. Skillfully maintaining an analogy between instinct and talent, i.e., never exposing himself to the reproach of having identified them, Fontenelle states that animal instinct achieves indeed admirable things, but never progresses: the beehive and the beavers' construction are today the same as at the beginning of time. Reason, on the contrary, develops constantly. "Peut-être viendra-t-il temps où les poëtes se piqueront d'être plus philosophes que poëtes, d'avoir plus d'esprit que de talent, et en seront loués. Tout est en mouvement dans l'univers, et à tout égard."

The two stages in history, the Ancients and the Moderns, do not present a static antithesis; there has been a progressive development from one to the other, and this progress has a marked orientation towards the future. Fontenelle's evolutionary conception of the human mind is not a general or abstract conception but supposes a slow, gradual development from a primitive stage of man's mentality where, as a result of ignorance, rudimentary thinking and limited experience in intellectual matters, and coarseness as well as savagery in moral matters, causality appears in the form of myths (Jupiter, Neptune, Eolus are personified causes) and history in the form of fables, to the full development of consciousness (the Cartesian *clare et distincte*) and the refinement of culture. In his *Discours sur les fables* this conception is developed by a comparison between various historically attested forms of primitive thinking: the myths and fables of Classical Antiquity are likened to those of savage tribes in Africa and America.

The criticism of the "images fabuleuses" and the hierarchy of images are thus linked with the great issues of Fontenelle's philosophy and of that of his time; the self-affirmation of Reason, the *Querelle des anciens et des modernes*, and the belief in progress. For the alliance between poetry and the humanities and for the backwards orientation of this alliance, he substitutes the alliance between poetry and philosophy and that between poetry and science. He firmly attached poetics, and more specifically the question of poetic expression, to the ideology of the Enlightenment. The *philosophes* who strove to reconcile the position of the Ancients with that of the Moderns found out how difficult it was to disengage poetics from the grip of this ideology.

Saint-Simon's Portrait of Louis XIV

Leo Spitzer

> *De ce tout il résulte qu'on admire et qu'on fuit.*
> —SAINT-SIMON, on Versailles

CHARACTER AND HISTORY

Saint-Simon's portrait of the *roi-soleil*, "toute cette longue digression sur le caractère, le règne et la vie journalière de Louis XIV" (Boislisle), is a huge expansion of an already extensive addition that he made to Dangeau's *Journal* under the date of 13 August 1715 (printed in Boislisle). A character-portrait of such enormous dimensions suggests a very particular conception of *character*. For Saint-Simon, character is the structure which arches over all the facts of history; it is the totality which embraces historical person-alities in their full extent and substance. Character is like some Trojan Horse concealing historical acts, events and customs, which can climb out of its belly and yet leave a clearly visible skeleton.

The résumé of the portrait given (in the Pléiade edition) at the head of chapter LI (but originally written in the margin throughout the manu-script) shows how the character of the king was conceived of as an all-embracing structure. It is out of his character that the history of his reign develops, and so history is built in to the character-portrait. The essential traits of the character unfold themselves in historical actions; the historian's art is to reinsert the chronological sequence of actions into the stable, static, sharply delineated contours of the character. Character is here the unmoved mover, the essence or Being from which the Becoming of history springs: individual historical events flow from individual aspects of Being as honey, so to speak, may flow from the separate cells of a single honeycomb. At the head of the résumé stands "Caractère de Louis XIV"; the character is formed by Mme de la Vallière, but immediately shows itself for what it is.

From *Essays on Seventeenth-Century French Literature*, edited by David Bellos. © 1983 by Cambridge University Press.

"*Le Roi hait les sujets, est petit, dupe, governé, en se piquant de tout le contraire.*"
Now come the facts: "*L'Espagne cède la préséance . . . Guerre de Hollande; paix d'Aix-la-Chapelle; siècle florissant. Conquêtes en Hollande et de la Franche-Comté,*" etc. The end-points of the first and second periods of the king's reign are indicated. But before the third period, which takes Louis from the full flowering of his reign to its ultimate decline, Saint-Simon brings out his psychology of the king: "*Vertus de Louis XIV; sa misérable éducation; sa profonde ignorance; il hait la naissance et les dignités; séduit par ses ministres.*" This allows Saint-Simon to incorporate the warmongering of the Louvois ministry and the events of the Spanish War of Succession up to the Peace of Utrecht into the overall structure of the character—as the result of Louis's hatred of true worth and of his vulnerability to ambitious ministers.

Saint-Simon does of course devote the bulk of his portrait to this third period, and he emphasises early on the contrast between a majestic exterior and the inner decay:

> Le troisième âge s'ouvrit par un comble de gloire et de prospérité inouie. Le temps en fut momentané. Il enivra et prépara d'étranges malheurs, dont l'issue a été un espèce de miracle.

At this point he repeats the formulation of the king's character given at the very beginning: "*L'esprit du roi était au-dessous du médiocre, mais très-capable de se former*" ("*Né avec un esprit au-dessous . . .*" etc.; the same formula occurs in the original addition to Dangeau).

The derivation of the historical facts from the psychological disposition of the king is expressed, in grammatical terms, by Saint-Simon's use of psychological qualities as the subjects of his sentences. . . . For example:

> *Ce même orgueil*, que Louvois sut si bien manier, épuisa le royaume par des guerres et par des fortifications innombrables.

> *Ce fut la même jalousie* qui écrasa la marine dans un royaume flanqué des deux mers . . . *Cette même jalousie* de Louvois contre Colbert dégoûta le Roi des négotiations.

> *L'orgueil du roi* voulut étonner l'Europe par la montre de sa puissance, . . . et l'étonna en effet. Telle fut la cause de ce fameux camp de Compiègne.

> *La même politique* continua le mystère de cet amour . . . *Le mystère* le fit durer . . .

(In the last example, the personifications of *politique* and *mystère* probably derive from the *précieux* jargon of love [see below, comments on *air*].). When the king's character suffers the blows of fate, Louis XIV is disaggregated into his component psychological parts, but restored almost immediately by an inclusive generalisation to a totality of personality and event:

Mais bientôt après le Roi fut attaqué par des coups bien plus sensibles: *son cœur*, que lui-même avait comme ignoré jusqu'alors, par la perte de cette charmante dauphine; *son repos*, par celle de l'incomparable dauphin; *sa tranquillité*, sur la succession à sa couronne, par la mort de l'héritier huit jours après . . .; *tous* ces coups frappés rapidement, *tous* avant la paix, presque *tous* durant les plus terribles périls du royaume.

Each blow of fate affects here a single psychological feature of the king. This disaggregation of character in decline is a corollary to Saint-Simon's general treatment of events as mere pretexts for the display of psychological properties, as for example "*Bientôt après, la mort du roi d'Espagne fit* saisir à ce jeune prince avide de gloire *une occasion de gloire*"; "Ce fut donc dans cette triste situation intérieure que *la fenêtre de Trianon* fit la guerre de 1688" (Louvois, insulted over a window being constructed under his supervision, declares war to make himself indispensable to Louis XIV).

To conclude these stylistic observations: Saint-Simon gives us history as chronology and development, but he always traps it in the static honeycomb structure of character.

In the third period, Louis is at the height of his power. Saint-Simon's résumé of chapter LIII: "*Bonheur du roi en tout genre. Autorité du Roi sans bornes; sa science de regner; sa politique sur le service, où il asservit tout et rend tout peuple.*" This levelling policy, designed to elevate the king above all else, results in extremely diverse acts of government—the introduction of *ancienneté*, "*la cour pour toujours à la campagne*," "*Le Roi veut une grosse cour*," "*Politique du plus grand luxe*," Versailles, Marly (résumé of chapter LIV), "*amours du roi*" (chapter LV)—and in the king's love-life, magnified beyond the limits of propriety by a lust for power, Mme de Maintenon establishes her huge enclave in Louis XIV's sphere of influence with historical effects that disturb the entire state. Madame de Maintenon is thus built in to the character-portrait of the king, and many historical actions—e.g. the revocation of the edict of Nantes, the foundation of Saint-Cyr, etc.—are reincorporated into the character of Mme de Maintenon ("goût de direction," "dévotion," etc.). The picture of Maintenon is constructed by analogy with that of Louis, the *mécanique* of her life is similarly depicted, as is her precise relationship to the great men of her time. Almost one-quarter of Saint-Simon's chapters on Louis XIV deal with the Maintenon enclave, with Maintenon as an excrescence or tumour on the king's character, with the debasement of the king at the hands of this woman, all of which sets in an advantageous light Louis's considerations on morality in the face of death. The death of the king should bring to an end Saint-Simon's representation of his character through the historical working-out of its imprinted forms, but the historian, who traces external actions and events from the inner dimensions of character, possesses an intermediate domain between the inner character and outer action of his subject: namely, the habits and customs that derive from character (they can "characterise princes") but which have nonetheless the material quality of external events. Saint-Simon calls this "l'écorce extérieure de la vie de ce monarque" or, elsewhere, "la mécanique [des temps et des heures]," and under this heading he gives us the daily routine that belongs to him and also to the public, which continues to serve after his death, without further historical development, making at the close out of his character once again a static and timeless phenomenon, an unmoving mover.

This reading of chapter LIX of the *Mémoires* involves rejecting the gloss given by Saint-Simon's editors on the phrase "tout ce qu'on a vu d'intérieur." It stands in opposition to "l'écorce extérieure de ce monarque" and refers not to the "internal life of the court" but to the inner life of the king. "Intérieur" is frequently used by Saint-Simon with reference to Louis:

> Louvois, qui était toujours bien informé de l'intérieur le plus intime, . . . sut les manèges de Mme de Maintenon pour se faire déclarer . . . et que la chose allait éclater.

There are also examples of "écorce" applied to outer life:

> le mystère de cet amour, qui ne le demeura que de nom, et tout au plus en très fine *écorce*.

> discerner la vérité des apparences, le necessaire de *l'écorce*.

> cet attachement pharisaïque à l'extérieur de la loi et à *l'écorce* de la religion.

[For similar usage in Spanish, see Gracián, *Criticón* I/II.] *Eclater*, on the other hand, means for Saint-Simon "to make known to other people," as in

> Bientôt après, elle [i.e. Maintenon's favour with the king] *éclata* par l'appartement qui lui fut donné à Versailles.

Saint-Simon's historical portrait is a unique attempt to compress the moving *course* of a life into a static *image* of a life and thus to explain what a man becomes by what a man is. The subject's Being is a nonderivative, composite but rationally graspable given which triumphs over the complexity of history. There is no concession to the formlessness and chaos of the stream of life, but lots of clearly labelled character-traits with their consequences in train, and no trace of impersonal or supraindividual forces. The only secret that remains is the personality, a balloon full to bursting point, producing deeds and habits, but simply standing there in its magnificent pregnancy. It is as if Saint-Simon's king-figure had been stuffed and bloated on the corpse of all those historical forces that go beyond the individual. The theory of history that underlies Saint-Simon's art of the portrait is a mystical belief in the breadth, substantiality and effective power of personality. He states this basis explicitly:

Ce peu d'historique, eu égard à un règne si long et si rempli, est
si lié au personnel du Roi qu'il ne se pouvait omettre pour bien
représenter ce monarque tel qu'il a véritablement été.

And by implication:

ce peu qui a été retracé du règne du feu Roi était nécessaire pour
mieux faire entendre ce qu'on va dire de sa personne.

Character is the stamped image of personality; it has, like a stamp, clear
edges; it is comprehensible and powerfully explicit. In such portraiture there
can be nothing left unsaid, vague or shaded. But such a conception of
character as a monstrously bloated *thing* also demands a very particular
type of composition that traces all the excrescences of the personality.

The claim that Saint-Simon did not compose is simply wrong. He
composed his portrait according to the relative importance of the parts for
the whole, and this accounts for the huge protuberance of Maintenon next
to the single page devoted to the first love, Mme de la Fayette, because
the revocation of the edict of Nantes is encapsulated in the Maintenon
section.

The organisation of character is significant in Saint-Simon also in the
sense that all qualities (and the deeds and events that follow from each
quality) are derived from a common denominator, reduced to a single fundamental trait. The virtuosity of the character-drawer consists therefore of
unravelling this fundamental trait in areas that seem utterly remote from
it: "Il faut montrer les progrès en tous genres de la même conduite dressé
sur le même point de vue." Louis XIV's basic trait is that he was born "avec
un esprit au-dessous du médiocre," and as this situation drives him to
"orgueil," he fears nobility of birth and intellect: "Il . . . craignait [la no-
blesse] autant que l'esprit." He requires the flattery of his ministers, gen-
erals, mistresses and courtiers, which produce the "superbe du roi, qui
forme le colosse de ses ministres sur la ruine de la noblesse." Further on,
Louis's involvement in all sorts of details is derived from his intellectual
limitations: "Son esprit, naturellement porté au petit, se plut en toutes
sortes de détails." The delight in minutiae, the grandeur of his ministers,
and the king's pleasure in his own greatness produce a series of consequences: the levelling-down of the power of functionaries in the state ("il
ne voulait de grandeur que par émanation de la sienne"), the king's choice
of "gens de rien" for high office, and his inaccessibility except through
official channels. The innate, quite clearly, forms the basis of the character
from which the details follow. Nonetheless Saint-Simon was not quite clear
about the distinction between nature and nurture. For if the king's less-
than-average mind *had* been capable of refinement, his education would
not have been as neglected as it was. Some qualities are given as acquired,
and at the same time inherited:

> Ce fut dans cet important et brillant tourbillon où le Roi se jeta d'abord, et où il *prit* cet air de politesse et de galanterie qu'il a toujours *su* conserver . . . On peut dire qu'il était *fait pour elle.*

Saint-Simon's reader is thus put in the same position as the spectator of a Racinian tragedy in which the most diverse consequences flow "naturally" from a character's circumstances like an example illustrating a mathematical rule: he must follow the unwinding of a clockwork machine, an indeflectible and logical sequence of events. But whilst the dramatist may think up a character and its logical derivates in abstract, Saint-Simon sees basic traits and consequences in concrete historical reality. The psychological feat of the historian is to have found in the multiform material of history precisely that basic feature which simplifies a complex picture into a line drawing, which reduces the disparate to a denominator. His function as historian is to make an order from the impenetrable, confused mass of facts—an order which he then buries and almost destroys by inserting his substantial concrete evidence into the cellular structure of his character-portrayal. That is why a superficial reader can easily arrive at a notion of Saint-Simon's description as disorder. Braunschvig's condensation of the whole enormous portrait of Louis XIV into a few pages (in his *Littérature française étudiée dans les textes*) certainly shows the high degree of organisation, composition, unity, order and clarity in Saint-Simon's work—all he lacks is precisely the historical substance, the concrete material, the unclear and the multiform from which Saint-Simon originally constructed his order. Here the whole enterprise of "littérature française étudiée dans les textes" shows itself to be of questionable utility and reveals its huge ignorance of artistic qualities because, although its approach is based on the "evidence" of "texts" alone, it leaves out all that which the text is evidence of, its imbrication in the whole, its value-content and its perspective within the whole . . .

The deductive form of the portrait is the product of Saint-Simon's organisation of the character, of his massing of individual traits and facts around a basic feature. That is why he uses expressions like *de là* together with a deleted verb (*vint*) to indicate the almost automatic nature of the deduction:

> De là [i.e. Louis's pride] ce désir de gloire qui l'arrachait par intervalles à l'amour; de là cette facilité à Louvois de l'engager en grandes guerres; . . . de là ce goût de revues.

> De là les secrétaires d'Etat et les ministres successivement à quitter le manteau, puis le rabat, après l'habit noir.

For transitions to such formulae, consider the following:

> De ces sources étrangères et pestilentielles lui vint cet orgueil, que . . .; témoin entre autres ces monuments si outrés . . .; et *de cet*

orgueil tout le reste, qui le perdit, dont on vient de voir tant d'effets funestes.

Other expressions having the same effect using *c'est ce qui,* etc.:

C'est ce qui donna tant d'autorité à ses ministres, par les occasions continuelles qu'ils avaient de l'encenser.

C'est là ce qui le faisait se complaire à faire régner ses ministres sur les plus élevés de ses sujets.

Introduction of new information as if it were "the same":

Ce *même* orgueil, que Louvois sut si bien manier, épuisa le royaume par des guerres et des fortifications innombrables.

Ce fut la *même* jalousie qui écrasa la marine dans un royaume flanqué de deux mers.

These formulae are all intended to work out, release and unfold things that are wrapped up in the basic conception of the character. In Saint-Simon, the character possesses an internal contradiction: Louis XIV is small, but wants to appear big. This produces a baroque dynamic, a pendulum rhythm within the portrait from the smallness that Louis wants to hide to the grandeur which he cannot impose entirely. The parvenu on the royal throne has not in reality "arrived," he has to fight continually to keep his position. The static quality of the portrait is not as absolute as I claimed to begin with; or, rather, the portrait is static, but the subject of portrayal is not: he is at pains throughout to appear other than what he is, and so the portraitist is obliged for his part to adjust the focus throughout and to uncover what lies behind the mask.

The organisation of character as the logical development of a basic feature would make an altogether too comforting image if Saint-Simon had not allowed his own search for truth to penetrate to the inner secret of Louis's being—if he had excluded his evaluation, or rather, his devaluation of his subject, and not devoted his art to the destruction of an idealised image.

CHARACTER-PORTRAYAL AND PANEGYRIC

One might expect a character-portrayal as extensive as this to deal with a model that is worthy of the historian's interest and emulation—after all, why take so long to depict a nullity? The opening sentence of chapter LI thus shocks the reader:

Ce fut un prince à qui on ne peut refuser beaucoup de bien, même de grand, en qui on ne peut méconnaître plus de petit et de mauvais, du quel il n'est pas possible de discerner ce qui était de lui et ce qui était emprunté.

Similarly, two paragraphs later:

> Né avec un esprit au-dessous du médiocre, mais un esprit capable de se former, de se limer, de se raffiner, d'emprunter d'autrui sans imitation et sans gêne, il profitait infiniment d'avoir toute sa vie vécu avec les personnes du monde qui toutes en avaient le plus.

Reflections of this sort occur throughout the portrait, which ends with the following paragraph in the section headed *Le Roi peu regretté:*

> Quel surprenant alliage! De la lumière avec les plus épaisses ténèbres . . . Quelle fin d'un règne si longuement admiré, et jusque dans ses derniers revers si étincelant de grandeur, de générosité, de courage et de force! et quel abîme de faiblesse, de misère, de honte, d'anéantissement, sentie, goûtée, savourée, abhorrée, et toutefois subie dans toute son étendue, et sans en avoir pu élargir ni soulager les liens! O Nabuchodonosor! Qui pourra sonder les jugements de Dieu, et qui osera ne pas s'anéantir en leur présence?

So it is a portrait of a less than mediocre prince, with more shade than light, who though feared and admired at first was not mourned at his end. The personality that Saint-Simon presents does not measure up to the dimensions of the portrait, appropriate to a panegyric or in any case an apologia. The subject turns out to be neither a hero nor a martyr, but just a little man raised *ad absurdum* by History, naked beneath his imperial garb. Though the drawing could not be fuller, its human subject is—empty; it is a lovingly detailed picture of an intellectual nonentity. And Saint-Simon does not lay bare one level after another to lead us progressively towards the inner emptiness of the man, but warns us from the first line on. We experience the unmasking of a "great" historical figure without enthusiasm and without false expectation: Louis XIV is taken up to his final *anéantissement* before God at the moment of death, but his character is reduced to nothing from the start. In Saint-Simon, the feeling for the mysterious "key" to a whole personality is not incompatible with the moral uncovering of the personality's mediocrity. In this pre-Rousseauistic mental world (the chapters on Louis XIV date from 1745), a character does not have to be an original genius to be worthy of a portrait, only the portrait must form "un tout," a closed entity. Saint-Simon's attitude towards his king is basically the same as Philippe de Commynes's towards his monarch: panegyric accompanied by unmasking, praise of his king's worldly glory alongside his moral nothingness before God. There are some striking parallels:

> Ce monarque si altier gémissait dans ses fers, lui qui avait tenu toute l'Europe.

> Est-il donc possible de tenir ung roy, pour le garder plus honnestement, en plus estroicte prison que luy mesmes se tenoit?
> (Commynes, *Mémoires*)

But the dualistic atmosphere of the late Middle Ages in the biography of Louis XI is replaced in the portrait of Louis XIV by the duplicity of the baroque courtier, half pagan and half Christian, convinced both of the power of personality and of its nothingness before God. Saint-Simon, the barometer of court life with aspirations to the status of a latter-day Bossuet, turns the panegyric or funeral oration (the portrait of Louis XIV is entered in the *Mémoires* under the year 1715, and its pretext is the king's death) into the unmasking of a character believed by others to be great. The portrait is not organic, it is not recounted or experienced from the inside of the subject's personality—it is a prejudged, predirected application of moral categories and impersonal criteria to a personality. In the very first sentence we are told: *bon, grand,* and *petit, mauvais;* and at the end: "Quel surprenant alliage! De la lumière avec les plus épaisses ténèbres!" The portraitist composes the picture from a set of features each carrying its specific consequences, but the character's features are extrapolations from Saint-Simon's general experience of men and life rather than derived from the individual, lived experience of the character of Louis XIV. The necessary basis for this kind of portraiture is coolness and distance between the painter and his model, of the sort made possible only by observation at short range, which was Saint-Simon's customary method and which he liked to invoke, as in the following:

> Après avoir exposé avec la vérité et la fidélité la plus exacte tout ce qui est venu à ma connaissance par moi-même, ou par ceux qui ont vu et manié les choses et les affaires pendant les vingt-deux dernières années de Louis XIV, et l'avoir montré tel qu'il a été, sans aucune passion.

Nothing could be less appropriate to such a style of portraiture than the image of the tree of life (paradoxically, so near to the metaphor of the "écorce extérieure de la vie de ce monarque")—there is no sense of the sap running through the personality of the king; on the contrary, the "good" branches and the "bad" are neatly sawn off in advance. Panegyric and unmasking *alternate* in the portrait, producing abrupt transitions between praise and criticism, even in the chapter résumés:

> *Vertus de Louis XIV; sa misérable éducation; sa profonde ignorance.* (chap. LI)

> *Politique du plus grand luxe; son mauvais goût.* (chap. LIV)

> *Malheurs des dernières années du Roi; le rendent plus dur et non moins dupe.* (chap. LVIII)

A particularly remarkable feature is the way praise is rendered hollow, as unmasking follows on the heels of a laudatory phrase—the opening sentence of the portrait quoted above being a good example. It leads up to "good" and "great" then falls without transition to "more that was small and bad" before concluding with the impossibility of distinguishing in Louis XIV what was his own from what was borrowed: not only is the king diminished, but he is deprived of all individuality. Another example:

> [A maxim of the king's] ce fut de gouverner par lui-même, qui fut la chose dont il se piqua le plus, dont on le loua et le flatta davantage, et qu'il exécuta le moins.

The sentence leads us to a climax (*dont il se piqua le plus*) which is then taken beyond its plausible limits (people praised the king for his personal government more than he even praised himself) and then plunges directly into a negative superlative (*qu'il exécuta le moins*). A similar trick:

> Il voulait régner par lui-même; sa jalousie là-dessus alla sans cesse jusqu'à la faiblesse. Il régna en effet dans le petit; dans le grand il ne put y atteindre et jusque dans le petit il fut gouverné.

By sleight of hand strength is turned to weakness, the strong king is made into a weak and trifling man.

Saint-Simon uses a whole variety of stylistic devices to undermine the character of Louis XIV. Perhaps the most perfidious type of transition from positive to negative is the (frequent) use of *Heureux si* + conditional clause, which raises a possibility only to withdraw it beyond reach, e.g. the king is said to be created for love:

> Heureux s'il n'eût eu que des maîtresses semblables à Mme de la Vallière . . .

but of course we know that he had other less reliable mistresses, and the beatification (*Heureux!*) turns into an anathema (other examples of the same device, "heureux s'il n'eût survécu" and "Heureux si, en adorant la main").

Another type of undermining involves the use of negative exclusive expressions:

> Jamais *personne* ne donna de meilleure grâce et n'augmenta tant par là le prix de ses bienfaits; jamais *personne* ne vendit mieux ses paroles, son souris même, jusqu'à ses regards.

Louis XIV is unequalled, but in the overpricing of his gifts and favours.

> Jamais *il ne lui échappa* de dire rien de désobligeant à personne, et, s'il avait à reprendre, à réprimander ou à corriger, ce qui était fort rare, c'était toujours avec un air plus ou moins de bonté, presque jamais avec sécheresse, jamais avec colère, si on excepte l'unique aventure de Courtenvaux . . . quoiqu'il ne fût pas exempt de colère, quelquefois avec un air de sévérité.

In this example, the irreproachably impassible and idealised façade of Louis XIV is loosened up by obvious modulators (*presque* jamais, *quelquefois* avec un air), by intensifiers that are actually delimiters (*fort rare*), by sliding scales (*plus ou moins* de bonté), by exceptions (*si on excepte*) and through concessive clauses which destroy what the main clause establishes (*quoiqu'*), letting in through the back what the front door shuts out.

In the next example, Saint-Simon gives the lie to Louis's "natural" courtesy by stressing the calculated graduation of the king's expressions of politeness:

> Jamais homme si naturellement poli, ni d'une politesse si fort me-
> surée, si fort par degrés, ni qui distinguât mieux l'âge, le mérite,
> le rang . . . Ces étages divers se marquaient exactement dans sa
> manière de saluer et de recevoir les révérences.

Note the colloquial, spoken-language register of this type of *jamais . . .* , which is quite common in Saint-Simon, e.g. "Ce dernier talent, il le poussa souvent jusqu'à la fausseté, mais avec cela *jamais de mensonge.*"

In the next example, Saint-Simon moves from praise to criticism without transition:

> Il aima en tout la splendeur, la magnificence, la profusion. Ce goût
> il le tourna en maxime par politique, et l'inspira en tout à sa cour
> . . . Il y trouvait encore la satisfaction de son orgueil par une cour
> superbe en tout, et par une plus grande confusion qui anéantissait
> de plus en plus les distinctions naturelles. C'est une plaie qui, une
> fois introduite, est devenue le cancer qui ronge tous les particuliers.

The uses of *Il* and *en tout* in this passage call for some remarks. The repetition of anaphoric subject pronouns is sometimes very extensive in Saint-Simon. . . . There is a similar constant repetition of *on*. In La Bruyère pronominal repetition of this sort is used to represent the "fâcheux," the "importun," irritatingly cropping up where he is not needed. In Saint-Simon it is more designed to portray the monotonous unity of the character of Louis XIV. As for *tout*, it has here a specific *panegyric* usage, perhaps deriving from religious discourse, depicting a generalised completeness, in contrast to its use as a precise quantifier appropriate to a factual description. Contrast for example

> [une galanterie] toujours majestueuse . . . et jamais devant le
> monde rien de déplacé, mais jusqu'au moindre geste, son marcher,
> son port, *toute* sa contenance, *tout* mesuré, *tout* décent, noble,
> grand, majestueux.

With the material restriction on *toujours* in the following:

> ses réponses en ces occasions étaient *toujours* courtes, justes,
> pleines, et *très rarement* sans quelque chose d'obligeant, *quelquefois*
> même de flatteur.

Saint-Simon's style is no different in the portrait of Mme de Maintenon. . . . Positive terms alternate, without transitions, with negative ones. She is "une femme de beaucoup d'esprit," "que la galanterie avait *achevé* de tourner au plus agréable." But in the very next sentence she has become "flatteuse, insinuante, complaisante, cherchant toujours à plaire." She possesses "une grâce incomparable à tout," "un air d'aisance," "un langage doux, juste, en bons termes," but her principal characteristic is "la dévotion" with which "la droiture et la franchise" are said to be incompatible. And so on: each quality is doubled and negated by a fault. There is perhaps no more perfidious style of description possible. An artist (I mean a real painter) presents us with an image that we perceive in a single moment; his picture allows us to see the advantages and drawbacks of a human being in a single sweep. But the writer, working with words that run on in a sequence in time, can parade advantages and drawbacks one after the other in the order that suits him or seems most appropriate—to fool the reader or to take him by surprise. In Saint-Simon, the venom of his character-portrayal creeps up behind the rosy embellishments of his introductory remarks. In the description of Mme de Maintenon we see first the wonderful *salon* lady, the virtuoso of sociability rising to her perfection ("d'abord avait été soufferte"—"achevé de tourner au plus agréable"), and then her drawbacks—duplicity and intrigue. Her intriguing was sometimes only an appearance, and sometimes she used it to work for other people, but she is nonetheless a schemer through and through, and her accomplishment can provide an aesthetic by-product (words like *les adresses* are charged even in this context with a positive value). Considered from the outside alone, the scheming lady of salon life stands before us as a picture of grace and tact, her low social origins (*sa longue bassesse*) quite imperceptible.

Saint-Simon's editor makes the critical point that "le précieux et le guindé" in Mme de Maintenon cannot be reconciled with her "grâce incomparable," her "langage juste, en bons termes et naturellement éloquent et court" and her "air d'aisance" (Boislisle). Now it is often unclear whether *air* should be understood as "a touch of" or as "adopted pose," whether in fact Saint-Simon means a real atmosphere or a hypocritical attitude when he uses this term. But this indecision between truth and fiction belongs essentially to the very *air* and atmosphere of *précieux* society, where the appearance of an atmosphere merges with the atmosphere itself in a social life treated as representation. The contradiction pointed out by Boislisle, though, is but one of several in a portrait built on contradictions, on the continuous countermanding of one character-trait by another. We are made to observe the development of Mme de Maintenon's "style guindé" and manneredness from something that simply hides her low origins into bigotry, into an assumed second identity which destroys all the rest of her being (*tout le reste y fut sacrifié sans réserve*). The verdict of falseness is mitigated, to be sure—she was perhaps not born false, but had falseness thrust upon her; she was perhaps more frivolous than false—but frivolity is the unmistakable, ineradicable trace of the low-born soul without a tradition to uphold, that has small thoughts and narrow feelings: Mme de Maintenon remains Mme Scarron and that is the import of the attack from which the scornful aristocrat, Saint-Simon *duc* and *pair*, cannot get away. The apparent rise of Mme de Maintenon was mere fiction. In reality she remained *abjecte, basse* and therefore *dangereuse*. All the panegyric and superlative expressions (*au plus agréable, incomparable, merveilleusement*, etc.) wither away at the final unmasking. Once again, Saint-Simon wraps the history of a life in the stillness of a portrait (external rise, internal fall or rather inconstancy of the king's favourite), but he also wraps in his motionless representation the inner dialectic of the character, which falls apart before the reader's eyes and displays its contradictions. The poles of this dialectic—Mme de Maintenon's *bourgeois* nature, and her *savoir-vivre* and position in life—conduct an underground battle in Saint-Simon's portrait, and the writer succeeds in showing in the end the bestially dangerous nature of putting a small personality in a position of greatness, just as he had shown in the ungreatness of Louis "the great" a disharmony of Being and destiny between which no synthesis could be sought or found. Never before had anyone depicted with such penetrating and profound vision or with such gruesome factuality the *petit-bourgeois* on the throne of power, exercising his majesty with all his *bourgeois* cravings and resentments, with false grandeur and real pettiness. What tragic desperation must have possessed Saint-Simon to make him show his king so hemmed in, so tightly hemmed in by his pettiness without any possibility of escape or transcendence—occupied solely with outer appearances, with the will to the appearance of grandeur in all the smallness of his being—hemmed in by the fate of seeking to be a big man whilst being small!

What is uncanny in these portraits is that Saint-Simon does not proceed in a straight line, so to speak, towards the revelation of his characters, but that he allows his moral destruction and intellectual judgment to break out from under expressions of admiration and praise: an uncanny juxtaposition, an amazing proximity of panegyric and character-revelation. "Il faut donc avouer [in respect of Louis XIV's gifts] que le Roi fut plus à plaindre que blâmable de se livrer à l'amour, et qu'il *mérite louange* d'avoir su s'en arracher par intervalles en faveur de la gloire"—praise for the king because he was able to tear himself away from love "from time to time"! Saint-Simon's praise is stranger and more uncanny than his blame. We cannot imagine how esteem can pass so abruptly into scorn. Nowadays, and especially for those who consider the mystical unity of the writer and his subject an absolute necessity for the artistic representation of a personality, there is something hardly thinkable about Saint-Simon's attitude. He seems as an observer of men to be quite monstrous, capable of sincere deference whilst gazing into the abyss; his perceptiveness comes from hatred, and yet he always seems to be just.

If one looks more closely at the values which Saint-Simon enters on the credit side of Louis's account, one finds (with the exception of the recognition of the king's religious behaviour on his death-bed) almost uniquely worldly, social values which constitute the personality's façade—and for us, who take purely human values much more seriously, the moral balance dips far deeper into the red than it would have done for the contemporaries of the *roi-soleil* and the age of rococo, more convinced as they were of the positive value of the sociable. Sociability, with its art of living on the edge of an abyss without showing it, with its ability to conceal the most hostile emotions behind a smooth outward surface, can lead to its own kind of gruesome horror, as Péguy discovered in his "gentle" Racine. In the portrait of Louis XIV the panegyric passages (*jamais . . .*) generally refer only to the king's outer attitudes—individual traits which in other people we would interpret as movements of the heart are in Louis XIV merely external attitudes taken up, out of calculation and the mentality of a ruler, in order to maintain decorum—like his taste for making gifts, or his love of splendour. The "vertus de Louis XIV" are public, his failings are private. Versailles represents for Saint-Simon a tyranny over nature: "la violence qui a été faite partout à la nature repousse et dégoûte malgré soi"; "de ce tout il résulte qu'on admire et qu'on fuit." Similarly, he examines Louis's character in terms of its naturalness. The character is aligned between the two poles of art and nature, and beneath the superficial artistry of the façade the truth of nature can be seen only through the few chinks that remain. Saint-Simon's involved manner of expression corresponds to the scant allowance made for a nature that cannot be seen at first glance. The observer is *per*-spic-ax, he "sees through it," he looks behind the disguises, masks and façades of his figures whose extension reaches down not into depths of feeling but into further concealment. Saint-Simon has a constant sense of the puzzle in personality; even in death the king's personality offers a puzzle: "Est-ce artifice? Est-ce tromperie? Est-ce dérision jusqu'en mourant? Quelle énigme à expliquer?" And he solves the enigma. His psychological glance must delve deep into the personality but in a rational and detective manner; Saint-Simon does not want to delve into recreated emotional "depth," but to show the monarch "as he really was"—"représenter ce monarque tel qu'il a véritablement été."

That is how Saint-Simon gets to those climax-like amplifications that occur when a failure is pointed out: the reader sees the surgeon's knife cutting into the wound, as in the portrait of Mme de Maintenon discussed above, that embroils us more and more deeply in her duplicity, or in these words on Louis XIV:

Ses ministres, ses généraux, ses maîtresses, ses courtisans s'aperçurent, bientôt après qu'il fut le maître, de *son faible plutôt que de son goût pour la gloire*. Ils le louèrent à l'envi et le gâtèrent. *Les louanges, disons mieux la flatterie*, lui plaisait à tel point, que *les plus*

> *grossières étaient bien reçues, les plus basses encore mieux savourées.* Ce n'était que par là qu'on s'approchait de lui . . . *La souplesse, la bassesse, l'air admirant, dépendant, rampant,* plus que tout l'air de néant sinon par lui, étaient les uniques voies de lui plaire.

Listings with climactic effects such as these are very typical of Saint-Simon's style. In the course of writing (or, more to the point, of talking) he gets into his subject, gets more excited and finds better and better descriptive terms. His text is not a finished written object, but we can see it "writing itself" before our eyes. In the following sentence Saint-Simon's rage at Louvois is aroused by the word *adresse*, which then unleashes the multiple list that follows:

> Tel fut l'aveuglement du Roi, telle fut l'*adresse*, la *hardiesse*, la *formidable autorité* d'un ministre.

In the following description of Louis's increasing powerlessness, there is a progressive, step-by-step movement towards the abyss, a drive towards self-destruction, a leap into the dark:

> . . . Une conviction entière de son injustice et de son impuissance, témoignée de sa bouche, *c'est trop peu dire*, décochée par ses propos à ses bâtards, et toutefois un abandon à eux et à leur gouvernante, devenue la sienne et celle de l'Etat, et *abandon si entier* qu'il ne lui permit pas de s'écarter d'un seul point de toutes leurs volontés; qui, presque content de s'être défendu en leur faisant sentir ses doutes et ses répugnances, leur immola tout, son Etat, sa famille, son unique rejeton, sa gloire, son honneur, sa raison, enfin sa personne, sa volonté, sa liberté, et *tout cela dans leur totalité entière*, sacrifice digne par son universalité d'être offert à Dieu seul, si par soi-même il n'eût pas été abominable.

In other places this attraction of *le néant* (revealing itself in this quotation in Louis's policy of levelling out differences of birth) is made apparent and palpable through the rhythm of the sentence structures:

> Mais cette dignité, il ne la voulait que pour lui, et que par rapport à lui; et celle-là, *même* relative, il la sapa presque toute pour mieux achever de ruiner toute autre et de la mettre, peu à peu, comme il fit, à l'unisson, en retranchant tant qu'il put toutes les cérémonies et les distinctions, dont il ne retint que l'ombre, et certaines trop marquées pour les détruire, en semant *même* dans celles-là des zizanies.

The two *même* point up stages in the downward movement, just as in the passage beginning "Piqué de n'oser égaler la nature" the stages are marked by *enfin, après, enfin* and reach a kind of inverted climax in *Ce ne fut pas tout. . . .*

Like Proust, Saint-Simon worked over his sentences and made secondary insertions in order to give a more appropriate and concrete form to Louis's "attraction towards the abyss." For example:

First draft (from the "Addition au *Journal* de Dangeau")	Final draft
Saint-Germain, lieu unique pour rassembler les merveilles de la vue, l'immense plain-pied d'une forêt unique par sa situation et sa beauté, l'avantage et la facilité des eaux, les agréments des hauteurs et des terrasses et les charmes de la Seine, il l'abandonna pour Versailles, le plus ingrat de tous les lieux, sans bois, sans eaux, sans terre (presque tout y est sable mouvant ou marécage), sans air par conséquent, qui n'y peut être bon. Boislisle	Saint-Germain, lieu unique pour rassembler les merveilles de la vue, l'immense plain-pied d'une forêt toute joignante, unique encore par la beauté de ses arbres, de son terrain, de sa situation, l'avantage et la facilité des eaux de source sur cette élévation, les agréments admirables des jardins, des hauteurs et des terrasses, qui les unes sur les autres se pouvaient si aisément conduire dans toute l'étendue qu'on aurait voulu, les charmes et les commodités de la Seine, enfin une ville toute faite, et que sa position entretenait par elle-même, il l'abandonna pour Versailles, le plus triste et le plus ingrat de tous les lieux, sans vue, sans bois, sans eau, sans terre, parce que tout y est sable mouvant ou marécage, sans air par conséquent, qui n'y peut être bon.

The move from Saint-Germain to Versailles, symbolic of the decline of France under Louis XIV, is made more drastic in the second draft by insertions which magnify the positive traits of Saint-Germain. Significantly, there is more strengthening of the positive aspects of Saint-Germain than of the negative ones of Versailles: the fall from the greatest height is adequately described by the depiction of the height itself (*enfin une ville toute faite*). And of course the rhythm of the sentence helps to make this clear. The description of Saint-Germain is ample, harmonious and linear; but Versailles is given in broken, mostly monosyllabic, polemical disorder.

Another point of stylistic interest is Saint-Simon's incorporation into his portraits of the speech and arguments of the subject of the portrait. Mme de Montespan's complaining about Mme de Maintenon is clearly *audible* in expressions like "une rivale abjecte," "une rivale si au-dessous," "cette suivante, pour ne pas dire servante" and so forth. The consuming cancer of Mme de Maintenon portrays itself through language and style, and Saint-Simon uses this image of a cancer explicitly to describe the king's love of splendour:

> C'est *une plaie* qui, une fois introduit, est devenue le *cancer* qui ronge tous les particuliers—parce que de la cour il s'est promptement communiqué à Paris et dans les provinces et les armées, où les gens en quelque place ne sont comptés qu'à proportion de leur table et de leur magnificence depuis cette malheureuse introduction—qui *ronge* tous les particuliers, qui force ceux d'un état à pouvoir voler à ne s'y épargner pour la plupart, dans la nécessité de soutenir leur dépense; et que la confusion des états, que l'orgueil, que jusqu'à la bienséance entretiennent, qui par la folie du gros va toujours en augmentant, dont les suites sont infinies, ne vont à rien moins qu'à la ruine et au renversement général.

This long sentence is itself an image of the progression of a cancer. It strides from the *particuliers* to the *général*, sketching in individual conditions (*états*) and temperaments; it is bloated by a parenthesis and bursts into a flood of different currents which swirl around the reader, drawing his glance towards the infinite and leading him finally "à la ruine et au renversement général."

It can now be understood how important the great black *background of Nothingness* was for Saint-Simon's type of portrait. The background puts all earthly grandeur beneath God: one simply does not know, at the end of Saint-Simon's work, whether Louis's dying submission to God is hypocrisy or true recognition. The correct unmasking of a man finally brings about only the revelation of God. It is He who crushes the great of this world and takes away the value of all appearances. The crowning of God—of whom no double portrait is possible and who recognises the vanity of pride—cannot in the end be left out of Saint-Simon's natural hierarchy; and it cannot be other than the rejection of a Caesar aspiring to divinity, his relegation to nothingness.

In Saint-Simon, "nothingness" (*le néant*) is both a social and a metaphysical-religious concept, since low birth is in his view of the world divinely ordained. He likes to scale the ladder from the bottom of the abyss to the summit of glory in a kind of baroque dynamic:

> On a vu . . . les divers degrés par lesquels les enfants du roi et de Mme de Montespan ont été successivement tirés du *profond et ténébreux néant* du double adultère, et portés plus qu'au juste et parfait *niveau* des princes du sang, et jusqu'au *sommet* de l'habilité de succéder à la couronne.

Louis XIV's presumption, vanity and *hubris* that take him near to rivalling God are stressed many times by Saint-Simon. Louis's upbringing is said to be responsible for "cet *orgueil*, que ce n'est point trop dire que, sans la crainte du Diable . . . il se serait fait adorer." His *orgueil* led him to become not only a "distributeur de couronnes, . . . châtieur de nations, . . . conquérant" but also "cet homme *immortel* pour qui on épuisait le marbre et le bronze, pour qui tout était à bout d'encens." Mme de Maintenon is part of God's design to bring *"au plus superbe des rois l'humiliation la plus profonde,"* and only the miracle of Louis's repentance (the realisation of his own nothingness) saves France from the complete *anéantissement* which the king's pride would have brought.

We are released from the Janus-like two-facedness of the portrait of a mortal man by contemplation of the heavenly Singular that wears no mask. Just as Molière's Tartuffe, rising to threaten the social order, requires the king as his counterpart and as the restorer of justice, so Saint-Simon's king, breaking into the realm of God, requires God as a *deus ex machina*. Or perhaps God is for Saint-Simon not *ex machina* but *ex natura*—the natural hierarchy of true values requiring, for him, a divine pinnacle.

PICTURE AND DEPICTION

From what was said in the first part of this essay it should be clear that Saint-Simon could not reproduce through language the flow of history. Again and again the mass of historical events coagulates—so to speak—into clots, clearly cut off from each other and each producing a separate picture. Or to put it another way: Saint-Simon leads us constantly to individual summits, gloriettes and watchtowers which afford a complete panorama. We are constantly reminded by this structure of the gardens of Versailles, ruled by man, by a landscape gardener. Representation in Saint-Simon is constantly rounded off into a medallion—historical representation is resolved into a series of medallions. So we get sections of Louis XIV's life all having precisely the same "circular" syntactic form. Everywhere in Saint-Simon we find sentences which present us with a totality: the author repeatedly reconstructs the character before our eyes, laying out in all the appositions and qualifications its whole content and extent, and competing in the *sequential* art of writing with the art of *juxtaposition*, the art of painting:

> Dans ces derniers temps, abattu sous le poids d'une guerre fatale, soulagé de personne par l'incapacité de ses ministres et de ses généraux, en proie tout entier à un obscur et artificieux domestique, pénétré de douleur, non de ses fautes, qu'il ne connaissait ni ne voulait connaître, mais de son impuissance contre toute l'Europe réunie contre lui, réduit aux plus tristes extrémités pour ses finances et ses frontières, il n'eut de ressources qu'à se reployer sur lui-même, et à appesantir sur sa famille, sur sa cour, sur les consciences, sur tout son malheureux royaume cette dure domination.

The attempt to achieve a total, static, rounded portrait within a single period leads Saint-Simon to use *anacoluthon* to an extent which (according to e.g.

Boislisle) is grammatically incorrect. For example, the sentence beginning "Déchiré au dedans par les catastrophes" goes on its second "leg" with "incapable d'ailleurs" and finally finds its grammatical subject with "cette constance, cette fermeté d'âme . . . c'est ce dont peu d'hommes auraient été capables." The following sentence, similarly, begins "La grandeur d'âme que montra constamment," but *ce roi*, the logical subject of the subordinate clause *que montra*, turns out to be the grammatical subject of the main verb "se vit enfin abandonné." In Racine, on the other hand, the complete subjectivisation of moral value-concepts does not allow anacoluthon, because the abstract forces are the real actors. Saint-Simon sees concrete figures, however, and moralises upon them, and this split vision has its grammatical expression in anacoluthon.

In one of the first "medallions" in the text Saint-Simon's fascination with his subject comes across clearly:

> Roi presque en naissant, étouffé par la politique d'une mère qui voulait gouverner, plus encore par le vif intérêt d'un pernicieux ministre, qui hasarda mille fois l'Etat pour son unique grandeur, et asservi sous ce joug tant que vécut ce premier ministre, c'est autant de retranché sur le règne de ce monarque.

It is as if he could not stop looking at this "almost great" small man "born to greatness," as if he were in thrall to the phenomenon of Louis XIV, as if the whole enormous portrait of the king owed its composition to Saint-Simon's bewitched resentment of the regal image.

This allows us to understand the *redites*, the repetitions that are so frequent, and frequently excused (*comme on le verra ailleurs*—*comme on l'a déjà vu*), in Saint-Simon. At every point in the *Mémoires* he wants to conjure up the figure of Louis in his historical totality, and the temporal flow slows and spreads as a river spreads when dammed. The author asks his audience not to take offence "s'ils s'y en trouve des redites, nécessaires pour mieux rassembler et former un tout"—an effort towards gathering in the total personality; he explains the *redites* by his striving to "expliquer assez en détail des curiosités que nous regrettons dans toutes les Histoires et dans presque tous les Mémoires des divers temps"—the anecdotal in the service of characterisation.

Saint-Simon's sentence structures are, in their breadth, roundedness and powerful self-enclosure, naturally destined to isolate historical medallions out of the flow of time. It is as if such "medallion-sentences" simply spring from Saint-Simon's pen as he writes: for example, when he talks of Louis's youth and young loves and opines that the king should have counted himself lucky if he had only had mistresses like Mme de Lavallière, a medallion of the lady follows quite automatically, as the grammatical attribute of the name Lavallière:

> Heureux s'il n'eût eu que des maîtresses semblables à Mme de la Vallière, arrachée à elle-même par ses propres yeux, honteuse de

l'être, encore plus des fruits de son amour, reconnus et élevés malgré elle, modeste, désinteressée, douce, bonne au dernier point, combattant sans cesse contre elle-même, victorieuse enfin de son désordre par les plus cruels effets de l'amour et de la jalousie, qui furent tout à la fois son tourment et sa ressource, qu'elle sut embrasser assez au milieu de ses douleurs pour s'arracher enfin, et se consacrer à la plus dure et la plus sainte pénitence!

The whole history of this woman's existence, from mistress to repentant sinner, is compressed into a portrait having the dimensions of a medallion.

One constantly comes across sentences which, although spoken about a specific situation, give the picture of the entire personality—as if Saint-Simon did not wish us to lose sight of the whole structure in any individual detail. On Louvois, for example, we get the following expansion:

Tel fut l'aveuglement du Roi, tel fut l'adresse, la hardiesse, la formidable autorité d'un ministre, le plus éminent pour les projets et pour les exécutions, mais le plus funeste pour diriger en premier; qui, sans être premier ministre, abattit tous les autres, sut mener le Roi où et comme il voulut, et devint en effet le maître.

The closed, atemporal implication of this sort of "compressed" portrait is in some sense in opposition to the flow of history, and so the next sentences come as a great surprise: "Il eut la joie de survivre à Colbert et à Seignalay, ses ennemis et longtemps ses rivaux. Elle fut de courte durée." The picture of lasting power is actually destroyed by that last short sentence, the effect of the portrait somehow suspended. Those then are the unresolved antimonies between picture and depiction in Saint-Simon.

Now we can see that Saint-Simon must constantly reach back to his beginning and use that style of repeated recapitulation so characteristic of Old French epic. A feeling that he has not expressed himself well enough in any single way, an otherwise quite un-French apprehension of stylistic incompleteness, drives him to a curiously repetitive procedure of retouching, of always saying the same thing in different formal variations and multiplications. That is to say, the writer never believes that his text is a finished product and has to stylise it afresh with new devices. Compare the "tirades" beginning with *jamais* in the depiction of the king's character (quoted above) with the *laisse*-like refrains beginning with *telles* . . . that represent Louis's last years:

Telles furent les dernières années de ce long règne de Louis XIV.

Telles furent les longues et cruelles circonstances des plus douloureux malheurs qui éprouvèrent la constance du roi.

Or the triple return introduced by *on:*

On a vu avec quelle adresse elle [Mme de Maintenon] se servit de la princesse des Ursins.

On ne répétera ce qu'on a vu pp. 776 . . . sur Godet, évêque de Chartres.

On a vu que Monsieur de Chartres était passionné sulpicien.

Saint-Simon repeatedly gathers his views into linguistic forms which remain unfinished, provisional and impressionistically unsettled. The *recommence-ment* is a linguistic "standing-in-for" that does not advance—Saint-Simon draws little sketches without ever reaching the "definitive" picture.

Let us now look at an extended example where these various techniques come together.

Prince heureux s'il en fût jamais, en figure unique, en force corporelle, en santé égale et ferme, et presque jamais interrompue, en siècle si fécond et si libéral pour lui en tous genres qu'il a pu en ce sens être comparé au siècle d'Auguste; en sujets adorateurs prodiguant leurs biens, leur sang, leurs talents, la plupart jusqu'à leur réputation, quelques-uns même leur honneur, et beaucoup trop leur conscience et leur religion, pour le servir, souvent même seulement pour lui plaire. Heureux surtout en famille, s'il n'en avait eu que de légitime; en mère contente des respects et d'un certain crédit; en frère dont la vie anéantie par de déplorables goûts, et d'ailleurs futile par elle-même, se noyait dans la bagatelle, se contentait d'argent, se retenait par sa propre crainte et par celle de ses favoris, et n'était guères moins bas courtisan que ceux qui voulaient faire leur fortune; une épouse vertueuse, amoureuse de lui, infatigablement patiente, devenue véritablement française, d'ailleurs absolument incapable; un fils unique toute sa vie à la lisière, qui à cinquante ans ne savait encore que gémir sous le poids de la contrainte et du discrédit, qui environné et éclairé de toutes parts, n'osait que ce que lui était permis, et qui, absorbé dans la matière, ne pouvait causer la plus légère inquiétude; en petit-fils dont l'âge et l'exemple du père . . . rassuraient . . . ; un neveu qui . . . tremblait devant lui . . . ; descendant plus bas, des princes du sang de même trempe, à commencer par le grand Condé, devenu la frayeur et la bassesse même . . . ; Monsieur le Prince son fils, le plus vil et le plus prostitué de tous les courtisans; Monsieur le Duc . . . hors de mesure de pouvoir se faire craindre . . . ; des deux princes de Conti . . . l'aîné mort si tôt, l'autre mourant de peur de tout, accablé sous la haine du Roi . . . ; les plus grands seigneurs lassés et ruinés . . . ; leurs successeurs séparés, désunis, livrés à l'ignorance . . . ; des parlements subjugués . . . ; nul corps ensemble, et par laps de temps, presque personne qui osât même à part soi avoir aucun dessein . . . ; enfin jusqu'à

la division des familles les plus proches . . ., l'entière méconnais-
sance des parents et des parentés . . .; peu à peu tous les devoirs
absorbés par un seul que la nécessité fit, qui fut de craindre et de
tâcher à plaire.

This cross-section of the entire state of France comes in a chapter headed
"Bonheur du Roi en tout genre." The "happiness" or rather pseudo-fortune
of the despot consists of the suppression of all forces that might have
threatened his own power. I do not need to mention the irony that illuminates and uncovers this "fortune" of the king in the qualifications and
subordinate clauses—"sujets adorateurs prodiguant . . . leur réputation
. . . leur honneur . . . leur conscience et leur religion"; "une épouse vertueuse . . . d'ailleurs absolument incapable," and so forth. What is of interest here is the gradation of the king's fortune by the echelons of the
kingdom's hierarchy. "Le bonheur du Roi en tout genre" is seen not from
the people's or the state's point of view but from the king's, and it flows
from the leader at the summit down to each lower level. What looks like
Augustan *fortuna* from the top is, seen from below, dissolution of the state,
oppression, and slavery. In this France the dominant view is the one from
above. The syntactic thread holding the passage together is *Heureux en . . .*,
because in this despotic state the decisive factor is the king's good fortune
with respect to this, that or the other. Even the construction *heureux en
famille . . . en mère. . . en frère* etc. on the same level as *heureux en santé* is
rather "regicentric" (if I may coin the term by analogy with "egocentric").
The physical good fortune of the king communicates itself to his whole
sphere of influence, and his family, his court and his entire state naturally
belong to that sphere. Saint-Simon could have found no better way of
depicting the debilitation of the body politic by the all-consuming power
of tyranny than this little preposition *en* that connects everything—men
and things—to the total fortune of the highest-born like items to be added
up in a column of figures. It is absolutely clear that Saint-Simon's conception
of character as a static entity, of history as the effect of character, together
with his belief in a natural order, could not but produce this sort of hierarchically graduated cross-section. What he shows in any case is the undermining of the old order by Louis XIV, burrowing and working through
the echelons and divisions created by the old order. The developments
brought about by the king's reign are given in passive past participles, as
faits accomplis: "les plus grands seigneurs *lassés* . . . leurs successeurs *séparés*
. . . des parlements *subjugués*," or in durative imperfects: "en frère dont la
vie . . . se noyait dans la bagatelle . . .; un fils . . . qui à cinquante ans ne
savait que gémir." It is the stasis of an Augustan age, but we had been
warned against it in the short, sharp sentence preceding: "La décadence
est arrivée à grands pas."

The picture of "the king's good fortune" stands as a pendant or balance
to the picture of the people's relief at the king's death given at the end of
the volume ("*Le Roi peu regretté*"). Here is the main skeleton of the sentence:

Louis ne fut regretté que de ses valets intérieurs, de peu d'autres gens, et des chefs de l'affaire de la Constitution. Son successeur n'en était pas en âge; Madame n'avait pour lui que de la crainte et de la bienséance; Mme la duchesse de Berry ne l'aimait pas, et comptait aller régner; M. le duc d'Orléans n'était pas payé pour le pleurer, et ceux qui l'étaient [= les bâtards] n'en firent pas leur charge. Mme de Maintenon était excédée du Roi depuis la perte de la Dauphine; . . . ainsi quoiqu'elle perdît en perdant le Roi, elle se sentit délivrée, et ne fut capable que de ce sentiment. . . . On a vu jusqu'à quelle joie, à quelle barbare indécence le prochain point de vue de la toute puissance jeta le duc du Maine. La tranquillité glacée de son frère ne s'en haussa ni baissa. Madame la Duchesse . . . n'avait plus besoin de l'appui du Roi . . . elle se trouva donc fort à son aise et en liberté. . . . Mme la duchesse d'Orléans . . . [cried and spent a few days in bed]. Pour les princes du sang, c'étaient des enfants. La duchesse de Ventadour et le maréchal de Villeroy donnèrent un peu la comédie, pas un autre n'en prit même la peine. Mais quelques vieux et plats courtisans . . . regrettèrent de n'avoir plus à se cuider . . . dans les raisonnements et l'amusement journalier d'une cour qui s'éteignait avec le Roi. Tout ce qui la composait était de deux sortes: les uns, en espérance de figurer, de se mêler, de s'introduire étaient ravis de voir finir un règne sous lequel il n'y avait rien pour eux à attendre; les autres, fatigués d'un joug pesant, toujours accablant . . . étaient charmés de se trouver au large; tous, en général, d'être délivrés d'une gêne continuelle, et amoureux des nouveautés. Paris, las d'une dépendance qui avait tout assujetti, respira dans l'espoir de quelque liberté, et dans la joie de voir finir l'autorité, de tant de gens qui en abusaient. Les provinces, au désespoir de leur ruine et de leur anéantissement, respirèrent et tressaillirent de joie, et les parlements et toute espèce de judicature anéantie par les édits et les évocations, . . . se flatta, les premiers de figurer, les autres de se trouver affranchis. Le peuple, ruiné, accablé, désespéré, rendit grâces à Dieu, avec un éclat scandaleux, d'une délivrance dont ses plus ardents désirs ne doutaient plus. Les étrangers, ravis d'être enfin . . . défaits d'un monarque qui leur avait si longuement imposé la loi . . . , se continrent avec plus de bienséance que les Français. . . . Pour nos ministres et les intendants des provinces, les financiers, et ce qu'on peut appeler la canaille, ceux-là sentirent toute l'étendue de leur perte.

That is truly a picture of the afterlife of a man who ruled over so many that it can be summed up in the phrase *omnis moriar*. It is a negative picture of fame, the inverse of a Renaissance *gloria*, graduated just as in some large historical group portrait with all the individual figures and forces in adoration of the Sun-king—but here they are doing something different from adoring! They approach with empty hands and without bending the knee. As in a large historical painting the individual figures are subtly distinguished from each other and it is Saint-Simon's virtuosity to indicate the specific attitude—and in this case of obligatory mourning, the specific pose—of each one, and finally to bring together a whole range of psychological attitudes into a single collective stance, that of "little regret." We saw earlier how the separate traits of the monarch's character composed a unity; here, in the same sense, the individual attitudes of the men destined to carry the king's "glory" further, compose a collective stance of rejection. Frozen as in the manner of a historical painting, this *historical* moment is grasped as a *static* one in which the pressure of the situation (or, rather, the removal of pressure on the king's underlings after his death) calls forth the true, underlying attitude and stance of the subject. It is an unmasking scene on a grand scale. Though Saint-Simon imposed the question of authenticity and falseness on his material elsewhere, here history itself offers him the opportunity to report in these terms the truth about the mood of the whole country. The dynamic which Saint-Simon had to work into an otherwise static portrait is in this instance something that was quite perceptible in history. Therefore Saint-Simon is fond of depicting such "revealing events" or moments of truth in all their multiple effects, and likes these snapshots of a whole historical moment (another example is the death of the Dauphin). And he surely enjoys the firm order in which the entire people of France in its social ranks expresses its opinion. Rather like some medieval dramatist, whose figures are restricted to their *mansions* on stage, and speak from their indicated places only, so the latter-day champion of medieval social ranks has the court, the *états* and the people take up a stance on Louis XIV's death "from their indicated places"; and the towering importance of Louis in his own lifetime, out of all proportion to his merits, is utterly flattened by his death, for his passing is regretted only by *la canaille!*

The conception of national attitude as a single block, cut like a stone into multiple facets of different kinds in the hierarchically ordered individual figures of history, is the psychological principle of order which Saint-Simon shares with Molière and Racine—the difference being of course that the historical portrait possesses the concrete fullness and breadth of frame that the playwrights neither have nor wish to have. That means that what destroys the king is finally the *people's judgment*, the judgment of the people that can only be hinted at as latent forces behind or beside the stage in classical drama. So Saint-Simon, champion of the medieval orders, is more modern than he knew; amazingly, for such a deep-dyed aristocrat, the spirit of what is spoken from the separate *mansions* of his stage is an egalitarian one. Freed from surveillance and fetters, France can now contemplate its past dispassionately, but also with a degree of cruelty towards itself, and formulate a bleak and cutting judgment. First, the view of the cold and calculating court: "Madame n'avait pour lui que de la crainte et de la bienséance; Mme la duchesse de Berry ne l'aimait pas et comptait aller régner." The further we descend towards the social depths, the more genuine, passionate, pathetic and insubordinate is the tone: the courtiers are merely "fatigués d'un joug pesant" or "amoureux des nouveautés," but Paris is "las d'une dépendance," the provinces are "au désespoir," the courts of justice feel "anéantie" and the people are "ruiné, accablé, déses-péré." In each *mansion* of the stage set there is a specific and particular shade of feeling; each of the represented personalities displays its "emo-tional" attitude, so to speak. An order rules over the complete insubor-dination of all concerned with the levelling and destruction of Louis XIV, for which they finally thank God "avec un éclat scandaleux." This is some kind of panopticon of frozen, upright figures, a "Last Judgment" taking place in this world and with rigid social ranks unchanged!

With his way of seeing and transforming the becoming of history into a set-piece stage and a gallery of medallion-portraits, Saint-Simon is a long way from the historical thought of the eighteenth century and remains much closer to the stable and hierarchical seventeenth century. Saint-Simon corresponds to the baroque counter-reformation of seventeenth-century Spain, whose literature sang of decay, defilement, disappointment and vanity in the most splendid formal beauty. Like the great Spanish portrayers of *desengaño* (disillusionment) he depicts life not as a mixed reality having both its ugliness and its beauty, but rather in an antithetical-polemical way, life as magnificent in its very nothingness. Thus he introduces a movement into the immobility of his edifice—the movement of inner subsidence, the worm in the apple. The impact of his writings is undecidable and ambig-uous, but in any case an intrinsically dynamic one: admiration and aversion together, as I tried to suggest in the epigraph of this essay. One recalls that Boileau saw Corneille's response to the precepts of Aristotle's poetics in the arousal not only of fear and pity but of admiration also (Boileau, *Lettre à Perrault*). Saint-Simon is the antidote to Corneille: his admiration leads without transition to disenchantment.

Montesquieu: Politics and History

Louis Althusser

Montesquieu's . . . method applied to his object is indisputably novel. But a method, even a novel one, may be in vain *if it fails to produce anything new*. What then are Montesquieu's positive discoveries?

"I have first of all considered mankind; and the result of my thoughts has been, that, amidst such an infinite diversity of laws and manners, they were not solely conducted by the caprice of fancy. I have laid down the first principles, and have found that the particular cases apply naturally to them; that the histories of all nations are only consequences of them; and that every particular law is connected with another law, or depends on some other of a more general extent" (SL, preface). (Quotations from the works of Montesquieu have in general been taken from the four-volume translation by Thomas Nugent entitled *The Works of Monsieur de Montesquieu*, published in London in 1777. References to the *Spirit of Laws* give the book number in Roman and the chapter number in Arabic numerals: thus, SL, VIII.9 means *The Spirit of Laws*, Book VIII, chapter 9.) Such is Montesquieu's discovery: not *particular ingenuities* but universal first principles making intelligible the whole of human history and *all its particulars*: "When once I had discovered my first principles, everything I sought for appeared" (ibid.).

What then are the principles which make history intelligible in this way? Once posed, this question raises a number of difficulties which directly involve the *make-up* of the *Spirit of Laws*. Montesquieu's great work, which opens with the pages I have just been discussing, does not indeed have the expected arrangement. First of all, from Book I to Book XIII, it contains a theory of governments and of the different laws that depend

From *Montesquieu, Rousseau, Marx: Politics and History,* translated by Ben Brewster.© 1959 by Presses Universitaires de France, translation © 1972 by NLB.

either on their natures or on their principles: in other words, a *typology*, which appears very abstract, although it is crammed with historical examples, and seems to constitute a whole isolated from the rest, "a complete master-piece within an incomplete master-piece" (J. J. Chevallier). After Book XIII we seem to enter another world. Everything should have been said about the governments, their types being known, but here we have the climate (Books XIV, XV, XVI, XVII), then the quality of the soil (Book XVIII), then manners and morals (Book XIX), and commerce (Books XX, XXI), and money (Book XXII), and population (Book XXIII) and finally religion (Books XXIV, XXV), which each in turn determine the laws whose secret has apparently already been provided. And to cap the confusion, four books of history, one discussing the development of the Roman laws of succession (Book XXVII), three expounding the origins of feudal laws (Books XXVIII, XXX, XXXI), and between them one book on the "manner of composing laws" (Book XXIX). Principles which claim to provide order for history ought at least to put some of it in the treatise which expounds them.

Where indeed are they to be found? The *Spirit of Laws* seems to be made up of three parts added on to one another, like ideas which have come up and that one does not want to lose. Where is the clear unity we expected? Should we seek Montesquieu's "principles" in the first thirteen books, and thus owe him the idea of *a pure typology of the forms of government*, the description of their peculiar dynamic, the deduction of laws as a function of their nature and principle? Suppose we agree. But then all the material about climate and the various factors, then the history, seem interesting certainly, but additional. Are the true principles on the contrary in the *second part*, in the idea that the laws are determined by different factors, some material (climate, soil, population, economy), others moral (manners and morals, religion)? But then what is the concealed argument linking these determinant principles with the first ideal principles and the final historical studies? Any attempt to maintain the whole in an impossible unity, the ideality of the types, the determinism of the material or moral environment, and the history, falls into irresoluble contradictions. Montesquieu could be said to be torn between a mechanistic materialism and a moral idealism, between atemporal structures and a historical genesis, etc. Which is a way of saying that if he did make *certain* discoveries, they are only linked by the disorder of his book, which proves against him that he did not make *the particular* discovery he thought he had made.

I should like to try to combat this impression and reveal between the different "truths" of the *Spirit of Laws* the *chain that links them to other truths* discussed in the Preface.

The first expression of Montesquieu's new principles is to be found in the few lines which distinguish between the *nature* and the *principle* of a government. Each government (republic, monarchy, despotism) has *its* *nature* and *its principle*. Its *nature* is "that by which it is constituted," its *principle* the passion "by which it is made to act" (SL, III.1).

What is to be understood by the *nature* of a government? The *nature* of the government answers the question: *who holds power? how does the holder of power exercise that power?* Thus, the *nature* of republican government implies that the body of the nation (or a part of the nation) has sovereign authority. The *nature* of monarchical government, that one alone governs, but by fixed and established laws. The *nature* of despotism, that one alone governs, but with neither laws nor rules. The retention and mode of exercise of power—all this remains purely legal, and when all is said and done, *formal*.

The *principle* takes us into life. For a government is not a pure form. It is the concrete form of existence of a society of men. For the men subject to a particular type of government to be precisely and lastingly subject to it, the mere imposition of a political form (*nature*) is not enough, they must also have a disposition to that form, a certain way of acting and reacting which will underpin that form. As Montesquieu puts it, there has to be a specific *passion*. Each form of government necessarily desires its own passion. The republic wants virtue, monarchy honour, and despotism fear. The principle of a government is drawn from its form, for it is a "natural" derivation of it. But this consequence is less its *effect* than its *precondition*. Take the example of the republic. The *principle* of the republic, virtue, answers the question: *on what condition can there be a government which gives power to the people and makes it exercise that power by the laws?*—On the condition that the citizens are *virtuous*, i.e. sacrifice themselves to the public good, and, in all circumstances, prefer the fatherland to their own passions. The same for monarchy and despotism. If the *principle* of the government is its *spring, that which makes it act,* that is because it is, as the life of the government, quite simply its condition of existence. The republic will only "go," to coin a phrase, on virtue, just as some motors will only go on petrol. Without virtue the republic will fall, as will monarchy without honour, despotism without fear.

Montesquieu has been accused of formalism because of his way of defining a government by its *nature*, which does indeed consist of a few words of pure constitutional law. But it is forgotten that *the nature of a government is formal for Montesquieu himself, so long as it is separated from its principle*. One should say: in a government a nature without a principle is inconceivable and non-existent. Only the *nature-principle totality* is conceivable, because it is real. And this totality is no longer formal, for it no longer designates a purely juridical form, but a political form engaged in its own life, in its own conditions of existence and survival. Although defined in one word, virtue, honour, fear, these conditions are highly concrete. Like passion in general, the passions may seem abstract, but *as principles they express politically the whole real life of the citizens*. The virtue of the citizen is his entire life devoted to the public good: this passion, dominant in the State, is, in one man, all his passions dominated. With the principle it is the concrete life of men, public and even private, that enters into the government. The *principle* is thus the intersection of the *nature* of the government (its political form) with the real life of men. It is thus *the point and aspect in which the real life of men has to be resumed in order to be inserted into the form of a government.* The principle is the concrete of that abstract, the nature. It is their unity, it is their totality, that is real. Where is the formalism?

This point will be conceded. But it is decisive if we are to grasp the full extent of Montesquieu's *discovery. In this idea of the totality of the nature and the principle of a government, Montesquieu is in fact proposing a new theoretical category,* one which gives him the key to an infinity of riddles. Before him political theorists had certainly tried to explain the multiplicity and diversity of the laws of a given government. But they had done little more than outline a logic of the *nature* of governments, even when they were not, as in most cases, satisfied by a mere description of elements *without any inner unity.* The immense majority of laws, such as those that determine education, division of lands, degree of property, techniques of justice, punishments and rewards, luxury, the condition of women, the conduct of war, etc. (SL, IV–VII), were excluded from this logic, because their *necessity* was not understood. Montesquieu here majestically closes this old debate, by *discovering and verifying in the facts the hypothesis that the State is a real totality and that all the particulars of its legislation, of its institutions and its customs are merely the effect and expression of its inner unity.* He submits these laws, which seem fortuitous and irrational, to a profound logic, and relates them to a single centre. I do not claim that Montesquieu was the first to think that the State should of itself constitute a *totality.* This idea is already lurking in Plato's reflection and we find it again at work in the thought of the theoreticians of natural law, at any rate in Hobbes. But before Montesquieu this idea only entered into the constitution of an *ideal* State, without lowering itself to the point of making *concrete* history intelligible. With Montesquieu, the totality, which was an *idea,* becomes a scientific *hypothesis,* intended to *explain the facts.* It becomes the fundamental category which makes it possible to think, no longer the reality of an ideal state, but the concrete and hitherto unintelligible diversity of the institutions of human history. History is no longer that infinite space in which are haphazardly scattered the innumerable works of caprice and accident, to the discouragement of the understanding, whose only possible conclusion is the insignificance of man and the greatness of God. This space has a structure. *It possesses concrete centres to which are related a whole local horizon of facts and institutions: the States. And at the core of these totalities, which are like living individuals, there is an inner reason, an inner unity, a fundamental primordial centre: the unity of nature and principle.* Hegel, who gave the category of the totality enormous scope well knew his own teacher when he expressed his gratitude for this discovery to Montesquieu's genius.

Here, however, formalism is still lying in wait for us. For it may well be that this category of the totality constituted the unity of the first books of the *Spirit of Laws.* But it may be said that it is restricted to them, and that it is marked by the error of these first books: that it concerns *pure models*, a truly republican republic, a truly monarchical monarchy and a truly despotic despotism only. In "Reflections on the Preceding Chapters" (SL, III.11), Montesquieu says: "Such are the principles of the three sorts of government: which does not imply, that, in a particular republic, they actually are, but that they ought to be, virtuous: nor does it prove, that, in a particular monarchy, they are actuated by honour; or, in a particular despotic government, by fear; but that they ought to be directed by these principles, otherwise the government is imperfect." Is this not to prove that *an idea which is only valid for pure models and perfect political forms* has been taken for a category applicable to all existing governments? Is it not to relapse into a theory of essences and into the ideal trap which was precisely what was to be avoided? Whereas one must, *as a historian*, necessarily explain *a certain* very imperfect republic or monarchy, not a *pure* republic or monarchy? If the totality is only valid for the purity, what use is the totality in history, which is impurity itself? Or, and this is the same aporia, how can one ever think history in a category attached in essence to pure atemporal models? We have come back to the difficulty of the disparity of the *Spirit of Laws*: how to unite the beginning and the end, the pure typology and the history?

I believe we should be careful not to judge Montesquieu by one sentence, but, as he forewarns us, take his work as a whole, without separating what he says in it from what he does. It is indeed very remarkable that this theoretician of pure models never (or hardly ever) in his work gives any but *impure* examples. Even in the history of Rome, which is for him truly the most perfect experimental subject, a kind of "pure substance" of historical experimentation, the ideal purity only had one moment, at the beginning, for all the rest of the time Rome lived in political impurity. It would surely be incredible if Montesquieu were unaware of such a contradiction. It must be that he does not think he is contradicting his principles, but that he is giving them a more profound meaning than they are attributed. I believe in fact that the category of the *totality* (and the *nature-principle* unity which is its core) is indeed a universal category, one which does not concern just the perfect adequacies: republic-virtue, monarchy-honour, despotism-fear. Manifestly, Montesquieu considers that *in any State, whether it is pure or impure, the law of this totality and its unity is supreme*. If the State is pure, the unity will be an *adequate* one. But if it is impure, it will be a *contradictory* one. All the impure majority of Montesquieu's historical examples are so many examples of this contradictory unity. Thus Rome, once the first period is over, and the first great conquests have occurred, lives in the State of a republic which will lose, loses and then has lost its principle: virtue. To say that therefore the nature-principle unity always survives but has become a contradiction is quite simply to state that *it is the relationship existing between the political form of a government and the passion then providing it with a content which governs the fate of that State*, its life, its survival, its future, and hence its historical essence. If this relationship is a *non-contra-dictory* one, i.e. if the republican form finds virtue in the men it governs, the republic will survive. But if this republican form is now only imposed on men who have abdicated all virtue and relapsed into private interests and passions, etc., then the relation will be a contradictory one. But it is precisely *this contradiction in the relation, i.e. the existing contradictory relation,* that decides the fate of the republic: it will perish. All this can be inferred from Montesquieu's historical studies, and in particular from *Considerations on the Causes of the Grandeur and Declension of the Roman Empire,* but it is also clearly stated in Book VIII of the *Spirit of Laws,* which deals with the corruption of governments. To say, as Montesquieu does, that a government which loses its principle is a lost government means quite clearly that the nature-principle unity is also supreme in the *impure* cases. If it were not, it would be impossible to understand how this broken unity could break its government.

Hence it is a strange mistake to doubt that Montesquieu has a sense of history, or to suspect that his typology diverted him from a theory of history, that he wrote books on history through a distraction which led him away from his principles. This mistake is no doubt rooted primarily in the fact that Montesquieu did not share the already widespread and soon to be dominant ideology, the belief that history has an end, is in pursuit of the realm of reason, liberty and "enlightenment." *Montesquieu was probably the first person before Marx who undertook to think history without attributing to it an end,* i.e. without projecting the consciousness of men and their hopes onto the time of history. This criticism is thus entirely to his credit. *He was the first to propose a positive principle of universal explanation for history;* a principle which is not just *static:* the totality explaining the diversity of the laws and institutions of a given government; but also *dynamic:* the law of the unity of nature and principle, a law making it possible to think the development of institutions and their transformations in real history, too. In the depth of the countless laws which come and go, he thus discovered a *constant connection* uniting the nature of a government to its principle; and at the core of this constant connection, he stated the inner variation of the relation, which, by the transitions of the unity from adequacy to inadequacy, from identity to contradiction, makes intelligible the changes and revolutions in the concrete totalities of history.

But Montesquieu was also the first to give an answer to a question which has become classic, the question of the *motor of history.* Let us look again at the law of historical development. It is completely governed by the *relation* existing between the nature and the principle in their very unity. If these two terms are in harmony (Republican Rome and virtuous Romans), the totality of the State is peaceful, men live in a history without crises. If the two terms are in contradiction (Republican Rome and Romans who have abandoned virtue), crisis breaks out. The principle is then no longer what is *wanted* by the nature of the government. Whence a chain reaction:

the form of the government tries blindly to reduce the contradiction, it changes, and its change drags the principle along with it, until, with the help of circumstances, a new harmony emerges (imperial-despotic Rome and Romans living in fear), or a catastrophe which is the end of this breathless chase (barbarian conquest). The dialectic of this process is quite clear: its extreme moments are, either peace between the two terms of the opposition, or their conflict; in their conflict, the interaction of the terms is clear, as is how each modification of one inevitably induces a modification of the other. Thus it is clear that *nature and principle are absolutely interdependent in the mobile but pregnant totality of the State.* But it is not clear where the first change comes from, nor the last one, either in the order of *time,* or in that of *causes.* It is not clear *which* of these two terms linked together in the fate of the totality *is the preponderant one.*

In his work on the *Philosophy of the Enlightenment,* Ernst Cassirer praises Montesquieu for having thus founded a quite modern "comprehensive" theory of history, i.e. for having thought history within the category of the *totality,* and the elements of this totality in a specific unity, *while precisely renouncing the idea that one element might be more important than the others,* i.e., that there might be a *motor of history.* History is simply a moving totality, whose unity can be *understood* and the *meaning* of whose inner movements can be grasped, but which can never be *explained,* i.e. its interactional movements can never be related to a determinant element. And in fact this view seems to accord with the letter of many passages from Montesquieu, who constantly turns from the form of the government to its principle, and from its principle to its form. It is the republican laws that produce the very virtue that enables them to be republican; the monarchical institutions that engender the honour that underpins them. As honour is for nobility, the principle is *both father and child of the form of government.* That is why every particular form produces in its principle its own conditions of existence, and always forestalls itself, although at the same time it is the principle which is expressed in that form. We would seem here to be in a real *circular expressive totality* in which each part is like the whole: *pars totalis.* And the movement of this sphere which we think is moved by a cause is no more than its displacement onto itself. With a rolling ball, each point on its sphere can move from top to bottom and return from there to the top, go back down again, and so on to infinity. But all its points do the same. There is neither top nor bottom in a sphere, entirely contained as it is in each of its points.

However, I believe that this slightly over-modern intuition does not express Montesquieu's most profound thought. For he intends there to be in the last instance *a determinant term: the principle.*

"The force of the principles draws everything to it." Such is the grand lesson of Book VIII, which opens with the sentence, "The Corruption of each government generally begins with that of the principles." Corruption (and thus the impure state I have been discussing) constitutes a sort of experimental situation which makes it possible to penetrate the indivisible nature-principle unity and decide *which is the decisive element of the opposition.* The result is that it is definitely the principle that governs the nature and gives it its meaning. "When once the principles of government are corrupted, the very best laws become bad, and turn against the state: but, when the principles are sound, even bad laws have the same effect as good" (SL, VIII.11). "A State may alter two different ways; either by the amendment, or by the corruption, of the constitution. If it has preserved its principles, and the constitution changes, this is owing to its amendment; if, upon changing the constitution, its principles are lost, this means that it has been corrupted" (SL, XI.13). This clearly shows the transition from the case of the experimental situation of corruption to the general case of any modification (to the good as well as to the bad) in the nature of the State. Thus it really is the principle which is, in the last resort, the cause of the development of forms and their meanings. To the point that the classic image of form and content (form being what informs, effectivity itself) has to be inverted. It is the principle that is, in this sense, the true form of that apparent form, the nature of the government. "There are very few laws which are not good, while the State retains its principles. Here I may apply what Epicurus said of riches: 'It is not the liquor, but the vessel, that is corrupted' " (SL, VIII.11).

Of course, this does not exclude *the effectivity of the nature on the principle,* but within certain limits. Otherwise it would be difficult to understand how Montesquieu could have imagined laws intended to preserve or reinforce the principle. The urgency of these laws is simply a confession of their *subordinate* character: they are only active in a domain which may escape them not only for a thousand accidental and external reasons, but also and above all for the fundamental reason that it reigns over them and decides even what they mean. There are thus limit situations in which laws that are intended to *provide manners and morals* are powerless against manners and morals themselves, and rebound against the end they were supposed to serve—the manners and morals rejecting laws opposed to their own goals. However hazardous a comparison it may be, and one that I put forward with all possible precautions, the type of this *determination in the last instance by the principle,* determination which nevertheless farms out a whole zone of subordinate effectivity to the *nature* of the government, can be compared with the type of determination which Marx attributes *in the last instance to the economy,* a determination which nevertheless farms out a zone of subordinate effectivity to *politics.* In both cases it is a matter of a unity which may be harmonious or contradictory; in both cases this determination does nonetheless cede to the determined element a whole region of effectivity, but subordinate effectivity.

Hence this interpretation reveals a real unity between the first and last parts of the *Spirit of Laws,* between the typology and the history. But there remains one difficulty: the so varied second part, which introduces climate,

soil, commerce, religion—surely it represents new principles, and het-
eroclite ones, which clash with the unity I have just demonstrated?

Let us first run through the new determinant factors suggested to us.
Before climate (Book XIV), there is another important element, referred to
on several occasions, and particularly in Book VIII: *the dimensions of the State.*
The nature of a government depends on the geographical extent of its
empire. A minute State will be republican, a moderate State monarchic and
an immense State despotic. Here is a determination that seems to overthrow
the laws of history, since geography decides its forms *directly.* Climate
reinforces this argument, since this time it is the temperature of the air that
distributes the empires, despotisms beneath violent skies, moderate governments beneath tender ones, and decides in advance which men will be
free and which slaves. We learn that "The empire of the climate is the first,
the most powerful of all empires" (SL, XIX.14), but at the same time that
this empire can be conquered by well-conceived laws leaning on its excesses
to protect men from its effects. A new cause then appears: *the nature of the
soil* occupied by a nation. According to whether it is fertile or arid, the
government there will be a government of one man or of many; according
to whether it is mountainous or a plain, a continent or an island, liberty
or slavery will be found to triumph there. But here again the causality
invoked can be counteracted: "Countries are not cultivated in proportion
to their fertility, but to their liberty" (SL, XVIII.3). But here are the *manners
and morals* (*moeurs*) or general spirit of a nation, which add their effectivities
to the others; then commerce and money, and finally religion. It is hard to
avoid an impression of disorder, as if Montesquieu wanted to exhaust a
series of principles he has discovered separately and then heaped together
for want of any better order. "Mankind are influenced by various causes;
by the climate, by the religion, by the laws, by the maxims of government,
by precedents, morals, and customs" (SL, XIX.4). The unity of a profound
law has turned into a plurality of causes. The totality is lost in a list.

I do not want to make it look as if I hoped to save Montesquieu from
himself by forcing this disorder to appear as an order. But I should like to
suggest briefly that in this disorder we can often glimpse something ap-
proaching an order which is not foreign to what has so far been established.

What is indeed remarkable in the majority of these factors, which either
determine the very nature of the government (e.g. geographical extent,
climate, soil) or a certain number of its laws, is the fact that they only act
on their object *indirectly.* Take the example of the climate. The torrid climate
does not produce the despot just like that, nor does the temperate the
monarch. The climate only acts on the *temperament* of men, by way of a
nice physiology which dilates or contracts the extremities and thereby affects the global sensitivity of the individual, imprinting on him peculiar
needs and leanings, down to his style of conduct. It is *the men thus constituted
and conditioned* who are apt for particular laws and governments. "It is the
variety of wants, in different climates, that first occasioned a difference in

the manner of living, and thus gave rise to a variety of laws" (SL, XIV.10). The *laws* produced by the climate are thus the *last effect* in a whole chain, whose *penultimate link*, the *product* of the climate and the cause of the laws, is the "customary life" (*manière de vivre*) which is the outside of the "manners and morals" (*moeurs*) (SL, XIX.16). Look at the *soil:* if fertile lands are good for the government of one man alone, that is because the peasant there is too busy and too well-paid by his efforts to raise his nose from the ground and his pence. *Commerce:* it does not act directly on the laws but via the intermediary of the manners: "Wherever there is commerce, there we meet with agreeable manners" (SL, XX.1)—hence the peaceful spirit of commerce, its suitability to certain governments, its repugnance for others. As for *religion* itself, it seems to be part of another world than these completely material factors, but it acts nonetheless in the same way: by giving a nation ways of living the law and practising morality; it only concerns government through the behaviour of citizens and subjects. It is its mastery of fear that makes the Mahometan religion so apt for despotism: it provides it with slaves, ripe for slavery. It is its mastery of morality that makes the Christian religion accord so well with moderate government: "We owe to Christianity, in government, a certain political law; and in war, a certain law of nations" (SL, XXIV.3). Thus just when they are acting on the government and determining certain of its essential laws, all these causes, apparently so radically disparate, converge *on a common point:* the customs, morals and manners of being, feeling and acting that they confer on the men who live within their empire.

From their conjunction arises what Montesquieu calls *the spirit of a nation.* He does write: "Mankind are influenced by various causes; by the climate, by the religion, etc.," but only so as to conclude: "from whence is formed a general spirit of the nation" (SL, XIX.4).

Hence it is the *result:* the manners and morals, the general spirit of a nation, which determines either the form of the government or a certain number of its laws. The question then arises, *is this not an already familiar determination?* Indeed, remember what I have said of the *principle* of a government and of the depths of the concrete life of men it expresses. Considered not from the viewpoint of the *form* of the government, i.e. of its political exigencies, but from the viewpoint of its *content,* i.e. of its origins, *the principle is really the political expression of the concrete behaviour of men,* i.e. of their manners and morals, and spirit. Of course, Montesquieu does not say in so many words that the manners and morals or spirit of a nation constitute the very essence of the *principle* of its government. But he does set out from principles as the pure forms of the government: their truth appears in their corruption. When the *principle* is lost, it is clear that *manners and morals effectively take the place of principle:* that they are its loss or salvation. Take the republic, abandoned by virtue: there is no longer any respect for magistrates there, nor for old age, nor even for . . . husbands. "No longer will there be any such things as manners, order, or virtue" (SL, VIII.2). It would be hard to say more clearly that the *principle* (virtue) is simply the expression of the *manners*. Look at Rome: in its trials and reverses, with events shaking all the forms, it held fast: "Rome was a ship held by two anchors, religion and manners, in the midst of a furious tempest" (SL, VIII.13). Finally, look at modern States: "Most of the European nations are still governed by manners and morals" (SL, VIII.8), which is what saves them from despotism, partly already master of their laws. How can it be doubted that the manners and morals, vaster and more extensive than the principle, are nonetheless its real foundation and seat, when the same dialectic can be seen outlined between the manners and morals and the laws as between the principles and the nature of a government? "Laws are established, manners are inspired; these proceed from a general spirit, those from a particular institution: now, it is as dangerous, nay, more so, to subvert the general spirit as to change a particular institution" (SL, XIX.12). It is hard to see why it would be *more* dangerous to change the manners and morals than the laws if the manners and morals did not have the same advantage over the laws as the principle has over the nature: *that of determining them in the last resort.* ("In all societies, which are simply a union of minds, a common character is formed. This universal soul adopts a way of thinking which is the effect of a chain of infinite causes which multiply and combine century by century. Once the tone has been given and received, it alone governs, and everything that sovereigns, magistrates, and peoples may do or imagine, whether it seems to conflict with the tone or to follow it, always relates to it, and it dominates even the total destruction [of the society]" [*Mes Pensées*].) Hence the idea that recurs so frequently of a sort of primitive virtue of manners and morals. If "a people always knows, loves and defends its manners more than its laws" (SL, X.11), that is because these manners are more profound and primordial. Thus, among the earliest Romans, "their manners were sufficient to secure the fidelity of their slaves; so that there was no necessity for laws" (SL, XV.16). Later, "as they then wanted manners and morals, they had need of laws." And among primitive peoples themselves, if manners precede laws and stand in for them (SL, XVIII.13), that is because in some sense they derive their "origin from nature." The form and style of conduct which are *expressed politically in the principle* can be reduced to this ultimate basis. This ultimate basis whose essential components Montesquieu lists as the climate, the soil, the religion, etc.

It seems to me that this substantial analogy between the manners and morals and the principle also explains the strange circular causality of these *factors*, which seem at first sight completely mechanical. It is true that the climate and the soil, etc., determine certain laws. But they can be counteracted by them, and all the art of the enlightened legislator consists of playing on this necessity in order to beat it. If this recourse is possible it is because this determination *is not direct but indirect,* and that it is completely gathered together and concentrated in the manners and spirit of a nation, entering via the *principle*, which is the political abstraction and expression of the manners and morals, into the totality of the State. But since within this totality there is a certain possible action of the nature on the principle, and hence of the laws on the manners and morals and consequently on their components and causes, *it is not surprising that climate may give way to the laws.*

I know that counter-quotations will be used against me and that I shall be accused of giving Montesquieu the benefit of the doubt. However, it seems to me that all the reservations one might express turn on no more than a single point: the ambiguity of the concepts of *principle* and *manners and morals*. But I believe that this ambiguity is *real* in Montesquieu himself. I should say that it expresses simultaneously his wish to introduce the utmost clarity and necessity into history, but also in some sense his inability—not to speak of his *choice*. For if the region of the *nature* of a government is always perfectly sharply defined, if the dialectic of the nature-principle unity and contradiction, and the thesis of the primacy of principle, both emerge clearly from his examples, the concept of principle and the concept of manners and morals remain vague.

I said that the principle expresses the condition of existence of a government, and has the real life of men as its concrete background. The parallel causalities of the second part of the *Spirit of Laws* reveal to us the components of this real life, i.e. the real material and moral conditions of the existence of a government—and summarize them in the manners and morals which come to the surface in the *principle*. But it is hard to see the transition from the manners and morals to the principle, from the real conditions to the political exigencies of the form of a government, which come together in the *principle*. The very terms I used, such as *the manners being expressed in the principles*, betray this difficulty—for this *expression* is in some sense torn between its origin (the manners and morals) and the exigencies of its end (the form of the government). All Montesquieu's ambiguity is linked to this tension. He did feel that the necessity of history could only be thought in the unity of its forms and their conditions of existence, and in the dialectic of that unity. But he grouped all these conditions, *on the one hand in the manners and morals*, which are indeed produced by real conditions, but whose concept remains vague (the synthesis of all these conditions in the manners and morals is no more than cumulative); and *on the other hand in the principle*, which, divided between its real origins and the exigencies of the political form it has to animate, *leans too often towards these exigencies alone.*

It will be said that this contradiction and this ambiguity are inevitable in a man who thinks in the concepts of his period and cannot transcend the limits of the then established knowledges, simply interrelating what he knows, and unable to seek in the conditions he is describing a deeper unity, which would presuppose a complete *political economy*. That is true. And it is already remarkable that Montesquieu should have defined and designated in advance in a brilliant conception of history an as yet obscure zone barely illuminated by a vague concept: the zone of *manners and morals* (*moeurs*), and behind it the zone of *the concrete behaviour of men in their relations with nature and with their past.*

But within him another man than the scientist took advantage of this ambiguity. The man of a political party which needed precisely the preeminence of the forms over their principles, and wanted there to be *three kinds of government*, in order that, protected by the necessities of climate, manners and morals, and religion, it could make its *choice* between them. There are thus three species of government. The republic, monarchy and despotism.

In the order of Montesquieu's definitions, despotism is the last of the governments. I hope to show that it is the first in his mind. Not according to his preference, which obviously goes to monarchy, but, what comes to the same thing, in his aversion. And that his object is to provide new arguments not only for choosing monarchy, but also for *re-establishing* it on its true foundations, by counterposing to it the spectacle of its downfall and bugbear.

What is despotism? Unlike the republic and like monarchy, it is an *existing* government. It is the government of the Turks, of the Persians, of Japan, of China and of most Asian countries. The government of immense countries with a voracious climate. The location of the despotic regimes already suggests their excess. Despotism is the government of extreme lands, of extreme extents beneath the most ardent skies. It is the limit government, and already the limit of government. It is easy to guess that the example of real countries is only providing Montesquieu with a pretext. Apparently, at the time of the 1948 conference, Turkish listeners, on mention of the famous statement that despotism is the government of the Turks, uttered "the most lively and most justifiable of protestations." M. Prélot has gravely related this incident ("Montesquieu et les formes de gouvernement"). But without being a Turk, one can suspect the political exoticism of a man who never went beyond Venice and the frontiers of Austria, and only knew the Orient by accounts among which he knew precisely the ones to choose. By 1778, in an admirable work on *Législation orientale*, Anquetil-Duperron was already opposing the real East to Montesquieu's oriental myth. But once the geographical myth of despotism has been denounced, there remains an *idea of despotism* that no Turkish protestation can refute. If the Persian does not exist, where does a French *gentilhomme*, born under Louis XIV, get the *idea* of him?

Despotism is certainly a political *idea*, the idea of absolute evil, the idea of the very limits of politics as such.

It is in fact insufficient to define despotism as the government "in which a single person, with neither rules nor laws, directs everything by his own will and caprice." For this definition remains a superficial one so long as the *concrete* life of such a regime has not been represented. How indeed could *a single person* really direct by his own caprice the immense empire of lands and peoples subject to his decree? This is the paradox that must be illuminated to discover the meaning of the idea.

The first feature of despotism is the fact that it is a political regime which has so to speak *no structure*. Neither legal-political nor social. Montesquieu repeats several times that despotism *has no laws*, and by that we should understand first of all *no fundamental laws*. I know that Montesquieu cites one when he argues that the tyrant delegates all his power to the grand vizir (SL, II.5), but this only has the appearance of a *political* law. In fact it is simply a law of passion, a psychological law which betrays the bestiality of the tyrant and the divine surprise which reveals to him, in the depths of his laziness, like the Pope Montesquieu cites who resigned the administration of his States to his nephew (ibid.), that the government of men is the art of a child: it is enough to let a third party govern them! In its pretension, this false law, which illegitimately converts passion into politics, suggests that *in despotism all politics can always be reduced entirely to passion*. We still have no structure. I know that there is nonetheless in despotism a substitute for a fundamental law: religion. It is indeed the only authority which is above authority, and can, in some circumstances, moderate the excesses of the prince's cruelty and the subjects' fear. But its essence, too, is passionate, since in despotism religion is itself despotic: "it is fear added to fear" (SL, V.14).

Hence neither in the vizirate nor in religion is there anything like an order of political and legal conditions transcending human passions. And in fact despotism knows no laws of succession. Nothing that designates tomorrow's despot to yesterday's subjects. Not even the arbitrary decree of the despot, which can be reduced to nothing by a palace revolution, a harem conspiracy or a popular rising. Nor does it know *political* laws other than the one that governs the strange transmission of power, always absolute, which descends from the prince to the last family head in the land, via the first vizir, the governors, the bashaws, repeating imperturbably from one end of the kingdom to the other the logic of passion: laziness on the one hand, delight in domination on the other. Nor does it know any *judiciary* laws. The only code of the cadi is his humour, the only procedure, his impatience. Hardly has he lent his ear to the parties than he decides, and distributes bastinados or chops off heads on the spot. Lastly, this strange regime does not even bother with that minimum of police that might regulate exchange and commerce. The "society of needs" is not even governed by the unconscious laws which constitute a market, an economic order transcending the practical life of men: no, the logic of the economy is the economy of logic, it reduces itself to the pure passions of men. The merchant himself lives *from one day to the next* for fear of losing tomorrow whatever surplus he might amass today, in his own way like the American savage cited by Rousseau who in the morning sells the bed he has just left, not thinking that there will be another night this evening. . . . Without political or legal transcendence, i.e. without past or future, despotism is the regime of the moment.

This precariousness is, if I may say so, ensured by the disappearance of any *social structure*. In a democracy, the magistrates have a statute, and property and even relative wealth are guaranteed by the law. In a monarchy, the nobility and the clergy are protected by the recognition of their privileges. In a despotism, nothing distinguishes between men: it is the realm of *extreme equality* which lowers all subjects to the same *uniformity* (SL, V.14). Here, says Montesquieu, all men are equal, not because they are everything, as in a democracy, but "because they are nothing" (SL, VI.2). It is the suppression of orders by a general levelling down. No hereditary order, no nobility: this sanguinary regime cannot tolerate greatness in blood. Nor greatness in goods: the tyrant cannot suffer the continuity of "families" that time enriches and the succession and effort of generations elevate in human society. Better, he cannot tolerate any of the greatnesses of establishment that he himself confers on certain of his subjects. For ultimately a vizir, governors, bashaws and cadis are needed! But this greatness is only occasional, taken back the moment it is conceded, almost evanescent. It is nothing the moment it has arrived. Every clerk may thus hold all the power of the despot, but his life is a postponed disgrace or assassination: that is all his freedom, that is all his security! It is as easy, says Montesquieu, to make of a prince a scullion, and of a scullion a prince (SL, V.19). The social distinctions that emerge from this egalitarian desert are no more than the appearance of a universal distinction. But even that body, so necessary to order or terror, the army, has no place in this regime: it would constitute too stable a body, and be too dangerous to the general instability. At most all that is needed is a guard of janissaries attached to the person of the prince, and which he sends out in lightning raids on someone's head, before locking it back up again in the night of the palace. Nothing that distinguishes between men, nothing that resembles in the slightest the outline of a social hierarchy or a social career, the organization of a social world, in which, in advance of and for all the time of the existence and for the growth of the generations, avenues open into the future—in which one may be sure of being noble for life if one is so by birth, of becoming bourgeois in life if one has deserved it by one's industry. No more than it knows any political and legal structure and transcendence, does despotism know any *social structure*.

This disposition gives a strange pace to the life of this regime. This government which reigns over vast spaces in some sense lacks any *social space*. This regime, which has lasted millennia in the Chinese example, is somehow stripped of all *duration*. Its social space and its political time are neutral and uniform. Space without places, time without duration. Kings, says Montesquieu, know the *differences* there are between provinces, and respect them. Despots not only do not know such differences, they destroy them. They reign only over empty uniformity, over the void constituted by the uncertainty of tomorrow, abandoned lands and a commerce that expires at its birth: over *deserts*. And it is the desert itself that despotism establishes at its frontiers, burning lands, even its own, to isolate itself from the world, to protect itself from the contagions and invasions from which nothing else can save it (SL, IX.4, 6). In fact, nothing that resists in the void: let a foreign army penetrate into the empire and nothing will stop it, neither strongpoint nor force, since there are none; it is thus necessary to weaken it before it ever reaches the frontier by opposing it with a first desert in which it will perish. The space of despotism is no more than the void: thinking he is governing an empire, the despot reigns only over a desert.

As for the *time* of despotism, it is the opposite of duration: the moment. Not only does despotism know no institutions, no orders and no families that *last*, but also its very own acts spurt out *in a moment*. The entire people is made in the image of the despot. The despot decides in a moment. Without reflecting, without comparing reasons, without weighing arguments, without "mediums" or "limitations" (SL, III.10). For it takes time to reflect, and a certain idea of the future. But the despot has no more idea of the future than the merchant who profits in order to eat and that is all. All his reflection comes down to deciding, and the legion of his precarious administrators *repeat* the same blind gesture to the end of the most remote province. What could they decide anyway? They are like judges without codes. They do not know the tyrant's reasons; he has none anyway. They have to decide! Hence they will follow his "subitaneous manner of willing" (SL, V.16). As "subitaneously" as they will be disgraced or butchered. Sharing in every respect the condition of their master, who would only learn of his future from his death, if he were not dying.

This logic of abstract immediacy, which contains extraordinary inklings of some of Hegel's critical themes, does nonetheless have a certain truth and content. For his regime that survives so to speak *beneath the political and the social*, restricted to the step below their generality and constancy, does at least live the lower life of this step. And this life is solely the life of *immediate* passion.

Perhaps it has not been sufficiently realized that the famous passions that constitute the *principles* of the different governments are not all of the same essence. Honour, for example, is not a simple passion, or, if you prefer, is not a "psychological" passion. Honour is capricious like all passions, but its caprices are *regulated*: it has its laws and its code. It would not require much pressure to make Montesquieu admit that the essence of monarchy is a disobedience, but a *regulated* disobedience. Honour is thus a reflected passion, even in its own intransigence. However "psychological," however immediate, honour is a passion highly educated by society, a cultivated passion, and, if the term can be suggested, a *cultural and social* passion.

The same is true of the passion of the republic. It, too, is a strange passion, one which has nothing immediate about it but sacrifices in man his own wishes to give him the general good as his object. Virtue is defined as the passion for the general. And Montesquieu obligingly shows us certain monks shifting to the generality of their order all the ardour of the particular passions they repress in themselves. Like honour, virtue thus has its code and its laws. Or rather it has *its law*, a single law: love of the fatherland. This passion for universality demands a universal education: the school of all life itself. Montesquieu answered the old Socratic question—can virtue educate itself?—by saying, it must, and the whole destiny of virtue is precisely to be taught.

The passion that sustains despotism knows not this duty. Fear, since it must be called by its name, needs no education, and the latter is, in despotism, "in some measure, needless" (SL, IV.3). It is not a compound or educated passion, nor a social passion. It knows neither codes nor laws. It is a passion without a career before it, and with no title behind it: a passion *in statu nascendi* which nothing will ever divert from its birth. A momentary passion which only ever repeats itself. Among the *political* passions it is the only one which is not political, but "psychological," because immediate. Nonetheless, this is the passion that constitutes the life of this strange regime.

If the tyrant resigns the exercise of government out of laziness and boredom, that is because he refuses to be a public man. It is because he does not want to pretend to that order of considered impersonality which constitutes a statesman. By a movement of private whim or lassitude, which dresses up in the trappings of solemnity, he divests himself of the public personage and hands it over to a third party, as a king hands his cloak to a valet, in order to abandon himself to the delights of private passions. The despot is no more than his desires. Hence the harem. *This abdication of the despot is the general form of the regime that renounces the order of the political in order to give itself up to the destiny of the passions alone.* It is hardly surprising therefore to see the same pattern repeated indefinitely in all the men making up the empire. The lowliest subject is a despot, at least over his wives, but also their prisoner: the prisoner of his passions. When he leaves his house, it is his desires that move him once more. This shows that in a despotism, the only desire that survives is a desire for the "conveniences of life" (SL, V.17, 18; VII.4. cf. IX.6: Despotism is the reign of "private interest"). But this is not a desire followed through: it does not have the time to compose itself a future. Thus the passions of despotism overturn into one another. The spring of despotism could be said to be desire as much as fear. For they are for themselves their own inverses, without any future, like two men tied back to back with no space between them, riveted to the spot by their chains. And it is this model of passion that gives despotism its style. That absence of duration, those sudden, irretrievable movements are precisely the attributes of these momentary and immediate passions which fall back on themselves like stones children hope to throw to heaven. If it is true, as Marx said in a youthful image, that politics is the heaven of private men, despotism can be described as a world without a heaven.

It is only too clear that what Montesquieu has been trying to represent in this picture of despotism is something quite different from the State in oriental regimes: it is *the abdication of politics itself*. This value-judgement explains its paradoxical character. In fact, despotism is always on the brink of being considered as a regime *which does not exist* but is the temptation and peril of the other regimes when corrupted; and yet as a regime *which does exist*, and can even *be corrupted*; although corrupt in essence, it can never fall into anything but corruption itself. No doubt that is the fate of all reprobate extremes: it is convenient to represent them as real in order to inspire disgust. It takes many pictures of the devil to uphold virtue. But it is also important to give the extremity all the features of the impossible and of negativity; to show that it is not what it claims; and to destroy in it even the appearances of the good that would be lost if one lapsed into it. That is why the image of despotism is justified by the example of the regimes of the East, at a time when the latter impressed itself and was refuted as an *idea*. Let us therefore leave the Turks and the Chinese in peace, and focus on the positive image for which this danger is the bugbear.

We have a sufficient number of texts and sufficiently categorical ones by Montesquieu and his contemporaries to suggest that despotism is only a geographical illusion because it is a historical allusion. It is *absolute monarchy* that is Montesquieu's target, or if not absolute monarchy in person, then at least the temptations to which it is prone. (Cf. the 37th Persian letter: A Portrait of Louis XIV. Usbeck: "He hath often been heard to say, that of all the governments in the world, that of the Turks, or of our august Sultan, pleased him best; so highly does he esteem the politics of the East.") As is well known, Montesquieu belonged by conviction to that right-wing oppositional party of feudal extraction which did not accept the political decline of its class and attacked the new political forms inaugurated since the fourteenth century for having supplanted the older ones. Fénelon, Boulainvilliers and Saint-Simon were of this party, which, until his death, set all its hopes on the Duc de Bourgogne, whom Montesquieu made his hero. It is to this party that we owe the most famous of the *doléances* against the excesses of Louis XIV's reign. The poverty of the peasantry, the horrors of war, the intrigues and usurpations of courtesans, these are the themes of its denunciations. All these famous texts acquired "liberal" overtones by their oppositional character, and I am afraid that they often feature in anthologies of *"la liberté"* alongside those of Montesquieu himself, and not without a well-established appearance of correctness, for this opposition took a unique part in the struggle against the feudal power really, and whatever they may have said, embodied by the absolute monarchy; but the purposes which inspired them had about as much relation to liberty as the ultras' clamour against capitalist society under the Restoration and the July Monarchy had with socialism. In denouncing "despotism," Montesquieu is not defending against the politics of absolutism so much *liberty in general* as the *particular liberties* of the feudal class, its individual security, the conditions of its lasting survival and its pretensions to return in new organs of power to the place which had been robbed from it by history.

No doubt "despotism" is a caricature. But its object is to terrify and to edify by its very horribleness. Here is a regime in which a single individual governs, in a palace he never leaves, prey to feminine passions and the intrigues of courtesans. A caricature of Versailles and the Court. Here is a tyrant who governs through his grand vizir. A caricature of the minister ("The two worst citizens France has known: Richelieu and Louvois" [*Mes Pensées*].) whom nothing, above all not his birth, entitles to that post save the prince's favour. And even in the all-powerful governors dispatched to the provinces, can we fail to recognize the grotesque masks of the intendants charged with the King's omnipotence in their domains? How could we fail to suspect in the regime of caprice a forced caricature of the regime of *"bon plaisir,"* in the tyrant who is *"tout l'État"* without saying it, a distorted echo of the Prince who had already said it, even if it was not yet completely true. But a cause has to be judged by its effects. Once we see the respective situations of the *great* and the *people* in despotism, we will realize the dangers against which it was meant to be a forewarning.

The paradox of despotism is to make such an effective attack on the *great*, whatever their extraction (and how could we fail to think of the nobility, the least revocable of the great?), that the people are in some sense spared. The despot has so much to do to defeat the great and destroy the threat of the rebirth of their condition, that the people, who know nothing of such things, are sheltered from this struggle unleashed over their heads. In a certain sense, despotism is the great brought down and the people tranquil in their passions and affairs. Sometimes, says Montesquieu, one sees torrents swollen by storms descend the mountain, ravaging all in their paths. But all around there are only green fields and grazing flocks. In the same way, despots sweep away the great, while the people, though poverty-stricken, know a kind of peace. I admit that this is only a "tranquillity" and indeed the tranquillity that reigns in a besieged town, since it is in these terms that Montesquieu criticizes it (SL, V.14), but who would not prefer it to the terror of the great, who live in the "pallor" of expected blows, if not death? When we come upon these passages, which Montesquieu almost seems to let slip (SL, XIII.12, 15, 19; III.9), it is clear that inadvertance has nothing to do with it. It is in fact a *warning* which has also the meaning of a reminder. The lesson is clear: the *great* have everything to fear from despotism, from terror to destruction. The people, however miserable they may be, are protected.

Protected. But also just as threatening in their own way. For despotism presents a second privilege: that it is *the regime of popular revolution*. No other government leaves the people to their passions alone, and God knows, the people are subject to them! These popular passions need the bridle of reflection: the notables elected in a republic; the intermediary bodies found in a monarchy. But in a despotism, in which passion reigns supreme, how are the people's instincts to be chained, in the absence of any order, legal or social, which they will accept? When passions dominate, the people, who are passion, always win in the end. Even if only for a day. But this day is enough to destroy everything. Enough at any rate to over-throw the tyrant in the shocks of a revolution. All this is plain to read in Book V, Chapter 11 of the *Spirit of Laws*. And it is hard to avoid drawing a *second lesson*, this time not addressed to the *great*, but to the *tyrants*, or by extension *to those modern monarchs tempted by despotism*. This second lesson clearly signifies: despotism is the sure road to popular revolutions. *Princes, avoid despotism if you would save your thrones from the people's violence!*

These two lessons together constitute *a third*: if the prince ruthlessly fights the *great*, the great will thereby lose their conditions of existence. But in doing so, the prince will have cleared the way for the people, who will turn against him, and nothing now protects him from their blows: he will thereby lose his crown and his life. *Hence let the prince understand that he needs the rampart provided by the great to defend his crown and his life against the people!* That is the basis for a fine and completely reasonable alliance based on mutual advantage. All he has to do to secure his throne is to recognize the nobility.

Such is despotism. An *existing regime*, certainly, but also and above all an *existing threat* which hangs over the other regime of the present day, monarchy. An existing regime, certainly, but also and above all a political lesson, a clear warning to a king tempted by absolute power. It is clear that despite its apparent detachment, the original list conceals a secret choice. Maybe there are *three species of government*. But one, the republic, does not exist except in historical memory. We are left with monarchy and despot-ism. But despotism is no more than abusive, perverted monarchy. We are thus left with monarchy alone, a monarchy to be protected from its perils. So much for the *present period*.

François Quesnay
and the Economic Society

Herbert Lüthy

A bizarre confusion of lines, figures, and formulas, seen as either entice-
ment or hobgoblin, flanks the approach to any study of Quesnay. The
Tableau économique, the first figurative model of the economic process, the
zigzag, the famous secret formula of the Physiocratic School that became
the butt of cruel and malicious jokes, was likewise the first popularization
of political economy, if we may be so bold as to use this expression for a
plan drawn up for the King in person to initiate him into the first principles
of the royal economy. When François Quesnay, ordinarily the physician
of the marquise de Pompadour, presented this curious scribbling in 1758
to Louis XV, ever in search of distractions, so that the monarch could print
it by his own hand in his tiny toy print shop which was decorated in gold,
mahogany, and tulipwood, he was applying the principle of pedagogy
which recommends that teaching be combined with amusement, a principle
as indispensable to courtiers as to tutors.

According to legend, Louis XV is supposed to have set up in type
almost half of the *Tableau*, for which he was also supposed to have conceived
a great admiration. Then this bored great lord turned his attention to amusements of a less abstract nature. But a small band of disciples of the new
science, which soon earned the sobriquet "the sect," gathered as an organized group in Dr. Quesnay's tiny apartment in the *entresol* of the château
at Versailles: Mirabeau père, Lemercier de la Rivière, Du Pont de Nemours,
G.-F. Le Trosne, the abbé Nicholas Baudeau, Turgot. Soon this secret meeting place became an intensely active literary and worldly propaganda center, the impact of which was felt over the whole of France, then throughout
Europe, reaching as far as Poland, Sweden, and Russia. It led to the es-

From *From Calvin to Rousseau: Tradition and Modernity in Socio-Political Thought from the Reformation to the French Revolution*, translated by Salvator Attanasio. © 1970 by Basic Books,
Inc.

tablishment everywhere of "economic societies" which corresponded with each other in order to spread the "doctrine." In the twilight of the *ancien régime*, the terms "economy" and "economist" designated the doctrines of Quesnay and his disciples, in contradistinction to the "commercial" doctrines deriving from mercantilism.

Quesnay's glory and that of his school was as shortlived as it had been great, lasting no more than fifteen years. The *Tableau économique* and the physiocratic view of social and economic structures dominated the thought of reformers in France, and well beyond her borders, during the last fifteen years of the reign of Louis XV. Then the doctrine sank into oblivion, almost overnight. During this brief period of fame, the *Tableau* cut a figure as a revelation which enabled its initiates to grasp in one sovereign glance the profound nature of the whole economic process with all its ramifications. On the morrow of its decline from glory it had become a piece of arcane twaddle, silly and absurd, a ridiculous nursery tale. It is rare in history to be able to put one's finger on the moral and spiritual end of a social order, but here the actual point of breakdown is strikingly evident. The *ancien régime* had already signed its act of abdication in 1776, when the direction of the kingdom's economy and financial policies was passed from the hands of the Physiocrat Turgot to those of the Genevan banker Necker, even though the regime was to drag on its existence for another fifteen years. It was not only the *Tableau économique* which had become an object of wonder and then of contempt; this fate befell the whole organization and structure of monarchical France.

Every French schoolboy has read *L'Homme aux quarantes écus*, the satire in which Voltaire pitilessly ridiculed the physiocratic theory of taxation according to which the land is the sole source of wealth and therefore the only taxable entity. Voltaire here recounts the story of a poverty-stricken small peasant proprietor crushed by bad harvests, stripped of his last *sou*, and thrown into prison by the Farmers-General, while an affluent merchant whose personal wealth is exempt from taxation, in conformity with the doctrine, regales the poor wretch with a string of philosophical reflections on the blessings of the land. This brilliant and facile persiflage has survived Quesnay's doctrine itself, and the literary public knows about physiocracy only by way of this caricature.

It was only around the middle of the nineteenth century that Quesnay and his theory were wrested from oblivion by the new discipline of the history of economic doctrines, which created an honorable niche for him in the pantheon of the pioneers of economic thought. The common opinion of historians of economic doctrines and of economists, generally expressed with infinite respect, can be summarized as follows: the *Tableau* was brilliant in conception, but wrong. Or, if you prefer, wrong admittedly but brilliantly so. It was brilliant as the first attempt at a comprehensive view of the economic process, wrong in all the assertions it made on this process, and on its operative factors and laws. Indeed, most often economists have dispensed with reading Quesnay himself, who as an author is often obscure and ponderous, in order to hold to the more polished and inoffensive version of his maxims elaborated by the followers for the sake of drawing rooms and ladies of wit. Despite the meritorious editions and commentaries of Eugène Daire and August Oncken, it was only in 1958, on the second centennial of the *Tableau économique*, that the National Institute of Demographic Studies published a complete text of Quesnay's economic writings—none too voluminous, incidentally—which finally enables us to extract his authentic doctrine from the tangle of misunderstandings and distortions that have grown up around it.

Quesnay was a peasant lost and out of his element in the artificial gardens of Versailles. Born in 1694, the same year as Voltaire, in Méré, a little village in the Ile-de-France, of a family of obscure husbandmen, he was self-taught, learning how to read and write from the village gardener, a man of some philosophical bent. His mother, who was widowed when François was thirteen, allowed him to go to Paris to earn his livelihood as an engraver of anatomical drawings while pursuing studies as a "practitioner" in surgery, a manual and despised auxiliary branch of medicine. He enjoyed a career as a rural surgeon and gradually acquired a bourgeois clientele, then a court clientele, being called to assist at deliveries which in the upper reaches of the society of the time often required secrecy and discretion. In addition to his skills as a surgeon and his rather rough and easygoing manner, it was precisely because of his virtues of discretion that many ladies of quality sent for Dr. Quesnay as their confidential physician, indeed almost as their father confessor, until the day when Mme de Pompadour summoned him to assist her with the burdensome task of distracting the King from his eternal ennui. Quesnay was loyal to the end to this protectress of the encyclopedists and economists, without ever worrying about whether he was in the good or bad graces of the King or of his entourage.

We shall not discuss Quesnay's medical treatises here, none of which has left its mark in history, nor his prodigious production of polemical writings in the great quarrel revolving around the precedence of the order of surgeons over that of physicians. But the title of his best-known medical work, *L'Essai physique sur l'économie animale*, is there to remind us of the exceedingly broad character of the term "economy," which embraces all the functions of a living organism.

The first reading, the first storehouse of knowledge for the young villager François Quesnay had been the old popular book, already famous, written by the physicians Charles Estienne and Jean Liébaut, *L'Agriculture ou la maison rustique*. It was a perfect example of that ancient household literature in which "domestic economy" extends to everything of interest to the concerned father of a family. It ranged from the proper administration of a happy household—from domestic morals and the education of the children—to husbandry and the making of tools, to medical advice respecting man and beast, to medicinal herbs and kitchen recipes. "Political" or "royal economy" was to be nothing else but household science extended to the kingdom. This peasant's son got the ambitious notion of becoming a surgeon after reading *La maison rustique*. But, no doubt, it was through this same book that he formed his first ideas of an economic order. Scholars have often tried to establish analogies between Quesnay's economic doctrine and his views on medicine, and especially between his *Tableau* and the system of the circulation of the blood. But the relation between them is deeper than a mere analogy. Physiocracy, that is, "the rule of nature," or the "natural order" as it was called, in reaction to administrative Colbertism, was the last powerful manifestation of the "organic" and "total" medieval view of society. A society that was nothing but the enlarged image of the House of the Father, where God has provided for all the needs of the body and the soul by the laws that He has given to nature. All that men have to do, and kings first of all, is to conform to them. But they cannot violate these same laws without drawing infinite evils upon themselves. In a very deep sense it was the last Catholic doctrine that was altogether coherent on the subject of economics. By virtue of his process of thought, Quesnay was the disciple of Malebranche and of the latter's occasionalist philosophy. According to this philosophy, ideas are not rationalizations achieved through the abstraction of our sense experiences, but pre-exist in us like the image of divine reason obscurely present in creation, and for which the experience of the senses is only the "occasional reason" that enables us to find evidence for the ideas in ourselves.

Quesnay's first nonmedical writing did not deal with political economy, but with philosophy: he made his contribution to the *Encyclopédie* in 1756 with the article "*Evidence*." His whole doctrine was to be constructed from such *evidence*, which he defined as "A certitude which is so clear and manifest that the mind cannot deny it." Those who grasped the doctrine in its central point found that all its details fell into place with perfect clarity; whereas those who had not grasped the first postulate saw it only as a tangle of obscurities and unproved affirmations. Whence ensued the inability of the Physiocrats to discuss the least particular proposition without referring to the "Whole" and without beginning again at every turn the complete exposition of the "Doctrine," which gave their school the character of an esoteric sect accessible only to the initiated.

The *Tableau économique*, in its brilliant apparent simplicity, became an inextricable labyrinth once commentators applied themselves to the task of deciphering its details; and the exegeses of its paths have filled libraries. Hence it will suffice to sum up its idea and formal aspect here. The *Tableau* claims to represent a complete cycle of the process of the production and the circulation of wealth, which according to Quesnay—quite naturally— begins with the annual harvest. The whole dynamic of the national economy of his time followed the same annual rhythm as the sowing and harvest seasons: the annual falling due of payments and of rents, seigneurial dues, etc., but also the annual arrival of fleets carrying silver bullion at Cádiz, the annual departure and return of expeditions for the East Indies, the annual return of international, regional, and local fairs, whose decreasing cycle marvelously corresponded to the zigzag line of the *Tableau*. The entire process starts out on the left from the sector of primary production, whose components remit their surplus product, their "net product," to a tax collector placed at the summit of society, which we shall provisionally call the sovereign power. It is only through the spending of the "net product" by this power group which appropriates the national revenue that the process of economic exchanges is set in motion. The zigzag aims to show how the "net product" expended at the summit in the purchase of the products of the different social classes returns directly, or by way of the detour of the industrial and artisan classes who spend their income in the purchase of foodstuffs and raw materials, to the primary production sector. Thus, its components can reconstitute their productive investments annually: the "renewal of annual advances" or a kind of "working capital" as we would say today, although the term does not exactly fit the circumstances.

It is obvious that any relative modification of the figures from which Quesnay starts out involves a modification of the other relations of magnitude and of their final product. If the primary production is burdened with rents and dues beyond its surplus "net product," or if the expenditure of the national product is badly managed, the primary production sector cannot reconstitute its capital. And this "agricultural disinvestment," to use a modern term, fatally involves a diminution of the product of the next annual cycle: it represents the waste and squandering of the nation's productive capital. Quesnay and Mirabeau employed this schema to demonstrate mathematically the ravages of a bad financial and fiscal policy, and to denounce the pernicious character of "Colbertism." By "Colbertism" they meant the artificial creation of industries to meet the sumptuary needs of luxury and prestige, artificially nurtured, subsidized, and privileged, at the expense of agriculture which alone was burdened with the weight of taxes and of seigneurial dues and crushed by the official ordinances weighing upon agricultural prices. In financial and political policy, Quesnay's fundamental principle asserts the primacy of agriculture: public investments should be directed toward agriculture as a matter of priority in order to increase its yield, and free trade and free exportation of cereals should permit the search for outlets at advantageous prices. As for industry and trade, they will defend themselves on their own in free competition, once a rich agricultural population, enjoying a high purchasing power, assures them a large market.

This polemic is the part of Quesnay's work which most markedly bears the stamp of the disputes of his age. But it is replete with striking insights into the particular nature of the "primary sector" which have basically retained their novelty to this day. For example, the observation that a low cost of living is the sign of a poor country, "such as in our provinces where produce is sold at a very low price, and where abundance co-exists with poverty"; that "agriculture, unlike trade, does not have a resource in credit" because the soil is not capital capable of liquidation since, although it can easily fall into debt, it cannot reimburse itself; that trading and industrial "republics" grow rich by rigorous savings, whereas "agricultural monarchies . . . increase their revenue through consumption" inasmuch as for them it can be said "as is the sale, so is the consumption." These are partial truths flowing from a fundamental thesis formulated in the *General Maxims of the Economic Government of an Agricultural Kingdom,* namely, the assertion that land is the pre-eminent fixed capital of the national economy, "which must be preserved with great care in order to ensure the production of taxes, revenue, and subsistence for all classes of citizens," and which cannot be subjected to the same rules of the economy of exchanges as can industrial and commercial capital.

As a method of visual initiation, the *Tableau* was a brilliant invention. But as for deducing, explaining, and proving the theses implicit in its conception, it was worthless. By wishing to be simultaneously—and contradictorily—a genetic model (in which everything is read in terms of agricultural production as the source of all wealth) and an analytic model of the functioning of a wholly constituted economic society (in which movement originates in the spending of the "net" social product), Quesnay presupposed what he wanted to prove at every point in his analysis. For his further demonstrations he had recourse to another graphic schema, the "Formula of the *Tableau*" which replaced the zigzag by a single series of exchanges of definite contingents. But here all the data are arbitrary, and there is no longer either a process or an annual cycle. Indeed, the Physiocrats always counselled their disciples not to persist in understanding this magic *Tableau,* but to make use of it as a simple visual support for reflection.

But the *Tableau* has not exhausted its virtues as such as optical support, nor as an intellectual brainteaser. It is precisely because it incites to contradiction while also fascinating us that it performs its pedagogical mission in provocatively placing before us the three fundamental theses of physiocracy: the theory of net product, the division of society into three classes, and the central role of the social group which determines the use that is to be made of the net product.

Let us be wary of beginning the discussion of the *Tableau* from its most controversial aspect, which has almost caused the conception as a whole to be forgotten: the division of working society into two classes, of which only one—that engaged in primary production—is called productive, whereas the other, including trade, industry, and the performance of services, is called sterile. By focusing on this pseudo problem of determining whether agriculture is truly the sole producer of economic values, the disciples and adversaries of physiocracy enthusiastically became bogged down in the most preposterous misunderstandings, and the discussion on this bizarre assertion ineluctably ended up with the conclusion that this old peasant Quesnay, despite his brilliant side, was a naïve rustic. In all of this, the way in which Quesnay posed the problem, and above all his conception of the social product, have remained incomprehensible because, in fact, they had become alien to the entire economic thought of the nineteenth century.

When Quesnay speaks of the "net product or revenue for the nation," he clearly specifies that this must not be confused "with the gain of merchants and entrepreneurs," which "must be placed on the rank of expenses for the nation" as well as farm products consumed on the spot by the farmers themselves. It is not a question of knowing whether this or that economic activity produces a benefit for him who produces it. What is at stake is that the social economy as a whole should produce a net surplus value above all the salaries, capital, and particular profits consumed in the economic process—a pure surplus above the expenses of subsistence and of reproduction and of the gains retained by the partners. It is the "net product" conceived as a freely disposable, excessive social product that the economic society remits to the noneconomic society. We shall return later to the question of what historical form this noneconomic society assumes in Quesnay's analysis, and precisely where he pinpoints the birth of this net product in the process he describes. The first decisive point is that Quesnay from the start assigns to economy, as such, an objective which goes beyond it. Consequently, this social "superstructure"—which appears in Adam Smith, in Jean-Baptiste Say, in Karl Marx, and in almost all the theorists of the nineteenth century only as a parasitic accessory of the economy—is for Quesnay the end and justification of the whole process. The whole mechanism analyzed by the *Tableau* is there only to support this "superstructure." The fact that this distinctive feature of the whole doctrine, which is glaringly apparent at first sight, has been cavalierly ignored by the dozens of learned dissertations of physiocracy shows strikingly how systematic thought is incapable of grasping a system other than its own.

This way of posing the problem is not familiar to us. We have not learned to consider political economy in terms of such a criterion. Its principle, perhaps, is more accessible to our historical sense than to our utilitarian economic reasoning. In fact, the history of any civilization and of any organized society, from the material point of view, is indeed the history of this social product not consumed by the productive classes. This product is deducted by the force of the authority to which they are subject, or by violence, so that it may be stored up in the courts of lords and princes, in the temples and treasuries of the clergy, and made available for ends other than those of physical subsistence: for the luxury and the art of living of a class of lords, for palaces, edifices for public worship and representation, and works of art, as well as for the deployment of the domineering power of the State. It was only the material disposal of a social produce, "the revenue of sovereignty," which made possible the establishment of an organized political order. The latter—unless it be a form of ephemeral brigandage doomed to perish of its own peculations—tended to favor in turn the growth of the "net product" on which it fed. It required the compartmentalization of the humane sciences, effected in the last century, to conceive of the idea of an economic process intelligible independently of the State, culture, and the juridical order, and of the idea of all the latter being independent of the economy.

In the history of civilizations we discern the meaning of this disposable social product, above the needs of subsistence and reproduction, which covers the noneconomic expenses of society in the way of luxury, prestige, or cultic religious practices. It is this surplus which bears the plus sign in Quesnay's *Tableau;* whereas in the economic theories of the nineteenth century, which recognized only an economic aim for economy, it was either wholly ignored or labelled with the minus sign as a nonproductive public expense. This explains why to a modern economist Quesnay's whole accounting system is topsy-turvy in its construction.

It seems to us that it is even more difficult to admit the physiocratic thesis, according to which the net product derives exclusively from primary production, whereas all other activity, commercial or industrial, is tributary to this surplus of the primary sector and merely shares in its consumption, being therefore sterile on the plane of social product level. I say primary production and not, as is customary, agriculture. In the "productive sector" of his *Tableau,* Quesnay expressly grouped together all the branches of the primary production of his age, including "forests, mines, fishing, etc."

At the outset, no doubt, we find ourselves confronting a myth of nature: only the good earth gives more than it receives, a grain of seed giving many grains, a tree bearing fruits, a flock reproducing itself. One manufactured article does not engender another, a table does not procreate other tables, a gold piece does not produce offspring. But the doctrinaire stubbornness with which Quesnay developed and hardened this initially hesitant thesis—in the *Tableau* the terms "productive" or "sterile" still were applied only to the different orders of public expenses, in a sense close to common acceptance—derives from his bellicose ardor against Colbertism. It was here that minds came to a separation of the ways: whoever admitted this peremptory assertion could count himself among the economists; whoever rejected it and recognized a productivity proper to trade and industry remained a mercantilist. In the final analysis, it was the formidable rise of trade and industry in the last third of the eighteenth century which suddenly made the whole physiocratic theory look absurd. Thenceforth it was considered as the simple doctrinaire reflection of a primitive agrarian stage of the economy which had been superseded. And this is how it figures today in the museum of economic doctrines.

It was Quesnay's disciples, in particular, who caused his teaching to fall into disrepute and ridicule. They degraded it by endowing it with the contours of a nostalgic feudal and romantic reaction to the rising industrial society. In the first place, Quesnay's doctrine had never been a naïve eulogy of rural life; it had nothing in common with the *bergeries de la Reine* of Versailles nor with a Rousseauist glorification of rustic and simple happiness. This legend is refuted in every line of his writings. On the contrary, Quesnay was an enthusiastic and radical propagandist of large-scale, rationalized, high-yield, and highly equipped farming, indeed, of industrialized farming, employing the least number of persons through the utilization of the farming techniques known to his time, "by means of animals, machines, rivers, etc." His model was contemporary England, the country of agricultural depopulation, where large landed estates administered by "capitalist" farmers, throwing their production on the market while at the same time driving the small peasantry toward the towns, created the conditions for rapid industrialization. For Quesnay, rural overpopulation, the distinctive sign of backward countries, was the cancer of the national economy, "the humble classes occupied in the countrysides, without profit for the State, with a bad cultivation from which they wrest a wretched subsistence" and which served mainly "to keep the population of a poor nation unfruitfully." Only an agriculture employing few persons and large amounts of capital furnishes this surplus production that enables the development of an urban economy and assures the "humbler classes" of the countryside jobs of a more useful character in the cities.

At this point in his reasoning it has been a game for satirists and pedants since Voltaire to accuse Quesnay of contradicting himself. But ultimately the quarrel revolved around words and terminology. Quesnay never claimed that nature was productive without the participation of man, or that machines could not increase this productivity of nature. He merely affirmed, with passionate stubbornness, that all labor and all the technical inventions could not produce a surplus over the single reproduction of invested force and material except by cooperating with the immanent productive force of nature. If he qualified as "sterile" all other forms of activity, it was due to the awkwardness of an amateur who had to forge his own terminology from scratch finding nothing usable in the mercantilist literature of his epoch, but who stubbornly persisted in his challenge so that he would have to surrender nothing in his thesis to the Colbertists: his assertion being that all enrichment and all differentiation in society must proceed from primary production and that any other industry can only add a secondary, complementary activity thereto; only the surplus of primary production furnishes the bases of the division of labor, specialization, and exchanges.

Expressed thus, it was a question of manifest historical fact, and if Quesnay had discovered the term "primary production," which he so laboriously strove to express with circumlocutions, he could have contented himself with the tautological assertion that primary production is certainly primary production—first, original, and fundamental—of which all the others are but extensions displacing, combining, and transforming the material that is furnished to them: through the coincidence of the signifying and the signified, any evidence in effect becomes tautology. This evidence has been rediscovered today; we find its modern expression in Colin Clark or in Fourastié, in the division of the economy into primary, secondary, and tertiary sectors, tillage of the soil and extraction of raw materials, processing industries, trade and services, each of these sectors obeying very different rhythms of technical progress and of the growth of productivity.

By the very fact of this disparity of progress, admittedly, the relations and orders of magnitude have changed entirely since two centuries ago. If in Quesnay's time the agricultural sector dominated, the following century in Western countries witnessed the astonishing advance of the secondary industrial sector. As for the tertiary sector, in which modern economists very democratically range all that is neither agricultural nor industrial—the charcoal seller and the chief of state, the priest, the porter, the waiter, the publicity agent, the musician, the hairdresser, the judge, the scholar, the striptease artist, the lawyer, and the man of letters—in short, the whole composite group defined by subtraction which satisfies those social needs not covered by agriculture and manufactured products, and which in modern societies tends to become the most numerous, evidently is no longer what it was in physiocratic society. Quesnay would have been flabbergasted to see the hierarchic summit of his *Tableau* and the rejects of his "sterile class" combined higgledy-piggledy in the same category. But this is a question of regime and not of economic terminology, and we can still prefer Quesnay's classification without fundamentally altering the analysis of the structural evolution.

What has dated in Quesnay is not the view of the fundamental articulations of economic society, but his material enumeration of the branches of primary production. Since the end of the eighteenth century, the very essence of the industrial revolution has been to place the "immanent forces of nature" in the service of an increasing number of activities which had up to then been in the hands of artisans. The enormous growth of material productivity over the past two centuries has progressed step by step with the utilization of motor forces and of the energy reserves of nature impounded by machines. Today a new Quesnay would find a place, perhaps, in the chapter entitled "Primary Production" for the production of hydraulic and thermal energy, for a great part of the chemical industry. And tomorrow, for the utilization of nuclear energy, and the whole industrial sector fed by these sources of energy, would be subsumed under the rubric "Productive Activities," leaving in the "sterile" class only the liberal, administrative, artistic professions and others, refractory to technical progress. All this would change nothing of his fundamental thesis (considered the most ridiculous physiocratic superstition), which asserts that human labor can create wealth only by allying itself with the immanent productive forces of the earth. What emerges from the economic process of the *Tableau* as the net social product placed at society's disposal is that which entered into this process as the productive force of nature, this "pure gift of the earth" which is added to man's labor and which is the bounteous (i.e., it comes as a gift, is not paid for) share, a common possession of society. Thus, the economic society produces a surplus which does not belong to the economy because it has incorporated a part which did not belong to it, formerly called the share of God. And because at the beginning of the process there is this "gift" or "advance" of nature, because society, like the individual, from its birth "spends" or consumes before producing, and because "everywhere expenditures precede the reproduction of expenditures," the whole economy of the *Tableau* can start out from the spending of the social revenue. Quesnay's economic science then becomes the science of proper spending.

To be sure, since Adam Smith serious economic science has ignored this sort of alchemy; it knew nothing of a collaboration or of a donation of nature and does not count them among the factors of production. At best, the encumbering problem of ground rent still recalls, like an erratic lump, a remote past subjugated to the soil. For the two great economic schools, liberal and socialist, work is the only factor productive of values. Capital—"produced means of production," according to Marx—is itself hoarded work, and these two incarnations of work, labor and capital, contend for the social product. This is where the boundary is drawn between two views of the world. The theory of value is the metaphysics of all economic doctrine, the realm of *a priori* definitions; and the economic metaphysics of the power of labor, creator of surplus value, is no less obscure than that of the creative force of nature of the Physiocrats. It merely displaces, without making it disappear, the irritating *non sequitur* which is produced in any economic system when, at the point in the social circuit of exchanges where all gain is balanced by an equivalent loss, there suddenly appears a surplus value, a value produced above the value consumed.

The gesture which, in a cobbler's workshop, sets into motion only a hammer or awl, consumes the same amount of force which, applied to a lever at a powerhouse, releases gigantic energies. If the labor power consumed alone enters into the product, then Marx's thesis—according to which the worker is defrauded of his right to the total product of his labor so that in our day, for example, the worker of the powerhouse is defrauded of the revenue of the millions of kilowatt hours he has produced, once the cost of the installation is paid off—is at least as plausible as the contrary arguments of the "capitalist apologia." Their philosophical postulate is fundamentally the same: for Adam Smith as for the economic science of the nineteenth century, liberal as well as Marxist, nature was offered gratuitously, *res nullius*, a windfall (for him who knew how to grab hold of a choice morsel) which entered economic accountancy only as an inexhaustible mine, and only the costs of exploitation, which figured on the balance sheet. We are no longer so sure, perhaps, that this philosophy, the most insipid that the world has known, has been the last word of wisdom.

As for the specific problems of primary production which occupied

Quesnay, the later economic science could calmly neglect them because Europe, following England, wanted to be the factory of the world. And for its primary production it rested upon those countries overseas which were "backward" or "in a state of nature" and which themselves were considered as *res nullius* offered gratuitously to him who could take, and as inexhaustible mines of raw materials. Today, it again finds these problems of a backward agriculture more than for a revolution, at times in Europe itself, but above all in the so-called "underdeveloped countries," precisely the countries of primary production which have arrived at this stage of veiled crisis that Quesnay had perceived in the France of Louis XV. The anatomical *Tableau* which he drew up from this, his theory of organic growth and differentiation, his polemic against the artificial grafting of industries catering to conspicuous consumption onto a stagnant and starveling rural economy, his fundamental intuition that industrialization must begin by way of the countryside, or—expressed in modern terms—the intuition that an industrial revolution can be successful only if it is based on an agricultural revolution: all this contains even more material for reflection for the experts and technicians of "economic development" than is offered by the whole corpus of "classic" liberal or Marxist literature.

It is not a question of returning as penitents to the wisdom of the old master, to his touching zigzag and his outdated terminology. His economic model clearly bears the stamp of his time, and it is only in this setting of the age of Louis XV that its originality is apparent. This noneconomic society, namely, one not occupied materially with earning its livelihood, which formed the all too high summit of the *Tableau*, which made disposal of the national net product, of the "revenue for the proprietors of the land, the Sovereign, and the tithe owners," and which by the way it spent it determined the totality of the economic circuit, was the royal constituted society of the *ancien régime* itself: the court, the nobility, the "proprietors" in the seigneurial sense, the "tithe-owning" clergy, and that numerous "bourgeoisie de robe" which had incorporated itself into the society by buying royal offices in the administration of justice and finance.

Here we pass from the economy per se to the political regime which, still more than a hierarchy of command, was a hierarchy of payees from the national revenue levied from the society of commoners. Quesnay does not leave a shadow of doubt as to the nature of this revenue, which was essentially seigneurial and which dispensed with any economic justification. Without the slightest equivocation, he defined the social and economic function of this society, which was to spend the social net product and, if possible, to spend it properly. "The proprietors are useful to the State only through their consumption; their revenues exempt them from labor; they produce nothing." This was really their sole function: the absolutist revolution of Louis XIV had guaranteed its seigneurial rights to the nobility, and in addition it had assured it the enormous revenues of the Church, as prebends for its younger sons; but it had stripped it of all public function, feudal, political, or administrative. But the *ancien régime* acquitted itself of the single function that remained to it, that of spending the national income, in an exemplary fashion and even with an excess of zeal, unto its own ruin. The whole brilliant, refined, and frivolous civilization of the eighteenth century, intellectual as well as material, cannot even be conceived outside this very large consumer society. It was indeed the exclusive consumer, of the national income; its occupation and burden were the art of living, of furnishing and ornamenting an almost artificial life; and it pushed refine-ment not only to generous patronage of literature and the arts but to the point where it treated itself to the mortal elegance of the subversive spirit.

The *Tableau* truly contains the key to the *ancien régime* at the zenith of the age of Louis XV. If historians had paid attention to it, cultural history and economic history would not have diverged from each other to the absurd point where the best economic and social histories examine under the microscope the development of trade, industry, and "capitalist" struc-tures in the eighteenth century, while ignoring (or almost) the existence of the King, the court, the nobility, the princes of the Church, the innumerable lawyers and owners of offices, and the swarming clientele of litterateurs, games-masters, favorites, and salon mistresses, as if all this society, because it was wholly consumer-oriented, had played no economic role. The truth, conforming with the *Tableau*, is that it determined the whole economic evolution, including the rise of the very forces which were to smash it. At a time when "the people" had a purchasing power which was practically nil and when, save for certain vitally necessary foodstuffs, there were by definition no mass consumption and no products designed for a nonexistent mass market, industrial specialization and large trade were almost exclu-sively pledged to the high consumption of luxury products, and the great manufactories were the creations of Colbertism—the *Manufacture Royal des Glaces*, the Gobelins, the porcelains, the fine linen of Abbeville—and the naval arsenals and shipyards, the armaments of war, luxury of kings. Out-side of some starveling village trades assuring the maintenance of a rudi-mentary equipment, rural and industrial economy were unaware of each other. The flow of exchanges was established exclusively through this high society, which was wholly consumer-oriented and which diverted its sei-gneurial and fiscal revenues toward luxury industries and the luxury trade, bringing luxury objects and foodstuffs from the fabulous Indies. As an historical description of this economic circuit, Quesnay's *Tableau* is as exact as a formula can be. With it, we can even put our finger on the distortions of the circuit and on those "unhealthy excrescenses" which ended up inev-itably by derailing it.

Dr. Quesnay did not call into question this regime which he knew so well, in all its splendor and its private misery by virtue of his office. He tried to demonstrate to the King that the regime could not with impunity hold in contempt its own vital laws and the sources of its wealth. Quesnay's lesson in political economy—and this is why it is so outdated in detail but so modern in its principle—aimed to be a lesson in economic policy. His fiscal theory, the most bitterly contested, ridiculed, and misunderstood part of his doctrine, was the crowning piece and the conclusion of an ineluctable logic. The "net product," which this whole privileged society at the summit of his *Tableau* consumed, was simply the disposable social product, the surplus taken from the commoners' economic society above its needs of subsistence and reproduction, and which "belongs as much to the State as to the proprietors" who "have only the enjoyment of it." It was exclusively on this net product that the public expenditures could be charged and taxes deducted, and this privileged society had to be blind and mad to have tried a second time, after having collected to its profit all the disposable social revenue, to shift the tax onto the rural and industrial classes who retained only the minimum wherewithal to keep them going. As Quesnay put it, it was like "levying a tax on the horses who work the soil." Such a fiscal system "would not be a tax, but a spoliation which reduces the people to forced saving on consumption, which halts labor, which extinguishes reproduction, and ends up by ruining the people and the Sovereign."

Thus Quesnay opened a frontal attack on the fiscal privileges of the nobility, clergy, and upper bourgeois officialdom, which ultimately led the *ancien régime* from financial breakdown to political bankruptcy, at the very moment when, in the first fatal years of the Seven Years' War, the lengthy fiscal quarrel flared up between the monarchy and its privileged members retrenched behind their parlements. The attack was conducted in a wholly didactic way, with a moderateness of terms which barely muffled the vehement tone of the reasoning. The conclusion that fiscal privileges had to be abolished emerges clearly from the *Tableau*, which seems to have been drawn up only in order to make this demonstration.

We see with what bad faith Voltaire, the feudal lord of Ferney, caricatured Quesnay's thesis in his famous satire: it was the approved method of hiding behind the poor little peasant when the privileges of the manorial lord were threatened. Nevertheless, the satire had fair game: Quesnay's disciples and epigoni, beginning with abbé Baudeau, and with the sole exception of Turgot, themselves worked hard to confuse this explosive conclusion and to drown it in confusion by transforming the feudal proprietors and the princes of the Church into honorary husbandmen. By this simple trick of prestidigitation, which destroyed the *Tableau*'s very structure by confusing what it had so neatly separated (namely, those who furnished and those who collected the "net product") the whole "doctrine" became a laughable imposture and fairy tale. All that remained of it, under the unwarranted title of physiocracy, was a pale idealization of rural life in the style of the *bergeries de la Reine* at Versailles, a sentimental and futile idyll perched on the edge of the abyss.

From Quesnay's doctrine, which was the crown and culmination of the whole literature of "household" economy, many subterranean paths lead to the present. When, in 1863, Karl Marx worked on the draft of the *Process of the Circulation of Capital,* he began with an attempt to construct an "Economic Tableau of the Process of Reproduction" conceived wholly on the model of Quesnay's *Tableau,* which he hailed as "the most brilliant finding ever made by political economy." But Marx meted out to Quesnay the same treatment which he meted out to all his teachers: he turned him on his head, while proclaiming, as he did with Hegel, that he was setting him on his feet again.

In the Marxian transposition, the lords of the country and of the land have become capitalists; the "sterile class"—purged of capitalists who, in Quesnay, formed part of it—is thenceforth the only productive class, and the net product deriving from the gift of the earth has become the surplus value extorted from this class of proletarians. As for primary production, it simply has disappeared as a particular category, annexed on the one hand to "the industry of the goods of production" for raw materials and on the other to the "industry of the goods of consumption" for alimentary products, so that the economy is reduced to two industrial sectors and society to two classes, the exploiters and the exploited.

Marx genuinely tried to resume Quesnay's "brilliant" idea, that is, to represent the whole functioning of the socioeconomic regime in a single tableau simultaneously showing the production and circulation of a surplus value in a single social process. But he could not succeed in so doing and finally dropped the project because it was impossible to transpose the idea of a social product arising from the economic circuit and freely disposable— disposable for whom?—to his view of a purely dualist society reduced to the antagonism between the proletarian and the capitalist, who is expropriating the surplus value for himself. Curiously, Marx does not seem even to have perceived—or he neglected it as a "feudal" anachronism—the key role allotted in Quesnay's *Tableau* to this central group which, independently of its historically ephemeral outline, represented *Power.* By suppressing this third term, through a vigorous simplification which at once makes for the polemical force and the historical weakness of his analysis, and by considering power—or the State—merely as the police appendage of the capitalist class, Marx, just like his liberal antipodes, constructed his socioeconomic model in an historical vacuum without institutions and without a frame of reference.

Two hundred years after Quesnay and a hundred years after Marx, it is striking to observe that the old *Tableau économique* of the Physiocrat physician, because it includes both the pre-economic sources of riches and the supra-economic institutions, remains capable of adaptation to all societal transformations. It would be easy, for example, to transpose it to Soviet society, with its strictly hierarchical summit which disposes of the social product and determines its distribution between the "productive" sector (heavy industry) and the "sterile" sector (consumer goods), whereas the classic Marxist and liberal models were only instantaneous abstracts from a state of local affairs at the middle of the nineteenth century.

Marx the economist (who is not Marx the philosopher nor Marx the historian of his time) was the twin brother of Manchesterian liberalism and thought along the same conceptual lines, while allotting them an inverse sign. But his enthusiasm for Quesnay's *Tableau* is significant of a profound nostalgia for an order that was more hieratic than the bourgeois materialist order of his time. And it should not surprise us that this dialectic mind proclaimed itself "materialist" out of anti-materialism. The same nostalgia is expressed at the beginning of the *Communist Manifesto*, in which Marx so curiously compares the "feudal, patriarchal, and idyllic relationship," those personal bonds "betwixt man and man," which the bourgeoisie has destroyed, to the "cold spirit of calculation" and to the "unscrupulous freedom of trade" and "unfeeling bookkeeping" of the capitalist economy. Perhaps without being overly aware of it, he projected this hardly ironic image of an ideal *ancien régime* into his future Society, which he never defined. The Marxian model of capitalism, a horrifying image of a social world without any interior cohesion or values other than of a commercial kind, returns to its negation, which was the physiocratic model from which he had started out, and which Quesnay had himself conceived in opposition to the "commercial doctrines" of mercantilism.

As an image opposed to the concept of an exclusively economic society, Quesnay's *Tableau* has never ceased to trouble and fascinate economists, and Marx is the most important link—but not the only one—between physiocracy and communitarian or totalitarian ideologies. To be sure, after two centuries of theoretical discussion and social upheaval, the contributions of all doctrines have been infinitely mixed. But in the two ideologies which today seem to confront each other apparently without possibility of compromise—Marxism, in which Marx would have difficulty in recognizing himself, and liberalism, whose evolutions would surely surprise its liberal ancestors—we could find dim shadows of the two great concepts which confronted each other in the eighteenth century. There, too, the disagreement over the premises of economic thought—the theory of value— made any mutual comprehension of accommodation impossible: the "household" doctrine, whose entire thought started out from the material and tangible social product, as opposed to the "commercial" doctrine, for which economy begins through exchange and receives its scale of values through the mechanism of the market. And behind this doctrinal opposition we can glimpse a *de facto* opposition, almost as old as history, between that of the authoritarian "agricultural monarchies" with fertile soil and a subject population, and the hustling and bustling "commercial republics," with a poor soil and free men.

This correlation between economic structure and political regime was so evident for Quesnay that, according to him, even in the Turkish capital "money, industry, and mercantile trade and illicit trading" constitute a kind of republic which "in the midst of despotism" gains "considerable ability and independence in its intercourse and in the free state of its commercial wealth." Further, he distinguished in the England of his time, with singular perspicacity, "a commercial republic which dominates this agricultural kingdom." In the crises of the "agricultural kingdom" of France, and in the face of the rise of the "commercial republic," Mme de Pompadour's physician tried to conceive a grand synthesis. Historically, it failed, but it remains the last doctrine in which the State and society, culture, economics, and nature, theory and history still constituted a single entity.

Rationality and the Text:
A Study of Voltaire's Historiography

Suzanne Gearhart

The object of this essay is to discuss the historical dimension of the definition of history. The necessity of such an approach is apparent in the fact that one cannot employ the most basic terms of the discussion—history and historiography—without becoming engaged in a conflict between various definitions coinciding with various phases in the history of the philosophy of history. If many contemporary historiographers have come to employ the word "history" solely in the sense of historiography, it is because they question the theoretical assumptions underlying the distinction between "history" understood as the events in themselves and "historiography," as a conscious presentation of those events; or between "history" as a simple narration and "historiography" as a methodologically conscious presentation. If we retain both terms, it is not because we too do not question the distinction between them, but because each is of a different value in discussing Voltaire's text. For Voltaire does frequently, though not always, employ the word "history" in two distinct senses. Our own use of the terms does not imply a hard and fast distinction between history and historiography, but a difference in emphasis depending on the context of our argument.

It seems evident that in order to discuss Voltaire's historiography, one must have at least a working definition of history. But the method for arriving at such a definition is less than evident. It would be naive to proceed as though we ourselves had no preconceptions concerning historiography, as though our view of the past were not influenced by contemporary historical method. But it would be equally naive to look to the present for a definition by which we could evaluate an eighteenth-century historiogra-

From *Studies on Voltaire and the Eighteenth Century* 140 (1975). © 1975 by Theodore Besterman. The Voltaire Foundation, 1975.

pher, for present historiography supplies us not with one, but with several definitions of history. An important aspect of the current effort to rethink the problem of history writing is a re-evaluation of past historiography. In general, the object of this re-evaluation is to guard against the continued use of certain naive assumptions common to many past historians and thus to permit the emergence of a new, more critical approach to history writing. Thus for many contemporary theorists, the term "history" has two meanings, one critical and one "naive." Michel Foucault calls history the "arrière-fond" of the social sciences, supplying them with their context and their content, but also serving as "une frontière qui les limite, et ruine d'entrée de jeu leur prétention à valoir dans l'élément de l'universalité." At the same time, history may be synonymous with "une lecture retrospective," that is, with the view that the past is an incomplete and inferior version of the present and that the sense of history is to be found in the notion of progress (*Les Mots et les choses*). Michel de Certeau makes an analagous distinction. For him, history may be a critical method for continually deconstructing theoretical models derived from the social sciences, by bringing to light exceptions to those models, or by fabricating "ces *différences pertinentes* que permettent de 'sortir' une rigueur plus grande dans les programmations et leur exploitation systématique." At the same time, according to Certeau, most history is produced and judged according to the standards of a university system which inhibits any direct reference to itself and to its particular ideology as the standard by which historiography is produced and judged ("L'Opération historique," in *Faire de l'histoire*). Summarizing the work of the *Annales* school, François Furet distinguishes between "l'histoire sérielle" and "l'histoire événementielle." The former implies a conscious construction of historical series which prohibits any illusions as to the "givenness" of the "facts" or to the universality of the conclusions they might support. The latter is characterized as an historicism whose preoccupation with an "événement" irreducible to any causal explanation goes hand in hand with the recuperation of the "événement" in the name of a teleology of progress, liberty, or reason ("Le Quantitif en histoire," in *Faire de l'histoire*).

For these thinkers, past historiography can be defined by what it excluded—that is, by questions about the validity of such notions as fact, event, reason, or progress—as well as by its positive content. Interestingly enough, although the sense of the exclusion is perhaps ultimately different, contemporary historiography too can be defined by what it hopes to exclude, that is, by certain naive assumptions about the "sense" of history. What makes this relationship of exclusion all the more interesting for us is the degree to which what is excluded from the present evokes Voltaire. Much distinguishes Voltaire from the historicist tradition of "l'histoire événementielle": he is not, he himself repeatedly states, interested in facts or events in themselves (*Histoire de Charles XII*, "Remarques sur l'histoire"). At the same time, his ideological affinity with positivist teleology (reason, liberty, progress, etc.) is clear. Certainly no one played a greater role in the diffusion of this ideology or is closer to its "original" sense than Voltaire. The evocation of a negative form of history—"l'histoire événementielle"—and of the ideologies that produced it by Certeau, Foucault, Furet, and others implies the hope that, once defined as a coherent system, this type of historiography can in some sense be put behind us, that it will become part of a past which no longer touches us directly; that by bringing to light the rules of a system which maintains itself through the repression of any open reference to those rules, that system can be relativized and its repressive force at least attenuated. At the same time, however, the exclusion from the present of "l'histoire événementielle" and of the ideologies that produced it implies that the latter form of historiography is indeed a part, however negative, of the present. Thus while we cannot evaluate Voltaire's historiography without being influenced by our experience of the present, our conception of the present is itself a part, however negative, of the past.

Hence our candour in reading Voltaire can be only relative. We cannot claim to approach his texts without preconception, but we cannot "clear our conscience" by admitting to a certain preconception (which one?) and using it openly as a standard for evaluating the texts. It is with a dilemma, rather than with a coherent set of assumptions, that we approach Voltaire's historiography. Indeed, if the coherence of our own position is undercut by its relation to past historiography, neither can we take for granted the coherence (or immanence) of Voltaire's historiography. The question to be asked is not, in the light of which criteria should the coherence of the text be revealed but, is the text coherent in any light? An obvious point of departure for such an inquiry are the passages in which Voltaire discusses the work of previous historians and presents his own view of what historiography should be. The question is, does the work conform to these programmatic statements and can they thus be considered as an expression of the coherence of the work? If the work does not conform to them, in what sense is the coherence of the work undercut?

Voltaire offers several criteria for determining whether or not a work is to be accepted as history. He begins his article on "l'histoire" in the *Dictionnaire philosophique* by distinguishing history from the fable: "L'histoire est le récit des faits donnés pour vrais, au contraire de la fable, qui est le récit des faits donnés pour faux." This definition proves to be idealistic, however, for in composing his own histories, Voltaire is constantly confronted with sources which in his own view are fables, but which are presented by their authors as history. Thus the essential question is not whether or not an account is given to be historical, but whether or not it is "vraisemblable." Philosophy "trouve des cérémonies, des faits, des monuments, établis pour constater des mensonges. . . . Les monuments ne prouvent les faits que quand ces faits vraisemblables nous sont transmis par des contemporains éclairés" (*Essai sur les mœurs*, cxcvii).

The "vraisemblable" is the ultimate standard of historiography, so much so that it takes precedence over the "vrai." It is conceivable for Voltaire that an event which is not "vraisemblable" could have taken place, but it would not be a proper object for history simply because it were true.

> Toutes ces aventures, qui tiennent du fabuleux, et qui sont pour-
> tant très-vraies, n'arrivent point chez les peuples policés qui ont
> une forme de gouvernement regulière.
>
> (*Essai*, cxc)

> Croyons les événements attestés par les registres publics, par le
> consentement des auteurs contemporains, vivant dans une capi-
> tale, éclairés les uns par les autres, et écrivant sous les yeux des
> principaux de la nation, Mais pour tous ces petits faits obscurs et
> romanesques, écrits par des hommes obscurs dans le fond de
> quelque province ignorante et barbare; pour ces contes chargés de
> circonstances; pour ces prodiges qui déshonorent l'histoire au lieu
> de l'embellir, renvoyons-les à Voraigne, au jésuite Causson, à
> Maimbourg, et à leurs semblables.
>
> (*Essai*, cxcvii)

The "vraisemblable" is not a category within the true, it is the true which is a category within the "vraisemblable." What is "vraisemblable" may not always be true, but if it is false, it will still participate in ultimate historical truth: "Il y a des erreurs historiques; il y a des mensonges his-toriques. . . . Quand on dit qu'un czar fit clouer le chapeau d'un ambas-sadeur sur sa tête, c'est un mensonge. Qu'on se trompe sur le nombre et la force des vaisseaux d'une armée navale, qu'on donne à une contrée plus ou moins d'étendue, ce n'est qu'une erreur, et une erreur très pardonnable" (*Histoire de Russie*, préface, viii). To err is to remain within the realm of historical truth. To "lie" is to be expelled to the barbarous realm of "contes absurdes" where the terms "truth" and "falsehood" can no longer have any meaning.

The "vraisemblable" is the fundamental category of history for Voltaire, but what, specifically, does it mean? As we have already seen, according to Voltaire, an event may take place without being "vraisemblable." History is not the faithful representation of all events, but only of certain events. The "vraisemblable" is thus not only a standard for determining the value of an historical work, but also, for determining which historical events and cultures are worthy of being treated by the historian. In a passage already cited (*Essai*, cxc) Voltaire declares that incidents unworthy of being called historical frequently occur that could not "chez les peuples policées qui ont une forme de gouvernement regulière." Only a "peuple policée" with a "regular" form of government is a proper object of history, for only this type of political structure maintains a relationship to time that Voltaire deems historical. For anyone outside such an order, time can only mean change—the purely negative principle often invoked by Voltaire to "explain," that is, to exclude from the realm of the historical all that cannot be labelled as rational: "Toutes ces coutumes, que le temps avait introduites, ont été abolies par le temps" (*Essai*, xlviii). Voltaire declares the impossibility of establishing any continuity between the present and previous historical ages, for the explanation of the present cannot be found in a past to which its only link is the purely negative movement of time: "C'est donc une idée bien vaine, un travail bien ingrat de vouloir tout rappeler aux usages antiques, et de vouloir fixer cette roue que le temps fait tourner d'un mouvement irrésistible. A quelle époque faudrait-il avoir recours . . . ? A quel siècle, à quelles lois faudrait-il remonter?" (*Essai*, lxxxv).

It is only with the modern era that history becomes possible for Voltaire, for it is only with the emergence of modern political systems of the type instituted by Louis XIV that change ceases to be quixotic and irrational and becomes instead rational change, progress, or history: before Louis XIV "pendant neuf cent années, le génie des Français a été presque toujours rétréci sous un gouvernement gothique, au milieu des divisions et des guerres civiles, n'ayant ni lois, ni coutumes fixes, changeant de deux siècles en deux siècles un langage toujours grossier" (*Le Siècle de Louis XIV*, i). (The close connection between what is rational in the political realm and what is rational in historiography is evident in Voltaire's use of the term "history." Though it is frequently evident from the context that Voltaire does recognize a semantic distinction corresponding to the difference between history as events "in themselves" and history as the narration of events, cases in which Voltaire's term "history" could have either meaning are equally frequent.) But while rational historiography cannot be discussed without a simultaneous discussion of the rational political order, the designation of the rational political order as the only realm in which rational historiography can be produced does not really enlighten us as to the nature of the rational or the "vraisemblable" itself. The *Essai sur les mœurs*, Voltaire's most comprehensive historical work, can be read as an attempt to give to the rational the positive content it lacks in his programmatic statements, for the *Essai* is both a chronicle of man's struggle to establish a rational form of social organization and an attempt to establish a point at which historiography could be said to have broken with the fabulous tradition of history writing which proceeded it, to become truly rational. What the *Essai* ultimately describes, however, is the successive failure of such attempts. "C'est ainsi que vous verrez, dans ce vaste tableau des démences humaines, les sentiments des théologiens, les superstitions des peuples, le fanatisme, variés sans cesse, mais toujours constants à plonger la terre dans l'abrutissement et la calamité, jusqu'au temps où quelques academiés, quelques sociétés éclairées, ont fait rougir nos contemporains de tant de siècles de barbarie" (lxii). Throughout the *Essai*, Voltaire is occupied less with pointing to the adumbrations of modern rationality than with the exclusion of past cultures and past historiography from the rational order.

For Voltaire, the possibility of a rational political order and of a rational historiography dates from the invention of speech by the intellectual elite whose presence in the state of nature guaranteed the immanence of rationality. But almost as soon as rational historiography becomes possible, it ceases to be. Oral historiography quickly degenerates into folk tales, for memory is imperfect and easily distorted by the imagination. (If Voltaire poses a difficulty to the modern reader, it is often not because his ideas seem antiquated and bizarre, but because they seem so self-evident as to be banal. Thus what is often required of the reader is not so much the restoration of a literary and cultural context in which the text could have made sense, as the acquisition of a distance from the text which permits its self-evidence to be questioned. Although the current political and intellectual climate is such that the ethnocentrism of Voltaire's view of history no longer appears justifiable, his judgement on the ahistoricity of cultures "sans écriture," which lends pseudoscientific support to that ethnocentrism, is still widely shared. In fact, the role of oral accounts and of memory in cultures "sans écriture" cannot be understood by considering their role in cultures that rely on writing for the transmission of all socially important knowledge. The complexity of the technical and cultural information transmitted from generation to generation in the former type of culture reveals that Voltaire's view of these cultures is far from self-evident.)

It is with the invention of writing that the defects of oral historiography are overcome, and Voltaire uses this date to establish anew the age of history: "Toute histoire est récente. Il n'est pas étonnant qu'on n'ait point d'histoire ancienne profane au-delà d'environ quatre mille années. Les révolutions de ce globe, la longue et universelle ignorance de cet art qui transmet les faits par l'écriture, en sont cause" (*Dictionnaire philosophique,* "Histoire"). But Voltaire is forced to retreat from this "new" position by the existence of different types of "écriture," each bearing a different relation to rational historiography. Voltaire calls hieroglyphs "des caractères parlantes." They represent an intermediate stage between the oral tradition and alphabetical writing, a stage through which all writing systems may have passed. But while the hieroglyph provides a logical link between speech and writing in what, for Voltaire, is the gradual perfection of the techniques of historiography, the historiography which the hieroglyph itself produced would be more accurately described as myth: "C'est à ces hiéroglyphes que nous devons les fables, qui furent les premiers écrits des hommes. La fable est bien plus ancienne que l'histoire" (*Essai,* Introduction, xliii).

For Voltaire, the Chinese and their "écriture symbolique" represent a more significant stage in the development of rationality. China is initially presented to the reader as the first culture to produce a wholly rational historiography, and so it seems, at least initially, that with the invention of "l'écriture symbolique" a clear-cut break with the irrationality of the fable has been made. The rationalization of historiography went hand in hand with the rationalization of Chinese social and political life: "Point d'histoire chez eux avant celle de leurs empereurs; presque point de fictions, aucun prodige, nul homme inspiré qui se dise demi-dieu, comme chez les Egyptiens et chez les Grecs: dès que ce peuple écrit, il écrit raisonnablement." (*Essai*, Introduction, xviii). "Nous avons remarqué que le corps de cet état subsiste avec splendeur depuis plus de quatre mille ans, sans que les lois, les moeurs, le langage, la manière même de s'habiller, aient souffert d'altération sensible (*Essai*, i). Indeed, Voltaire's China seems to conform in every respect to his ideal of an enlightened society. The Chinese are religious, but their religion has none of those features which lead to the fanatisme Voltaire despises. It has no priesthood and no religious hierarchy distinct from the political rulers. Confucius, the foremost of Chinese religious figures, did not teach the Chinese a new faith. He was a civil servant "qui enseignait les anciennes lois" (*Essai*, Introduction, xviii). Chinese society is hierarchical, but there is no "noblesse" in the European sense, government service being the only title to honours (*Essai*, ii).

Given Voltaire's admiration for the Chinese and the apparent similarity between China and enlightened European society, the way in which China and the historiography it produced are ultimately excluded from the historical realm is all the more interesting. In Voltaire's view, it is those same virtues which permitted the Chinese to form a rational government and to produce a rational historiography which have isolated China from the current of history, for they have impeded progress as well as prevented degeneration. "Si on cherche pourquoi tant d'arts et de sciences, cultivés sans interruption depuis si longtemps à la Chine, ont cependant fait si peu de progrès, il y en a peut-être deux raisons: l'une est le respect prodigieux que ces peuples ont pour ce qui leur est transmis par leurs péres, et qui rend parfait à leurs yeux tout ce qui est ancien; l'autre est la nature de leur langue, le premier principe de toutes les connaissances" (*Essai*, i). The respect of the Chinese for authority and for the ancient has prevented them from making the scientific discoveries which have characterized European progress. With regard to the question of language, this same respect for the ancient has prevented the Chinese from adopting western printing, for to do so, they would have to abandon symbolic writing in favour of the alphabet (*Essai*, 1). In Voltaire's view, so long as writing continues to be restricted to the small and inevitably elderly elite who has mastered the symbolic system only after years of study, the continued stagnation of China's political and intellectual life is assured. China, like the less rationally organized cultures which preceded it, is fundamentally ahistorical in Voltaire's terms, not because its culture and language are determined by accident, custom, sheer change, etc., but because it is closed to any modification. China has isolated itself from the purely negative effects of time, from pure change, but has succeeded too well, for in doing so has cut itself off from rational, historical time, or progress.

Voltaire's fundamental lack of appreciation for ancient history extends even to those ancient cultures which he seems at points to admire. Though ancient cultures are arranged by Voltaire on a scale placing those which most resemble modern Europe at the top, though one ancient culture might be progressive with regard to another, none guarantees the production of rational historiography and thus none provides a starting point for a rational history of mankind. Though the subject of the *Essai sur les mœurs* is the history of the world prior to the age of Louis XIV, the *Essai* only serves to confirm a remark by Voltaire in the introduction to the *Histoire de Charles XII* on the futility of most history:

> Il me semble que si l'on voulait mettre à profit le temps présent, on ne passerait point sa vie à s'infatuer des fables anciennes. Je conseillerais à un jeune homme d'avoir une légère teinture de ces temps resulés: mais je voudrais qu'on commençât une étude sérieuse de l'histoire au temps où elle devient véritablement intéressante pour nous: il me semble que c'est vers la fin du xve siècle. L'imprimerie, qu'on inventa en ce temps-là, commence à la rendre moins incertaine.
>
> (*Charles XII*, ''Remarques sur l'histoire'')

Voltaire renews his effort to establish an historical age starting with the invention of printing. By permitting the widespread diffusion of knowledge and of Enlightenment values, printing proves the superiority of the alphabet over other writing systems (for, among the systems discussed by Voltaire, only the alphabet is adapted to printing), and the superiority of modern Europe over ancient Greece and Rome. But Voltaire admits in his article on ''Langues'' in the *Dictionnaire philosophique* that no modern European language can perfectly express what he considers to be reality, and, in writing on modern history and historiography, Voltaire often declares that both have been less than what he would consider realistic or rational. This admission reveals the arbitrariness of Voltaire's exclusion from the historical realm of ancient cultures and writing systems. If all writing systems including the alphabet are only relatively faithful to the ''real,'' then the causes of ''irrationality'' do not lie in the systems themselves, but rather in the ideologies that dictate the various forms of historical discourse. In discussing the difficulties faced by the rational historiographer in the modern age, it is precisely these problems which Voltaire takes up. But he does so only after the exclusion of ancient cultures from the rational on grounds which he himself now implicitly rejects as inessential, that is, on the grounds that the ''pre-alphabetical'' writing systems are not technically ''advanced'' enough to ensure a rational representation of the real. For Voltaire, it is only the ''destructive'' forces undermining the rational which are ideological, and this view effectively precludes any discussion of the exclusion which founds the rational order. For Voltaire, ideology is only what others are prejudiced by.

Indeed, printing, which permits the broad diffusion of historiography, its public criticism, etc., and the resources of modern governments, which permit the printing and storing of chronicles and treaties (*Charles XII*, "Nouvelles Considérations sur l'histoire") do not in themselves guarantee that historiography is rational, even though they permit it to be factual. As we have already noted, in Voltaire's view facts alone do not constitute history: "Si on voulait faire usage de sa raison au lieu de sa mémoire, et examiner plus que transcrire, on ne multiplierait pas à l'infini les livres et les erreurs; il faudrait n'écrire que des choses neuves et vraies. Ce qui manquent d'ordinaire à ceux qui compilent l'histoire, c'est l'esprit philosophique" (*Charles XII*, "Remarques"). Once again Voltaire attempts to found an age of rational historiography, this time coinciding not merely with the modern age (post–fifteenth century) and the invention of printing, but with the advent of what he calls philosophy: "Chez toutes les nations l'histoire est défigurée par la fable, jusqu'à ce qu'enfin la philosophie arrive au milieu de ces ténèbres" (*Essai*, cxcvii).

Like all previous guarantees of the rationality of historiography, philosophy is threatened from all sides. Speculation on the broader sense of history does not, for Voltaire, necessarily represent an advance over mere fact-finding. In attempting to go beyond factual accuracy the historian risks being caught up in his own speculations to such an extent that they no longer reflect historical reality, but rather, become an intellectual fiction of the philosopher-historian's creation. This, it seems, was the case of Boulainvilliers, described by Voltaire as "le plus savant gentilhomme du royaume dans l'histoire, et le plus capable d'écrire celle de la France, s'il n'avait pas été trop systématique" (*Louis XIV*, "Catalogue des écrivains français"). The overly systematic historian is, for Voltaire, a more sophisticated version of the providential historian who interprets history from a narrow cultural or religious perspective. Such, according to Voltaire, were the Jewish historians who could interpret world-shaking events only as being for their particular edification, and such are the European historians who blithely ignore the four-thousand-year-old Chinese empire to assert that the monarchy who is paying them to write its history is the oldest in the world.

Furthermore, not all of Voltaire's contemporaries shared his philosopher's view that the principal value of ancient historiography, which Voltaire considers "aussi faux qu'obscur et dégoûtant" (*Essai*, Introduction, lii) is to heighten the reader's thankfulness to be living in the age of Enlightenment. Traces of their opinions can be found in Voltaire's attacks on them. Some, though they too may have perceived past historiography as largely unscientific, still felt that these "fables" deserved the attention of rational historiographers as documents of past values. In Voltaire's view, those who believe the "fables" recounted by ancient history are bad enough—"insensé et imbécile"—but "peut-être les plus insensés de tous ont été ceux qui ont voulu trouver un sens à ces fables absurdes, et mettre de la raison dans la folie" (*Essai*, Introduction, vi). Still others, more critical of present institutions, looked to the past for models which might serve for reform. Voltaire accuses them of desiring the impossible—that history would reverse itself

(*Essai*, lxxxv). For Voltaire, the only rational attitude toward the past is one of rejection: "Quel plus grand fruit pouvons-nous retirer de toutes les vicissitudes recueillies dans cet Essai sur les moeurs que de nous convaincre que toute nation a toujours été malheureuse jusqu'à ce que les lois et le pouvoir législatif aient été établis sans contradiction?" (*Essai*, lxxxii).

Thus even the historiography of his contemporaries has been, by Voltaire's definition, largely irrational. If rational historiography is possible, it is possible only in the future or, rather, in the present in which Voltaire himself is writing. It is impossible for Voltaire to live up to his own definition of rational historiography in the greater part of the *Essai sur les mœurs*, for its subject is the ancient and feudal cultures which, both as producers of historiography and as subjects for later historiographers, are sources of irrationality. In the age of Louis XIV Voltaire finds a subject worthy of the rational historiographer, and thus it is only with the *Siècle de Louis XIV* that it becomes possible for Voltaire to live up to his programmatic statements concerning rational historiography.

One of Voltaire's most frequent criticisms of existing historiography is its preoccupation with events of primary concern to the aristocracy and the monarchy, and of little importance to the larger audience which Voltaire designates as "mankind" (Such a conception of "mankind" would not include the peasants, who, in the eighteenth century were the vast majority of France's population, but whose illiteracy "naturally" excluded them from Voltaire's audience.):

> Je considère donc ici en général le sort des hommes plutôt que les révolutions du trône. C'est au genre humain qu'il eut fallu faire attention dans l'histoire: c'est là que chaque écrivain eût du dire *homo sum*; mais la plupart des historiens ont décrit des batailles.
>
> (*Essai*, lxxxiv)

> Je voudrais découvrir quelle était alors la société des hommes, comment on vivait dans l'intérieur des familles, quels arts étaient cultivés, plutôt que de répéter tant de malheurs et tant de combats.
>
> (*Essai*, lxxxi)

The notion that true history is made by the class of people engaged in commerce, industry, the arts and sciences is directly contradicted by the notion that Louis XIV was the cause of the great political and intellectual achievements of his day. Voltaire's project of describing the state of "mankind" in the preceding century is at odds with his decision to characterize the century in question as that of Louis XIV: "Mais surtout soyez un peu moins fâché contre moi de ce que j'appelle le siècle dernier le siècle de Louis XIV. . . . Non seulement il s'est fait de grandes choses sous son règne, mais c'est lui que les faisait" (*Lettre à milord Hervey*).

Voltaire's insistence that the role of Louis XIV is all-important in rationalizing intellectual and political life contradicts his claims concerning the historical importance of the middle class. It is very much in keeping, however, with his claim that the rational can only be introduced by means of a radical rupture with an irrational past. For Voltaire Louis XIV embodies just such a break with the past. René Pomeau (ed. Voltaire, *Oeuvres historiques*) notes that Voltaire minimizes the accomplishments of previous governments in order to portray Louis XIV as the originator of all institutional reform. By the same logic, Voltaire never portrays the change instituted by Louis XIV as the result of a prolonged struggle between the monarch and reactionary historical forces. The reforms which initiate rational history cannot be themselves historical, they must be immediate if rationality is to be established without contradiction. Voltaire portrays the most radical political changes as coinciding with the will of Louis XIV. He speaks once and the parliament of Paris, a perennial fomentor of destructive, factional disputes, is silenced for an indefinite period. He dominates the nobility—a constant source, in Voltaire's view, of violence and political irrationality—by bringing them all to Versailles where they are wholly under his influence. He wills it, and, with Colbert as his instrument, French trade and industry flourish and a navy is created overnight. Indeed, Voltaire argues that Colbert's accomplishments were not his own, but should be credited to Louis XIV: "qu'eût fait un Colbert sous un autre prince?" (*Lettre à milord Hervey*).

Ironically, Louis XIV's patronage of commerce, science, arts and letters comes to justify the importance of his actions in spheres which for Voltaire himself are only indirectly, or even negatively, related to the former. The preponderant role ascribed to Louis XIV in the "positive" achievements of his reign, forces Voltaire to emphasize the military and aristocratic matters which, much more than the arts and sciences, or even commerce, preoccupied Louis XIV. Thus by far the better part of the *Siècle de Louis XIV* deals with aspects of history which, according to Voltaire, have already received too much attention and from the point of view of which the age of Louis XIV is much like any other. Though Voltaire frequently laments the fact that "la plupart des historiens n'ont décrit que des batailles," the first twenty-four of a total of thirty-nine chapters comprising the *Siècle de Louis XIV* are concerned with military history. Voltaire himself seems aware of this apparent incongruity when he writes at the beginning of chapter xi: "On croit nécessaire de dire à ceux qui pourront lire cet ouvrage qu'ils doivent se souvenir que ce n'est point ici une simple relation de campagnes, mais plutôt une histoire des mœurs des hommes." Indeed, it is necessary for Voltaire to state what is far from obvious, for aside from his protestation to the contrary, nothing substantial distinguishes his relation of Louis XIV's conquests and reverses from the military history he declares to be irrelevant to rational historiography: "Après avoir lu trois ou quatre mille descriptions de batailles, et la teneur de quelques centaines de traités, j'ai trouvé que je n'étais guère plus instruit au fond. . . . Je ne connais pas plus les Français et les Sarrasins par la bataille de Charles Martel, que je ne connais les

Tartares et les Turcs par la victoire que Tamerlan remporta sur Bajazet" (*Charles XII*, "Nouvelles Considérations").

Four out of the thirty-nine chapters are devoted to anecdotes. And yet in his "Nouvelles considérations sur l'histoire" Voltaire himself declares they are only of ephemeral interest:

> Il y a des livres qui m'apprennent les anecdotes vraies ou fausses d'une cour. Quiconque a vu les cours, ou a eu envie de les voir, est aussi avide de ces illustres bagatelles qu'une femme de province aime à savoir les nouvelles de sa petite ville: c'est au fond la même chose et le même mérite. . . . Toutes ces petites miniatures se conservent une génération ou deux, et périssent ensuite pour jamais.
>
> (*Charles XII*, "Nouvelles Considérations")

According to Voltaire, anecdotes, like battles, are all alike. Once again, Voltaire reveals an awareness that he is including material which does not support his contentions about the rationality of Louis XIV's reign. At the same time he attempts to justify himself by invoking a uniqueness of Louis XIV that the anecdotes themselves cannot reveal: "Je croirais même que ces intrigues de cour, étrangères à l'État, ne devraient point entrer dans l'histoire si le grand siècle de Louis XIV ne rendait tout intéressant" (*Louis XIV*, 26).

Five chapters of the *Siècle de Louis XIV* are devoted to religious disputes. Here Voltaire himself points up the contradiction between what he sees as the enlightenment of the age and the ignorance and narrowness of the antagonists. These disputes cannot simply be dismissed as historically insignificant in view of the role of Louis XIV himself in aggravating them. Voltaire views Louis XIV's role in the debate surrounding Jansenism as of little consequence, for he viewed Jansenism itself as more or less impotent (*Louis XIV*, 37). But the violence of the government's policy against the Huguenots, culminating in the *dragonnade*, and the active role of Louis XIV in the formulation of that policy are, even for Voltaire, very real:

> C'était un étrange contraste, que, du sein d'une cour voluptueuse où regnaient la douceur des moeurs, les grâces, les charmes de la société, il partît des ordres si durs et si impitoyables. . . . "Sa Majesté veut qu'on fasse éprouver les dernières rigueurs à ceux qui ne voudront pas se faire de sa religion; et ceux qui auront la sotte gloire de vouloir demeurer les derniers doivent être poussés jusqu'à la dernière extrémité."
>
> (*Louis XIV*, xxxvi)

The conflict between Louis XIV's interests and those Voltaire is promoting as those of "mankind" persists in the chapters on government finances and the arts which are in principle devoted to the positive accomplishments of Louis XIV's reign. In Voltaire's view, the wars conducted by

Louis XIV had an ultimately negative effect on France's economy: "Depuis les anciens Romains, je ne connais aucune nation qui se soit enrichie par des victoires. . . . Parmi les nations de l'Europe, la guerre, au bout de quelques années, rend le vainqueur presque aussi malheureux que le vaincu" (*Louis XIV*, xxx). In many cases, the exigencies of war brought about the abolition of reforms made in the early years of Louis XIV's reign. Though elsewhere Voltaire insists that Louis XIV deserved ultimate credit for the accomplishments of Colbert, the chapters on finances show Colbert time and again "emporté hors de ses mésures," that is, resorting to economic practices he deplored in order to finance Louis XIV's grandeur: "Colbert, pour fournir à la fois aux dépenses des guerres, des bâtiments, et des plaisirs, fut obligé de rétablir, vers l'an 1672, ce qu'il avait voulu d'abord abolir pour jamais: impôts en parti, rentes, charges nouvelles, augmentation de gages, enfin ce qui soutient l'État quelque temps, et l'obère pour des siècles" (*Louis XIV*, xxx). Louis XIV's preoccupation with his grandeur had a negative effect on art and architecture analogous to its effect on finances and the economy. Though Voltaire claimed that the consumption of articles "de luxe" had a stimulating effect on French industry, he deplored Louis XIV's decision to concentrate art and luxury at his own capital, Versailles, rather than at Paris, where the result would have been accessible to a greater number of citizens (*Louis XIV*, xxix). Like the wars conducted by Louis XIV, Versailles, the symbol of his grandeur, became "un gouffre où tous les canaux de l'abondance s'engloutissent" (*Louis XIV*, xxx).

Voltaire declares that the age of Louis XIV was "celui . . . qui approche le plus de la perfection" and that Louis XIV was directly responsible for the great accomplishments of his age. What the *Siècle de Louis XIV* reveals is that the specific actions and preoccupations of Louis XIV were, more often than not, in conflict with the philosopher's notion of perfection or rationality. In the light of this conflict, Voltaire tries to retrieve the ultimate sense of Louis XIV and his reign by maintaining that Louis XIV's relationship to the projects which exalted him at the expense of the "nation"—the third estate—was one of fundamental detachment, that is, that his essence as rational monarch was not fundamentally implicated in any of the specific actions or policies which were in apparent conflict with the ideal of rationality.

There is a parallel to be drawn between the rational historiographer and the rational monarch. In principle, the former produces an historiography free of ideological distortion. He scrupulously avoids interposing his personal point of view or any speculation which would be the product of his imagination and not a faithful reflection of the "real." To do otherwise would be to lose his objectivity, to become implicated in an ideology and, thereby, to cease to be rational. According to Voltaire, the rational historiographer must "peindre au lieu de juger," and he finds in a painting of Pope Gregory VII the model which the rational historiographer must strive to imitate: "Tous les portraits, ou flatteurs ou odieux, que tant d'écrivains ont fait de lui, se trouvent dans le tableau d'un peintre napolitan, qui peignit Grégoire tenant une houlette dans une main et un fouet dans l'autre, foulant des sceptres à ses pieds et ayant à côte de lui les filets et les poissons de saint Pierre" (*Essai*, xlvi).

It is only the rational order over which Louis XIV rules that maintains a relationship to itself through time which, in Voltaire's view, can be termed historical. Thus in maintaining the rational order, Louis XIV produces history in much the same way that the philosopher produces historiography. His production, like that of the rational historiographer, must be free of any ideological distortion which might result from the predominance of one faction within the political order. Though there may be an apparent divergence between the interests of his grandeur and those of the nation, he must maintain that, in fact, his grandeur and the interests of the state are one, that his relationship to the rational order is perfectly disinterested. The rational order, which takes the form of a tableau when presented by the philosopher-historian, also takes a visual form when presented by the monarch. The reign of Louis XIV is a spectacle played to all of Europe. His marriage is celebrated by the representation of an Italian opera in which the king and queen both dance. In 1662 a carousel is presented across from the Tuileries in which the king figures prominently. Louis plans his military expeditions much as he stages these spectacles. Taste and magnificence are evident even in his military camps. The military début of Monseigneur is carefully staged by his father: "On avait tout prévu et tout disposé pour que le fils de Louis XIV, contribuant à cette expédition de son nom et de sa présence, ne reçut pas un affront. Le maréchal de Duras commandait réellement l'armée"(*Louis XIV*, xvi). His own campaigns are equally well-staged: "Le roi, avec tant d'avantages, sur de sa fortune et de sa gloire, menait avec lui un historien qui devait écrire ses victoires" (*Louis XIV*, x). But though he may participate in the historical spectacle that is his reign, Voltaire assures us that Louis XIV himself is never caught up in the spectacle; his participation never endangers his absolute status as monarch. In this sense, Voltaire's portrait of Louis XIV contrasts explicitly with that of Charles XII of Sweden. The latter best typifies Voltaire's definition of the "glorieux" or the ruler who can achieve only a "vaine" or "fausse gloire" because he has become excessively enamoured of "l'appareil de la representation" (*Dictionnaire philosophique*, "Glorieux"). Charles XII seeks out the most dangerous situation on a given battlefield in order to better demonstrate his own heroism. His ardour contrasts with Louis XIV's detachment: "On ne lui voyait point, dans les travaux de la guerre, ce courage emporté de François Ier et de Henri IV, qui cherchaient toutes les espèces de dangers. Il se contentait de ne les pas craindre, et d'engager tout le monde à s'y précipiter pour lui avec ardeur" (*Louis XIV*, ix). Charles XII abandoned his specific duties as ruler of Sweden in his quest for personal glory. But the brilliant court amusements which reflect Louis XIV's personal glory "ne dérobaient rien aux travaux continuels du monarque" (*Louis XIV*, xxv). Significantly, as soon as it occurs to Louis XIV that his participation as an actor in the plays and operas produced for the amusement of the court detracts from his dignity as sovereign, he ceases to appear on the stage.

It is not the specific policies he may or may not have implemented which distinguish Louis XIV from the monarchs who have preceded him. There is no essential difference between his wars, his court, his personal intrigues, and the wars, courts, and intrigues of rulers of the less rational political orders portrayed in the *Essai sur les mœurs*. The rationality of Louis XIV's monarchy lies in Voltaire's affirmation—which echoes the affirmation of Louis XIV himself—that Louis XIV's actions were fundamentally disinterested, that he represented, not himself, or a class, but the state. In the final analysis, Louis XIV's reality and rationality are purely formal, for no specific action or long-term policy can negate the rational, nothing concrete can disprove the purity of Louis XIV's intentions.

By Voltaire's definition, the *Siècle de Louis XIV* represents a privileged moment in history and historiography, one in which the rational and the "vraisemblable" are more than ideally conceivable as the organizers of "history." But in fact, nothing concrete distinguishes Louis XIV from other monarchs, and there is no substantial thematic difference between the *Siècle de Louis XIV* and the *Essai*. As Voltaire's text reveals, the "historical" is a term devoid of any specific content. Its only reality is formal, that is, its only reality consists in the infinite exclusion of any alterity or content. The various terms—the rational, the "vraisemblable," the historical, the perfectability of man—which are key terms in Voltaire's theory of history are only negatively connected to the texts of Voltaire's histories, which are chronicles of the irrational, the "invraisemblable," and the persistent misery of an "inhuman" mankind. In this sense, the work itself contradicts the claims Voltaire makes on its behalf. It bears witness that the order posited by rational historiography is only the relatively valid "system" which another faction imposes on the "real," and that its claim to universal validity is simply false.

The coherence of Voltaire's text does not lie in the consistency between his programmatic statements and the historical content of the text. At the same time, it must be pointed out that the "real" or content which contests the formal claims of rationality is itself defined and determined by the text. It is the rational order itself which names the elements it excludes—the "irrational," the "fanatical," the "absurd," etc. From this point of view Voltaire's failure to invest the rational-historical with any positive content can do nothing to invalidate the rational, just as no concrete action can disprove the disinterestedness of the rational monarch. The ultimate vindication of the rational would not lie in its success or failure as a programme, but in the fact that it is the rational which determines what is "success" and what is "failure." The pure formality of the conception of history at work in the *Essai sur les mœurs* and the *Siècle de Louis XIV* conveys their ideological message. Seen in this light, the programmatic statements do in fact express the ultimate coherence of the work as a product of ideology.

From the point of view of its ideological coherence, Voltaire's work is part of a past which no longer touches us directly. The formal rules determining the text as a mechanism of exclusion can be brought to light, understood, and thereby cease to determine historiography in the present. A break with the Voltairean past becomes possible. Indeed, one cannot be aware of the ideological and theoretical limitations of Voltaire's view of history without hoping that it will in some sense be gone beyond—however much the example of Voltaire's manipulation of the notion of progress may cause us to relativize our conception of the difference between the present and the future. At the same time, no amount of critical distance from Voltaire which the present might provide can guarantee our ability to produce a text which would not also be a mechanism of ideological exclusion. At the very least, a text making such a claim would exclude "Voltaire," and with him, an important segment of the "eighteenth century." If we argue that Voltaire's view of history is still relevant, it is not in the name of a universally valid conception of history of the Voltairean type, but in the name of the same ideological considerations which make apparent the relativity of Voltaire's rationalist, universalist claims. While our own notion of ideological coherence implies a critical distance from the ideology in question, it would be naive to conclude that any amount of distance could automatically guarantee the distinction between our notion of coherence and Voltaire's conception of the rational.

Thus if Voltaire's historiography is still readable for us, it is not because that historiography is coherent in any simple sense. There is a distance between Voltaire's texts and ourselves in the light of which they appear ideologically coherent and part of an irrevocable past which is no longer directly pertinent. At the same time, there is a potential similarity between the relationship of Voltaire's text to the elements it excludes and the relationship of contemporary historiography to the historical context which defines it and which it defines. In this sense, Voltaire's text is neither simply past nor simply contemporary. And while this dual status constrains us as we approach the text, it is this same dual status which permits us to read Voltaire.

La Mettrie: The Robot
and the Automaton

Blair Campbell

Historians of social and political thought generally regard the eighteenth century as the last age in which intelligent men seriously undertook to propound "philosophies of life." The *philosophes* of the French Enlightenment represent western man's last attempt to impose ethical coherence upon his life by means of his reason. And, though some view this enterprise with misgiving, the general tendency is to treat the *philosophes* with great sympathy and veneration. Our admiration for their philosophic quest of the humane (if not the good) life is so pronounced that we tend to use it as a criterion in determining which of the French thinkers are worthy of our remembrance. For instance, most historians would agree that while such men as Voltaire, Diderot, d'Holbach, and Helvétius were superficially conversant with the major intellectual currents of their time, they were not particularly astute as philosophers; their doctrines are often shallow and unoriginal. Yet their philosophic ambitions are more important to us than their doctrines. The latter were but means, instruments for their admirable task of humanizing man's social and political institutions.

Such a perspective is useful, and perhaps even necessary for our understanding of the *philosophes*, but it has often had the unfortunate consequence of equating humanitarian philosophizing with a sweeping dilettantism. And, in at least one instance—that of Julien La Mettrie—an influential Enlightenment thinker whose name is associated with a particular doctrine has been unjustly ignored. Because of his apparently exclusive preoccupation with biology, La Mettrie's role as a *philosophe* has been overlooked; he has been understood as a minor figure, of interest only within the specialized confines of the history of science. This results in undue

From *Journal of the History of Ideas* 31, no. 4 (October–December 1970). © 1970 by Journal of the History of Ideas, Inc.

narrowness of our understanding, not merely of La Mettrie, but of the general problems encountered by humanitarian Enlightenment thinkers as well.

La Mettrie is remembered today as a biological theorist, a specialized protoscientist. He is significant, according to our contemporary understanding of him, because of his agency in the evolution of Cartesianism. He completed the last stage in the transformation of this dualistic system into a materialist monism congenial to biological speculation. While this interpretation is correct as far as it goes, it is too restrictive. La Mettrie was a scientist, but unless we see that there is more to him than that, we are forced to ignore certain facts about his reception among his contemporaries and about his thinking.

Although his major work, *L'Homme machine*, made La Mettrie an object of loathing and outrage among most of his contemporaries, it earned him great respect from the *philosophes*; indeed Voltaire openly borrowed from him. But as a result of his later writings, La Mettrie was ostracized even by the *philosophes*. It is doubtful that a mere scientist would have provoked such scorn and ridicule as were directed against La Mettrie by cleric and *philosophe* alike.

If we read *L'Homme machine* without preconception, we cannot fail to see that it is more than a biological treatise. Its biological aspect is presented in the most cursory fashion; the man-machine hypothesis relinquishes space to other themes concerning the nature of reason, the good life, and the good society. The La Mettrie-as-scientist interpretation requires that we dismiss these other themes as the irrelevant effusions of an undisciplined mind.

There is little doubt that La Mettrie viewed himself as a *philosophe*, as well as a scientist. In eulogizing Descartes, he was careful to distinguish science from philosophy: "without him the field of philosophy, like the field of science without Newton, might perhaps be still uncultivated" (*Man a Machine*). Newton was the founder of modern science, yet it is Descartes whom La Mettrie praises. Moreover, La Mettrie decorates the frontispiece of *L'Homme machine* with a quotation from Voltaire. It is unlikely that the author would have considered a poet's *bons mots* an effective eye catcher for a scientific audience. If we accept La Mettrie's own apparent conception of his role, then we acquire a more coherent perspective concerning his aims and procedures. For instance, the exuberant blasts at superstition and human presumption, that otherwise seem so extraneous in *L'Homme machine*, acquire significance.

If the La Mettrie-as-*philosophe* perspective is helpful in elucidating *L'Homme machine*, it becomes indispensable if we are to attribute any coherence to the whole of his writings. In the first place, his works range a gamut—from the arid scholasticism of the *Traité de l'âme* to the sensual exuberance of the *Discours sur le bonheur*—far too broad to be encompassed by an interpretation which attempts to maintain the integrity of a given doctrine. Secondly, the "man-machine" undergoes a metamorphosis in La Mettrie's writings, a change much like that wrought upon Hawthorne's scarlet letter. In *L'Homme machine* it is used to annul the uniqueness and spontaneity of the individual in his relationship to society (or culture): mechanism hangs upon the human personality as a symbol of humiliation, an invitation for society to chastise all elements of individuality. But in La Mettrie's later writings, the same doctrine is used to opposite effect. The man-machine now asserts his individuality: mechanism no longer represents the defeat, but rather the triumph, of personality. The formerly chastised individual becomes superior to, somehow more untrammeled than, his culture. A purely scientific understanding of the "man-machine" must blind us to this metamorphosis as completely as would a calligraphic interpretation of Hawthorne's "A." Only when understood as a *philosophe* does La Mettrie's thought acquire coherence. But let us make certain that we are aware of the consequence of accepting a La Mettrie-as-*philosophe* interpretation: we are to understand his doctrines (especially the man-machine notion), not primarily as self-justifying intellectual constructs, but as weapons; weapons which always remain subordinate to the overriding purpose of the *philosophe*.

If, however, we are to understand La Mettrie—or, for that matter, the French Enlightenment—we must remember that philosophic humanitarianism was not without its dilemmas. The task of humanizing politics and society was insoluble until a prior problem was solved, that of politicizing and socializing humanity. Enlightenment thinkers had inherited an egocentric anthropology from their seventeenth-century predecessors who appeared impervious to their ideals of civility. Unleashed, perhaps, by the Reformation and secularized by laymen such as Montaigne and the libertines, egocentrism had gradually come to be enshrined on all secular fronts. Whether we turn to the satire of La Rochefoucauld or Swift, the harsh political philosophy of Hobbes, or the comprehensive system of Descartes, we encounter a conception of human nature inimical to the traditional forms of civil persuasion.

Descartes' influence was perhaps greatest in transmitting egocentrism to the eighteenth century. It was he who offered the world its first secular framework for total comprehension and, concomitantly, the most unequivocally secular conception of human dignity ever asserted in the West. For the first time in western history, the individual was freed from the oppressive demands of conscience in his pursuit of manhood: he could accept his own thought and desires—even his passions—without qualm or hesitation, if he but subjected them to methodical self-discipline. But Descartes had also held out the promise of social order and harmony: he had proclaimed ethics to be the highest branch in his tree of knowledge. And ethics, as the term has been used throughout history (certainly as Descartes' Enlightenment progeny understood it), places the beholder in a perspective which demands that he look askance at exclusively egocentric behavior.

Ethics involves the individual in a relationship of obligation to others; it requires that the subject venture beyond himself in interests and fundamental commitments, that he be genuinely other-regarding. Thus Descartes had the effect, however unintentionally, of offering two mutually exclusive goals for behavior. The Cartesian promise becomes a dilemma. Since there appeared to be no solution for the dilemma, it was necessary for the *philosophe* to grasp one of its horns. If he wished to seize that horn provided by the Cartesian ethical promise, then he had to attempt to undo, to deny, the "facts" of Cartesian egocentrism.

La Mettrie's thinking acquires continuity if we understand it as an alternative seizing of both horns of the dilemma. In *L'Homme machine* he seizes the ethical horn. The man-machine doctrine, seen in conjunction with the other themes of the book, is not merely a scientific description of man, but primarily a propagandistic device for attacking the prevalent conception of egocentrism. At this first stage of his thinking, the man-machine is a mere robot, a gadget directed by the impersonal forces of society or culture. The next paragraph describes this phase of La Mettrie's thought. But La Mettrie pays far too high a price for sociability (he goes much further than the other *philosophes* in depriving man of his spontaneity). In subsequent works, he rejects his own creation. He then seizes the other horn of the dilemma, exulting in the individual. The man-machine is transformed from a culture-directed robot to an automaton; a machine no less determined than his sociable progenitor, but determined by the vast forces which govern the universe, rather than by the forces of culture. More importantly, his governing forces operate upon him in a unique manner as a result of variations in the generic organizational pattern of man. Destiny thus confirms him in his individuality. Culture now becomes his oppressor rather than his director. The final section describes this metamorphosis.

If an attack on egocentrism is to be effective, it must strike at the root level: it must attempt to erode that mysterious inner force, the ego or soul. Such an assault presents a problem, however, since this inner force emanates from a feeling, rather than from an intellectual persuasion; a feeling or an intuition that the individual has within him an unlimited source of creativity, an irreducible and inexplicable potency. Because it is, in essence, noncognitive, it eludes rationalistic attack; like Proteus it can change from one conceptual form to another with the utmost facility. Assault the "cogito," it emerges as "will"; charge "will" and it becomes simply "*moi*": these are but echoes of a hidden voice. How does one destroy an intuition? Perhaps there is no effective way. But the dogged aggressor must begin somewhere: he examines the immediate emotional-ideational milieu of this feeling. What notions seem to be most cherished by this inner force? Spontaneity and unity are two such notions. Man, for Descartes, was like God in his capacity for spontaneity, and his "*moi*" was a homogeneous unit. Is it possible to play these predicates against each other? One must first devise a framework that is no less related to the ego's milieu.

The mechanistic framework seemed to fit the requirements. Descartes himself formulated it and it had since acquired scientific legitimacy. If it could be broadened to include man, its range of appeal could be extended beyond the realm of science. A perspective which would allow us to approach man, not as an enigma, but rather as a puzzle—a collection of pieces cut to a determined pattern—would be both aesthetically and intellectually gratifying. Moreover, such a perspective would fulfil the need for unity even more than Descartes' formulation. Not merely the ego, but all of man would be homogeneous. And best of all, this conception of unity could be used against the more dangerous feeling of spontaneity, since it would entail determinism.

Mechanism as a critical perspective or framework is quite different from mechanism as a positive doctrine, however. As a positive doctrine, it must be presented in cogent form. As a critical perspective one can either take its cogency for granted, or rely on its appeal within a broader frame of reference, in order to get down to cases. And it is primarily as a critical perspective that La Mettrie utilizes mechanism. He is not concerned to describe and defend the case of the man-machine, but rather to wield it; to wield it against the ego and its conceptual forms. The reader of *L'Homme machine* searches in vain for a detailed description of the working of the human mechanism. Instead, he finds numerous examples of bodily states such as disease and old age, exercising an influence upon our mental condition. Since these are invariably examples of negative influence, they are not adequate even to substantiate his modest conclusion that "the diverse states of the soul are always correlative with those of the body." And La Mettrie is careful to point out that he is speaking only of correlation, rather than causation:

> . . . we must confess that our weak understanding, limited to the coarsest observations, cannot see the bonds that exist between cause and effects. This is a kind of harmony that philosophers will never know.

As it stands, the argument would be acceptable to the most conservative of clerics. No one will deny that a relation exists between old age and senescence, or between fever and delirium. And here the argument for mechanism stops; henceforth it must rest on its own appeal. The conclusions, however, are quite different from what we would expect. Having argued half-heartedly for the probability of the man-machine notion, La Mettrie launches his attack on the ego:

> The soul is therefore but an empty word, of which no one has any idea, and which an enlightened man should use only to signify the part of us that thinks. Given the least principle of motion, animated bodies will have all that is necessary for moving, feeling, thinking, repenting, or in a word for conducting themselves in the physical realm, and in the moral realm which depends upon it.

The sense of inner prowess is gone, replaced by a simple principle of motion. Motion is universal, conceptual, predictable and therefore necessary; the soul functions consequently upon the same principle as the most insignificant dust particle. Knowledge is universal—since knowledge must be of motion—and man is unified.

La Mettrie is no less relentless in his attack on other manifestations of the egocentric self. He scourges it when it appears as "will" and when it assumes its most fundamental, cognitive form, that of "cogito." Of course, will is easily dispatched: it vanishes as a direct consequence of the determinist postulate:

> In vain you fall back on the power of the will, since for one order that the will gives, it bows a hundred times to the yoke. . . . Beautiful the soul, and powerful the will which cannot act save by permission of the bodily conditions, and whose tastes change with age and fever!

Cogito, however, must be approached more gingerly. Descartes had fortified it strongly with a bulwark of indefinability, insisting that it was a primal reality. Yet if it could be successfully assaulted, egocentrism would suffer most heavily, for the thinking function was its fountainhead, providing the justification for the individual's self-esteem. La Mettrie approaches *cogito* from several angles. He makes several isolated sniper's forays, such as this rather cryptic attempt to drive a wedge between reason and happiness:

> We were not originally made to be learned; we have become so perhaps by a sort of abuse of our organic faculties, and at the expense of the State which nourishes a host of sluggards whom vanity has adorned with the name of philosophers. Nature has created us solely to be happy.

He repeatedly disparages knowledge; all human lore is but a "huge mass of words and figures." Moreover, he removes God as the source of certainty for *cogito*, since God's existence is a "theoretical" truth of little "practical" value. His most concerted assault against *cogito*, however, is found in his theory of the imagination, his own peculiar version of empiricism. All of man's intellectual activities are reducible to the functioning of the imagination:

> Thus, judgment, reason, and memory are not absolute parts of the soul, but merely modifications of this kind of medullary screen upon which images of the objects painted in the eye are projected as by a magic lantern.

La Mettrie never describes this sensory screen in detail but the emphasis is upon its role as passive receptacle, rather than as a modifier. By "modification" he apparently means intuitions of similarity and dissimilarity, as well as other elementary perceptual and logical rules. Modification, however, is far removed from the dynamic effects Descartes had ascribed to *cogito*. This passive faculty constitutes the soul in its entirety, since it performs all the soul's functions: "imagination" provides the muse for the artist as well as the philosopher's *cogito*. In order to appreciate fully the ego-annulling function of La Mettrie's conception of intellect, we must compare Descartes' version of intellectual discipline with La Mettrie's. For Descartes, it was self-discipline: one deliberately disciplined oneself. Secondly, the emphasis on discipline was for Descartes a positive one: one disciplined oneself, not against, but for. For La Mettrie, on the contrary, discipline is enforced, and is negative. Discipline is against; against one's own impetuosity and vivacity:

> . . . if the imagination be trained from childhood to bridle itself and to keep from being carried away by its own impetuosity—an impetuosity which creates only brilliant enthusiasts—and to check, to restrain, its ideas, to examine them in all their aspects in order to see all sides of an object, then the imagination, ready in judgment, will comprehend the greatest possible sphere of objects, through reasoning; and its vivacity (always so good a sign in children, and only needing to be regulated by study and training) will be only a far-seeing insight without which little progress can be made in the sciences.

Discipline thus becomes a form of gentle, though ineluctable, oppression, a systematic extirpation of nascent spontaneity; the self has its wings clipped almost from birth. For a child subjected to such a regimen, the soul would be, no doubt, an "empty word."

La Mettrie cannot confine his attack on human self-esteem to a denial of the worth of the individual, however, if he is to vitiate the force of egocentrism. Persuade the egocentric individual that he possesses no intrinsic worth and he will respond in the style of Voltaire's Babouc: however lowly their status and however determined their behavior, the collective achievements wrought by the egocentric pursuits of myriads of individuals nonetheless justify human self-esteem. In order to preclude even this left-handed justification, La Mettrie attacks the value humanity places on itself. Man's sense of his uniqueness as a species must be brought into doubt. The seeds for this doubt have been sown, in the principle of unity. The fact that man's essence consists of motion, the principle which governs the entire universe, is in itself sufficient ground for the statement: "Man is not moulded from a costlier clay; nature has used but one dough, and has merely varied the leaven." But La Mettrie desires more than this. Merely to inform egocentric man that he is at one with the universe would be to upgrade, rather than to downgrade, him in his own eyes, for his *amour-propre* would no doubt lead him to compare himself with the heavens rather than the earthworms. La Mettrie requires some method of forcing men to look downward, and:

. . . to confess that these proud and vain beings, more distinguished by their pride than by the name of men however much
they may wish to exalt themselves, are at bottom only animals
and machines which, though upright, go on all fours.

He requires a persuasive means for belittling humanity and he has it, for
La Mettrie is a scientist. In order to illustrate the soul's dependence upon
the body, La Mettrie suggests, let us examine the bare organs of man and
animals, for: "How can human nature be known, if we may not derive any
light from an exact comparison of the structure of man and of animals?"
This comparison not only unseats man from his position of superiority over
animals, it actually teaches him that he does himself an unmerited honor
in placing himself even in a position of equality with animals, "For, truly,
up to a certain age, he is more of an animal than they, since at birth he
has less instinct." The comparative study of brains affords us little reason
to vaunt our uniqueness. Our brains are but a little larger and of a little
higher quality. Also, as La Mettrie ascends the zoological scale, he notes
an increase in intelligence and a loss in instinct, although he is not certain
whether this represents a gain or a loss. There is, however, a significant
moral to be drawn from this neurological sweep: "1st, that the fiercer [*plus
farouches*] animals are, the less brain they have; 2nd, that this organ seems
to increase in size in proportion to the gentleness [*docilité*] of the animal."
Thus man sits at the apex of the zoological heap by virtue of a sole, most
unegocentric, quality: his docility. His claim to distinction consists not in
a unique capacity, but rather in his incapacity for ferocity. La Mettrie has
thus deprived egocentrism of another of its manifestations by denying the
force of human passion. Descartes was right in suggesting that language
provides us with a behavioral distinction between man and beast, but he
was wrong to interpret this distinction as presenting an unbridgeable gulf.
La Mettrie has "very little doubt" that, with the proper training, an ape
could be taught a language. Such a possibility renders esteem for humanity
a real come-uppance, for:

Then he would no longer be a wild man, but he would be a perfect
man, a little gentleman, with as much matter or muscle as we
have, for thinking and profiting by his education.

Not just in intellect, but in morality as well, is man scarcely distin-
guishable from the beasts. Enlightenment conceptions of natural law such
as Voltaire's were, in La Mettrie's estimate, absurdly species-bound. It is
true that, in order to be happy, nature has given us natural law, "a feeling
that teaches us what we should not do, because we would not wish it to
be done to us." But this natural law is not lodged uniquely within the
human heart, as Voltaire naively had believed; it dwells rather in all varieties
of protoplasm. Since animals as well as humans evince symptoms of repentance, "what is there absurd in thinking that beings, almost as perfect

machines as ourselves, are like us, made to understand and to feel nature?" Thus, in any quality that man values—his will, his morality—he is but slightly above the beasts, indeed, from the most lowly of beasts: "we are veritable moles in the field of nature; we achieve little more than the mole's journey and it is our pride which prescribes limits to the limitless."

But La Mettrie has overstated his case. His man-machine is no mere rodent, no ordinary animal; he is rather a highly trained organism. Culture has come to him, however adventitiously, and wrought an indelible effect on his natural docility. Having reduced man to a puppet, La Mettrie gives him social strings. If man's "preeminent advantage is his organism," it is nonetheless true that the best brain would be but a cipher without education, "just as the best constituted man would be but a common peasant, without knowledge of the ways of the world." It is education that confers on intellect its prowess; an educated brain can "bring forth a hundredfold what it has received." The empty receptacle of imagination is "raised by art to the rare and beautiful dignity of genius." It is this cultural training that elevates man beyond his natural status as an unusually stupid animal, bereft of instinct—an animal who "saw only colors and shapes without being able to distinguish between them"; who "lisped out his sensations and his needs." La Mettrie cannot ascertain the source of culture: words, languages, laws, and the fine arts have simply "come." But it is certain that culture could not have been spontaneously generated by the robot. Hollow humanity could not rise to such a feat. On the question of cultural genesis—as in the case of all fundamental questions—we must "submit to an invincible ignorance on which our happiness depends"; we can no more know our origin than we can our destiny.

La Mettrie does not submit, however. Instead, he presents us with a "great man" theory of culture, and, in the process, gives us an anticipatory glimpse of the overhauled man-machine. At some point in human history there must have existed splendid geniuses whose spontaneity, or "superior organization" permitted them to create culture *ex nihilo*. Man owes his distinctiveness, his humanity, to these remote founders. But they were of a different stuff, and their memory has been lost "in the night of time." Consequently, the man-machine owes his humanity in fact to an impersonal culture, an alien force.

Man is thus willy-nilly a sociable creature. His will is as non-existent as his ego, his *cogito* a cultural artifact. His morality, itself presupposing the existence of society, also imposes sociability upon him. The natural law governs his moral behavior in the strictest sense of the word, for he is compelled to obey its dictates. This law cannot be destroyed, even by the most ferocious outbursts of passion. One obeys, not from any sense of obligation, but rather to avoid self-torment, for one experiences suffering as a result of inflicting it. To say that we "ought" to obey such a law is like saying that we ought to obey the laws governing the functioning of the alimentary canal; to disobey them is to suffer intense discomfort. But in order for the law to be obeyed, it must be known: hence the justification for *L'Homme machine*. La Mettrie closes his gospel of sociability with a series of beatitudes for the man-machine who truly believes:

> He who so thinks will be wise, just, tranquil about his fate, and therefore happy. He will await death without either fear or desire, and will cherish life. . . . More than that! Full of humanity, this man will love human character even in his enemies. Judge how he will treat others. He will pity the wicked without hating them; in his eyes they will be but mismade men. . . . In short, the materialist, convinced, in spite of the protests of his vanity, that he is but a machine or an animal, will not maltreat his kind, for he will know too well the nature of those actions, whose humanity is always in proportion to the degree of the analogy proved above [between human beings and animals].

This interpretation of the man-machine as a *philosophe*'s weapon has left an important question unanswered. What position did it occupy in La Mettrie's private convictions? Was it a ruse, a sort of conspiracy to utilize philosophy for quasi-religious aims; an attempt to reduce sinful egocentric man to social submission? There is some evidence to this effect. He obviously accepted the compatibility of the "ruse" or noble lie with philosophic grandeur. He betrays this acceptance in his eulogy on Descartes. Descartes's dualistic conception of nature had been "but a trick of skill, a ruse of style, to make theologians swallow a poison, hidden in the shade of an analogy." Elsewhere he makes the following statement: "I say of truth in general what M. de Fontenelle says of certain truths in particular, that we must sacrifice it in order to remain on good terms with society." But this explanation is inadequate when we consider the transformation which the man-machine subsequently underwent, since it is unlikely that discretion to the point of mendacity is readily reversible. If La Mettrie began *L'Homme machine* as a ruse, he must, at some point, have fallen under his own spell. Having envisioned his world of robots, he apparently decided that the goal of social order was not worth such anthropological Procrusteanism. Egocentric man finally triumphs against La Mettrie's vapid caricature of humanity.

If La Mettrie was concerned to empty man of his individuality in his *L'Homme machine*, he was no less concerned to replace it in such works as *La Volupté* and *L'Art de jouir*. Here he invites the man-machine to redirect his attention; to turn away from externals, away from his socio-biological machine shop, in order to look inward. Obediently erasing the impersonal images of motion and organs and natural law from his medullary screen, the robot discovers that the magic lantern has become magic indeed! Strange new images appear, images of emotions: pleasant, exuberant emotions; emotions that only *he* can feel. Arriving in this hitherto unsuspected wonderland, he discovers that the old rules governing his behavior no longer apply, for he finds a new master: "Pleasure, sovereign master of men and gods, before which all vanishes; even reason itself" (*L'Art de jouir*). La Mettrie has had his fill of docility; man is capable of more worthy adjustments. The machine discovers that he dwells not in a zoo but rather in a garden, and he has tasted the fruit of happiness. In order for the man-machine to remain in his new wonderland, however, La Mettrie must dismantle the machine shop: he must insure that all disappears before pleasure. He performs this task in his *Anti-Sénèque, ou discours sur le bonheur*.

In the *Discours* we find La Mettrie's man-machine no less determined than in *L'Homme machine*. But there is a change, for now the emphasis is on the subjective aspects of his determinants: determinism means not so much that we *are* what we must be, as that we *feel* what we must. And with determinism comes acceptance. Just as *L'Homme machine* informs us that society with its law of nature determines our essence and is therefore legitimate, so it is in the *Discours* with the feelings. In contrasting his own thought with the Stoic philosophy, La Mettrie demonstrates his new use of determinism. Viewing themselves as spiritual beings, the Stoics dispensed with their bodies. We who view ourselves as corporeal entities, declares La Mettrie, would dispense, in turn, with our souls.

> The Stoics showed themselves to be inaccessible to pleasure and pain; we would pride ourselves in feeling both. We would not dispose of that which governs us, nor would we presume to command our sensations; avowing their empire and our slavery, we would seek to render them agreeable, persuaded that it is in this that the happiness of life consists.

The argument is the same as that of *L'Homme machine*: submit to the force which makes of you a man. Only the terms have changed, yet the transformation is cataclysmic. Society is replaced by the passions as the determing force; "man" ceases to be a taxonomical label: he takes on life as the individual self. La Mettrie's use of "sensations" here is revealing. In *L'Homme machine* sensations were only perceptions of external data upon a screen; the object or source of sensations was its reality. La Mettrie now equates sensation with feeling. Sensations in this sense operate upon the passions, and passion becomes the "sovereign mistress" of the will. The passions, those sirens of egocentrism, had been appropriately excluded from *L'Homme machine*. They now enter, not merely to embellish the man-machine, but to govern him. La Mettrie seldom refers to the external determinant of man's behavior in his later writings. Remote and obscure—frequently personified as "Nature"—it serves the same function, in effect, as Descartes's God: it passively holds the key to man's mainspring after having wound him. Accepting his passions as given facts of his nature, the automaton is free to follow their dictates without legitimate external constraint. His imagination, even, ceases to serve as a reflecting screen for his environment; it becomes, instead, the passions' handmaiden. Thus equipped, the man-machine possesses both the motive (happiness) and the means for an autonomy so complete as to inspire even Descartes with envy.

> Nothing troubles a well-constituted man. Patient and tranquil (to the extent that it is possible) in pain, it can scarcely disturb him in his bearing. Judge whether he is firm in adversity! He laughs to see that Fortune has duped herself in having believed she could trouble him: he makes sport of her, as pyrrhonism does with truth. I have seen some of these characters who were in better humor when ill than when healthy, when poor than when rich.

Determinism in all its forms—Fate, Society, and Body—are scorned by this spontaneous creature equipped with the *daemon* of imagination. Sick or well, sleeping or waking, his imagination can render him content. Neither bodily states nor external sensations are relevant to his pleasure. Thus La Mettrie uses the same facet of the self (imagination) first to reduce man to a state of passive social-directedness and then to confer spontaneous inner-directedness upon him.

Along with La Mettrie's discovery of a distinctly human nature comes a new conception of morality. It is absurd to think that man shares his moral dimension with the beasts, for he alone is capable of attaching moral significance to his behavior. His human nature ceases to be an object upon which extraneous moral forces operate; his nature *is* morality: "Let us only be men and we will be virtuous. Let us enter anew into ourselves and we will find virtue: it is not in the temples, it dwells in our own heart." Moral rules are unique in kind as well as scope; they cease to be the laws of nature which had governed the robot without reference to his inclinations and purposes. Morality still exercises a determinative influence on man, but in a new way. It has its source in the exigencies of our social situation rather than in our animal nature, and is thus a human artifact. The above quotation continues: "It is not some natural law unrecognized by nature; it is rather the wisest of men who have inscribed it there, and have there placed the most useful fundamentals." Since morality is a human creation, it forfeits its quality of absoluteness; it becomes relative to society.

La Mettrie's emphasis on the personal element of morality is deceiving, however. Virtue is not an individual value; he is not asking the individual to seek his morality within his own heart, but rather in his society. And society makes demands quite different from those posed by the heart. La Mettrie never relinquishes his view of society as a superhuman mechanic engaged in the task of assembling faceless robots. However much he exalts the abstract individual, social man remains for him as heteronomous as in *L'Homme machine*. La Mettrie's hypothetical account of the genesis of society is, at the same time, a description of the taming of the automaton. Natural man, at some point in his development, finds himself in a conflicting situation. He discovers that liaisons with other people are necessary; yet, considered from a social point of view, he is a rather wicked creature: proud, impetuous and indomitable. He devises political institutions in order to reconcile these antagonistic elements of his nature. The emerging political leaders fabricate, in turn, a system of morality. They deem "virtuous" those acts which enhance the cause of society and political order; those acts which impede this cause, they stigmatize with the rubric "vice." Virtues do not acquire their force by appealing to any innate sense of decency or morality. Social virtue is so alien to man's nature that it never acquires stability within the individual. It rests upon man like a bird upon a branch, ready to fly away with the slightest provocation: so fragile and inconstant is it that incessant education and innumerable rewards are required in order to reinforce it. Virtue's power resides foremost in human vanity: our self-esteem requires other people's admiration, and virtue provides us with the requisite avenue. Thus the more noble of human drives, such as the desire for honor and glory, have been designated to follow in the cortege of social morality. And if vanity is an insufficient sanction for society, it has the powerful assistance of religion:

> Men having formed the plan to live together, it was necessary to form a system of political practices [*moeurs*] for the surety of their commerce, and since they were intractable animals, difficult to subjugate, and were spontaneously pursuing their own being . . . those who, by virtue of their sagacity and their genius, had been designated to be placed at the head of the others, had wisely summoned religion to the aid of the rules and the laws, very sensibly, in order to be able to assert an absolute authority over the impetuous imagination of turbulent and frivolous people.
>
> (*Discours préliminaire*)

Thus far La Mettrie has played his role as *philosophe* to the letter: egocentric man has been neatly socialized. Of course, it was necessary to employ a ruse, a noble lie, but the price was a small one. His moral and religious seduction did him no harm; indeed he benefited greatly from it, for his commerce was thereby secured. Society provides him with innumerable compensations; it can even help him to overcome his natural deficiencies. For instance, suppose that he has an ugly daughter. The state of nature would be for her a state of utter misery, for natural man, cruelly lacking in subtlety of judgment, would spurn her. But society can remedy this unfortunate situation; it places value on more plastic qualities than physical appearance, and it can provide her with the means for acquiring them. The ugly girl can make her way among sociable men by virtue of her wit, for example (*Anti-Sénèque*). Surely this is ample reward for sociability.

But La Mettrie's task is not complete. He has recast, rather than resolved, the Cartesian dilemma. His argument for sociability is persuasive only for those who are in a chronic state of dependency upon others, such as defectives and those who dwell in the symbiotic web of the marketplace. But these are not typical of humanity, they are not La Mettrie's individual.

What about *him*—the well-constituted, indomitable automaton? Why should he submit to the heteronomy of society? Or, if this question is unanswerable, why does he *in fact* submit? La Mettrie does not attempt to answer the moral question. He explains the fact of submission by describing the process of socialization in terms every bit as harsh as Freud's. Society ceases to be the humanizing force so venerated by the *philosophes*; it becomes instead a cruel oppressor of our human individuality.

The individual obeys the laws of his country because he has been taught to fear, rather than to respect, them. The state does not postpone its function of punishing antisocial acts until its citizen has reached adulthood, nor does it confine its scrutiny to the realm of action. Starting from our earliest infancy, it makes us suffer for our innermost feelings of independence. It is not so gauche as to utilize corporeal chastisement at this early stage; its technique is more subtle, more painful and enduring. It instills its hangman within our very souls in the form of anxiety or remorse. It comes to us at first as a feeling, a nebulous specter; slowly it builds within us until it is strongly imprinted on our brains as a signet stamped in soft beeswax. Finally, the child reaches a point where he discovers that his passions are of no avail against this strange new force. They can mitigate it only for brief intervals; it always resumes its sway, haunting us as a troublesome reminiscence throughout our lives. Sociability is thus internalized as a destructive passion; it exists first as a censor then as an aspiring surrogate for the passions of individuality. Remorse never succeeds completely in suppressing the voice of selfhood, however: the automaton remains, a struggling captive. Man pays the price of endless psychological conflict for his sociability. His individuality bids him to "live for himself alone, and to be unto himself parents, friends, and the entire universe"; his remorse demands that he be "useful," that he "live for others." Remorse is entirely destructive in its influence; it is ineffectual in restraining man from vice, for it only arises after he has acted or felt in an antisocial direction. Society emerges profoundly intolerable; in seeking the means for assuring his commerce, man has created an entity that has the destruction of personality as its aim. There is no doubt that for La Mettrie, the psychological waste affected by society more than offsets its advantages:

> Man, especially the good man: was he made to be handed over to hangmen; he whom nature has sought to attach to life with so many allurements. . . . For every rascal who has ceased being unhappy, resuming an unmerited relationship of peace and tranquility with other men, how many wise and virtuous persons, unseasonably tormented in the midst of a sweet, innocent and delicious life . . . and having a delicious pleasure replaced by a devouring tedium?

La Mettrie is reluctant to press the message of the *Discours sur le bonheur* to its ultimate, anarchic conclusion. Instead he exhumes Descartes's egocentric argument for sociability as an alternative to remorse. The enlightened man must realize that his happiness is augmented in the process of sharing and communicating it: he enriches himself in sharing his happiness, and he also participates in the pleasure he produces for others. This perspective, however, will only appeal to the "well-born." For the rest, an unseen hand works its benevolent effect:

> Solely occupied with completing the narrow circle of existence, we find ourself all the more happy that we live not only for ourself, but for our country, for our king, and, in general, for the humanity that we proudly serve. We create social happiness along with our own.

These arguments, however, are but pale alternatives to anarchy when we recall the harsh facts of socialization. Confronted with the indomitable individual, society necessarily must use his own passions against him. A more thorough La Mettrie would have faced the issue, choosing between society and the individual. The choice that such a La Mettrie might make may be inferred from a casual sentence: "Socrates preferred death to exile; I am not so intensely afflicted with this *maladie du pays.*"

La Mettrie was aware of the anarchic implications of the *Discours sur le bonheur*. In the *Discours préliminaire* which he attaches to his philosophic works, he feels it necessary to defend himself against the charge that he had undermined society and the state. In conducting his defense, he completely forfeits his role as a *philosophe*. Although philosophy leads us to antisocial conclusions, he informs his reader, philosophy, after all, is not relevant to the real concerns of life. It is rather ideal or metaphysical, a game utterly devoid of existential force; consequently philosophy will not, cannot, break the chains of society. One has only to look at the example of the *philosophe* in order to appreciate the existential impotency of philosophy. He regulates his passions; while he may lapse periodically into voluptuousness, he never indulges in crime and disorder. He is a paragon of humanity, candor, gentleness, and probity. Thus his gentleness serves to offset his vile doctrines. While writing against natural law, he follows it vigorously; in disputing justice, he is nonetheless just in his dealings with society. The great disputes of philosophy, in short, are of no more real significance than those conducted in a sophomore's dormitory. He concludes in the manner of a man from whom a great secret has been wrenched: "Tell me, vulgar souls, what more do you require?"

The *philosophes* were doubly justified in despising La Mettrie. In suggesting that society was inimical to personality, he raised serious doubts as to the humanitarian quality of their enterprise; then in order to exonerate himself, he tossed reason, their beloved weapon, to the mob. But it was only the later La Mettrie that they rejected; La Mettrie of *L'Homme machine* was to exercise an enduring influence upon the French Enlightenment.

Promises (Rousseau's *Social Contract*)

Paul de Man

The connection between the political and the religious writings of Rousseau is enigmatic and, at first sight, entirely contradictory. Rousseau's theology and his political theory seem to lead in opposite directions. There have been excellent books written about Rousseau's political theory that don't even mention his religious concerns, and vice versa. Yet the second part of the *Nouvelle Héloïse* combines the discussion of political institutions with theological considerations and at least suggests a close, albeit unformulated, interrelationship between both. And the *Social Contract*, which obviously proposes a model for political institutions and reflects on the authority of legal language, has to reintroduce religious themes at at least one crucial point. (Particularly in the section on the lawgiver [*Social Contract*, book 2, chapter 7] and in the penultimate section of the text [*Social Contract*, book 4, chapter 8]). The difficulty may well stem from the use of such thematic terms as "political" or "religious," as if their referential status were clearly established and could be understood without regard for the rhetorical mode of their utilization.

It may be just as difficult to decide upon the rhetorical status of theoretical texts such as the *Profession de foi* and the *Social Contract* as on a fiction such as the *Nouvelle Héloïse*. The difference between a fictional and a theoretical text carries very little weight in the case of Rousseau. By reading the unreadability of the *Profession de foi*, we found it to be structured exactly like the *Nouvelle Héloïse*: the deconstruction of a metaphorical model (called "love" in the *Nouvelle Héloïse*, "judgment" in the *Profession*) leads to its replacement by homological text systems whose referential authority is both asserted and undermined by their figural logic. The resulting "meanings" can be said to be ethical, religious, or eudaemonic, but each of these

From *Critical Inquiry* 2, no. 4 (Summer 1976). © 1976 by The University of Chicago Press.

thematic categories is torn apart by the aporia that constitutes it, thus making the categories effective to the precise extent that they eliminate the value system in which their classification is grounded. If we choose to call this pattern an allegory of unreadability or simply an allegory, then it should be clear that the *Profession de foi*, like *Julie*, is an allegory and that no distinction can be made between both texts from the point of view of a genre theory based on rhetorical models. The fact that one narrates concepts whereas the other narrates something called characters is irrelevant from a rhetorical perspective.

But if the *Profession de foi* is an allegory of (non)signification, can the same still be said of the *Social Contract*? Again, no reliable answer can be given by merely quoting or paraphrasing the text without reading it. And to read the *Social Contract* is, for instance and among other things, to determine the relationship between general will and particular will, two notions that obviously play a predominant part in the organization of the text.

A first difficulty in the use of the polarity between the general and the particular will is lexicological and stems from the apparently interchangeable use of the terms "natural" (as in *religion naturelle, droit naturel*, etc.) and "particular" or "individual," both used in opposition to "civil" or "collective." Rousseau follows common usage in speaking of natural law, natural religion, or natural freedom; he does not use "volonté naturelle" however, but would rather have chosen, in opposition to "volonté générale," the term "volonté particulière." (The specific expression "volonté particulière" occurs rarely or not at all in this form, but Rousseau speaks frequently of "fait," "droit," "objet" or "acte" "particulier" in a way that leaves no doubt that what is in conflict when "man" is opposed to "citizen" are the categories of particularity and generality. The same polarity opposes private to public in such expressions as "personne publique" and "personne privée.") Yet, taken literally, "particular" is clearly not the same as "natural"; if we say, for example, that the first part of the *Nouvelle Héloïse* deals with the particular, or individual, relationships between Julie and Saint-Preux in contrast to the second part which, at least at times, deals with public, collective relationships between the inhabitants of Clarens, it does not follow that, in the first three books, Julie and Saint-Preux are in the state of nature as the term is used in the *Second Discourse*. A certain amount of confusion results from Rousseau's interchangeable use of "natural" and "particular," especially since his sense of the complexities of selfhood puts the individuals he portrays far beyond the simplicity of the state of nature. This is true of fictional entities such as the "characters" of the *Nouvelle Héloïse* (if one wishes to consider them as such) as well as of actual human beings, including Rousseau himself, in the autobiographical writings. It would be absurd, for instance, to consider the *Confessions* as more "natural" than the *Social Contract* because it deals with individual experiences rather than with societies. The case of *Emile* is somewhat different, since the diegetic narrative is suppose to follow the history of an empirical human being from the start and along chronological lines (a problem that does not arise in the *Second Discourse* where the natural origin of mankind is a fiction and the diachrony of the narrative only exists on the level of the signifier). This forces upon us the contrast between a "natural" child and a corrupted citizen, an antithetical pattern of innocence and experience. The rhetorical mode of *Emile* produces the opposition between nature and society as a textual necessity. No such polarity functions in the *Confessions*, since Rousseau never claims to narrate anything about the child Jean-Jacques that is not directly remembered by him. He is thus at least twice removed from the preconscious condition of nature: the experiences of a highly self-conscious and "dénaturé" child are told by the disfigured figure of a highly self-conscious narrator.

The lexicological confusion between "natural" and "particular" thus has only limited theoretical interest, although it certainly has been responsible for many aberrations in the interpretation of Rousseau. It nevertheless provides a point of entrance into the remarkably smooth and homogeneous textual surface of the *Social Contract*. For it again attracts attention to the danger of hypostatizing such concepts as "nature," "individual" or "society" as if they were the designation of substantial entities. Rousseau can legitimately shift these terms around and confuse the names of two such divergent semantic fields as those covered by "nature" and "particularity" because they designate relational properties, patterns of relational integration or disintegration, and not units or modes of being. This may be easier to admit in the case of superstructures such as civil society, or the arts, or technology, but it pertains to the term nature as well. Rousseau calls natural any stage of relational integration that precedes in degree the stage presently under examination. In the analysis of conceptualization, the "natural" stage that precedes the concept is denomination; in the analysis of metaphor, the natural figure would be metonymy; in the critique of judgment, it is sensation or perception; in the case of generality, any previous mode of particularity, etc. The deconstruction of a system of relationships always reveals a more fragmented stage that can be called natural with regard to the system that is being undone. Because it also functions as the negative truth of the deconstructive process, the "natural" pattern authoritatively substitutes its relational system for the one it helped to dissolve. In so doing, it conceals the fact that it is itself one system of relations among others, and it presents itself as the sole and true order of things, as nature and not as structure. But since a deconstruction always has for its target to reveal the existence of hidden articulations and fragmentations within assumedly monadic totalities, nature turns out to be a self-deconstructive term. It engenders endless other "natures" in an eternally repeated pattern of regression. Nature deconstructs nature, hence the ambiguous valorization of the term throughout Rousseau's works. Far from denoting a homogeneous mode of being, "nature" connotes a process of deconstruction redoubled by its own fallacious retotalization. In the opposition between private and public, or particular and general, the first term is the "natural" counterpart of the second, provided one reads "natural" as has just been suggested. We conclude that there is no structural difference between the couple linking "volonté particulière" to "volonté générale" and, on the other hand, such pairings as "droit" or "religion naturelle" "de l'homme" with "droit" or "religion civile" "du citoyen."

Any Rousseau text that puts such polarities into play will therefore have to set up the fiction of a natural process that functions both as a deconstructive instrument and as the outcome of the deconstruction. Frequently enough, the fiction is provided by a contemporary or traditional text written by someone else: in the *Profession de foi*, it was primarily Helvétius and Quesnay that were thus being used; in the first version of the *Social Contract*, Diderot's *Encyclopédie* entry on "Droit naturel" furnishes the appropriate target. Lacking a suitable formulation, Rousseau sets one up himself, thus conveying an impression of self-contradiction that has considerably enriched, if not clarified, the history of his interpretation. This is in part what happens in the *Second Discourse*, where neither Hobbes, nor Condillac, nor any of the other polemical opponents, provides an adequate natural model and where Rousseau therefore has to invent one himself. A similar, somewhat more complex instance of the same strategy occurs in a text that has close affinities with some aspects of the *Social Contract*, the fragment that the editors of the Pléiade edition have included under the title "Du bonheur public."

Although the fragmentary state of "Du bonheur public" (as well as the fact that it originated as an occasional improvisation in reply to a questionnaire sent out by the Société économique de Berne) makes a sustained reading difficult, the notes nevertheless illustrate the odd logical shape of Rousseau's political discourse. And because it deals with the opposition between private and public values as they relate to the political constitution of the State, the brief text is like a blueprint for the more elaborate structure that supports the *Social Contract*. In truth, "Du bonheur public" is not based on a dialectic of private as opposed to public or social identity; it considers the possibility of a readable semiology of private happiness that would be based on analogies between inside feelings and their outside manifestations only in order to reject it out of hand: "Happiness is not pleasure; it is not a fleeting stirring of the soul, but a permanent and entirely inward feeling, that can only be evaluated by the person who experiences it. No one can therefore decide with certainty if someone else is happy, nor can he, as a result of this, come to know with certainty the *signs* that bear witness to the happiness of individuals." (A little further in the text, Rousseau also speaks of "the true *signs* that might characterize the well-being of a people" [my italics].) Consequently, there can be no easy metaphorical totalization from personal to social well-being, based on an analogical resemblance between both: "It is . . . not by the feeling that the citizens have of their happiness, not consequently by their happiness itself that one can judge the prosperity of the State," or: "If I had deduced the idea of happiness collectively from the particular state of happiness of every citizen that makes up the State, I could have said something that would have been easier to grasp for many readers, but aside from the fact that no conclusions could ever have been drawn from these metaphysical notions that depend on the way of thinking, the mood and the disposition of each individual, I would have given a very inaccurate definition." The text takes the deconstruction of a private inwardness that could be equated with a natural inwardness for granted; the spontaneous manifestations of the happy consciousness are so unnatural as to be entirely unfathomable and beyond observation. The actual evocation of private happiness, so freely developed in many other Rousseau texts such as the *Confessions* or the *Rêveries,* does not even require formulation here. Yet it operates as a totalizing power based on natural properties, and it at once replaces the dismissed, natural affectivity of the individual subject by a natural affectivity of the group that can be interpreted precisely as the self has just been shown *not* to be. Natural societies in which "men [will be] social [*civils*] by nature" are assumed to exist or (what amounts to the same thing) to have existed or to be conceivable in the future. In such societies, the semantics of affectivity, opaque in the case of individuals, are transparent and reliable: "[The] virtues [and the] vices [of political societies] are all apparent and visible, their inner feeling is a public one. . . . For any eye that can see, they are what they seem to be, and one can safely evaluate [*juger*] their moral being." This being granted, the totalization is bound to ensue without further delay: "[men] will be united, they will be virtuous, they will be happy, and their felicity will be the well-being of the Republic; for since they receive all their being from the State, they owe everything to the State. The Republic will own all they own and will be all they are" ("car n'étant rien que par la république ils ne seront rien que pour elle, elle aura tout ce qu'ils ont et sera tout ce qu'ils sont"). Such sentences automatically fall back into the familiar direction of "all" and "nothing," or "all" and "one," in the reconciliation "schon längst Eines und Alles genannt" (Hölderlin) of the pantheistic *hen kai pan.* The model for this utopia is the reconciliation of the most natural of groups, the family, with the State: "The family, pointing to its children, will say: it is in them that I flourish." It also reconciles moral virtue with economic wealth and makes property innocent by making it collective; the word "bien" can be used in its ethical register (as the opposite of "mal") as well as in the economic sense of "real" estate. That, in the sentence which speaks of "les biens, les maux" of political societies, "biens" also means wealth is clear from its use a few lines further on: "au trésor public, vous aurez joint les *biens* des particuliers" (my italics).

As it denies the validity of the metaphor that unites the self with society, the text, by the same token, elaborates a new metaphor, the "natural" political society or family which, in its turn, fulfills the totalization that was denied to the first binary pair. But the logic of totalization works both ways, toward the *one* as well as toward the *all,* and the welfare of the natural society is bound to restore the well-being of the individual who relates to it as part relates to whole in an organic synecdoche, as the "member" relates to the "body" in the political unit. Therefore Rousseau has to state the very opposite of his initial assertion: "do not imagine that the State could be happy when all its members are in distress. This ethical fiction that you call public happiness is, by itself, a chimera: if the feeling of well-being is not felt by anyone, it has no existence and no family can flourish if its children do not prosper." This is stated in the paragraph immediately following the one which denied the significance of any individual well-being for the society as a whole, and it will be followed, not much further, by the equally categorical assertion: "[that it is] therefore not by [the] happiness [of the citizens] that one can measure the prosperity of the State."

The occurrence of such contradictions within the confines of a few lines obviously does not have the same effect in a tentative, unfinished and disjointed text as in a more continuous argument. On the other hand, one may well wonder, with equally good reason, whether the pattern of contradiction in this fragmented composition does not represent a more faithful outline of Rousseau's thought patterns, simply because the narrative developments and transitions that conceal incompatible affirmations merely by putting some space between them are lacking in this case. A text such as this one bears a close resemblance to what is generally referred to, rather inaccurately, as Nietzsche's aphoristic manner, as we know it from *Human All Too Human* on. This discontinuous format goes back, in Rousseau, at least as far as the notes to the *Second Discourse* and represents probably the most characteristic dimension of his style.

The reading of "Du bonheur public" is not completed when the figural pattern of contradiction has been pointed out. Short as it is, the text contains the elements necessary to the second deconstruction that can be grafted onto the first undoing of the "natural" metaphor, and that raises its figural status to the second power, making it into the figural deconstruction of the prior deconstruction of a figure. For the text also states, this time truly in the form of an aphorism, without further context: "The moral condition of a people is less the result of the absolute condition of its members than of the relationships among them." One is reminded of the structure of judgment as a posited relationship (in the *Profession de foi*) and also of the statement about love in the *Nouvelle Héloïse:* "the source of happiness does not reside wholly in the desired object nor in the heart that possesses it, but in the relationship of the one to the other." An entirely different principle of organization is introduced by this description. If the principle of collectivization or generalization that constitutes what is here called a "people" does *not* operate between part and whole but is determined by the relationship that the different parts, as parts, establish between each other, then the rhetorical structure is no longer the same as in binary structures. The principle of differentiation no longer operates between two entities whose difference is both redundant (since it is posited from the start) and transcended (since it is suspended at the end); it now operates to reveal differences where a metaphorical totalization had created the illusion of an identity, a delusive generality in such words as "man," "self," "people," or "State," all of which suggest that, to the extent that they are men, or people, or States, all men, people, and States are essentially the same. Groups constituted on the basis of relationships which no longer claim to be natural engender different systems of interaction, in relation to themselves as well as to other groups or entities. Since the principle that establishes their *general* character as group is no longer a principle of necessity, but the result of an uncertain act of judgment ratified by convention, it follows that the principle of generalization that constituted it is by no means unique. The same entity can thus be inscribed within diverse systems that are not necessarily compatible. They can be considered from different points of view without necessarily allowing for a coordination of these various perspectives. Neither does their interference with other systems necessarily allow for specular exchanges or integrations.

The shift from a (deconstructed) binary model to this still unidentified "other" model occurs in "Du bonheur public" when Rousseau abruptly changes ground, abandons the binary model that seeks to derive political well-being from private happiness altogether, and affirms, as a "very general idea . . . to which no reasonable man could, I believe, refuse his assent" that "the happiest nation is the one that can most easily dispense with all others and the most flourishing the one the others can least dispense with" ("la nation la plus heureuse est celle qui peut le plus aisément se passer de toutes les autres, et la plus florissante est celle dont les autres peuvent le moins se passer".) The language shifts from the qualitative and unfathomable "will to happiness" to an outspoken will to power quantified in terms of economic and military interests. The decisive relationship is no longer between constituting and constituted elements. Within a political entity, no necessary link connects individual to collective well-being; to pursue the problem of this relationship (as "Du bonheur public" set out by doing) is to pursue a false problem. It is not irrelevant to raise the question of the "happiness" of a political entity such as a State, but it can only be considered in terms of the relationship of one State to another. The very concept of a political entity, be it a State, a class or a person, also changes: an entity can be called political, not because it is collective (constituted by a plurality of similar units), but precisely because it is not, because it sets up relationships with other entities on a nonconstitutive basis. The encounter between one political unit and another is not a generalization in which a structure is extended on the basis of a principle of similarity (or of a proximity considered as similarity) to include both under its common aegis. Just as the unit itself is not the outcome of such a generalization, the relationships of the units among each other are not stated in terms of affinities, analogies, common properties or any other principle of metaphorical exchange. They depend instead on the ability of one entity, regardless of similarities, to keep the relationship to another contingent, "to be able to dispense with all other [nations]." If this degree of autarchy is achieved, relationships with other States are still possible, and perhaps desireable, but they are no longer compulsory. To the extent that a less fortunate State is unable to achieve this and remains dependent for its existence on necessary links, it is not a truly political entity, not really a State at all. In other words, the structure postulates the necessary existence of radical estrangement between political entities. Autarchy, as it is here conceived, is not a principle of autonomy, still less of totalization. The accent does not fall on freedom as a positive force but on the ability to dispense with others; the worst that can happen politically is having to have recourse to "strangers." Such patterns of estrangement are an inevitable aspect of political structures; it is well known, for instance, that Rousseau refused to believe in perpetual peace and that, by consistently arguing against Hobbes that the state of war is not a natural state, he had to see war as a necessary moment in the political process: "far from being natural to man, the state of war, is born from peace, or at the least from the precautions men had to take in order to insure themselves of a durable peace. (*Ecrits sur l'Abbé de Saint-Pierre.* See also: "Hobbes' error is not to have assumed that this is the natural condition of the species, and to have made it the cause of the vices of which it is the effect" [*Social Contract*, first version]. Kant's famous text *On Perpetual Peace* [1795] is of course highly relevant here.)

In its stress on separation and solitude, on the fragmented differentiation of entities rather than on their unity, the condition of political estrangement is reminiscent of the state of nature. This is not surprising, since the fiction of a natural "state" results from the deconstruction of metaphorical patterns based on binary models—which is exactly how Rousseau's definition of political happiness here comes into being, after the antithetical system that deduces public from private happiness has been allowed to destroy itself by running its course. For the same reason, the rediscovery of differential moments, such as those suggested by the term estrangement, also signals the inevitable relapse into patterns of totalization. The sentence that asserts the differentiation ("the happiest nation is the one that can most easily dispense with all others") also asserts the simultaneous reconstruction of an aberrant totality: "the most flourishing is the one the others can least dispense with." The shift from qualitative happiness [*nation heureuse*] to quantitative prosperity [*nation florissante*] is revealing. The synonymy of both terms is asserted as part of the system: "if money makes the rich happy, it is less by its immediate possession than because it enables them, first to satisfy their needs and to carry out their will in all things, without having to depend on anyone, and second to exercise command over others and keep them in their dependence." (The point is further developed, in terms of a semiology of money, in the fragment "Le luxe, le commerce et les arts." See also *Discours sur les richesses*.) Yet a shift is implied by the quantification, which is also a surreptitious reintroduction of conceptual number metaphors into the deconstructed system. The "happy" State is entirely self-sufficient and does not need to establish relationships with any other nation, but the very strength resulting from this independence allows it, almost in spite of itself, to assert its power over others and make them in turn aware of their dependency:

> The security, the conservation [of the State] require that it become more powerful than all its neighbors. It can only augment, nourish and exercise its power at their expense, and although it does not have to look for subsistence beyond its boundaries, it nevertheless always seeks for new members that reinforce its own strength [*qui lui donnent une consistance plus inébranlable*].
>
> (*Ecrits sur l'Abbé de Saint-Pierre*)

The political power does not remain in its condition of fragmented isolation in which it is satisfied to consider the other State as a pure stranger. Carried by the metaphorical structure of the number system, it enters into relationships of comparison that necessarily lead back to totalizations from part to whole:

> Since the size of the political body is entirely relative, it is forced to enter steadily into comparison in order to know itself; it depends on everything that surrounds it, and must take an interest in everything that happens outside, although it would want to remain self-confined, without gains or losses. . . . Its very strength, making its relationships to others more constant, makes all its actions further-reaching and all its quarrels more dangerous.
>
> (*Ecrits sur l'Abbé de Saint-Pierre*)

Consciousness of selfhood [*se connaître*], whether individual or political, is itself dependent on a relationship of power and originates with this relationship. The danger of the situation is not only the actual damage done to the others, but the reintroduction of a master/slave relationship of mutual dependency within a system that had come into being by overcoming the fallacies of this model. ("The war [between two nations] can only cease when both of them freely proclaim their renunciation of war. It follows that, as a consequence of the relationship between master and slave, they continue even in spite of themselves, of being in a state of war" [*Ecrits sur l'Abbé de Saint-Pierre*].) The fact that the strong and "happy" State comes to depend on the dependency of the other as if it were a necessity dissolves the structure to which it owed its existence. For the master/slave relationship is not the (non)relationship of pure estrangement that was posited as the necessary condition for a political entity to come into being. It clearly is a polarity susceptible of dialectical exchange: master and slave are no strangers to each other, as little as the conquered State remains a stranger to its conqueror. "Du bonheur public," like all the other allegorical Rousseau texts, reintroduces the metaphorical model whose deconstruction had been the reason for its own elaboration. It is therefore just as "unreadable" as the other allegories we have considered.

Does this mean that it can, without further qualification, be equated with such previously considered texts as *Julie* or the *Profession de foi?* It would then differ from them only thematically, by its political "content," but not rhetorically. If we are correct in assuming that the logical structure of "Du bonheur public" also operates as the organizing principle of the *Social Contract*—a point that remains to be shown—it would follow that the *Social Contract* could be called an allegory of the same type and for the same reason as the *Profession de foi*. This conclusion would, in a sense, make the consideration of the *Social Contract* and of Rousseau's political texts in general redundant for the rhetorical analysis of his work as a whole. It would merely confirm what we already know, that Rousseau's fictional as well as his discursive writings are allegories of (non)signification or of unreadability, allegories of the deconstruction and the reintroduction of metaphorical models. We would merely have gained yet another version of this same insight. This would not lead to a refinement of the question that remained precariously suspended at the end of the reading of the *Profession de foi*, when the referential power of the allegorical narrative seemed to be at its most effective when its epistemological authority was most thoroughly discredited. The political question would then only have a digressive importance in the reading of Rousseau; like the metaphor of selfhood, it would have no privileged interpretative function. Such a conclusion is not without consequence: for example, the naïve [*impensé*] distinction between a "literary" and a "political" Rousseau from which we started out as from the empirical *donnée* provided by the present state of Rousseau studies has, to a considerable extent, been overcome. It no longer makes sense to consider *Julie* as more or less "literary" than the *Social Contract*; neither can the assumed inconsistencies and contradictions of the political theorist be explained away by calling them "literary" and attributing them to the discrepancies between "l'analyse intellectuelle" and "l'élan du coeur." (The expression is by Pierre Burgelin in his introduction to the edition of the *Profession de foi du vicaire savoyard* [*Oeuvres complètes*, vol. 4, Gallimard: Pléiade, 1959–64].) One can no longer call Rousseau an "admirable" writer and dismiss the political theorist or, conversely, praise the rational rigor of the political analyses while writing off the more disquieting aspects of the imaginative and autobiographical writings as more or less accidental pathology. The rhetorical reading leaves these fallacies behind by accounting, at least to some degree, for their predictable occurrence. With the assistance of the political writings, it may however be possible to take one further step.

"Du bonheur public" appears to be "privileged" in at least one respect:

it isolates a model for the elaboration and the comportment of political entities that is more rigorous and systematic than the models we have encountered up till now. It is true that this model never asserts itself as an actual state of being (in all the meanings of the term "state," be it as state of nature, state of war, the State, etc.). It is at once overtaken by other rhetorical patterns, similar in structure to conceptual metaphors. But the question remains what is being overtaken and how this "relapse" is to be understood. The *Social Contract,* the most complete section of Rousseau's planned treatise on political institutions, provides information on this point. We are not here concerned with the technically political significance of this text, still less with an evaluation of the political and ethical praxis that can be derived from it. Our reading merely tries to define the rhetorical patterns that organize the distribution and the movement of the key terms—while contending that questions of valorization can be relevantly considered only after the rhetorical status of the text has been clarified.

That the *Social Contract* implies a deconstruction of a binary metaphorical system similar to that operating between personal and public happiness in "Du bonheur public" is hardly apparent in the final text but becomes much more noticeable if one takes into account the earlier version known as the *manuscrit de Genéve* (Pléiade, vol. 3). This version begins with a genetic section that sets out to investigate "d'où *naît* la nécessité des institutions politiques" (my italics). The section was subsequently omitted from the final version, and this omission has not made the interpretation of the *Social Contract* any easier. It has made it difficult, for example, to see in what way the structure of the political entity established on a contractual basis differs from that of an empirical or natural entity. The principle of totalization that organizes the first formal definition of the contract seems, in all respects, to be similar in kind to the organic link that binds part to whole in a metaphorical synecdoche. The social pact is determined as follows: "Everyone puts his will, his property, his strength, and his person in common, under the direction of the general will, and we receive as a body [*en corps*] each member as an inalienable part of the whole." The final version retains this definition, with some changes in wording that do not detract from its assumed holism. The metaphorical system that unites limb to body, one to all, individual to group, seems firmly established. A few paragraphs earlier in the same version, Rousseau has described a similar system: "There would exist a kind of common sensorium that would control the correspondence of all the parts; public good and evil would not only be the sum of particular virtues and vices as in a simple juxtaposition [*une simple aggrégation*], but it would reside in the link that unites them. It would therefore be larger than the sum, and far from having public well-being derive from the happiness of individuals, it would be its source." (The passage is crossed out in the manuscript for reasons on which one can speculate. Its suppression is certainly not caused by a divergence with the general thrust of the argument, within which it fits perfectly well.) The distinction between metonymic aggregates and metaphorical totalities, based on the presence, within the latter, of a "necessary link" that is lacking in the former, is characteristic of all metaphorical systems, as in the equation of this principle of totalization with *natural* process. After the deconstruction of the metaphorical model has taken place, the attribute of naturalness shifts from the metaphorical totality to the metonymic aggregate, as was the case for the "state of nature" in the *Second Discourse* or for "sensation" in the *Profession de foi*. However, at this point in the argument, the evocation of this natural synthesis—Rousseau makes the comparison with chemical compounds, whose properties are distinct from the properties of their components—is not held up as the desirable wholeness that political units must try to emulate, but as the very opposite: they are precisely the misleading model after which no sound political system should be patterned. The synesthetic illusion of the common sensorium, just as the concomitant illusions of a universal language and a golden age, ("The happy existence of a golden age was always alien to the race of man, either for not having known it when it was within reach or for having lost it when they were capable of knowledge."), is a mythical aberration of judgment devoid of truth and of virtue. It becomes pernicious when it is used as the foundation of a political society: the entire polemic with Diderot, in the *manuscrit de Genève*, is directed toward the necessity of devising a model for a political order that is not natural, in this sense of the term. Hence the categorical rejection, more explicit in the early version than in the final text, of the family as a suitable political model, precisely because the family is based on natural ties. (*Social Contract*, first version. The final version [chap. 2, "Des premières sociétés"] seems to reverse this when it states: "The family is, if one so wishes [*si l'on veut*], the first model of political societies." But the passage uses the same metaphor of the "link" negatively ["Still, the children remain linked (*liés*) to the father for only as long as they need him in order to survive. As soon as this need ceases, the natural link dissolves"] and concludes that actual families are in fact not natural but political institutions: "If they remain together, it is no longer for natural reasons but by their own will, and the family itself remains in existence only by convention.") In this respect, the family is no better model for legality than imperialistic conquest or the enslavement of prisoners in time of war, and it is discussed under the same rubric as these anarchic manifestations of power. The same is true of the god-centered systems that occupy such a prominent place in the *Profession de foi* and that, in this context, begin by being dismissed altogether (although they will reappear in a different form later on in the *Social contract*): the idea of a natural religion is as absurd as the idea of a natural law, and the text seems to be an even sharper attack on the vicar of the *Profession de foi* than on Diderot: "if the notions of a great being and of natural law were *innate* in all hearts, it would be quite superfluous to instruct people in either of them. . . . Let us therefore discard the sacred precepts of the various religions. Their abuse has caused as many crimes as their use can prevent, and let us give back to the Philosopher a question that the Theologian has treated only at the expense of mankind." The deconstruction of metaphorical totalities which, in "Du bonheur public," starts out from the relationship between private and public well-being here has a wider scope that encompasses all organic and theotropic ideologies. It is not carried out in a detailed analysis, as was the case in some of the other texts, but asserted sweepingly, as if it could be taken for granted. If the formal definition of the contract then seems to relapse into the figure which has just been decisively condemned, then this can certainly not be true without further qualification. The definition is far from telling all there is to tell about the structure of the contract, perhaps because a degree of complexity has been reached that no longer allows for definitional language.

As the mechanics of the contractual convention are being elaborated in more detail, it becomes apparent that the constitutive power of the contract, the manner in which it engenders entities, is no dialectical synthesis or any other system of totalization. The general will is by no means a synthesis of particular volitions. Rousseau starts out instead from the opposite assertion and postulates the incompatibility between collective and individual needs and interests, the absence of any links between the two sets of forces: the general will is "a pure act of reason that operates without regard for the passions [*dans le silence des passions*]" but "where is the person who can thus sever himself from his own desires and . . . can he be forced to consider the species in general in order to impose upon himself duties of which he cannot perceive the link with his own, particular constitution?" It is clear that when Rousseau, in the next paragraph, speaks of "the art of generalizing ideas" in order to orient them toward the general will, the act of generalizing must then have a very different figural structure than such metaphorical processes as, for example, conceptualization, love, or even judgment.

The simplest way to gain insight into the process or function that is being described may be by way of its most naive, spatial version, in the section of the *Social Contract* entitled, in the *manuscrit de Genève*, "Du domaine réel." Considered from a geopolitical point of view, the State is not primarily a set of individuals, but a specific piece of land; Rousseau praises the wisdom implied in the modern custom of calling a monarch King *of France*, or *of England*, rather, than, as was the case in Antiquity, King of the Persians or of the Macedonians. "By thus holding the land, [the kings] are certain to hold its inhabitants." This terminology is said to be more precise because the original possesion of the land is, in fact, arbitrary and "natural," in the anarchic sense of the term. One could call it metonymic, simply based on the fact that one happened to be in the proximity of this particular piece of terrain, and this "right of first occupancy" may be "less absurd, less repellent than the right of conquest" but nevertheless, "on close examination . . . it is not more legitimate."

A specific piece of landed property within the State is the result of a contractual convention that involves both the citizen and the State; it is only when the State is thus involved that one can speak of property rather than of mere possession. Although property, unlike possession, will exist and function within a legal context that is no longer based on mere physical inequality, it is not in itself more legitimate, if only because the State itself, on which it depends, is such an arbitrary entity: "since the powers of the State are incomparably larger than those of each individual, public possession is, in practice, stronger and more irrevocable, without being more legitimate." The contractual instrument that is thus constituted exists as a paradoxical juxtaposition or interference of relational networks. On the one hand, as private property, objects of possession used for the fulfillment of individual needs and desires [*jouissance*], the relationship between the owner and the land, or dwelling, is entirely literal. It is perfectly defined in its identity by its objective dimensions, and the inscribed signs by means of which these dimensions are designated (be it as a fence, or as a "non-trespassing" sign) is semantically unambiguous. A principle of functional identification between the owning subject and the owned object is implied. This identification, as we saw, is not natural and legitimate, but contractual. There is nothing legitimate about property, but the rhetoric of property confers the illusion of legitimacy. The contract is self-reflective; it is an agreement *du même au même* in which the land defines the owner and the owner defines the land. One could say, with equal justice, that the private owner contracts with himself or that the private property contracts with itself; the identity of the owner is defined by the identity of the land. Thus it is that Marcel, in Proust's novel, understands the fascination of the *proper* names of the aristocracy because it is impossible to distinguish their names from the geographical names of their landed estate. There can be no more seductive form of onomastic identification. The fascination of the model is not so much that it feeds fantasies of material possession (though it does this too, of course) but that it satisfies semiological fantasies about the adequation of sign to meaning seductive enough to tolerate extreme forms of economic oppression.

On the other hand, Rousseau stresses that property can also be considered from a public point of view as part of the rights and duties of the State: "This is how the united and contiguous land of private owners becomes public territory, and how rights of sovereignty, extending from the subjects to the land they occupy, become both 'real' and personal. But the relationship that governs the public aspect of the property is not the same as the one that determines its private identity. The difference becomes apparent in the way in which the property's "inside" relates to what lies beyond its boundaries. When considered from the private point of view, this relationship is still governed by patterns of genuine similarity. The relation of one private property to another is a relationship between two units that are similarly constituted, and it therefore suffices to respect the principle of this constitution in order to have a reliable system of arbitration available in the adjudication of any conflict that may arise between the two owners. Neighbors can have any number of conflicts with each other, but whether they want it or not, they remain neighbors and not strangers; as far as their mutual property rights are concerned, they can always be derived from the propietary status they have in common, in the form of a deed or any other instrument of ownership. Local obscurities in the phrasing of the deed can be clarified and the deed is, in principle, a denominative text that is entirely readable to all parties. Therefore, though it is never guaranteed, peace between neighbors is at least legally conceivable. But the same is not true when the property is considered within a context of public interests, especially when they involve the interests of the State with regard to other States. The contractual constitution of a State may or may not be similar to that of another, but this question is irrelevant with regard to territorial conflict and integrity. From that point of view, the other State is, per definition, a hostile stranger: "the Greeks often called peace treaties the treaties established between two people who were not at war. The words for stranger and for enemy have long been synonyms for many ancient people, including the Romans." When considered privately, property is a structure based on similarity and on the integration of shared needs and desires; when considered publicly, the same property functions as a structure of necessary estrangement and conflict. This hostility is the foundation of the State's political integrity and can therefore be valorized positively: it protects property "with all its strength against the outsider [*contre l'Etranger*]" and it enables Rousseau to speak approvingly of "what is admirable in this alienation."

From a rhetorical perspective, the interest of the structure is that the same single entity (a specific piece of land) can be considered as the referent of two entirely divergent texts, the first based on the proper meaning engendered by a consistent conceptual system, the second on the radical discontinuity and estrangement of noncomparable systems of relationship that allow for no acts of judgment and, consequently, for no stable meaning or identity. The semiological systems at work within each of these systems are entirely different: the one is monological and controlled in all its articulations, the second at the mercy of contingencies more arbitrary even than the strength based on numerical power. Yet, in its absence, the first could never have come into being. The power of property is vested "in the distinction between the rights that the sovereign and the owner have over the same fund." Behind the stability and the decorum of private law lurk the "brigands" and the "pirates" whose acts shape the realities of politics between nations, the most difficult adjustment being the necessity of considering these mixed standards as entirely honorable.

The pattern may seem crude and literal when it is applied to material property, but it pervades all aspects of the political society. The social contract is best characterized, not by the conceptual language of its formal definition, but by the *double rapport* that we found operative in the determination of property rights and that also characterizes the pact in its most fundamental form, of which property is only a derived, particular version. The expression *double rapport* is used in a difficult and controversial passage that formulates a distinction in the degree to which the contract is binding for the individual citizen as compared to the degree to which it is binding for the sovereign: "the act of original confederation includes a reciprocal commitment between the public and the private sector. Each individual, contracting so to speak with himself, is committed in a double relationship, namely as member of the sovereign authority with regard to individuals and as member of the State with regard to the sovereign authority. We know from empirical experience that the individual is subjected to a more stringent legal control than the executive power which has much more leeway in its actions and initiatives, in international politics, for example, where it is expected to resort to war and to violence in a manner that could not be tolerated in relationships between individuals. Rousseau accounts for this by stressing that the private interests of the individual (which can be called this commitments toward himself) have nothing in common with his political, public interests and obligations. The former do precisely *not* derive from the latter as part derives from whole; the sentence "there is considerable difference between a commitment toward oneself and a commitment toward a whole of which one is a part" is true because no metaphorical totalization is allowed to intervene. The double relationship of the individual toward the State is thus based on the coexistence of two distinct rhetorical models, the first self-reflective or specular, the other estranged. But what the individual is estranged from is precisely the executive activity of his own State as *souverain*. This power is unlike him and foreign to him because it does not have the same double and self-contradictory structure and therefore does not share in his problems and tensions. The *souverain* can consider himself "under one single and identical relationship" and, with regard to any outsider, including the individual citizen, it can become "a single Being or an individual" ("à l'égard de l'étranger, il devient un Etre simple ou un individu." Unlike the "individual," who is always divided within himself, the executive is truly in-dividual, undivided.

The passage becomes clearer in its implications if one takes into account the precise meaning of the terminology. What Rousseau calls the "souverain" (which can, with some historical hindsight, be translated as the executive power) is, of course, not a person but specifically the political body when it is active as distinct from this same body as a mere entity, the carrier, or ground, as it were, of the action that it makes possible by its existence: "the sovereign authority, by its very nature, is only a moral person, whose existence can only be abstract and collective. The idea that is linked to this term cannot be equated with that of a single individual." "This public person thus constituted by the union of all the others . . . is called by its members the *State* [*Etat*] when it is passive, the *Sovereign* [*Souverain*] when it is active." The individual's private will (like his private property) is clear and comprehensible in itself, but devoid of any general interest or signification beyond himself. The same is still true of the relationship between several private volitions. Only with the "double relationship" does the possibility of generalization come into being but, at the same moment, the continuity between purpose and action that remained preserved on the private level is disrupted. It follows that the divergence which prevails, within the State, in the relationship between the citizen and the executive is in fact an unavoidable estrangement between political rights and laws on the one hand, and political action and history on the other. The grounds for this alienation are best understood in terms of the rhetorical structure that separates the one domain from the other. The passage, as is well known, was to be one of the main considerations in condemning Rousseau as politically subversive. It proves however that he had a much more developed sense of political praxis than the magistrates of the city of Geneva; he certainly never meant to imply that the executive has the right to change the constitution at its own will, but merely to caution against the fact that it would always be tempted and have the power to do just that, and that therefore the State needs legislation to protect it against the persistent threat of its own executive branch. And, as his admiration of Moses indicates, Rousseau is equally convinced of the need for durable institutions or States. But precisely because it is not rooted in the contract itself, durability has to be legislated. The *Social Contract* does not warrant belief in a suprahistorical political model that, in the words of the 1738 *Edit de Médiation* of the State of Geneva, would make the political State "perpetual." For this would reduce the double structure of the constitutional text to a monological signification and cause the State to relapse into the kind of aberrant natural model of which the end of the *Second Discourse* gives a fictional description. The declaration of the "permanence" of the State would thus greatly hasten its dissolution. It follows however that the meaning of the contractual text has to remain suspended and undecidable: "there can be no fundamental Law that is binding for the entire body of the people" and "since the decisions of the executive, as executive, concern only itself, it is always free to change them." Revolution and legality by no means cancel each other out, since the text of the law is, per definition, in a condition of unpredictable change. Its mode of existence is necessarily temporal and historical, though in a strictly nonteleological sense.

The structure of the entity with which we are concerned (be it as property, as national State or any other political institution) is most clearly revealed when it is considered as the general form that subsumes all these particular versions, namely as legal *text*. The first characteristic of such a text is its generality: "the object of the Law must be general, like the will that dictates it. It is this double universality that determines the legality of the Law." At first sight, it seems that this generality is rooted in the selective applicability of the law to the part that makes up the political whole, as the exclusion of the part that does not partake of this whole: "This is why the general will of an entire people is not general for a foreign individual [*un particulier étranger*], for this individual is not a member of this people." But it turns out that the estrangement is not (as it still misleadingly appeared to be in the case of territorial property models) the result of some spatial, temporal, or psychological nonpresence, but that it is implied by the very notion of particularity itself. To the extent that he is particular, *any* individual is, as individual, alienated from a law that, on the other hand, exists only in relation to his individual being. "For at the moment that a people consider a particular object, *even if it be one of its own members*, a relation is created between whole and part that makes them into two separate beings. The part is one of these beings, the whole minus this part the other. But the whole minus a part is not the whole and as long as the relationship persists, there is no whole, only two unequal parts." This statement is repeated whenever the mode of applicability of the law to particular citizens is under discussion. "There is no general will acting upon a particular object" but the particularity of the legal subject, to which the law is made to apply, is independent of its being inside or outside the precinct of the State; the categories of inside and outside do not function as the determining principle of an unavoidable estrangement. That the *extra-muros* individual is estranged from the law is obvious: "If [the particular object] is outside the State, a will that is estranged from him is not general in relation to him"(*Social Contract*). But the same applies necessarily to the individual *intra-muros*, simply because he is individual or particular: "Indeed, this particular object is either within the State, or without it. . . . If the object is within the State, then it is a part of it. A relation is then created between the whole and the part that makes them into two separate beings. The part is one of them, the whole minus the part the other. But the whole minus a part is not the whole . . . etc."

From the point of view of the legal text, it is this generality which ruthlessly rejects any particularization, which allows for the possibility of its coming into being. Within the textual model, particularization corresponds to reference, since reference is the application of an undetermined, general potential for meaning to a specific unit. The indifference of the text with regard to its referential meaning is what allows the legal text to proliferate, exactly as the preordained, coded repetition of a specific gesture or set of gestures allows Helen to weave the story of the war into the epic. As a text, the *Social Contract* is unusual among Rousseau's works because of its impersonal, machinelike systematicity: it takes a few key terms, programs a relationship between them, and lets mere syntax take its course. It is, for instance, the only Rousseau text to make explicit and repeated use of mathematical ratios. By suppressing the genealogy of the key terms from the final version, this quasi-mechanical pattern becomes even more evident. "I shall go directly to my subject without first demonstrating its importance"

Rousseau announces at the start of the final text, but the early version still felt the need to make explicit what is taken for granted later on: "I describe the mainsprings [of the social body] and its various parts, and I assemble them into place. I make the machine ready to go to work; others, wiser than I am, will regulate its movements."

We have moved closer and closer to the "definition" of *text*, the entity we are trying to circumscribe, a law being, in its facticity, more like an actual text than a piece of property or a State. The system of relationships that generates the text and that functions independently of its referential meaning is its grammar. To the extent that a text is grammatical, it is a logical code or a machine. And there can be no agrammatical texts, as the most grammatical of poets, Mallarmé, was the first to acknowledge. Any nongrammatical text will always be read as a deviation from an assumed grammatical norm. But just as no text is conceivable without grammar, no grammar is conceivable without the suspension of referential meaning. Just as no law can ever be written unless one suspends any consideration of applicability to a particular entity including, of course, oneself, grammatical logic can function only if its referential consequences are disregarded.

On the other hand, no law is a law unless it also applies to particular individuals. It cannot be left hanging in the air, in the abstraction of its generality. Only by thus referring it back to particular praxis can the *justice* of the law be tested, exactly as the *justesse* of any statement can only be tested by referential verifiability, or by deviation from this verification. For how is justice to be determined if not by particular reference?

> Why is the general will always right, and why do all citizens constantly desire the well-being of each, if it were not for the fact that no one exists who does not secretly appropriate the term *each* and think of himself when he votes for all [*il n'y a personne qui ne s'approprie en secret ce mot* chacun *et qui ne songe à lui-même en votant pour tous*]? Which proves that the equality of right and the notion of justice that follows from it derive from the preference that each man gives to himself, and therefore from the nature of man.
>
> (*Social Contract*, first version)

(Rousseau suppressed the all-important specification "en secret" in "s'approprier [en secret] ce mot *chacun*" in the final version. The self-censorship that operates between earlier and later versions of texts can, in cases such as this, reveal more than it conceals: how could one be more secretive than by trying to hide "the secret"?) There can be no text without grammar: the logic of grammar generates texts only in the absence of referential meaning, but every text generates a referent that subverts the grammatical principle to which it owed its constitution. What remains hidden in the everyday use of language, the fundamental incompatibility between grammar and meaning, becomes explicit when the linguistic structures are stated, as in the case here, in political terms. The preceding passage makes clear that the incompatibility between the elaboration of the law and its application (or justice) can only be bridged by an act of deceit. "S'approprier en secret ce mot *chacun*" is to steal from the text the very meaning to which, according to this text, we are not entitled, the particular *I* which destroys its generality; hence the deceitful, covert gesture "en secret," in the foolish hope that the theft will go unnoticed. Justice is unjust; no wonder that the language of justice is also the language of guilt and that, as we know from the *Confessions*, we never lie as much as when we want to do full justice to ourselves, especially in self-accusation. The divergence between grammar and referential meaning is what we call the figural dimension of language. This dimension accounts for the fact that two enunciations that are lexicologically and grammatically identical (the one being, so to speak, the quotation of the other and vice versa) can, regardless of context, have two entirely divergent meanings. In exactly the same way Rousseau defines the State or the law as a "double relationship" that, at closer examination, turns out to be as self-destructive as it is unavoidable. In the description of the structure of political society, the "definition" of a text as the contradictory interference of the grammatical with the figural field emerges in its most systematic form. This is not unexpected, since the political model is necessarily diaphoric and cannot pretend to ignore the referential moment entirely. We call *text* any entity that can be considered from such a double perspective: as a generative, open-ended, nonreferential grammatical system and as a figural system closed off by a transcendental signification that subverts the grammatical code to which the text owes its existence. The "definition" of the text also states the impossibility of its existence and prefigures the allegorical narratives of this impossibility.

In the *Social Contract*, the model for the structural description of textuality derives from the incompatibility between the formulation and the application of the law, reiterating the estrangement that exists between the sovereign as an active, and the State as a static, principle. The distinction, which is not a polarity, can therefore also be phrased in terms of the difference between political action and political prescription. The tension between figural and grammatical language is duplicated in the differentiation between the State as a defined entity (Etat) and the State as a principle of action (Souverain) or, in linguistic terms, between the constative and the performative function of language. A text is defined by the necessity of considering a statement, at the same time, as performative and constative, and the logical tension between figure and grammar is repeated in the impossibility of distinguishing between two linguistic functions which are not necessarily compatible. It seems that as soon as a text knows what it states, it can only act deceptively, like the thieving lawmaker in the *Social Contract*, and if a text does not act, it cannot state what it knows. The distinction between a text as narrative and a text as theory also belongs to this field of tension.

Especially in the final version, with the conceptual genealogy and the metaphorical deconstruction omitted, the *Social Contract* does not seem to be a narrative but a thoery, a constitutional machine to which Rousseau was to resort for the elaboration of specific constitutions. If this were the case, then the text of the law and the law of the text would fully coincide and generate both the *Social Contract,* as a master text, and a set of contractual rules on which the constitution of any State could be founded, or from which the suitability of a given territory to be made into a State could be deduced. It turns out, however, that the "law of the text" is too devious to allow for such a simple relationship between model and example, and the theory of politics inevitably turns into the history, the allegory of its inability to achieve the status of a science. The passage from constative theory to performative history is very clear in evidence in the *Social Contract.* The text can be considered as the theoretical description of the State, considered as a contractual and legal model, but also as the disintegration of this same model as soon as it is put in motion. And since the contract is both statutory and operative, it will have to be considered from this double perspective.

The legal machine, it turns out, never works exactly as it was programmed to do. It always produces a little more or a little less than the original, theoretical input. When it produces more, things go almost too well for the State: "the more [the] natural forces [of man] are withered away and eliminated, and the more his acquired forces are stable and powerful, the more solid and perfect the institution will be. Legislation reaches the highest point it can reach when each citizen can act only through the others and when *the acquired power of the whole is equal or superior* to the sum of the natural forces of all individuals" (*Social Contract,* first version, my italics). The result of this supplementary efficiency of the political process is stated in (metaphorical) terms that are not entirely reassuring, neither physically nor epistemologically, since they suggest a substitutive process that is far from harmless: to found a State is "to substitute a fragmentary and moral existence for a physical and autonomous one," and this reductive substitution is called to kill, to annihilate, and "to mutilate, so to speak, the human constitution in order to strengthen it" ("mutiler en quelque sorte la constitution de l'homme pour la renforcer"). (The final version deletes "mutiler" and replaces it by the innocuous "altérer.") A somewhat cryptic and isolated note by Rousseau would seem to fit the situation: "I created a people, and I was unable to create men" ("J'ai fait un peuple et n'ai pu faire des hommes") (fragment "Des lois"). The thing to worry about is perhaps not so much the redoubtable power that the State can generate as the fact that this power is not necessarily equal to the power that went into its production. For at other moments, the supplementary or differential structure of the input/output relationship can take on a negative as well as a positive sign:

> The general will is rarely that of all, and the public strength is always less than the sum of individual strengths. As a result, we find in the wheels of the State an equivalent of the principle of

inertia in machines [*on trouve dans les ressorts de l'état un equivalent aux frottements des machines*]. This counterforce has to be kept to a minimum or, at the very least, it must be computed and deducted beforehand from the total power in order to set up a proper ratio between the means one uses and the effect one wishes to produce. ("One cannot avoid, in politics as in mechanics, acting weakly or slowly, and losing strength or time" [*Social contract,* first version].)

The transformation of the generative power of theory and of grammar into a quantitative economy of *loss,* a kind of political thermodynamics governed by a debilitating entropy, illustrates the practical consequences of a linguistic structure in which grammar and figure, statement and speech act do not converge.

Regardless of whether the differentiation engenders excess or default, it always results in an increasing deviation of the law of the State from the state of the law, between constitutional prescription and political action. As in the *Profession de foi,* this differential structure engenders an affectivity and a valorization, but since the difference is one of epistemological divergence between a statement and its meaning, the affect can never be a reliable criterion of political value judgment. As we already know from "Du bonheur public," the eudaemony of politics is not an exact science: "In order for everyone to want to do what he has to do according to the commitment of the social contract, everyone has to know what he should want. What he should want is the common good; what he should avoid is public evil. But since the existence of the State is only ideal and conventional, its members possess no common and natural sensibility through which, without mediation, they are forewarned by a pleasurable impression of what is useful to the State and by a painful impression of what could harm it" ("ses membres n'ont aucune sensibilité naturelle et commune, par laquelle, immédiatement avertis, ils reçoivent une impression agréable de ce qui lui est utile, et une impression douloureuse sitôt qu'il est offensé"). The affective code is unreadable, which is equivalent to stating that it is not, or not merely, a code.

The discrepancy within the contractual model (here claimed to be the linguistic model in general) will necessarily manifest itself phenomenologically, since it is defined, in part, as the passage, however unreliable, from "pure" theory to an empirical phenomenon. The noncoincidence of the theoretical statement with its phenomenal manifestation implies that the mode of existence of the contract is temporal, or that time is the phenomenal category produced by the discrepancy. Considered performatively, the speech act of the contractual text never refers to a situation that exists in the present, but signals toward a hypothetical future: "Far from preventing the evils that attack the State, [the members of the State] are rarely on time to remedy them when they begin to perceive their effects. One has to foresee them well in advance in order to avoid or to cure them" (*Social*

Contract, first version). All laws are future-oriented and prospective; their illocutionary mode is that of the *promise*. On the other hand, every promise assumes a date at which the promise is made and without which it would have no validity; laws are promissory notes in which the present of the promise is always a past with regard to its realization: "the law of today should not be an act of yesterday's general will but of today's; we have not committed ourselves to do what the people wanted but what they want. It follows that when the Law speaks in the name of the people, it is in the name of the people of today and not of the past." The definition of this "people of today" is impossible, however, for the eternal present of the contract can never apply as such to any particular present.

The situation is without solution. In the absence of an *état présent*, the general will is quite literally voiceless. The people are a helpless and "mutilated" giant, a distant and weakened echo of the Polyphemos we first encountered in the *Second Discourse*. "Does the body political possess an organ with which it can state [*énoncer*] the will of the people? Who will give it the necessary foresight to shape the people's actions and to announce them in advance, and how will it pronounce them when the need arises? How could a blind mob, which often does not know what it wants because it rarely knows its own good, carry out by itself as huge and difficult an enterprise as the promulgation of a system of Law?" Yet it is this blind and mute monster which has to articulate the promise that will restore its voice and its sight: "The people subject to the Law must be the authors of the Law" (*Social Contract*). Only a subterfuge can put this paralysis in motion. Since the system itself had to be based on deceit, the mainspring of its movement has to be deceitful as well.

The impostor is clearly enough identified: Rosseau calls him the "lawgiver." It has to be an individual, since only an individual can have the sight and the voice that the people lack. But this individual is also a rhetorical figure, for his ability to promise depends on the metaleptic reversal of cause and effect: "For a people to appreciate the sound maxims of politics and to follow the fundamental rules of political reason [*la raison d'Etat*], effect should become cause, and the social spirit that the institutions are to produce should preside over their elaboration. Men should be, prior to the laws, what they are to become through them." The metaphor engendered by this metalepsis is equally predictable. It can only be God, since the temporal and causal reversal that puts the realization of the promise before its utterance can only occur within a teleological system oriented toward the convergence of figure and meaning. Since the *Social Contract* is nothing of the sort, it is entirely consistent that it should introduce the notion of divine authority at this particular point and have to define it as a simulacrum: "If prideful philosophy and blind partisan spirit continue to regard [the lawgiver] as a fortunate impostor, true political minds admire in the institutions they created, the forceful genius that presides over enduring laws." When the truly political mind is also a philosopher, he will no longer be "prideful," but this lawgiver will be no less of an impostor, albeit no longer a fortunate one. The metaphorical substitution of one's own for the divine voice is blasphemous, although the necessity for this deceit is as implacable as its eventual denunciation, in the future undoing of any State or any political institution.

Is Rousseau himself the "lawgiver" of the *Social Contract* and his treatise the Deuteronomy of the modern State? If this were the case, then the *Social Contract* would become a monological referential statement. It could not be called an allegory, nor a text in our sense, since the exposure of the deceit would have to come from outside evidence not provided by the text itself. Since it implicitly and explicitly denies, in chapter 7 of book 2 ("Du législateur") and again in the related chapter 8 of book 4 ("De la religion civile"), any form of divine inspiration for itself, it is clear that Rousseau does not identify himself with any of the major legislators, be it Moses, Lycurgus, or Christ; instead, by raising the suspicion that the Sermon on the Mount may be the Machiavellian invention of a master politician, he clearly undermines the authority of his own legislative discourse. Would we then have to conclude that the *Social Contract* is a deconstructive narrative like the *Second Discourse*? But this is not the case either, because the *Social Contract* is clearly productive and generative as well as deconstructive in a manner that the *Second Discourse* is not. To the extent that it never ceases to advocate the necessity for political legislation and to elaborate the principles on which such a legislation could be based, it resorts to the principles of authority that it undermines. We know this structure to be characteristic of what we have called allegories of unreadability. Such an allegory is metafigural: it is an allegory of a figure (for example, metaphor) which relapses into the figure it deconstructs. The *Social Contract* falls under this heading to the extent that it is indeed structured like an aporia: it persists in performing what it has shown to be impossible to do. As such, we can call it an allegory. But is it the allegory of a figure? The question can be answered by asking what it is the *Social Contract* performs, what it keeps doing despite the fact that it has established that it could not be done. What the *Profession de foi* keeps doing is to assert the metaphorical analogy between mind and nature against which the text has generated its own argument; it keeps listening, in other words, to the voice of conscience (or of God) affectively, although it no longer can believe it. What Julie keeps doing, at the end of part 3 of the novel, is to "love" Saint-Preux and God as if they were interchangeable. To listen and to love are referential transitive acts that are not self-positing. What the *Social Contract* keeps doing however is to promise, that is, to perform the very illocutionary speech act which it has discredited and to perform it in all its textual ambiguity, as a statement of which the constative and the performative functions cannot be distinguished or reconciled.

That the *Social Contract* denies the right to promise is clear from the fact that the legislator has to invent a transcendental principle of signification called God in order to perform the metalepsis that reverses the temporal pattern of all promissory and legal statements. Since God is said to be, within this perspective, a subterfuge, it follows that the *Social Contract* has lost the right to promise anything. Yet it promises a great deal. For example: "far from thinking that we can have neither virtue nor happiness and that providence [*le ciel*] has abandoned us without shelter to the degradation of the species, let us extract from evil itself the remedy that must cure it. Let us if possible improve by new institutions [*de nouvelles associations*] the shortcomings of society in general. . . . Let our interlocutor see in a better constitution of things the reward for virtuous deeds, the punishment of evil and the harmonious accord of justice and well-being" (first version). Or: "it becomes obvious that individuals do not really give up anything when they enter into the social contract. Their new situation is genuinely preferable to the old one, before the contract. Instead of an alienation, they have exchanged an uncertain and precarious way of life against a better and more secure one; instead of natural independence, they now have freedom; instead of the power to harm others, they now have their own security; and instead of their individual strength, which others might overcome, they now have rights which the social union makes invincible" (second version). Several other instances could be quoted, some explicit, some all the more suggestive because they are all-pervasive in their connotations; it is impossible to read the *Social Contract* without experiencing the exhilarating feeling inspired by a firm promise.

The reintroduction of the promise, despite the fact that its impossibility has been established (the pattern that identifies the *Social Contract* as a *textual* allegory), does not occur at the discretion of the writer. We are not merely pointing out an inconsistency, a weakness in the text of the *Social Contract* that could have been avoided by simply omitting sentimental or demagogical passages. The point is not that the *Social Contract* relapses into textual activism because it does so explicitly, in sections and passages that can be isolated and quoted by themselves. Even without these passages, the *Social Contract* would still promise by inference, perhaps more effectively than if Rousseau had not had the naïveté, or the good faith, to promise openly. The redoubtable efficacy of the text is due to the rhetorical model of which it is a version. This model is a fact of language over which Rousseau himself has no control. Just as any other reader, he is bound to misread his text as a promise of political change. The error is not within the reader; language itself dissociates the cognition from the act. *Die Sprache verspricht* (*sich*); to the extent that is necessarily misleading, language just as necessarily conveys the promise of its own truth. This is also why textual allegories on this level of rhetorical complexity generate history.

Toward a Supreme Fiction: Genre and Beholder in the Art Criticism of Diderot and His Contemporaries

Michael Fried

How are we to understand the renewed importance given to the sister doctrines of the hierarchy of genres and the supremacy of history painting in French criticism and theory of painting in the second half of the eighteenth century? As Rensselaer Lee and others have shown, both doctrines were implicit in humanist theory of painting from Alberti onwards, received explicit formulation in the writings and institutions of the Académie Royale de Peinture, and were central to the classical system that dominated artistic thinking in France until the death of Louis XIV. Both were eclipsed in practice by the rise of the Rococo, whose emphases on intimacy, sensuousness, and decoration effected a sharp though only partly conscious revision of classical values. And both became crucial once more shortly before the middle of the eighteenth century when a powerful reaction against the Rococo in the name of artistic and moral reform began to take shape along a broad front.

Locquin and subsequent scholars have shown that the anti-Rococo movement was promoted at the highest levels of the government by the Directeurs Généraux des Bâtiments du Roi Lenormant de Tournehem and Marigny, in part as a deliberate attempt to recreate the grandeur of the reign of Louis XIV. For example, the official scale of fees was altered so that artists would be paid more for history paintings than for portraits; a new Ecole Royale was established to provide young painters with the background and knowledge history painting required; and altogether royal patronage was exploited to encourage history painting over other genres. As Locquin recognized, however, the reactivation of the doctrines of the hierarchy of genres and the supremacy of history painting was not simply

From *New Literary History* 6, no. 3 (Spring 1975). © 1975 by *New Literary History*, The University of Virginia, Charlottesville, Virginia.

the result of official policy. From the start of the reaction against the Rococo in the late 1740s the leading critics and theorists of the period, men as intellectually heterodox as La Font de Saint-Yenne, Laugier, Grimm, and Diderot himself, insisted upon the axiomatic importance of those doctrines and characterized the almost complete lapse of history painting in the decades before mid-century as a cultural disaster. At the same time they and other anti-Rococo writers responded positively to outstanding paintings in "lesser" genres: Diderot's praise of Chardin's still lifes in his *Salons* of the 1760s is only the most famous instance of a general state of affairs. But their appreciation of work other than history painting in no sense undercuts their often passionate advocacy of the doctrines in question. If anything it makes the fact of that advocacy all the more compelling.

Historians of eighteenth-century art have without exception interpreted the doctrines of the hierarchy of genres and the supremacy of history painting in terms of an underlying and in effect determining hierarchy of categories of subject matter; while some historians, going further, have represented the adherence to those doctrines on the part of anti-Rococo critics and theorists as a mistake, a glaring example of misconceived and retardataire academicism (or, alternatively, of the substitution of literary and moralistic qualities and values for authentically pictorial ones). In this connection the gradual abandonment of both doctrines by nineteenth-century painters has been portrayed as an unmasking of their inessentialness if not indeed of their fallaciousness, and the achievement of Chardin has been invoked as evidence that they were without relevance to the best and most progressive painting of the time.

The trouble with this interpretation, whose authority within art history has perhaps begun to expire, is that it is anachronistic. It projects upon an earlier and radically different state of affairs a vision of painting and in particular of the neutrality of subject matter precipitated by Impressionism and Post-Impressionism and ratified by subsequent developments. It fails to give sufficient weight to the fact that the history of modern painting is traditionally (and rightly) seen as having begun with David's masterpieces of the 1780s, most importantly the *Oath of the Horatii* (1784, exhibited 1785), which at once established itself as paradigmatic for ambitious painting: as exemplifying, down to the smallest details of its execution, what painting had to do and be if it were to realize the highest aims open to it. Now the *Horatii*, like the *Belisarius* (1781) that preceded it and the *Death of Socrates* (1787) and the *Lictors Returning to Brutus the Bodies of His Sons* (1789) that followed it, was a history painting according to the most rigorous current definition of the genre; and it is inconceivable that any canvases that were *not* history paintings could have had a comparably profound impact on contemporary sensibility and subsequent artistic practice. (Certainly Chardin's still lifes, for all their marvelous quality and wide renown in their own time, did not have that significance for painters that came after him.) This suggests that, far from having been retardataire in its implications, the adherence to the doctrines by anti-Rococo critics and theorists ought instead to be seen as having been progressive—as having anticipated, perhaps as having helped prepare, the next major phase in the evolution of French painting.

It is true that the critics and theorists I shall be discussing viewed their undertaking in quite other terms. They believed that the conception of the nature and function of painting put forward in their writings consisted essentially in the recovery, after a period of decadence, of fundamental principles discovered by the ancients and embodied in the work of the greatest sixteenth- and seventeenth-century painters (e.g., Raphael, Domenichino, Poussin, Lesueur, Le Brun). But the fact that they saw themselves in this light, looked to a canon of previous masters in this way, and, as we shall see, openly derived many of their basic ideas from the writings of classical theorists does not mean that their conception of painting was merely a reformulation of earlier assumptions and imperatives. And the fact that the principles they believed they found in the art of those masters are seen in retrospect to have been not absolute or universal but historically conditioned hardly implies that the principles themselves were without urgent relevance to the actual situation of French painting in their time.

This is not to deny the close connection of the sister doctrines of the hierarchy of genres and the supremacy of history painting with the idea of a hierarchy of categories of subject matter. In their classical versions the sister doctrines had been grounded in the conviction, derived from Aristotle and stated forcefully by Alberti, that the art of painting at its highest consisted in the representation of significant human action; and with their reinstitution shortly before 1750 that conviction too became important once more.

The terms in which it was reasserted owed a great deal to the Abbé Du Bos, whose *Réflexions critiques sur la poésie et sur la peinture* (1719) strongly influenced French artistic thought of the second half of the century. Du Bos had argued on empirical grounds that a painting's power to move the beholder and thereby to command his attention (and ultimately to divert him from *ennui*) was a function of the power of its subject matter to do so in real life. The effect of this argument was inevitably to exalt the subject matter of history painting as traditionally conceived, in which significant action and strong passions were primary, and to downgrade subject matter wholly devoid of these, such as bowls of fruit, views of countryside without human figures, portraits of unknown men and women, genre scenes in which humble persons engage in trivial activities and, so on. "La plus grande imprudence que le Peintre ou le Poëte puissent faire," Du Bos wrote, "c'est de prendre pour l'objet principal de leur imitation des choses que nous regarderions avec indifférence dans la nature." He did not claim that paintings of still life, landscape, or genre subjects were in all cases literally unable to interest the beholder. But he argued that the beholder's interest could be elicited only by their technique, not their subject matter, and that consequently their power to command his attention was much weaker than that of an equally well-executed painting of action and passion.

The imprint of Du Bos' arguments on the thought of anti-Rococo critics and theorists is unmistakable. Thus we find the Comte de Caylus, in a lecture of 1748 to the painters of the Académie Royale, criticizing Watteau, under whom he had studied as a very young man, for the aimlessness, almost the subjectlessness, of all but a few of his paintings: "[Most of his compositions] n'ont aucun objet. Elles n'expriment le concours d'aucune passion, et, par conséquent, elles sont dépourvues d'une des plus piquantes parties de la peinture, je veux dire l'action. Ce genre de la peinture, surtout dans l'héroique [i.e., history painting], est le sublime de votre art; c'est la partie qui parle à l'esprit, qui l'entraine, l'occupe, l'attache et le détourne de toute autre idée" ("Vie d'Antoine Watteau," in *Vies d'artistes du XVIIIe siècle, discours sur la peinture et la sculpture, salons de 1751 et 1753, lettre à Lagrenée*, edited by André Fontaine). A year earlier, La Font de Saint-Yenne, the first truly independent critic of painting and one of Diderot's chief predecessors had said: "De tous les genres de la Peinture, le premier sans difficulté est celui de l'Histoire. Le Peintre Historien est seul le peintre de l'âme [that is, of passions of the soul as they are manifested in action], les autres ne peignent que pour les yeux" (*Réflexions sur quelques causes de l'état présent de la peinture en France*). As for Diderot, whose familiarity with Du Bos' thought cannot be doubted, the same priorities are directly or indirectly affirmed on almost every page of the *Salons, Essai sur la peinture*, and *Pensées détachées sur la peinture*. "La peinture est l'art d'aller à l'âme par l'entremise des yeux," he wrote in the *Salon de 1765*. "Si l'effet s'arrête aux yeux, le peintre n'a fait que la moindre partie du chemin." And in his view the actions and passions of human beings were inherently more compelling, more attuned to the natural interests of the soul, than any other class of subject matter.

Diderot's admiration for Chardin, often construed as a sign of inconsistency in this regard, is in fact nothing of the sort. For Diderot as for others among his contemporaries, Chardin's greatness consisted preeminently in his ability to overcome the triviality of his subject matter by virtue of an unprecedented mastery of the means of imitation, an all but miraculous power to evoke the reality of objects, space, and air. "Si le sublime du technique n'y étoit pas," Diderot wrote with characteristic vigor, "l'idéal de Chardin seroit misérable" (ibid.). Conversely he held that history paintings that were not well executed could nevertheless manage to hold the spectator's attention on the strength of their subject matter and overall conception. Even his proposed revision of the traditional distinctions among genres, far from expressing uneasiness with these priorities, radically confirmed them. For example, he maintained that Greuze and Joseph Vernet, both of whom were officially classed as painters of genre subjects, ought instead to be considered history painters because of their mastery of the representation of action. More generally, he suggested reducing the traditional multiplicity of genres to a single basic opposition, between works that imitated "la nature brute et morte," to be called genre painting, and works that imitated "la nature sensible et vivante," to be called history painting (*Essai*): the chief virtue of that simplification being that it would have encouraged painters who ordinarily did not think of themselves as history painters to recognize the primary of considerations of action for their own work. (Neither suggestion broke in principle with the notion of a hierarchy of genres; and in later writings Diderot backed away from the simplifications he had earlier proposed.)

All this may be summed up by saying that for Diderot and his contemporaries, as for the Albertian tradition generally, the human body *in action* was the best picture of the human soul; and the representation of action and passion was therefore felt to provide, if not quite a sure means of reaching the soul of the beholder, at any rate a pictorial resource of potentially enormous efficacy which the painter could neglect only at his peril.

But far more was at stake in the doctrines of the hierarchy of genres and the supremacy of history painting as they were held by anti-Rococo critics and theorists than simply a hierarchy of categories of subject matter. While the importance to their thought of such a hierarchy, and more broadly of considerations of subject matter, cannot be denied, the question remains whether that hierarchy and those considerations were truly fundamental, as most historians of the period have supposed, or whether they were largely determined by other, pictorially prior, and in that sense more fundamental concerns and imperatives. I believe that the latter is the case, and in the pages that follow I shall distinguish three functionally interdependent and in my view progressively more fundamental contexts of concern which bear directly on the opening question of this essay. A summary of these contexts of concern will serve as a guide to the argument I now wish to pursue:

(1) The repeated assertions of the primacy of subject matter of action and passion in the writings of the major critics and theorists of the anti-Rococo reaction is to be seen as one expression of a new *explicitly dramatic* conception of painting. That conception tended naturally to entail the representation of action and passion—hence the exaltation of these in contemporary criticism and theory—but cannot reciprocally be understood in terms of subject matter alone. In other words the doctrines of the hierarchy of genres and the supremacy of history painting as they were then held evince the priority not so much of a class of subject matter as of a class of values and effects, the values and effects of the dramatic as such.

(2) The new dramatic conception of painting is to be understood in turn as the expression of a yet more fundamental preoccupation with *pictorial unity*. As I shall try to show, French criticism and theory of the period insisted from the outset on the need for painting to achieve what might be called an absolutely perspicuous mode of pictorial unity, one in which the

causal necessity of every element and relationship in the painting would be strikingly and instantaneously apparent. And that mode of unity, with its emphasis on compulsion, intelligibility, and instantaneousness, called for realization in and through the dramatic representation of a single moment in a single heroic or pathetic action.

(3) Finally, the preoccupation with unity is itself to be seen in terms of the accomplishment of a pictorially and ontologically prior relationship, at once literal and fictive, *between painting and beholder*. The nature of that relationship was grasped and articulated only by Diderot, but his account of it enables us to understand much that appears obscure, arbitrary, or otherwise inexplicable not merely in the criticism and theory of the age but in its painting as well.

Here I might remark that throughout the present essay Diderot's writings on painting receive more attention by far than those of anyone else. There are two reasons for this. First, Diderot was without question the greatest critical intelligence of his age and nation. Second, although his *Salons* and related writings are the most extreme expression of what I think of as the radical wing of the anti-Rococo movement, the conception of painting those writings expound was in large measure characteristic of the movement as a whole. This is not to impugn the originality of his views, as is sometimes done. But it is to insist that the magnitude and nature of his originality become clear only within the context of his agreement with others. Unlike Baudelaire's art criticism, which for all its brilliance and fascination represents an eccentric or at least idiosyncratic point of view, Diderot's gives us access to a vision of painting that was held almost communally, though in crucial respects unconsciously, by a score of contemporaries—painters as well as writers on painting. It is as though almost before his debut as a *salonnier* Diderot pursued to their logical and expressive conclusions a body of assumptions about the nature and purposes of painting that were widely shared but which in the writings of all but a handful of his colleagues remained mostly unexamined, undeveloped, and so to speak divorced from their profoundest implications.

I. THE DRAMATIC CONCEPTION OF PAINTING

The new explicitly dramatic conception of painting that began to emerge in France around 1750 had important sources in previous theory. Here for example is a characteristic passage from Antoine Coypel: "Aristote dit que la tragédie est une imitation d'une action, et par conséquent elle est principalement une imitation de personnes qui agissent. Ce que ce philosophe dit de la tragédie convient également à la peinture, qui doit par l'action et par les gestes exprimer tout ce qui est du sujet qu'elle représente" ("Sur l'Esthétique du peintre," *Conférences de l'Académie Royale de Peinture et de Sculpture,* edited by Henry Jouin; [hereafter referred to as Jouin, *Conférences*]). Or, to take another example, here is Du Bos' explanation of why, despite what he believed to be painting's greater power over the soul, tragedies in the theater often made one weep whereas paintings with very rare exceptions did not: "Une Tragédie renferme une infinité de tableaux. Le Peintre qui fait un tableau du sacrifice d'Iphigénie, ne nous représente sur la toile qu'un instant de l'action. La Tragédie de Racine met sous nos yeux plusieurs instans de cette action, & ces différens incidens se rendent réciproquement les uns les autres plus pathétiques" (*Réflexions critiques*). In Roger De Piles' succinct formulation: "On doit considérer un tableau comme une scène, où chaque figure joue son rôle" (*Eléments de peinture pratique*).

More broadly, the view that "expressive movement is the life blood of all great painting" had been central to the critical tradition of classicism in Italy and had been codified and adapted to prevailing Cartesian ideas by the theorists of the Académie Royale. But there is nothing in the writings of Coypel and Du Bos, or Dufresnoy, Fréart de Chambray, Le Brun, Testelin, Félibien, and De Piles, or for that matter the Englishmen Shaftesbury, Richardson, and Harris, that more than prepared the ground for the comprehensive rapprochement between the aims of painting and drama that took place in France in the second half of the eighteenth century. Greuze's multi-figure paintings from 1755 onwards mark a crucial sequence of phases in that rapprochement within painting itself. In criticism the *Salons* of Grimm (1753, 1755, and 1757) and Laugier (1753) are early statements whose historical significance has never really been appreciated. But is is in Diderot's writings of the 1750s and 1760s that the new relations between painting and drama received their fullest and most influential aritculation, and in the interests of economy of exposition I shall restrict myself to them.

Diderot's vision of those relations is expounded in his two early treatises on the theater, the *Entretiens sur le Fils naturel* (1757) and the *Discours de la poésie dramatique* (1758), in which he called for the development of a new stage dramaturgy that would find in painting, or in certain exemplary paintings, the inspiration for a more convincing representation of action than any provided by the theater of his time. (The single painting that seems to have meant most to him in that regard was Poussin's *Testament of Eudamidas*, a work that came to have almost talismanic significance for ambitious painters in the 1760s and after.) Specifically, Diderot urged playwrights to give up contriving elaborate *coups de théâtre* (surprising turns of plot, reversals, revelations), whose effect he judged shallow and fleeting at best, and instead to seek what he called *tableaux* (visually satisfying, essentially silent, apparently accidental groupings of figures), which if properly managed he believed could move an audience to the depths of its collective being. The spectator in the theater, he maintained, ought to be thought of as before a canvas, on which a series of such *tableaux* follow one another as if by magic (*Poésie dramatique*). Accordingly he stressed the values of pantomime as opposed to declamation, of expressive movement or stillness as opposed to mere proliferation of incident, and called for the institution of a stage space devoid of spectators which in conjunction with painted scenery would allow separate but related actions to proceed simultaneously, thereby providing a more intense because more pictorial dramatic experience than the French theater had hitherto envisaged. The *Entretiens* and the *Poésie dramatique* were not Diderot's first explorations of these ideas. As early as 1751, in the great *Lettre sur les sourds et muets*, he put forward a notion of the gestural or situational sublime, citing as an example Lady Macbeth walking in her sleep and obsessively washing her hands: "Il y a des gestes sublimes que toute l'éloquence oratoire ne rendra jamais. . . . La somnambule Mackbett s'avance en silence & les yeux fermés sur la scene, imitant l'action d'une personne qui se lave les mains, comme si les siennes eussent encore été teintes du sang. . . . Je ne sais rien de si pathétique en discours que le silence & le mouvement des mains de cette femme. Quelle image du remords!" He went on to compare the position of a beholder of a painting with that of a deaf person watching mutes converse among themselves by sign language on subjects known to him, and recounted how when he wanted to gauge the expressive power of actors' gestures he would attend a performance of a play familiar to him, sit far back in the hall, and stop his ears.

Diderot's first *Salon* was written for Grimm's *Correspondance littéraire* in 1759, the year after the composition of the *Poésie dramatique*, and as historians have long been aware the same emphases and priorities that characterize his writings on theater inform his criticism of painting. Probably the most striking of these is his abhorrence of the conventional, mannered, and declamatory and his unqualified insistence that representations of action, gesture, and facial expression actually convey what they ostensibly signify (for more on this see part III below). That insistence stood in implicit opposition to Academic practice, which despite profuse verbal acknowledgment of the virtues of naturalness and truth of expression by Academic theorists tended mostly to perpetuate a limited repertory of postures and attitudes derived from the work of a few sixteenth- and seventeenth-century painters, notably Raphael and Poussin. And it signalled a major difference between Diderot's dramatic conception of painting on the one hand and late seventeenth- and early eighteenth-century equations of painting and tragedy on the other. Far from agreeing with Coypel that "tout contribue dans les spectacles à l'instruction du peintre," a claim advanced just a few paragraphs before the passage quoted above (Jouin, *Conférences*), Diderot held that the actual influence on painting of traditional theatrical conventions was catastrophic, and called for the reform of the theater through a conception of the pictorial which although based in part on a canon of works by the same sixteenth- and seventeenth-century masters affirmed as never before the radical primacy of dramatic and expressive considerations. Similarly, when Du Bos wrote that "une Tragédie renferme une infinité de tableaux" he meant by *tableaux* simply the visual component of the stage action at different points in the play, whereas Diderot felt that the stage conventions of the classical theater resulted in artificial, inexpressive, and undramatic groupings of figures, groupings that were the antithesis of what the concept of the *tableau* meant to him. And this too affirmed the primacy of dramatic and expressive considerations for painting at least as much as it asserted the importance of visual or pictorial considerations for drama.

The new and largely anticlassical emphasis on violent emotion and extreme effects that characterizes Diderot's writings on painting almost from the first is chiefly to be seen in this light. "On peut, on doit en sacrifier un peu au technique," he wrote in the *Essai*. "Jusqu'où? je ne sais rien. Mais je ne veux pas qu'il en coûte la moindre chose à l'expression, à l'effet du sujet. Touche-moi, étonne-moi, déchire-moi; fais-moi tressaillir, pleurer, frémir, m'indigner d'abord; tu récréeras mes yeux après, si tu peux." Thus his attraction to subject matter verging on the horrific, such as scenes of Christian martyrdom, and in general his taste for subjects and effects which modern scholars are perhaps too quick to call melodramatic; his recommendation that the passions be represented at their most extreme relative to a given subject (*Pensées detachées*); his claim that in every genre extravagance is preferable to coldness; his involvement as early as the *Lettre sur les sourds et muets* with notions of the sublime; and his admiration for the "verve brulante" and "chaleur d'âme," the innate dramatic and expressive powers, of artists like Vernet, Van Loo at his best, Greuze, the Fragonard of *Corésus et Callirhoé*, Deshays, Doyen, Casanove, Loutherbourg, Durameau, and the young David. I suggest too that his insistence that a painting be an *exemplum virtutis* or lesson in virtue, a position usually taken at face value as indicating a moralistic if not grossly sentimental attitude towards art, ought instead to be understood as urging a body of subject matter and an approach toward that subject matter which together not only allowed but demanded maximum intensity of dramatic effect. As Diderot had Dorval argue in the *Entretiens:* since the object of a dramatic composition was to inspire in men a love of virtue and a horror of vice, "dire qu'il ne faut les émouvoir que jusqu'à un certain point, c'est prétendre qu'il ne faut pas qu'ils sortent d'un spectacle, trop épris de la vertu, trop éloignés du vice. Il n'y aurait point de poétique pour un peuple qui serait aussi pusillanime. Que serait-ce que le goût; et que l'art deviendrait-il, si l'on se refusait à son énergie, et si l'on posait des barrières arbitraires à ses effets?"

Moreover, the morality that such a view of art entailed was not exactly that of ordinary life. As Diderot wrote in the *Salon de 1767*: "Nous aimons mieux voir sur la scène l'homme de bien souffrant que le méchant puni, et sur le théâtre du monde, au contraire, le méchant puni que l'homme de bien souffrant. C'est un beau spectacle que celui de la vertu sous les grandes épreuves; les efforts les plus terribles tournés contre elle ne nous déplaisent pas." Indeed his feeling for the dramatic conflict of moral opposites had even more unorthodox, not to say Balzacian, consequences: "Je hais toutes ces petites bassesses qui ne montre qu'une âme abjecte; mais je ne hais pas les grands crimes: premièrement, parce qu'on en fait de beaux tableaux et de belles tragédies; et puis, c'est que les grandes et sublimes actions et les grands crimes, portent le même caractère d'énergie" (*Salon de 1765*). And in a striking passage he embraced the possibility that the morality of artistic creation itself was perhaps the reverse of ordinary morality:

> J'ai bien peur que l'homme n'allât droit au malheur par la voie qui conduit l'imitateur de Nature au sublime. Se jetter dans les extrêmes, voilà la règle du poëte, garder en tout un juste milieu, voilà la règle du bonheur. Il ne faut point faire de poésie dans la vie. Les héros, les amants romanesques, les grands patriotes, les magistrats inflexibles, les apôtres de religion, les philosophes à toute outrance, tous ces rares et divins insensés font de la poésie dans la vie, de là leur malheur. Ce sont eux qui fournissent après leur mort aux grands tableaux, ils sont excellens à peindre.
>
> (*Salon de 1767*)

Of course moral considerations mattered to Diderot in their own right. But his advocacy of the moral mission of painting must also be understood in the context of his dramatic conception of painting, a conception that was itself far from unambiguously moral in its implications.

The reach of that conception was not limited to representations of action and passion. It extended even to the genre of still life, improbable though this may seem. "Il y a une loi pour la peinture de genre et pour les groupes d'objets pêle-mêle entassés," he wrote in the *Pensées détachées*, no doubt thinking of Chardin. "Il faudrait leur supposer de la vie, et les distribuer comme s'ils s'étaient arrangés d'eux-mêmes, c'est-à-dire avec le moins de gêne et le plus d'avantage pour chacun d'eux." In other words the still life painter had to persuade the beholder that the objects in his painting had arrived as if without intervention at their own best expression; and this, it is clear, amounted to an essentially dramatic illusion. In the *Salons* themselves the dramatic core of Diderot's vision of Chardin's still lifes is manifest in his attempts to describe—more accurately, to evoke—the latter by giving directions for *staging* them. "Choisissez son site; disposez sur ce site les objets comme je vais vous les indiquer, et soyez sûr que vous aurez vu ses tableaux," he wrote in the *Salon de 1765*, and went on to recreate several paintings by these means. The same *Salon* contains Grimm's announcement, in an editorial aside, that he had seen "des sociétés choisies, rassemblées à la campagne, s'amuser pendant les soirées d'automne à un jeu tout-à-fait intéressant et agréable. C'est d'imiter les compositions de tableaux connus avec des figures vivantes." Diderot's evocations of Chardin's still lifes in the *Salon de 1765* may be read as directions for staging them as *tableaux vivants,* just as the contemporary practice of staging *tableaux vivants* may be seen in turn as an expression of the same instinctive demand for the dramatization of painting active in Diderot's artistic thought from the beginning.

Finally, his strong distaste for symmetry in painting expresses that demand in almost abstract terms. As he argued in the *Pensées détachées*: "La symmétrie, essentielle dans l'architecture, est bannie de tout genre de peinture. La symmétrie des parties de l'homme y est toujours détruite par la variété des actions et des positions; elle n'existe pas même dans une figure vue de face et qui présente ses deux bras étendus." The close connection, as Diderot saw it, between asymmetry on the one hand and action and movement on the other could not be more explicit; and this strongly suggests that his call for the banishment of symmetry from all genres of painting, including those from which the human figure is absent, is a further index of the primacy of dramatic considerations in his vision of painting altogether. Not surprisingly, however, such a vision tended principally to seek fulfillment in and through the representation of action and passion, the raw materials of drama par excellence, and therefore to affirm the doctrine of a genre hierarchy rather than to grant all genres equal status.

II. THE DEMAND FOR UNITY

The demand for unity, expressed in concepts derived from classical drama, had been a cornerstone of seventeenth- and early eighteenth-century pictorial theory in France. As Lee has remarked, Academicians like Le Brun and Testelin habitually analyzed pictures "in terms of the logical dramatic relationship of each figure in the painting to the cause of his emotion," on the principle that "every element in a painting whether formal or expressive must . . . unfailingly contribute to the demonstration of a central thematic idea." Thus Le Brun praised Poussin's *Israelites Gathering Manna* for its unity of action, which he seems to have regarded as all the more impressive because of the painting's many figures and diversity of actions and expressions. "Comme l'auteur de cette peinture est admirable dans la diversité des mouvements," Le Brun is reported to have said, "et qu'il sait de quelle sorte il faut donner la vie à ses figures, il a fait que toutes leurs diverses actions et leurs expressions différentes ont des causes particulières qui se rapportent à son principal sujet," (Jouin, *Conferences*). The notion of unity of action was closely linked to one of unity of time, which like the first was based on an analogy with drama. Roughly, a painter was held to be limited to the representation of a single moment in an action, an idea that brought certain crucial differences between the two arts if not yet into focus at least into view. Classical theorists were by no means in complete agreement as to the strictness with which this law was to be observed. By and large, however, what was felt to be important was not the apparent instantaneousness of the representation but rather that the painter, having made the best possible choice among the principal phases of the action, confine himself to that phase and not trespass upon the others more than was absolutely necessary for the most effective presentation of his subject. Above all the juxtaposition within the same canvas of manifestly incompatible or contradictory phases of the same action was to be avoided in the interests of *vraisemblance*. Failure to observe these strictures resulted in a loss not only of unity but of intelligibility. Shaftesbury for example held as axiomatic "that what is principal or chief, should immediately shew itself, without leaving the mind in any uncertainty." And this was plainly not the case when the beholder was "left in doubt, and unable to determine readily, which of the distinct successive parts of the history or action is represented in the design," ("A Notion of the Historical Draught or Tablature of the Judgment of Hercules," in *Second Characters, or The Language of Forms,* edited by Benjamin Rand). (Unity of action and of time were inconceivable apart from unity of place, which is probably why that notion, as distinguished from questions of the historical or archaeological accuracy of particular sites, appears to have been taken more or less for granted by classical writers.) Intelligibility also depended in large measure on the beholder's familiarity with the subject represented, as Du Bos recognized perhaps more clearly than any theorist before him. In addition, classical writers, especially De Piles, stressed the role of *clair-obscur,* chiaroscuro, in promoting unity of effect.

All these concerns were shared by critics and theorists of the anti-Rococo reaction, whose preoccupation with unity was an extension of the views of their classical predecessors. But there is a shift of emphasis and in particular an assertion of the claims of actual experience in the writings of the later men that signal not just a revised order of priorities but a transformed vision of the aims and essence of painting. Diderot's conception of unity of action, indebted as it was to earlier ideas, is a case in point. In contrast for example to Le Brun and Du Bos he called for the elimination of all incident, however compelling in its own right, that did not contribute directly and so to speak indispensably to the most dramatic and expressive presentation of the subject that could be imagined:

> Les groupes qui multiplient communément les actions particulières doivent aussi communément distraire de la scène principale. Avec un peu d'imagination et de fécondité, il s'en présente de si heureuses qu'on ne saurait y renoncer; qu'arrive-t-il alors? c'est qu'une idée accessoire donne la loi à l'ensemble au lieu de la recevoir. Quand on a le courage de faire le sacrifice de ces épisodes intéressans, on est vraiment un grand maître, un homme d'un jugement profond; on s'attache à la scène générale qui en devient tout autrement énergique, naturelle, grande, imposante et forte.
>
> (*Salon de 1767*)

A composition, he argued in the *Essai,* could not afford "aucune figure oisive, aucun accessoire superflu. Que le subjet en soit un." In that spirit he praised an oil sketch by Carle Van Loo for having "un intérêt, un, une action, une. Tous les points de la toile disent la même chose: chacun à sa façon" (*Salon de 1765*). And in the *Pensées détachées* he summed up one of the major themes of his criticism in the statement: "Rien n'est beau sans unité; et il n'y a point d'unité sans subordination. Cela semble contradictoire, mais cela ne l'est pas." Any failure to declare the unity of action as strongly and as perspicuously as possible amounted, in Diderot's view, to a failure of composition, a term that comprised considerations of action and expression, though not necessarily to a failure of *ordonnace*, which concerned the arrangement of figures and objects across the surface of the canvas. That distinction, under various names, was fundamental to seventeenth- and eighteenth-century criticism and theory but disappeared in the nineteenth. In Diderot's writing the distinction is underscored and at the same time rendered almost otiose by his assertion of the absolute primacy of drama and expression: "On a prétendu que l'ordonnance était inséparable de l'expression. Il me semble qu'il peut y avoir de l'ordonnance sans expression, et que rien même n'est si commun. Pour de l'expression sans ordonnance, la chose me paraît plus rare, surtout quand je considère que le moindre accessoire superflu nuit à l'expression, ne fût-ce qu'un chien, un cheval, un bout de colonne, une urne" (*Essai*). The point is not simply that in his view compositional unity entailed unity of *ordonnance* whereas the reverse was not the case. It is also that for Diderot, as to a greater or lesser degree for other anti-Rococo critics and theorists, a painting had to do more than demonstrate a central dramatic idea: it had to set that idea in motion, in dramatic action, right before his eyes. And the question he seems always to have asked himself was not whether a particular painting could be shown to possess an internal rationale that justified and in that sense bound together the different actions, incidents, and facial expressions represented in it, but whether his actual experience of the painting, an experience prior to any conscious act of intellection, persuaded him beyond all doubt of its dramatic and expressive unity.

Perhaps the sharpest difference between Diderot's and the classical theorists' respective conceptions of pictorial unity concerned the idea of causality, which as already noted played a major role in French Academic thought (cf. Le Brun's remarks on Poussin quoted above). "La principale idée [of a painting], bein conçue, doit exercer son despotisme sur toutes les autres." Diderot wrote in the *Essai*. "C'est la force motrice de la machine qui, semblable à celle qui retient les corps célestes dans leurs orbes et les entraîne, agit en raison d'inverse de la distance." The machine-painting analogy was a traditional one, as in De Piles' statement that a painting ought to be regarded "comme une machine dont les pièces doivent être l'une pour l'autre & ne produire toutes ensembles qu'un même effet" ("Conversations sur la peinture"). But for De Piles and other classical writers the point of the simile was chiefly the idea of an internal accord and mutual adjustment of parts; and in general what in classical theory were characterized as causes are ostensible occasions for the action or expression of individual figures or groups of figures. Whereas for Diderot unity of action and beyond that the unity of the painting as a whole involved nothing less than an illusion of the inherent dynamism, directedness, and compulsive force of causation itself. "Une composition doit être ordonnée de manière à me persuader qu'elle n'a pu s'ordonner autrement," he wrote in one of the most important of the *Pensées détachées*, "une figure doit agir ou se reposer, de manière à me persuader qu'elle n'a pu agir autrement." He craved persuasion not demonstration, determinism not logic.

Moreover, as Diderot's reference to the celestial bodies and the force of gravity suggests, there was in his view a strict parallel between nature and art, or rather between what nature is and what art ought to be. An explicit and wholly characteristic statement to that effect appears in his review of Watelet's didactic poem, *L'Art de peindre* (1760): "Tout détruit l'ensemble dans une figure supposée parfaite; l'exercise, la passion, le genre de vie, la maladie. . . . Mais ne peut-on pas dire, en prenant l'ensemble sous un point de vue plus pittoresque, qu'il n'est jamais détruit ni dans la nature où tout est nécessaire, ni dans l'art, lorsqu'il sait introduire dans ses productions cette nécessité? . . . Cette nécessité introduite fait le sublime." (The review appeared in the *Correspondance littéraire* for 15 March, 1760.) The implications of this view for the representation of the human figure were irrevocably opposed both to any abstract or ideal canon of proportions and to any excessive demonstration of anatomical knowledge. In Dieckmann's summary:

> Chaque fonction que le corps remplit exerce un effet non seulement sur une de ses parties, mais sur le corps tout entier. Il y a une "conspiration générale des mouvements", une interdépendance de toutes les parties, que l'artiste doit connaître et sentir pour les représenter. . . . Ce qui est 'imité', c'est la manifestation de certaines lois, l'expression de certaines fonctions; l'une et l'autre n'existent que pour celui qui sait former l'idée d'un tout, d'un ensemble de causes et d'effets.
>
> (*Cinq leçons sur Diderot*)

And as Diderot insisted, the painting as a whole had also to be just such a dramatic and expressive system of causes and effects: "L'on dit l'ensemble d'une figure; on dit aussi l'ensemble d'une composition. L'ensemble de la figure consiste dans la loi de nécessité de nature, étendue d'une de ses parties à l'autre. L'ensemble d'une composition, dans la même nécessité, dont on étend la loi à toutes les figures combinées" (from his review of Watelet in the *Correspondance littéraire*). In short, for Diderot pictorial unity was a kind of microcosm of the causal system of nature, of the universe itself; and conversely the unity of nature, apprehended by man, was, like that of painting, at bottom dramatic and expressive.

It is in this connection that Diderot's account of the dramatic significance of *clair-obscur* ought chiefly to be seen. Its principal function, he wrote, was "d'empêcher l'oeil de s'égarer, en le fixant sur certains objets" (*Pensées détachées*): thus a few large and strong contrasts of light and dark were vastly preferable to a multiplicity of smaller ones, which produced the attention-dispersing effect known as *papillotage*. Once again Diderot went further than pre-Rococo theorists, and further too than his contemporaries, in his characterization of *clair-obscur* as a medium of the unity of dramatic effect of nature itself, for example in a remarkable passage that describes the play of late afternoon light and shadow among actual trees, branches, and leaves, and concludes:

> Nos pas s'arrêtent involontairement; nos regards se promènent sur la toile magique, et nous nous écrions: Quel tableau! Oh! que cela est beau! Il semble que nous considérions la nature comme le résultat de l'art; et, réciproquement, s'il arrive que le peintre nous répète le même enchantement sur la toile, il semble que nous regardions l'effet de l'art comme celui de la nature. Ce n'est pas au Salon, c'est dans le fond d'une forêt, parmi les montagnes que le soleil ombre et éclaire, que Loutherbourg et Vernet sont grands. (*Essai*)

What made so powerful and enthralling an experience possible was the conviction of absolute necessity elicited by painting through the management of *clair-obscur* and by nature through its infinitely subtle and of course causally determined effects of light and shade. For the most part, however, this illusion lay beyond the power of the landscape painter's art. And in general Diderot's causal conception of pictorial unity tended overwhelmingly to reinforce the doctrines of the hierarchy of genres and the supremacy of history painting, for the simple reason that subjects involving action and passion lent themselves far more readily than any others to an overtly dramatic and expressive presentation both of causal relations in their multifariousness and of the entire subsumption of those relations in a necessary whole.

If Diderot's contemporaries could not match his vision of the relationship between pictorial unity and causality, he and they were of one mind in demanding that pictorial unity be instantaneously apprehensible and in maintaining that to the extent that a painting failed to reach this condition the painter had fallen far short of his proper goal. As Caylus argues in "De la Composition" (1750): "[La composition] n'a qu'un instant pour objet, auquel il est nécessaire que tout se rapporte et que tout concoure, mais si parfaitement que rien ne peut excuser les altérations de ce rapport; l'oeil le moins sévère ne peut les pardonner; dès l'instant que ce même oeil aperçoit, il doit tout embrasser" (*Vies d'artistes*). And in the *Correspondance littéraire* for 15 December 1756 Grimm expanded on the double theme of unity and instantaneousness in a long passage whose importance has to my knowledge never been recognized:

> Les grandes machines en peinture et en poésie m'ont toujours déplu. S'il est vrai que les arts en imitant la nature n'ont pour but

que de toucher et de plaire, il faut convenir que l'artiste s'en écarte aussi souvent qu'il entreprend des poëmes épiques, des plafonds, des galeries immenses, en un mot, ces ouvrages compliqués auxquels on a prodigué dans tous les temps des éloges si peu sensés. La simplicité du sujet, l'unité de l'action, sont non-seulement ce qu'il y a de plus difficile en fait de génie et d'invention, mais encore ce qu'il y a de plus indispensable pour l'effet. Notre esprit ne peut embrasser beaucoup d'objets, ni beaucoup de situations à la fois. . . . Il veut être saisi au premier coup d'oeil par un certain ensemble, sans embarras et une manière forte. Si vous manquez ce premier instant, vous n'en obtiendrez que ces éloges raisonnés et tranquilles qui sont la satire et le désespoir du génie. . . . Pour moi, j'avoue franchement que jamais je n'ai vu une galerie ou un plafond, ni lu un poëme épique sans une certaine fatigue et sans sentir diminuer cette vivacité avec laquelle nous recevons les impressions de la beauté.

Grimm's remarks signal the end of the Renaissance and Baroque (and Rococo) elision of easel painting and decoration. The new emphasis on unity and instantaneousness was by its very nature an emphasis on the *tableau*, the portable and self-sufficient picture that could be taken in all at once as opposed to the "environmental," architecture-dependent, often episodic decorative project that could not.

Furthermore, as the passages just quoted suggest, the demand that pictorial unity be apprehended all at once, in a single *coup d'oeil*, was implicitly a demand that the painting as a whole be instantaneously and within reasonable limits, universally intelligible.

Indeed what might be called radical intelligibility is a major theme of anti-Rococo criticism and theory, though once again the implications of that theme are developed more fully by Diderot than by anyone else. "Une composition, qui doit être exposée aux yeux d'une foule de toutes sortes de spectateurs, sera vicieuse, si elle n'est pas intelligible pour un homme de bon sens tout court," he wrote in the *Essai*. This was rarely true of allegorical paintings, which Diderot along with others among his contemporaries, and unlike almost all pre-Rococo writers, found cold, obscure, and uninteresting: "Je tourne le dos à un peintre qui me propose un emblème, un logogriphe à déchiffrer. Si la scène est une, claire, simple et liée, j'en saisirai l'ensemble d'un coup d'oeil" (*Essai*). His point however was not just that allegorical paintings made use of abstruse symbolism whereas historical subjects, chosen with care, could be taken as known. It was also that historical subject matter provided the context required for the representation of action and gesture to assume the fullness and precision of meaning without which true dramatic unity was unrealizable. "Quand le sujet d'une proposition oratoire ou gesticulée n'est pas annoncé," Diderot wrote in the *Lettre sur les sourds et muets*, "l'application des autres signes reste suspendue." Or as he remarked in the article "Encyclopédie" (1754), "c'est à l'histoire à lever l'équivoque." A few years later he might have said morality as well.

"Tout morceau de sculpture ou de peinture doit être l'expression d'une grande maxime, une leçon pour le spectateur; sans quoi il est muet," he stated in the *Pensées détachées*. This is always cited as proof of the moralistic bias of his vision of art. But it may also be read as calling for the achievement in painting of the decisiveness, memorability, and sententiousness—in short the radical intelligibility—epitomized in discourse by maxims of conduct, and as implying that any work of visual art not directed to a moral end must inevitably fall short in those respects.

Finally, the anti-Rococo preoccupation with unity and intelligibility was accompanied by a far more rigorous conception of the unity of time than any envisaged by classical writers. This is implicit in the passage from Caylus quoted above as well as in Diderot's equation of pictorial unity with the continuously changing and essentially instantaneous causal unity of nature. One might say that for Diderot a painter's failure to declare the singleness and instantaneousness of his chosen moment with sufficient clarity undermined and often destroyed the dramatic illusion of causal necessity on which the conviction of unity depended. More generally, the demand that pictorial unity be made instantaneously apprehensible found natural expression in the almost universal tendency among anti-Rococo critics and theorists to define the essence of painting in terms of instantaneousness as such; and that tendency reinforced still further the primacy of subject matter of action and expression, which far more than any other class of subject matter was suited to the specification and perspicuous representation of a single instant.

Two more points might be mentioned very briefly before bringing this section to a close. First, the new, more rigorous conception of unity of time was attended by a far more rigorous conception of unity of place than had hitherto been entertained. Thus Diderot noted of Doyen's *Miracle des Ardens* that few people would be able to grasp the exact nature of its setting (the front porch of a hospital) and surmised that the painter had first imagined separate scenes of terror and only afterwards had devised a *local* capable of bringing them together (*Salon de 1767*). Second, no doubt influenced by Shaftesbury but going far beyond him, Diderot added to the traditional unities of action, time, and place, a fourth unity, that of point of view, which he built into his definition of pictorial composition from the start and articulated most forcefully in the *Essai*: "Toute scène a un aspect, un point de vue plus intéressant qu'aucun autre; c'est de là qu'il faut la voir. Sacrifiez à cet aspect, à ce point de vue, tous les aspects, ou points de vue subordonnés; c'est le mieux."

It is I think hardly necessary to add that point of view so conceived is essentially dramatic. There is nothing abstract, ideal, or otherwise a priori about the beholder's relation to what is represented. Rather the specific character of both action and moment determines that relation and so to speak positions the beholder before the painted scene. And reciprocally it is in and through the representation of action and moment that point of view so conceived is made most strongly felt.

III. PAINTING AND BEHOLDER

We are now in a position to try to define the relationship between painting and beholder mentioned earlier, a relationship which I believe lies at the heart of the anti-Rococo conception of painting. For Diderot and his colleagues, as we have seen, the painter's task was above all to reach the beholder's soul by way of his eyes. This traditional formulation was amplified by another, which like the first was widely shared: a painting, it was claimed, had first to attract (*attirer, appeller*) and then to arrest (*arrêter*) and finally to enthrall (*attacher*) the beholder, that is, a painting had to call to someone, bring him to a halt in front of itself, and hold him there as if spellbound and unable to move. The terms themselves derived from previous writers—in particular De Piles, who emphasized the need for paintings to attract, surprise, and stop the beholder, and Du Bos, who was chiefly concerned with their power to command his attention—but it was in the writings of Diderot and some of his contemporaries that they first assumed critical as distinguished from mainly rhetorical significance: that the idea that a painting must attract, arrest, and enthrall the beholder was for the first time taken literally and matched against the actual experience of specific pictures. (The results of the comparison were not flattering to painting. As the reader of Diderot's *Salons* quickly becomes aware, the number of canvases that seemed to him to pass this almost behavioristic test was relatively small.)

This new emphasis on the responsiveness of a painting to a beholder may not entitle us to say that until a particular moment and place the presence of the beholder (though not his enthrallment) could be taken for granted (and thus exploited or disregarded, as the painter chose). But it seems clear that starting at about the middle of the eighteenth century in France the beholder's presence before the painting came increasingly to be conceived by critics and theorists as something that had to be accomplished or a least powerfully affirmed by the painting itself; and more generally that the existence of the beholder—which is to say the primordial convention that paintings are made to be beheld—emerged as problematic for painting as never before.

From a slightly different perspective this development may be seen as yet another aspect of the rapprochement between the aims of painting and drama that took place in France during these years. The recognition that the art of painting was inescapably addressed to an audience that must be gathered corresponds to the exactly concurrent recognition that the theater's audience was inescapably a gathering not simply of auditors but of beholders. In both cases what was recognized had been glimpsed earlier in the century by Du Bos but until now had not presented problems of a fundamental character. And in both cases the problems were to be resolved through the instrumentality of the *tableau*, whose significance for each art was in a sense complementary to its significance for the other. Thus unity of point of view, implicit in the construction of the dramatic *tableau*, was in the theater almost a logical consequence of the fact that the audience was already gathered; while in painting it had explicitly to be built into the depicted scene in order to position the beholder not just before that scene but in front of the painting, the *tableau*, itself. ("Deux qualités essentielles à l'artiste, la morale et la perspective," Diderot noted in the *Pensées détachées*.) By the same token Diderot was not thinking of the theater when he argued that compositional unity consisted in the law of the necessity of nature extended to the interaction of the various figures in the painting. But his emphasis on necessity was in effect an emphasis on manifest dramatic motivation; and it was only by persuading the theatrical audience of such motivation via the *tableau* that the visuality of the audience, which had come to threaten the very possibility of drama, could be made to serve its ends.

I have so far described merely the literal or situational component of the relationship between painting and beholder I am seeking to define. Just as important, and still more fundamental, is what might be called the fictive component of that relationship. By now the reader will not be surprised to learn that the first extended discussions of the latter are to be found in Diderot, in the *Entretiens* and the *Poésie dramatique*, or that those discussions chiefly concerned the conditions necessary for dramatic illusion as such. The basic idea was first stated in the *Entretiens* in connection with Diderot's campaign against the classical *tirade*: "Dans une représentation dramatique, il ne s'agit non plus du spectateur que s'il n'existait pas. Y a-t-il quelque chose qui s'adresse à lui? L'auteur est sorti de son sujet, l'acteur entraîné hors de son rôle. Ils descendent tous les deux du théâtre. Je les vois dans le parterre; et tant que dure la tirade, l'action est suspendue pour moi, et la scène reste vide." This was expanded and its ramifications explored in the *Poésie dramatique*:

> Si l'on avait conçu que, quoiqu'un ouvrage dramatique ait été fait pour être représenté, il fallait cependant que l'auteur et l'acteur oubliassent le spectateur, et que tout l'intérêt fût relatif aux personnages, on ne lirait pas si souvent dans les poétiques: Si vous faites ceci ou cela, vous affecterez ainsi ou autrement votre spectateur. On y lirait au contraire: Si vous faites ceci ou cela, voici ce qui en résultera parmi vos personnages.
>
> Ceux qui ont écrit de l'art dramatique ressemblent à un homme qui, s'occupant des moyens de remplir de trouble toute une famille, au lieu de peser ces moyens par rapport au trouble de la

famille, les pèserait relativement à ce qu'en diront les voisins. Eh! laissez là les voisins; tourmentez vos personnages; et soyez sûr que ceux-ci n'éprouveront aucune peine, que les autres ne partagent.

The penalties for violating this fundamental principle were severe: "Et l'acteur, que deviendra-t-il, si vous êtes occupé du spectateur? Croyez-vous qu'il ne sentira pas que ce que vous avez placé dans cet endroit et dans celui-ci n'a pas été imaginé pour lui? Vous avez pensé au spectateur, il s'y adressera. Vous avez voulu qu'on vous applaudît, il voudra qu'on l'applaudisse; et je ne sais plus ce que l'illusion deviendra" (ibid.). The conclusion was obvious: "Soit donc que vous composiez, soit que vous jouiez, ne pensez non plus au spectateur que s'il n'existait pas. Imaginez, sur le bord du théâtre, un grand mur qui vous sépare du parterre; jouez comme si la toile ne se levait pas" (ibid.). Throughout the remainder of the essay Diderot returned to this theme. On the subject of extravagant costumes he remarked: "Si c'est pour le spectateur que vous vous ruinez en habits, acteurs, vous n'avez point de goût; et vous oubliez que le spectateur n'est rien pour vous." He praised the members of the Comédie Italienne for performing more freely than their French counterparts: "Ils font moins du cas du spectateur. Il y a cent moments où il en est tout à fait oublié." And he explained why actors who played subordinate characters tended in his view to remain true to their roles while those who played principal characters did not: "La raison, ce me semble, c'est qu'ils sont contenus par la présence d'un autre qui les commande: c'est à cet autre qu'ils s'adressent; c'est là que toute leur action est tournée." Whereas the leading actors, who of course were free of that constraint, "s'arrangent en rond; ils arrivent à pas comptés et mesurés; ils quêtent des applaudissements, ils sortent de l'action; ils s'adressent au parterre; ils lui parlent, et ils deviennent maussades et faux."

Diderot's advocacy of *tableaux* as opposed to *coups de théâtre* is to be understood chiefly in this light. "Un incident imprévu qui se passe en action, et qui change subitement l'état des personnages, est un coup de théâtre," he wrote in the *Entretiens*. "Une disposition de ces personnages sur la scene, si naturelle et si vrai, que, rendue fidèlement par un peintre, elle me plairait sur la toile, est un tableau." In other words a *coup de théâtre* took place as it were *within* the action and marked a sudden change in the consciousness of the characters involved; whereas the grouping of figures and stage properties that constituted a *tableau* stood *outside* the action, with the result that the characters themselves were ostensibly unaware of its existence and hence of its effect on the audience. "Celui qui agit et celui qui regarde, sont deux êtres très différents," Diderot observed in the opening pages of the *Entretiens*. The concept of the *tableau* at once hypostatized that difference and defined it as above all one of point of view. A *tableau* was visible, it could be said to exist, only from the beholder's point of view.

But precisely because that was so, it helped to persuade the beholder that the actors themselves were unconscious even of his presence.

The usual reading of Diderot's concept of the *tableau*, as asserting the importance of visual considerations in the achievement of dramatic illusion, and moreover as implying an exaltation of vision itself, is therefore somewhat misleading. The primary function of the *tableau* as Diderot conceived it was not to excite or even to exploit the visuality of the theatrical audience so much as to neutralize that visuality, to wall it off from the action taking place on stage, to put it out of mind for the *dramatis personae* and the audience alike. Similarly, Diderot's dramaturgy is often seen as calling for stage realism pure and simple. But it would be truer to say that it called primarily for the illusion that the audience did not exist, that it was not really there or at the very least had not been taken into account. In the absence of that illusion no amount of realism could provide the dramatic experience Diderot sought.

As might be expected, the same dramaturgical principle was fundamental to Diderot's vision of painting. He wrote in the *Pensées détachées*:

> Lairesse prétend qu'il est permis à l'artiste de faire entrer le spectateur dans la scène de son tableau. Je n'en crois rien; et il y a si peu d'exceptions, que je ferais volontiers une règle générale du contraire. Cela me semblerait d'aussi mauvais goût que le jeu d'un acteur qui s'adresserait au parterre. La toile renferme tout l'espace, et il n'y a personne au delà. Lorsque Suzanne s'expose nue à mes regards, en opposant aux regards des vieillards tous les voiles qui l'enveloppaient, Suzanne est chaste et le peintre aussi; ni l'un ni l'autre ne me savaient là.

The subject of *Susannah and the Elders* presented special problems because beholding, specifically illicit beholding, belonged to its theme. It therefore threatened to call attention to the actual beholder and in effect to implicate him along with the elders: "Je regarde *Suzanne*; et loin de ressentir de l'horreur pour les vieillards, peut-être ai-je désiré d'être à leur place." The solution that Diderot advocated and to which he referred in the passage just quoted engaged directly with that threat: "Un peintre italien a composé trés-ingénieusement ce sujet. Il a placé les deux vieillards du même côté. La Susanne porte toute sa draperie de ce côté, et pour se dérober aux regards des vieillards, elle se livre entièrement aux yeux du spectateur. Cette composition est très-libre, et personne n'en est blessé. C'est que l'intention évidente sauve tout, et que le spectateur n'est jamais du sujet" (*Salon de 1765*).

Another subject that raised the issue of the beholder's presence with special acuteness was the one popularly known as *Roman Charity*, in which a woman nourished her aged and imprisoned father at her breast. "Je ne veux pas absolument que ce malheureux vieillard, ni cette femme charitable, soupçonnent qu'on les observe," Diderot wrote in the *Salon de 1765*. "Ce soupçon arrête l'action et détruit le sujet." And a few pages further on he remarked: "Cette frayeur dénature le sujet, en ôte l'intérêt, le pathétique, et ce n'est plus une charité." Somewhat more generally he observed in the *Pensées détachées:* "Toutes les scènes délicieuses d'amour, d'amitié, de bien-faisance, de générosité, d'effusion de coeur se passent au bout du monde." By *au bout du monde* he meant a setting that conveyed an impression of silence, solitude, and—most important—the absence of witnesses, of beholders.

The crucial point is not the special problems that came with these subjects but the general principle that gave rise to them in the first place: "Ne pensez non plus au spectateur que s'il n'existait pas." And: "La toile renferme tout l'espace, et il n'y a personne au delà." Or as Diderot remarked in the *Salon de 1767:* "Une scene représentée sur la toile, ou sur les planches, ne suppose pas de témoins." This more than anything else was the basis of his abhorrence both in painting and in the theater of the mannered working up of physical gesture and facial expression that he called *grimace.* "Ne voyez-vous pas que la douleur de cette femme est fausse, hypocrite," he wrote of a figure in a picture by Lagrenée, "qu'elle fait tout ce qu'elle peut pour pleurer et qu'elle ne fait que grimacer?" (*Salon de 1767*). The desire to make an impression on an audience also led both painter and actor to exaggerate their effects, and this too Diderot found unbearable. "Je ne saurais supporter les caricatures, soit en beau, soit en laid," he wrote in the *Poésie dramatique,* "car la bonté et la méchanceté peuvent être égale-ment outrées"; while in the *Essai sur la peinture* he argued that *dessin,* color, and *clair-obscur* were all liable to be caricatured and that "toute caricature est de mauvais goût." In a similar spirit of revulsion he observed in the essay "De la manière" that whereas ugliness was natural "et n'annonce par elle-même aucune prétention, aucun ridicule, aucun travers d'esprit," *la manière* was unnatural, hypocritical, and concerned exclusively with ap-pearances, all of which made it "plus insupportable à l'homme de goût que la laideur." This was a principal ground of his antagonism to the art of the Rococo, which in his view clearly reflected the manners and con-ventions of polite society: "La politesse, cette qualité si aimable, si douce, si estimable dans le monde, est maussade dans les arts d'imitation. Une femme ne peut plier les genoux, un homme ne peut déployer son bras, prendre son chapeau sur sa tête, et tirer un pied en arrière, que sur un écran. Je sais bien qu'on m'objectera les tableaux de Watteau; mais je m'en moque, et je persiste" (*Essai*). Once again the object of his distaste was not exaggeration or caricature or *politesse* as such but the awareness of an au-dience, of being beheld, that they implied. And it was above all else the apparent extinction of that awareness, for example by virtue of a figure's absolute absorption in an action or activity, that he demanded of works of pictorial art: "Il est rare qu'un être qui n'est pas tout entier à son action ne soit pas *maniéré.* . . . Tout personnage qui semble vous dire: 'Voyez comme je pleure bien, comme je me fâche bien, comme je supplie bien', est faux et *maniéré*" ("De la manière"). As he wrote in the *Essai:* "Si vous perdez le sentiment de la différence de l'homme qui se présente en compagnie et de l'homme intéressé qui agit, de l'homme qui est seul et de l'homme qu'on regarde, jetez vos pinceaux dans le feu. Vous académiserez, vous redresserez, vous guinderez toutes vos figures." In the event the painting was no longer "une rue, une place publique, un temple"; it became "un théâtre," that is, an artificial construction in which persuasiveness was sacrificed and dramatic illusion vitiated in the attempt to impress the beholder and solicit his applause.

Diderot's use of the term *théâtre* in this connection reveals the depth of his revulsion against the conventions then prevailing in the dramatic arts. But it also suggests that he may have despaired that those conventions, and the consciousness of the beholder they embodied, could ever fully be overcome once and for all. This appears to be the implication of his next remark: "On n'a point encore fait, et l'on ne fera jamais un morceau de peinture supportable, d'après une scene théâtrale" (*Essai*). Presumably Diderot felt that if the theater were to be reformed along the lines proposed in the *Entretiens* and the *Poésie dramatique* painters would be able to look to the stage for inspiration without dooming themselves to mediocrity or worse. But throughout his writings on painting he continued to express his despair of the theater as he knew it, and used the term *le théâtral*, the theatrical, implying consciousness of being beheld, as synonymous with falseness. The opposite of the grimacing, the mannered, and the theatrical was *le naïf*, which Diderot characterized in the *Pensées détachées* as "tout voisin du sublime" and summed up in the phrase: "C'est la chose, mais la chose pure, sans la moindre altération. L'art n'y est plus." By this he meant something more striking or perspicuous than ordinary fidelity to appearances: "Tout ce qui est vrai n'est pas naïf, mais tout ce qui est naïf est vrai, mais d'une vérité piquante, originale et rare. Presque toutes les figures du Poussin sont naïves, c'est-à-dire parfaitement et purement ce qu'elles doivent être. Presque tous les vieillards de Raphaël, ses femmes, ses enfants, ses anges, sont naïfs, c'est-à-dire qu'ils ont une certaine originalité de nature, une grâce avec laquelle ils sont nés, que l'institution ne leur a point donnée" (*Pensées détachées*). In sum naïveté was the distinctive mode of expression of the causal unity of nature, or at any rate the hallmark of that unity in art. (The definition of grace in the *Essai* as "cette rigoureuse et précise conformité des membres avec la nature de l'action" is entirely consistent with this idea.) Conversely the pictorial expression of the causal unity of nature entailed negating the beholder's presence before the painting—or, more positively, creating the illusion that "il n'y a personne au delà."

I am for my part convinced that the insistence by anti-Rococo critics and theorists that painters achieve what I have called an absolutely perspicuous mode of pictorial unity was ultimately an expression of the prior or more fundamental demand that not just each figure but the painting as a whole, the painting itself, declare its unconsciousness or obliviousness of the beholder. I realize, however, that only Diderot among the writers of his time actually formulated that demand, and that he cannot be said to have made its connection with unity fully explicit.

These considerations lie behind the distinction drawn in the *Essai* between actions and attitudes: "Autre chose est une attitude, autre chose une action. Les attitudes sont fausses et petites, les actions toutes belles et vraies." Nothing quite like this can be found in the writings of Diderot's predecessors or contemporaries. It had of course always been recognized that individual painters were to a greater or lesser degree masters of action and expression. But Diderot's distinction between actions and attitudes asserted a difference not of degree but of kind, i.e., between natural, spontaneous, largely automatic realizations of an intention or expressions of a passion on the one hand and mannered, conventional, and (in the pejorative sense of the term just given) theatrical simulacra of these on the other: so that to describe something as an action was already to have passed a favorable, though not necessarily a final or complete, judgment upon it. (Significantly, each of the three major sources of what might be called the attitudinization of action singled out by Diderot in the *Essai*—the Academic pedagogy of drawing from a model holding a fixed pose, the false ideal of grace taught by dancing masters like Marcel, and the Academic principle of deliberately arranged contrast between figures in a painting, and even between the limbs of individual figures—institutionalized the consciousness of being beheld that he deplored.)

Diderot's originality, as well as his alignment with the main impulse of the anti-Rococo movement, become evident if his thought is compared with Caylus'. As early as 1747, in his "Réflexions sur la peinture," Caylus distinguished between two sorts of studies of the human figure: "La figure que nous appelons *académie* n'a été posée que pour l'exercice du dessin en général, le professeur n'a eu avec raison d'autre objet en la posant que celui de présenter un beau choix, un heureux contraste dans les parties, d'y répandre une belle lumière avec un beau jeu de muscles, tandis que la figure que nous connaissons sous le nom d'*étude* posée pour un sujet déterminé, est remplie d'une intention et d'une action qui parle à l'esprit" (*Vies d'artistes*). By emphasizing the importance of considerations of action and intention Caylus' distinction anticipated Diderot's. But Caylus used the term *posée* in connection with both sorts of studies, and in fact never questioned the value of working from a model who held a stationary pose or attitude. More generally, both Diderot and Caylus advocated a return to truth and nature after what they regarded as the mannerism of the Rococo. But there is a world of difference between Caylus' exhortation, "Songeons que toute la nature est à nous et qu'elle pose continuellement pour augmenter nos connaissances" ("Sur l'Harmonie et sur la couleur," ibid.), or his reference to "la Nature, toujours prête *à poser*" (*Tableaux tirés de l'Iliade,* the italics are Caylus'), and Diderot's vision of nature as intelligible to man in its causal unity only to the extent that it is *not* represented as posing for him, as existing to be beheld.

Why, it may be asked, did not Diderot's antagonism to the theatrical militate against the doctrines of the hierarchy of genres and the supremacy of history painting? In particular why was he not led to extol the virtues of still life painting, whose subject matter was inanimate and therefore literally incapable of evincing awareness of the beholder? The answer is implicit in much that has gone before: inanimate subject matter made the artistic and presentational aspects *of the painting itself* all the more apparent by imposing almost desperate demands on technique and by calling attention to the fact that the objects depicted by the painter were chosen by him, arranged by him, illuminated by him, and in general exhibited to the beholder at his direction. Whereas in the case of history painting the beholder's vastly greater interest in the actions and passions of human beings minimized the pressure on technique; the illusion that the *dramatis personae* had arrived by themselves at their positions and groupings was on the face of it more plausible; and at least in principle the painter could aim to engross or absorb his figures in action or feeling—to render each "tout entier à son action"—and thereby to declare their aloneness relative to the beholder or at any rate their obliviousness of his presence.

The last point is especially important. The problems which, in Diderot's view, the still life painter faced—and which only Chardin among his contemporaries seemed to him to transcend—suggest that simply disregarding the beholder was not enough. It was necessary to obliviate him, to deny his presence, to establish positively insofar as that was feasible that he had not been taken into account. And Diderot seems clearly to have felt that there was no more powerful or effective means to that end than to take as subject matter the deeds and sufferings of conscious agents who were, to say the least, fully *capable* of evincing awareness of the beholder, and then to overcome or extinguish all traces of such awareness in and through the dramatic representation of their actions and passions. Furthermore, I have suggested that the demand for an absolutely perspicuous mode of pictorial unity was at bottom a demand for the negation of the beholder's presence before the painting; and since, as I have tried to show, subject matter of action and passion lent itself far more readily than any other to the achievement of that unity, the history painter was on these grounds also better equipped than his colleagues in other genres to bring the negation about. All this may be summed up by saying that Diderot's conception of painting rested ultimately upon the supreme fiction that the beholder did not exist, that he was not really there, standing before the canvas; and that the dramatic representation of action and passion, and the causal and instantaneous mode of unity that came with it, provided the best available medium for establishing that fiction in the painting itself.

We have reached an apparent contradiction, or paradox. As we have seen, the recognition that paintings were made to be beheld and therefore presupposed the existence of the beholder led to the demand for the actualization of his presence: a painting, it was insisted, had to attract the beholder, to stop him in front of itself, and to hold him there in a perfect trance of involvement. At the same time, taking Diderot's writings as the definitive formulation of a conception of painting that up to a point was widely shared, it was only by negating the beholder's presence that this could be achieved: only by establishing the fiction of his absence or nonexistence could his actual placement before and enthrallment by the painting be secured. This paradox directs attention to the problematic character not only of the painting-beholder relationship but of something more fundamental—the *object*-beholder (one is tempted to say object-*subject*) relationship which the painting-beholder relationship epitomizes. It suggests that by the middle of the eighteenth century in France the object-beholder relationship as such, the very condition of spectatordom, had emerged as theatrical, a medium of dislocation and estrangement rather than of access to truth and conviction. The essential task of the painter as construed by Diderot, and to a degree by other anti-Rococo critics and theorists, was to undo that state of affairs, to *de-theatricalize beholding* and so make it once again a medium of absorption, sympathy, and self-transcendence. (The antidualistic implications of this project are obvious, and wholly consistent with the dominant tendency of Diderot's thought in all fields.)

Put simply and assertively: the criticism and theory that we have been considering expressed an implicit apprehension of the self's disjunction from the objects of its beholding; insisted on the need for painters to overcome the disjunction in their work if painting was to be restored to its former status as a major art; and propounded a strategy by which this could be accomplished. That strategy involved the reactivation of the doctrines of the hierarchy of genres and the supremacy of history painting which had fallen into desuetude with the rise of the Rococo. But the meaning of those doctrines in the writings of Diderot and his contemporaries was fundamentally different from the meaning they had had in late seventeenth- and early eighteenth-century Academic theory. So their reactivation must be understood not as a return to an intellectualist and by then outdated ideal, and not as a confusion about the proper aims of painting, but as a cogent, deeply motivated, and, as events were to prove, entirely progressive adaptation of traditional materials to a radically transformed structure of pictorial priorities.

IV. POSTSCRIPT

A few brief remarks in conclusion:

(1) If one asks why beholding or spectatordom emerged as problematic and specifically as theatrical in France around the middle of the eighteenth

century, one cannot expect an answer in terms of painting alone. For what underlay that development was at once a new consciousness of the self and a new experience of the role of beholding in the stabilizing (and undermining) of that consciousness. The ultimate sources of the theatricalization of beholding must be sought in the social, political, and economic reality of the age—in all that bears on the history of the self.

(2) I have said nothing about the actual practice of painting during the period. I believe however that the priorities and imperatives outlined in these pages, in particular the insistence upon the need to establish the painting's obliviousness to the beholder (and ultimately to undo the theatricalization of beholding), correspond to the central preoccupations of French painters between the start of the reaction against the Rococo and the emergence of David as the leader of his generation in the second half of the 1780s. Crucial figures in that development include Chardin, Carle Van Loo, Greuze, Vien, Fragonard, and David himself. In fact David's artistic development from the *Belisarius* (1781) through the *Leonidas at Thermopylae* (begun c. 1800, completed 1814) reveals an ongoing and largely conscious preoccupation with the considerations of drama, unity, and antagonism to the theatrical discussed above.

(3) For most of the period just mentioned the correspondence between criticism and theory on the one hand and actual paintings on the other does not authorize us to infer the influence of the first upon the second. By the time we reach David, however, the question of this influence cannot be ignored. I cannot address that question here. It is worth noting though that the possibility of significant relation between David's canvases and Diderot's writings on painting has never received the consideration it merits for the simple reason that the *Salons* began to be published only in 1796, too late to have played a role in the formation of David's conception of his enterprise. But Diderot's views on painting were in restricted circulation in France before that date; and in any case the *Entretiens* and *Poésie dramatique*, which contain the essence of his pictorial dramaturgy, were published in 1757 and 1758 respectively. Moreover, between 1769 and 1775 the young David resided with the playwright Michel-Jean Sedaine, whose *Le Philosophe sans le savoir* (1765) exemplified Diderot's dramatic theories and was hailed by him as a masterpiece. The playwright and the philosopher became fast friends, and under Sedaine's sponsorship the young David had ample opportunity to meet Diderot socially and to become exposed to his ideas.

(4) The problem of the theatrical remained central to painting in France (and only there) until well into the second half of the nineteenth century. And I claim that the chief current of French painting between the start of the reaction against the Rococo and Manet's masterpieces of the 1860s, traditionally analyzed in terms of style and subject matter and presented as a sequence of ill-defined and disjunct movements, may be grasped as a single development whose guiding preoccupation was to come to grips

with one primitive condition of the art of painting—that its objects necessarily imply the presence before them of the beholder. My claim is not that the traditional art-historical categories of style and subject matter are irrelevant to our understanding of the art of David, Gros, Géricault, Delacroix, Daumier, Couture, Courbet, and Manet. But the effort to construct a convincing account of the development of French painting between 1747 and 1870 in terms of these categories must be acknowledged to have failed.

(5) With the advent of Realism in the 1850s the sister doctrines of the hierarchy of genres and the supremacy of history painting lost, or lost again, their fundamental importance. The deeper issues of theatricality and the relation of painting to beholder no longer required the instrumentality of those doctrines for their resolution. But it was only after Manet's paradigmatic canvases of the 1860s that ambitious painting found it possible to ignore genre considerations entirely.

The Archeology of the Frivolous: Reading Condillac

Jacques Derrida

After all, Voltaire is only a man of letters. . . . The true eighteenth-century metaphysician is the abbé de Condillac. . . .

Condillac's most salient qualities are his clearness and precision, a certain analytic force, and with that some finesse and spirit. Considerable flaws are joined to these valuable qualities. Condillac lacks a sense of reality. He knows neither man nor mankind, neither life nor society. Common sense never restrains him. His mind is penetrating but narrow. Headstrong in an excessive love of simplicity, he sacrifices everything for the frivolous benefit of reducing everything to a unique principle. Left without any spirit for observation, he feels more comfortable with word or figure combinations than in faithful and detailed descriptions of facts. From that comes his dry and precise style, of excellent quality but without grandeur, which little by little is credited among us as the true style of philosophy.

—VICTOR COUSIN, *Histoire générale de la philosophie*

Metaphysics had become insipid. In the very year in which Malebranche and Arnauld, the last great French metaphysicians of the seventeenth century, died, Helvétius and Condillac *were born. . . . Besides the negative refutation of seventeenth-century theology and metaphysics, a* positive, anti-metaphysical *system was required. A book was needed which would systematise and theoretically substantiate the life practice of that time.* Locke's *treatise* An Essay concerning Humane Understanding *came from across the Channel as if in answer to a call. . . . Is* Locke *perhaps a disciple of* Spinoza? *"Profane" history can answer: Materialism is the* natural-born *son of* Great Britain. *. . . Locke's* immediate *pupil,* Condillac, *who translated him into* French, *at once applied Locke's sensualism against seventeenth-century* metaphysics. *He proved that the French had rightly rejected this metaphysics as a mere botch work of fancy and theological prejudice. . . . It was only by* eclectic *philosophy that Condillac was ousted from the French schools.*

—KARL MARX, "Critical Battle against French Materialism," *The Holy Family*

I. THE SECOND FIRST—METAPHYSICS

This book, *An Essay on the Origin of Human Knowledge,* should have opened the doors to a nameless science.

From *The Archaeology of the Frivolous: Reading Condillac,* translated by John P. Leavey, Jr. © 1980 by Duquesne University Press.

341

It used to be possible to criticize metaphysics only *as such*. This book does that—which regularly amounts to founding *a* new metaphysics. This book lacks nothing in that respect either—which implies a rigorous and inveterate distinction between *two* metaphysics. We are going to verify this.

"We must distinguish two sorts of metaphysics." For the metaphysics of essences and causes, Condillac very promptly proposes substituting a metaphysics of phenomena and relations ("connections"). For the metaphysics of the hidden, a metaphysics of the open—we could say a phenomenology of the things themselves—and a critical science of limits. One "wants to search into every mystery; into the nature and essence of beings, and the most hidden causes; all these she [metaphysics] promises to discover to her admirers, who are pleased with the flattering idea. The other more reserved, proportions her researches to the weakness of the human understanding [*esprit*] . . . only trying to see things as they in fact are" (*Essay*, Introduction [modified]).

Since such a new science was created to give ideas their names, it will consequently have some trouble finding its own name.

What particular name could we assign to a *general* science ending nowhere and utilizing a universal analysis, an analysis that leads us back in all fields of knowledge to the simplest, most elementary ideas and that also defines their laws of connection, combination, complication, substitution, repetition? But also—*a problem of principle*—their laws of generation? Will this general theory truly be metaphysics?

Paleonymy: at the beginning of his *Essay*, Condillac seems very calmly resolved to preserve the old name, provided we "distinguish two sorts of metaphysics." The opposition of the two metaphysics, therefore, is analogous to that between the hidden essence and the proffered phenomenon. In returning to the latter, we reproduce its generation, we "retrace" (one of the two chief words in the *Essay*) its origin, we go back there, repeat the origin, and analyze it. Thus, since "good" metaphysics is the science of origins and true beginnings (and augurs *La Langue des calculs*: "I begin at the beginning." "That is why I begin where no one has ever begun before."), we might feel that "good" metaphysics should also be presented as first philosophy.

But that is not at all the case! The science of beginnings—the metaphysics of the simple, of combination and generation—the new philosophy, will be irreducibly *second*. Such is its condition.

Long after the *Essay*, Condillac is more prudent and more uncomfortable than ever about using the word *metaphysics*. Above all he is anxious to avoid the stumbling-block of *philosophia prote*. His metaphysics will not be first philosophy. Or theology. We must do what Descartes did not succeed in doing, break with the Aristotelian tradition:

> Perhaps it will seem surprising that I had forgotten to give the history of metaphysics, but that is because I do not know what

this word means. Aristotle, thinking to create a science, took it upon himself to gather together all the general and abstract ideas, such as being, substance, principle, causes, relations, and other resemblances. He will consider all these ideas in a preliminary treatise, which he called *first wisdom, first philosophy, theology,* and so on. After him, Theophrastus or some other peripatetic gave the name metaphysics: a science which proposes to treat everything in general before having observed anything in particular, i.e., to speak about everything before having learned anything: a vain science which bears on nothing and leads to nothing. Since we ourselves raise some particular ideas to general notions, general notions could not be the object of the first science. (*Cours d'études pour l'instruction du Prince de Parme: Histoire moderne,* Book 20, chap. xii, "Des progrès de l'art de raisonner")

Consequently, the new metaphysics will be second only by returning to the principle's true generation, to its actual production. The new metaphysics will resemble empiricism—without any doubt. But what Condillac denounces in Aristotle's first philosophy is as well an unconscious empiricism, one that takes derived generalities for premises, products for seeds or origins [*germes*]: as a second philosophy incapable of establishing itself as such, it is an irresponsible empiricism. Through a chiasmus effect the new metaphysics, by advancing itself as second philosophy, will methodically reconstitute the generative principles, the primordial production of the general starting from real singularities. The new metaphysics will be called metaphysics only by *analogy* (it follows that *analogy,* its fundamental operative, will be analogous only to the analogy of the Aristotelian tradition, and here we have the matrix of an infinite set of problems) and will be properly named *analysis,* or analytic method. By retracing the true generation of knowledge, by going back to the principles, an actually inaugural practice of analysis can finally dissolve, destroy, decompose the first first philosophy. That means, in the end: replace the first first philosophy while inheriting its name. Or better still: "supply" it (*suppléer* is the second chief word of the *Essay*).

Since we need to analyze objects in order to elevate ourselves to true knowledge, it is absolutely necessary to order our ideas by distributing them into different classes and by giving each of them names by which we may be able to recognize them. There lies all the artifice of more or less general notions. If the analyses have been done well, they lead us from discovery to discovery; because, in showing us how we succeeded, they teach us how we can succeed again. The characteristic of analysis is to lead us by the simplest and shortest means. This analysis is not one science separated from the others. It belongs to all the sciences, it is their true method, their soul. I will call this analysis metaphysics, provided you do not confuse it with the first science of Aristotle.

(ibid.)

We need to pursue promptly this *division* of metaphysics. Undertaken from the first page of the *Essay*, this division nevertheless continually complicates the *Essay*'s space and operation.

On the one hand, in fact, "bad" metaphysics has consisted of bad linguistic use coupled with a bad philosophy of language. This "bad" metaphysics can only be corrected, then, by elaborating another theory of signs and words, by using another language. That is the *Essay*'s constant and most obvious intent. For example: "all this quarter of metaphysics has hitherto lain involved in such obscurity and confusion, that I have been obliged to frame to myself, in some measure, a new language. It was impossible for me to be exact, and at the same time to employ such undeterminate signs as vulgar use has adopted" (*Essay*, I.2). *La Langue des calculs* will develop this very project: the constitution of a rigorously arbitrary, formal, and conventional language. But once again the task of establishing this language's *grammar* amounts to metaphysics properly so called—to metaphysics and not to the algebraists' technique of calculation. The philosophical intent is continually reaffirmed when the question is the handling of language and its rules. We could say, the handling of discourse: "I dwelled a long time on the question that the calculators never imagined to treat, because these questions are metaphysical ones and because the calculators are not metaphysicians. They do not know that algebra is only a language, that this language still has no grammar at all, and that metaphysics alone can give it one" (*La Langue des calculs*). (Just as there are two origins, two metaphysics, and so on, there are two barbarisms, "two sorts of barbarism: one which succeeds enlightened centuries, the other which precedes them; and they do not at all resemble each other. Both suppose a great ignorance, but a people who have always been barbarian do not have as many vices as a people who become such after having known the luxurious arts [*les arts de luxe*]" [*Cours d'études:* "Introduction à l'étude de l'histoire,"].)

But, on the other hand, if good metaphysics must be stated in an absolutely artificial grammar, since metaphysics is the very thing that grammar will have instituted, isn't that in order to guide itself by "another" good metaphysics—this time, the most natural one, that which will have preceded all language in general? Isn't that in order to make amends through language for language's misdeeds, to push artifice to that limit which leads back to nature: "There is the advantage that algebra will have; it will make us speak like nature, and we will believe we have made a great discovery" (ibid.)? In guiding its extreme formalization by the necessity of the simple, the language of calculus must reconstitute metaphysics's prelinguistic and natural base. Good metaphysics *will have been* natural and mute: in the end—physics. "Good metaphysics began before languages; and the latter owe to the former the best things they possess. But those metaphysics were at first less a science than an instinct. It was nature that led men without their knowledge, and metaphysics have only become a science, when they ceased to be good and rational" (*Logic*).

Science must *cure*, in the transitive and the intransitive senses of this word. Science must cure—(must be cured of) science. Consequently—another displacement and reinscription of duality—there will again be two metaphysics in the very heart of the new science. Once more use will have to distinguish between two metaphysics within the metaphysics Condillac intends to elaborate. Renouncing knowledge of essences and causes and bent back onto the experience of ideas (i.e., effects), the new "metaphysics" (whose "sole object is the human mind [*esprit*]") will articulate in itself these two metaphysics: not the good and the bad, this time, but the good in the form of the "prelinguistic" origin, "instinct," or "feeling," and the good in the form of the highest linguistic elaboration, new language, and "reflection." *De l'art de raisonner* organizes this double system; it gives the rule which must relate to each other the metaphysics of natural instinct and metaphysics as such, the second science which cures.

Metaphysics as such must *develop* and not degrade the metaphysics of natural instinct; metaphysics as such must even reproduce *within* language the relation it has, as language, to what precedes all language. In the order of the human mind, the values of *feeling* and *reflection* define the law of this relation. The first comes to the second in this statement:

> When its sole object is the human mind, metaphysics can be distinguished into two kinds: the one, reflection; the other, feeling. The first disentangles all our faculties. It sees their principle and their generation and accordingly dictates rules to direct them: reflection is acquired by force of study. The second feels our faculties; obeys their action; follows principles which it does not know; is acquired without appearing to be acquired, because fortuitous circumstances have made it natural; is the lot of just minds; is, so to speak, their instinct. Thus the metaphysics of reflection is only a theory which develops, in its principle and its effects, everything that the metaphysics of feeling practices. For example, the latter creates languages, the former explains their system: the one forms orators and poets; the other gives the theory of eloquence and of poetry.
>
> (*Cours d'études: De l'art de raisonner*)

This will have been remarked: although these two metaphysics oppose each other, they succeed one another and develop like practice and theory. The primacy of the practical instance [*instance*] is the most decisive and invariable trait of this new critical metaphysics. But it will resemble less a philosophy of *praxis* than a metaphysics of *fact*.

The first consequence for the *Essay*: since this general theory is no longer a first science or a preliminary method, and in order to take into account and reap the consequences of the development or the acquisition of knowledge, the general theory comes *after* the development or acquisition of knowledge ("in showing us how we succeeded, they teach us how we can succeed again"). The general theory *succeeds* some particular history of science. De facto and de jure, it presupposes the scientific *fact* (as we are going to see), just as the general idea is constructed starting from particular ideas. Like the theoretical, the general is always engendered. To submit both to analysis is to return to the practical conditions for emergence and to the genetic processes of their constitution. This is not only to decompose a combination into simple elements, to separate the particles of a calculus, but also, by the same movement (yet will it be the same?), to retrace a genesis and reactivate a chain of psychic operations. Would the *Essay* thus be a treatise of practical *psychology*?

But like metaphysics, the word psychology is also outside usage, outside good use, of course: "Even this metaphysics is not the first science. For will it be possible to analyze clearly all our ideas, if we do not know what they are and how they are formed? Before all, then, we must know their origin and generation. But the science attending to this object still has no name, as it is younger. I would call it psychology, if I knew any good work under this title" (*Cours d'études: Histoire moderne*).

Attentive to becoming, more precisely to "progress," Condillac is always interested in the conditions of the historical possibility of his undertaking. Truly, this historic reflection never lets itself be separated from the undertaking itself; it analyzes some particular conditions and situations but only in order to have posited first the general law of historicity. If philosophy—theoretical metaphysics, the general method—is essentially historical, that is because it always comes *after* the practice of cognition, *after* the upshot or the discovery of a science. Philosophy is always late with respect to an operation of cognition and its occurrence [*fait*].

Thus the general method proposed by Condillac—and so, already, his concept of method, the generalization of the rule after the fact [*après coup*]—can be established only after a discovery—or stroke [*coup*] of genius (a value we will determine farther on). In the philosophic order, this discovery already transposes a discovery, a scientific stroke of genius.

So the *Essay* is engaged on a trail marked out by Locke and Newton. And it draws its lesson from this fact by generalizing the concept of method. "I cannot help thinking, but that a method which has conducted us to one truth may lead us to a second, and that the best must be the same for all sciences. It is therefore sufficient to reflect on the discoveries already made, in order to proceed in the exercise of our inventive powers" (*Essay*, II.27). No doubt Condillac would have subscribed to the words of D'Alembert: by his criticism of innate ideas, his descriptions of the generation and connection of ideas, Locke "created metaphysics, almost as Newton had created physics" (*Preliminary Discourse to the Encyclopedia of Diderot*). Consequently, the content of a method and the concept of method suppose the *marked out trail*. Given the principle of observing nature, the "path of truth is finally opened: it is carved out to the extent that we advance further. . . . Of all philosophers, Newton is certainly the one who knew this route the best, who traces a series of truths tied to one another" (*Cours d'études: Histoire moderne*). The great principle of analogy authorizes the same statement in the order of human studies [*la science de l'esprit*]:

> Just as we have formed good grammars or poetics only after having had good writers in prose and verse, it happened that we have known the art of reasoning only to the extent that we have good minds, which have thoroughly reasoned in different genres. Thereby you can judge that this art made its greatest progress in the seventeenth and eighteenth centuries. In fact, the true method is due to these two centuries. It was first known in the sciences, wherein ideas are naturally formed and determined almost without difficulty. Mathematics is the proof of this. . . . If some Tartars wanted to create a poetics, you think indeed that it would be bad because they have no good poets. The same goes for the various logics created before the seventeenth century. Then there was only one way to learn to reason: it was to consider the origin and the progress of the sciences. After the discoveries already made, it was necessary to find the means to make new ones; and to learn, by observing human mental aberrations, not to be engaged in the routes which lead to error.
>
> (ibid.)

Since method is "first known in the sciences," the philosopher who marks out a trail is the one who repeats (by generalizing) the fact of an earlier rupture, which both transposes and extends that fact. Thus Locke inaugurates—but *after* Bacon and Newton.

Condillac inaugurates *after* Locke.

Before Locke, philosophers and scientists did not recognize Bacon—a lapse of genius, which also *means*, as we will see, by reason of their historical situation.

> They should have studied Bacon. This latter philosopher regretted that nobody had yet undertaken to efface all our ideas and to engrave more exact ones on human understanding. . . . Locke no longer gave way to any similar regrets. Convinced that the mind can only be known through observation, he himself opened and marked out a route which had not been frequented before him. While considering the progress the sciences of his time owed to experience and observation, he could form this plan and try to execute it. But to his credit his discoveries were not pre-

pared by any of those who had written before him on human understanding.

(ibid.)

For the moment let us leave to one side the criticisms that Condillac will also direct to Locke. We will consider Locke our model, since Condillac so often invites us to do so. How could Locke carve out a trail while contenting himself to develop, indeed repeat, an earlier rupture? This question forms the paradigm of a much more general set of problems, which can be dug out (with little transposition) of each page of the *Essay*. Trying to answer this question involves interpreting the whole.

If Locke opened a trail by recommencing an operation, it is undoubtedly because he applied a general law to a particular domain. Better still, he discovered, produced, and recognized this field for the first time: that of human understanding. The operation of transposition and of application to which he devoted himself was at the same time productive or constitutive. By proceeding analogically, he discovered an unknown. Invention by analogy, perhaps, is the most general formula of this logic. What is true of analogy (analogy in general or the mathematical analogy of proportion) is also true of analysis. New "objects" are constituted by transposing or proportioning, as well as analyzing, a given. That is why the progress of science, the enrichment of knowledge, can always proceed—as Condillac unrelentingly affirms—by "identical propositions," by analytical judgments.

Under these conditions, Condillac's relation to Locke will be analogous to Locke's relation to his predecessors. The science of human understanding, as properly inaugurated by Locke, is repeated, corrected, and completed by Condillac—particularly concerning the decisive question of language. But he will do nothing less than found it: finally and for the first time. For we must not forget that the *Essay on the Origin of Human Knowledge* concerns itself with [*garde*] a very narrowly delimited object: not even the human spirit, not even the operations of the soul that could as well be related to the will as to the understanding: "The subject of this essay plainly shews that my purpose is to consider [the operations of the soul] only in the relation they bear to the understanding" (*Essay*, I.2).

It is by no means fortuitous that, in the *Logic*, the most explicit text on this matter first concerns analogy, the identical proposition, and the history of science. This text explains the productive functioning of analogy by the principle of a difference of degree ("In analogy we must therefore distinguish different degrees" [*Logic*].). In order to understand that in Condillac's system *the combinative is an energetics and the taxonomic element a germinal power*, we must continually associate this principle of difference of degree with the economic principle of force, vivacity, or quantity of connection ("according as the combinations vary, there is more or less connexion between the ideas. I may therefore suppose a combination in which the connexion is as great as it possibly can be. . . . But let me consider an object on that side which is most connected with the ideas I am investigating, the whole shall be fully discovered to my view" [*Essay*, II.2.39].).

This analogy [concerning the Earth's double revolution] supposes that the same effects have the same causes; a supposition which, being confirmed by new analogies and new observations can no longer be called in question. It is thus that good philosophers conducted their reasonings. If we want to learn to reason like them, the best means is to study the discoveries which have been made from Galileo down to Newton. . . .

It is thus also that we have tried to reason in this work. We have observed nature and learned analysis from it. With this method we studied ourselves; and having discovered, by a series of identical propositions, that our ideas and faculties are nothing but sensation which takes different forms, we assured ourselves of the origin and generation of both.

We remarked that the unfolding of our ideas and faculties is only operated by the medium of signs, and could not take place without their assistance; that consequently our manner of reasoning can only be rendered complete by correcting the language, and that the whole art amounts to the accurate or perfect formation of the language of every science.

Finally, we proved that the first languages, in their origin, were well formed, because metaphysics which presided over their formation, was not a science as it is in our times, but an instinct given by nature.

(Logic)

From a distance of thirty years, the *Logic* gives the general rule of the *Essay*—after the fact, but, in proportion to this generality, without the slightest alteration. The rule of the "identical proposition," the analytic rule, implies the genealogical return to the simple—and that progressive development can only be done by combining or modifying a material unmodifiable in itself. Here sensation. That is the first material: informed, transformed, combined, associated, it engenders all knowledge. And the whole *Essay* is organized according to this opposition of material and employment ("The sensations therefore, and the operations of the mind [*l'âme*], are the materials of all our knowledge; materials which our reflection employs when it searches throughout some combinations for the relations that the materials contain" [*Essay*, I.1.5 (modified)].). His theory of understanding is a theory of sensation, of employment, and of information modifying this first material ("it can be included that the operations of the understanding are only sensation itself, which is transformed by attention, comparison, judgment, reflection" [*Cours d'études*: "Précis des leçons préliminaires"]).

Thus there would exist a mute first material, an irreducible core of immediate presence to which some secondary modifications supervene, modifications which would enter into combinations, relations, connections, and so on. And yet this metaphysics (we have seen in what sense it was still a metaphysics), this sensationalist metaphysics—this characteristic cannot be refused it—would also be throughout a metaphysics of the sign and a philosophy of language. If we want to read Condillac and not close ourselves off from his text, if we do not want to be immobilized before a grid of constituted and supervenient oppositions, we must accede to its logic, rather to its *analogic*, which develops a sensationalism into a semiotism. This is indeed a development—not an identity from coincidence, but a development through "identical propositions"—for sensation is not only a simple element, but also a *germ*.

This biological, vitalist, or organicist "metaphor" is constant in Condillac. The whole preamble to *De l'art de penser*, to which we are referred, develops the likewise germinal sentence of the book: "The germ of the art of thinking is in our sensations." And the development of this sentence is the analogical description of thought's development, which *resembles* an animal's.

Similarly, in order to explain the division of the *Essay*, Condillac interprets its theory of signs and language as the system of what develops or "employs" the sensible and elementary, material germ, the subject of the first part: "And yet I have thought proper to make this same subject [the theory of language] a considerable part of the following work, as well because it may be viewed in a new and more extensive light, as because I am convinced that the use of signs is the principle which unfolds [*développe*] the germ of all our ideas" (*Essay*, introduction [modified]).

The opposition of germ and development overlaps that of content (material) and form (employment). The principle of analogy, the analogical analytic, assures the passage, the unity, the synthetic power between both terms of this opposition. Our inquiry should bear on this principle. And if the concept of analogy bears the concept of *metaphor*, still nothing will be said, for example, about the germ when qualified as "metaphor." Preliminarily, Condillac's rhetoric and rhetorical philosophy would have to be reconstituted in order to uphold such a proposition. I will try to do that elsewhere. [Here Derrida is referring to a book he once planned to write, entitled *Le Calcul des langues*. He has abandoned the project for now.—Trans.]

What obstinately keeps together the generative and the combinative exigencies can seem in Condillac to be a contradiction, indeed a "deficiency," the opening to "epistemological myths." But that appears to be the case only in comparison with an old philosophical opposition which prohibits thinking these two exigencies other than according to the category of exclusion or (speculative) dialectical synthesis. And perhaps the notion of "epistemological myth" is far from amenable to being reduced to that completely negative and unproductive concept of deficiency. What is the status of all the "epistemological myths" in the history of science? Perhaps the maintenance of *both exigencies* resists, in a nondialectical way, the metaphysical opposition of calculus and genesis. And now we need to ask ourselves under what conditions a text can be found (in this perspective, up to a certain point, and according to determinable axes) relevant to the irruptions of a scientific modernity (for example, biology, genetics, linguistics, or psychoanalysis), in which neither "author" nor "production" are "contemporaneous": what uproots such a text—but also every other, provided we recognize this division [*coupe*]—both from its author (this is the first condition of this expropriation) and from the all-powerful constraint of a mythic *episteme*.

What the mythic *episteme* implies of the finite code belongs still and solely to the representation that can be given a determined *episteme*. The imaginary of *one episteme* is the terrain and the condition for the upsurging of the general theory of *epistemes* which alone would make the table, the finite code, and taxonomy its determining norm.

What, given a classic metaphysics grid (which Condillac undoubtedly must also reckon with), is debated, even up to the point of not being able to ascertain any categorical overhang; what will be perceived as an internal opposition, contradiction, or deficiency, or as the impotent hesitation between two models (for example, the algebraic and the biological)—indeed, to us, today, this seems to constitute the force and interest of such a text.

That Condillac "himself" had not *laid down* the rule of this debate is no doubt not insignificant, and we must take it into account.

At least we must take into consideration some of the effects this can have in his text and its history.

But provided we know how to limit consequentially the authority of an "author" over his very "own" *corpus*, what works (over) such a text, for all that, ought not be misjudged: a traditional opposition, to be sure (and even older than a so-called Classical "*episteme*"), but also a lever of disorganization.

The lever works at ruining this alternative between genesis and calculus, at ruining the whole system with which the alternative is interrelated—but not in just any way. On the contrary, this lever works with a disconcerting regularity which, without a doubt, can give itself to be read only after the fact—and in a determined situation.

II. GENIUS'S DEFERRED ACTION [L'APRÈS-COUP]

To dissolve the alternative opposition: that is a motif which, defining the system's working (that on which it works as much as what works on it), undoubtedly has not been able to find the literal rule of its statement. This explains, at least in part, the disposability, if not the vulnerability, the openness of a corpus exposed to historical blows, to those violent and self-serving operations that are innocently termed lapses in reading.

Of course, the most remarkable example of this is the interpretation of Maine de Biran.

It forms a kind of routine.

Once the debt is recognized, and it was immense, Biran rejects both materialist, determinist sensationalism (the insistence on the simple passivity and the unique principle of experience) and idealism, which is also an abstract algebraism.

The grid of this reading will be very useful.

Handling it becomes even easier when Condillac's "contradictions" or "hesitations" can be adjusted to states or stages in the development, as is said, of his thought. Doing so, Maine de Biran meanwhile completely reserves for himself two possible readings of contradiction: sometimes it is a matter of systematic incoherence, sometimes of historic succession. "Thus his doctrine was not uniform" (*De la décomposition de la pensée*). From this statement Biran draws two kinds of conclusions, simultaneously or alternately. On the one hand, Condillac has left us a bad system, a double system ("his doctrine is double," "Condillac's double theory")—an unusual argument on the part of a philosopher who has made duplicity a theme and a norm of his own discourse, who relentlessly sets the structure of the double root and of *homo duplex* over against every "alchemy" of the unique principle. According to Biran, the system can be corrected, can be made more homogeneous and simpler only after Condillac. "Thus his doctrine was not uniform; but it remained susceptible of a new simplification and admitted a more perfect homogeneity. Such is the end that one of Condillac's most famous disciples has proposed since then." (This concerns Tracy whom, it must be added, Biran criticizes immediately afterwards.)

On the other hand, however, Condillac himself would have parceled out or reduced, from one stage to the other, from one book to the other, the systematic contradiction. Thus this contradiction is no more than historical slippage [*décalage*]—which also is not ordered as simple progress. The systematic vice (which still remains) can provoke relapses or can manifest, at the end of the account, its true constraint. All this is stated in a note:

> While composing the *Traité des systèmes*, Condillac was struck, above all, with the danger that abstractions had to be realized, since that is where he found the common source of all metaphysicians' aberrations. This is also probably what led him to try out a new theory, wherein he could separate the supposed abstract idea of a substantial *ego* (distinct from its accidental modifications) and that of a cause (or productive force internal or external to the same modifications). Expressing in that way only passive effects

or modes and transforming the literal [*propre*] idea of faculties, he could also dispense with *reflection*, which, following Locke, he had admitted in his first work as a *specific source of ideas*. Thus did he compose the *Treatise on the Sensations*. . . . The success of his attempt, the clarity and the precision that it seemed to carry with it in the theory of intellectual faculties—all these strongly predisposed him in favor of an exclusive application of his new method. Now since this method consisted uniquely in forming *a language* (see the first chapter of *Treatise on the Sensations*), i.e., in expressing (and consequently deducing) precisely the simple or compound results of his hypotheses or conventions, he was more and more inclined to believe that it was all there, whatever besides was the object of a science. That is also the degree of simplicity to which he finally brought his doctrine, as can be judged from the *language of calculus*.

It has often been noted that Condillac had never systematized all his doctrine. In fact, it is very easy, when the various works of this philosopher have been read and compared with the attention they merit, it is easy, I say, to notice that his doctrine is double. And as a result, he presents two completely different systems of philosophy, wherein everything which rallies to the doctrine of the *Treatise on the Sensations* cannot be reconciled with the principles of the *Essai sur l'origine de nos connaissances* [*sic*]. Indeed, it would be proper to mark all the points where this division occurs, as well as to make an exact abstract of all the important changes the author brought to bear since then on his *Treatise on the Sensations*. Perhaps there we would recognize the need such a brilliant mind felt to give more to the activity of *sentient* and *motor* being, which at first he had considered exclusively under nothing but a single one of its relations to the other.

(ibid.)

But everything that would drive Condillac from the simple principle of passive sensibility (his progress, according to Biran, starting from the *Essay*—would unfortunately push him toward semiological activism, algebraic artificialism, linguistic formalization. The system is such that no progress is possible for it; its central deficiency will always make it hesitate between two lapses. The model of the "modern" reading is fixed: within another historico-theoretical configuration. This affords thought.

Such would be, will have been, for Biran, the ultimate truth of Condillac's enterprise, just as its end—*La Langue des calculs*—opened the way for him:

I confess that I have long been searching in vain for the word for this enigma of *transformed sensation*; and that the decomposition of the faculty of thinking, likened to that of an equation (see *Logic*, Part I, ch. vii, and Part II, ch. viii), has often tired my mind. . . . I never thought I held the key to this theory until I had read *La Langue des calculs* and meditated on the foundation of an assertion like the following: everything is reduced to language and its transformations, whatever the object of reasoning, and so on. . . . Then I understood that our philosophy, since it starts with the supposition of the animated statue and according to this fantastic model forms the ideas that are truly archetypes of diverse faculties, could believe itself authorized to compose and decompose the terms by following its own definitions or transforming its language after them: it seems that *La Langue des calculs* had produced the *Logic* and the *Treatise on the Sensations*. However, I think the case is just the reverse. . . . By composing the *Traité des systèmes*, Condillac must have learned to keep himself more on guard against the danger of realized abstractions. This probably induces him to try out a theory wherein he could set aside even [Biran added in his own hand: the use of the term or of] the idea of an incomprehensible substance endowed, outside of present impressions, with some feeling of itself, with some power or *virtuality*, and so on; wherein he could also dispense with reflection which, following Locke, he had admitted in his first work. The success of Condillac's attempt (and the clarity it had appeared, for him, to shed on the theory of intellectual faculties) must have strongly predisposed him in favor of the sound quality of his method. Now as his method consisted principally (in the *Treatise on the Sensations* or at least in its first chapter) in expressing the simple results of its very own conventions, and to deduce accordingly, he was inclined more and more to think that everything could be reduced to this point, whatever the object of the science.

Once this reading machine is recognized, it is no longer surprising to see it spew out its critical cards, successively or simultaneously, against *too much* or *too little* freedom.

First, the *too much* in the *Notes* of the *Cahier-Journal* on the *Essay*: "Condillac does not give enough, it seems to me, to the physical mechanism of ideas. He seems to suggest that we produce ideas by an act of our will, and to believe that they are not the results of the movement of brain fibers or something similar." Then, indirectly, in all the renewed questionings of algebraism or artificialism, of the arbitrary in general, of everything that amounts to "constructing science thus with some artificial or logical elements, as algebraic formulas are constructed," to "reasoning as exactly and surely with the signs of metaphysics as with those of algebra. Indeed, Condillac seems to have founded nearly all his doctrine on this opinion, to which he shows himself very consistent in his *Treatise on the Sensations*, his *Logic,* and above all his *Langue des calculs*" (*Essai sur les fondements de la psychologie*).

This criticism of the arbitrary forms a system with the criticism of rationalism, of alchemism (*reduction* to the gold of an abstract, simple, fundamental element), of idealism. ("Chiefly I am speaking of [Condillac's doctrine] in the *Treatise on the Sensations* . . . which then does not rest on any principle of fact. . . . There he already tacitly and above all presupposed the existence of the personality or *ego,* which preexists in the very nature of the soul or sentient subject, as the alchemists believed" [*Essai sur les fondements de la psychologie*]. "Condillac's doctrine can lead to a kind of idealism wherein the ego would remain alone in the purely subjective world of its very own modifications" [*De la décomposition de la pensée*].)

The *too little:* "The way in which Condillac and his school consider these faculties excludes any idea of free activity in them; by subjecting them to any kind of influence whatever from external objects or to the particular *dispositions* of sensibility, they are removed from a mode of culture or of moral development which would tend, as is proper, to free these faculties from their dependence on sensible objects" (*Essai sur les fondements de la psychologie*). (Biran began by calling for a "Condillac of the will" who would do for the activity of willing what the *Essay* had done for the understanding: "It would be advantageous to desire a man accustomed to being circumspect to analyze the will, as Condillac has analyzed the understanding" [*Cahier-Journal*].)

But no more than in Condillac is the question here one of "hesitation," a confused notion which always marks a reading's empiricist limit. Such as Maine de Biran's reading of Condillac, no doubt, but of which we must consequently twice beware.

Customary and insufficiently shaken or disturbed [*sollicitée*], the opposition of activity and passivity forms the hinge. In relying on the evidence of the value of passivity, Biran turns, lets turn the criticism of idealism as an effect of passivity into a criticism of idealism as activism, artificialism, formalism, and so on. This is because the ego remains enclosed in itself only to the extent of its passivity, and too much freedom is the other side of too little freedom: "a kind of idealism wherein the ego would remain alone in the purely subjective world of its very own modifications, while, on the other hand, these modifications (since they are all passive) necessarily presuppose the objective reality of organs which receive them and of bodies which produce them. We cannot, I believe, escape these contradictions without going back to the foundation of a twofold observation, or to the first fact of consciousness and to the primitive condition on which it is founded" (*De la décomposition de la pensée*).

Of what does the operation of reading consist, reading which, here for example, amounts to constituting as a formal contradiction, hesitation, or systematic incoherence what, in the other, is claimed or assumed to be duplicity? Why would the couple activity/passivity give rise to a contradiction in Condillac, but to the analysis of a duplicity in Biran? Do rigorous criteria of reading exist to decide this? This question (the relations between textuality on one hand, dialectic and meaning on the other) is specified in this space through that of *repetition*—such would be the economy of the reading proposed here. In Condillac as in Biran (and in the whole textual field indicated by these names), the constant recourse to a value of repetition—whose law and possibility are never questioned—jumbles the opposition activity/passivity, without the rule of this indecision ever coming to conception [*au concept*]. No doubt the limit here is not *a* concept but, with regard to the structure of repetition, *the* concept.

Undoubtedly this simplifying criticism, of which Condillac's philosophy was already the object in the nineteenth century, necessarily bore, simultaneously or alternately, on his materialism *and* his idealism or spiritualism, on his empiricism *and* his formalism, on his sensationalist or geneticist psychologism *and* his logicist algebraism. In France the history of the reading of Condillac is also, according to a relation not at all external or contingent, that of the formation of a university and its models of philosophical teaching. The system of this relation should be analyzed very closely. At the end of a complex and necessary process, Condillac's thought is often limited (in the imagination of so many undergraduates) to a statute's petrified hardheadedness and the evanescence of a rose's scent.

Might Condillac have been surprised? In any case he had no love for the university of his time.

Let us consider the *dissolution of the alternative* at the point where it concerns less a determined object or a particular domain than the very project of the science to which it gives rise. Here the question is of a *new* science which, however, would only set in order (by generalizing through analogy) the acquisition of knowledge in order to administer its consequence. Neither a generative model nor a combinative one can, taken separately, account for this *fact*.

The fact that "new combinations" exist. The invention of a science is at once the example and the discovery of this, the production of one of those events and the concept of this law. The *Essay* attributes invention to genius rather than to talent. But let us not pretend to understand what *genius* means. First, we would have to consider *trailblazing* [frayage]: the possibility of a new combination, a creation "in some measure." We are still far from that.

> We do not properly create any ideas; we only combine, by composing and decomposing, those which we receive by the senses. Invention consists in knowing how to make new combinations: there are two kinds of it; talent, and genius.
>
> Talent combines the ideas of an art, or of a science, in such a manner as is proper to produce those effects, which should naturally be expected from it. Sometimes it requires more imagination,

sometimes more analysis. Genius adds to talent the idea in some measure of a creative mind. It invents new arts, or in the same art, new branches equal, and even sometimes superior to those already known. It examines things in a point of view peculiar to itself; it gives birth to a new science; or in those already cultivated it carves out a road to truths, which it never expected to reach.

(*Essay*, I.2.104 [modified])

The concept of *generation*, indispensable to the *Essay*'s structure [*l'édifice*] and to the whole criticism of innatism, is itself a combinative concept, provided novelty is admitted there. The innatist philosophers are blind to this novelty and believe they must choose between the classification of innate ideas and the empiricism of genesis, between calculus and engendering: "The obscurity and confusion which prevails in the writings of philosophers, arises from their not suspecting that there are any ideas which are the workmanship of the mind, or if they suspect it, from an incapacity of discovering their real origin, their generation. . . . Hence, let me beg leave to repeat it, there is a necessity of making a new combination of ideas" (ibid., II.2.32 [modified]).

As this paragraph from the *Essay* clearly indicates, "a new combination of ideas" designates both a general possibility (new combinations of ideas can be produced) and the concept of this possibility: the philosopher must form a new combination of ideas concerning the combination of ideas. He must produce another concept of the order and the generation of ideas: "Hence, let me beg leave to repeat it, there is a necessity of making a new combination of ideas, beginning with the most simple ideas transmitted by the senses, and framing them into complex notions, which combined in their turn, will be productive of others, and so on."

This lays claim to a new logic: the addition of the new arises from the sole association or complication—analogical connection—of a finite number of simple givens.

As an example of itself, this logic is new, since it is said to belong to a historical configuration breaking with all the past. And yet this logic does nothing but recompose a series of elementary philosophemes belonging to the oldest funds of metaphysics. The example of this logic not only resists the major opposition of continuist or discontinuist, evolutionist or epigeneticist histories (of culture, ideology, philosophy, science), indeed it resists the major option of taxonomy and history. Already capable of these oppositions, more powerful than they (potentially in them [*en puissance d'elles*]), this logic should not be able to become the object of a discipline (traditional or modern and whatever its name) governed by these categories, these criteria of cutting out [*découpage*] and of articulation. This logic thwarts and deconstructs them almost by itself; it is already no longer there when we naively believe we have captured it in a wide-mesh net.

In effect, Condillac not only claims to engender—perhaps we would have to say generate—a new science, or at least bring about a singular contribution to a generation which is one of his "time": he simultaneously proposes a general interpretation, a theory of the general conditions for the upsurge of a theory.

This double gesture, this sort of "historic" reflectivity folds itself over its very own description.

Apparently, everything returns to a theory of genius. The advent of a new science depends on the stroke of genius, and of an individual genius. Genius's essential quality seems to be imagination. But imagination only invents what it must in order to follow nature's dictate and to know which way to begin. This motif is at work from the *Essay* onward (this can be verified), but *La Langue des calculs* strikes its best formulation: "*To invent, people say, is to find something new through the force of one's imagination. This definition is completely wrong.*" And after he substituted the power of *analysis* for it: "What then is genius? A simple mind who finds what no one knew how to find before it. Nature, which puts all of us on the path of discoveries, seems to watch over it so that it never strays or deviates. Genius begins at the beginning and goes forward from there. That is all its art, a simple art, which for this reason will not be hidden" (*La Langue des calculs*, Book II: "Des opérations du calcul avec les chiffres et avec les lettres," chap. 1: "L'analogie considérée comme méthode d'invention"). "And, when I say *men of genius*, I do not exclude nature whose favorite disciples they are" (ibid., Introduction).

What resembles a theoretical decree or a presupposition at once mystical, naturalistic, psychologistic, obscurantistic, and ahistoric, does not limit opening up historical kinds of questions. Such is even a rule of the system of constraints—on these grounds do we retain here the example from this—which binds Condillac's course: the presupposition is put in place in order to set free, as from its own proper limit, the establishment of questions and hypotheses, of inquiries on the conditions of possibility. The concepts of sensibility and experience, which define the field of those possibles and open questioning about origins, are constituted thus starting from an article of faith. ("Whenever therefore I happen to say, *that we have no ideas but what come from the senses,* it must be remembered, that I speak only of the state into which we are fallen by sin. This proposition applied to the soul before the fall, or after its separation from the body, would be absolutely false. I do not treat of the knowledge of the soul in the two extreme states; because I cannot reason but from experience. . . . Our only view must be to consult experience, and to reason only from facts, which no one can call in question" [*Essay*, I.1.8].)

Thus the genius who "finds what no one knew how to find before it" nevertheless finds only on certain conditions. The origin of one science is not the origin of science itself. The distinctions proposed by the *Dictionnaire des synonymes* between *find, discover, invent, come or light upon* [*rencontrer*], clearly show that for Condillac a scientific discovery, indeed the institution of a new science, belongs to the complex chain of a history in which fact, hypothesis, concept, theory, and so on, are not homogeneous and contemporaneous "novelties." These definitions take as their example—but it is at one blow more than an example—one of the two discoveries that Condillac will consider (in a sense still to be stated precisely) to be the "models" and the conditions for exercising his own discourse: that of Newton. "In the birth of the arts and sciences, more things are *come upon* than *discovered*. In the last century more was *discovered* than *come upon*. Only by reflecting on what has been *come upon* has one begun to make any *discoveries*. Some individuals before Newton *came upon* the attraction which he discovered and which Descartes could not find" (*Dictionnaire des synonymes*; also see *La Langue des calculs*).

The medium of the conditions for discovery is always the history of language, the history of sign systems.

This history, which itself has natural conditions that are analyzed in the *Essay*, always prepares the stroke of genius. This stroke cannot be produced before the constitution of a certain state of language, of certain semiotic possibilities in general. The least natural language, algebra, and the language of calculus, at once science and language, remain *historical* possibilities. They have a history and they open up a history.

> The circumstances favourable to the displaying of genius, are always to be come upon in a nation, when the language begins to have fixed principles and a settled standard: such a period is therefore the epocha of great men. . . .
>
> If we recollect that the habit of the imagination and memory depends intirely on the connexion of ideas, and that the latter is formed by the relation and analogy of signs; we shall be convinced that the less a language abounds in analogous expressions, the less assistance it gives to the memory and the imagination. Therefore it is not at all proper for the exertion or display of talents. It is with languages as with geometrical figures; they give a new insight into things, and dilate the mind in proportion as they are more perfect. Sir Isaac Newton's extraordinary success was due to the choice which had been already made of signs, together with the contrivance of methods of calculation. Had he appeared earlier, he might have been a great man for the age he would have lived in, but he would not have been the admiration of ours. It is the same in every other branch of learning. The success of geniuses who have had the happiness even of the best organization, depends intirely on the progress of the language in regard to the age in which they live; for words answer to geometrical signs, and the manner of using them to methods of calculation. In a language

therefore defective in words, or whose construction is not sufficiently easy and convenient, we should meet with the same obstacles as occurred in geometry before the invention of algebra.
(*Essay*, II.1.146–47 [modified]; also see *Cours d'études:
Histoire moderne*)

But if genius is borne by language, by a certain state of the analogy of
signs, it is also defined by the science of that language and state. This
science is a science of combination, and of the "new combination." This
science takes into account both a historical development of the analogy of
signs and the peculiar genius of language, which is itself only a particular
manner of combining: "I would fain know whether it be not natural for
every nation to combine their ideas according to their own peculiar genius;
and to connect a certain fund of principal ideas with different adventitious
notions, according as they are differently affected. Now these combinations
authorized by time and custom, are properly what constitutes the genius
of a language" (*Essay*, II.1.160 [modified]).

Yet nothing of all this seems to make history. The word and even more
the notion of history seem incompatible with this conception of development, progress, of changes of every kind. The order of nature limits them
on every side. Condillac speaks of "this historical account of the progress
of language" (ibid., 162 [modified]), of "the history of language" (ibid.,
I.2.49), of "the history of the human spirit" (*Cours d'études: Histoire moderne*),
but the question concerns history as a narrative retracting a prescribed
progress, a natural progress. History is only the development of a natural
order. On one hand, certainly, the role of genius is never obliterated.
Language furnishes it elementary conditions which it has no more than to
recognize in order to bring them into play. But genius keeps in its own
right some power that it in turn gives to language: "Though it be true that
great men partake, in some sense or other, of the character of their nation,
yet they have still something that distinguishes them from the crowd. They
see and feel in a manner peculiar to themselves, which they cannot communicate without imagining *new turns of expression within the rules of analogy,
or at least so as to deviate from them as little as possible.* Hence they *conform to
the genius of their language, to which at the same time they communicate their
own*" (*Essay*, II.1.153 [modified]; my emphasis). ("So as to deviate from
them as little as possible." The archeology of the frivolous is this deviation
of genius: "After having shewn the causes of the last improvements of
language, it will be proper to inquire into those of its decline: they are
indeed the same." The man "of genius" tries a new road. But as every
style analogous to the character of the language, and to his own, hath been
already used by preceding writers, he has nothing left but to deviate from
analogy. Thus in order to be an original, he is obliged to contribute to the
ruin of a language, which a century sooner he would have helped to improve. Though such writers may be criticised, their superior abilities must

still command success. The ease there is in copying their defects, soon persuades men of indifferent capacities, that they shall acquire the same degree of reputation. Then begins the reign of subtil and strained conceits, of affected antitheses, of specious paradoxes, of frivolous turns, or far-fetched expressions, of new-fangled words, and in short of the jargon of persons whose understandings have been debauched by bad metaphysics. The public applauds: frivolous and ridiculous writings, the beings of the day, are surprisingly multiplied" [*Essay*, II.1.158–59 (modified)].)

III. IMAGINING—CONCEPTUAL STAND-IN AND THE NOVEL OF FORCE

If there were only (natural or national) genius and the progress of language, we might think there would not be any history. Individual genius, the "new combination," the "new turns of expression within the rules of analogy," and idiomatic deviation, all these make history, so far as history involves the unforeseeable novelty of the event. Conversely, if individual genius, its event, cannot be reduced to its own conditions, we might think there is no more history, only gaps [*écarts*], irruptions, discontinuities referred to a power of singular imagination. But, as we have already seen, invention no more depends on imagination than imagination has the ability to create anything whatever. The fact is, production of the new—and imagination—are only productions: by analogical connection and repetition, they bring to light what, without being there, *will have been* there.

All this leads us back to the time of repetition, to the status of imagination as described in the *Essay*. Imagination is what *retraces*, what produces as reproduction the lost object of perception, the moment attention (of which imagination is nevertheless only the first modification) no longer suffices to make the object of perception *subsist*, the moment the first modification of attention breaks with perception and regulates passing from weak presence to absence. Such is the case [*instance*] of the sign and then of the historic milieu in general, the element of deviation [*écart*] wherein individual genius and the progress of languages are interchanged.

> Experience shews that the first effect of attention is to make those perceptions which are occasioned by their objects to subsist still in the mind, when those objects are absent. They are preserved, generally speaking, in the same order in which the objects presented them. By this means a chain or connexion is formed amongst them, from whence several operations, as well as reminiscence, derive their origin. The first is imagination, which takes place when a perception, by the force alone of the connexion which attention has established between it and the object, is retraced at the sight of this object. Sometimes, for instance, the bare mentioning of the name of a thing is sufficient to represent it to one's self, as if it were really present. (*Essay*, I.2.17 [modified])

First let us remark the value of the "force of connection." Condillac does not insist on this, but it is an active spring of all his discourse. The passage (continuity and/or rupture) from one operation or structure to another and the articulation, then, of their concepts always amount to a difference of force, of the quantity of force. But—such is the universal law of analogy which dominates this whole set of problems—quantity of force is always quantity of connection. . . .

Force is first determined as force of connection and its quantity as quantity of connection.

What is a quantity of connection?

Perhaps this question, which Condillac never seems to answer, could guide a deconstructive reading of the *Essay*. The "new" of a combination arises from the analysis of a certain—the greatest—"quantity of connection":

> It has been already observed that the analytic method is the only mean or instrument of invention. But some perhaps will ask me, by what mean or instrument are we to discover the analytic method itself? I answer, by the connexion of ideas. When I want to reflect upon an object, in the first place I observe that the ideas I have of it are connected with those I have not, and which I am in search after. I observe next, that the one and the other may be combined a great many ways, and according as the combinations vary, there is more or less connexion between the ideas. I may therefore suppose a combination in which the connexion is as great as it possibly can be; and several others in which the connexion gradually diminishes, till it ceases to be sensible. If I view an object on that side which has no sensible connexion with the ideas I am seeking, I shall find nothing. If the connexion is superficial, I shall discover very little; my conceptions shall seem to be no more than the consequence of a violent application, or even the effect of chance, and a discovery of this nature will afford me very little assistance towards making any further progress. But let me consider an object on that side which is most connected with the ideas I am investigating, the whole shall be fully discovered to my view.
>
> (*Essay*, II.2.39 [modified])

The quantity of connection between a known and an unknown, analysis as the analogical process (eventually of proportionality), innovation as revelation, the energy connecting the present to the absent, difference of degree as a structural opposition, discontinuous continuity—all these increase and articulate themselves in the concept of force as the force of repetition (retracing, supplying).

In this reading, we can ascertain that the system of this articulation or this increase regularly produces a silent explosion of the whole text and introduces a kind of fissure, rather fission, within each concept as well as each statement. In the context occupying us here, there are two examples.

(1) The explanation gets carried away, disappropriates itself, since it overplays the notion of force whose obscurantist effect or "metaphoric" value Condillac denounces elsewhere. The metaphoric, hence analogical value: the force of connection, the analogical energy can, itself, give rise only to an analogical concept. Here we must refer to the *Dictionnaire des synonymes* (the natural product of a philosophy of analogy and the application of a metaphoristic theory of language), to the article on *attraction*, the physical model of the universal connection that is transferred by analogy into the realm of ideas:

> ATTRACTION. n.
> Name given to a cause no more known than impulse.
> [It is a force which draws just as impulse is a force which pushes. Now the word *force* is a name given to a cause we do not know at all; see *force*]. *Attraction* is universal and in some cases the laws it follows are known. But my plan does not include dwelling on words of this kind. I only speak of attraction because it is the cause of weight, of gravity, and so on, about which I have been able to create an article. Yet I could predict that this word will be used figuratively when Newton's system will be more generally known. In fact, for example, why wouldn't one say: there is an *attraction* between man, but it acts only at the point of contact, or at most at a small distance.

Now read the article on *force*. Just as everything he did while criticizing this value in the article on *attraction*, Condillac in advance outmaneuvers, captures Biran's object on the flank. The primitive sense proceeds from the internal feeling of effort and is, like every primitive sense, sensible, physical, of the order of one's own body. This sense is transferred and "figuratively" extended by metaphor and analogy—such is the rule which organizes this whole dictionary of synonyms:

> We owe to internal feeling or consciousness the first idea of what we call *force*. This quality is what makes us able to move and carry our bodies, to overcome what resists us, to resist what acts on us. . . . From the body this word has been transferred to the mind and the soul. . . . *Forces* are taken for the multitude of things of which they are the effect. . . . This word was also transferred to inanimate things. But then it is the name of a cause of which we have no idea and which we know only by effects; indeed this cause has occasioned various verbal disputes among those who thought they had discovered it and consequently caused rather absurd things to be said. See what the natural philosophers [*les physiciens*] have said about the *force* of bodies. . . . In addition, we

say the *force* of a thought, an expression, an argument, a discourse;
but analogy enlightens us on these examples and on all the others.

(*Dictionnaire*)

Thus only in the realm of physics, the science of inanimate bodies, is *force* the name of a cause of which we have no idea. But *force* does not recover its primitive sense when passing from inanimate bodies to spiritual animation, to thought, mind, or idea: this last case still concerns a metaphor ("From the body this word has been transferred to the mind and the soul. . . . In addition, we say the *force* of a thought . . . a discourse; but analogy enlightens us"). The "first idea," the primitive sense, then, is reserved for one's own internal, bodily experience, to the sensible "internal feeling or consciousness." But here we are short of all definition. Since Condillac refers in the *Essay* to "the force alone of the connexion" to define the relation between a presence and an absence, a perception and all its others; since he refers to beginning with attention and imagination, in what sense must we understand the word *force*? To what sense must we extend it? Reserve it? And if, the organizing thesis of this discourse, language is primordially metaphorical; if the primitive is figured, where is force found? Here we only want to begin considering this question.

(2) Another disappropriation, another fission: this tampers with the very concept of what disappropriates, what produces the "new combination," what opens up the given; it tampers then with the whole system which links repetition (retracing-supplying), sign, time, analogy.

It concerns imagination.

First of all, in chapter II (*Essay*, I.2), imagination is purely *reproductive*, it "retraces" the perceived. In this sense, imagination invents or innovates nothing; it only combines in relation to each other the given's finite presences. But the force connecting the present to the absent sets free production of the "new."

Productive force is also called imagination.

This name will not be equivocal provided we know how to regulate its use; however, it is the name of what (along with analogy, metaphor, the connection of known to unknown, of presence to absence) will introduce into all language the risk of ambiguity.

We can say that all the problems of the *Essay* are spread out between the two senses of the word *imagination*, the reproductive imagination which retraces (connection is in some way tied to this) and the productive imagination which, in order to supply, adds something more. Its *freedom* is defined some chapters farther on and occasions a note:

> From the power we have of reviving our perceptions in the absence
> of objects, is derived that of reuniting and connecting the most
> distant ideas. Every thing is capable of assuming a new form in
> our imagination. By the freedom with which it transfers the qual-
> ities of one subject to another, it unites in one only the perfections

which nature would judge sufficient for the embellishment of many. Nothing at first sight seems more contrary to truth, than this manner in which the imagination disposes of our ideas. And indeed if we do not render ourselves masters of this operation, it will infallibly mislead us; whereas if we learn how to subject it to rule, it will prove one of the principal sources of all our knowledge.

(*Essay*, I.2.75 [modified])

The note is called for right here. Before we cite it, let us remark that the freedom is only one of transfer (a displacement of predicates from one subject to another and a metaphorical operation), and that there are not only two concepts of imagination: the productive imagination itself has two possible values or effects: truth and nontruth.

The note:

Hitherto I have taken the imagination for that operation only which revives the perceptions in the absence of objects: but now that I consider the effects of this operation, I find no inconveniency in following the common acceptation; nay, I am obliged to do it. Hence it is that in the present chapter I take the imagination for an operation, which by reviving our ideas, forms new combinations of them at will. Thus the word *imagination* shall henceforward have two different significations with me: but this shall not occasion any equivocation or ambiguity, because the circumstances in which I use it, will determine each time my particular meaning.

(ibid.)

(A remarkable index, the imagination appears twice, in two places, under two different titles on the second to last page of the *Essay*: at the same time as material and as employment, as content and as form. "The senses are the source of human knowledge. The different sensations, perception, consciousness, reminiscence, attention and imagination, the two last considered as not yet subject to our controul, are its materials: memory, imagination, as subject to controul, reflexion, and the other operations, employ these materials: the signs to which we are indebted for the habit [*l'exercise*] of these very operations, are the instruments they make use of: and the connexion of ideas is the first spring which puts all the rest into motion" [*Essay*, II.2.53].

The opposition material/employment thus traverses and divides the concept of imagination which is consequently its element or environment. Correlatively, the opposition which internally marks the imagination is also that of nonmastery to mastery, of *noncontrol* to *control*, of *disposition* to *nondisposition*. This opposition furrows and orders the whole *Essay*. The sign, signification is the operation of mastery, the *putting-under-the-control-of*, at once [as we have just seen] as the condition and the instrument of exercising. If there are two concepts of imagination, there are two concepts or values of the sign, and that will not be without consequence.)

"If we render ourselves masters of this operation": we can verify that, in the *Essay*, "to render oneself master of," "to dispose of," is the final sense of every operation. If action and the language of action are at the beginning, Condillac always determines them axiomatically as mastery or as the movement toward mastery. With imagination's duplicity functioning as a hinge, to render oneself master of, to control the ambiguity and risks, is the major strategic operation of mastery—we could almost say, mastery itself.

But since mastery, in order to be what it is, must take possession of what is not, of nothing then, to be sure it is never itself. Mastery, *if there is any*, does not exist.

The imaginations constitute the place of history and the "progress of language." The narrative we can construct will have to be probable but, in the milieu of imagination, of language on language, always risks *resembling* a fable. Its affinity with the novel or romance, indeed with a mythic epistemology, remains congenital to the narrative. ("Ignorance always rushes its judgments and treats as impossible everything it does not understand. The history of our faculties and ideas seems a completely chimerical romance to minds which lack any penetration: it would be easier to reduce them to silence than to enlighten them. In physics and astronomy, how many discoveries were judged impossible by ignorant people of former times!" [*De l'art de raisonner*].)

> From this historical account of the progress of language every body may see, that to a person well acquainted with languages, they are a painting of the character and genius of every nation. He may see in what manner the imagination first made a combination of ideas from prejudice and passion. . . . But if the manners of a people influenced language, the latter, as soon as its rules were ascertained by celebrated writers, had in its turn an influence on manners, and for a long time preserved to each people their peculiar characteristic.
>
> Some perhaps will look upon this whole history as a romance: but they cannot at least deny its probability.
>
> (*Essay*, II.1.162–63 [modified])

Voltaire had written on Locke: "Such a multitude of reasoners having written the romance of the soul, a sage at last arose who gave, with an air of the greatest modesty, the history of it." (*Lettres philosophiques*.) The *Essay* regularly defines Locke's enterprise as a model, but as one to be corrected and completed, still a fable to be made more historical, more probable.

What Newton has accomplished to perfection in the realm of physical science, Locke has only roughed out in the field of psychology.

The *Essay* makes two major references to this. Newton understood the order of truths in the science of the physical universe. But in doing this, he not only gave Condillac an example to transpose, the particular model of a methodical and formal success in a different domain. Condillac now has access to a universal content: the idea of a simple and unique principle ruling the connection of things among themselves on the basis of one fundamental property.

What did Newton discover? Condillac explains in *De l'art de raisonner* by advancing a "comparison," a technical comparison to bring into view a physical truth. If the beam of a balance is placed on the tip of a needle, and if the farthest bodies are made to turn around the same center, we will have "the image of the universe." The machine, the balance or lever, is the principle of all other machines, simple (wheel, pulley, inclined plane, pendulum) or compound.

> The identity is sensible; the machines take different forms in order to produce more conveniently different effects, but in the beginning they are all only one same machine. Now our universe is only a great balance. . . . [The] point of suspension, fulcrum, and the center of gravity are at bottom the same thing. This comparison is enough for us to make comprehensible how all these masses are regulated in their course by that same force which makes this notebook fall if you stop holding it up. . . . For if there is fundamentally only one machine, there is fundamentally only one property.

This unique property assures discourse of the power to proceed by identical propositions, that is, self-evidentially [*dans l'évidence*], since identity is "the only sign of evidence." "So identity is the sign by which a proposition is recognized as self-evident; and identity is recognized when a proposition can be translated into terms which return to those very terms, *the same is the same*" (ibid.; see also *Logic*).

The principle of evidence which alone "must exclude every kind of doubt" is the ultimate appeal. Here recourse to the identical (nontautological) proposition follows the rule of the evidence of reason that Condillac distinguished from evidence of fact and evidence of feeling (ibid.).

In transposing the Newtonian discovery into the psychological order, Condillac also submits the *Essay* to the criterion of evidence and of a non-Cartesian indubitability ("our only aim should be to discover a fundamental experience which no one can question, and will be sufficient to explain all the rest" [*Essay*, Introduction (modified)]). In combining and overseeing the three types of evidence, he studies as well the universal connection (of idea among themselves, of ideas and signs, of signs among themselves in analogy). He leads all experience back to a first property which knows itself and which does nothing then but modify itself: sensibility.

Although the *Essay* only treats the understanding, it implies the later proposition of the *Treatise on the Sensations*: "Judgment, reflexion, desires, passions, etc. are only sensation itself differently transformed" (dedication [modified]). The *Essay* states: "The perception or the impression caused in the mind [*l'âme*] by the agitation of the senses, is the first operation of the understanding. The idea of it cannot be acquired by any discourse or words whatsoever; nothing can convey it to us but the reflexion on what passes within us, when we are affected by some extraneous impression on the senses" (I.2.1).

The general principle of analogy authorizes this transposition of Newtonian discourse. No doubt this principle, like every philosophy of metaphor which proceeds from it, gives rise to an ambiguous axiology. Analogy can also mislead us, but then that is because the analogy is weak, the "quantity of connection" is not great enough. Analogy creates language and method. Analogy makes possible and homogeneous the passage from one place of discourse to another, the transfer of a scientific model into another field. Analogy is itself the unity of method, it is *the* method.

Although Condillac often criticized the mathematism of certain philosophers, he accepts consideration of the mathematical object and method as models, but as models of language included in the general field of science as particular domains. This fundamental homogeneity of the scientific field in general depends not only on discursive analogy but also on the fact that this analogy is natural, forms a sequence with nature. Analogy never does anything but extend natural productions. The continuity of this observation can be verified from the *Essay* to *La Langue des calculs*:

> The first expressions of the language of action are given by nature, since they are a continuation of our organization: the first expressions are given, analogy forms the others and extends this language, which little by little becomes suited to representing our ideas of whatever kind.
>
> Nature, which starts everything, starts the language of articulated sounds, just as it has begun the language of action; and analogy, which completes languages, forms them correctly, if it continues as nature has begun.
>
> Analogy is properly a relation of resemblance: then a thing can be expressed in many ways, since there is nothing which does not resemble many other things.
>
> But different expressions represent the same thing under different relations, and the mental aspects, i.e., the relations under which we consider something, determine the choice we should make. . . .
>
> Languages are all the more imperfect since they seem more arbitrary; but remark that they seem to be less so in good writers. When a thought is well rendered, everything is founded on reason, even up to the placement of each word. Thus are the men of genius who have made everything that is good in languages; and, when I say *men of genius*, I do not exclude nature whose favorite disciples they are.
>
> Algebra is a well-made language, and it is the only one: nothing

there appears arbitrary. Analogy, which never gets away, leads sensibly from expression to expression. Here usage has no authority. Our concern is not to speak like the others; we must speak according to the greatest analogy in order to come to the greatest precision. Those who made this language have felt that stylistic simplicity makes all its elegance: a truth less well-known in vulgar languages.

As soon as algebra is a language that analogy constructs, analogy which forms language forms the methods: or rather, the method of invention is only analogy itself.

Analogy: that then is what all the art of reasoning is reduced to, as is all the art of speaking; and in this single word we see how we can instruct ourselves of others' discoveries and how we can make some of them ourselves. . . .

Mathematics is a well-discussed science, whose language is algebra. So let us see how analogy makes us speak in this science, and we will know how it ought to make us speak in the others. That is what I propose. Thus mathematics, which I will treat, is in this work an object subordinated to a much greater object. The question is showing how this exactitude can be given to all the sciences, an exactitude believed to be the exclusive lot of mathematics.

(La Langue des calculs)

This situation of mathematics (as model and included object) results from the unlimited generality of the principle of analogy: the types of analogy (sensible, natural resemblance, proportionality, and so on) are analogous among themselves (ibid.). If the end of the *Essay* seems to criticize philosophical mathematism and even, as is thought, the mathematical in general, it aims to make them only the confused transposition of what is the least mathematical: geometry, the geometer's preference for synthesis ("Geometricians themselves, who of all philosophers ought to be best acquainted with the advantages of the analytic method, give the preference very frequently to the synthetic. Hence it is that when they quit their calculations to enter into researches of a different nature, we find they have neither the same clearness, nor precision, nor the same extent of comprehension. Of four celebrated metaphysicians, Des Cartes, Mallebranche, Leibnitz, and Locke, the latter is the only one that was not a geometrician, and yet how vastly superior is he to the rest!" [*Essay*, II.2.52]. The program of *La Langue des calculs* is on the other hand very clearly opened.

The status of the two models differs. Newton must be transposed, Locke must be completed and corrected. On numerous points, which all seem reducible to this: Locke missed the sign because he lacked order. He did not recognize the principle of the germ's development ("the use of signs is the principle which unfolds the germ of all our ideas" [ibid., introduction (modified)]), because he did not radically analyze the germ or seed.

Lack of order. If there has been historical progress, for example from Locke to Condillac, that is because the natural order had been perverted. If that order had been immediately perceived, there would not have been any historical density. But even more so, not without a return to the natural order. We will have to take these two motifs into account.

They not only explain Condillac's interpretation of his own relation to Locke's discovery, but also Condillac's lineage in relation to himself; also the "progress" of his own thought: first within the *Essay*, then from the *Essay* to subsequent works, in particular to the *Treatise on the Sensations*. Condillac multiplies the considerations of history in his own discourse. He does not hold them as marginal. They must be part of the discourse itself which, marking out the trail, must be recounted, must explain its steps (if not its faux-pas), the rules it followed or those it should have followed.

That such analyses are part of the principal discourse undoubtedly indicates their importance and seriousness. But simultaneously we are ordered not to trust this too much: these analyses tell us what Condillac was thinking of doing, or rather thought he had done. This ensemble of rules had to constitute method (and the general concept of method) after the fact, as the reflection of a success; a method which should allow successors to repeat the science and multiply its discoveries. The *methodological* operation is in some way a *revolutionary* operation. A rare merit is accorded Descartes, in a passage of the *Essay* which will be, like so many others, literally reproduced by *De l'art de penser*: "Philosophers would have supplied our general incapacity of self-reflexion, if they had left us the history of the progress of their minds. Des Cartes indeed has done it, and this is one of the great obligations we owe him. . . . I am apt to think that this contrivance greatly contributed to the revolution occasioned by this philosopher" (*Essay*, II.2.41). If the *Essay's* "truth," its possibility, then its limits have twice appeared after the fact; if the system is unfolded, *explained* in a history, that is because there was a lack of order, because the natural order of ideas was violated. The retrospective evidence first occurs within the *Essay*, in the course of its exposition.

But this exposition is not the outside of his labor. What, up to the end of the book, will have been hidden by a fault of composition, by a lapse in the order of didactic linking, is precisely the extent of "the principle of the connexion of ideas." This principle is nothing but the principle of order itself, of order conforming to nature. What the lack of order will have hidden—not any particular object or moment determined in the consequence—is the principle of consequence: this principle then "abysses" [*s'abyme*] or shows some of itself. In short, Condillac explains that, had he followed order itself in composing the *Essay*, he would have discovered more quickly the principle of order. A sentence which, since it can be inverted, encircles history within nature. But look at the considerations on the order of exposition in the *Essay* (I.2.107; and II.2.45ff.). Among other things that will be brought into relief is Condillac's silence on the sense of that error which for a long time limited or delayed the generalization of his discovery: "With regard to philosophic works, nothing but order will enable an author to perceive some things that have been forgotten, or others which have not been sufficiently examined. This I have often myself experienced. The present essay, for example, was finished, and yet I did not even then understand the principle of the connexion of ideas in its full extent. This was owing intirely to a passage of about two pages, which was not in its right place" (ibid., II.2.47). What is the status of this remark, inscribed in the book only when the "present essay, for example, was finished?"

Condillac never retouched the *Essay*.

What two pages were these? Why doesn't Condillac tell us? If these pages here are made to open and not close our reading, must we stop at this point?

The Rhetoric of Enlightenment: D'Alembert

Peter France

Like Montesquieu, d'Alembert was an academician. He was indeed a member of several academies. He was only twenty-one when he made his first communication to the Académie des Sciences, where his mathematical and scientific work soon won him a place as *adjoint* and then *associé*. In the 1740s he produced a series of works on dynamics and related subjects which gave him a European reputation; before long he was a member of the Royal Society of London and the Royal Academy of Prussia. But after beginning his career strictly as a scientist, he became joint editor of the *Encyclopédie* and a frequenter of the *salons*. The author of the Preliminary Discourse of the *Encyclopédie* became identified with the *philosophe* movement, and it was as a *philosophe* that in 1753 he allowed his name to be put forward, strongly backed by Madame du Deffand, for a seat in the Académie française. He was elected in 1754 and quickly made his mark as a conscientious member, ready to perform all sorts of relatively trivial duties of a mainly literary kind, such as speeches of adjudication and prize-giving for competitions of poetry or prose eloquence.

D'Alembert's two French academies pursued quite different ends: the encouragement of good writing and speech, and the advancement of scientific learning. They had, it is true, a good deal in common. The Académie des Sciences, in particular, seems to have felt itself obliged in public session to comply with some of the standards of eloquence upheld by its sister academy. This was not a two-way process, however. Before d'Alembert's time, the Académie française took little interest in philosophy or science; he himself worked hard to give some philosophical body to its dignified proceedings. Thus, although we should not talk in sensational terms of a

From *Rhetoric and Truth in France: Descartes to Diderot.* © 1972 by Oxford University Press. Clarendon Press, 1972.

great gap between two cultures in eighteenth-century France, it may be said that d'Alembert moved in two different worlds. His successor as secretary of the Académie française, Marmontel, himself only a *littérateur*, gives us a glimpse of this double life as it appeared round about 1750: "J'étais content, j'étais heureux, lorsque dans la petite chambre de d'Alembert, chez sa bonne vitrière, faisant avec lui tête à tête un dîner frugal, je l'entendais, après avoir chiffré tout le matin de sa haute géométrie, me parler en homme de lettres, plein de goût, d'esprit et de lumières."

"Sa haute géométrie"—this was what had made d'Alembert's name, and it appears that, for all his literary activities, this continued to be the work he valued most. Indeed, if we are to believe Condorcet's *Eloge*, it was the only work he valued, the rest being hardly more than a frivolous pastime:

> Ses ouvrages mathématiques étaient les seuls auxquels il attachât une importance sérieuse; il disait, il répétait souvent qu'il n'y avait de réel que ces vérités; et tandis que les savants lui reprochaient son goût pour la littérature, et le prix qu'il mettait à l'art d'écrire, souvent il offensait les littérateurs, en laissant échapper son opinion secrète sur le mérite ou l'utilité de leurs travaux.

If, then, we are to study the rhetoric of d'Alembert's writings, we should look first of all at his most serious work, the *Traité de dynamique* (1743), which sets out the principle for which his name is still known to scientists.

The *Traité* opens with a preliminary discourse which is quite separate from the body of the work and which d'Alembert later incorporated with some alterations in his *Eléments de philosophie*. I shall discuss this work later, so for the moment I shall confine my attention to the treatise itself—but it should be remembered that it did in fact appear in public with an introduction which is much more accessible to the average reader than what follows it. The *Traité* proper is written to be read by experts; it makes few concessions to the demands of literary taste. It is, however, written in French rather than Latin, which is already something of a concession. D'Alembert states the case for scientific Latin in his essay *Sur la latinité des modernes*:

> Mais autant il serait à souhaiter qu'on n'écrivît jamais des ouvrages *de goût* que dans sa propre langue, autant il serait utile que les ouvrages *de science*, comme de géométrie, de physique, de médecine, d'érudition même, ne fussent écrits qu'en langue latine, c'est-à-dire dans une langue qu'il n'est pas nécessaire en ces cas-là de parler élégamment, mais qui est familière à presque tous ceux qui s'appliquent à ces sciences, en quelque pays qu'ils soient placés.

But as he admitted, most scientists did in fact use their own vernacular by 1750, and he himself invariably does so. By so doing he was consenting to be governed by the norms of correct and even elegant French usage; he declares in his *Réflexions sur l'élocution oratoire* that although the style of the orator, the historian, and the philosopher may differ, "l'élocution n'a pour tous qu'une même règle; c'est d'être claire, précise, harmonieuse, et surtout facile et naturelle."

Clarity and precision, rather than harmony and ease, are the dominant qualities of the *Traité*. It begins impeccably with a set of basic definitions, of impenetrability, body, place, rest, and so on. The "définitions et notions préliminaires" are given in a language accessible to any educated man. The French is correct, unpretentious, and as clear as the subject allows. Gradually the reader is led to more complex notions; at the same time the language departs from that written or spoken by those who are not mathematicians or scientists. This is evident in the growing frequency of mathematical symbols, which are at first placed mainly in the notes, but quite soon make up an integral and unavoidable part of the argument. It is in this above all that d'Alembert reveals that he is writing for colleagues and not for the general public. Nevertheless, these colleagues were academicians and they too appreciated good writing—and indeed good speaking, for it is interesting to note that a good deal of the *Traité* was in fact read out in front of the Académie des Sciences. The academicians could hardly object to equations, but they naturally expected a speaker's prose to be correct, and as clear and easy on the ear as possible. And this is more or less what they got; to take an example free from mathematical symbols, we read:

Du mouvement en lignes courbes et des forces centrales

33. Comme un corps tend de lui-même à se mouvoir en ligne droite, il ne peut décrire une ligne courbe qu'en vertu de l'action d'une puissance qui le détourne continuellement de sa direction naturelle. On peut déduire de l'article précédent les principes du mouvement d'un corps sur une courbe.

Il est démontré qu'un arc infiniment petit d'une courbe quelconque peut être pris pour un arc de cercle, dont le rayon serait égal au rayon de la développée de cet arc de la courbe. On réduit par ce moyen le mouvement d'un corps sur une courbe quelconque au mouvement de ce même corps sur un cercle dont le rayon change à chaque instant.

The exposition proceeds steadily and logically; the sentences are well formed and grammatically irreproachable. This is the admirable basic scientific style of the eighteenth century. It can best be characterized in negative terms—the language of ordinary speech, but pruned of a number of undesirable elements.

The first of these undesirable elements is the trope. The didactic or illustrative simile and the ennobling metaphor and metonymy are all virtually excluded from the *Traité*. Neither is there any place for the elegant periphrasis or euphemism. D'Alembert believes in avoiding technical terms where this can be done without detriment to the scientific value of his work: "on ne doit pas surtout exprimer d'une manière savante ce qu'on dira aussi bien par un terme que tout le monde peut entendre. On ne saurait rendre la langue de la raison trop simple et trop populaire." In this treatise, however, there can be no question of avoiding the technical. I have already noted the heavy reliance on the symbols of algebra. Similarly, d'Alembert attaches the appropriate formal labels to the different sections of his demonstration—"loi," "corollaire," "remarque," "théorème," "scolie," "lemme"—and numbers his paragraphs. The reader must also have some acquaintance with mathematical terminology; in the passage just quoted we have "développée," "arc," and "rayon." Obviously no elegant circumlocution could replace these.

As undesirable as the tropes are those figures of speech which organize language so as to affect the ear, the pattern figures. This does not mean that the speaker must try to sound unpleasant, but that he must avoid any turns of phrase which might appear to be stylistic frills. . . . In the passage quoted above the sentences march forward, without any of the figures which make language dance by setting up a balance between one clause and another. Consider, for instance, the first sentence with its series of three clauses which merely follow one another, without there being any attempt to build them up to a climax. The sentences in these two paragraphs are all reasonably short and thus avoid any disagreeable awkwardness, but in other places d'Alembert is led by his argument into long and even graceless sentences which run counter to the norms of classical rhetoric. But if symmetrical patterns are avoided, so too are the deliberately irregular constructions which were often used for oratorical effect—anacoluthon, asyndeton, inversion, and others. It will be remembered that for the *philosophes* one of the virtues of French was precisely the "natural" word-order (subject-verb-predicate), which distinguished it from the ancient languages. It is not surprising, therefore, if d'Alembert constructs almost all his sentences on the approved model.

Inversion and similar turns of phrase were to be avoided because they were unnatural, but also because they were associated with the emotive style of poetry and oratory. Similarly, we shall not expect to find in a book like the *Traité* any of the exclamations, apostrophes, and other figures which were the normal vehicle for the *chaleur* which d'Alembert distrusted. It is worth noting, however, that the didactic question appears from time to time; the author takes into account the facts of communication and attempts to forestall the response of the reader:

On pourrait faire ici une difficulté qu'il est bon de prévenir . . .
Comment accorder ces deux propositions? La réponse est très simple.

Here the tone becomes slightly less impersonal for a moment; the same is true of the passages where the normal "on" or "nous" gives way to "je." "Je" is in fact quite frequent in this work (more so than it would be in an equivalent work written today), but it is still a fairly impersonal pronoun. "Je" is the author of the treatise, who explains why he has set out his material in this or that way ("Je ne m'étendrai pas davantage sur les lois de l'équilibre dans cette première partie"). It is a hand holding a pen, never a man with an existence outside the field of mathematics. That sort of "je" could only confuse things.

In a word, then, the *Traité de dynamique* does without rhetoric, if by rhetoric we understand the system of departures from an imagined norm which was taught in the schools of eighteenth-century France. D'Alembert more than once dismisses schoolroom rhetoric, most forcefully in his *Encyclopédie* article "Collège." It was easy enough to ridicule the subject. It was more difficult, however, not to conform in some respects to its teaching, particularly when you were writing for a wider public than that which could understand the *Traité de dynamique*.

D'Alembert was an academician, an encyclopedist, and an enlightener. For all his love of higher mathematics, he was more committed than most of his contemporaries to spreading the new philosophy among amateurs. It was for them that he wrote many of his most famous works, notably the *Eléments de philosophie*, the Preliminary Discourse of the *Encyclopédie*, and the *Eloges* of dead academicians. He was as aware as anyone of the dangers of popularization. . . . Above all, he feared the influence of the great and warned eloquently against it in his *Essai sur la société des gens de lettres avec les grands* (1753), which reflects its author's experience as a favourite of the Paris *salons*. According to d'Alembert, great men were still inclined, even in this age of philosophy, to treat men of letters as entertainers. They were, moreover, poor judges of literary productions and, worse still, had a bad influence on French style, encouraging frivolity, servility, and affectation. Little wonder that in the *Encyclopédie* article, "Figure de la terre," d'Alembert excludes from his readership "cette partie du public indifférente et creuse, qui, plus avide du nouveau que du vrai, use tout en se contentant de tout effleurer."

It is the same with the *Eléments de philosophie* (1759). His readers are, he supposes, "des personnes à qui d'autres occupations ne permettent pas de s'appliquer à ces sciences et d'en faire leur objet." His duty, therefore, as he says in the "Avertissement," is to write in a language both intelligible and acceptable to the non-specialist. This does not, however, open the door to the dilettante: "On croit devoir avertir ceux qui ne cherchent qu'à s'amuser dans leurs lectures, qu'ils peuvent se dispenser d'entreprendre celle de ce volume." So while d'Alembert is willing elsewhere to admit that it is necessary for the Académie française to preserve purity of language and good taste, and even (albeit ironically) that the courtier members of the Academy have their value in maintaining taste by talking elegant nothings, his insistence in his own philosophical popularization is always on the austere truth. He distinguishes again and again between the "ouvrage de goût" and the "ouvrage philosophique," between the orator and the philosopher—thus on the crucial question of harmony:

> L'arrangement harmonique des mots ne peut quelquefois se concilier avec leur arrangement logique; quel parti faut-il prendre alors? un philosophe rigide ne balancerait pas; la raison est son maître, je dirais presque son tyran. L'orateur soumis à l'oreille autant que le philosophe l'est à la raison, sacrifie suivant le cas, tantôt l'harmonie, tantôt la justesse.
>
> (*Réflexions sur l'élocution oratoire et sur le style en général*)

Whatever the orator or poet may be allowed to do, the philosopher is the servant of truth. If he is eloquent, d'Alembert insists that his eloquence will come from his subject alone, not from any added graces. Neither will he allow himself that personal warmth which gives a spurious persuasive force to arguments. Thinking perhaps of Jean-Jacques, whom he sometimes cites as an example of fraudulent enthusiasm, he distances himself from such tricks in the "Avertissement" to the *Eléments de philosophie*:

> On ne parle aujourd'hui que de *chaleur;* on en veut jusque dans les écrits qui ne sont destinés qu'à instruire. . . . Pour moi . . . je n'ai jamais eu pour point de vue dans mes écrits que ces deux mots, *clarté* et *vérité;* et je me tiendrais fort heureux d'avoir rempli cette devise, persuadé que la vérité seule donne le sceau de la durée aux ouvrages philosophiques; qu'un écrivain qui s'annonce pour parler à des hommes ne doit pas se borner à étourdir ou amuser des enfants; et que l'éloquence est bientôt oubliée quand elle n'est employée qu'à orner des chimères.

Note the characteristic comparison of the child and the adult; d'Alembert knows all too well which is the world for him.

There is, inevitably, a certain variety in the rhetoric of the *Eléments*. Predictably, the opening pages contain more clearly than the body of the work the sort of writing that a non-specialist audience may have expected from d'Alembert. Similarly, he writes in a "nobler," more animated way when dealing with general philosophical questions than when he is on his home ground of mathematics. If we look at the chapter entitled "Mécanique," which is a slightly modified version of his original Preliminary Discourse to the *Traité de dynamique*, we find that although there are no mathematical symbols and not many technical terms, there is also very little of the rhetorical embellishment whose absence we noted in the *Traité* itself. It is the honest, clear style of the philosopher. At most, one might point to a certain care for the sound of the sentences; there are no elaborate verbal patterns, but there is often a sober harmony which is not so easily to be found in the *Traité*. Take the following paragraph:

Comme le rapport des parties du temps nous est inconnu en lui-même, l'unique moyen que nous puissions employer pour découvrir ce rapport, c'est d'en chercher quelque autre plus sensible et mieux connu, auquel nous puissions le comparer. On aura donc trouvé la mesure du temps la plus simple, si on vient à bout de comparer, de la manière la plus simple qu'il soit possible, le rapport des parties du temps avec celui de tous les rapports qu'on connaît le mieux. De là il résulte que le mouvement uniforme est la mesure du temps la plus simple. Car, d'un côté, le rapport des parties d'une ligne droite est celui que nous saisissons le plus facilement: et de l'autre il n'est point de rapports plus aisés à comparer entre eux, que des rapports égaux. Or, dans le mouvement uniforme, le rapport des parties du temps est égal à celui des parties correspondantes de la ligne parcourue. Le mouvement uniforme nous donne donc tout à la fois le moyen, et de comparer le rapport des parties du temps au rapport qui nous est le plus sensible, et de faire cette comparaison de la manière la plus simple; nous trouvons donc dans le mouvement uniforme la mesure la plus simple du temps.

There is certainly no suspect "chaleur" here, but there is a dignified and reassuring balance of clauses and at the same time the variety (short sentences and long sentences) which rhetoric always recommended. The first two sentences, solid and steady, lead up to an emphatic short sentence which contains the central assertion of the paragraph. This is then expanded and explained in a series of symmetrical sentences, which lead again to the satisfying reappearance of the main theme: "nous trouvons donc dans le mouvement uniforme la mesure la plus simple du temps." The whole paragraph is built of two blocks, the one seeming to echo the other; within this division other discreet but agreeable symmetries find their place. It can be read aloud with satisfaction. And all this is done without any sacrifice of truth; there can be no question of "fausses fenêtres pour la symétrie," but the patterning may be felt as a bonus by the stylistically conscious reader.

In other places d'Alembert goes a little further—and particularly at the beginning of the work, where his aim is to capture the interest of the reader. In the "Avertissement," as we have seen, he issues stern warnings to the frivolous, but even so the first few chapters do make certain concessions, if not to frivolity, then at least to fine writing. There is still nothing that could really be called "chaleur," no attempt on the author's part to rouse our emotions by showing his own involvement with the subject. The tone remains agreeably cool, with a slight tendency, much less pronounced than in Montesquieu, to the witty turn of phrase—thus on metaphysics, in the tradition of Voltaire but with less sparkle: "On peut dire en un sens de la métaphysique que tout le monde la sait ou personne, ou pour parler plus exactement, que tout le monde ignore celle que tout le monde ne peut savoir." But it is the metaphor and the simile which are the chief mark of fine writing here. D'Alembert uses these figures in a completely unoriginal way; the same old comparisons occur, used in the same old ways, their function being not to illuminate the argument, but to give dignity to the proceedings. Thus history, which he feels obliged to say something about, even though it is far from the centre of his interests, calls forth images of this sort: "Les hommes placés sur la scène du monde sont appréciés par le sage comme témoins, ou jugés comme acteurs." It is at such points in the *Eléments* that the voice of the honest philosopher gives way to the more pompous voice of the public speaker, that d'Alembert becomes, in the words of an enemy, "un joli pédant, géomètre orateur."

What we see then in the *Traité* and the *Eléments* is a limited hierarchy of styles, ranging from the rebarbatively technical to the grandly general. We can extend this range by considering works which are less narrowly philosophical, the Preliminary Discourse of the *Encyclopédie* and the *Eloges* of former academicians. These were all part of d'Alembert's campaign for the new philosophy. The *Discours préliminaire* is intended not only to explain the plan of the *Encyclopédie*, but equally to provide an imposing entrance gate and to fire readers for the greatness of the cause. Thus d'Alembert is led to depart yet further from the plain writing which is his staple. Noting the different ways in which Buffon and Fontenelle had made philosophy attractive, he himself writes up for the occasion. Not unduly so, of course; the *Discours* displays primarily the good sense of a philosopher talking to *honnêtes gens*, explaining elegantly, but not too wittily, the foundations of the encyclopedic enterprise. There are moments, however, when the subject calls forth in d'Alembert something not far removed from the suspect "chaleur." Significantly, this is less apparent in the methodological section of the *Discours* (which resembles the *Eléments*) than in the historical sketch of the progress of philosophy. Here d'Alembert is drawn towards the oratorical style of the traditional historian. Francis Bacon, the hero of the encyclopedists, is introduced in these terms:

> A la tête de ces illustres personnages doit être placé l'immortel chancelier d'Angleterre, François Bacon, dont les ouvrages si justement estimés, et plus estimés pourtant qu'ils ne sont connus, méritent encore plus notre lecture que nos éloges. A considérer les vues saines et étendues de ce grand homme, la multitude d'objets sur lesquels son esprit s'est porté, la hardiesse de son style qui réunit partout les plus sublimes images avec la précision la plus rigoureuse, on serait tenté de le regarder comme le plus grand, le plus universel, et le plus éloquent des philosophes. Bacon, né dans le sein de la nuit la plus profonde, sentit que la philosophie n'était pas encore, quoique bien des gens sans doute se flattassent d'y exceller; car plus un siècle est grossier, plus il se croit instruit de tout ce qu'il peut savoir.

The language is a long way from the modest honesty which d'Alembert tends to recommend. We notice the nobly abstract vocabulary, the banal epithets of greatness ("immortel," "illustre," "sublime"), and the conventional images, particularly that of "la nuit la plus profonde," which helps to emphasize the struggle of light and darkness that is the dominant metaphorical theme of the *Discours*. But it is the oratorical patterning which above all gives this passage its grandiose tone. Like any public speaker, d'Alembert arranges his sentences according to the traditional symmetry, which centres round the alternation of antithetical constructions and three-fold enumerations. Most typically, two ternary constructions balance one another; the enumeration of "les vues saines . . . la multitude d'objets . . . la hardiesse de son style" is set against the threefold glorification of Bacon, "le plus grand, le plus universel, et le plus éloquent des philosophes."

In an essay on style, d'Alembert speaks scornfully of "ce langage figuré, poétique, chargé de métaphores et d'antithèses, qu'on appelle, je ne sais par quelle raison, *style académique*, quoique les plus illustres membres de l'Académie Française l'aient évité avec soin et proscrit hautement dans leurs ouvrages," and goes on to assert, in his partisan way, that "on l'appellerait avec bien plus de raison *style de la chaire*." Nevertheless, we can identify the praise of Bacon as a mild example of this style, whether we call it academic or not. That it has something to do with academies, and with the Académie française in particular, is suggested by a reading of d'Alembert's *Eloges*.

The majority of these were designed to be included in a history of the Academy which d'Alembert undertook as its secretary, and were read out by their author at fashionable open sessions. Condorcet notes that these pieces are less uniformly noble in tone than earlier "éloges," such as that of Montesquieu, which were composed shortly after the death of their subject, and that they include anecdotes and "traits plaisants" which certain readers considered misplaced. Since the subjects had been dead for many years, the author was less tied to the solemnity of the funeral oration and did what he could to enliven a potentially monotonous series of panegyrics. He tells us in his *Réflexions sur les éloges* that he has deliberately varied his style and, more generally, "je n'ai rien négligé pour soutenir et intéresser l'attention des gens de lettres." The *Eloges* are usually built on a foundation of dignified but straightforward narration, the standard style of historical writing. This is constantly enlivened, however, by anecdotes, jokes, and a familiar tone, or embellished by the noble ornaments and even the would-be "chaleur" of what d'Alembert would have had to call the "style de la chaire." In the *Réflexions* he himself says that in some of his panegyrics he had adopted the style of his subject; in this way, after several rather chatty portraits of minor seventeenth-century academicians, he lets himself go in a flood of traditional rhetoric to honour the great orator Bossuet.

The *Eloge de Bossuet* is a good example of the way in which eloquence comes in to fill gaps, even for d'Alembert. (In the *Encyclopédie* article "Elocution," after stating that all true eloquence is natural, d'Alembert admits that rhetoric may have a minor role to fulfil: "les règles de l'élocution n'ont lieu, à proprement parler, et ne sont vraiment nécessaires que pour les morceaux qui ne sont pas proprement éloquents, que l'orateur compose plus à froid, et où la nature a besoin de l'art." In the same way, rhetoric helps the philosopher to talk about subjects which are really beneath his interest.) We have reason to suppose that Bossuet was not an object of true admiration for him, but the job had to be done and the panegyrist goes dutifully through the motions of the sublime—seasoned, however, with a few anecdotes. Bossuet's religious controversies, which seemed puerile to d'Alembert the philosopher, gave d'Alembert the academic secretary an opportunity to show that he too could speak like an angel:

> Là, on le voit sans cesse aux prises, soit avec l'incrédulité, soit avec l'hérésie, bravant et repoussant l'une et l'autre, et couvrant l'Église de son égide contre ce double ennemi qui cherche à l'a-néantir. Son goût pour la guerre semble le poursuivre jusque dans les pièces qu'il a consacrées à l'éloquence; il oublie quelquefois qu'il est orateur, pour se livrer à cette controverse qu'il chérit tant; et du trône où il tonne, daignant descendre dans l'arène, il quitte, si on peut parler ainsi, la foudre pour le ceste: mais il reprend bientôt cette foudre, et le dieu fait oublier l'athlète.

Here it appears that the academic rhetoric of symmetry and metaphor is the product of d'Alembert's lack of interest, or even embarrassment; it serves at the same time to conceal his true feelings from those who do not want to take the hint and to convey an ironic judgement to those who are willing to accept it.

The *Eloges* display their author's stylistic versatility. They are almost his furthest venture away from the plain style of the honest philosopher. The furthest ventures of all are probably the two short pieces in memory of Julie de Lespinasse, *Aux mânes de Mademoiselle de Lespinasse* and *Sur la tombe de Mademoiselle de Lespinasse*, both written in 1776. There is nothing philosophical about these pieces; they are highly personal, full of the "je" who had to be excluded from philosophy, and aiming to express what we must presume to be genuine emotions of love, regret, and jealousy with all the "chaleur" that their author felt. But if the subject is personal, the style is literary; d'Alembert not only quotes freely from the modern classics (Racine in particular), but he adopts all the ways of classical tragic rhetoric, apostrophe, exclamation, repetition, and indeed all the elements whose absence we noted in the *Traité de dynamique*: "Adieu, adieu, pour jamais! hélas, pour jamais! ma chère et infortunée Julie!" Only the alexandrines are missing.

D'Alembert was not a versifier. Grimm said of him that he had no style. He himself characterized his style as "serré, clair et précis, ordinaire-ment facile, sans prétention quoique châtié, quelquefois un peu sec, mais jamais de mauvais goût . . . plus d'énergie que de chaleur, plus de justesse que d'imagination, plus de noblesse que de grâce"—and it is remarkable how close this is to the definition of the ideal style of philosophical communication which he gives when talking about Malebranche in the preface to his *Eloges*, "méthodique sans sécheresse, développé sans verbiage, intéressant et sensible sans fausse chaleur, grand sans effort, et noble sans enflure." It is impossible to pick out any of his different styles as his "true" style—in speech he appears to have been far more of an individualist, far more witty and disconcerting than he ever is on paper. (An exception to this generalization is provided by his letters, for instance, those addressed to Voltaire, where he is seen as the lively, clever cynic, speaking with a voice quite different from any we hear in his published writings. Clearly, for d'Alembert, publication implied a seriousness which is strange in one whose professed faith [to Voltaire] was that the world is only fit for laughing at. D'Alembert was good at wearing different hats.) Where he is writing on his own subjects, as in most of the *Eléments*, his style is much as he describes it; at most one might question the word "énergie." Like a true academician, however, he was prepared to dress up for the occasion, as we have seen in the *Discours préliminaire* and the *Eloges*. But he stops short of verse, which was for him the final step in rhetorical embellishment. Yet if he did not actually write verse, he was led by his academic life to think and write *about* it, and what he says on the subject is both curious and characteristic of the man and his times.

Reading d'Alembert on philosophy and poetry is rather like reading a modern exposition of the "two cultures" question. He was first and foremost a scientist, anxious to defend the value of science and the "esprit philosophique." One of his aims was to conquer the Academy for the new philosophy, but he knew that poetry and oratory occupied a place of eminence; moreover, as a member of the Académie française, he became interested in gaining a reputation as a man of taste and eloquence. He therefore set out to reconcile the two enemies. (A title of one of his typical academic performances is : *Dialogue entre la poésie et la philosophie, pour servir de préliminaire et de base à un traité de paix et d'amitié perpétuelle entre l'une et l'autre.*) In order to do this, he must show that philosophers can appreciate poetry, that the vogue of scientific philosophy is not detrimental to literature (though he does in fact admit this charge in his *Discours préliminaire*), and that the philosopher has qualities which the man of letters should respect.

Basically, for him, the appeal of poetry lay in difficulty conquered. He believed that it was the ability to dance gracefully in chains which distinguished the good poet: "moins nous adoucirons la rigueur de nos lois poétiques, plus il y aura de gloire à les surmonter" (*Réflexions sur la poésie*). Pleasing the reader of taste is like running an obstacle-race: "On impose au poète les lois les plus sévères; et pour comble de rigueur, on lui défend de laisser voir ce qu'il lui en a coûté pour s'y soumettre" (*Suite des réflexions sur la poésie, et sur l'ode en particulier*). But this pleasure in the harmony of a virtuoso performance is not enough to satisfy the adult reader. D'Alembert notes repeatedly—though perhaps not correctly—that poetry has fallen out of favour in his century; this is because philosophy has taught men that a poem must be judged not only by its own standards of beauty, but by the standards of sense which apply equally to prose writing. So, as well as being pretty, poetry must be worth reading for its ideas, taking "ideas" in its broadest sense; the most valuable poet (and Virgil and Homer do badly on this test) is the one who best survives translation:

> Les vers qu'on retient avec facilité, qu'on se rappelle avec plaisir, sont ceux dont le mérite ne se borne pas à l'arrangement harmonieux des paroles. Un sentiment confus semble nous dire, qu'il ne faut pas mettre à exprimer les choses plus de peine et de soin qu'elles ne valent; et que ce qui paraîtrait commun en prose, ne mérite pas l'appareil de la versification. Toute poésie, on en convient, perd à être traduite; mais la plus belle peut-être est celle qui y perd le moins.

The way to reconcile poetry and philosophy is therefore to make poetry philosophical. Although d'Alembert is anxious not to put his case too crudely or to condemn pleasant novelties, his real preference is for instructive verse; here is the doctrine expressed in its classic form:

> C'est avec cette sévérité que le philosophe examine et juge les ouvrages de poésie. Pour lui le premier mérite et le plus indispensable dans tout écrivain, est celui des pensées: la poésie ajoute à ce mérite celui de la difficulté vaincue dans l'expression; mais ce second mérite, très estimable quand il se joint au premier, n'est plus qu'un effort puéril dès qu'il est prodigué en pure perte et sur des objets futiles.
>
> *(Réflexions sur la poésie)*

There is a note of contempt here and elsewhere which makes one suspect that the praise which d'Alembert of the Académie française gives to poetry is often but patronizing lip-service. Just as he is willing to go through the motions of eloquence in his own popularization, so he is willing to allow publicly the value of an activity which he really rather despises. His attitude is not unlike that of the adult Descartes—but Descartes had the good fortune not to be an academician. And it is perhaps the same with the theatre. Although he went along with Voltaire in calling for a theatre in Geneva, d'Alembert seems to have had a low opinion of dramatic art; his defence of it is to describe it as a toy for sick children. The child needs toys, plays and poems; the adult philosopher will not mind humouring the child. One understands why Diderot exclaimed in exasperation, after hearing about one of his colleague's ventures into literary theory: "Qu'il s'en tienne aux équations. C'est son lot."

Turgot on Progress, Sociology, and Economics

Ronald L. Meek

There are minds to whom nature has given a memory which is capable of assembling together a large number of pieces of knowledge, a power of exact reasoning which is capable of comparing them and arranging them in a manner which puts them in their full light, but to whom at the same time she has denied that fire of genius which invents and which opens up new roads for itself. Created to unite past discoveries under one point of view, to clarify and even to perfect them, if they are not torches which shine with their own light, they are diamonds which brilliantly reflect a borrowed light, but which total darkness would confound with the meanest stones.

—TURGOT, *Philosophical Review*

THE "PHILOSOPHICAL REVIEW" AND "ON UNIVERSAL HISTORY"

Turgot was fond of this comparison between "torches which shine with their own light" and "diamonds which brilliantly reflect a borrowed light." The particular version quoted above is from the discourse which he read at the *Maison de Sorbonne* in December 1750. But we find it earlier than this, in a set of notes on "The Causes of the Progress and Decline of the Sciences and the Arts" which he apparently wrote in 1748; and later than this, in almost the same form, in his notes on "Universal History" which probably date from 1751. Whether he had himself in mind when he wrote this passage we do not know, but the description fits him so admirably that this may not be beyond the bounds of possibility.

Certainly, at any rate, Turgot set out from the beginning with the conscious intention of becoming a polymath rather than a specialist in one particular field of enquiry. There is extant an extraordinary "List of Works to be Written" which he apparently prepared at the outset of his career. It begins with "*The Barmecides*, a tragedy" and ends with "*On luxury*, political reflections"; and in between these are forty-eight others, including works on universal history, the origin of languages, love and marriage, political geography, natural theology, morality, and economics, as well as numerous translations from foreign languages, literary works, and treatises on scientific subjects. Even making allowances for the natural ebullience and optimism of an extremely gifted and precocious young man, this list of subjects is remarkable; but what is even more remarkable is the fact that Turgot managed, during his short life of only fifty-four years (1727–81), to make some kind of contribution to so many of them, or at least to retain an active and intelligent interest in them.

Turgot's notes, mentioned above, on "The Causes of the Progress and Decline of the Sciences and the Arts," were probably written in 1748, at any rate if we are to judge from a marginal note referring to a prize to be offered early in 1749 by the Academy of Soissons for a discourse on this subject. It is clear from these fragmentary but quite extensive notes that many of the views which Turgot was later to express in the *Philosophical Review* and *On Universal History* were already formed before he entered the Sorbonne: the notes obviously constituted part of the raw material upon which he drew when he was writing these two pieces. A number of the more picturesque analogies used in the latter are to be found already in the notes; there are distinct traces of the "materialist" approach which he was later to employ much more extensively; the critique of Montesquieu's theory of the influence of climate which appears in *On Universal History* is present in the notes in embryo; and there, too, is the famous prophecy about the coming revolt of the American colonies. But three major unifying constituents of the later works are still lacking. First, although there is a passing reference to Locke's notion that "all our ideas come to us from the senses," there is no indication of the important role which this notion was later to play in Turgot's thinking. Second, although the notes contain several references to different arts and sciences being "perfected," no general doctrine of perfectibility is explicitly stated. And third, there is no indication of the stadial theory of socio-economic development which was to become part of the framework of *On Universal History*.

In a critique which Turgot wrote in March 1750 of a book on the origin of languages by Maupertuis, however, the sensationalist theory of Locke pervades the whole, and, even more important, the outlines of a stadial theory of the development of early society are fairly clearly delineated. "Thence arose the different languages," Turgot writes, "according to whether the people were hunters, shepherds, or husbandmen. . . . The hunter would have few words, very vivid, not closely linked together, and progress would be slow; the shepherd, with his peaceful life, would construct a gentler and more refined language; the husbandman, one that was colder and more coherent. The general idea implied here—that early society proceeds naturally and successively through the hunting, pastoral, and agricultural stages, each with its own "superstructure" of languages, laws, customs, etc.—was destined to be of great importance, not only for Turgot's own work, but also for the emergence and development of social science as a whole in the eighteenth century.

It is possible that the inspiration for this seminal idea came to Turgot from Montesquieu. At the end of Book I of *L'Esprit des lois*, Montesquieu says that the laws ought to be related to (*inter alia*) "the principal occupation of the natives, whether husbandmen, huntsmen, or shepherds"; and in Book XVIII ("Of Laws in the Relation they Bear to the Nature of the Soil") we find the following statement:

The laws have a very great relation to the manner in which the several nations procure their subsistence. There should be a code of laws of a much larger extent for a nation attached to trade and navigation than for people who are content with cultivating the earth. There should be a much greater for the latter than for those who subsist by their flocks and herds. There must be a still greater for these than for such as live by hunting.

These statements, and some of the rather haphazard comments which follow, may well have seized Turgot's imagination. But it must be emphasised that the clarity with which Turgot expressed the idea, the way in which he refined and developed it, and the uses to which he put it, mark him and not Montesquieu out as the one who really deserves the name of innovator.

On 3 July 1750, in his capacity as *prieur*, Turgot gave the first of his two discourses at the Sorbonne, under the title *The Advantages which the Establishment of Christianity has Procured for the Human Race*. This rather over-eloquent piece is usually compared unfavourably with his second discourse of 11 December 1750—the famous *Philosophical Review of the Successive Advances of the Human Mind*. . . . But the 3 July discourse is rather more significant than it is usually made out to be. In it, Turgot sets out to show how the doctrines of Christianity have helped to temper human passions, to perfect governments, and to make men better and happier. He begins by considering the effects of the Christian religion on men considered in themselves, concentrating here on such matters as the preservation of classical literature by the monks, the abolition of cruel customs such as the exposure of children, and, generally, the way in which Christianity has improved morals and manners and made men more humane. He then goes on, in the second and more interesting part of the discourse, "to examine the progress of the art of government, and to show how Christianity has contributed to it." After a diatribe against great legislators, whose laws have a tendency to "acquire a fatal immutability," he goes on to say this:

> More happy are the nations whose laws have not been established by such great geniuses; they are at any rate perfected, although slowly and through a thousand detours, without principles, without perspectives, without a fixed plan; chance and circumstances have often led to wiser laws than have the researches and efforts of the human mind; an abuse which had been observed would give rise to a law; the abuse of that law would give rise to a second which modified it: by passing successively from one excess to the opposite excess, men little by little drew nearer to the happy medium.

The important thing here, of course, is that it is not Christianity—nor, apparently, even the Deity—which produces "these slow and successive advances." They occur, as it were, of themselves, and the role of Christianity is confined to eradicating injustices from the laws, spreading the idea that men—and nations—are brothers, and moderating the potentially despotic behaviour of monarchs.

In the discourse of 11 December 1750 these "slow and successive advances" become in effect the main theme, and the part played by Christianity in the historical process of attaining perfection is summarised in a single paragraph. And by the time one reaches this paragraph, with its question "Holy religion, could it be that I should forget you?", one feels strongly not only that it could, but also that it almost was. Perhaps this is unfair to Turgot: it could be argued that the two discourses are in fact all of a piece—both are about progress and perfection, but the first deals with their sacred and the second with their secular aspects. There is an interesting parallel here with Bossuet's *Discours sur l'Histoire Universelle*, by which Turgot was greatly (if perversely) influenced: in that book, a sacred history (mainly of the Jews) is followed by a completely separate secular history entitled "The Empires." Possibly what appears at first sight to be a conflict between Turgot's 3 July and 11 December discourses is merely another example of this kind of conscious and disciplined compartmentalisation. But it is rather more probable, I think, that the conflict was, at least in part, a real one, reflecting a mental struggle which was going on in his mind in the months immediately before he announced that he was abandoning his ecclesiastical career.

"The whole human race, through alternate periods of rest and unrest, of weal and woe, goes on advancing, although at a slow pace, towards greater perfection." This is the main theme of Turgot's 11 December discourse, in which the idea of progress which we particularly associate with the second half of the eighteenth century was put forward for the first time. The oratorical flights are sometimes tiresome, and the ritualistic passages at the end sound rather strangely in modern ears, but for all that the new message is clear enough. The keynote is sounded in the first two paragraphs. The "succession of mankind," says Turgot, "affords from age to age an ever-changing spectacle. . . . All the ages are bound up with one another by a succession of causes and effects . . . . Thus the human race, considered over the period since its origin, appears to the eye of a philosopher as one vast whole, which itself, like each individual, has its infancy and its advancement." And this "advancement," as the next paragraph makes clear, is "towards greater perfection."

The aim of the discourse, then, is to illustrate this idea by indicating "the main lines of the progress of the human mind," with particular reference to the development of the arts and sciences. The aim is, of course, overambitious, and it is often difficult to discern these "main lines" beneath the wealth of detail and apostrophes. The unifying theme, however, is the Lockean notion that "the senses constitute the unique source of our ideas," and the associated notion that "the need perfects the tool." Turgot's argument seems to be that since all men have the same organs and senses, the spectacle of the same universe has always given them the same ideas; and since their needs and inclinations are broadly the same, they have always originated and perfected the same arts, and have proceeded through roughly the same stages of development from barbarism to refinement. But "they do not all move forward at the same rate along the road which is marked out for them." Turgot argues that "circumstances" either encourage or discourage development, and it is the infinite variety of these "circumstances" which brings about the manifest inequality in the progress of nations.

Given his general aim and this conceptual framework, then, Turgot is obliged to deal with two main questions—first, what exactly are these "circumstances" which either increase or decrease the rate of progress; and second, why exactly is it that the general long-run tendency is in fact towards "greater perfection" rather than towards, say, the reverse? Turgot does not clearly distinguish between these two questions, and his answer to the second and more important one is by no means fully worked out. The elements of his answer to it, however, may with a little effort be disentangled from the rest. First, the general process of the growth and development of societies is a *natural* process, comparable to the process of growth of the individual from infancy to adulthood, or that of the plant from seed to flower. Second, the main (although by no means the only) reasons why societies tend in the long run to develop towards "greater perfection" are to be sought in the *economic* sphere. In the discourse, Turgot emphasises in this connection (*a*) the crucial importance of the emergence in the agricultural stage of development of a *social surplus*, which not only makes possible the development of "towns, trade, the useful arts and accomplishments, the division of occupations," etc., but also facilitates the creation of a leisured class which "bends all its strength to the cultivation of the arts"; (*b*) the way in which the development of commerce is associated with the perfection of "astronomy, navigation, and geography"; (*c*) the important role of the towns—"the centres of trade and the backbone of society"—in preventing the decline of the arts and sciences in periods of barbarism; and (*d*) the way in which the "mechanical arts" are preserved in times of general decline by the "needs of life," and are developed in the long run merely by virtue of the fact that time passes. To describe Turgot's argument in these terms is not, I think, to misrepresent it, although one is bound to look at it to some extent with the hindsight afforded by one's knowledge of his later work in this field.

All these ideas were clarified and developed further in *On Universal History,* which, together with its companion work *On Political Geography,* was written by Turgot (according to Du Pont) "while he was at the Sorbonne, or shortly after he left it." Du Pont tells us that Turgot was planning a succession of three works, of which the first would have been Universal History, the second Political Geography, and the third a treatise on the Science of Government. *On Political Geography* is interesting not only as further evidence of the extraordinary breadth and novelty of the young Turgot's interests and ideas, but also because it contains an important development of the "three stages" theory. Turgot's notes consist essentially of a description of five "political maps of the world," the first of which would contain details of (*inter alia*) the following:

> The successive changes in the manner of life of men, and the order in which they have followed one another: peoples who are shepherds, hunters, husbandmen.
>
> The causes which have been able to keep certain peoples for longer periods in the state of hunters, then shepherds. The differences which result from these three states, in relation to the number of men, to the movements of nations, to the greater or lesser degree of ease in surmounting the barriers by which nature has, so to speak, assigned to different societies their portion of the terrestrial globe, to communications, to the greater or lesser degree of ease with which peoples are intermingled.

And the second "political map of the world," similarly, would contain details of:

> The first formation of governments among peoples who are savages, hunters, shepherds, husbandmen. The variations relative to these three manners of life.

The "three stages" theory which is expressed so clearly here by Turgot was, as I have already said, of great importance in the subsequent development of social science in the eighteenth century. Not only did it enable a plausible explanation of *differences* between societies to be given; but it also facilitated the formulation of a general theory of the *development* of society from lower to higher levels.

In *On Universal History*, Turgot makes a much more extensive use of the "three stages" theory than in any of his earlier works. After a short introduction in which he describes the aim of "universal history" as he understands it, he proceeds in the first of the two "discourses" of which the work consists to consider the state of mankind immediately after the Flood. In the beginning, when men could devote themselves to nothing but obtaining their subsistence, they were primarily hunters, in much the same situation as the savages of America. But in countries where certain animals like oxen, sheep, and horses were to be found, "the pastoral way of life" was introduced, resulting in an increase in wealth and a greater understanding of "the idea of property." Eventually, in fertile countries, pastoral peoples moved on to the state of agriculture, and as a result of the surplus which agriculture was able to generate there arose "towns, trade, and all the useful arts and accomplishments," a leisured class, and so on. Within this conceptual framework, Turgot sets an account of wars and conquests among early peoples, the ways in which different nations were led to intermingle, and the overall effects of this intermingling.

Immediately after this section there is an important passage in which Turgot comes very close to the idea, later to be used so effectively by the members of the Scottish Historical School, that the development of society is essentially a kind of unintended by-product of the conflict of human wills and actions which are often directed towards quite different ends. The passions of ambitious men, says Turgot, "have led them on their way without their being aware of where they were going. . . . They were, so to speak, the leading-strings with which nature and its Author guided the human race in its infancy. . . . It is only through upheavals and ravages that nations have been extended, and that order and government have in the long run been perfected."

> I seem to see [Turgot says] a huge army, every movement of which is directed by some mighty genius. When the military signals are given, when the trumpets sound tumultuously and the drums beat, whole squadrons of cavalry move off, the very horses are filled with a passion which has no aim, and each part of the army makes its way through the obstacles without knowing what may result from it: the leader alone sees the combined effect of all these different movements. Thus the passions have led to the multiplication of ideas, the extension of knowledge, and the perfection of the mind, in the absence of that reason whose day had not yet come and which would been less powerful if its reign had arrived earlier.

One feels very strongly here that when Turgot speaks of the way in which, through this kind of mechanism, "nature and its Author" guided the human race, it is nature rather than its Author to which he is mainly referring— that he is, in fact, feeling his way towards the idea that social development is due to the unfolding of certain immanent laws of history rather than to the conscious intervention of the Deity. This is a point on which I shall have something more to say later.

In the remaining part of the first "discourse," Turgot is concerned in the main with the development of different forms of government—as related in particular to the size and geographical situation of the nation concerned—and with the formation and conflicts of empires. These sections, although they contain many stimulating insights, are perhaps not as well organised as the earlier ones. A number of interesting themes are developed however, notably the association of the "spirit of equality" with the "spirit of commerce," and the idea that knowledge and reason almost always, in one way or another, prevail over force. And towards the end, when Turgot comes on to the subject of slavery, the "three stages" idea is brought in once again as a conceptual framework.

In the second "discourse," Turgot is concerned mainly with progress in the arts and sciences. He begins with a fairly detailed account of the sensationalist psychology which, as we have already seen, was one of his great unifying themes, and, closely linked with this, a sketch of his theory of language. He then propounds a kind of "law of uneven development" of the human mind comparable to the similar law relating to human society which he has in effect put forward in the first "discourse," the basic idea here being that genius is spread evenly throughout all peoples, but that "the chances of education and of events" either develop it or leave it buried in obscurity. The inequality in the development of knowledge which results from this is closely associated—both as cause and as effect—with that inequality in the general development of the nations concerned, which Montesquieu tries mistakenly to account for in terms of differences in climate.

In the wide-ranging accounts of the development of music, dance, poetry, history, metaphysics, physics, mathematics, logic, the arts of taste, and eloquence which follow this introduction, a number of the themes which Turgot has used before—including the "three stages" theory—reappear yet again. The most pervasive theme, perhaps, is the simple idea that the arts and sciences come to man not from heaven but from earth—from his sensations, from his psychological and economic needs, from experiences "which are common to and within the reach of all men," and that they change as these sensations, needs, and experiences change. This theme is prominent in Turgot's account of the way in which the needs of tillage and navigation developed astronomy; the primitive origins of music, dance, and poetry; the reason why the fables of all peoples resemble one another; the origins of design, sculpture, and painting; the origin of mathematics; the "god-making" activities of early peoples; the reason why the English have not been able to produce any great painters; the connection between trade and taste; the reasons for the continuation of the mechanical arts when letters and taste have fallen; the necessity for the cultivation and perfection of the mechanical arts in order that "real physics and the higher philosophy" could arise; and in a dozen other places as well. Turgot is not consistent in his use of this theme, and it appears side by side with a number of others, but it would be absurd to pretend that it does not exist or that it is not important.

The final point I want to make about *On Universal History* is that in it Turgot goes some way towards clarifying his views about the state of perfection towards which society is advancing in the Age of Reason. In the *Philosophical Review* the general picture we get is one of an infinite advance on all fronts, of everlasting progress in every sphere, and we are apt to pass over the following significant paragraph:

> Knowledge of nature and of truth is as infinite as they are: the arts, whose aim is to please us, are as limited as we are. Time constantly brings to light new discoveries in the sciences; but poetry, painting, and music have a fixed limit which the genius of

languages, the imitation of nature, and the limited sensibility of our organs determine, which they attain by slow steps and which they cannot surpass. The great men of the Augustan age reached it, and are still our models.

In *On Universal History* this idea is repeated and expanded a little. In particular, Turgot describes in a very interesting way the manner in which poetry, although it has already reached perfection in certain basic respects, will continue to change and progress in certain other respects as time goes on.

On Universal History finishes in midstream, just at the point where Turgot is embarking upon an interesting discussion of the way in which progress in the sciences depends upon "inventions and technical processes"; and the great plan of a geographical-cum-sociological-cum-political treatise was never achieved. Turgot became a civil servant and statesman, and his intellectual interests turned more and more in the direction of economics. (It is curious—and perhaps significant—that one of his economic works contains the first clear statement of the law of diminishing returns in agriculture, which was later to be used by Malthus and some of his contemporaries as a weapon *against* the "perfectibilists" of their time.) Echoes of his early perfectibilist views, and, more particularly, of the theory of history with which they were associated, are however to be found scattered among some of his later works on language and literature, in some of his letters to friends, and in his economic work—notably, as we shall see, in the *Reflections*. Turgot gradually became known, at any rate among a small circle, as a pioneer perfectibilist, and the verbal tradition was handed on by men like Du Pont and, more importantly, Condorcet. In his *Life of Turgot,* which appeared in 1786, Condorcet described Turgot's view concerning the unbounded perfectibility of the human understanding and the limitless progress of the sciences as "one of the great principles of his philosophy," which he "never once abandoned." And when, a few years later, in the shadow of the guillotine, Condorcet came to write his own great work on the advances of the human mind, he gave Turgot his full due, placing him together with Price and Priestley as "the first and most illustrious apostles" of the doctrine of the limitless perfectibility of the human species—that new doctrine which, in Condorcet's words, was to give "the final blow to the already tottering structure of prejudice" (*Esquisse d'un tableau historique des progrès de l'esprit humain*). Bliss was it indeed, in that dawn, to be alive.

THE "REFLECTIONS"

I have done a lot of scribbling since I saw you last [wrote Turgot to Du Pont on 9 December 1766]. . . . I have drawn up some *Questions* for the two Chinese about whom I have spoken to you, and, in order to make their object and meaning clear, I have prefaced them with a kind of analytical sketch of the work of society and of the distribution of wealth. I have not put any algebra at all in it, and there is nothing of the *Tableau Économique* but the metaphysical part; moreover, I have left on one side a large number of questions which would have to be dealt with in order to make the work complete, but I have dealt pretty thoroughly with what concerns the formation and course of capitals, interest on money, etc.; it is a kind of groundwork.

The "two Chinese" mentioned by Turgot, according to Du Pont, were MM. Ko and Yang, two clever young men who, after having been brought up in France by the Jesuits, were being sent back to Canton with a pension from the Crown so that they could carry on a correspondence about Chinese literature and science. Turgot gave them books, valuable instruments, the *Questions* referred to, and the *Reflections* (presumably in manuscript form). But the departure of MM. Ko and Yang, who were thus unknowingly immortalised, was of course only the occasion and not the cause of the production of the *Reflections*. Even though Turgot himself described the work in a letter to Du Pont some years later as having had "no other object than to render intelligible the questions I put to the Chinese about their country," there is no need to take this too literally: Turgot was adept at finding pegs on which to hang important works, and if Ko and Yang had not conveniently presented themselves he would no doubt have found some other occasion for summarising the great system of economic theory at which he had arrived by the end of 1766.

This system cannot be fully understood, I believe, without an appreciation of the way in which its leading propositions were connected with Turgot's historical and sociological theories. But let us leave this on one side for the time being, and consider briefly the development of Turgot's main *economic* ideas up to 1766.

Among the "works to be written" in the extraordinary list mentioned above was a "Treatise on circulation; interest, banking, Law's system, credit, exchange, and commerce;" and among Turgot's papers there is a manuscript, apparently written about 1753–54, entitled "Plan of a Work on Commerce, the Circulation and Interest of Money, the Wealth of States," which was presumably intended as a first step in the realisation of this part of his programme. This document is interesting partly because of the absence from it of any peculiarly "Physiocratic" principles, and partly because of the presence in it of (*a*) a very clear statement of the way in which supply and demand determine the equilibrium price of a commodity, which can be regarded as a first sketch of the rather more developed treatment of this subject in the *Reflections* (XXXI and XXXII; numbering refers to Meek translation); (*b*) a clear statement in favour of free competition and against the regulation of prices; and (*c*) a fairly clear statement, remarkable enough for its time, to the effect that free competition would establish a price for all commodities which was sufficient to cover not only the vendor's subsistence and paid-out costs, but also "the interest on the advances which their trade requires." Even if the "vendors" referred to in the latter statement are assumed to be merchants (in the narrow sense) rather than producers, the statement when read in its context may be regarded as the germ of the *general* theory of returns to capital which was later to be used with such striking effect in the *Reflections*.

In 1759, when the celebrated Vincent de Gournay died and Marmontel asked Turgot (who had known Gournay well and been greatly influenced by him) to provide some notes about him for an obituary, Turgot wrote an *Eloge* which purported to summarise Gournay's economic beliefs. Whether the summary was a wholly accurate one so far as Gournay's views were concerned is rather doubtful, but there is very little doubt that it represented Turgot's own views at the time. The work is noteworthy for an elaborate and uncompromising statement of the *laissez-faire* principle, and for a number of passages which indicate that Quesnay's influence, as well as that of Gournay, was already becoming important. Near the beginning of the piece, Turgot ascribes to Gournay the view that "a worker who manufactures a piece of material adds real wealth to the total wealth of the State"; and a few pages further on he similarly ascribes to him the view that "the only real wealth which the State possesses is the annual product of its land *and of the industry of its inhabitants*," and that the sum of the revenues produced annually in the State consists of "the net revenue of each piece of land *and the net product of the industry of each individual*." These non-Physiocratic (or perhaps deliberately anti-Physiocratic) statements, however, are followed shortly afterwards by three distinct bows in the Physiocratic direction: a favourable reference to Quesnay's article *Corn*; a statement that it is "agriculture and commerce, *or rather agriculture animated by commerce*" which is the source of the revenue accruing to the State; and, more important, a rather implausible ascription to Gournay of the view that "all taxes, of whatever kind, are always in the last analysis paid by the proprietor of land." The latter statement, and the advocacy of a single tax on land rent which accompanies it, would seem at first sight to be logically incompatible with the views ascribed to Gournay earlier in the piece—and this was indeed a real problem, with which Turgot was later to wrestle in the *Reflections*. Even more important, however, is a statement in the *Eloge* to the effect that a high rate of interest "excludes the nation from all branches of commerce of which the product is not one or two per cent above the current rate of interest"—a statement which was to reappear in a generalised and more accurate form in the *Reflections* (LXXXIX), and which suggests that by 1759 Turgot had already advanced a considerable way towards his general theory of the returns to capital.

Between 1759 and 1766, the date of the writing of the *Reflections*, the main intellectual influence on Turgot was of course that of Physiocracy.

He would almost certainly have seen a copy of the "third edition" of the *Tableau Economique* when Quesnay distributed it privately in 1759; and, the period from 1759 to 1766 was precisely that in which almost all of the most important economic works of Quesnay and Mirabeau were published. The basic economic idea of the Physiocrats, upon which a great deal of the remainder of their system depended, was their doctrine of the exclusive "productivity" of agriculture. It was only agriculture, they claimed, which was inherently capable of yielding a disposable surplus over necessary cost—the famous "net product," which according to them crystallised out into land rent. Manufacture and commerce, they argued, were *not* "productive" *in this sense*—i.e., they were not inherently capable of yielding a disposable surplus over necessary cost. Turgot was evidently very impressed by this doctrine, although his own interpretation of it, and the uses to which he put it, were appreciably different from Quesnay's.

But the feature of Quesnay's work which obviously impressed Turgot more than anything else was its emphasis on the necessity of *capital* in agriculture. "M. Quesnay," wrote Turgot in his "Plan of a *Mémoire* on Taxes," "has dealt with the mechanism of cultivation, wholly based on very large *original advances* and demanding *annually other advances* which are equally necessary." And in the same document, Turgot gave Quesnay the credit for having been the first to lay down clearly the true distinction between *gross product* and *net product*, and "to exclude from the *net product* the profits of the cultivator, which are the inducement, the unique and indispensable cause of cultivation." It is very significant that Turgot should have singled out the latter point, because it was precisely on this that Quesnay was *not* clear. What was now required, Turgot came to believe, was (*a*) a generalisation of Quesnay's concept of "advances," and its use as the basis for an explanation of the economic "mechanism" *as a whole*— i.e., not simply for an explanation of the "mechanism of cultivation"; and (*b*) a clarification and development of the idea that the profit of the entrepreneur who makes the "advances" is part of the absolutely necessary expenses of production. Both these themes begin to appear in Turgot's work from about 1763 onwards. By 1766 he is talking clearly about the existence and crucial importance of an entrepreneurial class—that "precious species of men" who turn their capitals to account not only in agriculture but also "in every other kind of commerce." What still appears to be missing is a clear recognition that "commerce" in this connection includes not only "commerce" in the strict sense—i.e. buying and selling—but also manufacturing. Turgot is still talking about enterprises "in agriculture and commerce": it is not until the *Reflections* that he begins to talk clearly and consistently about "agricultural, manufacturing, and commercial enterprises."

In this respect, an important influence on Turgot on the eve of his composition of the *Reflections* may possibly have been that of Hume, most of whose economic essays (with which Turgot was of course quite familiar) had been published as early as 1752, and who was himself in Paris from October 1763 to January 1766. In the latter half of 1766, Turgot corresponded with Hume on the question of the incidence of taxation, and in particular on the question of the validity or otherwise of the proposition that all taxes are ultimately paid by the landowners. In one of Hume's letters to Turgot, which was apparently written in late September 1766, he made the following point:

> I beg you also to consider, that, besides the Proprietors of Land and the labouring Poor, there is in every civilized Community a very large and a very opulent Body who employ their Stocks in Commerce and who enjoy a great Revenue from their giving Labour to the poorer sort. I am perswaded that in France and England the Revenue of this kind is much greater than that which arises from Land: For besides Merchants, properly speaking, I comprehend in this Class all Shop-Keepers and Master-Tradesmen of every Species. Now it is very just, that these shoud pay for the Support of the Community, which can only be where Taxes are lay'd on Consumptions. There seems to me no Pretence for saying that this order of Men are necessitated to throw their Taxes on the Proprietors of Land, since their Profits and Income can surely bear Retrenchment.

Hume's explicit division of that "very opulent Body who employ their Stocks in Commerce" into "Merchants, properly speaking" on the one hand and "all Shop-Keepers and Master-Tradesmen of every Species" on the other was quite remarkable for its time, and may well have helped to supply Turgot with an essential constituent of his system.

We do not know why Turgot kept the *Reflections* by him for three years before sending it to Du Pont for publication, or whether the work was changed and developed in any way during those three years. So far as the first question is concerned, it is possible that Turgot was waiting to see how *Ephémérides* would progress under Du Pont's editorship; but it seems rather more likely that he was hoping that he might find time to "make something passable" of a piece which, however much thought may have gone into the making of its basic propositions, was no doubt written down hastily and with perhaps a little more than passing reference to the occasion of the departure of MM. Ko and Yang. On the second question, it would seem unlikely that any really substantial changes were made in the work during the period concerned. The significant thing here is that during those three years Turgot's ideas on a number of the subjects treated in the *Reflections* underwent a certain amount of development. In his notes on the *mémoires* which Graslin and Saint-Péravy submitted in 1767 for a prize offered by the Royal Agricultural Society of Limoges, for example, Turgot not only put forward his famous statement of the law of diminishing returns, but also appreciably clarified his analysis of the nature of entrepreneurial profit—an analysis carried to a still higher stage in his letters of October–December 1770 to Terray on the corn trade. Yet there is no real trace of any of these developments in the *Reflections*.

Turning now to the *Reflections* itself, one of the most interesting things about it is the way in which the staggeringly "modern" theory of capital in which it culminates, and the basic "Physiocratic" theory of production of which it makes use, are both set within the context of a broad historical and sociological analysis, deriving from Turgot's early works of the Sorbonne period. Turgot's intellectual development in this respect mirrored that of his great contemporary Adam Smith and anticipated that of Marx: all three began with some kind of "materialist" theory of history, and then went on to develop from this a system of economics which in one way or another embodied or made use of its basic propositions. It is perfectly possible, of course, if one wishes, to abstract Turgot's theory of capital from its context and present it purely as an anticipation of the best nineteenth-century analytical work in this field—which it indeed was. But by doing this alone, one tends to underestimate the brilliance of Turgot's achievement, and cuts oneself off from any hope of understanding the way in which the "modern" and "Physiocratic" parts of his analysis were related to one another.

Turgot's main aim in the *Reflections* was to investigate the way in which the economic "machine" operated in a society where there were three main classes or "orders" of economic agents—landowners, wage-earners, *and capitalist entrepreneurs*. His very postulation of an entrepreneurial society of this kind was a highly remarkable achievement, given the time and place in which he was working: Turgot evidently possessed to the full that peculiar feature of genius which sometimes allows it not only to observe what *is* typical, but also to discern and analyse what is *becoming* typical. But even more remarkable was the way in which he appreciated, whether consciously or unconsciously, that one could arrive at an understanding in depth of such a society by beginning with an analysis of the working of the "machine" *in the type of society which historically preceded it*, and then asking oneself what alterations in its working were brought about when a new class of capitalist entrepreneurs entered upon the historic scene. This is a methodological device which was later to be used very effectively by Smith, Ricardo, and Marx; the only real difference between their approach and Turgot's—and it is indeed a significant difference—is that whereas the preceding state of society which they postulated was one in which there were neither landlords nor capitalists, so that the labourer owned what Smith called "the whole produce of his labour," that which Turgot postulated was one in which landlords—although not of course capitalists— *did* exist.

What Turgot did, in effect, was to accept the view—already adumbrated by Quesnay and Mirabeau in their *Philosophie Rurale* and later to be developed by the Scottish Historical School—that after the hunting, pastoral, and agricultural stages society proceeded to a fourth stage—the so-called "commercial" stage; to assume that in this fourth stage a capitalist or entrepreneurial form of organisation was paramount; and to analyse this form of society by examining the way in which it arose from and impinged upon the "agricultural" stage and altered the basic relations which were characteristic of it.

Turgot's starting-point in the *Reflections*, then, is a society which has already proceeded through the hunting and pastoral stages (LIV) to the *agricultural stage*. This society is characterised (*a*) by the social division of labour and the mutual exchange of the products of the different kinds of labour (I–IV); (*b*) by a basic social division between the class of cultivators, which is "productive" in the sense that the fertility of the soil enables it to produce a surplus over subsistence, and the class of artisans, which is "stipendiary" in the sense that it is in effect supported by this surplus (V–VIII); (*c*) by the eventual emergence of a "disposable" class of private landowners, to whom the surplus or "net product" of the land accrues in the form of "revenue" (IX–XVIII); and (*d*) by the existence of various different arrangements which the landowners may make with the cultivators in order to get their land cultivated and to ensure that they receive the "net product" (XIX–XXVIII). These arrangements, which are dealt with in more or less the order in which they actually appeared on the historic scene, culminate in "tenant-farming, or the letting-out of Land" (XXVI). The importance of the latter kind of arrangement, as the sequel shows, is that the farmers to whom the land is leased are *capitalist entrepreneurs*, who make all the "advances" involved in cultivation and pay the landowners the "net product" in the form of an annual rent.

Having at last—one quarter of the way through the book—introduced the concept of *capital*, Turgot proceeds immediately (XXIX) to the subject of "capitals in general, and of the revenue of money," thereby making the vital transition from the agricultural society which was his historical (and analytical) starting-point to the specifically *capitalist* or *entrepreneurial* society which it was his main concern to examine. He begins with what may appear at first sight to be a digression (XXX–XLVIII) on the use of gold and silver on commerce and the general principles according to which the prices of exchangeable commodities are determined in a competitive market. A "digression" of this kind, however, over-long though it may perhaps be, was essential in order to set the stage for much of what was to follow. *Capitals* are then reintroduced, and the historical process of their accumulation—at first in the form of various items of "movable wealth" and then in the form of money—is briefly discussed (XLIX–L).

The ordering of the sections which immediately follow leaves something to be desired: it is not always easy, as Turgot found at this point, to make history and analysis run hand in hand. But the main lines of his argument are clear enough. "Advances" in the form of movable wealth are necessary in every occupation (LI). They are necessary, first, in *agriculture*, where thay have historically taken various different forms (LII–LV), and where the demands of large-scale cultivation (LXIV) lead to the separation of the broad class of cultivators into ordinary wage-earners and "Entrepreneurs or Capitalists who make all the advances" (LXV), the latter necessarily receiving, over and above the return of their capital, their "wages," and compensation for their various costs, "a profit equal to the revenue they could acquire with their capital without any labour" (LXII–LXIII). They are necessary, second, in *manufacture and industry* (LIX), where large-scale production leads similarly to the separation of the industrial stipendiary class into "ordinary Workmen" and "capitalist Entrepreneurs" (LX–LXI), each of the latter necessarily receiving, over and above the return of his capital, his "wages," and compensation for his various costs, "a profit sufficient to compensate him for what his money would have been worth to him if he had employed it in the acquisition of an estate" (LX). And they are necessary, finally, in *commerce*, in respect of which a similar analysis leads to similar conclusions (LXVI–LXVII). This picture of a society in which, behind the veil of money, we see the whole of agriculture, industry, and commerce depending upon the continual advance and return of capitals owned by a great entrepreneurial class (LXVIII–LXX), was extraordinarily advanced for its time.

In a society of this kind, Turgot explains, capital may be invested not only in agricultural, industrial, and commercial enterprises, but also in the purchase of *land*, the revenue from which will then in effect constitute the return on the capital so invested (LVI–LVIII, LXXXIII, and LXXXV). Or, alternatively, the capital may simply be lent out to a borrower in return for interest on it at an agreed rate (LXXI). This loan transaction, in essence, is one in which the *use of money* is bought and sold; and the price of this use of money is determined, like the prices of all other commodities, "by the haggling which takes place between the seller and buyer, by the balance of supply and demand" (LXXI–LXXII), and not, as a number of earlier economists had believed, by the quantity of money (LXXVII–LXXIX). The receipt of interest is morally justifiable, in spite of the contrary view expressed by certain theologians (LXXIII–LXXV); and the level of the rate of interest ought never to be fixed by law (LXXVI). Turgot's theory of interest, with its clear recognition that "the rate of interest is relative to the quantity of values accumulated and put into reserve in order to create capitals" (LXXX–LXXXII), represents a considerable advance over Hume's theory; and there is some substance in Schumpeter's claim that it was "not only by far the greatest performance in the field of interest theory the eighteenth century produced but it clearly foreshadowed much of the best thought of the last decades of the nineteenth (*History of Economic Analysis*).

After a "recapitulation of the five different methods of employing capitals" (LXXXIII), Turgot goes on to explain the way in which the returns to capital in these different employments are, as he puts it, "mutually limited by one another" (LXXXIV). The basic idea lying behind the four sections which follow would seem to be that if there were no differences in the trouble and risk involved in the different uses of capital, an equilibrium situation would be reached in which the rates of return on capital were equal in all these uses. Since there are in fact marked differences in the trouble and risk involved, however, the equilibrium situation actually reached is characterised not by an equality but by an inequality of returns— capital invested in land bringing in the least (LXXXV), capital lent out at interest bringing in a little more (LXXXVI), and capital invested in agricultural, manufacturing, and commercial enterprises bringing in the most (LXXXVII), so that equilibrium is perfectly compatible with inequality of returns and indeed necessarily produces it (LXXXVIII). It follows, according to Turgot, that the rate of interest is the "thermometer" of the extent to which production will be carried: if interest were at five per cent, for example, no agricultural, manufacturing, or commercial enterprises which were incapable of yielding a net return higher than this would in fact be undertaken (LXXXIX–XC)—once again a very "modern" proposition.

After two sections dealing with certain problems of social accounting (XCI–XCII), Turgot proceeds to his final task—to ask what essential difference, if any, was made to the basic relations characteristic of the simple "agricultural" society with which he had started by the impingement upon it of the new class of capitalist entrepreneurs. The coming of the new class had certainly resulted in the division of the productive class and the stipendiary class into capitalists and labourers: but did this necessarily mean that the basic relations previously existing between the productive class as a whole and the stipendiary class as a whole, and between these two classes and the disposable class, now no longer existed? The way in which Turgot himself formulated the question was simply this: "Let us now see how what we have just said about the different methods of employing capitals squares with what we previously laid down about the division of all the members of Society into three classes—the productive class, or that of agriculturists, the industrial or commercial class, and the disposable class, or that of proprietors" (XCIII).

In the agricultural society, it will be remembered, the product of the labour of the (undifferentiated) productive class had been sufficient not only to provide its own wages, but also to provide a *net* product, or revenue, which accrued in one form or another to the proprietors of the land. This revenue alone was "disposable" (XIV), in the sense that it did not have to be earmarked for use in the reproduction of the annual product at the same level in the following year (Turgot's clearest definition of "disposable" in this connection is to be found not in the *Reflections* but in his fifth letter to Terray [14 November 1770], where he says that "it is only this net product which is *disposable;* it is only this portion of the fruits of the earth which is indispensably earmarked (*affectée*) for the reproduction of the following year."); and the class of proprietors which received it was itself also "disposable," in the sense that its members were not "earmarked" for any particular kind of work (XV). And it was the expenditure of this revenue by the proprietors, together with the expenditure of the cultivators, which was conceived to generate the incomes of the third social class (XVII), which for this reason was called the stipendiary class (XV).

How, then, is this picture altered when capitals and capitalist entrepreneurs are introduced? At first sight the alterations would seem to be very radical indeed. For, in the first place, if agriculture, manufacture, and commerce are to be maintained, the entrepreneurs in these occupations must now receive a return which is sufficient not only to secure for them their subsistence, the refund of their capital, and compensation for their paid-out costs, but also to provide a net "profit" sufficiently high to prevent them from transferring their capital out of the particular sector concerned and either investing it in the purchase of land or lending it out at interest. Turgot's discussions of this "profit" are somewhat vague: there are hardly two places in which he describes it in exactly the same way, and one is never really clear what precisely it is supposed to be a reward *for*, or indeed whether it can be said to be a "reward" at all. (His clearest and most useful description is probably that in the fifth letter to Terray. Some commentators have seized on Turgot's use of the verb *attendre* at one point in LX to ascribe a "waiting" theory to him, but this seems to me to be unduly selective: one might just as easily father an "exploitation" theory upon him on the basis of the wording in LXI.) But whatever it actually is, and wherever it actually comes from, there is no doubt that its level will be sufficiently high to enable its recipients to live at well above the subsistence level; and the question therefore arises as to whether this part of the entrepreneur's income is in fact "disposable," so that in the entrepreneurial society the rent of land is no longer the *only* "disposable" (and taxable) form of income (XCV). And, in the second place, the interest on money placed on loan, and the recipient of this interest, would both also appear at first sight to be "disposable," thereby raising a rather similar problem (XCIV–XCVIII).

The problem of the entrepreneurs' "profit," Turgot believed, was fairly easy to deal with. If we define a "disposable" income as one whose receipt is not absolutely necessary in order to ensure that an enterprise carries on its operations next year at the same level (at least) as it is carrying them on this year, then the "profit" of the entrepreneur is definitely *not* "disposable," since if it is not received the enterprise will not be carried on at all. What Turgot was doing here, in effect, was to argue that in an entrepreneurial society the "absolutely necessary" receipts must be taken to include not only compensation for paid-out and subsistence costs (which was all that they normally included in a simple agricultural society), but also a risk and "special ability" premium, and compensation for the *opportunity cost* involved in employing one's capital in the enterprise concerned rather than investing it in the purchase of land or lending it out at interest.

The problem of interest was more difficult, because the recipient of interest, unlike the entrepreneur, is indeed clearly "disposable" so far as his person is concerned (XCIV); and at first sight it would appear that the interest itself is also "disposable," since "the entrepreneur and the enterprise can do without it" (XCV). The way in which Turgot gets over this is simple enough, in essence, although his argument becomes rather tortuous at this point. What he does, in effect, is to put a further gloss on the concept of "absolutely necessary" receipts. If the operations of enterprises over the economy as a whole are to be maintained at their existing level, then it is not only "absolutely necessary" that each entrepreneur should receive a sufficient amount of "profit" to prevent him from closing down his enterprise and becoming a landowner or money-lender, but it is also "absolutely necessary" that the class of money-lenders should receive a rate of interest which is not artificially reduced below its market level (e.g. by taxing it). For, says Turgot, if this interest is "encroached upon," the rate charged on advances to all enterprises will increase, thereby causing the operations of the enterprises themselves to be reduced (XCVI). Thus the interest received by money-lending capitalists is very different from the revenue received by landowners (XCVII–XCVIII), and the latter is revealed as being still the only *truly* "disposable" (and therefore taxable) form of income in the entrepreneurial society (XCIX). It also still remains true that the wages and profits of the industrial and commercial classes are "paid either by the proprietor out of his revenue, or by the agents of the productive class out of the part which is earmarked for their needs" (XCIX), so that the adjective "stipendiary" still correctly describes them; and there is even a sense— although a somewhat rarefied one—in which capitals themselves "come from the land" (C).

How far does all this make Turgot a Physiocrat? He certainly used a great deal of the Physiocrats' economic terminology—although he clearly objected to the use of the unnecessarily inflammatory adjective "sterile" to describe the industrial and commercial classes. He accepted Quesnay's crucial concept of "advances"—although he generalised and developed it out of all recognition. He accepted the Physiocrats' basic class stratification—although not really as much more than a kind of historical and logical starting-point. He accepted, in a sense, the quite basic Physiocratic doctrine that land rent was the only "disposable" (and taxable) income—although the arguments which enabled him to reach this conclusion for an entrepreneurial (as distinct from an agricultural) society owed relatively little to Physiocratic inspiration, and were in some respects anti-Physiocratic. Finally, he accepted the Physiocratic idea that the incomes of the industrial and commercial classes were "paid" by agriculture—although he put a distinctive gloss of his own on this idea too. To describe him as a Physiocrat, then, would be as wrong as to describe him as a non-Physiocrat, or for that matter as anything else. "I may be wrong," wrote Turgot to Du Pont in 1770, "but everyone wants to be himself, and not another. . . . All your additions tend to make me out to be an economist, something which I do not want to be any more than an encyclopedist." ("Economist" was used at this time not in its modern sense, but as the equivalent of "Physiocrat.") So although he himself was prepared to say that he was a disciple of Quesnay *and Gournay*, he would probably have preferred not to be regarded as anyone's disciple. "Would you care to join my following?" asked the Comte de Guiche. "No sir," answered Cyrano de Bergerac, "I do not follow."

SOCIOLOGY, ECONOMICS, AND PROGRESS

Turgot's *On Universal History*, as we have seen, stopped short at the point where he had begun enlarging upon the role of the "mechanical arts" in the development of society, and the great work on geography, sociology, and politics which he had projected was never in fact achieved. What emerged instead was the theory of an entrepreneurial economy which he sketched out in the *Reflections*. In this respect, as I have already said, Turgot's intellectual development was very similar to that of Smith and Marx: all three thinkers began by working out the elements of a universal "sociological" system, embodying a theory of history which laid emphasis on economic causes, and then developed *from* these "sociological" systems the great systems of economic theory by which we mainly know them today.

The basic concept which united the "sociological" and "economic" systems, in the case of all three thinkers, was the revolutionary idea that the historical processes of social development, and the manner in which any particular society (or economy) operated, were not arbitrary, but were in an important sense "subject to law." What had happened in history, and what was happening in contemporary society, reflected the working of certain law-governed, almost mechanistic processes, which operated independently of the wills of individual men, and which it was the task of the social scientist to analyse and explain. In Turgot's sociology, we see the beginnings of this idea in, for example, his account of the way in which the evil passions of ambitious princes promoted progress; in his theory that the mathematical frequency of the appearance of geniuses was constant; and in a number of his biological and mechanical analogies. In his economics, we see the idea again in a rather different form: the concept of the economy as a kind of great "machine," always tending of itself to bring about a situation of "equilibrium," becomes quite central. It emerges very clearly, for example, in a letter which Turgot wrote to Hume on 25 March 1767, where he speaks of "a kind of equilibrium" which establishes itself between certain economic quantities; of the way in which, if one of the "weights" is changed, "it is impossible that there should not result from this in the whole of the machine a movement which tends to re-establish the old equilibrium"; and of the way in which "in every complicated machine, there are frictions which delay the results most infallibly demonstrated by theory."

It remained true, of course, that society and its history were made by human beings; but the important point was that they were not, in general, made consciously, but emerged as what I have called above a kind of unintended by-product of the conflict of human wills and actions which were often directed towards quite different ends. There is already an inkling of this in a passage in *L'Esprit des lois,* where Montesquieu, talking about the principle of monarchy, says:

> It is with this kind of government as with the system of the universe, in which there is a power that constantly repels all bodies from the centre, and a power of gravitation that attracts them to it. Honor sets all the parts of the body politic in motion, and by its very action connects them; thus each individual advances the public good, while he only thinks of promoting his own interest.

And there is much more than an inkling of it, as we have seen, in Turgot's analogy of the army "directed by some mighty genius."

The fact that men in their social and economic life were "subject to law" did not of course mean, in Turgot's view, that free will was an illusion. Nor did it mean that the heavens were empty. Providence still existed, and still in a sense worked through men, but it did so in a much more remote and roundabout way than most of the ecclesiastical practitioners of "universal history" had thought. Bossuet, for example, in his celebrated *Discourse on Universal History,* had argued that God controlled human affairs in part directly, by influencing great men on strategic occasions, and in part indirectly, by bringing it about that all the parts of the whole depended upon one another, and by "preparing the effects in the most distant causes." Even though this account left the "particular causes" of historical events as a worth-while subject of study, Turgot felt that it still gave far too much weight to the influence of Providence. The most that it could be assumed that the latter had done was to create a law-governed universe in which the complex interplay of cause and effect was likely to produce a long-run—but often very slow and unsteady—tendency towards perfection. It was only in this rather attenuated sense, then, that the world could be said to be "the most glorious witness to the wisdom which presides over it." And the purpose of social science was simply to analyse the processes whereby history, as it were, made itself and the economy ran itself. If the results of this analysis turned out to justify the ways of God to man, then that was all to the good, but it was not the primary object of the exercise.

Up to a point, then, it is true to say that Turgot's theory of history was put forward as an alternative to the "Providential" theories of men like Bossuet. And it is also no doubt true that Turgot, like all of us on such occasions, was influenced more than he knew by the very doctrines which he was combating. The parallels between Turgot's and Bossuet's work are certainly quite striking. Bossuet had talked in terms of a succession of religious "epochs"; Turgot talked in terms of a succession of socio-economic "stages." Bossuet had emphasised the way in which God worked through individual law-givers and conquerors, so that although they made history they did not make it as they wished; Turgot emphasised the way in which certain historical laws and necessities worked through them, with much the same kind of result. Bossuet had proclaimed that "all the great empires which we have seen on earth have led in different ways towards the good of religion and the glory of God"; Turgot proclaimed that through all its vicissitudes mankind in the long run advances towards greater perfection.

But there is no need to go all the way with Professor Baillie, who has described the eighteenth-century doctrine of progress as "essentially a re-disposition of the Christian ideas which it seeks to replace" (*The Belief in Progress*). There is no doubt that Turgot's version of the doctrine of progress was influenced in an important way by these "Christian ideas," but there were other important influences as well. One, obviously, was the spectacular progress of the sciences in the seventeenth and eighteenth centuries, which led many others beside Turgot to conclude that no bounds could be put to their further development. Another, perhaps equally important, was the stimulus afforded by the succession of studies of the Indian tribes of North America which had appeared earlier in the century. If, as everyone soon came to appreciate, "our ancestors and the Pelasgians who preceded the Greeks were like the savages of America," then it was fairly obvious that something which most people would want to call "progress" had been taking place since the time of the Pelasgians.

If we want to regard Turgot as the unconscious vehicle of some kind of *zeitgeist*, surely we would be on safer ground looking in his work for "bourgeois" rather than for "Christian" currents. Professor Pollard has gone so far as to say that Turgot "personifies the French bourgeoisie in the full flower of its hope" (*The Idea of Progress*); and it is certainly true that if we look at his life's work as a whole—not only his sociology and his economic theory, but also his practical work as an administrator—it appears more of a piece when looked at from this viewpoint than from any other. Even if one is not prepared to see anything distinctively "bourgeois" in his respect for English rights and liberties, his worship of science, his faith in reason, and his immense optimism about the future of mankind, one can surely not deny the aptness of the label when applied, say, to his numerous statements to the effect that "the State has the greatest interest in conserving the mass of capitals," and above all, to the theoretical system of the *Reflections*.

There is no doubt that the system of the *Reflections* is basically "capitalist," and that the particular form of "capitalism" which it envisages and analyses is by no means a primitive one. This can be brought home if one contrasts Turgot's system with Cantillon's, which was certainly the most advanced prior to Turgot's and from which Turgot may well have learned a great deal. Chapter XIII of Part One of Cantillon's *Essay on the Nature of Commerce in General*, indeed, reads at first sight rather like a concise summary of the *Reflections*. The very heading of the chapter—"The circulation and exchange of produce and commodities, as well as their production, are carried on in Europe by Entrepreneurs, and at a risk"—is reminiscent enough; and the content of the chapter, with its distinction between entrepreneurs and hired people, its emphasis on the way in which all entrepreneurs bear risks, and its association (in certain cases) of entrepreneurship with capital (usually *fond* or *fonds*, rarely *capital*), is even more so. When one looks into it, however, the differences between Cantillon's and Turgot's accounts are seen to be rather more striking than the resemblances. With Cantillon, the "entrepreneurs" include those who are "Entrepreneurs of their own labour without any capital"—chimney sweeps, water carriers, and even beggars and robbers; with Turgot, all entrepreneurs are assumed to be employers of labour, and independent workmen and artisans do not enter the picture at all. With Cantillon, although the fact that an entrepreneur may set himself up with a capital to conduct his enterprise is quite often mentioned, it is not particularly emphasised; with Turgot, the large capitals or "advances" assumed to be employed by entrepreneurs are constantly emphasised and play a crucial role in the working of the system as a whole. With Cantillon, finally, the "profit" of the entrepreneur seems to be regarded as a kind of superior but unfixed wage; with Turgot, there is a much sharper differentiation between the profit of the entrepreneur and the wage of the hired workman. Clearly Cantillon is analysing a society where the capitalist entrepreneur is just beginning to separate himself out from the ranks of the independent workmen; Turgot on the other hand is analysing a society where it is assumed that this process has been completed and that the capitalist system has consolidated itself in all fields of economic activity.

Now the interesting and important thing about all this is that in contemporary France, and even in contemporary England, a capitalist system of this kind was very far from having in fact emerged: at most, it was in the process of emerging. And Turgot, of course, was well aware of this: having spent thirteen years of his life working in the backward but not untypical provinces of Limousin and Angoumois he could hardly have been under any illusions about it. In Turgot's France, capitalism had some hold in agriculture, but only in certain areas; it had very little hold in "manufacture," which was quite largely carried on by independent workmen; and competition was seriously restricted in almost every field of activity. Yet in the *Reflections* we have a clear picture of an economy in which capitalism embraces all spheres of production; in which the "industrious" classes are divided sharply into entrepreneurs and wage-earners; in which free competition is universal and there appears to be no monopoly whatsoever; in which even landownership seems to be little more than just another form of investment of capital; and in which there is no possibility of a "general glut of commodities" because savings are transformed immediately into investment.

This marked gap between the model and contemporary reality would not have appeared in any way mysterious to Turgot's readers, assuming that the latter were by this time familiar with the writings of the Physiocrats. Quesnay, in order to draw attention in a striking way to the backwardness of the contemporary economy, had adopted the device of beginning with an analytical model of the economy in what he called "a state of prosperity." This model was in part descriptive, in the sense that it contained certain elements which were already evident on the surface of contemporary reality; in part predictive, in the sense that it embodied the assumption that certain current trends had continued and intensified; and in part a kind of ideal, in the sense that it was assumed to represent a highly desirable state of affairs towards the attainment of which government policies should properly be directed. Turgot's model of an entrepreneurial society in the *Reflections* was of precisely the same general type, and would have been clearly recognised as such by the majority of his readers, at any rate in France. They would also have recognised the essential difference between Quesnay's model and Turgot's—that in the former capitalism was assumed to be paramount only in agriculture, whereas in the latter it was assumed to be paramount in every field of economic activity. And they would not have been misled by the absence in the *Reflections* of any elaborate panegyrics in praise of the postulated system into believing that the model was intended to be merely descriptive and predictive, and not in addition an ideal to which Turgot felt it was quite practicable and eminently desirable that society should endeavour to attain. As such, they would almost certainly have regarded it as part and parcel of Turgot's general doctrine of progress.

But before we ourselves accept it as such, and as yet another reflection of the views of "the French bourgeoisie in the full flower of its hope," there are two qualifications which must be made. In the first place, we do not get any clear picture in the *Reflections* of an economy which is capable of continuous and indefinite advance: rather, we get a picture of an economy which, in some respects at any rate, has reached a kind of ceiling—even if a very high one—and which is subject to certain important constraints on further development. For example, "the wage of the Workman is limited to what is necessary in order to enable him to procure his subsistence" (VI), and there is no suggestion that he can ever expect any more than this. There appears to be no guarantee that the rate of interest fixed by the market will be low enough to enable a nation to carry its industry and agriculture to the full extent of its potential (LXXXIX–XC). There is no built-in specification about technological progress, and the main emphasis in the model is more on its static than on its dynamic aspects. And if we incorporate into the model, as we probably should, the law of diminishing returns in agriculture which Turgot formulated in 1767, it becomes even more evident that his optimism and hope were tempered by a fairly healthy sense of realism.

In the second place, although Turgot's "capitalism" was relatively advanced as compared with Cantillon's, it was still relatively backward as compared with Adam Smith's. Smith's capitalists, generally speaking, are not themselves "industrious": they use their capital to employ labour, and receive, over and above the return of their paid-out costs and interest on their capital at the normal rate, a *net* income, profit, which is as it were exuded by the capital-labour relationship, and which bears a regular proportion not to the effort, if any, which they expend but to the value of the capital they have invested. Turgot's capitalists, on the other hand, are definitely "industrious," and the "profit" which they receive from their enterprises is not clearly differentiated from the wages of their labour or the interest on their capital. Nor is this "profit" exuded by the capital-labour relationship: basically, it is simply a risk and "special ability" premium plus compensation for an opportunity cost whose level is determined by the general demand-and-supply situation. Smith's capitalists, again, are an independent class, standing on their own, whose income is as it were original rather than derived. Turgot's industrial and commercial capitalists, on the other hand, are still a "stipendiary" class, and their incomes are "paid either by the proprietor out of his revenue, or by the agents of the productive class." Clearly Turgot was unable completely to transcend the limitations of the "agricultural" framework within which the analysis in the first part of the *Reflections* was set. The flower of the French bourgeoisie's hope was still rooted—even if only loosely—in feudal soil.

Scientism, Elitism, and Liberalism: The Case of Condorcet

Keith M. Baker

If we are to believe La Harpe, Condorcet's reception speech at the *Académie française* in 1782 was not a striking success. "Il roule sur l'utilité des sciences et de l'esprit philosophique, sujet usé que le récipiendaire n'a pas rajeuni," announced the *Correspondance littéraire*. "C'est une suite de lieux communs débités dans un style froidement grave, souvent abstrait, pénible, obscur, denué de mouvement, de grâce et d'intérêt." Condorcet was naturally of a somewhat different opinion. While perhaps willing to accept La Harpe's evaluation of the literary merits of his discourse as a victory of sorts, on scientific principle, he was never one to put his trust in eloquence and later came to regard it as one of the chief obstacles to a rational politics—he had no doubts as to its substance. Indeed, some measure of the significance he attached to this speech may be derived from the fact that he prepared the notes for a revised edition which still remain among his papers in the Bibliothèque de l'Institut de France. Admitted to the academy only at the cost of dividing the forty in one of the more bitterly disputed and closely fought elections in a period not noted for peaceful ones, Condorcet evidently intended an important manifesto of his philosophical creed. A foremost principle of this creed, one which he hastened to bring to the attention of his audience with all the force of his authority as perpetual secretary of the Académie des sciences, was the conviction, as Condorcet put it, that "En méditant sur la nature des sciences morales, on ne peut, en effet, s'empêcher de voir qu'appuyées comme les sciences physiques sur l'observation des faits, elles doivent suivre la même méthode, acquérir une langue également exacte et précise, atteindre au même degré de certitude."

Condorcet was perpetual secretary of the Académie des sciences at one

From *Studies on Voltaire and the Eighteenth Century* 55 (1967). © 1967 by Theodore Besterman. The Voltaire Foundation, 1967.

of the most vigorously productive periods of its existence. As such, he witnessed and himself experienced a marked increase of interest in the necessity and the possibility of bringing to social and political affairs the methods and techniques of the sciences. In this respect, the confidence of scientists in the applicability of their method to all important matters combined with the growing needs of government for exact information on social questions. Turgot, Condorcet's political mentor, drew heavily on the talents of scientists of his acquaintance to gain expert information on administrative matters during his brief reforming ministry. (Condorcet was himself appointed by Turgot to the position of *Inspecteur des Monnaies* and accepted—with d'Alembert and Bossut—the task of directing the improvement of the canals and internal waterways of France as *directeur de la navigation.*) He shared with Condorcet a fundamental intellectual aim: that of bringing to moral and political questions the attitudes and methods found valid in the physical sciences, thereby creating the social science that was to be the necessary condition of a rational social order. It was with such a science in mind that Condorcet demanded in his *Eloge de Turgot* "pourquoi la politique, fondée, comme toutes les autres sciences, sur l'observation et le raisonnement, ne se perfectionnerait-elle pas à mesure que l'on porterait dans les observations plus de finesse et d'exactitude, dans le raisonnement plus de précision, de profondeur et de la justesse?"

For Condorcet, the whole edifice of the moral and political sciences—"ces sciences, presque créées de nos jours, dont l'objet est l'homme même, dont le but direct est le bonheur de l'homme"—was to be based, like the physical sciences, upon the Baconian foundations of positive fact; raised, like the sublime architecture of Newton, by the Lockean method of *analyse*; bound, like Lavoisier's chemistry, by the mortar of a precise, well-determined language. Such a construction, he prophesied in 1782, would be no less secure than the lofty mansions of Newtonian science. Sharing the methods of the natural sciences, the moral and political sciences must necessarily attain the same degree of certainty.

But what degree of certainty did the natural sciences enjoy? Condorcet answered this point in one of the most interesting of the notes he prepared to develop the themes of his reception speech. In the case of all scientific statements except the self-evident truths of pure mathematics and the certain propositions of metaphysics, he argued there, it is necessary to distinguish between the internal coherence of propositions and their correspondence with observable reality. Considered as axioms in an analytical system, correctly established scientific propositions are—as logical statements—as precise and evident as the certain truths of mathematics. As descriptions of empirical reality, however, they depend for their validity upon an observed correlation with an order of facts. As truths of experience they are only probable. They possess "cette espèce de degré de certitude qui est une véritable probabilité exprimée à la manière des géomètres. Cette certitude diffère essentiellement de la certitude strictement dite des géomètres."

The degree of validity to which the sciences of observation attain thus depends upon the greater or lesser constancy of the order of facts observed, the greater or lesser probability that these facts have a common cause, the greater or lesser probability that the fact regarded as a cause is indeed the cause. This is as true of the moral sciences, Condorcet remarked, as of the physical. To the extent that observation of facts is more difficult in the social world, the results of the moral sciences will be less probable than those of the physical sciences. But the probability of all truths of experience can be expressed and evaluated mathematically within probability theory. A phenomenon which has occurred 100,000 times, for example, is less likely to recur than one observed 200,000 times. But while the probabilities involved are different, Condorcet insisted, the mathematical evaluation of these probabilities is in both cases equally valid. "La science en général est aussi certaine puisque je connais exactement le degré de certitude que j'obtiens mais le degré de certitude du résultat n'est pas le même" (ibid.).

Condorcet's claims for the certainty of the moral sciences hinge upon this distinction between the certainty of a science and the certainty of its results. At any given time, he argued, the results of the moral sciences may be less probable than those of the physical. If the observation of facts is more difficult in human affairs, and their order consequently less easy to elicit, the moral sciences may in given cases acquire fewer precise truths. If the order of observed facts is itself less constant in the moral sciences than in the physical sciences, then the actual results of the former will be less probable than those of the latter. It nevertheless remains true that these results may be expressed and evaluated mathematically within probability theory; and in this form the propositions of the moral sciences are as certain—"pour la science en général"—as the truths of the physical sciences themselves.

Thus Condorcet seized upon the calculus of probabilities as the essential epistemological link between the moral and the physical sciences. His aim was to recover for science—and to integrate into a predominately mathematical conception of science—even those areas of knowledge thrown to the sceptical dogs by Descartes. Like the author of another major eighteenth-century attempt to establish the validity of social science, Giambattista Vico, he achieved his aim by first establishing that the truths of the physical sciences are merely probable. But while Vico accordingly rejected the model of the physical sciences in search of a category of historical understanding that would offer man the certain knowledge he could no longer expect to find in the physical world, Condorcet put his probabilistic evaluation of the physical sciences to more positive use. Taking up the demand of Leibniz in his *Nouveaux essais de l'entendement humain* for a new logic based on the calculus of probabilities, Condorcet bound the moral and the physical sciences together in a unified conception of science applicable to the whole realm of human experience. All those who have attacked the certainty of human knowledge have committed the same fault, Condorcet argued in the notes to his edition of the *Pensées de Pascal* in 1776.

They have established that in matters of experience we cannot attain the rigorous certitude of geometrical propositions; but they have been mistaken in concluding, with Pascal, that man has no sure rule on which to base his opinions and his conduct in these matters. Mitigated by the application of the calculus of probabilities, such scepticism no longer issued in the social quietism of Pascal—the great threat to the *philosophes'* philosophy of action—but proved to be *la vraie philosophie*. It provided a certain means of evaluating the greater or lesser validity of our opinions, the greater or lesser probability of our expectations. It bound the moral and the physical sciences together on a sliding scale of probabilities that could at all times be evaluated with mathematical certainty. It issued, in short, in a science of conduct applicable—in the words of Condorcet's first biographer, Sylvestre François Lacroix—to "tout ce qui tient aux connaissances et aux déterminations vraiment essentielles à notre existence et à notre conservation" (*Notice historique sur la vie et les ouvrages de Condorcet*).

Condorcet vindicated his claim that the moral sciences could attain the certainty of the physical sciences, then, by demoting the latter from the realm of the certain and demonstrating that they are, like the moral sciences, only probable. It is important to bear this point in mind in returning to his reception speech to the *Académie française*. "Tout serait égal entre elles pour un être qui, étranger à notre espèce, étudierait la société humaine comme nous étudions celle des castors ou des abeilles," he explained, after insisting that the moral sciences must share the methods and attain the certainty of the natural sciences: "Mais ici, l'observateur fait partie lui-même de la société qu'il observe, et la vérité ne peut avoir que des juges ou prévenus ou séduits."

At first sight, it would appear that Condorcet is here raising a final, insuperable obstacle to the claims of the moral sciences. Laboulle, in discussing this passage, credited him with the revolutionary realization that man cannot conceive of himself outside the conceptual framework imposed by the society which has given birth to him; that reason is not immutable, but a changing part of the social process. This interpretation is clearly anachronistic. Condorcet's purpose is not to contrast the objective nature of natural science with the essential subjectivity of the sciences of man; nor to assert, on the basis of this contrast, that the truths of the moral sciences must, after all, be less certain than those of the physical. His conception of scientific knowledge is at once more traditional and more sophisticated than such an interpretation would suggest. For the distinction that he is attempting to draw in this passage is not that between the greater or lesser objectivity of the truths of the moral and of the physical sciences, but that between the greater or lesser objectivity with which their truths are received by "juges ou prévenus ou séduits." Condorcet intended to make absolutely clear in his notes that he was referring not to the advance of the moral sciences towards objective truth, but to the propagation of these truths among the people. "L'auteur a paru confondre ici les progrès réels d'une science avec la propagation des vérités qu'elle établit, ce qui est ici très important à distinguer." Furthermore, it is clear from his analysis of causality that Condorcet regarded the laws of the natural sciences as interpretations imposed upon nature according to the more or less probable experience of the observer, rather than objective, external relations existing in nature. From this point of view, as we have seen, there is no distinction to be made between the objectivity of the natural and of the moral sciences.

Because they are concerned with human affairs, however, the findings of the moral sciences are far more likely than the physical to be the subject of passion, prejudice and vested interests which will resist the popularization of their truths. The clergy and those who exercise political authority have arrogated to themselves the right to judge of these truths, Condorcet maintained; and discoveries in these sciences never fail to excite their opposition. To the obstacles raised by the vested interests of such powerful elites, however, must be added those arising from the contrary claims of popular opinion. Condorcet made this point strongly in a letter to Turgot in 1779: "Je suis bien dégoûté de tout ce qui se dit et tout ce qui se fait, excepté en physique. Je crois que vous avez deviné la véritable raison de la ténacité des opinions populaires dans les sciences morales, et qu'elle tient réellement à ce que chacun croyant les entendre veut être juge."

The truths of the physical sciences are generally recognized as soon as they are discovered, simply because physical scientists are alone regarded as qualified to examine them and pronounce a judgment as to their validity. The same is far from true of the moral sciences, Condorcet insisted. Their aim is to deal precisely with matters that all men know vaguely and imprecisely; and everyone believes he can understand them. They employ a language taken from ordinary human affairs; and no one feels obliged to seek therein the precision of an exact, scientific terminology. Furthermore, they are concerned with social affairs; and men therefore have a right to judge of their validity: "Elles intéressent directement tous les hommes, et c'est un de leurs droits d'en être juges."

But was this social right to judge of the truths of the moral and political sciences to be admitted even at the cost of its adverse effects upon their progress? In 1786, reconstructing from conversation the unwritten *summa* of his master Turgot, Condorcet made an important distinction in this respect. The right of all members of society to express an opinion upon social affairs should not be confused, he insisted, with the right to pronounce upon the validity of a proposition in the moral and political sciences: a privilege which in these sciences, as in the physical sciences, must be the sole prerogative of the enlightened. "Chacun s'y croit juge; on n'imagine pas qu'une science qui n'emploie que des mots de la langue usuelle ait besoin d'être apprise; on confond le droit social d'avoir un avis sur ce qui intéresse la société, avec celui de prononcer sur la vérité d'une proposition, droit que les lumières seules peuvent donner. On veut juger, et on se trompe." Here Condorcet raised one of the cardinal issues in the history of the idea of social science. He revealed the latent tension involved in that idea between an authoritarian conception of society administered by a scientific elite upon the basis of an unequivocal scientific plan, and that of a libertarian society guided by the public interplay of subjective political action and often uninformed interests. Turgot and Condorcet assimilated politics to physics: could they do so without entailing the Comtean conclusion that since liberty of opinion is inapplicable to physics it is irrelevant to politics?

The following remarks will analyze the treatment of this fundamental issue in three of Condorcet's works most immediately relevant to his developing conception of social science. The first and most important for our purposes, the monumental *Essai sur l'application de l'analyse à la probabilité des décisions rendues à la pluralité des voix*, was the work that Condorcet valued perhaps more highly than any other of his scientific writings. It was specifically undertaken in 1785 to demonstrate the truth of the contention that the moral and political sciences are susceptible of mathematical treatment. The second, the *Tableau général de la science qui a pour objet l'application du calcul aux sciences politiques et morales*, appeared in 1793 in a popular journal dedicated to the instruction of the people in the rational conduct of politics. (The dating and historical context of this document are important. See below. On the basis of what must have been a printing error in the Arago edition, it has often been assumed that the work appeared posthumously in 1795.) It remained unfinished when the journal was discontinued and Condorcet disappeared into hiding in the rue Servandoni. The final work to which brief attention will be given, the *Fragment sur l'Atlantide, ou efforts combinés de l'espèce humaine pour le progrès des sciences*, was one of the most important fragments on the progress of the human mind that Condorcet prepared, while in hiding, for the never completed *Tableau historique des progrès de l'esprit humain*. Like the *Essai* it has only recently attracted the critical attention it deserves.

There are, however, certain difficulties involved in analysing these works, especially as regards the *Essai*. It will be necessary, in the first place, to abandon the judicious advice recently proffered by a distinguished student of the history of political ideas: to "beware of political philosophers who use mathematics, no matter how simple, to illustrate their meaning! God will forgive them, for they know what they do, but we shall not understand them" (J. Plamenatz, *Man and Society*). As if this warning were not enough, it will also be necessary to proceed in the face of the even more menacing judgment of a historian of mathematics, that "the obscurity and self contradiction [of the *Essai*] are without any parallel, so far as our experience of mathematical works extends . . . no amount of examples can convey an adequate impression of the extent of the evils. We believe that the work has been very little studied, for we have not observed any recognition of the repulsive peculiarities by which it is so undesirably distinguished (I. Todhunter, *History of the Mathematical Theory of Probability from the Time of Pascal to That of Laplace*). Fortunately, more recent mathematicians have penetrated beyond the peculiarities so repulsive to Todhunter to find in the *Essai* a remarkably modern approach; but it is impossible—and in any case unnecessary—to follow them here. Paradoxically perhaps, the *siècle des lumières* was already well acquainted with the problem of the two cultures. We shall therefore be in distinguished company if we attempt to follow the course proposed by Condorcet to another non-mathematician, Frederick the great, in limiting ourselves to the preliminary discourse of the *Essai*, in which the principal conclusions are presented as far as possible *dégagés de tout l'appareil du calcul.*

The principal object of the *Essai* was to answer the following question: under what conditions will there be a degree of probability that the majority decision of an assembly or tribunal is true, which is adequate to justify the obligation of the rest of society to that decision? The manner in which the question is posed needs some explanation. Condorcet saw the process of political decision-making not as a means of ascertaining the strongest among a number of opposing parties—not, that is, as a mere expression of will—but as a method for the collective discovery of truth. Among the ancients, he argued, great affairs were decided either by a general assembly of all the citizens or by a body which had secured itself in sovereign power. The expressed will of this body—whether just or unjust; founded on truth or error—necessarily had the backing of force; and to propose means of subjecting that will to reason would have been to invite citizens to set chains to their liberty and limits to their authority and independence. In such circumstances, political decision-making was an expression of will and not an articulation of reason: "ils cherchèrent beaucoup plus à contrebalancer les intérêts et les passions des différents Corps qui entraient dans la constitution d'un Etat, qu'à obtenir de leurs décisions des résultats conformes à la vérité" (*Essai*).

In modern times, however, political decision-making has a very different locus and should have an entirely different purpose. Among the populous modern nations, Condorcet maintained, affairs are most often decided by a body of representatives or officers chosen either by the nation or the prince. It is in the interests of the people as the ultimate source of public power that such power be employed only in support of decisions conformable to reason; that representative or deliberative bodies be composed, and their procedures be directed, in such a way as to ensure the correctness and rationality of their decisions.

This formulation of the problem has important bearings on Condorcet's conception of social science, since it helps to define the social or political field to which his scientism was meant to apply. Condorcet, like Rousseau, rejected the conception of politics as the interplay of the corporate wills expressed by various social groups within the state. Nor, of course, was this merely an abstract point. In eighteenth-century France, if politics existed at all, it did so in the traditional fashion as a series of accommodations between the government and the separate, constituted bodies within a corporate society. As such, it took on a character that may be described for our purposes as still "semi-private" rather than fully "public": semi-private, in the sense that the government dealt with the various social bodies as individual entities within corporate society, and governed by reaching (or imposing) separate accommodations in each case; rather than fully public, in the sense that acceptable and legitimate political decisions were taken in the interests and on behalf of a citizen body as a whole, and held to apply to individuals as members of that citizen body without differentiation of rank or estate. By mid-century, however, this traditional pattern of politics was already breaking down in France as the result of the endemic political conflicts between the crown and the spokesmen of corporate society in parlements, church and provincial estates. In this respect, of course, France was unusual only in the intensity of the conflict. Throughout Europe, administrative needs obliged governments to penetrate more deeply into the traditional societies at the head of which they found themselves; growing states created citizens before public law, as they were forced by military and financial necessity to prise individuals slowly (and reluctantly) from their corporate moorings in traditional society. The government of Louis XV, forced to demand changes in the structure of taxation that threatened the very privileges defining the social status of these corporate bodies, was yet powerless to put down their counter-offensive. In such a situation, when neither side of the traditional political equation was able to impose its will upon the other, and the issue could therefore no longer be decided in terms of that equation, politics broke out of the narrow traditional circle of consensus (whether achieved or enforced) and became a matter of public interest in several senses.

It became public, first, in the sense that these conflicts took place before an educated audience denied active participation in politics but by no means indifferent to the issues involved. Pamphlets appealed to this public on all sides; men of letters conceived the task of teaching it the language of public political discussion. Mathiez long ago pointed out that, from *De l'esprit des lois* to *Du contrat social* the most important publications of the *philosophes* coincided with this period of intense political conflict in France; and it is clearly impossible to understand their political thinking outside this context. ("Les philosophes et le pouvoir au milieu du XVIIIe siècle," *Annales Historiques de la Révolution Française* 12 [1935]). But in becoming a matter of public concern in this way, politics—or rather, political theory—also became public in mid-century France in a second and more fundamental sense. The refusal of the clergy and nobility to abandon their privileges relating to taxation—to take but the most obvious example—raised fundamental questions concerning the nature of their corporate contribution to society and, indeed, the nature of the society to which they could justifiably be regarded as contributing as corporate entities. By 1748 Montesquieu had already answered these questions by producing the most powerful justification of the politics of corporate society as the only defense against encroaching royal despotism. For many of the *philosophes,* however—including those who also served as government officials—these questions could be answered only in terms of the language of the fully public interest as previously defined: only, that is, in terms of the relationship of the totality of individuals, defined politically as citizens and not socially as members of corporate social groups, to the public authority that was gradually seeking to detach them from their traditional social moorings. The task of developing such a conception of citizenship was the greatest challenge to, and the greatest achievement of, the political thinkers of the French Enlightenment. It emerges clearly, for example, in Turgot's celebrated article "Fondations," where public utility—the supreme law—is defined as the common interest of the individual citizens comprising society, while corporate bodies have no rights—and, indeed, no existence—beyond those of the individuals composing them. It emerges most powerfully, of course, in Rousseau's conception of the general will: the clearest and most abstract formulation that the century witnessed of the state as the true *res publica,* and of politics as the common activity of individuals as citizens.

When Condorcet insisted in the introduction to the *Essai* that modern political decision-making was a matter of the articulation of public reason and not the expression of an aggregate of the partial corporate wills within society, he was following Rousseau and, more directly, Turgot in defining the ideal field of politics as the public action of individual citizens equal before the law. It was in terms of this ideal field, moreover, that he intended to elaborate his conviction concerning the applicability of the scientific method to the conduct of human affairs. Montesquieu arrived at what might be called a radically sociological view of the social universe by objectifying the corporate society of the *ancien regime* for its defence against the absolutist state. The conservative model of society he developed—taken up after the French Revolution by Bonald and Maistre and transmuted into sociology by Saint-Simon and Comte—stressed the primacy of the social over the political, the organic structure of society and the functional interplay—according to characteristic laws—of such social entities as estates, corporations or (as they came to be redefined after the Revolution) classes. The social science that emerged from the application of the scientistic conviction to this social field was historical in its approach, organic and functionalist in its orientation and generally conservative in its import. For Condorcet, on the other hand, the attitudes and methods of science were to be applied to a very different conception of society. Montesquieu may be said to have "sociologized" society by objectifying it as the autonomous field of interaction between constituted social bodies. Condorcet "politicized" society by regarding it as the continuum of political and social decisions made by the individual citizens of which he held it to be essentially composed. As we have seen, he brought to this liberal-individualistic conception of society a mathematical model: a model, indeed, that was entirely appropriate to it.

The close association in Condorcet's social science between an individual conception of society and a mathematical model of science is of some historical significance. The later social theorists usually associated with the origins of sociology followed Montesquieu in reacting to the strain of social and political conflict in eighteenth- and nineteenth-century France. They did so by elaborating a historical sociology that contained an implicit demand for a return to the closed society of the old regime. Condorcet, in contrast, developed a liberal social science appropriate to the model of the open society elaborated by the political theorists of the Enlightenment. His sense in relying on a mathematical model of science in this respect was entirely sure: the open society, as Popper remarked in putting forward the term, is characterized by abstract, depersonalized relationships which are clearly very susceptible of mathematical treatment (*The Open Society and Its Enemies*); and it is significant that it is precisely the theorists in search of a methodology appropriate to the abstract relationships of contemporary open societies who have recently signalled the rich significance of Condorcet's social mathematics in this context.

But in addition to the theoretical reasons for the link between Condorcet's definition of the social field and his view of the scientific method appropriate to it, there are important historical reasons. It is significant that the development of political arithmetic—or social mathematics, as Condorcet later came to call it—was closely associated with the expanding administrative efforts of states to which we have already referred. Wishing to tap the full human and financial resources of their societies, governments had need of accurate, extensive social statistics; and many of the important demographic investigations of eighteenth-century France were carried on by royal officials. Forced to raise money to meet an inflated budget by the practice of selling life-annuity contracts, governments required precise information concerning the probable life-expectancies of their subjects; and it was with this as a prime purpose in mind that the calculus of probabilities was first applied by mathematicians to the contingencies of man's social existence. Thus as the state penetrated more deeply into traditional society to bring individuals within the purview of public political authority as citizens, it was also obliged to quantify them. As citizens, indeed, individuals were quantifiable and interchangeable units in a way that they were not as members of corporate social orders; as political units, each—as Rousseau emphasized—counted for one. There is thus a fundamental continuity in administrative practice—as in political theory—between citizenship and quantifiability. Nor should it be forgotten that, as a scientific expert, Condorcet was closely associated with financial administration under the old regime and the Revolution. He not only defined the social field to which his scientism applied by drawing the full political implications from the conflict between state and corporate society in eighteenth-century France. Perhaps more significantly, he also elaborated the scientific methodology appropriate to that field by generalizing the mathematical techniques largely developed in terms of the administration of states to fit his conception of society as a whole. He regarded it as the task of his new social science to rationalize the social process of decision-making in such a way that the public good would emerge from the totality of individual choices.

Rousseau had appeared to argue in *Du contrat social*, however, that the true expression of the general will—and therefore the true achievement of the public good—was politically impossible in terms of the representative institutions that Condorcet regarded as necessary in populous modern nations. It was accordingly to this question that Condorcet addressed himself in the *Essai sur l'application de l'analyse*. His intention was to apply mathematical reasoning to the general problem of political obligation in the context of representative—or even fiduciary—institutions. On what grounds can it be justifiable to subject citizens to a law that has not been unanimously voted, or to a decision that they believe goes against their own interest? How can the right of the individual citizen to defend the oppressed be reconciled with the duty of the state to punish offenders condemned by the decision of a judicial tribunal. In both cases, Condorcet found the answer to these questions in a mathematical guarantee: "une très grande probabilité de cette décision est le seul motif raisonnable et juste d'après lequel on puisse exiger d'eux une pareille soumission" (*Essai*).

The purpose of the *Essai* was to lay the mathematical goundwork for a system of representative institutions that would embody this guarantee to the represented.

> Nous devons donc chercher principalement ici quelle est la probabilité qui donne une assurance de la bonté d'une loi admise à la plus petite pluralité, telle qu'on puisse croire qu'il n'est pas injuste d'assujettir les autres à cette loi, et qu'il est utile pour soi de s'y soumettre . . . alors le citoyen, en obéissant à la même loi, sentirait que s'étant soumis, par une condition nécessaire dans l'ordre social, à ne pas se conduire conformément à sa raison seule dans une certaine classe de ses actions, il a du moins l'avantage de ne suivre que des opinions, qu'en faisant abstraction de son jugement, il doit regarder comme ayant le degré de probabilité suffisant pour diriger sa conduite.

It is important to note in this context that Condorcet regarded the represented citizen possessed of this mathematical assurance as in a position very similar to that of the dissenting citizen of *Du contrat social*. All men, Rousseau and Condorcet agreed, have the right to follow their own opinion. But reason dictates that on entering political society they consent to submit to the general will—or, in Condorcet's phrase, *la raison commune*—those of their actions that must be governed for all according to the same principles. In submitting himself to a law contrary to his own opinion, the dissenting citizen of Rousseau and the represented citizen of Condorcet are both following the same reasoning: "Il ne s'agit pas ici de moi seul, mais de tous; je ne dois donc pas me conduire d'après ce que je crois être raisonnable mais d'après ce que tous, en faisant comme moi, abstraction de leur opinion, doivent regarder comme étant conforme à la raison et la vérité." This quotation is taken from the *Essai sur l'application de l'analyse* but it would not come strangely from the pages of *Du contrat social*. There is more of a similarity between Condorcet's conception of *la raison commune* and Rousseau's idea of *la volonté générale* than might at first be expected from their very different terminology. Rousseau's first claim for the general will, of course, was that it was "right," not that it was "true." In so far as he meant by this that the general will emanated from the sovereignty of the assembled people and was the unanswerable expression of their will, the conception obviously goes beyond Condorcet's dichotomy between will and reason. It was on exactly this basis that the two writers differed as to the legitimacy of representation. But despite this fundamental difference, there is still an important similarity between the conceptions of *volonté générale* and *raison commune*. The general will not only expressed the will of the assembled people, but their will for the public good; and it is essential to the concept that in so far as it was a correct appreciation of the public good it was also the articulation of the public reason: "l'union de l'entendement et de la volonté dans le corps social" (*Contrat* 2.6).

Thus Rousseau and Condorcet approached decision-making with essentially the same problem. Both regarded voting as more than a device to ascertain the will of the strongest party within the assembly; both were faced with the problem of ensuring the emergence of an enlightened decision from the majority vote. Indeed, it is difficult to resist the suspicion that Condorcet set himself to answer the very question to which Rousseau was unable to give an entirely satisfactory answer in *Du contrat social*: namely, under what conditions can the majority of an assembly be regarded as expressing the appropriate decision? Such an interpretation of the *Essai sur l'application de l'analyse* is strikingly supported by the fact that Rousseau himself seems to have attempted to offer the dissenting voter a quasi-mathematical guarantee that he would be obliged to follow the general will and not the will of all; that he would only, indeed, be forced to be free. Rousseau distinguished the general will from the will of all in mathematical terms: "Il y a souvent bien de différence entre la volonté de tous et la volonté générale: celle-ci ne regarde qu'à l'intérêt commun; l'autre regarde à l'intérêt privé, et n'est qu'une somme de volontés particulières: mais ôtez de ces mêmes volontés les plus et les moins qui s'entre-détruisent, reste pour somme des différences la volonté générale" (*Contrat* 2.3). There is here, perhaps, an awareness of statistical probability, an implicit assumption of the law of the probability of errors to which mathematicians of the time were turning their interest, that may well have engaged and directed Condorcet's attention.

Armed, then, with the calculus of probabilities, Condorcet set out to discover under what conditions there will be an adequate guarantee that the majority decision of an assembly or tribunal is true. The probability of a voter's opinion may be expressed as greater than one half if he is more likely to make a correct than an erroneous judgment and less than one half if he is more inclined to error than to truth. Now if in an assembly the probability of each voter's opinion is greater than one half, it follows that the probability of the truth of a decision passed by a simple majority increases with the number of voters. Conversely, if it is less than one half, the larger an assembly the smaller the probability that a majority decision will be true (*Essai*). Condorcet derived important political conclusions from this principle. Under modern conditions, he argued, a very numerous, popular assembly cannot be composed only of enlightened men. It is very probable that those who swell its numbers will bring to many questions prejudices no less misleading than the ignorance from which they stem. Since popular ignorance and prejudice extend to many important political issues, there will be a large number of questions upon which—the probability of the voter's opinions falling to below one half—a popular assembly will involve a considerable risk of false decision. Such a risk can be minimized by demanding complicated combinations of assemblies or majorities proportional to the number of voters—but only at the cost of increasing the danger of reaching no decision at all. Condorcet concluded that "il peut être dangereux de donner une constitution démocratique à un peuple sans lumières . . . cette forme d'assemblées devient nuisible, à moins qu'elles ne bornent l'exercice de leur pouvoir à la décision de ce qui intéresse immédiatement le maintien de la sûreté, de la liberté, de la propriété; objets sur lesquels un intérêt personnel direct peut suffisamment éclairer tous les esprits."

Unless the members of an assembly are enlightened—and the more enlightened, as the questions which they have to decide are complicated— the form of decision required to prevent a false decision will serve only to perpetuate abuses and bad laws. "Ainsi la forme des assemblées qui décident du sort des hommes, est bien moins importante pour leur bonheur que les lumières de ceux qui les composent; et les progrès de la raison contribueront plus au bien des Peuples que la forme des constitutions politiques."

Although Condorcet was careful to direct Frederick the great to this conclusion as one of the two most important results of his analysis, it seems at first sight to fall incongruously from a work which treats the forms of political organization in such laborious detail. In fact, it defines the limits and provides the final justification of the whole *Essai*. In Condorcet's view, the pure democracy envisaged by Rousseau was applicable only to the most primitive and the most fully developed societies, in neither of which is there justification for limiting the exercise of the right to vote. In the first stages of society, where men are equal in their ignorance and where there can be no great probability of reaching true decisions in any case, there is no legitimate motive for limiting the number of voters and subjecting the greatest number to the will of the few. In fully developed societies, on the other hand, where men are fully and equally enlightened on matters of public interest, wise laws and prudent decisions can be expected from a numerous popular assembly; and there is once again no justification for limiting the exercise of the vote. But Condorcet clearly regarded such a society as not yet in existence anywhere: "Une démocratie pure ne pourrait même convenir qu'à un peuple beaucoup plus éclairé, beaucoup plus exempt de préjugés qu'aucun de ceux que nous connaissons par l'histoire" (*Essai*).

Only monarchical or representative institutions, then, are appropriate to societies on the long road from ignorance to enlightenment; and only such institutions as are appropriate to the position of each particular society on the historical scale of enlightenment. While public happiness is ultimately determined by the progress of reason, it is nevertheless the case that the actual achievement of the maximum public happiness at any given stage of social development depends upon the elaboration of political institutions appropriate to the degree and distribution of enlightenment within the country. Condorcet concluded that in a society in which enlightenment was not widespread although there were some enlightened men—and it is surely justifiable to see in these conditions a description of the France of his day—it would be possible to give a mathematical guarantee to the represented by entrusting deliberations of importance to a small assembly of enlightened representatives, but impossible—or, at least, very difficult—to do so by means of a large assembly. "Ainsi, pourvu que dans une société il y ait un grand nombre d'hommes éclairés et sans préjugés, *et pourvu que le droit du grand nombre qui n'a pas assez des lumières, se borne à choisir ceux qu'il juge les plus instruits et les plus sages*, et auxquels en conséquence les citoyens remettent le droit de prononcer sur les objets qu'eux-mêmes ne seraient pas en état de décider, on peut parvenir à une assurance suffisante d'avoir des décisions conformes à la vérité et à la raison" (*Essai*; my italics).

What are the implications of these conclusions for Condorcet's liberalism? At first sight, it might appear that the elitism inherent in his scientism has been responsible for introducing the canker of political elitism into the very heart of his liberal thinking. It might seem that it is but a short step from Condorcet's attempt—in any case unrealisable in practice—to guarantee politically that decisions will be "rational" by entrusting them to an enlightened elite, to Comte's assertion that the "rational" or "positive" decisions of a scientific elite are their own guarantee. But such an interpretation, while appealing, would be premature. For the problem of elitism was by no means new to liberalism by the eighteenth century: the reliance of the author of the *Vindiciae contra Tyrannos* (Junius Brutus [pseudonym]) on the political initiative of the duly constituted magistrates; the similar weight attached by John Locke to the opinions of the "industrious and rational," are enough to indicate an important strand of elitism in traditional liberal thinking which quite clearly antedates Condorcet's scientism. Nor is this particularly surprising. Both Locke and the author of the *Vindiciae* were concerned with the problem of revolution from above: their aim was to defend the inherited constitutional rights of their respective kingdoms from the despotism of royal encroachment and to hammer out the right of the people—but only when called to arms by an elite, for these authors were careful to hedge the right of rebellion with safeguards—to defend the constitutional integrity of the various "parts and portions of the kingdom" (*A Defence of Liberty against Tyrants*, edited by H. Laski). However in eighteenth-century France, as we have seen, liberal political theory was less concerned with the defense of parts and portions of the kingdom from revolution from above, than with the more general—more public—implications of the endemic political conflict between the crown and the constituted bodies. In rejecting representation—the heart of liberal political theory as it emerged from the constitutional struggles of the sixteenth and seventeenth centuries—Rousseau was of course also rejecting the traditional constitutional locus of elitism in liberal thought.

It is in this context that the relationship between scientism, elitism and liberalism in Condorcet's thinking becomes more clear. Condorcet's fundamental aim—like that of Rousseau—was to envisage a system of political institutions that would rationalize public political decision-making for the public good. He accomplished this aim by recovering the earlier liberal reliance on the functions of an elite in terms of the scientistic argument that, in the existing state of enlightenment, rational (or "scientific") political decisions could be made only by the rational and enlightened few. To this extent, the effect of Condorcet's scientism was to replace an elite previously defined in political or economic terms by one now in principle defined in intellectual or scientific terms. But Condorcet's aim was also to justify the traditional liberal reliance upon the special abilities of an elite in the face of—and, to a large degree, in the very terms of—the radically democratic doctrines of Rousseau. He saw the application of mathematical reasoning to the process of political decision-making as providing a means of reconciling the specific functions and responsibilities of an enlightened elite with the general democratic principle of universal consent. If, then, the criterion of democratic theory is to be found not in a rejection of the special functions of an elite, but in the procedures by which that elite attains its power and is held responsible to the people, the *Essai sur l'application de l'analyse* deserves more notice in the history of liberalism than it has so far received. For, far from looking forward to Comte's vision of a society administered by an authoritarian scientific elite, Condorcet sought to achieve constitutionally what Locke had hoped to achieve by the admission of the extraconstitutional right of revolt: the elaboration, as a recent interpreter has put it, of "a division of labour between the more and the less enlightened members of society" (M. Seliger, "Locke's Natural Law and the Foundation of Politics," *Journal of the History of Ideas* 24 [1963]). Far from introducing an alien element of elitism into his liberal political thinking, therefore,

Condorcet's scientism made it possible for him to redefine the traditional elitist strand of liberalism in keeping with the more radical demands of eighteenth century democratic theory.

Nevertheless, a tension remained. Condorcet had argued forcefully in the *Essai* that political arrangements were to be appropriate to the distribution of enlightenment in any given country; that it might be useful in certain cases—"mais c'est seulement comme une hypothèse propre à donner un exemple, et non que nous admettions cette opinion, surtout pour une législation permanente"—to restrict unenlightened citizens temporarily in the full exercise of their natural political rights, while still offering them a mathematical guarantee of the truth of political decisions taken on their behalf. But he was irrevocably opposed to the existence of an enlightened elite that maintained itself in power by keeping the people perpetually in ignorance. If the advance of the moral sciences is impeded by the unsubstantiated claims of the majority to understand them, he argued in the *Eloge de Turgot*, the ultimate means of accelerating their progress lies in seeking to substantiate these claims rather than in rejecting them. If the right to judge of the validity of a social-scientific proposition is the prerogative of enlightenment, then it must be made available to all through public instruction. Thus the educational schemes that Condorcet produced during the revolutionary period gave the greatest prominence to the teaching of the physical sciences: not with the intention of accustoming men to accept the dictates of the "scientist," but precisely because the physical sciences— accepting no authority but that of fact—developed the critical faculties to the highest degree. They stressed the importance of developing a precise, scientific language for instruction in the moral and political sciences: not as a linguistic shield for an esoteric doctrine, but to render reason general; to dispel the social and political effects of the unfortunate contrast between the exact terminology of the philosopher-scientist and the vague formulations of the common man.

Condorcet was never more convinced of the deleterious results of such a gap than in 1793 when—his constitutional schemes rejected in the Convention by the radicals of the Mountain—he turned with Sieyès and a lesser-known figure, Jules Michel Duhamel, to the publication of the *Journal d'instruction sociale*. Convinced that their failure in the assembly—together with all the excesses, all the misfortunes of the Revolution—had been the result of the ignorance of the people in the face of political charlatans, and the consequent inability of the people to choose enlightened leaders, Condorcet and Sieyès took up Duhamel's suggestion for a popular journal of social instruction as the only means of saving the people and the Revolution from the despotism of extremists. The avowed aim of the *Journal d'instruction sociale* was popularization: it made its appeal not to an elite of scientists and statesmen but to the people as a whole. Prejudices long ago destroyed among the enlightened elite still continue to subject the nations, Condorcet maintained in the prospectus that announced the new journal: new truths continually enrich the fund of human knowledge, but remain of no use to the happiness of the mass of those who do not know them. There can be no true liberty, no justice, in a society in which equality is not real. Nor can there be true equality unless all are able to acquire well-reasoned ideas concerning the questions of social and political conduct. "Toute société qui n'est pas éclairée par des philosophes, est trompée par des charlatans," Condorcet insisted in the prospectus: "Jamais la tyrannie ne s'est établie, ni maintenue que par l'erreur, et parce que les moyens ou le courage de détromper le peuple ont manqué aux amis de la liberté."

In the eyes of its founders, then, the aim of the *Journal d'instruction sociale* was to free men from the ignorance which subjects them to *les charlatans politiques*. Its object was not to inculcate a political dogma, but to teach men to submit social and political questions to the authority of their own reason. On the grounds that one of the principal causes of the lack of progress of the moral and political sciences was the imperfection of their language, the *Prospectus* also promised an analysis of political vocabulary. This indeed, may be regarded as the primary and fundamental purpose of the journal. "Alors il se forme, en quelque manière, une science nouvelle," reported the *Chronique de Paris* (18 May 1793) in its analysis of the prospectus, "dont le peuple a besoin d'étudier les principes, la doctrine, et surtout les expressions, ces mots déjà usités dans le langage, mais dont le sens nouveau doit être parfaitement entendu, si l'on ne veut que le peuple tombe dans de grandes et dangereuses erreurs."

It is important to note from this point of view—as did the *Chronique de Paris*—that Duhamel's association with the *Institution nationale des sourde-muets* was far from coincidental. "On ne pouvait mieux choisir, pour ce genre nouveau de travail qu'un homme accoutumé à démontrer à des sourds la métaphysique du langage . . . les sourds ne se paient pas de mots; on leur parle par des signes, et pour faire entendre d'eux, il faut absolument les leur expliquer."

In a century preoccupied with linguistic questions and fascinated by the possibility of achieving a precise, unambiguous and universal language, the invention of a means of communicating with deaf-mutes was heralded as a significant step towards this end. In his reception speech to the Académie Française, Condorcet celebrated the application of *analyse* to the language of the deaf and dumb as another monument to the philosophical advance of the eighteenth century. It had elevated these unfortunates, he argued, *au rang des hommes et des citoyens utiles*. In 1793, he saw the application of philosophical analysis to everyday political language as the primary means of restoring the mass of the people *au rang des hommes et des citoyens utiles* in a political sense; and it is hardly surprising, therefore, that he turned to Duhamel for help in the achievement of this goal. Duhamel addressed himself to the task of analysing the more common terms of the political vocabulary, while Sieyès and Condorcet applied themselves to developing the principles of *droit naturel et politique, économie publique* and *art social (Prospectus)*. The most important article printed in the *Journal* for our purposes, however, is the unfinished *Tableau général de la science*.

Condorcet had for some time been thinking in terms of a general introductory work on the applications of mathematics to the moral and political sciences. He had made it clear to the marquis Lucchesini in 1785 that he intended the *Essai sur l'application de l'analyse* and further similar treatises on political arithmetic to be followed by such a work: "un ouvrage élémentaire et méthodique sur cette science,qui n'existe que par fragments." It is nevertheless of some interest to ask why this general introduction finally appeared—although it was never finished—in 1793 and within the pages of the *Journal d'instruction sociale*. In Condorcet's view, mathematical reasoning and calculation formed an integral part of rational political conduct. "La raison suffit tant qu'on n'a besoin que d'une observation vague des événements," he had concluded in the *Essai*, "le calcul devient nécessaire aussitôt que la vérité dépend d'observations exactes et précises."

The abstract general truths of the moral and political sciences are often vague and inapplicable in practice, he insisted in the *Tableau*. They do not extend beyond a statement of first principles in matters which require precise observation and measurement or are susceptible of numerous mathematical combinations. Reliance upon reasoning not supplemented by calculation is therefore likely to lead to error: either by giving some maxims a generality which they do not possess, or deducing from them consequences which are not properly their result. "Enfin, l'on arriverait bientôt au terme où tout progrès devient impossible, sans l'application des méthodes rigoureuses du calcul et de la science des combinaisons, et la marche des sciences morales et politiques, comme celle des sciences physiques, serait bientôt arrêtée."

Furthermore, Condorcet maintained, almost all our opinions and all the judgments which direct our conduct enjoy a greater or lesser degree of probability, which we normally evaluate "d'après un sentiment vague et presque machinal, ou des aperçus incertains et grossiers." In all his conduct, man is a gambler: he automatically and instinctively balances the probability of one opinion against that of another, the desired goal of future action against its probable results. Although Condorcet's ideas are by no means fully developed in the fragmentary *Tableau*, he seems to have envisaged the applications of the calculus of probabilities to the science he now called *mathématique sociale* under two general heads. In the first place, he regarded it as the foundation of a science of man which would describe the statistical frequency of the natural and social causes influencing human life and social existence and the economic contingencies of the market place. Such a study, as Granger has clearly shown, was intended not only as an objective description of social behaviour but as a scientific basis for individual conduct. In Condorcet's view, the individual who is able to evaluate the contingencies of human conduct mathematically and on the basis of an observed science of man—even though it may be impossible for him to do so in all cases and on all occasions—will have an advantage similar to that which the card player who learns to calculate his game has over an opponent who only plays by instinct and routine.

Nor is this merely a question of personal advantage: it is clear from his references to instinct and routine, to *sentiments presque machinals*, that Condorcet once again saw the issue largely in terms of reason and consciousness. For in addition to its sociological applications, the calculus of probabilities had a logical or psychological aspect. It provided a means of assessing the grounds of credibility and of choice by evaluating the probability of our judgments and our opinions. There is no one, Condorcet had argued in the *Essai*, who has not at some time found his opinions changing, not as a result of new motives or a revised argument but according to the impressions of time, circumstance and events. However, if we were able to substitute for this habitual and instinctive process of adjustment the precise evaluation of motives and beliefs, "notre raison cesserait d'être l'esclave de nos impressions" (*Essai*). The application of the calculus of probabilities to such questions, Condorcet argued in the *Tableau*, would shed the light of reason "sur des objets trop longtemps abandonnés aux influences séductrices de l'imagination, de l'intérêt ou des passions.

Au lieu de céder machinalement à la force de certaines impressions, on saura la calculer et l'apprécier."

There is thus a fundamental continuity between the naive political etymologies with which Duhamel filled much of the *Journal d'instruction sociale* and Condorcet's unfinished *Tableau*. Condorcet saw the calculus of probabilities as the essential foundation of the rational science of political conduct at which the journal aimed. Social mathematics could only be developed, he argued, by "les géomètres qui ont approfondi les sciences sociales." But its utility was no more limited to the mathematicians who cultivated it than was the use of the lunar tables widely employed by sailors for navigational purposes. It was possible to present the new science in such a way that its applications were within the competence of anyone with elementary mathematical knowledge. "Ce n'est donc pas d'une science occulte, dont le secret soit renfermé entre quelques adeptes, qu'il s'agit ici; c'est d'une science usuelle et commune."

It is important to underline the essential significance of this passage. Frank Manuel, in a stimulating essay on Condorcet, quotes from the *Tableau* to support the suggestion that Condorcet based the application of the calculus of probabilities to social science on the Benthamite assumption that individual pains and pleasures are comparable and calculable. "Comme tous les hommes qui habitent un même pays, ont à peu près les mêmes besoins, qu'ils ont aussi en général les mêmes goûts, les mêmes idées d'utilité, ce qui a une *valeur* pour l'un d'eux en a généralement pour tous." He concludes from this passage that Condorcet expected the state to estimate the probabilities of desire within the aggregate of individuals and to legislate accordingly. "With the accumulation of sufficient data and the application of the calculus of probabilities the state could be run by social mathematics—without debates. With one leap, the first sociologist of scientific creativity traversed the age of middle-class parliamentarism and arrived at the ideal of the all-knowing scientific technician as the ruler of society" (Manuel, *The Prophets of Paris*).

But to argue in this way is to misinterpret the essential meaning of Condorcet's conception of social mathematics. The passage from the *Tableau* quoted in this context by Manuel attempts nothing more than a definition of economic value (as the context and Condorcet's underlining of *valeur* make quite clear) and should not be regarded as providing the methodological groundwork for an authoritarian social mechanics. As we have seen, Condorcet envisaged social mathematics as a science of individual conduct: a common, everyday science that would extend the bounds of reason in social affairs. Almost all individual violations of ethics are the result of an erroneous appreciation of our own interests, he argued in the *Esquisse*. For each harmful action committed in a fit of violent passion, a thousand occur as the result of false calculation of interest. It was for this reason that Condorcet insisted in the *Fragment de l'histoire de la Xe époque* that general instruction should be extended far enough for each individual to determine the distant and durable consequences of his actions "et même juger la probabilité de ces conséquences." Despite its close historical association with the growth of administrative techniques, Condorcet did not draw technocratic implications from the newly created discipline of social mathematics. Far from being the instrument of the scientific technician who would rule over society, he intended it to provide the basis for a liberal social science oriented towards a conception of rational individual conduct in the open society.

This aspect of social mathematics is closely linked with another one. In discussing the method to be followed in electing the scientists who would preside over the formulation of his New Atlantis, Condorcet maintained that this was best carried out in writing and by avoiding any large meeting. "Il faut en général éviter toute réunion nombreuse: c'est le seul moyen d'obtenir une égalité véritable, d'éviter l'influence de l'intrigue, de la charlatanerie et du verbiage; de conserver à la simple vérité tout son empire, d'être conduit par les lumières, et non par les passions." But while there is certainly evidence here—as Manuel has suggested—that "Condorcet the scientific expert was becoming uneasy about democratic parliamentary procedures," there is no necessary indication that he was thereby becoming hostile to democracy as such. Condorcet had long tended to equate the written word with reason and science and the spoken word with passion and prejudice; and his provisions in this respect suggest nothing more than a further attempt on his part to arrive at a process of decision-making that, being more rational, would thereby preserve "une égalité véritable." Condorcet clearly shared with Saint-Simon the desire to replace the political conflicts of the revolutionary period by a "scientific politics": but while for

Saint-Simon this involved exiling politics in favour of the scientific admin-istration of things, Condorcet envisaged only the dissipation of the passion and prejudice that nourished the demagogue and the institution of pro-cesses of political decision-making that were at once rational and democratic.

With this conclusion in mind, it is necessary to look briefly at Con-dorcet's treatment of the relationship between science and social organi-zation in the *Fragment sur l'Atlantide*. For it is in this fragment—to which, embittered by the defeat of his constitutional project at the hands of the *Convention* and doubtless appalled by the anti-scientific emotions which his educational schemes had engendered in the assemblies, he committed his final plans for the organization of scientific activity—that the elitist aspects of his scientism are at once most apparent and their limits yet most clearly defined. Bacon had conceived of a means of hastening the knowledge and consequent social progress of mankind by mastering a weapon so powerful that Nature had seemed to reserve it to herself: the weapon of *time*. The main thesis of the *Fragment sur l'Atlantide* was that the establishment of the French republic had finally made possible the first, national step towards realizing the Baconian vision of a vast society of scholars united in an effort to prise open the secrets of nature by constant observation through all parts of the world and over the course of many generations. In an unenlightened age, Bacon had still hoped that a king would flatter himself to establish such a society. But the ethos of monarchy—Condorcet argued in 1793—could never have supported the disinterested search for truth over many generations which such an enterprise implied. Nor, indeed, could such a project be the responsibility of any public power, even in a republic. "L'es-prit d'égalité dégénère souvent en une basse envie. . . . Plus les hommes qui gouvernent restent au niveau des citoyens, plus leur autorité est pas-sagère, partagée et bornée, et plus la supériorité personnelle que donnent le génie et les lumières, offense leur orgueil."

Even if those appointed to govern did not prefer "la charlatanerie qui flatte et qui rampe, au mérite qui se tient à sa place et qui sait y mettre les autres," Condorcet argued in a burst of Cartesian fury, one could not look to the constant flux that operates in the political world for a perpetual programme of ordered scientific research. A good method of election and an adequate level of public instruction were sufficient to ensure that the democratic choice of the people fell upon men capable of making political decisions which would be right in the eyes of those with superior intelli-gence. But the collective means by which the scientific elite was to arrive at new truths could never have the people—or its leaders—as judge, and should not be submitted to its direction.

The New Atlantis could be built, then, only as the result of the vol-untary co-operation and co-ordination of the activities of the scientific elite, independent of all governmental direction. But Condorcet not only at-tempted to safeguard the organization of scientific activity from the meddling of the people. He was also careful to entrust the direction of the general plan of research only to an elite among scientists, and then subject to the achievement of certain pluralities among them. Manuel has rightly stressed the importance of this emphasis on the organizational aspects of science in the *Fragment sur l'Atlantide*, suggesting that it contains the germs of the antagonism between freedom and organization which became one of the dominant themes of nineteenth-century social thought. This argument is of considerable importance. The institutional guarantees against erroneous administration and alteration of the scientific plan that Condorcet built into the organization of his New Atlantis are similar in general outline to those suggested in political terms in the *Essai sur l'application de l'analyse*, with the single exception that the elite of scientists entrusted with decision-making in this respect was to be chosen on the basis of its expert qualifications and not specifically by election. It would appear that the tension in Condorcet's treatment of decision-making between the vote as the articulation of reason and the expression of mere will was finally resolved in the case of scientific organization—always closest to Condorcet's heart—by limiting the power of decision indefinitely to a most enlightened elite of experts. It was clearly only necessary for Condorcet to take one further step—that of applying this model of scientific organization to the administration of society—to arrive at the fully technocratic conception of social science reached by Saint-Simon and Comte.

Yet Condorcet resolutely refused to take this step. The aim of a scientific organization and that of a political society is by no means the same, he argued: "celui d'une société est le maintien des droits égaux de chacun des membres dans leur plus grande étendue; celui d'une association scientifique est le progrès des sciences. . . . Dans l'une, une décision fausse peut violer les droits les plus importants ou des commetants, ou de la minorité; dans l'autre, elle ne peut en violer aucun, puisque chacun est entré volontairement. . . . Dans l'une, une influence égale est un droit pour chacun, et dans toutes les décisions; dans l'autre l'inégalité peut être conforme à la raison." The predominance of the experts over the rank and file scientists was to be made a condition of association in the New Atlantis and was therefore not subject to the further will or choice of individuals, once they were members. In political society, on the other hand, while there were objects upon which a majority decision was often likely to be erroneous and against the common interest, Condorcet maintained that it was always the right of the majority to decide on the nature of the objects to be reserved for the consideration of a more enlightened elite, and to set up appropriate means of guaranteeing that a correct decision would be made concerning them. "Sans doute, il est des objets sur lesquels la majorité prononcerait peut-être plus souvent en faveur de l'erreur et contre l'intérêt commun de tous; mais c'est encore à elle à décider quels sont ces objects . . . , c'est à elle à déterminer qui seront ceux dont elle croit devoir substituer la raison à la vérité; et elle ne peut abdiquer l'autorité de prononcer si leurs décisions n'ont point blessé les droits commun à tous."

Condorcet's mathematical attempt to reconcile the advantages of expert decisions in social affairs with the political necessity for democratic control was at once the most precarious and the most short-lived aspect of his liberalism. However, it reveals that there was a greater maturity to his thought and a greater depth to his liberal convictions than has sometimes been regarded as the case. Scientism and democratic liberalism are but two aspects of the Enlightenment inheritance that must still be reconciled. In his attempts to reconcile them, Condorcet may be regarded as the founder of a liberal social science by no means irrelevant to modern preoccupations.

Rousseau in Robespierre and Saint-Just's Language of Politics

Carol Blum

The significance of Maximilien Robespierre's political career has been the subject of nearly two hundred years of frequently acrimonious debate. As Georges Rudé has pointed out, however, most serious observers have agreed about at least one thing: "he was a man of unshakable principles." Rudé defined those basic tenets of Robespierre's thought as follows: "the end of politics must be the embodiment of morality in government; that morality, or goodness or 'virtue', emanates from the people and from the people alone; and, therefore, it is the people's will, and not that of their fallible and corruptible rulers, that must be sovereign and prevail."

Rudé then went on to pose the questions that such declarations evoke: "But what is 'virtue'; what is 'sovereignty'; and who indeed are 'the people'?"

> To Robespierre virtue is essentially that which contributes to the public good: love of country and the subjection of the private to the public interest. To promote public good . . . sovereignty must be undivided and exercised by the people as a whole. Yet some people, he believed, were more trustworthy as depositories of virtue and therefore more fit to exercise sovereignty than others. And the main purpose of the Revolution, as Robespierre conceived it, must be to create a republic of such socially independent citizens, exercising a common sovereignty and restored by good government to their natural and inalienable rights of personal freedom, political equality and the pursuit of happiness.
> (*Robespierre: Portrait of a Revolutionary Democrat*)

From *Rousseau and the Republic of Virtue: The Language of Politics in the French Revolution.* © 1986 by Cornell University Press.

Rudé charted the cardinal points of Robespierre's public discourse: "virtue," "sovereignty," and "the people." He states that in Robespierre's intellectual development "the greatest debt of all he owed to Rousseau." In his history of Robespierre's political activities, however, he has tended to reduce the role of these conceptions to a large degree or to bring their definitions more closely in line with the mainstream of revolutionary thinking. Where Robespierre's speeches have struck observers as peculiarly inappropriate, as somehow grounded in an alien worldview, Rudé has tried to normalize their meaning, to neutralize the oddly galvanizing effect of certain passages, to fit Robespierre into the mold of a reality-oriented politician. Yet, if we examine how Robespierre used the words "sovereignty," "people," and above all, "virtue," in the volumes of his collected works representing his speeches before the assemblies and the Jacobins, his correspondence, and his contributions to journals, a coherent vision emerges, and it is one of a figure engaged in an intense, heroic effort to render real and concrete an exaltation of virtue which he had found in Rousseau.

Alfred Cobban also credited "Rousseauistic inspiration" for Robespierre's basic conceptions, which he enumerated as follows:

> The constant relating of political to ethical ends, the definition of utilitarianism in terms of morality, the emotional deism expressed later in the Cult of the Supreme Being, faith in the natural goodness of the people, the assertion of the sovereignty of the people and the General Will, emphasis on the idea of equality, suspicion of the rich and powerful, combination of the idea of sovereignty with separation of functions in government, supremacy of the legislative power, hostility to representation . . . above all, there was a Rousseauistic quality in his mind.
>
> (*Aspects of the French Revolution*)

Cobban, however, noted that for all these similarities and references to Rousseau in his speeches and writings, Robespierre hardly mentioned the *Contrat social* and "it is remarkable also that there is no evidence in Robespierre of any acquaintance with the political writings of Rousseau other than the *Contrat social*."

Cobban claims that "the interest in the career and ideas of Robespierre for the historian, and particularly the historian of political ideas, lies in their value as illustrating the theoretical and practical difficulties involved in the application of the principle of democratic sovereignty." While this may be true when his career and ideas are interpreted externally—that is, from the vantage point of the historical development of representative institutions—"popular sovereignty" for Robespierre, Saint-Just, and some of their colleagues figures only as an ancillary issue to the essential problem of the state, which they explicitly labeled "virtue," not democracy. When the same idea and career are viewed from within the rather alien context of that set of semantic postulates, different values emerge, of no less interest to the historian of ideas.

Besides Robespierre's eight volumes of political texts, a number of parallel and complementary documents produced by such figures as Jean-Paul Marat, Jacques-Nicolas Billaud-Varenne, Georges Couthon, Philippe Le Bas, Gheslain Lebon, and Anacharsis Cloots bore witness to the commitment to "making virtue reign." During a few crucial years this florid production of texts dedicated to "Rousseauvian virtue" seems to have corresponded to a deeply felt need in France; that moment past, the nation went on to other business as did most of the political figures who had taken it up for opportunistic reasons. But for the self-representations Robespierre and Saint-Just created there was no other business, and when the "reign of virtue" ceased to speak to the vitals of a significant part of the French population, their time had come to an end. In the following chapters we will examine not the political careers of the leaders of the Jacobins, but the expression of their dominant idea as it was tested in the arena of the French Revolution.

Robespierre was born in Arras four months after his parents' marriage. His father abandoned him when he was eight years old, shortly after his mother had died in childbirth. "His family circumstances," Norman Hampson suggests, "were oddly reminiscent of those of Rousseau" (*Will and Circumstance: Montesquieu, Rousseau, and the French Revolution*). It is possible that these similarities between his background and Rousseau's contributed to the intense feelings of identification he experienced in reading the *Confessions*.

In his "Dedication to Jean-Jacques Rousseau" he addressed himself to Rousseau as follows:

> Divine man, you taught me to know myself: while I was still young you made me appreciate the dignity of my nature and reflect upon the great principles of the social order. The old edifice is crumbling: the portico of a new edifice is rising upon its ruins, and, thanks to you, I have brought my stone to it. Receive my homage; as weak as it is, it must please you: I have never flattered the living. I saw you in your last days, and this memory is for me the source of proud joy, I contemplated your august features; I saw in them the imprint of the dark grief to which the injustices of men had condemned you. From that moment on I understood all the pains of a noble life devoted to the cult of truth. They did not frighten me. The consciousness of having wanted the good of his fellow beings is the recompense of the virtuous man; then comes the gratitude of the peoples who surround his memory with the honors due to him . . . even when he purchases them at the price of a premature death.

Called upon to play a role in the midst of the greatest events which have ever agitated the world, witness to the death of despotism and the awakening of real sovereignty; on the verge of seeing break forth the storms building up on all sides, storms the results of which no human intelligence can predict, I owe to myself, I shall soon owe my fellow citizens, an accounting of my thoughts and of my acts. Your example is there, before my eyes, your admirable *Confessions*, that free and courageous emanation of the purest soul, will go on to posterity less as a model of art than as a prodigy of virtue. I wish to follow your venerable footsteps, even if I were to leave only a name which fails to interest the centuries to come: happy if, in the perilous career that an unprecedented revolution just opened before us, I remain constantly faithful to the inspirations I found in your texts!

This dedication is quoted in its entirety because several important aspects of Robespierre's Rousseauvian self-representation emerge from it. He calls Rousseau "divine," and this attribution of superhuman quality is no mere hyperbole on Robespierre's part, for, as we have seen, he was not alone in assigning a supernatural significance to the career of his mentor. What he gleaned from his study of Rousseau, it is to be noted, was not originally a political theory or a set of principles regarding the state; what he learned was to know himself. The significance of the revelation is clear: through Rousseau he learned "to appreciate the value" of his nature and it was that appreciation which led him to "reflect upon the great principles of the social order." Thus, politics, for Robespierre as he described himself, began with the discovery of his own worth, and from that vantage point of heightened self-approbation he was able to understand the fundamentals of society. It was not the political writings that brought Robespierre to his recognition, it was the *Confessions*, and the aspect of the *Confessions* that was meaningful to him was the virtue he discovered there. Robespierre, like Rousseau, alluded to his conviction of his own inner goodness: "I have never known jealousy except by hearsay. Never will a vile sentiment approach my heart." Assured of his own goodness, he displayed himself in his role as legislator of the nation. "The first thing the legislator must know," he said, "is that *le peuple* is good."

Thus Robespierre began, in a metaphysical rather than chronological sense, with Rousseau's two postulates: a statement of belief in his own goodness, dependent in some way on that of Rousseau, and an affirmation of belief in the goodness of *le peuple*. "I tell you that I have understood this great moral and political truth announced by Jean-Jacques, that men never sincerely love anyone who does not love them, that *le peuple* alone is good, just, and magnanimous and that corruption and tyranny are the exclusive appanage of those who disdain *le peuple*." Contempt for the people was an attribute of evil whereas love for the people was a sign of goodness. "Vile egoists," Robespierre wrote in the *Défenseur de la Constitution*, "insist on slandering the people, they attempt to degrade the people, they slaughter the people when they can . . . they render divine homage to the people's executioners." Thus the "people's enemies" were vicious; the "people," however, was "closer to nature and less depraved." (In French, as opposed to English, the word "peuple" is singular, and this attribute facilitates conceptualizing the people as if they constituted one single being, rather than a group of individuals. In order to respect that nuance, I shall use the French word "peuple" in the appropriate quotations rather than the English "people," which does not carry identical connotations.)

It must be understood that the "people" was not any specific person or group of persons. On the contrary, particular human beings were by definition not the "people." This aspect of Robespierre's lexicon has occasioned confusion, with attempts being made to determine whether "the people" meant the poor alone, or the petty bourgeois, or some other externally identifiable group. "Le peuple" in his discourses, however, was a single figure of goodness with which it was possible to fuse in imagination. "I understand by that word all the French," he said. To the extent that someone distinguished himself from that figure, he was not "the people" any more. "The morality which has disappeared in most individuals can be found only in the mass of people and in the general interest" (June 11, 1790). As François Furet pointed out, this question of the actual identity of the "people" was at the heart of much of the philosophical and political problem raised by the collapse of the *ancien régime*. "Which group, which assembly, which meeting, which consensus is the depositary for the word of the people? It is around this deadly question that the modalities of action and the distribution of power organize themselves" (*Penser la Révolution française*). "Individuals" and "the people" were antithetical terms: "*Le peuple* is always worth more than the individuals*," Robespierre proclaimed. To the extent that his own goodness was extended outward, it included humanity, the people, and "all Frenchmen," indiscriminately. "Man is good," he said, "leaving the hands of nature; whoever denies this principle must not think of instituting man."

Robespierre identified with the great undifferentiated body of "the people," and when he was accused of leading them astray he responded angrily: "You dare to accuse me of wishing to mislead and flatter the people. How could I! I am neither the courtier, nor the moderator, nor the defender of the people; I am (the) people myself! (Je suis peuple moi-même!)" The people, however, was also the sovereign. There was no separate body ruling a passive citizenry; in Robespierre's text, the nation and the legislature, the agent and the patient were one. This was the difficulty with revolutionary governments; "they saw the people only as subject and never as sovereign." To remedy this the National Convention should adopt:

purer and more democratic principles. It will adopt them, no doubt, and the portrait of the Legislator traced by the most eloquent of our philosophers must not frighten us: "It would take a superior intelligence, which sees all the passions and experiences none of them; which, aiming for a distant glory in the progress of time, could work in one century and enjoy in another. It would take Gods to give laws to men."

(J.-J. Rousseau, *Le Contrat social*, VII)

Robespierre recognized and enunciated the same "strange loop" Rousseau had identified: that in order to create a state of virtue, people would have already to be virtuous. "In order to form our political institutions," he said, "we would have to have the morals that those institutions must someday give us." Robespierre, then, defined his role in the Assembly and later in the Convention, not as that of a "representative" or as a "spokesman," but as a Legislator, in the same sense that Rousseau had intended.

"The first thing the legislator must know," he said, "is that *le peuple* is good: the first feeling he must experience is the need to avenge the people's insults and give the people back all its dignity." Thus love for the "people," on the one hand, was wed to a program of reprisals against the "people's" enemies, and the primary need of *le peuple* was a sense of its own worth, always refuted by those who willfully separated themselves from it. "If you wish to be happy and free," Robespierre wrote, "*le peuple* must believe in its own virtue." It was that very belief which formed the Republic, not some group of elected representatives or legal formulas. "Republic is not a vain word; it is the character of the citizens, it is virtue, that is, love of the Fatherland."

Thus Robespierre was not talking about a political organization in the ordinary sense, he was invoking a state of emotional fusion between his good self and the emanation of that self which he called "the people," or "the Republic" or "the Fatherland." "The soul of the republic is virtue," he said, "that is to say love of the fatherland, the magnanimous devotion which merges all private interests in the general interest."

Robespierre's political fortunes were linked with those of the Mountain, which he defined as:

> a part of the room in the Constituant Assembly where, from the beginning of the Revolution, sat the small number of deputies who defended the cause of the people to the end with the most consistency and fidelity. It is known that the opposite side, called the right side, was always occupied by men of a diametrically opposite character. . . . Solon of Athens had observed that his country contained three classes of inhabitants whose characters were different: those of the mountain, who were lively, courageous, and born of the republic, those of the plain, who were quieter and more moderate, those of the seashore who were harder and inclined toward aristocracy. I blame Solon for having made bad laws to please those two classes of half-breed Athenians; he

should have brought them all together to the principles of liberty
and to the eternal laws of reason and justice, engraved in the hearts
of all men. Solon was a "feuillant," who fondled all the parties.

Like Rousseau, Robespierre extolled the rigorous Spartan constitution over
the corruption he found in Athens, and described his role as Legislator,
together with his fellow Montagnards, as creating a state which would
make all citizens "men of the mountain." Democracy did not signify the
compromises arrived at by a motley amalgam of alien individuals and
groups, but rather the one pure will of the truly virtuous people whose
spokesman was Robespierre.

"Virtue," said J. M. Thompson, "was Saint-Just's point of contact with
Robespierre" (*Leaders of the French Revolution*). Saint-Just's brief revolutionary career, beginning with his election to the National Convention in September 1792, until his execution on 9 thermidor, year II, was inseparably
bound to that of Robespierre, with whom he shared mastery of a common
moral vision derived from Rousseau. Like Robespierre, Saint-Just presented
himself as a man free from any taint of evil: "certainly," he remarked, "no
one ever hoped that I would lend my pure hands to inequity." In a work
entitled *L'Esprit de la Révolution et de la constitution en France*, which Saint-
Just published in 1791, before being elected to office, he described the
Revolution from the point of view of virtue: "So many men have spoken
of this revolution, and most of them have said nothing. I do not know that
anyone, until now, has put himself to searching, deep in his heart, for
virtue in order to know what he deserves from liberty. I do not claim to
accuse anyone; each man does well to think what he thinks, but whoever
speaks or writes owes an accounting of his virtue to the city." Saint-Just
described how he had evaluated the first assemblies: "as a member of the
sovereign I wanted to know if I was free." He concluded that he had found
reason to believe that in the new laws "I would be obeying only my virtue."

Thus, from the very beginning, Saint-Just depicted his role as that of
the man of virtue who would find in the new government not negotiations
or coalitions between the various elements which constituted France, but
his own inner value externalized to become the law of the land. At the
conclusion of the work he commented on the decision to erect a monument
to Rousseau. "France finally just honored Jean-Jacques Rousseau with a
statue. Ah, why is this great man dead?" The National Assembly, he said,
had a mission, which it:

> would not exercise like Lycurgus, Mohammed, and Jesus Christ,
> in the name of heaven; heaven was no longer in men's hearts,
> they needed another lure more in conformity with human interest.
> As virtue is still a marvel among arrogant and corrupt mortals,
> . . . everyone became intoxicated with the rights of man, and phi-
> losophy and pride found no fewer disciples than the immortal
> gods. However, under the simple name of national assembly, the

legislator, speaking to men only of themselves, struck them with a holy vertigo and made them happy.

Rousseau's dream of virtue, therefore, was the touchstone of the new republic, replacing the Christian heaven that had served the monarchy long and well. Unlike the priestly caste of the *ancien régime*, however, the legislator would not speak to men about God, but about themselves, causing immediate bliss for all rather than describing the possibility of beatitude for some.

Saint-Just, like Robespierre and Rousseau, stated as axiomatic the innate goodness of man or the "peuple." "Each *peuple* is right for virtue," he said, and only those who wish to tyrannize over others see wickedness as natural to the human race. "I combat this pretext used by tyrants, of the natural violence of man, in order to dominate him." Man is what his government makes him, morally speaking. "The virtue of Lacedemonia was in the heart of Lycurgus." "Our corruption under the monarchy was in the heart of all the kings, corruption is not natural to peoples."

Saint-Just never wavered from his statement that "le peuple" was good, although sometimes "too simple, too pure, too poor." As object, the people's goodness was its passive nature: " 'le peuple,' is good and credulous, because the people is without ambition and without intrigue."

The word "people" could then signify, as Annie Geoffroy demonstrated, not any *existing* human beings, but "an ideal political unity," and as she pointed out, this single body was characterized by poverty and passivity ("Le 'Peuple' selon Saint-Just"). *Le peuple* spoke through Saint-Just; it was he who found the laconic pronouncements that expressed its goodness and its concomitant pathos.

Le peuple, however, was capable of an alternate manifestation, in which it played the role of protagonist in its struggle with "the enemies of the people." Saint-Just described *le peuple* in its active phase as the "revolutionary man," whom he envisaged in the following terms:

A revolutionary man is inflexible, but he is sensible, he is frugal; he is simple without advertising false modesty; he is the irreconcilable enemy of all lies, all indulgence, all affectation. As his aim is to see the Revolution triumph, he never criticizes it, but he condemns its enemies without enveloping them with the Revolution; he does not exaggerate it, but he enlightens it, and jealous of its purity, he watches himself when he speaks of it, out of respect for it; he claims less to be the equal of authority, which is the law, than the equal of men, and above all of the unfortunate. . . . The revolutionary man pursues the guilty and defends innocence in the courtroom; he tells the truth in order that it instruct, not for it to do damage; he knows that in order for the Revolution to affirm itself, people must be as good as they used to be wicked; his probity is not an intellectual *finesse*, but a quality of the heart.

Marat was kind at home, he threatened only traitors. J.-J. Rousseau was a revolutionary and certainly was not insolent: I conclude from this that a revolutionary man is a hero of good sense and probity.

(26 germinal, year II)

Saint-Just's thought was so close to Rousseau's and it was expressed so elliptically that it would often be incomprehensible without that referent. Frequently, however, on certain questions, he assumed an ultra-Rousseauvian posture and he did so in the name of virtue. In this way he consistently went beyond Rousseau in the pursuit of a Rousseauvian argument by denying one of the balancing considerations which his mentor invoked. Thus, in the paragraph cited above, Saint-Just refused the "legislator" supernatural powers, in defiance of Rousseau's suggestion in Book 2, chapter 7 of the *Contrat social,* but he did so to bolster the importance of *virtue* and it alone as the standard of society. Similarly, Rousseau had accepted, with reservations, the principle of capital punishment in the *Contrat social.* In his *Esprit de la Révolution,* Saint-Just refuted Rousseau on the grounds that a truly good government would create a citizenry *so good* that it would be incapable of serious crime, so that a capital offense would, in reality, condemn the government, not the offender.

Whatever veneration the authority of J.-J. Rousseau imposes, I do not pardon you, oh great man, for having justified the death penalty. . . . Before consenting to death the contract must consent to be altered, because crime is but the result of that alteration; now, how does the contract come to be corrupt? By the abuse of laws which permit the passions to awaken and open the door to slavery. Arm yourself against the corruption of laws, if you arm yourself against crime you are taking the fact for the right. . . . The social treaty, Rousseau says, aims to conserve the contractants; now, they are conserved by virtue and not by force.

By means of this logic, Saint-Just showed that the only possible crime was the act committed against *le peuple* and its virtue. Since it was the government, under any form of polity, which was defined as opposed to *le peuple,* only individuals with political power could ever be guilty.

In his role as a member of the Committee of Public Safety, Saint-Just has been accused of switching sides on the question of the death penalty. As we shall see, however, he came to prove the necessity for capital punishment by means of exactly the same argument he had used against it: the "corruption of laws" was the enemy needing to be punished, not individual criminals, who were victims of a corrupt state. Man was born good, and in an ideal state "the sovereign consists of all the hearts yearning for virtue." This definition of the "sovereign" (*le souverain*) as a collective sentimental mystery, distinct from "sovereignty" (*la souveraineté*), the exercise of the "common will," follows Rousseau. Two aspects of the same phenomenon, the good people fuse together to form a sovereign state of virtue which exercises its sovereignty by creating good people. In this way the good state was defined as virtue, and the state which was not good was wickedness itself. "The monarchy," said Saint-Just (8 ventôse, II), "is not a king, it is crime; the Republic is not a senate, it is virtue."

That Saint-Just spoke in terms of the familiar tenets of morality his generation had absorbed from Rousseau in no way made him unusual. Where Saint-Just was innovative, however, and what lent tremendous power to his oratory, was the distinct persona he assumed in relation to the "people" and the government. Although he spoke first as a representative to the National Convention and later as a member of the Committee of Public Safety, he always took the position that he spoke for a single, undifferentiated body called the people, or the fatherland, which was surrounded by enemies, principal among whom was the government itself. This was his most disconcerting and effective rhetorical weapon in the constant political infighting that marked the failure of the Convention to achieve stable functioning. Rousseau had aligned himself with nature, with antique virtue, and with the simple goodness of the humble artisan in order to humiliate those whose claim to influence was based on birth, money, or achievement. Now, in a representative government, Saint-Just took the same attitude toward his fellow deputies, other elected officials, and the entire bureaucratic organization of the state.

The anger that sometimes emerged in Rousseau's writing as for example, at the end of the *Confessions* when he declared that any reader who didn't respect the author "deserves to be strangled," was closely linked, for Saint-Just, with the idea of his own role in bringing the people to their own goodness. Two passages, one from the beginning of his career and one from the day before the end, serve to illustrate this connection.

In a letter to an associate, Daubigny, Saint-Just expressed his feelings about being too young for election to the Legislative Assembly. It was July 1792, he was twenty-four years old, and he had just published his *Esprit de la Révolution.* He had apparently been to Paris, had an unsatisfactory meeting with Camille Desmoulins, and returned to Noyon.

> It is unfortunate that I cannot stay in Paris. I feel that I have it in me to leave my mark on this century. Go see Desmoulins, embrace him for me and tell him that he will never see me again, that I esteem his patriotism but I despise him, because I have seen through his soul. . . . He does not in the least possess the audacity of magnanimous virtue. Adieu, I am above misfortune. I shall endure everything, but I will tell the truth. My palm will rise, however, and perhaps it will put you in the shade. Wrench out my heart and eat it; you will become what you are not, great! O Gods! must Brutus languish forgotten by Rome! My mind is made up however; if Brutus does not kill others, he will kill himself.

This passage is of especial interest not only because it demonstrates the rage which charged assertions of moral superiority with tremendous energies, but also because of the conclusion: failure to destroy "others" necessitated destruction of the self.

Usually reticent to a remarkable degree about personal matters, even in his private notes, Saint-Just commented once more on his role in a set of fragments entitled "Sur les institutions Républicaines": "The day when I become convinced that it is impossible to give the French people morals which will be gentle, energetic, sensitive, and inexorable toward tyranny and injustice, I shall stab myself."

A rhetorical position which placed the speaker outside the framework of the representative organization to which he belonged, which permitted him to assume a posture of alienation through identification with "the people" in virtue, and which was based upon a declaration to kill either the opposition or himself, these were the elements which Saint-Just brought to the National Convention and with which he rapidly established himself as revolutionary legislator capable of influencing opinion.

It was during the trial of Louis XVI that Saint-Just forged the special moral vocabulary which he and so many of his generation had absorbed from Rousseau into an instrument of oratorical power. The reader will recall the conflicts that threatened France and the Revolution in the summer of 1792. The constitution of 1791 had become a cumbersome legal fiction, impossible to respect, extremely difficult to undo. After the king's aborted flight to Varennes in June 1791, the fact that France remained a monarchy at all enraged the left, while those still attached to the crown found the notion of a captive king insufferable. The government, since April under the Girondist leadership of Roland, Mme Roland, and a coterie of close friends, issued pronouncements in which lofty moral superiority toward both the king and the Mountain was coupled with verbal incitements to violence on behalf of virtue. Much of the early rhetorical shift toward a bloody moral polarization of political life must be attributed to the Gironde. Mme Roland was, in Gita May's words, "one of the first to advocate methods of intimidation and repression against all suspicious elements" (*Madame Roland and the Age of Revolution*).

The Legislative Assembly, led by the bourgeois but bellicose Gironde, had lost authority. The presence of *sans-culottes* from the Paris sections, lining the corridors leading to the Assembly hall and within the hall itself, functioned to shape the discourse pronounced at the podium. The sections were at once an audience to whom words were addressed, a symbolic chorus enacting the role of the *peuple* of whom the orators were speaking, and ultimately the judges and guarantors of the Assembly's legitimacy. This triple function structured the dynamics of political oratory for speakers of every political persuasion.

Robespierre, no longer part of the government, was devoting his energies to the Paris Commune which, on August 10, invaded the Tuileries in search of the "tyrant Capet." Louis, the queen, and their children crossed the Tuileries on foot and took refuge in the Assembly itself. The representatives moved to incarcerate the king and the royal family in the Temple.

According to Jean Jaurès, "The last phase of the Legislative's authority was a subordinate one. But would the Commune limit its power to Paris?" It quickly became apparent that the Parisian patriots had no such intention; the Commune sent "commissars" to the eighty-three departments, and "that was the Paris Commune's seizure of all of France."

The Commune suspended liberty of the press, arrested and imprisoned known monarchists as well as a number of obscure individuals, and closed convents and monasteries. Philippe Buonarroti characterized that period in the following terms: "To the value of the conceptions of Jean-Jacques [the men of August 10] added the boldness of applying them to a society of twenty-five million men" (Jaurès).

In Jaurès' words, however, "it was Robespierre who by means of the Commune was the true mayor of Paris." By the end of August a sort of reaction seemed to be setting in, and members of the Legislative began to express their disapproval of the continuing usurpation of the elected body's authority by the insurgent group.

On September 2 the more radical sections, excited by the successes of their direct action, both encouraging and encouraged by popular fear of foreign invasion, sounded the tocsin. *Sans-culottes* broke into the prisons and executed the prisoners, including a number of suspect priests who were said to be in league with enemies of the nation. Eleven hundred persons were killed in Paris in four days.

The way in which the massacres were described throws light on the workings of the emerging dominant morality. Those who participated in the assassinations and those who directed them were not to be considered immoral. On the contrary, they expressed hurt at being criticized. A member of the surveillance committee, Antoine-François Sergent, who had signed the order to "judge all the prisoners of the Abbaye," complained only four days later that the assassins were being accused of stealing the deceased's belongings. He reacted by wishing to reassure the assassins that their virtue was appreciated. "M. Sergent told about the odious means employed to slander the people, . . . he proposed that to make some virtuous, it is necessary to appear to believe in his virtue, he demanded that the General Council [of the Commune] put forth a proclamation which, by making the people feel its virtue, would make them fear to tarnish it." Sergent's request underlines how essential it was for many revolutionaries to experience themselves and their actions as legitimized by a widely accepted morality. The people could rise to the assassination of conspirators with pride; to label them petty thieves was to destroy their self-esteem and reduce them once again to rabble.

Restif de la Bretonne, that intrepid observer of life in revolutionary Paris, expressed a feeling which underlies much of the ambivalence toward the massacres. In a truly democratic state, in the absence of a transcendental theory, was the group impulse not always right? If the masses, incarnating the people, felt inclined to kill the representatives of a discredited religion or political system, who was to blame them? "No," he commented in the *Nuits révolutionnaires*, "no, I do not pity them, those fanatical priests, they have done too much harm to the fatherland. The minority is always guilty, I repeat, even if it is morally in the right." The notion that "the minority is always guilty" and hence subject to execution was in the air during the election (as the massacres were taking place) of the National Convention and had its effect upon the results of that selection process.

By September 20, the Assembly had been replaced by the new ruling body. It included no overt royalists, the Paris delegation was entirely Jacobin, the Republic was proclaimed, and a whole new political and moral frame of reference had come into existence. The Convention quickly revealed, however, the same three-way split characteristic of all the Revolution's governing bodies, which Robespierre described. Girondins elected entirely by the provinces, now displayed ambivalence toward extralegal violence, advocating it in the case of the king, but protesting it when threatened themselves. Despite Brissot's cry: "No peace with the Bourbons!" the Girondins' policy seemed inconsistent; as Albert Soboul commented, their stance as war party, on the one hand, was incompatible with their "policy of social reaction" (*Le Procès de Louis XVI*). Thus weakened, they were pushed to the right by the numerically inferior Mountain, spiritually in touch with the Commune on the left. In between was the uncommitted Plain.

This then, was the context in which the question of judging the king arose: the Commune was pressing the Convention to relinquish its royal prey to popular justice. The Mountain had decided to champion the cause of his prosecution. Deliberately associating itself with the Commune, the Mountain now faced an unfocused but embittered oppositional majority. The legislative body settled into a complicated debate on the unprecedented constitutional problems of prosecuting a king, a dispute that the majority of delegates did not seem eager to see end. Some members of the legislative body, still reeling from the implications of the prison massacres and Robespierre's threats against the Gironde, found the notion of expressing solidarity with the *septembriseurs* by means of an official political execution frightening. The legal grounds for the Convention to accuse and try Louis were uncertain. The constitution had specifically labeled the king inviolable; for the Convention both to accuse the dethroned monarch and then to judge him was venturing onto the shaky ground of unprecedented jurisprudence. The uneasy majority, however, had one essential maneuver at its disposal: it could stall for time indefinitely by introducing a series of obfuscating diversions.

In the midst of this factional jousting sat Saint-Just, at last twenty-five years old and elected to take his seat at the Convention as delegate from l'Aisne. On November 13 he rose to deliver his maiden speech, one which set Louis's fate in the new moral framework and in some way established the speaker's moral authority over the assembled deputies. In his address of December 27 on the same topic, he completed his brilliant dialectical conquest of the Convention.

No other revolutionary leader was able to pose the vital questions of France's destiny on such an exalted plane and maintain the tone. After his trenchant formulations of the issues, other orators sounded verbose and compromised, as if mere humanity were incapable of rising to the realm inhabited by the leader who bore the evocative name of Saint-Just.

The simple but deadly argument which Saint-Just elaborated before the Convention was based on the logical extension of meanings Rousseau had attached to the word "innocence" and the word "guilt," but denuded, as was Saint-Just's habit, of the qualifications with which Rousseau hedged the terms. "Innocence," in Saint-Just's Rousseauvian vocabulary, was an essential attribute of the "people," while "guilt" was the inescapable lot of the "people's enemies." Saint-Just was impatient at the Conventionals' difficulty in grasping the vital distinction. "Defenders of the king," he asked, "what do you want for him? If he is innocent, *le peuple* is guilty" (December 27, 1792).

As Saint-Just spoke, groups of *sans-culottes*, armed with pikes, were wandering freely in the *Manège*, punctuating the speaker's words with enthusiastic applause. Saint-Just had discovered a potent technique for leading the Convention. Rather than objecting to the "manifestations of popular will" organized by the Commune, he explicated them before the delegates, so that they could be more responsive to the people's wishes. "*Le peuple*," he told his colleagues, "is innocent and good." Saint-Just did not presume to speak for the "poor people"; rather that body was speaking through him.

In the course of these two speeches, Saint-Just took a major ontological step; he disassociated himself from the government and identified himself completely with the carefully defined entity he called the people. Until his execution some twenty months later, although with Robespierre, he came to dominate the Committee of Public Safety and through it the operations of the government, he presented himself as a powerless emanation of the axiomatically pure people. He did not speak as a representative of a separate body called the government. He frequently alluded to his conviction that "a people has but one dangerous enemy: its government."

Jean-Paul Gross comments, in regard to the kind of aura surrounding Saint-Just, that "it is not as 'archangel of death,' but as talented young politician that Saint-Just first made himself known to his contemporaries" ("Saint-Just en mission"). While it is true that the Saint-Just of the Committee of Public Safety and of the missions to the army became a mythical figure of his own making, the essential operative elements of the legend were all in place at the time of the trial: the peculiarly trenchant speech with its metaphysical oppositions between goodness and evil, life and death; the skillful use of implicit menace, in this instance, the grandstands filled with *sans-culottes* recalling fresh memories of the September massacres. At the front, Gross points out, Saint-Just used exemplary instant executions to achieve the same electrifying results.

Saint-Just explained that the French had been frivolous and depraved before the Revolution, but since the people had become sovereign, the reign of egotism was over. Now the wishes of the people could immediately become law, provided that the Convention itself was not treacherous, and an era of justice would be born. The iniquitous past was over, its order of value reversed: "an unfortunate is superior to the government and the powers of the earth; he must speak to them as a master."

Thus Saint-Just developed the possibilities of Rousseau abrogation of original sin; the "republic of virtue" offered the humble what Christianity never did: power over the great *in the present,* not some theoretical preference over them in the world to come. If the "government and the powers of the earth" were not sufficiently responsive, *"arm the people,* the people must reign."

The king and the government were separated from the "people" and to the extent that they actively ruled they were culpable. To reign was to impose a will upon a people distinct from its own, to direct its activities toward some mediated goal, to mark distinctions between men. A legitimate leader would lose himself in the people, he would merge with the fatherland, and, far from crossing the will of the sovereign people, he would express it, putting into words the inchoate volition of the masses which he discovered by looking into his own heart. Saint-Just explained that traitors often tried to fool the people with complicated intellectual arguments. As for himself, however, "I know only *just* and *unjust*; these words are understood by all consciences. All definitions must submit to the conscience: the mind is a sophist which leads virtue to the scaffold."

A reigning monarch was irrevocably separated from a people, and its innate purity. Saint-Just's celebrated aphorism, "no one can reign innocently," condemned Louis as the negation of the innocent people, and hence essentially guilty. His rhetoric cut through the complex legal knots the Convention was busily tying in its efforts to avoid pronouncing on Louis's fate. Contemptuously dismissing the squabbling over technicalities, Saint-Just declared the king a being apart, for whom the laws applying to the people were invalid. He then reasoned from Louis's separation to the necessity of his execution: "Since the French *peuple* has demonstrated its will [by invading the Tuileries], everything outside the sovereign is the enemy. . . . Between the people and its enemies there is nothing in common but the blade." Louis, the "enemy of the people," was a different species from the French people, he was *outside* the city, a "barbarian." The rules that applied to the citizenry were not to be taken into consideration for the outsider. In all of France he was the exceptional one, no appeals to justice could be accepted from him. "Louis," said Saint-Just, "is a stranger in our midst."

Camille Desmoulins, the clever and frequently impudent journalist whose role it was for a time to express the same ideas as Saint-Just and Robespierre in cruder form, commented: "You know very well that to the Republican all men are equal. I am mistaken, you know very well that there is only one man whom the true Republican cannot regard as a man [but] a two-legged cannibal, and that enemy beast is a king."

Saint-Just spoke from a still world of absolutes, he denied process as he denied compromise. Events could reveal the nature of certain persons, they could "lift the mask," or "rend the veil," but they could not be used to judge moral attributes. Just as the people was innocent in Saint-Just's world of existential stasis, the king was guilty, not of this crime or that, but of having been king. It was not the specific acts of treason with which Louis XVI was charged that interested Saint-Just in the least; it was the culpable nature of his being. The handsome, self-possessed, young delegate urged his colleagues to close the gap between themselves and the people by acting directly upon the person of the king, by becoming not only Louis's prosecutor and judge but his executioner as well. "Someday they will be astonished that in the eighteenth century people were less advanced than in Caesar's time: then the tyrant was immolated in the middle of the senate with no more formality than twenty-three strokes of a dagger, and no other law than Roman liberty."

Saint-Just squeezed the Convention between his strangely abstract logic on the one hand, and on the other, his exegesis of the noisy throng in the galleries, evoking the picture of a Commune poised once more to run amok. The delegates, in their extended debates, had been reaching for some sort of compromise formulation among the half-dozen positions to be taken on the question of Louis XVI. Saint-Just denounced conciliation and reduced the delegates to two choices: "I see no middle ground," he told them. "This man must reign or die." The tacit corollary of this maxim, that the delegates themselves might die if the king reigned, was underscored by the restless crowds outside the *Manège* and in the grandstands, imposing their presence on the deputies. Albert Soboul comments: "That the Convention deliberated under the menacing gaze of the galleries, there can be no doubt. What is more, by their applause, or their murmurs, they intervened in the debates."

Some of the bolder representatives complained of the ominous mobs at their elbows. Saint-Just answered them by praising the openness of the trial: "kings used to prosecute virtue in the dark; us, we judge kings before the universe! Our deliberations are public so that no one accuses us of unseemly behavior." When Saint-Just said "we," the referent was not "we representatives." The "we" of whom he spoke was himself, at the podium, and the "people" in the gallery. His colleagues in the Convention were a distant "they," or "those who," as in a statement from his notebook after the trial and execution of the Gironde delegates: "Those who govern must be frightened, *le peuple* is never to be frightened."

In Saint-Just's pursuit of the guilty Louis XVI, he had to combat the implicit accusation that the Mountain, using the *sans-culottes* as a weapon, was plotting coward's revenge on a defeated man, rather than planning an act of republican morality. The king had been a virtual prisoner for more than a year, during which time it was said that he and his family were reviled and threatened. Moreover, there were certain ambiguities attached to his actions in office, if not to his general ineptitude. From various accounts Michelet assembled a picture of how Louis appeared on December 11, as his formal arraignment was about to begin: he was "a man like so many others, he seemed like a bourgeois, living off his investments, a family man; he had a simple air about him, a bit near-sighted, his skin already pale from prison; he was sensing death" (*Histoire de la Révolution française*).

The lonely figure of the former king, amid the vociferous throng, aroused some compassion. Louis, the ineffectual, the worried, the fat, utterly lacking the legendary Bourbon panache, seemed to some observers less like a tyrant than a martyr. Proposals were aired to pardon him as a gesture of the generosity of a great Republic, and Saint-Just was challenged to wrest moral superiority from the middle and harness it to the guillotine. To do this he had to overcome the obstacle of Louis's pathos. To vote, in cold blood, to decapitate a man whose actions were open to so many interpretations was difficult for many of the delegates. The task was rendered still more delicate by the fact that they were, by and large, imbued with Rousseau's belief in the moral significance of pity. Man's instinctive, nonintellectual sympathy for the sufferer, to Rousseau, was nature's basic virtue. "What is generosity, clemency, humanity, if not pity applied to the weak, the guilty, the human species in general?" Rousseau had asked. The men of the Convention knew that spontaneous sympathy for the sufferer was the sign of a superior soul. How then could this large assembly vote the death of Louis and still experience itself as one with the "innocent people"?

The answer Saint-Just found in his mentor was that pity was aroused naturally, and hence legitimately, only by the poor, the humble, and the good. As for the wicked, "the pity they inspire is never very keen," Rousseau had pointed out. For Rousseau, the only authentic pity was that aroused by suffering innocence; to sympathize with the guilty was to sacrifice the people for the sake of one individual, since "pity for the wicked is a great cruelty toward men."

In his *Lettres à ses commettans* Robespierre put forth Rousseau's argument that pity was the natural principle underlying clemency, and used it to condemn Louis XVI. The king, by violating the "political pact," had entered a state of nature and had to obey its law. But what was the law of nature?

> It imposes a double duty upon men; the first is that of seeing to their own conservation, from which derives the right to punish all those who attack their liberty or their security; the second is to help our oppressed fellow men, from which, again, is derived the right to punish those who oppress them. Because next to the penchant which leads us to defend our existence, nature has placed the imperious feeling of compassion, which is but an emanation of the first penchant.

Rousseau's dual-instinct theory is recognizable here; compassion is only an "emanation" of the impulse toward self-protection, and the self empathizes with the one he perceives to be the victim. Thus, Robespierre insisted, one must not ask the question: "Is it necessary to inflict punishment upon Louis, dethroned, powerless, abandoned at this hour?" The real question was: "Have not all nations until now been granted the right to strike tyrants down, and has not the admiration of the centuries put such courageous acts on the level of the most sublime characteristics of virtue?"

Saint-Just, whose discourses were in philosophic harmony with Robespierre's, denounced pity for Louis as aristocratic wickedness toward the people. Counterrevolutionaries "try to stir up pity, soon they will buy some tears, they will do anything to touch our sympathies, to corrupt us." The spontaneous sympathy natural to the people was being exploited by the enemy, who used it against them: "This humanity they talk to you about is cruelty toward the people; this pardon they are looking to suggest is the death sentence of liberty."

Since Louis was a priori guilty because of his separation from the "people," Saint-Just showed that his actions were irrelevant to his trial. Whatever Louis did was *by definition* intended to harm the people. Acts of kindness toward his subjects only demonstrated that he was a hypocrite as well as a tyrant. That Louis used to distribute alms to the poor—by late eighteenth-century standards an act of exemplary virtue—only betrayed his corrupt essence. Saint-Just pointed out how Louis's charity could be but a sham, one so vile as to cast a shadow on virtue itself. "Louis insulted virtue," he said, "to whom will it ever appear innocent again?"

Distinguishing act from intention, Saint-Just reserved moral judgments exclusively for the latter. Intention alone was the criterion of guilt or innocence, and intentions, one's own or other people's, were known by reference to the "public conscience," moral analogue of the "general will." The public conscience was "composed of the people's inclination toward the general good. Respect the mind, but rely on the heart." Those delegates whose hearts were attuned to the public conscience would realize that Louis was an unusually cruel tyrant precisely because he behaved so well. His reign was "the first under the sun, in recorded history, [where] the system of the king's tyranny was sweetness and the appearance of goodness; everywhere he put himself in the place of the fatherland and tried to alienate affection belonging only to it."

Saint-Just demonstrated that the king's only authentic existence was as the people's enemy. The people fused to form one innocent body, the fatherland, menaced by its archetypal Nemesis incarnate in Louis XVI. Saint-Just described the day of August 10, when Louis sought refuge in the Assembly itself. Rather than seeing him as a fugitive from a mob, Saint-Just reversed the situation so that it was the king who brutalized the body politic: "He forced his way into the bowels of the Fatherland with blows of his sword," said Saint-Just, "in order to hide himself inside."

Saint-Just's rhetoric transcended itself in this passage: the body of the fatherland, passive and patient in its innocence, had been violated by the aggression of the hated stranger. The galleries, according to Michelet's rather romantic account, were effectively aroused by Saint-Just's eloquence: "they felt the hand of a master and trembled with joy." Saint-Just drew the necessary conclusions from his argument; the Convention had to choose between a corrupt sentimental pity for the king as man, and its duty to punish a being whose very essence was tyranny. "The Fatherland is in your midst," he said, "choose between it and the king, between the exercise of the people's justice and the exercise of your personal weakness."

It is interesting to note how the king's defense attorney, De Seze, attempted to answer the charges brought against the prisoner: "Here is my response," he said, "I read in Jean-Jacques Rousseau these words: 'Neither the law which condemns nor the judge who sentences can abide by the general will because the general will cannot, as general will, pronounce upon either a man or an act.' Thus spoke Louis before the bar, thus spoke Rousseau, instructing the peoples about liberty."

Despite the appeal of Rousseau's authority, of 749 delegates, 387 voted to behead Louis. The age of despotism was over, France was about to embark upon an era of peace and unity. "With the kings," said Saint-Just, "all systems of violence have been destroyed."

The trial and execution of Louis XVI are of interest from a variety of perspectives. The question of whether he was legally guilty, or whether the actions of the Convention were appropriate, of what results the verdict had for the future of the Revolution have been disputed since the trial began. What is significant, . . . however, is the nature of the argument put forth most effectively by Saint-Just and the way this model of justice was to gain ascendancy over previous standards in the months to come. The essential quality of the accused, as evaluated by the hearts of pure patriots, would come to be the criterion of guilt or innocence, and behavior would not only be discounted, but labeled a subversive consideration. Cobban comments: "The trial and execution of the King proved to be the first of a long series of political trials and condemnations, in the course of which all ideas of judicial impartiality vanish." The very expression, "judicial impartiality," implies a set of cold, intellectualized, procedure-ridden attitudes which the republic of virtue wished to replace with a more emotionally immediate and hence morally superior method of justice.

Biographical Notes

Michel Eyquem de Montaigne was born outside Bordeaux in 1533. His father, later mayor of Bordeaux, had his son's education conducted solely in Latin. He became a member of the Parlement of Bordeaux in 1557 and shortly afterwards became close friends with Etienne de la Boétie, who died in 1563. Montaigne's first published work was his translation of Raymond de Sebond's *Theologia Naturalis,* done at the request of his father. In 1570 Montaigne retired from the Parlement and began to work on his *Essais,* of which the first two books were published in 1580. At this time, Montaigne made his Italian voyage, returning when he was named mayor of Bordeaux, a post he held until 1585. In 1588 a fourth edition of the *Essais* appeared, containing a third book and hundreds of additions. Montaigne died in 1592.

René Descartes was born in 1596 in Brittany and educated at the Royal Jesuit College of La Flèche. He initially studied law, but began pursuing independent studies in geometry in 1619. The next nine years were devoted to the composition of the *Regulae ad Directionem Ingenii* (published posthumously). In 1637 Descartes published three scientific essays (*La Dioptique, Les Météores,* and *La Géométrie*), preceded by the *Discours de la méthode.* In 1641 he published the more technical *Meditationes de Prima Philosophia,* together with a series of objections formulated by Mersenne, Arnauld, Hobbes, and others, as well as his own responses. He expounded his physics in the *Principia Philosophiae* (1644). Descartes died in Stockholm in 1650 while visiting the court of Queen Christina.

Les messieurs de Port-Royal was the collective pseudonym for Antoine Arnauld (1612–94), Claude Lancelot (1615–95), and Pierre Nicole (1625–95), who came together as solitaries at the Jansenist abbey of Port-Royal des Champs. The school founded there by Saint-Cyran included Racine among its pupils. Lancelot's work was concentrated upon pedagogics, from his *Nouvelle méthode pour apprendre la langue grecque* (1644) and *Nouvelle méthode . . . latine* (1655) to his work with Arnauld on the famous *Grammaire générale et raisonnée* (1660). Arnauld was a philosopher and theologian, carrying on correspondance with Descartes, Mersenne, and Leibniz. He was a constant polemicist for the Jansenist cause, as seen in works such as *De la fréquente communion* (1643) and in the controversy over *droit* and *fait* after the Pope's condemnation of the Five Propositions in 1653. He and Nicole were the coauthors of *La Logique; ou, l'art de penser* (1662). Nicole also devoted much of his life to practical theology and polemics, collected in the *Essais de morale.*

455

François, duc de La Rochefoucauld (*François de Marcillac*) was born in 1613; he inherited the name de La Rochefoucauld after his father's death in 1650. He was married at the age of fifteen and enlisted in his first military campaign, in Italy, in 1630. Much of his life at the court of Louis XIII was spent in various intrigues involving the queen, the minister Richelieu, and, later, Mazarin. After the end of the Fronde and the establishment of authority by Louis XIV, La Rochefoucauld restricted his activities to literary ones. He frequented the salons of Mme de Sablé and Mme de La Fayette, and devoted himself to the composition of the *Maximes*, which were first published in 1665. La Rochefoucauld died in 1680.

Blaise Pascal was born in Auvergne in 1623; in 1631 his family moved to Paris, then to Rouen in 1640. As a youth Pascal seems to have been a scientific prodigy; his *Essai sur les sections coniques* was published in 1640 and the *Nouvelles expériences concernant le vide* in 1647. Pascal's family was converted to Jansenism in 1646 and his sister Jacqueline entered the convent of Port-Royal in 1652. In 1654 Pascal had the visionary experience known as the second conversion and retreated to the abbey of Port-Royal des Champs. He defended the Jansenist movement against its Jesuit opponents in the *Lettres provinciales* and began keeping the notes for an apology for the Christian religion which became the *Pensées* (first published by Arnauld and Nicole in 1670). Pascal died in 1662.

Madame de Sévigné (*Marie de Rabutin Chantal*) was born to a noble family in Paris in 1626. Orphaned as a young girl and raised by relatives, she married Charles de Sévigné at the age of eighteen. The alliance produced two children, Françoise Marguerite (later Mme de Grignan) and Charles, before the death of M. de Sévigné in a duel in 1651. The remaining years of Mme de Sévigné's life were split between fashionable society—her friends included la Rochefoucauld, Mme de La Fayette, Corneille, Boileau, and Mme de Maintenon (the royal mistress)—and her letters. The greatest number of these are addressed to her daughter, from whom she was separated from 1671 onwards. Mme de Sévigné died in 1696; her letters circulated in manuscript form in her lifetime and were published posthumously.

Jacques-Bénigne Bossuet was born at Dijon in 1627. He was dedicated to the priesthood at an early age and studied theology at the Collège de Navarre in Paris. He gained a great reputation as a preacher, especially for his funeral orations. He was named bishop of Condom in 1669 and became tutor to the Dauphin in 1670, holding the position until 1680. In 1671 he was elected to the Académie française, and published his *Exposition de la doctrine catholique sur les matières de controverse*. In 1681 Bossuet published the *Discours sur l'histoire universelle* and was named archbishop of Meaux. His reputation and importance as a preacher continued to grow, culminating in the *Oraison funèbre du prince de Condé* (1687). In 1688 he published his *Histoire des variations des Eglises protestantes*. The major works of the rest of his career are the *Maximes et réflexions sur la comédie* (1694), *Instruction sur les états d'oraison* (1697), and the *Relation sur le quiétisme* (1698). Bossuet died in 1704.

Charles Perrault was born in Paris in 1628. A somewhat irregular student, he withdrew from school as an adolescent to read on his own and later gained a law degree of questionable value. In 1654 he took the first of a series of civil-service posts under his brother, the Receiver-General of Paris. In 1663 he became an architectural consultant to the minister Colbert; his association with the latter lasted until 1683. Perrault became a member of the Académie française in 1671, but his literary career did not truly begin until his retirement from civil service. In 1687 he published his *Siècle de Louis le Grand* and in 1688 the first three volumes of his *Parallèle des Anciens et des Modernes* (the fourth and final volume appeared in 1697). He is best known for his 1697 collection of the *Contes de ma Mère l'Oye*. Perrault died in 1703.

François de Salignac de La Mothe-Fénelon was born in the Périgord on August 6, 1651.

After the death of his father he was brought to Paris by his uncle Antoine in 1666, where he studied philosophy at the Collège du Plessis and trained for the priesthood at Saint-Sulpice. Fénelon was ordained in 1674 or 1675; following the revocation of the Edict of Nantes in 1685 he was entrusted with missionary work in the conversion of Protestants. In 1689 he was appointed preceptor to the duc de Bourgogne, the grandson of Louis XIV. In this capacity he composed many of his most famous works, including the *Dialogue des morts* and *Télémaque* (both published in 1699). Through his friendship with Madame Guyon he became involved in the Quietism controversy, and, following the publication of his *Maximes des saints sur la vie intérieure* (1697, condemned by the Vatican in 1699), he was exiled to his archbishopric at Cambrai and deprived of his title of preceptor. He spent the rest of his life in Cambrai, writing the *Traité de l'existence et des attributs de Dieu* (1712), the *Lettres sur divers sujets de métaphysique et de religion* (1713), and the *Lettre à l'Académie* (1714). Fénelon died on January 7, 1715.

Jean de La Bruyère was born into a bourgeois Parisian family in 1645. In 1673 he joined the petty nobility by purchasing the office of treasurer at Caen, and in 1684, sponsored by Bossuet, he became tutor to the grandson of the Prince de Condé, remaining part of the Condé household for many years. The first edition of his *Caractères* was published in 1688; eight further editions, with extensive revisions and additions, appeared in his lifetime. After a bitter struggle, he was elected to the Académie française with the support of Boileau in 1693. His *Discours à l'Académie* was one of the more divisive contributions to the *Querelle des Anciens et des Modernes*. La Bruyère died in 1696 while at work on the *Dialogues sur le quiétisme*.

Bernard Le Bovier, Sieur de Fontenelle was born in Rouen in 1657. His literary reputation was established by works of the 1680s such as the *Dialogues des morts*, the *Entretiens sur la pluralité des mondes*, the *Histoire des oracles*, and the *Digression sur les Anciens et les Modernes*. After four unsuccessful candidacies, Fontenelle was elected to the Académie française in 1691. He became the secretary of the Académie des Sciences in 1697 and held that position until 1740. During that period, he wrote *éloges* of all the members and the *Histoire de l'Académie des Sciences*. Fontenelle died in 1757.

Louis de Rouvroy, duc de Saint-Simon was born in 1675. His father, a one-time favorite of Lous XII and later exiled by Richelieu, first presented him at the court of Louis XIV in 1691. In 1694 Saint-Simon began to keep the notes that would become his *Mémoires*. Following the death of Louis XIV in 1715, Saint-Simon was an important counselor to the Regent, the duc d'Orléans. After the death of Orléans in 1723, Saint-Simon retired from the court and devoted himself to the composition of his *Mémoires*, which he finished four years before his death in 1755. The *Mémoires* were not published until 1830.

Charles Louis de Secondat, baron de La Brède et de Montesquieu was born at La Brède, near Bordeaux, in 1689. After studying law, he became a counselor in the Parlement of Bordeaux in 1714, and inherited his uncle's position as *président à mortier* in the Parlement of Bordeaux along with the name Montesquieu. He was a founding member of the Bordeaux Académie des Sciences and in 1721 he published the immensely popular satirical novel *Les lettres persanes*. After selling his position in the Bordeaux Parlement, he published the *Temple de Gnide* and became a member of the Académie française in 1728. For the next decade he traveled throughout Europe, becoming a member of the Royal Society in 1730 during his stay in England. In 1734 he published the *Considérations sur la grandeur et la décadence des romains*, and, in 1748, *De l'esprit des lois*, which was placed on the Vatican Index in 1751. Montesquieu died in Paris in 1755.

François Quesnay was born in 1694 to a peasant family in the village of Méré in the Ile-de-

France and was trained as a rural surgeon. His major medical publication is the *Essai physique sur l'économie animale* of 1736. In 1750 he became the personal physician to Mme de Pompadour, mistress of Louis XV, and moved to Versailles. In 1756 and 1757 he contributed five articles to Diderot's *Encyclopédie*. At the same time he met the marquis de Mirabeau, who became his disciple, collaborator, and spokesman. In 1758 they published an edition of the "Tableau économique" with an explanation and a series of economic maxims. Mirabeau gave further explanations of Quesnay's physiocratic system in *L'Ami des hommes* (1757–59) and *La Philosophie rurale* (1763). Quesnay himself regularly published articles of a polemical nature in the *Journal de l'agriculture, du commerce, et des finances*. Quesnay died in 1774 at Versailles.

Voltaire (François-Marie Arouet) was born in Paris in 1694. His first great literary success came in 1718 with the production of his play *Oedipe*, at which time he adopted the name Voltaire. In 1726, following a quarrel with the chevalier de Rohan, Voltaire was forced into exile in England. There he published the *Henriade* (1728). On his to return in 1729 he produced the plays *Brutus* (1729) and *Zaïre* (1732), and published the *Histoire de Charles XII* (1731) and the *Lettres philosophiques* (1733). The banning of this work forced him to leave Paris for Cirey with Mme du Châtelet. In 1738 he published *Eléments de la philosophie de Newton*, and first met Frederick II. His plays (*Mahomet* [1742] and *Mérope* [1743]) continued to meet with great success, and in 1745 Voltaire was appointed royal histographer, and then elected to the Académie française in 1746. The following year, he published *Zadig*. In 1750 Voltaire moved to Berlin, where he published *Le siècle de Louis XIV*. He returned to France in 1753, but upon the publication of a pirated edition of *L'Essai sur les moeurs*, Voltaire was once again exiled. He then moved to Geneva and purchased *Les Délices*. In 1759 he published *Candide*. Much of the rest of his life was devoted to establishing cooperative industries on his Swiss properties and championing the victims of *l'infâme*. Voltaire died in 1778 in Paris.

Julien Offray de La Mettrie was born in Saint-Malo in Normandy in 1709. He received a degree in medicine in 1725, and in 1733 went to Leyden to study with Boerhaave; his first published work was a translation of Boerhaave's *Aphrodisiacus*. In 1745, while a military doctor, La Mettrie published his *Histoire naturelle de l'âme*, whose materialism caused enough ire among theologians to force him to leave France. The similar reception accorded to his *L'Homme machine* of 1748 forced him to seek refuge at the court of Frederick II in Berlin, where he died in 1751.

Jean-Jacques Rousseau was born in Geneva in 1712. He left Geneva in 1728, traveled, and found employment as a servant. He moved to Paris in 1742, where he became friends with Diderot and Condillac. His first published work, *Discours sur les sciences et les arts*, was published in response to a prize question of the Academy of Dijon. His operetta, *Le Devin de village* (1753), was a great success at court. In 1754 Rousseau published the *Discours sur l'origine et les fondements de l'inégalité parmi les hommes*, again in response to a prize question from the Academy of Dijon. Rousseau returned to Geneva at this time. In 1758 the *Lettre à d'Alembert sur les spectacles* was published in response to the article "Genève." This same period saw the composition of *Julie, ou la nouvelle Héloïse* (1761), and *Du contrat social* and *Emile* (1762). The novel was a tremendous popular success, but both treatises were burned in Geneva and banned in Paris. From 1765 to 1769, Rousseau, often in hiding, wrote his *Confessions*, which were read aloud to a Parisian audience in 1771. In 1772 Rousseau began the *Dialogues, Rousseau juge de Jean-Jacques*, and from 1776 until his death in 1778 he wrote the *Rêveries d'un promeneur solitaire*.

Denis Diderot was born in 1713, the son of a prosperous cutler in the provincial town of

Langres. He moved to Paris as a student and in the 1740s became friendly with Rousseau and Condillac. In 1746 he was named coeditor, with d'Alembert, of the *Encyclopédie*. His writings of the period—*Pensées philosophiques* (1746), *Les Bijoux indiscrets* (1748), and *Lettre sur les aveugles* (1749)—were considered atheistic and subversive enough for Diderot to be imprisoned at Vincennes in 1749. After his release, he published two more philosophical essays, the *Lettre sur les sourds et les muets* (1752) and the *Pensées sur l'interprétation de la nature* (1753), before turning to drama (*Le Fils naturel* [1757] and *Le Père de famille* [1758]) and dramatic theory (*Entretiens sur le Fils naturel* [1757] and *Discours sur la poésie dramatique* [1758]). In 1759 he began to publish accounts of the annual *Salons* in Grimm's *Correspondance littéraire*. The greatest portion of the rest of Diderot's literary output, however, appeared posthumously—the "novels" *La Religieuse* (1760), *Le Neveu de Rameau* (begun 1760), and *Jacques le fataliste* (begun 1771), as well as the philosophical essays *Le Rêve de d'Alembert* (1769) and *Supplément au voyage de Bougainville*. In 1773 Diderot journeyed to Russia to visit the court of his patroness Catherine the Great. He died in 1784.

Etienne Bonnot de Condillac was born in 1714 at Grenoble. He was raised by his brothers, one of whom, the socialist abbé de Mably, brought him to Paris and introduced him to salon society. His first book, *Essai sur l'origine des connaissances humaines*, was published in 1746, followed by the *Traité des systèmes* of 1749, the year Condillac was elected to the Academy of Sciences of Berlin. Following the publication of the *Traité des sensations* (1754), Condillac became tutor to the Prince of Parma, a position he held until 1767. In this capacity he produced a *Cours d'études* (published 1775), including an *Art d'écrire*, an *Art de penser*, an *Histoire ancienne et moderne*, and the *Dictionnaire des synonymes*. Condillac was elected to the Académie française in 1768. His last work, *La Langue des calculs*, was published posthumously. Condillac died in 1780.

Jean Le Rond d'Alembert was born in 1717, the illegitimate son of Mme de Tencin. He was christened Jean Le Rond after the Parisian church where he was left as a foundling; he took the name d'Alembert while a student. His studies led him to mathematics and he first became an adjunct member of the Académie des Sciences in 1745. His early scientific works include the *Traité de dynamique* (1743) and the *Traité de l'équilibre et du mouvement des fluides* (1746). In 1745 he was named coeditor, with Diderot, of the *Encyclopédie*. D'Alembert was responsible for the scientific portion of the work; he also contributed the *Discours préliminaire* to the first volume (1751) and numerous general articles. In 1757–58 the furor caused by his article "Genève" led to his resignation from the enterprise and contributed to the suppression of the *Encyclopédie* in 1759. D'Alembert died in 1783.

Anne-Robert-Jacques Turgot was born in Normandy in 1727. He originally studied for the priesthood. His earliest sociological text, *Tableau philosophique des progrès successifs de l'esprit humain*, was addressed to his fellow theology students at the Sorbonne in 1750. At the same time Turgot wrote the *Remarques critiques sur l'origine des langues et la signification des mots*, and the notes *Sur l'histoire universelle*. In 1751 he renounced the priesthood and entered the civil service. He contributed five articles to the *Encyclopédie* in 1756–57. In 1761 he became the intendant of Limoges; while in this post he composed his major works on economics, *Réflexions sur la formation et la distribution des richesses* (1769), *Valeur et monnaie* (published posthumously), and *Lettres sur le commerce des grains* (1770). In 1774 Turgot was appointed *Contrôleur général des finances*, but was dismissed in 1776. He died in 1781.

Marie-Jean-Antoine-Nicholas Caritat, marquis de Condorcet, was born in Picardy in 1743. He became a member of the Académie des Sciences in 1769 on the strength of his *Essai sur le calcul intégral* (1765) and *Essai d'analyse* (1767–68). In 1773 he became secretary of this body and in this capacity wrote a number of éloges, such as the *Vie de Turgot* (1786). In 1785 he published the *Essai sur l'application de l'analyse à la probabilité des décisions redues à la pluralité des voix*. He was a prolific political pamphleteer, and in 1790 was elected to the legislative assembly. While a member of that body, he wrote *Mémoires sur l'instruction publique* (1793) and a project for educational reform; he was also the architect of a (rejected) project for a new constitution. In 1793 he broke with the Jacobins and was forced into hiding, where he wrote the *Esquisse d'un tableau historique des progrès de l'esprit humain*. Condorcet was denounced and arrested in 1794 and died in prison, possibly a suicide.

Maximilien-Marie-Isidore de Robespierre was born in Arras on May 6, 1758. From a family of lawyers, he too studied law in Paris, and practiced in Arras from 1781 to 1789. He was elected a delegate of the third estate from Arras for the *Etats généraux*, the first constituted body of the Revolution. He was subsequently a member of the Constituent Assembly and the National Convention, the Paris Revolutionary Commune, and, finally, in July 1793, he became a member of the Committee of Public Safety. Robespierre, through his speeches at the Convention and at the Jacobin Club, was long one of the most powerful men of the Revolution, setting the policies of the late war effort and the General Maximum, and was closely involved in the Reign of Terror. He fell from power in Thermidor and was guillotined on July 28, 1794.

Louis-Antoine de Saint-Just was born at Décize on August 25, 1767. He studied law at the University of Reims. In 1789 he published a long and somewhat scandalous poem, *Organt*, composed while held in detention. He became active in politics with the beginning of the Revolution, publishing *L'Esprit de la Révolution* in 1791 and in 1792 being elected to the National Convention. The youngest member of that body, he first came to prominence with his speech of November 13, 1792, in favor of the execution of Louis XVI. In May 1793, he became a member of the Committee of Public Safety; in this capacity he undertook a number of military and agricultural missions, as well as playing a crucial role in the Reign of Terror. Saint-Just was the author of the most important of the indictments. He fell with Robespierre in Thermidor and was guillotined on July 28, 1794.

Contributors

Harold Bloom, Sterling Professor of the Humanities at Yale University, is the author of *The Anxiety of Influence, Poetry and Repression*, and many other volumes of literary criticism. A MacArthur Prize Fellow, he is general editor of five series of literary criticism published by Chelsea House. During 1987–88, he served as Charles Eliot Norton Professor of Poetry at Harvard University.

Timothy J. Reiss is Professor of French and Comparative Literature and Associate Professor of Philosophy at Emory University. He is the author of *Toward Dramatic Illusion, Tragedy and Truth, The Discourse of Modernism*, and *The Meaning of Literature*.

Jean-Luc Nancy is a French philosopher teaching at the University of Strasbourg. He has also taught at the University of California at San Diego and at Berkeley. He has collaborated with Philippe Lacoue-Labarthe on *L'Absolu littéraire* and *Le Titre de la lettre*. He is also the author of *Ego Sum, La Remarque spéculative, Le Discours de la syncope*, and *L'Impératif catégorique*.

Noam Chomsky is Institute Professor of Linguistics at the Massachusetts Institute of Technology. He is known both for his works in linguistics and generative grammar such as *Aspects of the Theory of Syntax* and *On Government and Binding* and for his political studies such as *The Washington Connection and Third World Fascism* (with Edward S. Herman) and *Towards a New Cold War*.

Philip E. Lewis is Associate Professor of French in the Department of Romance Languages at Cornell University. He is the author of *La Rochefoucauld: The Art of Abstraction* and is the editor of *Diacritics*.

Paul de Man was, until his death in 1983, Sterling Professor of Comparative

461

Literature at Yale University. He is the author of *Blindness and Insight: Essays in Contemporary Criticism; Allegories of Reading: Figural Language in Rousseau, Nietzsche, Rilke, and Proust;* and *The Rhetoric of Romanticism;* and posthumously of the forthcoming collections *The Resistance to Theory, Aesthetic Ideology,* and *Fugitive Essays.*

Louise K. Horowitz is Associate Professor of French at Rutgers University. She is the author of *Honoré d'Urfe* and *Love and Language: A Study of the Classical French Moralist Writers.*

Domna C. Stanton is Professor of French in the Department of Romance Languages at the University of Michigan. She is the author of *The Aristocrat as Art* as well as the collections *The Defiant Muse: French Feminist Poems from the Middle Ages to the Present* and *The Female Autograph.*

Kirsti Simonsuuri is a senior research fellow at the University of Iceland and has been a Fulbright Exchange Scholar at Harvard University. She has translated numerous books into Finnish, and is the author of three collections of verse and a volume of prose in addition to the study *Homer's Original Genius: Eighteenth-Century Notions of the Greek Epic.*

Wilbur Samuel Howell is Professor Emeritus of Rhetoric and Poetry at Princeton University. He is the author of *Poetics, Rhetoric, and Logic: Studies in the Basic Disciplines of Criticism; Eighteenth-Century British Logic and Rhetoric;* and *Logic and Rhetoric in England 1500–1700;* and is the translator of *Fénelon's Dialogues on Eloquence.*

Roland Barthes, the preeminent French literary critic since Sartre, is best remembered for *Writing Degree Zero, S/Z, Mythologies,* and *The Pleasure of the Text.*

Herbert Dieckmann is one of the leading philologists and textual scholars on the French eighteenth century. His interpretations have been published in *Cing leçons sur Diderot, Die kunsterlich Form des Rêve de d'Alembert,* and in journals of many countries and several languages.

Leo Spitzer was an American linguist and philosopher. His books include *Linguistics and Literary History, Essays in Historical Semantics,* and *Essays on English and American Literature.*

Louis Althusser is an influential French Marxist philosopher. His works include *For Marx, Reading* Capital (with Etienne Balibar), *Lenin and Philosophy,* and *Essays in Self-Criticism.*

Herbert Lüthy is a Swiss historian. He has translated Montaigne into German, and is the author of *France against Herself, La banque protestante en France,* and *Wozu Geschichte?*

Suzanne Gearhart teaches in the Department of Literature at the University of California, San Diego. She is the author of *The Open Boundary of History and Fiction: A Critical Approach to the French Enlightenment* and has published a number of articles on contemporary literary theory.

Blair Campbell teaches political science at the University of California, Los Angeles. He has published articles on Plato, Montaigne, and Rousseau.

Michael Fried is Professor of Humanities and History of Art and Director of the Humanities Center at Johns Hopkins University. He is the author of *Absorption and Theatricality: Painting and Beholder in the Age of Diderot; Realism, Writing, Disfiguration: On Thomas Eakins and Stephen Crane;* and of monographs on Manet and Morris Louis. His forthcoming book is a study of Courbet.

Jacques Derrida is Directeur d'Etudes at the École des Hautes Études en Sciences Sociales in Paris, Visiting Professor in the Humanities at Yale University, and Andrew D. White Professor-at-large at Cornell University. He has written two books on Nietzsche, *Otobiographies* and *Spurs/Eperons,* and is the author of many articles and books including *La voix et le phenomene* (*Speech and Phenomena*), *La Dissemination* (*Disseminations*), *Les Marges* (*Margins*), *Glas,* and *La Carte postale.*

Peter France teaches in the Department of French at the University of Edinburgh. He is the author of *Poets of Modern Russia, Racine's Rhetoric,* and studies of Diderot and Rousseau.

Ronald L. Meek was Tyler Professor of Economics at the University of Leicester until his death in 1978. His books include *Studies in the Labor Theory of Value, The Rise and Fall of the Concept of the Economic Machine, Economics and Ideology and Other Essays,* and *Smith, Marx and After.* He also edited the writings of Quesnay, Turgot, Adam Smith, and others.

Keith M. Baker teaches history at the University of Chicago. He is the author of a full-length study of Condorcet, *Condorcet: From Natural Philosophy to Social Mathematics,* and of numerous articles on Enlightenment intellectual history.

Carol Blum is Associate Professor of French at the State University of New York, Stony Brook. She is the author of *Rousseau and the Republic of Virtue: The Language of Politics in the French Revolution.*

Bibliography

GENERAL

Andresen, Julie T. "From Condillac to Condorcet: The Algebra of History." In *Progress in Linguistic Historiography*, edited by Konrad Koerner, 187–97. Amsterdam: Benjamins, 1980.

Auerbach, Erich. *Mimesis: The Representation of Reality in Western Literature*. Translated by Willard R. Trask. Princeton: Princeton University Press, 1953.

Barber, W. H., et al., eds. *The Age of Enlightenment: Studies Presented to Theodore Besterman*. London: Oliver & Boyd/University Court of the University of St. Andrews, 1967.

Bringham, Alfred, and Virgil W. Topazio, eds. *Enlightenment Studies in Honour of Lester G. Crocker*. Oxford: The Voltaire Foundation at the Taylor Institution, 1979.

Brody, Jules, ed. *French Classicism: A Critical Miscellany*. Englewood Cliffs, N.J.: Prentice-Hall, 1966.

Brunschwicg, Leon. *Descartes et Pascal, lecteurs de Montaigne*. Neuchâtel: La Baconnière, 1945.

Cassirer, Ernst. *The Philosophy of the Enlightenment*. Translated by Fritz C. A. Koelln and James P. Pettegrave. Princeton: Princeton University Press, 1951.

Cognet, Louis. *Crépuscule des mystères: Bossuet, Fénelon*. Tournai, Belgium: Desclée, 1958.

Coulet, Henri, ed. *L'Histoire au dix-huitième siècle*. Aix-en-Provence: EDISUD, 1980.

Davidson, Hugh M. "Fontenelle, Perrault, and the Realignment of the Arts." In *Literature and History in the Age of Ideas: Essays in the French Enlightenment Presented to George R. Havens*, edited by Charles G. S. Williams, 3–13. Columbus: Ohio University Press, 1975.

Dieckmann, Herbert. "Esthetic Theory and Criticism in the Enlightenment: Some Examples of Modern Trends." In *Introduction to Modernity: A Symposium on Eighteenth-Century Thought*, edited by Robert Mollenauer, 63–105. Austin: University of Texas Press, 1966.

———. "An Interpretation of the Eighteenth Century." *Modern Language Quarterly* 15 (1954): 295–311.

————. "Natural History from Bacon to Diderot: A Few Guideposts." In *Essays on the Age of Enlightenment in Honor of Ira O. Wade,* edited by Jean Macary, 93–112. Geneva: Droz, 1977.

Foucault, Michel. *The Order of Things: An Archaeology of the Human Sciences.* New York: Pantheon, 1971.

Fox-Genovese, Elizabeth, ed. *French Women and the Age of Enlightenment.* Bloomington: Indiana University Press, 1984.

France, Peter. *Rhetoric and Truth in France, Descartes to Diderot.* Oxford: Clarendon Press 1972.

Frankel, Charles. *The Faith of Reason: The Idea of Progress in the French Enlightenment.* New York: King's Crown Press, 1948.

Friedenthal, Richard. *Entdecker des Ich: Montaigne, Pascal, Diderot.* Munich: Piper, 1969.

Gay, Peter. *The Party of Humanity.* New York: Knopf, 1964.

————. *The Englightenment: An Interpretation.* 2 vols. New York: Knopf, 1966, 1969.

Gearhart, Suzanne. *The Open Boundary of History and Fiction: A Critical Approach to the French Enlightenment.* Princeton: Princeton University Press, 1984.

Gossman, Lionel. *Medievalism and the Ideologies of the Enlightenment: The World and Work of LaCurne de Sainte-Palaye.* Baltimore: Johns Hopkins University Press, 1968.

Grimsley, Ronald. *From Montesquieu to Laclos: Studies on the French Enlightenment.* Geneva: Droz, 1974.

Hampson, Norman. *Will and Circumstance: Montesquieu, Rousseau, and the French Revolution.* London: Duckworth, 1983.

Hazard, Paul. *European Thought in the Eighteenth Century: From Montesquieu to Lessing.* Translated by J. Lewis May. New Haven: Yale University Press, 1954.

Hobson, Marian. *The Object of Art: The Treatment of Illusion in Eighteenth-Century France.* Cambridge: Cambridge University Press, 1982.

Horowitz, Louise. *Love and Language: A Study of the Classical French Moralist Writers.* Columbus: Ohio State University Press, 1977.

Juolowitz, Dalia. *Subjectivity and Representation: The Origins of Modern Thought in Descartes.* Cambridge: Cambridge University Press, 1986.

Lüthy, Herbert. *From Calvin to Rousseau: Tradition and Modernity in Socio-Political Thought from the Reformation to the Revolution.* Translated by Salvator Attanasio. New York: Basic Books, 1970.

McDonald, Christie V. *The Dialogue of Writing: Essays in Eighteenth-Century French Literature.* Waterloo, Ont.: Wilfrid Laurier University Press, 1984.

Manuel, Frank E. *The Prophets of Paris.* Cambridge, Mass: Harvard University Press, 1962.

Moore, W. G. *French Classical Literature.* London: Oxford University Press, 1961.

Morgues, Odette de. *Two French Moralists: La Rochefoucauld and La Bruyère.* Cambridge: Cambridge University Press, 1978.

Rigault, Hippolyte. *Histoire de la querelle des Anciens et des Modernes.* Paris: L. Hachette, 1856.

Vartanian, Aram. *Diderot and Descartes: A Study of Scientific naturalism in the Enlightenment.* Princeton: Princeton University Press, 1953.

Voegelin, Eric. *From Enlightenment to Revolution.* Edited by John H. Halliwell. Durham, N.C.: Duke University Press, 1975.

Wade, Ira O. *The Structure and Form of the French Enlightenment.* 2 vols. Princeton: Princeton University Press, 1977.

White, R. J. *The Anti-Philosophers: A Study of the Philosophes in Eighteenth-Century France.* London: Macmillan; New York: St. Martin's Press, 1970.

MICHEL DE MONTAIGNE

Bauschatz, Cathleen M. "Montaigne's Conception of Reading in the Context of Renaissance Poetics and Modern Criticism." In *The Reader in the Text: Essays on Audience and Interpretation*, edited by Susan R. Suleiman and Inge Crosman, 264–91. Princeton: Princeton University Press, 1980.

Beaujour, Michel. "Speculum, Method, and Self-Portrayal: Some Epistemological Problems." In *Mimesis: From Mirror to Method, Augustine to Descartes*, edited by John D. Lyons and Stephen G. Nichols, Jr., 188–96. Hanover, N.H.: University Press of New England for Dartmouth College, 1982.

Blanchard, Jean Marc. "Of Cannibalism and Autobiography." *MLN* 93 (1978): 654–76.

Bloom, Harold, ed. *Modern Critical Interpretations: Montaigne's Essais*. New Haven: Chelsea House, 1987.

———. *Modern Critical Views: Montaigne*. New Haven: Chelsea House, 1987.

Boase, Alan M. *The Fortunes of Montaigne: A History of the Essais in France, 1580–1669*. London: Methuen, 1935.

Bowen, Barbara C. *The Age of Bluff: Paradox and Ambiguity in Rabelais and Montaigne*. Urbana: University of Illinois Press, 1972.

———. "Montaigne's Anti-*Phaedrus*: 'Sur des vers de Virgile' (*Essais*, III, v)." *Journal of Medieval and Renaissance Studies* 5 (1975): 107–21.

Brody, Jules. "Les Oreilles de Montaigne." *Romanic Review* 74 (1983): 121–35.

Brown, Frieda S. *Religious and Political Conservatism in the Essais of Montaigne*. Geneva: Droz, 1963.

Brush, Craig B. "The Essayist Is Learned: Montaigne's *Journal de voyage* and the *Essais*." *Romanic Review* 62 (1971): 16–27.

———. "Reflections on Montaigne's Concept of Being." In *From Marot to Montaigne: Essays on French Renaissance Literature*, edited by Raymond C. La Charité, 147–66. *Kentucky Romance Quarterly* 19, supplement no. 1, 1972.

Bulletin de la Société des Amis de Montaigne 1– (1913–   ).

Butor, Michel. *Essais sur les Essais*. Paris: Gallimard, 1968.

Cameron, Keith, ed. *Montaigne and His Age*. Exeter: University of Exeter, 1981.

Cave, Terence. "Montaigne." In *The Cornucopian Text: Problems of Writing in the French Renaissance*, 271–321. Oxford: Clarendon Press, 1979.

Clark, Carol. *The Web of Metaphor: Studies in the Imagery of Montaigne's Essais*. Lexington, Ky.: French Forum Publishers, 1978.

Coleman, D. G. "Montaigne's 'Sur des vers de Virgile': Taboo Subject, Taboo Author." In *Classical Influences on European Culture, A.D. 1500–1700*, edited by R. R. Bolgar, 135–40. Cambridge: Cambridge University Press, 1976.

Compagnon, Antoine. *Nous, Michel de Montaigne*. Paris: Editions du Seuil, 1980.

———. *La Seconde Main ou le travail de la citation*. Paris: Editions du Seuil, 1979.

Cottrell, Robert D. *Sexuality/Textuality: A Study of the Fabric of Montaigne's Essais*. Columbus: Ohio State University Press, 1981.

de Man, Paul. "Montaigne and Transcendence." In *Fugitive Essays*, edited by Lindsay Waters. Minneapolis: University of Minnesota Press, forthcoming.

Dow, Neal. *The Concept and Term "Nature" in Montaigne's Essais*. Philadelphia: University of Pennsylvania, 1940.

Duval, Edwin M. "Lessons of the New World: Design and Measuring in Montaigne's 'Des Cannibales' (I, 31) and 'Des Coches' (III, 6)." *Yale French Studies* no. 64 (1983): 95–112.

———. "Montaigne's Conversions: Compositional Strategies in the *Essais*." *French Forum* 7 (1982): 5–22.

Emerson, Ralph Waldo. "Montaigne; or, The Skeptic." In *Representative Men: Seven Lectures*, 148–84. Boston: Phillips, Sampson, 1850.

L'Esprit créateur 8, no. 3 (Fall 1968). Special Montaigne issue.

Frame, Donald M. "Did Montaigne Betray Sebond?" *Romanic Review* 38 (1947): 297–329.

———. *Montaigne: A Biography*. New York: Harcourt, Brace & World, 1965.

———. *Montaigne's Discovery of Man: The Humanization of a Humanist*. New York: Columbia University Press, 1955.

———. *Montaigne's Essais: A Study*. Englewood Cliffs, N.J.: Prentice-Hall, 1969.

———, and Mary B. McKinley, eds. *Columbia Montaigne Conference Papers*. Lexington, Ky.: French Forum Publishers, 1981.

Friedrich, Hugo. *Montaigne*. Bern: Franke, 1949.

Gide, André. "Montaigne." *Yale Review* 28 (1939): 572–93.

Glauser, Alfred. *La Balance de Montaigne: Exagium/essai*. Paris: A.-G. Nizet, 1972.

———. "Montaigne and Sebond: The Rhetoric of Paradox." *French Studies* 28 (1974): 134–45.

———. *Montaigne paradoxal*. Paris: A.-G. Nizet, 1972.

Greenberg, Mitchell. "Montaigne at the Crossroads: Textual Conundrums in the *Essais*." *Stanford French Review* 6 (1982): 21–34.

Hallie, Philip P. *The Scar of Montaigne: An Essay in Personal Philosophy*. Middletown, Conn.: Wesleyan University Press, 1966.

Harth, Erica. " 'Sur des vers de Virgile' (III, 5): Antinomy and Totality in Montaigne." *French Forum* 2 (1977): 3–21.

Horkheimer, Max. "Montaigne und die Funktion der Skepsis." In *Kritische Theorie: Eine Dokumentation*, edited by Alfred Schmidt, vol. 2, 201–59. Frankfurt a.M.: S. Fischer Verlag, 1968.

Hunt, R. N. Carew. "Montaigne and the State." *Edinburgh Review* 246 (1927): 259–72.

Kritzman, Lawrence D. *Destruction/découverte: Le Fonctionnement de la rhétorique dans les* Essais *de Montaigne*. Lexington, Ky.: French Forum Publishers, 1980.

La Charité, Raymond C. *The Concept of Judgement in Montaigne*. The Hague: Martinus Nijhoff, 1968.

———, ed. *O un amy! Essays on Montaigne in Honor of Donald M. Frame*. Lexington, Ky.: French Forum Publishers, 1977.

Lanson, Gustave. *Les* Essais *de Montaigne: Etude et analyse*. Paris: Mellotée, 1930.

Larkin, Neil M. "Montaigne's Last Words." *L'Esprit Créateur* 15, nos. 1–2 (Spring–Summer 1975): 21–38.

Lüthy, Herbert. "Montaigne, or the Art of Being Truthful." *Encounter* 1, no. 2 (November 1953): 33–44.

McFarlane, Ian D. "Montaigne and the Concept of the Imagination." In *The French Renaissance and Its Heritage: Essays Presented to Alan M. Boase*, edited by D. R. Haggis et al., 117–37. London: Methuen, 1968.

———, and Ian Maclean, eds. *Montaigne: Essays in Memory of Richard Sayce*. Oxford: Clarendon Press, 1982.

McGowan, Margaret. *Montaigne's Deceits: The Art of Persuasion in the* Essais. London: University of London Press, 1974.

McKinley, Mary B. *Words in a Corner: Studies in Montaigne's Latin Quotations*. Lexington, Ky.: French Forum Publishers, 1981.

Marin, Louis. "Montaigne's Tomb; or, Autobiographical Discourse." *Oxford Literary Review* 4, no. 3 (1981): 43–58.

Mehlman, Geoffrey. "La Boetie's Montaigne." *Oxford Literary Review* 4, no. 1 (1981): 45–61.

Merleau-Ponty, Maurice. "Reading Montaigne." In *Signs,* translated by Richard C. McCleary, 198–210. Evanston, Ill.: Northwestern University Press, 1964.

Moore, W. G. "Montaigne's Notion of Experience." In *The French Mind: Studies in Honour of Gustave Radler,* edited by W. G. Moore, 34–52. Oxford: Clarendon Press, 1952.

Norton, Glyn P. *Montaigne and the Introspective Mind.* The Hague: Mouton, 1975.

O'Neill, John. *Essaying Montaigne: A Study of the Renaissance Institution of Reading and Writing.* London: Routledge & Kegan Paul, 1982.

Pouilloux, Jean-Yves. *Lire les* Essais *de Montaigne.* Paris: Maspero, 1969.

Poulet, Georges. "Montaigne." In *Studies in Human Time,* translated by Elliot Coleman, 39–49. Baltimore: Johns Hopkins University Press, 1956.

Regosin, Richard L. *The Matter of My Book: Montaigne's* Essais *as the Book of the Self.* Berkeley: University of California Press, 1977.

Rendall, Steven. "*Mus in pice:* Montaigne and Interpretation." *MLN* 94 (1979): 1056–71.

———. "The Rhetoric of Montaigne's Self-Portrait." *Studies in Philology* 73 (1976): 285–301.

Rider, Frederick. *The Dialectic of Selfhood in Montaigne.* Palo Alto: Stanford University Press, 1973.

Rigolot, François. "Montaigne's Maxims: From a Discourse of the Other to the Expression of Self." *L'Esprit Créateur* 22, no. 3 (Fall 1982): 8–18.

Samaras, Zoe. *The Comic Element in Montaigne's Style.* Paris: A.-G. Nizet, 1970.

Sayce, Richard A. *The* Essays *of Montaigne: A Critical Exploration.* London: Weidenfeld & Nicholson, 1972.

Screech, M. A. *Montaigne and Melancholy: The Wisdom of the* Essays. London: Duckworth, 1983.

Starobinski, Jean. *Montaigne in Motion.* Translated by Arthur Goldhammer. Chicago: University of Chicago Press, 1985.

Strowski, Fortunat. *Montaigne.* 2d ed. Paris: F. Alcan, 1931.

Tetel, Marcel, ed. *Actes du colloque international: Montaigne (1580–1980).* Paris: A.-G. Nizet, 1983.

Villey, Pierre. *Les Sources et l'évolution des* Essais *de Montaigne.* 2 vols. Paris: Hachette, 1908.

Wilden, Anthony. "Montaigne on the Paradoxes of Individualism: A Communication about Communication." In *System and Structure: Essays in Communication and Exchange,* 88–105. London: Tavistock, 1972.

———. " 'Par divers moyens on arrive à pareille fin': A Reading of Montaigne." *MLN* 83 (1968): 577–97.

Winter, Ian J. *Montaigne's Self-Portrait and Its Influence in France 1580–1630.* Lexington, Ky.: French Forum Publishers, 1976.

Yale French Studies no. 64 (1983). Special Montaigne issue.

RENÉ DESCARTES

Bruns, Gerald L. "A Literary Man's Guide to the *Discourse on Method.*" *Boundary 2* 8, no. 2 (1980): 141–64.

Butler, R. J., ed. *Cartesian Studies.* New York: Barnes & Noble, 1972.

Cahne, Pierre. "Saint Augustin et les philosophes au XVIIe siècle: Ontologie et autobiographie." *Dix-septième siècle* no. 135 (April–June 1982): 121–32.

Carter, Richard B. *Descartes' Medical Philosophy: The Organic Solution to the Mind-Body Problem.* Baltimore: Johns Hopkins University Press, 1983.

Caton, Hiram Pendleton. *The Origin of Subjectivity: An Essay on Descartes*. New Haven: Yale University Press, 1973.

Derrida, Jacques. "Cogito and the History of Madness." In *Writing and Difference*, translated by Alan Bass, 31–63. Chicago: University of Chicago Press, 1978.

———. "Languages and Institutions of Philosophy." *Semiotic Inquiry/Recherches Sémiotiques* 4, no. 2 (June 1984): 91–154.

Doney, Willis, ed. *Descartes: A Collection of Critical Essays*. Garden City, N.Y.: Doubleday (Anchor), 1967.

Flores, Ralph. "Delusions of Self: Descartes' Authorial Burden." *Kentucky Romance Quarterly* 25 (1978): 283–95.

Frankfurt, Harry G. *Demons, Dreamers, and Madmen: The Defense of Reason in Descartes' Meditations*. Indianapolis: Bobbs-Merrill, 1970.

Gankroger, Stephen, ed. *Descartes: Philosophy, Mathematics, and Physics*. Totowa, N.J.: Barnes & Noble, 1980.

Gilson, Etienne. *René Descartes*, Discours de la méthode: *Texte et commentaire*. 3d ed. Paris: J. Vrin, 1962.

Harries, Karsten. "Descartes, Perspective, and the Angelic Eye." *Yale French Studies* no. 49 (1973): 28–42.

Hooker, Michael, ed. *Descartes: Critical and Interpretive Essays*. Baltimore: Johns Hopkins University Press, 1978.

Kennington, Richard. "Descartes and the Mastery of Nature." In *Organism, Medicine, and Metaphysics: Essays in Honor of Hans Jonas on His 75th Birthday, May 10, 1978*, edited by Stuart F. Spicker. Dordrecht: Reidel, 1978.

Koyre, Alexandre. "Descartes After Three Hundred Years." *University of Buffalo Studies* 19 (1951): 1–37.

Lyons, John D. "Subjectivity and Imitation in the *Discours de la méthode*." *Neophilologus* 66 (1982): 508–24.

Magnus, Bernd, and James B. Wilbur, eds. *Cartesian Essays: A Collection of Critical Studies*. The Hague: Martinus Nijhoff, 1969.

Margolis, Joseph, ed. *Fact and Existence*. Oxford: Basil Blackwell, 1969.

Nancy, Jean-Luc. "Dum Scribo." *Oxford Literary Review* 3, no. 2 (1978): 6–21.

———. *Ego Sum*. Paris: Aubier-Flammarion, 1979.

———. "Larvatus Pro Deo." *Glyph* 2 (1977): 14–36.

Siebers, Tobin. "The Blind Spot in Descartes' *La Dioptrique*." *MLN* 94 (1979): 836–43.

Sievert, Donald. "Descartes' Self-Doubt." *Philosophical Review* 84 (1975): 51–69.

LES MESSIEURS DE PORT-ROYAL

(Antoine Arnauld, Pierre Nicole, Claude Lancelot)

Abercrombie, Nigel. *The Origins of Jansenism*. Oxford: Clarendon Press, 1936.

Chomsky, Noam. *Cartesian Linguistics: A Chapter in the History of Rationalist Thought*. New York: Harper & Row, 1966.

Foucault, Michel. *The Order of Things: An Archaeology of the Human Sciences*. New York: Pantheon, 1971.

James, Edward Donald. *Pierre Nicole, Jansenist and Humanist: A Study of His Thought*. The Hague: Martinus Nijhoff, 1972.

———. "The Political and Social Theory of Pierre Nicole." *French Studies* 14 (1960): 117–28.

Marin, Louis. *La Critique de discours: Sur la* Logique de Port-Royal *et les* Pensées *de Pascal*. Paris: Editions du Minuit, 1975.

Norman, Buford. "Nicole's *Essais de morale*: Logic and Persuasion." *French Literature Series* 9 (1982): 9–17.

Ogle, Richard. "Two Port-Royal Theories of Natural Order." In *Progress in Linguistic Historiography*, edited by Konrad Koerner, 102–12. Amsterdam: Benjamins, 1980.

Pariente, Jean Claude. *L'Analyse du langage à Port-Royal: Six études logico-grammaticales*. Paris: Editions du Minuit, 1985.

Sainte-Beuve, Charles Augustin. *Port-Royal*. 3 vols. Paris: Gallimard (Pléiade), 1952–55.

Shackleton, Robert. "Jansenism and the Englightenment." *Studies on Voltaire and the Eighteenth Century* 57 (1967): 1387–97.

Tavenaux, René. "Presentation." In *Jansénisme et politique*, 7–50. Paris: Armand Colin, 1965.

FRANÇOIS, DUC DE LA ROCHEFOUCAULD

Baker, Susan R. "La Rochefoucauld and the Art of the Self-Portrait." *Romanic Review* 65 (1974): 13–30.

Barthes, Roland. "Introduction." In *Maximes et Réflexions de La Rochefoucauld*, edited by Roland Barthes. Paris: Le Club Français du Livre, 1961.

Bénichou, Paul. "L'Intention des *Maximes*." In *L'Ecrivain et ses travaux*. Paris: José Corti, 1967.

Coulet, Henri. "La Rochefoucauld ou la peur d'être dupe." In *Hommage au Doyen Etienne Gros*, 105–12. Aix-en-Provence: Gap, 1959.

Culler, Johnathan. "Paradox and the Language of Morals in La Rochefoucauld." *Modern Language Review* 68 (1973): 28–39.

Fine, Peter Martin. *Vauvenargues and La Rochefoucauld*. Manchester: Manchester University Press; Totowa, N.J.: Rowman & Littlefield, 1974.

Freudmann, Felix R. "La Rochefoucauld and the Concept of Time." *Romance Notes* 3 (1962): 33–37.

Frey, Hans-Jost. "La Rochefoucauld und die Wahrheit." *Schweizer Monatshefte* 47 (1967): 388–94.

Green, Robert. "Lost Paradise and Self-Delusion in the *Maxims* of La Rochefoucauld." *French Review* 48 (1974): 321–30.

Lafond, Jean. *La Rochefoucauld: Augustinisme et littérature*. Paris: Klincksieck, 1977.

Lewis, Philip E. *La Rochefoucauld: The Art of Abstraction*. Ithaca: Cornell University Press, 1977.

Meleuc, Serge. "Structure de la maxime." *Langages* 13 (1969): 69–99.

Moore, Will G. *La Rochefoucauld: His Mind and Art*. Oxford: Clarendon Press, 1969.

Mourgues, Odette de. *Two French Moralists: La Rochefoucauld and La Bruyère*. Cambridge: Cambridge University Press, 1978.

Norman, Buford. "Knowledge, Meaning, and Style in Variants of La Rochefoucauld's *Maximes*." *Papers on French Seventeenth-Century Literature* no. 14(1) (1981): 19–31.

Pierssens, Michel. "Fonction et champ de la maxime." *Sub-Stance* 1 (1971): 1–9.

Starobinski, Jean. "Complexité de La Rochefoucauld." *Preuves* no. 135 (May 1962): 33–40.

———. "La Rochefoucauld et les morales substitutives." *Nouvelle revue française* no. 163 (July 1966): 16–43 and no. 164 (August 1966): 211–29.

Sutcliffe, F. E. "The System of La Rochefoucauld." *Bulletin of the John Rylands Library* 49 (Autumn 1966): 233–45.

Thweatt, Vivien. *La Rochefoucauld and the Seventeenth-Century Concept of the Self*. Geneva: Droz, 1980.

Weber, Joseph G. "The Personae in the Style of La Rochefoucauld's *Maximes*." *PMLA* 89 (1974): 250–55.

Zeller, M. F. *New Aspects of Style in the* Maxims *of La Rochefoucauld*. Washington, D.C.: Catholic University of America Press, 1954.

BLAISE PASCAL

Auerbach, Erich. "On the Political Theory of Pascal." In *Scenes from the Drama of European Literature*, 101–29. New York Meridian Books, 1959.
Baird, A. W. S. "Pascal's Idea of Nature." *Isis* 61 (1970): 297–320.
———. *Studies in Pascal's Ethics*. International Archives of the History of Ideas, no. 16. The Hague: Martinus Nijhoff, 1975.
Barker, John. *Strange Contrarieties: Pascal in England during the Age of Reason*. Montreal and London: McGill–Queen's University Press, 1975.
Beitzinger, A. J. "Pascal on Justice, Force, and Law." *Review of Politics* 46 (1984): 212–43.
Bishop, Morris. *Pascal: The Life of Genius*. New York: Reynal & Hitchcock, 1936.
Blaise Pascal, l'homme et l'oeuvre. Cahiers du Royaumont, Philosophie, vol. 1. Paris: Editions du Minuit, 1956.
Broome, J. H. *Pascal*. New York: Barnes & Noble, 1965.
Brunet, Georges. *Le Génie de Pascal*. Paris: Hachette, 1924.
———. *Le Pari de Pascal*. Paris: Desclée, de Brouwer, 1956.
Chambers, Frank M. "Pascal's Montaigne." *PMLA* 65 (1950): 790–804.
Chevalier, Jacques. *Pascal*. Translated by Lilian A. Clare. London: Sheed & Ward, 1930.
Davidson, Hugh M. *The Origins of Certainty: Means and Meanings in Pascal's Pensées*. Chicago: University of Chicago Press, 1979.
Demorest, Jean-Jacques. *Dans Pascal: Essai en partant de son style*. Paris: Editions du Minuit, 1953.
———. "Pascal's Sophistry and the Sin of Poesy." In *Studies in Seventeenth-Century French Literature Presented to Morris Bishop*, edited by Jean-Jacques Demorest, 132–52. Garden City, N.Y.: Anchor Doubleday, (1966).
Demorest, Jean-Jacques, and Lise Leibacher-Ouvrard, eds. *Pascal; Corneille: Désert, retraite, engagement*. Paris: Papers on French Seventeenth-Century Literature, 1984.
Dijksterhuis, E. J. "Pneumatics: Blaise Pascal." In *The Mechanization of the World Picture*, translated by C. Dikshoorn, 44–45. Oxford: Clarendon Press, 1961.
Eastwood, D. M. *The Revival of Pascal*. Oxford: Clarendon Press, 1936.
Eliot, T. S. "The *Pensées* of Pascal." In *Selected Essays*, 355–68. New ed. New York: Harcourt, Brace, 1950.
L'Esprit Créateur 2, no. 2 (Summer 1962). Special Pascal issue.
Europe nos. 597–98 (January–February 1979). Special Pascal issue.
Ferreyrolles, Gérard. *Pascal et la raison du politique*. Paris: Presses Universitaires de France, 1984.
Fletcher, Frank Thomas Herbert. *Pascal and the Mystical Tradition*. New York: Philosophical Library, 1954.
Goldmann, Lucien. *The Hidden God: A Study of the Tragic Vision in the Pensées of Pascal and the Tragedies of Racine*. Translated by Philip Thody. London: Routledge & Kegan Paul; New York: Humanities Press, 1964.
Howe, Virginia K. "*Les Pensées*: Paradox and Signification." *Yale French Studies* no. 49 (1973): 120–31.
Hubert, Sister Marie-Louise. *Pascal's Unfinished Apology*. New Haven: Yale University Press, 1952.
La Charité, Raymond C. "Pascal's Ambivalence towards Montaigne." *Studies in Philology* 70 (1973): 187–98.

Lafuma, Louis. *Histoire des* Pensées *de Pascal.* Paris: Editions du Luxembourg, 1954.
————. *Recherches pascaliennes.* Paris: Delmas, 1949.
Le Guern, Michel. *L'Image dans l'oeuvre de Pascal.* Paris: A. Colin, 1969.
Lewis, Phillip. "Dialogic Impasse in Pascal's *Provinciales.*" *Canadian Review of Comparative Literature* 3 (1976): 27–38.
MacKenzie, L. A. "To the Brink: The Dialectic of Anxiety in the *Pensées.*" *Yale French Studies* no. 66 (1984): 57–66.
Marin, Louis. *La Critique de discours: Sur la* Logique *de Port-Royal et les* Pensées *de Pascal.* Paris: Editions du Minuit, 1975.
————. "Discourse of Power—Power of Discourse: Pascalian Notes." In *Philosophy in France Today,* edited by Alan Montefiore, 155–74. Cambridge: Cambridge University Press, 1983.
————. "On the Interpretation of Ordinary Language: A Parable of Pascal." In *Textual Strategies: Perspectives in Post-Structuralist Criticism,* edited by Josue V. Harari, 239–59. Ithaca: Cornell University Press, 1979.
————. " 'Pascal': Text, Author, Discourse. . . ." *Yale French Studies* no. 52 (1975): 129–51.
Melzer, Sara E. *Discourses of the Fall: A Study of Pascal's* Pensées. Berkeley: University of California Press, 1986.
Mesnard, Jean. *Pascal.* Translated by Claude and Marcia Abraham. University: University of Alabama Press, 1969.
————. *Pascal: His Life and Works.* Translated by Ronald Knox. New York: Philosophical Library, 1952.
————, ed. *Méthodes chez Pascal: Actes du colloque tenu a Clermont-Ferrand, 10–13 juin 1976.* Paris: Presses Universitaires de France, 1979.
Miel, Jan. *Pascal and Theology.* Baltimore: Johns Hopkins University Press, 1969.
Mortimer, Ernest. *Blaise Pascal: The Life and Work of a Realist.* London: Methuen, 1959.
Mueller, Gustav E. "Pascal's Dialectical Philosophy and His Discovery of Liberalism." *Journal of the History of Ideas* 6 (1945): 67–80.
Nelson, Robert James. *Pascal: Adversary and Advocate.* Cambridge, Mass.: Harvard University Press, 1981.
Poulet, Georges. "Pascal." In *Studies in Human Time,* translated by Elliot Coleman, 74–96. Baltimore: Johns Hopkins University Press, 1956.
————. "Pascal." In *The Metamorphoses of the Circle,* translated by Carley Dawson and Elliot Coleman in collaboration with the author, 32–49. Baltimore: Johns Hopkins University Press, 1966.
Sellier, Philippe. *Pascal et Saint Augustin.* Paris: A. Colin, 1970.
Stanton, Domna C. "Pascal's Fragmentary Thoughts: Dis-Order and Its Over-Determination." *Semiotica* 51 (1984): 211–35.
Stewart, H. F. *The Holiness of Pascal.* Cambridge: Cambridge University Press, 1915.
————. *The Secret of Pascal.* Cambridge: Cambridge University Press, 1941.
Topliss, Patricia. *The Rhetoric of Pascal: A Study of His Art of Persuasion in the Provinciales and the* Pensées. Leicester: Leicester University Press, 1966.
Valéry, Paul. "Variations on a 'Pensée.' " In *Masters and Friends (Collected Works,* vol. 9), translated by Martin Turnell, 86–107. Princeton: Princeton University Press, 1968.
Webb, Clement C. J. *Pascal's Philosophy of Religion.* Oxford: Clarendon Press, 1929.
Wetsel, David. *L'Écriture et le reste: The* Pensées *of Pascal in the Exegetical Tradition of Port-Royal.* Columbus: Ohio State University Press, 1981.

MADAME DE SÉVIGNÉ

Allentuch, Harriet Ray. *Madame de Sévigné: A Portrait in Letters.* Baltimore: Johns Hopkins University Press, 1963.

————. "My Daughter/Myself: Emotional Roots of Madame de Sévigné's Art." *Modern Language Quarterly* 43 (1982): 121–37.

Bray, Bernard. *L'Art de la lettre amoureuse.* Hague: Mouton, 1967.

————. "Quelques aspects du système épistolaire de Mme de Sévigné." *Revue d'Histoire Littéraire de la France* 69 (1969): 491–505.

Cordelier, Jean. *Mme de Sévigné par elle-même.* Paris: Editions du Seuil, 1967.

Duchêne, Roger. *Ecrire au temps de Mme de Sévigné: Lettres et texte littéraire.* Paris: J. Vrin, 1981.

————. *Madame de Sévigné, ou, la chance d'être femme.* Paris: Fayard, 1982.

————. *Réalité vécue et art épistolaire: Madame de Sévigné et la lettre d'amour.* Paris: Bordas, 1970.

Goldsmith, Elizabeth C. "Giving Weight to Words: Madame de Sévigné's Letters to Her Daughter." *New York Literary Forum* 12–13 (1984): 107–15.

————. "Madame de Sévigné's Epistolary Retreat." *L'Esprit Créateur* 23, no. 2 (Summer 1983): 70–79.

Guenon, Solange. "Correspondance et paradoxe." *Papers on French Seventeenth-Century Literature* no. 15(2) (1981): 137–52.

Marcu, Eva. "Madame de Sévigné and Her Daughter." *Romanic Review* 51 (1960): 182–91.

Mossiker, Frances. *Madame de Sévigné: A Life and Letters.* New York: Knopf, 1983.

Nicolich, Robert. "Life as Theatre in the Letters of Madame de Sévigné." *Romance Notes.* (1975): 376–82.

Stanton, Domna C. "On Female Portraiture in Sévigné's Letters." *Papers on French Seventeenth-Century Literature* no. 15(2) (1981): 88–94.

Woolf, Virginia. "Madame de Sévigné." In *The Death of the Moth,* 51–57. New York: Harcourt, Brace, 1942.

JACQUES-BÉNIGNE BOSSUET

Bayley, Peter. "The Art of the *Pointe* in Bossuet." In *The Equilibrium of Wit: Essays for Odette de Morgues,* edited by Peter Bayley and Dorothy Gale Coleman, 262–79. Lexington, Ky.: French Forum Publishers, 1982.

Christofides, C. G. "Bossuet and Jansenism." *Romance Notes* 1 (1960): 141–45.

————. "Bossuet on Dramatic Theory." *Symposium* 16 (1962): 225–27.

France, Peter. "Bossuet: The Word and the World." In *Rhetoric and Truth in France,* 116–48. Oxford: Clarendon Press, 1972.

Goyet, Thérèse. *L'Humanisme de Bossuet.* 2 vols. Paris: Klincksieck, 1965.

Goyet, Thérèse, and Jean-Pierre Collinet, eds. *Journées Bossuet: La Prédication au XVIIᵉ siècle: Actes du colloque tenu à Dijon les 2, 3, et 4 décembre pour le trois cent cinquantième anniversaire de la naissance de Bossuet.* Paris: A.-G. Nizet, 1980.

Grosheintz, Oscar. *L'Esthétique oratoire de Bossuet.* Zurich: Imprimerie Leemann frères, 1914.

Hesbert, René-Jean. *Echo de Tertullian: Bossuet.* Paris: Nouvelles Éditions Latines, 1980.

Lanson, Gustave. *Bossuet.* Paris: Lecène, Oudin, 1891.

Reynolds, Ernest Edwin. *Bossuet.* Garden City, N.Y.: Doubleday, 1963.

Stanton, Domna C. "The Predicatory Mouth: Problematics of Communication in Bossuet's *Oeuvres oratoires.*" *Papers on French Seventeenth-Century Literature* no. 16(1) (1982): 103–21.

Terstegge, Georgiana. *Providence as idée maîtresse in the Works of Bossuet: Theme and Stylistic Motif.* Washington, D.C.: Catholic University of America Press, 1948.

Truchet, J. *La Predication de Bossuet: Etude des Thèmes.* 2 vols. Paris: Editions du Cerf, 1960.

Vernet, Max. "Théatre et usurpation du sujet: 'Le monde et son image' dans les *Maximes et réflexions sur la comédie* de Bossuet." *Etudes Françaises* 15, nos. 3–4 (October 1979): 149–74.

CHARLES PERRAULT

Berg, Elizabeth L. "Recognizing Differences: Perrault's Modernist Aesthetic in the *Parallèle des anciens et des modernes.*" *Papers on French Seventeenth-Century Literature* no. 18 (1983): 135–48.

Bonnefon, Paul. "Charles Perrault, littérateur et académicien." *Revue d'Histoire Littéraire de la France* 12 (1905): 549–610.

Howells, R. J. "Dialogue and Speakers in the *Parallèle des anciens et des modernes.*" *Modern Language Review* 78 (1983): 793–803.

Jauss, Hans Robert. "Ästhetische Normen und geschichtliche Reflexion in der 'Querelle des Anciens et des Modernes.'" In *Parallèle des anciens et des modernes en ce qui regarde les arts et les sciences,* by Charles Perrault, edited by Hans Robert Jauss, 8–64. Munich: Eidos Verlag, 1964.

Kortum, Hans. *Charles Perrault und Nicolas Boileau: Der Antike-Streit im Zeitalter der klassischen französischen Literatur.* Berlin: Rutten & Loenig, 1966.

Rigault, Hippolyte. *Histoire de la querelle des ancients et des modernes.* Paris: L. Hachette, 1856.

Simonsuuri, Kirsti. *Homer's Original Genuis: Eighteenth-Century Notions of the Greek Epic.* Cambridge: Cambridge University Press, 1979.

Soriano, Marc. *Le Dossier Perrault.* Paris: Hachette, 1972.

FRANÇOIS DE SALIGNAC DE LA MOTHE-FÉNELON

Alcover, Madeleine. "The Indecency of Knowledge." *Rice University Studies* 64, no. 1 (Winter 1978): 25–39.

Boulvé, Léon. *De l'hellénisme chez Fénelon.* Geneva: Slatkine, 1970.

Carcassone, Elie. *Fénelon, l'homme et l'oeuvre.* Paris: Hatier-Boivin, 1955.

Cherel, Albert. *Fénelon et la religion du pur amour.* Paris: Denoël & Steele, 1934.

Clark, Priscilla P. "Leçons du grand siècle: The Aesthetics of Education in *Télémaque.*" *Papers on French Seventeenth-Century Literature* no. 6 (Winter 1976–77): 23–35.

Cognet, Louis. *Crépuscule des mystiques: Bossuet, Fénelon.* Tournai: Desclée, 1958.

Cor, M. Antonia. "The Shield of Télémaque." *Romance Notes* 23 (1982): 17–21.

Cosentini, John. "The Literary Art of Fénelon's *Dialogue des morts.*" *Thought Patterns* 6 (1959): 29–61.

Davis, James Herbert, Jr. *Fénelon.* Boston: Twayne, 1979.

De La Bedoyère, Michael. *The Archbishop and the Lady: The Story of Fénelon and Madame Guyon.* New York: Pantheon, 1956.

Dru, Alexander. "Fénelon in History." *Downside Review* no. 282 (January 1968): 1–12.

Dupriez, Bernard Marie. *Fénelon et la Bible: Les Origines du mysticisme fénelonïen.* Paris: Bloud & Gay, 1961.

Finch, Robert. "Fénelon: Qualities Rather than Forms." In *The Sixth Sense: Individualism in French Poetry,* 37–55. Toronto: University of Toronto Press, 1966.

Goré, Jeanne Lydie. *L'Itinéraire de Fénelon: Humanisme et spiritualité.* Paris: Presses Universitaires de France, 1957.

———. *La Notion d'indifférence chez Fénelon, et ses sources*. Paris: Presses Universitaires de France, 1956.

Gouhier, Henri. *Fénelon philosophe*. Paris: J. Vrin, 1977.

Granderoute, Robert. *Le Roman pédagogique de Fénelon à Rousseau*. 2 vols. Geneva: Slatkine, 1985.

Haillant, Marguerite. *Culture et imagination dans les oeuvres de Fénelon "ad usum Delphini."* Paris: Les Belles Lettres, 1983.

———. *Fénelon et la prédication*. Paris: Klincksieck, 1969.

Hess, M. Whitcomb. "Fénelon, the Dauphin's Tutor." *Contemporary Review* 197 (1960): 207–9.

Hillenaar, Henk. *Fénelon et les Jésuites*. The Hague: Martinus Nijhoff, 1967.

Little, Katherine Day. *François de Fénelon: Study of a Personality*. New York: Harper, 1951.

Lombard, Alfred. *Fénelon et le retour à l'antique au XVIIIe siècle*. Neuchâtel: Secrétariat de l'Université, 1954.

Maurer, Karl. "Fénelon's 'Futile' Criticism of French Classicism and the Emancipation of German Literature from Neo-Classicist Rules." In *Proceedings of the Xth Congress of the International Comparative Literature Association, New York, 1982*. Vol. 1, *General Problems of Literary History*, edited by Anna Balakian et al., 469–75. New York: Garland, 1985.

May, James Lewis. *Fénelon: A Study*. London: Burns, Oates & Washbourne, 1938.

Mohr, Eva. *Fénelon und der Staat*. Bern: Lang, 1971.

Raymond, Marcel. *Fénelon*. Paris: Desclée, De Brouwer, 1967.

Varillon, François. *Fénelon et le pur amour*. Paris: Editions du Seuil, 1957.

Warnick, Barbara, ed. *Fénelon's Letter to the French Academy*. Lanham, Md.: University Press of America, 1984.

JEAN DE LA BRUYÈRE

Brody, Jules. "Sur le style de La Bruyère." *L'Esprit Créateur* 11, no. 2 (Summer 1971): 154–68.

Campion, Edmund J. "Rhetorical Theory in *Les Caractères*." *Papers on French Seventeenth-Century Literature* no. 15(2) (1981): 227–38.

Harthes, Erica. "Classical Disproportion: La Bruyère's *Caractères*." *L'Esprit Créateur* 15, nos. 1–2 (Spring–Summer 1975): 189–210.

Horowitz, Louise K. "La Bruyère: The Limits of Characterization." *French Forum* 1 (1976): 127–38.

Kirsch, Doris. *La Bruyère; ou, le style cruel*. Montréal: Presses de l'Université de Montréal, 1977.

Koppisch, Michael S. *The Dissolution of Character: Changing Perspectives in La Bruyère's Caractères*. Lexington, Ky.: French Forum Publishers, 1981.

Wohinsky, Barbara R. "Shattered Speech, La Bruyère, *De la cour*, 81." *Papers on French Seventeenth-Century Literature* no. 15(2) (1981): 210–26.

BERNARD LE BOVIER, SIEUR DE FONTENELLE

Birkett, Mary Ellen. "The Ironic Cartography of Fontenelle's 'Description de l'Empire de la Poésie.' " *Modern Language Studies* 15 (1985): 157–64.

Carré, Jean R. *La Philosophie de Fontenelle, ou le sourire de la raison*. Paris: F. Alcan, 1932.

Cosentini, John W. *Fontenelle's Art of Dialogue*. New York: King's Crown Press, 1952.

Grégoire, F. *Fontenelle, une philosophie désabusée.* Nancy: Imprimerie Georges Thomas, 1947.

Krauss, Werner. "Vorwort." In *Fontenelle und die Aufklärung,* edited by Werner Krauss, 7–69. Munich: W. Fink, 1969.

Marsak, Leonard M. "Bernard de Fontenelle: The Idea of Science in the French Enlightenment." *Transactions of the American Philosophical Society* n.s. 49, no. 7 (1959): 5–64.

LOUIS DE ROUVROY, DUC DE SAINT-SIMON

Boislisle, A. de, ed. *Saint-Simon, Mémoires.* Paris: Hachette, 1916.

Brancourt, Jean-Pierre. *Le Duc de Saint-Simon et la monarchie.* Paris: Cujas, 1971.

Brody, Jules, and Leo Spitzer. *Approches textuelles des* Mémoires *de Saint-Simon.* Tübingen: Gunter Narr; Paris: J.-M. Place, 1980.

Coirault, Yves. "La Forme et le miroir dans les *Mémoires* de Saint-Simon." *Dix-septième Siècle* 94–95 (1971): 167–87.

———. " 'Un morceau si curieux . . . ': La Stylisation historique dans les *Mémoires* de Saint-Simon." *Revue d'Histoire Littéraire de la France* 71 (1971): 207–25.

———. *L'Optique de Saint-Simon: Essai sur les formes de son imagination et de sa sensibilité d'après les* Mémoires. Paris: Armand Colin, 1965.

De Ley, Herbert. *Saint-Simon, Memorialist.* Sherbrooke, Que.: Editions Namaan, 1975.

Elden, D. J. H. van. *Esprits fins et esprits géométriques dans les portraits de Saint-Simon.* International Archives of the History of Ideas, no. 50. The Hague: Martinus Nijhoff, 1975.

Europe, nos. 609–610 (January–February 1980). Special Saint-Simon issue.

Goyet, Thérèse. "Histoire et charité: L'Écriture sainte de Saint-Simon." *Dix-septième Siècle* 94–95 (1971): 139–51.

Himmelfarb, Hélène. "Culture historique et création littéraire: Saint-Simon lecteur d'histoire et de mémoires." *Dix-septième Siècle* 94–95 (1971): 153–66.

Le Roy Ladurie, Emmanuel. "Système de la cour (Versailles vers 1709)." *L'Arc* 65 (1976): 21–35.

Scott, Simone. "Saint-Simon et ses premiers lecteurs." *Stanford French Review* 5 (1981): 35–50.

Van der Cruysse, Dirk. *La Mort dans les* Mémoires *de Saint-Simon.* Paris: A.-G. Nizet, 1981.

———. *Le Portrait dans les* Mémoires *du duc de Saint-Simon.* Paris: A.-G. Nizet, 1971.

CHARLES DE SECONDAT, BARON DE LA BRÈDE ET DE MONTESQUIEU

Baum, John Allen. *Montesquieu and Social Theory.* New York: Pergamon Press, 1979.

Cox, Iris. *Montesquieu and the History of French Law. Studies on Voltaire and the Eighteenth Century* 218. Oxford: The Voltaire Foundation at the Taylor Institution, 1983.

Dargan, Edwin Preston. *The Aesthetic Doctrine of Montesquieu: Its Application in His Writings.* Baltimore: J. H. Furst, 1907.

Ehrard, Jean. *Montesquieu critique d'art.* Paris: Presses Universitaires de France, 1965.

Europe no. 574 (February 1977). Special Montesquieu issue.

Goyard-Fabre, Simone. *La Philosophie du droit de Montesquieu*. Paris: Klincksieck, 1973.

Hulliung, Mark. *Montesquieu and the Old Regime*. Berkeley: University of California Press, 1976.

Karimi, M. H. "Persia in the Writings of Montesquieu." Translated by F. R. C. Bagley. *Durham University Journal* 38 (1977): 231–37.

McLelland, Jane Kyle. "Metaphor in Montesquieu's Theoretical Writings." *Studies on Voltaire and the Eighteenth Century* 199 (1981): 205–24.

Mason, Sheila Mary. *Montesquieu's Idea of Justice*. International Archives of the History of Ideas, no. 79. The Hague: Martinus Nijhoff, 1975.

Merry, Henry J. *Montesquieu's System of Natural Government*. West Lafayette, Ind.: Purdue University Studies, 1970.

Morgan, Charles. *The Liberty of Thought and the Separation of Powers: A Modern Problem Considered in the Context of Montesquieu*. Oxford: Clarendon Press, 1948.

Prélot, M. "Montesquieu et les formes de gouvernement." In *Recueil Sirey du bicentenaire de L'Esprit des lois*. Collectif. Paris: L. Audiat, 1952.

Proust, Jacques. "Poétique de *L'Esprit des lois*." *Spicilegio Moderno: Saggi et Ricerche di Letterature e Lingue Straniere* 9 (1978): 3–17.

Shackleton, Robert. *Montesquieu: A Critical Biography*. London: Oxford University Press, 1963.

Stark, Werner. *Montesquieu, Pioneer of the Sociology of Knowledge*. London: Routledge & Kegan Paul, 1960.

Todorov, Tzvetan. "Droit naturel et formes de gouvernement dans *L'Esprit des lois*." *Esprit* 75 (March 1983): 35–48.

Vlachos, Georges. *La Politique de Montesquieu: Notion et méthode*. Paris: Editions Montchrestien, 1974.

Weddicor, Mark H. *Montesquieu and the Philosophy of Natural Law*. International Archives of the History of Ideas, no. 37. The Hague: Martinus Nijhoff, 1970.

FRANÇOIS QUESNAY

Beer, Max. *An Inquiry into Physiocracy*. London: George Allen & Unwin, 1939.

Einaudi, Mario. *The Physiocratic Doctrine of Judicial Control*. Cambridge, Mass.: Harvard University Press, 1938.

Eltis, Walter A. "François Quesnay: A Reinterpretation." *Oxford Economic Papers* 27, no. 2 (July 1975): 167–200 and 27, no. 3 (November 1975): 327–51.

Fox-Genovese, Elizabeth. *The Origins of Physiocracy: Economic Revolution and Social Order in Eighteenth-Century France*. Ithaca, N.Y.: Cornell University Press, 1976.

Haufle, Heinrich. *Aufklärung und Oekonomie: Zur Position der Physiokraten im Siècle des Lumières*. Munich: W. Fink, 1978.

Higgs, Henry. *The Physiocrats, Six Lectures on the French Economistes of the Eighteenth Century*. New York: Langland Press, 1952.

Kiernan, Colm. "Happiness and a Science of Economics in the French Enlightenment." *Studies on Voltaire and the Eighteenth Century* 153 (1976): 1189–1220.

Marx, Karl. *Theories of Surplus-Value*. Vol. 1. Translated by Emile Burns. Moscow: Progress Publishers, 1963.

Meek, Ronald L. *The Economics of Physiocracy*. Cambridge, Mass.: Harvard University Press, 1963.

Neill, Thomas P. "Quesnay and Physiocracy." *Journal of the History of Ideas* 9 (1948): 153–73.

Tribe, Keith. "The Structure of Political Economy." In *Land, Labor, and Economic Discourse*, 80–109. London: Routledge & Kegan Paul, 1978.

FRANÇOIS-MARIE AROUET—VOLTAIRE

Ages, Arnold. "The Technique of Biblical Criticism: An Inquiry into Voltaire's Approach in *La Bible enfin expliquée*." *Symposium* 19 (1965): 67–79.

Barthes, Roland. "The Last Happy Writer." In *Critical Essays*, translated by Richard Howard, 83–89. Evanston, Ill.: Northwestern University Press, 1972.

Besterman, Theodore. *Voltaire*. New York: Harcourt, Brace & World, 1969.

———. "Voltaire, Absolute Monarchy, and the Enlightened Monarch." *Studies on Voltaire and the Eighteenth Century* 32 (1965): 7–22.

———. *Voltaire Essays, and Another*. London: Oxford University Press, 1962.

Bottiglia, William F., ed. *Voltaire: A Collection of Critical Essays*. Englewood Cliffs, N.J.: Prentice-Hall, 1968.

Brooks, Richard A. *Voltaire and Leibniz*. Geneva: Droz, 1964.

Brumfitt, J. H. *Voltaire Historian*. Oxford: Oxford University Press, 1958.

Davidson, Hugh M. "Voltaire Explains Newton: An Episode in the History of Rhetoric." In *The Dialectic of Discovery: Essays on the Teaching and Interpretation of Literature Presented to Lawrence E. Harvey*, edited by John D. Lyons and Nancy Vickers, 72–82. Lexington, Ky.: French Forum Publishers, 1984.

Epstein, Julia L. "Voltaire's Myth of Newton." *Pacific Coast Philology* 14 (1979): 27–33.

———. "Voltaire's Ventriloquism: Voices in the First *Lettre philosophique*." *Studies on Voltaire and the Eighteenth Century* 182 (1979): 219–35.

Gay, Peter. *Voltaire's Politics: The Poet as Realist*. 2nd ed. New Haven: Yale University Press, 1988.

Gossman, Lionel. "Voltaire's Charles XII: History into Art." *Studies on Voltaire and the Eighteenth Century* 25 (1963): 691–720.

Lanson, Gustave. *Voltaire*. Translated by Richard A. Wagoner. New York: John Wiley & Sons, 1966.

Mason, Hadyn T. *Pierre Bayle and Voltaire*. London: Oxford University Press, 1963.

Monty, Jeanne R. *Etude sur le style polémique de Voltaire: Le Dictionnaire philosophique*. *Studies on Voltaire and the Eighteenth Century* 44. Geneva: Institut et Musée Voltaire, 1966.

Moreaux, Jose-Michel. "Ordre et désordre dans *Le dictionnaire philosophique*." *Dix-huitième Siècle* 12 (1980): 381–400.

O'Meara, Maureen F. "Linguistic Power-Play: Voltaire's Considerations on the Evolution, Use, and Abuse of Language." *Studies on Voltaire and the Eighteenth Century* 219 (1983): 93–103.

———. "Toward a Typology of Historical Discourse: The Case of Voltaire." *MLN* 93 (1978): 938–62.

Perkins, Merle L. *Voltaire's Concept of International Order*. *Studies on Voltaire and the Eighteenth Century* 36. Geneva: Institut et Musée Voltaire, 1956.

———. "Voltaire's Principles of Political Thought." *Modern Language Quarterly* 17 (1956): 289–300.

Reisler, Marsha. "Rhetoric and Dialectic in Voltaire's *Lettres philosophiques*." *L'Esprit Créateur* 17, no. 3 (Fall 1977): 311–24.

Rowe, Constance. *Voltaire and the State*. New York: Columbia University Press, 1955.

Schwarzbach, Bertram Eugene. *Voltaire's Old Testament Criticism*. Geneva: Droz, 1971.

Topazio, Virgil W. *Voltaire: A Critical Study of His Major Works*. New York: Random House, 1967.

Walters, Robert L., ed. *Colloque 76: Voltaire*. London, Ont.: Department of French, University of Western Ontario, 1983.

Williams, David. *Voltaire as Literary Critic. Studies on Voltaire and the Eighteenth Century* 48. Geneva: Institut et Musée Voltaire, 1966.

JULIEN OFFRAY DE LA METTRIE

Deprun, Jean. "La Mettrie et l'immoralisme sadien." *Annales de Bretagne et des Pays de l'Ouest (Anjou, Maine, Touraine)* 83 (1976): 745–50.
Falvey, John F. "The Aesthetics of La Mettrie." *Studies on Voltaire and the Eighteenth Century* 87 (1972): 397–479.
———. "The Individualism of La Mettrie." *Nottingham French Studies* 4, no. 1 (May 1965): 15–27 and no. 2 (October 1965): 66–78.
———. "Women and Sexuality in the Thought of La Mettrie." In *Women and Society in Eighteenth-Century France: Essays in Honor of John Stephenson Spink,* edited by Eva Jacobs et al., 55–68. London: Athlone Press, 1979.
Honoré, Lionel. "The Philosophical Satire of La Mettrie." *Studies on Voltaire and the Eighteenth Century* 215 (1982): 175–222.
Lange, Friedrich A. *History of Materialism.* Translated by E. J. Thomas. 3 vols. London: Trübner & Co., 1877–80.
Rosenfield, L. *From Beast-Machine to Man-Machine.* New York: Oxford University Press, 1941.
Thomson, Ann. "L'Art de jouir de La Mettrie à Sade." In *Aimer en France: 1760–1860. Actes du colloque international de Clermont-Ferrand,* edited by Paul Viallaneix and Jean Ehrard, vol. 2, 315–22. Clermont-Ferrand: Association des Publications de la Faculté des Lettres et Sciences Humaines, 1980.
———. *Materialism and Society in the Mid-Eighteenth Century: La Mettrie's* Discours préliminaire. Geneva: Droz, 1981.
Vartanian, Aram. L'Homme machine: *A Study in the Origins of an Idea.* Princeton: Princeton University Press, 1960.

JEAN-JACQUES ROUSSEAU

Althusser, Louis. "Rousseau: *The Social Contract* (The Discrepancies)." In *Montesquieu, Rousseau, Marx: Politics and History,* translated by Ben Brewster, 113–60. London: NLB, 1972.
Annales de la Société Jean-Jacques Rousseau 1– (1905–).
Baczko, Bronislaw. *Rousseau: Solitude et communauté.* Translated by Claire Brendhel-Lamhout. The Hague: Mouton, 1974.
Barish, Jonas A. "The Anti-Theatricalism of Rousseau." *Stanford French Review* 1 (1977): 167–90.
Baud-Bovy, Samuel, ed. *Jean-Jacques Rousseau.* Neuchâtel: La Baconnière, 1962.
Bloom, Harold, ed. *Modern Critical Views: Jean-Jacques Rousseau.* New Haven: Chelsea House, 1987.
Brooks, Richard A. "Rousseau's Anti-Feminism in the *Lettre à d'Alembert* and *Emile.*" In *Literature and History in the Age of Ideas: Essays on the French Enlightenment Presented to George Remington Havens,* edited by Charles G. S. Williams, 208–27. Columbus: Ohio State University Press, 1975.
Broome, Jack Howard. *Rousseau: A Study of His Thought.* New York: Barnes & Noble, 1963.
Burt, E. S. "Developments in Character: Reading and Interpretation in 'The Children's Punishment' and 'The Broken Comb.'" *Yale French Studies* no. 69 (1985): 192–210.
———. "Rousseau the Scribe." *Studies in Romanticism* 18 (1979): 629–82.

Cameron, David R. *The Social Thought of Rousseau and Burke: A Comparative Study*. London: Weidenfeld & Nicholson, 1973.

Carroll, Robert C. "Rousseau's Bookish Ontology." *Studies on Voltaire and the Eighteenth Century* 79 (1971): 103–52.

Cassirer, Ernst. *The Question of Jean-Jacques Rousseau*. Translated by Peter Gay. New York: Columbia University Press, 1954.

Chapman, John William. *Rousseau—Totalitarian or Liberal?* New York: Columbia University Press, 1956.

Charvet, John. *The Social Problem in the Philosophy of Rousseau*. Cambridge: Cambridge University Press, 1974.

Cobban, Alfred. *Rousseau and the Modern State*. London: George Allen & Unwin, 1934.

Coleman, Patrick. "Characterizing Rousseau's *Emile*." *MLN* 92 (1977): 761–78.

———. *Rousseau's Political Imagination: Rule and Representation in the* Lettre à d'Alembert. Geneva: Droz, 1984.

Colletti, Lucio. *From Rousseau to Lenin: Studies in Ideology and Society*. Translated by John Merrington and Judith White. London: NLB, 1972.

Cranston, Maurice, and Richard S. Peters, eds. *Hobbes and Rousseau: A Collection of Critical Essays*. Garden City, N.Y.: Doubleday (Anchor), 1972.

Crocker, Lester Gilbert. *Jean-Jacques Rousseau*. Vol. 1, *The Quest;* Vol. 2, *The Prophetic Voice*. New York: Macmillan, 1968, 1973.

———. *Rousseau's* Contrat social: *An Interpretive Essay*. Cleveland: Case Western Reserve University Press, 1968.

Daedalus 107 (1978). Special Rousseau issue.

de Man, Paul. *Allegories of Reading: Figural Language in Rousseau, Nietzsche, Rilke, and Proust*. New Haven: Yale University Press, 1979.

———. "The Rhetoric of Blindness: Jacques Derrida's Reading of Rousseau." In *Blindness and Insight: Essays in the Rhetoric of Contemporary Criticism*, 102–41. 2d ed., rev. Minneapolis: University of Minnesota Press, 1983.

Derathé, Robert. *Jean-Jacques Rousseau et la science politique de son temps*. Paris: Presses Universitaires de France, 1950.

———. *Le Rationnalisme de J.-J. Rousseau*. Paris: Presses Universitaires de France, 1948.

Derrida, Jacques. *Of Grammatology*. Translated by Gayatri Chakravorty Spivak. Baltimore: Johns Hopkins University Press, 1976.

Einaudi, Mario. *The Early Rousseau*. Ithaca: Cornell University Press, 1967.

Ellenburg, Stephen. *Rousseau's Political Philosophy: An Interpretation from Within*. Ithaca: Cornell University Press, 1976.

Fralin, Richard. *Rousseau and Representation: A Study of the Development of His Concept of Political Institutions*. New York: Columbia University Press, 1978.

Gans, Eric. "The Victim as Subject: The Esthetico-Ethical System of Rousseau's *Rêveries*." *Studies in Romanticism* 21 (1982): 3–31.

Genette, Gérard, and Tzvetan Todorov, eds. *Pensée de Rousseau*. Paris: Editions du Seuil, 1984.

Gilden, Hilail. "Revolution and the Formation of Political Society in the *Social Contract*." *Interpretation: A Journal of Political Philosophy* 5 (1976): 247–65.

Goldschmidt, Victor. *Anthropologie et politique: Les Principes du système de Rousseau*. Paris: J. Vrin, 1974.

Gossman, Lionel. "Time and History in Rousseau." *Studies on Voltaire and the Eighteenth Century* 30 (1964): 311–49.

Gouhier, Henri Gaston. *Les Méditations métaphysiques de Jean-Jacques Rousseau*. Paris: J. Vrin, 1970.

Grimsley, Ronald. *Jean-Jacques Rousseau: A Study in Self-Awareness*. 2d ed. Cardiff: University of Wales Press, 1969.

————. *The Philosophy of Rousseau*. London: Oxford University Press, 1973.

Guehenno, Jean. *Jean-Jacques Rousseau*. 2 vols. Translated by John and Doreen Wightman. London: Routledge & Kegan Paul; New York: Columbia University Press, 1966.

Hamilton, James F. *Rousseau's Theory of Literature: The Poetics of Art and Nature*. York, S.C.: French Literature Publications, 1979.

Hampson, Norman. *Will and Circumstance: Montesquieu, Rousseau, and the French Revolution*. London: Duckworth, 1983.

Harari, Josue V. "Therapeutic Pedagogy: Rousseau's *Emile.*" *MLN* 97 (1982): 787–809.

Harvey, Simon, et al., eds. *Reappraisals of Rousseau: Studies in Honour of R. A. Leigh*. Manchester: Manchester University Press, 1980.

Kumbier, William A. "Rousseau's *Lettre sur la musique française.*" *Stanford French Review* 6 (1982): 221–37.

Leigh, R. A., ed. *Rousseau After Two Hundred Years*. Cambridge: Cambridge University Press, 1982.

MacCannell, Juliet Flower. "History and Self-Portrait in Rousseau's Autobiography." *Studies in Romanticism* 13 (1974): 279–98.

————. "Nature and Self-Love: A Reinterpretation of Rousseau's 'Passion primitive.' " *PMLA* 92 (1977): 890–902.

Mercken-Spaas, Godelieve. "The Social Anthropology of Rousseau's *Emile.*" *Studies on Voltaire and the Eighteenth Century* 132 (1975): 137–81.

Noone, John B. *Rousseau's* Social Contract: *A Conceptual Analysis*. London: G. Prior, 1981.

Perkins, Jean A. "Justification and Excuses in Rousseau." *Studies on Voltaire and the Eighteenth Century* 89 (1972): 1277–92.

Perkins, Merle A. *Jean-Jacques Rousseau on the Individual and Society*. Lexington: University of Kentucky Press, 1974.

Plattner, Mark F. *Rousseau's State of Nature: An Interpretation of the* Discourse on Inequality. DeKalb: Northern Illinois University Press, 1979.

Polin, Raymond. *La Politique de la solitude: Essai sur Rousseau*. Paris: Sirey, 1971.

Raymond, Marcel. *Jean-Jacques Rousseau: La Quête de soi et la rêverie*. Paris: J. Corti, 1962.

Robinson, Philip. "La Conscience: A Perceptual Problem in Rousseau." *Studies on Voltaire and the Eighteenth Century* 90 (1972): 1377–94.

Scanlan, Timothy M. "Manners, Morals, and Maxims in Rousseau's *Lettre à Christophe de Beaumont.*" *Neophilologus* 65 (1981): 366–74.

Schwartz, Joel. *The Sexual Politics of Jean-Jacques Rousseau*. Chicago: University of Chicago Press, 1984.

Senior, Nancy J. "Sophie and the State of Nature." *French Forum* 2 (1977): 134–46.

Shell, Marc. "The Lie of the Fox: Rousseau's Theory of Verbal, Monetary, and Political Representation." *Sub-Stance* 10 (1974): 111–23.

Shklar, Judith N. *Men and Citizens: A Study of Rousseau's Social Theory*. Cambridge: Cambridge University Press, 1969.

Spengeman, William C. "Philosophical Autobiography: The *Confessions* of Rousseau." In *The Forms of Autobiography*, 62–72. New Haven: Yale University Press, 1980.

Starobinski, Jean. *Jean-Jacques Rousseau, la transparence et l'obstacle: Suivi de sept essais sur Rousseau*. Paris: Gallimard, 1971.

————. *L'Oeil vivant*. Paris: Gallimard, 1961.

————. "Rousseau's Happy Days." *New Literary History* 11 (1979–80): 147–66.

Starobinski, Jean, et al. *Jean-Jacques Rousseau: Quatre Études*. Neuchâtel: La Baconnière, 1978.

Strauss, Leo. "On the Intention of Rousseau." *Social Research* 14 (1947): 455–87.

Studies in Romanticism 10 (1971). Special Rousseau issue.

Tanner, Tony. "Rousseau's *La Nouvelle Héloise.*" In *Adultery in the Novel: Contract and Transgression,* 113–78. Baltimore: Johns Hopkins University Press, 1979.

Williams, Huntington. *Rousseau and Romantic Autobiography.* Oxford: Clarendon Press, 1983.

Wilson, Nelly. "Discourses on Method and Professions of Faith: Rousseau's Debt to Descartes." *French Studies* 37 (1983): 157–67.

Wokler, Robert. "Rousseau on Rameau and Revolution." *Studies in the Eighteenth Century* 4 (1979): 251–83.

Wood, Ellen Meiskins. "The State and Popular Sovereignty in French Political Thought: A Genealogy of Rousseau's 'General Will.' " *History of Political Thought* 4 (1983): 281–315.

Yale French Studies no. 28 (1961–62). Special Rousseau issue.

DENIS DIDEROT

Betts, C. J. "The Function of Analogy in Diderot's *Rêve de d'Alembert.*" *Studies on Voltaire and the Eighteenth Century* 185 (1980): 267–81.

Chambart, Elaine. "The Function of the 'Lecteur' in Diderot's Non-Fiction." *Essays in Literature (Western Illinois University)* 1 (1974): 227–35.

Crocker, Lester G. *Diderot's Chaotic Order.* Princeton: Princeton University Press, 1974.

―――. *Two Diderot Studies: Ethics and Esthetics.* Baltimore: Johns Hopkins University Press, 1952.

Diderot Studies 17 (1973). Special issue on the *Rêve de d'Alembert.*

Dieckmann, Herbert. *Cinq leçons sur Diderot.* Geneva: Droz, 1959.

Doolittle, James. "Hieroglyph and Emblem in Diderot's *Lettre sur les sourds et les muets.*" *Diderot Studies* 2 (1952): 148–67.

L'Esprit Créateur 8, no. 1 (Spring 1968) and 24, no. 1 (Spring 1984). Special Diderot issues.

Fontenay, Elizabeth de. *Diderot, Reason and Resonance.* Translated by Jeffrey Mehlman. New York: Braziller, 1982.

France, Peter. *Diderot.* Oxford: Oxford University Press, 1983.

Funt, David. "Diderot and the Esthetics of the Enlightenment." *Diderot Studies* 11. Geneva: Droz, 1968.

Goodman, Dena. "The Structure of Political Argument in Diderot's *Supplément au Voyage de Bougainville.*" *Diderot Studies* 21 (1983): 123–38.

Guerlac, Suzanne. "The *Tableau* and Authority in Diderot's Aesthetics." *Studies on Voltaire and the Eighteenth Century* 219 (1983): 183–94.

Hill, Emita. "Materialism and Monsters in *Le Rêve de d'Alembert.*" *Diderot Studies* 10 (1968): 67–94.

Hobson, Marian. "La *Lettre sur les sourds et les muets* de Diderot: Labyrinthe et langage." *Semiotica* 16 (1976): 291–328.

Jauss, Hans Robert. "Diderots Paradox über das Schauspiel (Entretiens sur le 'Fils Naturel')." *Germanisch-Romanische Monatsschrift* 11 (1961): 380–413.

Lacoue-Labarthe, Philippe. "Diderot, le paradoxe et la mimesis." *Poetique* 11 (1980): 267–81.

Mehlman, Jeffrey. *Cataract: A Study in Diderot.* Middletown, Conn.: Wesleyan University Press, 1979.

Meyer, Paul H. "The *Lettre sur les sourds et les muets* and Diderot's Emerging Concept of the Critic." *Diderot Studies* 6 (1964): 133–56.

Seznec, Jean. "Diderot and Historical Painting." In *Aspects of the Eighteenth Century*, edited by Earl Wasserman, 129–42. Baltimore: Johns Hopkins University Press, 1965.

Stanford French Review 8 (Fall 1984). Special Diderot issue.

Strugnell, A. *Diderot's Politics: A Study of the Evolution of Diderot's Political Thought After the* Encyclopedie. International Archives of the History of Ideas, no. 62. The Hague: Martinus Nijhoff, 1973.

Swain, Virginia Edith. "Diderot's *Paradoxe sur le comedien:* The Paradox of Reading." *Studies on Voltaire and the Eighteenth Century* 208 (1982): 1–71.

Szondi, Peter. "*Tableau* and *Coup de théatre:* On the Social Psychology of Diderot's Bourgeois Tragedy." *New Literary History* 11 (1979–80): 323–43.

Undank, Jack, and Herbert Josephs, eds. *Diderot: Digression and Dispersion: A Bicentennial Tribute*. Lexington, Ky.: French Forum Publishers, 1984.

Vartanian, Aram. "Diderot and the Phenomenology of the Dream." *Diderot Studies* 8 (1966): 217–53.

———. "From Deist to Atheist: Diderot's Philosophical Orientation, 1746–1749." *Diderot Studies* 1 (1949): 46–63.

Wachs, Morris. "Diderot's 'Parallèle de César et de Frédéric.' " *Diderot Studies* 14 (1971): 259–65.

Wartofsky, Max. "Diderot and the Development of Materialist Monism." *Diderot Studies* 2 (1952): 279–329.

ETIENNE BONNOT DE CONDILLAC

Derrida, Jacques. *The Archaeology of the Frivolous: Reading Condillac*. Translated by John P. Leavey. Pittsburgh: Duquesne University Press, 1980.

Hine, Ellen McNiven. "Condillac and the Problem of Language." *Studies on Voltaire and the Eighteenth Century* 106 (1973): 21–63.

———. *A Critical Study of Condillac's* Traité des systèmes. International Archives of the History of Ideas, no. 93. The Hague: Martinus Nijhoff, 1979.

Lefèvre, Roger. *Condillac ou la joie de vivre*. Paris: Seghers, 1966.

Mosconi, Jean. "Analyse et genèse: Regards sur la théorie du devenir de l'entendement au XVIIIᵉ siècle." *Cahiers pour l'analyse* 4 (September–October 1966): 47–82.

O'Meara, Maureen F. "The Language of History and the Place of Power: Male and Female Versions of Condillac's *Histoire ancienne et moderne.*" In *Discours et pouvoir*, edited by Ross Chambers, 177–204. Ann Arbor: Department of Romance Languages, University of Michigan, 1982.

Rosenfield, L. "Condillac's Influence on French Scientific Thought." In *The Triumph of Culture: Eighteenth-Century Perspectives*, edited by Paul Fritz and David Williams, 157–68. Toronto: A. M. Hakkert, 1972.

Sgard, Jean, ed. *Condillac et les problèmes du langage*. Geneva: Slatkine, 1982.

Stam, James H. "Condillac's Epistemolinguistic Question." In *Psychology of Language and Thought: Essays on the History and Theory of Psycholinguistics*, edited by R. W. Rieber, 77–90. New York: Plenum, 1980.

JEAN LE ROND D'ALEMBERT

Briggs, Morton J., Jr. "D'Alembert: Philosophy and Mechanics in the Eighteenth Century." *University of Colorado Studies, Series in History* 3 (1964): 38–56.

Butts, Robert E. "Rationalism in Modern Science: D'Alembert and the 'esprit simpliste.' " *Bucknell Review* 8 (1958–59): 127–39.

Dix-huitième Siècle 16 (1984). Special d'Alembert issue.

Dugas, René. *A History of Mechanics.* Translated by J. R. Maddox. London: Routledge & Kegan Paul, 1957.

Essar, Dennis F. *The Language Theory, Epistemology, and Aesthetics of Jean Le Rond d'Alembert. Studies on Voltaire and the Eighteenth Century* 159. Oxford: The Voltaire Foundation at the Taylor Institution, 1976.

Grimsley, Ronald. *Jean d'Alembert.* Oxford: Oxford University Press, 1963.

Hawkins, Thomas L. "D'Alembert and the Great Chain of Being." *Actes du XIIe congrès international de l'histoire des sciences* 3B (1968): 41–44.

———. *Jean d'Alembert, Science, and the Enlightenment.* Oxford: Clarendon Press, 1970.

Iltis, Carolyn. "D'Alembert and the *vis viva* Controversy." *Studies in History and Philosophy of Science* 1 (1970): 135–44.

Ley, H. "Sur l'importance de d'Alembert." *Pensée* 44 (1952): 49–57 and 46 (1953): 39–50.

Moser, Walter. "D'Alembert: L'ordre philosophique de ce *Discours.*" *MLN* 91 (1976): 722–33.

Pappas, John N. "Diderot, d'Alembert, et l'*Encyclopédie.*" *Diderot Studies* 4 (1963): 191–208.

———. "L'Esprit de finesse contre l'esprit de géometrie: Un Débat entre Diderot et d'Alembert." *Studies on Voltaire and the Eighteenth Century* 89 (1972): 1229–53.

———. "La Poétique de d'Alembert." In *Beitrage zur französischen Auflakrung und zur spanischen Literatur: Festgabe für Werner Krauss zum 70. Geburtstage,* edited by Werner Bahner, 257–70. Berlin: Akademie-Verlag, 1971.

———. *Voltaire and d'Alembert.* Bloomington: Indiana University Press, 1962.

Shklar, Judith N. "Jean d'Alembert and the Rehabilitation of History." *Journal of the History of Ideas* 42 (1981): 643–64.

ANNE-ROBERT-JACQUES TURGOT

Bordes, Christian and Jean Morange, eds. *Turgot, économiste et administrateur.* Paris: Presses Universitaires de France, 1982.

Cavanaugh, Gerald C. "Turgot and the *Encyclopédie.*" *Diderot Studies* 10 (1968): 23–33.

Dakin, D. *Turgot and the Ancien Régime in France.* London: Methuen, 1939.

Faure, Edgar. *La Disgrace de Turgot.* Paris: Gallimard, 1961.

Grimsley, Ronald. "Turgot's Article 'Existence' in the *Encyclopédie.*" In *The French Mind: Studies in Honour of Gustave Radler,* edited by Will Moore et al., 126–51. Oxford: Clarendon Press, 1952.

Groenewegen, Gerald C. "A Reappraisal of Turgot's Theory of Value, Exchange, and Price Determination." *History of Political Economy* 2 (1970): 177–96.

———. "A Reinterpretation of Turgot's Theory of Capital and Interest." *Economic Journal* 81 (1971): 327–40.

Meek, Ronald L. "Introduction." In *Turgot on Progress, Sociology, and Economics.* Cambridge: Cambridge University Press, 1973.

ANTOINE-NICOLAS DE CONDORCET

Alengry, Franck. *Condorcet, guide de la Révolution française.* Paris: V. Giard & E. Brière, 1904.

Baker, Keith Michael. *Condorcet: From Natural Philosophy to Social Mathematics.* Chicago: University of Chicago Press, 1975.

————. "Scientism, Elitism, Liberalism." *Studies on Voltaire and the Eighteenth Century* 55 (1967): 129–65.

Bouissounouse, Janine. *Condorcet: Le Philosophe dans la Révolution*. Paris: Hachette, 1963.

Cazes, Bernard. "Condorcet's True Paradox, or The Liberal Transformed into Social Engineer." *Daedalus* 105 (1976): 47–58.

Frazer, Sir James George. *Condorcet on the Progress of the Human Mind*. Oxford: Clarendon Press, 1933.

Granger, Gaston G. *La Mathématique sociale du marquis de Condorcet*. Paris: Presses Universitaires de France, 1958.

Keohane, Nannerl O. "The Enlightenment Idea of Progress Revisited." In *Progress and Its Discontents*, edited by Gabriel A. Almond and Marvin Chodorow, 21–40. Berkeley: University of California Press, 1982.

Kintzler, Catherine. *Condorcet: L'instruction publique et la naissance du citoyen*. Paris: Le Sycomore, 1984.

Koyré, Alexandre. "Condorcet." *Journal of the History of Ideas* 9 (1948): 131–52.

Laboulle, M. J. J. "La Mathématique sociale: Condorcet et ses prédécesseurs." *Revue d'Histoire Littéraire de la France* 46 (1939): 33–55.

Rosenfield, Leonora Cohen, ed. *Condorcet Studies, vol. 1*. Atlantic Highlands, N.J.: Humanities Press, 1984.

Schapiro, J. Salwyn. *Condorcet and the Rise of Liberalism*. New York: Harcourt, Brace, 1934.

Williams, David. "Condorcet, Feminism, and the Egalitarian Principle." *Studies on Voltaire and the Eighteenth Century* 153 (1976): 151–63.

REVOLUTIONARY ORATORS
(SAINT-JUST, ROBESPIERRE, MARAT)

Abensour, Miguel. "La Philosophie politique de Saint-Just." *Annales Historiques de la Révolution Française* no. 183 (January–March 1966): 1–32 and no. 185 (July–September 1966): 341–58.

Actes du colloque Saint-Just. Sorbonne, 25 June 1967. Paris: Société des Etudes Robespierristes, 1968.

Barny, Roger. "Rousseau dans la Révolution." *Dix-huitième Siècle* 6 (1974): 59–98.

Blanchard, Jean-Marc. "The French Revolution: A Political Line or a Language Circle?" *Yale French Studies* 39 (1967): 64–76.

————. "*Organt* de Saint-Just et le destin." *Nouvelle Revue Française* no. 196 (April 1969): 571–75.

Blanchot, Maurice. "The Main Impropriety." *Yale French Studies* no. 39 (1967): 50–63.

Blum, Carol. *Rousseau and the Republic of Virtue: The Language of Politics in the French Revolution*. Ithaca: Cornell University Press, 1986.

Bruun, Geoffrey. *Saint-Just: Apostle of the Terror*. Boston: Houghton Mifflin, 1932.

D'Astorg, Bertrand. *Introduction au monde de la terreur*. Paris: Editions du Seuil, 1945.

Dispot, Laurent. *La Machine à terreur: Révolution française et terrorismes*. Paris: Grasset, 1978.

Eli Blanchard, Marc. *La Révolution dans les mots: Saint-Just et cie*. Paris: A.-G. Nizet, 1980.

Fortunet, Françoise. "L'Amitié et le droit selon Saint-Just." *Annales Historiques de la Révolution Française* 54 no. 248 (April–June 1982): 181–95.

France, Peter. "Eloquence révolutionnaire et rhétorique traditionelle: Etude d'une séance de la convention." *Saggi e ricerche di letteratura francese* n.s. 24 (1985): 141–76.

Furet, François. *Penser la Révolution française.* Paris: Gallimard, 1978.

Goldschläger, Alain. "Marat, lecteur de Rousseau." *Revue de l'Université d'Ottawa* 51, no. 1 (January–March 1981): 151–58.

Goulet, Jacques. "Robespierre: La Peine de mort et la terreur." *Annales Historiques de la Révolution Française* no. 244 (April–June 1981): 219–38 and no. 251 (January–March 1983): 38–64.

Huet, Marie-Hélène. *Rehearsing the Revolution: The Staging of Marat's Death, 1793–1797.* Berkeley: University of California Press, 1982.

———. "La signature de l'histoire." *MLN* 100 (1985): 715–27.

Ipotési, Monique. "Robespierre et le mythe des anciens." *Annali della Facoltà di Lettere e Filosofia dell'Università degli Studi di Bari* 23 (1980): 239–62.

———. *Saint-Just et l'antiquité.* Paris: A.-G. Nizet, 1984.

Kelly, George Armstrong. "Conceptual Sources of the Terror." *Eighteenth-Century Studies* 14 (1980): 18–36.

Mathiez, Albert. *Etudes sur Robespierre.* Paris: Editions Sociales, 1958.

———. *The French Revolution.* Translated by Catherine Alison Phillips. New York: Knopf, 1928.

Matrat, Jean. *Robespierre, or The Tyranny of the Majority.* Translated by Alan Kendall. New York: Scribner's, 1975.

Philenko, Alexis. "Réflections sur Saint-Just et l'existence légendaire." *Revue de Métaphysique et de Morale* 77 (1972): 339–55.

Scherer, René. "La Queue de Robespierre (Sur le langage de la terreur)." *L'Homme et la Société* 63–64 (January–June 1982): 27–51.

Soboul, Albert. "Robespierre et les contradictions du jacobinisme." *Annales Historiques de la Révolution Française* 50, no. 231 (January–March 1978): 1–19.

Tamine, Joëlle. "Les Métaphores chez Saint-Just et Robespierre." *Langue Française* 15 (September 1972): 47–55.

Torjussen, Serena. " 'Arlequin Diogène,' comédie de Saint-Just." *Annales Historiques de la Révolution Française* no. 237 (July–September 1979): 475–85.

———. "Fonction de la création littéraire dans l'évolution de la pensée de Saint-Just (D'*Organt* à *De la nature*)." *La Pensée* 215 (October 1980): 151–60.

———. "Saint-Just et ses biographes." *Annales Historiques de la Révolution Française* no. 236 (April–June 1979): 234–49.

Acknowledgments

"Montaigne and the Subject of Polity" by Timothy J. Reiss from *Literary Theory/Renaissance Texts*, edited by Patricia Parker and David Quint, © 1986 by The Johns Hopkins University Press. Reprinted by permission.

"Descartes: *Mundus Est Fabula*" (originally titled "*Mundus Est Fabula*") by Jean-Luc Nancy from *MLN* (French Issue) 93, no. 4 (May 1978), © 1978 by The Johns Hopkins University Press. Reprinted by permission.

"Deep and Surface Structure in the Port-Royal *Grammar* and *Logic*" (originally titled "Deep and Surface Structure") by Noam Chomsky from *Cartesian Linguistics: A Chapter in the History of Rationalist Thought* by Noam Chomsky, © 1966 by Noam Chomsky. Reprinted by permission of Harper & Row, Publishers, Inc.

"The Social Ethic of '*Honnêteté*' in La Rochefoucauld's *Maximes* and *Réflexions*" (originally titled "The Social Ethic of *Honnêteté*") by Philip E. Lewis from *La Rochefoucauld: The Art of Abstraction* by Philip E. Lewis, © 1977 by Cornell University. Reprinted by permission of Cornell University Press.

"Pascal's Allegory of Persuasion" by Paul de Man from *Allegory and Representation: Selected Papers from the English Institute 1979–1980*, edited by Stephen J. Greenblatt, © 1981 by the English Institute. Reprinted by permission of The Johns Hopkins University Press.

"Madame de Sévigné" by Louise K. Horowitz from *Love and Language: A Study of the Classical French Moralist Writers* by Louise K. Horowitz, © 1977 by the Ohio State University Press. Reprinted by permission.

"The Predicatory Mouth: Problematics of Communication in Bossuet's *Oeuvres oratoires*" by Domna C. Stanton from *Papers on French Seventeenth-Century Literature* no. 16, Part 1 (1982), © 1982 by *Papers on French Seventeenth-Century Literature*. Reprinted by permission.

"Opposition to Antiquity: Charles Perrault" (originally titled "Ancients and Moderns: The Problem of Cultural Progress" and "Opposition to Antiquity: Charles Perrault") by Kirsti Simonsuuri from *Homer's Original Genius: Eighteenth-Century Notions of the Early Greek Epic (1688–1798)* by Kirsti Simonsuuri, © 1979 by Cambridge University Press. Reprinted by permission.

"Oratory and Poetry in Fénelon's Literary Theory" by Wilbur Samuel Howell from *Quarterly Journal of Speech* 37, no. 1 (February 1951), © 1951 by the Speech Communication Association. Reprinted by permission of *Quarterly Journal of Speech*.

"La Bruyère" by Roland Barthes from *Critical Essays* by Roland Barthes, translated by Richard Howard, © 1972 by Northwestern University Press. Reprinted by permission.

"Fontenelle's Theory of Poetic Expression" (originally titled "Esthetic Theory and Criticism in the Enlightenment: Some Examples of Modern Trends") by Herbert Dieckmann from *Introduction to Modernity: A Symposium on Eighteenth-Century Thought*, edited by Robert Mollenauer, © 1965 by the University of Texas Press. Reprinted by permission of University of Texas Press and the author.

"Saint-Simon's Portrait of Louis XIV" by Leo Spitzer from *Essays on Seventeenth-Century Literature*, edited by David Bellos, © 1983 by Cambridge University Press. Reprinted by permission.

"Montesquieu: Politics and History" by Louis Althusser from *Montesquieu, Rousseau, Marx: Politics and History* by Louis Althusser, © 1959 by Presses Universitaires de France, translation © 1972 by NLB. Reprinted by permission of Verso.

"François Quesnay and the Economic Society" by Herbert Lüthy from *Calvin to Rousseau: Tradition and Modernity in Socio-Political Thought from the Reformation to the French Revolution* by Herbert Lüthy, translated by Salvator Attanosio, © 1970 by Basic Books, Inc. Reprinted by permission.

"Rationality and the Text: A Study of Voltaire's Historiography" by Suzanne Gearhart from *Studies on Voltaire and the Eighteenth Century* 140 (1975), © 1975 by Theodore Besterman. Reprinted by permission.

"La Mettrie: The Robot and the Automaton" by Blair Campbell from *Journal of the History of Ideas*, 31, no. 4 (October–December 1970), © 1970 by *Journal of the History of Ideas*, Inc. Reprinted by permission.

"Promises (Rousseau's *Social Contract*)" (originally titled "Political Allegory in Rousseau") by Paul de Man from *Critical Inquiry* 2, no. 4 (Summer 1976), © 1976 by The University of Chicago Press. Reprinted by permission.

"Toward a Supreme Fiction: Genre and Beholder in the Art Criticism of Diderot and His Contemporaries" by Michael Fried from *New Literary History* 6, no. 3 (Spring 1975), © 1975 by *New Literary History*, The University of Virginia, Charlottesville, Virginia. Reprinted by permission of The Johns Hopkins University Press.

"The Archaeology of the Frivolous: Reading Condillac" by Jacques Derrida from *The Archaeology of the Frivolous: Reading Condillac* by Jacques Derrida, translated by John P. Leavey, Jr., © 1980 by Duquesne University Press, © 1986 by University of Nebraska Press. Reprinted by permission of the University of Nebraska Press.

"The Rhetoric of Enlightenment: D'Alembert" by Peter France from *Rhetoric and Truth in France: Descartes to Diderot* by Peter France, © 1972 by Oxford University Press. Reprinted by permission.

"Turgot on Progress, Sociology, and Economics" (originally titled "Introduction") by Ronald L. Meek from *Turgot on Progress, Sociology, and Economics* by Ronald L. Meek, © 1973 by Cambridge University Press. Reprinted by permission.

"Scientism, Elitism, and Liberalism: The Case of Condorcet" by Keith M. Baker from *Studies on Voltaire and the Eighteenth Century* 55 (1967), © 1967 by Theodore Besterman. Reprinted by permission of The Voltaire Foundation, University of Oxford.

"Rousseau in Robespierre and Saint-Just's Language of Politics" (originally titled "Rousseau and Saint-Just" and "The Trial of the King") by Carol Blum from *Rousseau and the Republic of Virtue: The Language of Politics in the French Revolution* by Carol Blum, © 1986 by Cornell University Press. Reprinted by permission.

Index